THE PAPERS OF ULYSSES S. GRANT

THE PAPERS OF

ULYSSES S. GRANT

Volume 11: June 1–August 15, 1864

Edited by John Y. Simon

ASSOCIATE EDITOR

David L. Wilson

EDITORIAL ASSISTANT

Sue E. Dotson

═══

SOUTHERN ILLINOIS UNIVERSITY PRESS

CARBONDALE AND EDWARDSVILLE

Library of Congress Cataloging in Publication Data (*Revised*)
Grant, Ulysses Simpson, Pres. U.S., 1822–1885.
 The papers of Ulysses S. Grant.

 Prepared under the auspices of the Ulysses S. Grant Association.
 Bibliographical footnotes.
 CONTENTS: v. 1. 1837–1861—v. 2. April–September 1861.
—v. 3. October 1, 1861–January 7, 1862.—v. 4. January 8–March 31,
1862.—v. 5. April 1–August 31, 1862.—v. 6. September 1–December 8, 1862.—v. 7. December 9, 1862–March 31, 1863.—v. 8.
April 1–July 6, 1863.—v. 9. July 7–December 31, 1863.—v. 10.
January 1–May 31, 1864.—v. 11. June 1–August 15, 1864.

 1. Grant, Ulysses Simpson, Pres. U.S., 1822–1885. 2. United
States—History—Civil War, 1861–1865—Campaigns and battles
—Sources. 3. United States—Politics and government—1869–1877
—Sources. 4. Presidents—United States—Biography. 5. Generals—
United States—Biography. I. Simon, John Y., ed. II. Wilson, David
L. 1943–. III. Ulysses S. Grant Association.
E660.G756 1967 973.8'2'0924 67–10725
ISBN 0-8093-1117-8 (v. 11)

To T. Harry Williams (1909–1979)

Contents

―――

Maps and Illustrations

Introduction

===

THE CORRESPONDENCE of Ulysses S. Grant in this
volume covers a period of missed opportunities, disappointments, and
failures, perhaps the low point of the entire campaign against Richmond which began on the Rapidan and ended at Appomattox. By June
1, 1864, Grant had brought the Army of the Potomac closer to Richmond than it had been for nearly two years through a series of bloody
battles followed by flanking movements. Now he probed the Confederate defense line at Cold Harbor with enough success to order a major
assault for the following day. Delay in massing troops, however, led
him to postpone the assault for twenty-four hours, and by June 3 General Robert E. Lee's Army of Northern Virginia was adequately entrenched. At the close of his life, Grant still regretted his decision to
assault, which led to a decisive repulse, costly in lives and morale.

Yet Grant immediately demonstrated his customary resilience by
continuing his campaign against Richmond, making his boldest move
to date. He planned to take his entire army south of the James River to
unite with forces under Major General Benjamin F. Butler for a combined assault on Lee's diminished army. As a diversion to prevent Confederate concentration he sent infantry in the Shenandoah Valley under
Major General David Hunter east toward Lynchburg, Va., to be joined
if possible by cavalry under Major General Philip H. Sheridan from
Cold Harbor. In a brilliant operation, Grant disengaged his forces from
Lee, crossed a major river, and on June 15, Major General William F.
Smith assaulted Petersburg before Confederates knew where Grant
would strike. The failure of Smith to press his advantage that day gave

his opponents time to prepare, and may represent the greatest single military failure of the Civil War.

By June 18, operations before Petersburg had settled into a siege destined to continue until virtually the close of the Civil War. Yet Grant's forces were far from idle; they continued to probe Confederate defenses, and Grant conducted offensives both north and south of the James for the purpose of extending siege lines and attempting to cut off Confederate supplies. To relieve the pressure, Lee sent forces under Lieutenant General Jubal A. Early to the Shenandoah Valley, which eventually threatened Washington, D.C., in July, forcing Grant to send two corps to the capital.

At the end of July, U.S. forces exploded a huge mine beneath the Petersburg defenses, taking Confederates by surprise, then failed to follow through promptly and effectively, allowing Confederates to win the ensuing battle of the Crater. Earlier that month, Grant had commented: "I am the only one at Head Quarters who has not had a days sickness since the campaign commenced." A few days after the battle of the Crater, however, his staff reported him ill, presumably as a result of his bitter disappointment.

The pressure of failure took its toll among the commanders. Smith and Butler clashed so violently that at least one had to go, and Butler remained. Smith had also criticized both Major General George G. Meade and Major General Winfield S. Hancock, and Grant gave serious consideration to transferring Meade. Beyond the Army of the Potomac, Grant was successful in replacing Major General Franz Sigel in the Shenandoah Valley, unsuccessful in ousting Major General William S. Rosecrans in Missouri. Grant's placement of Sheridan in the Shenandoah Valley proved the most fateful of his command decisions that summer.

By August 15, all the key elements for final victory were in place: Major General William T. Sherman in Georgia, Sheridan in the Shenandoah Valley, Grant before Petersburg. As Grant had crossed the James, President Abraham Lincoln telegraphed: "I begin to see it. You will succeed. God bless you all." On August 15, Grant telegraphed to Washington about the necessity of keeping his army at Petersburg. Lincoln replied: "I have seen your despatch expressing your unwillingness to break your hold where you are. Neither am I willing. Hold on with a bull-dog gripe, and chew & choke, as much as possible." Lincoln and Grant had reached a vital understanding.

We are indebted to W. Neil Franklin and Karl L. Trever for searching the National Archives; to Mary Giunta, Anne Harris Henry, and Sara Dunlap Jackson for further assistance in the National Archives; to Harriet Simon for proofreading, and to Judy Anderson, Tamara Melia, and Eric A. Topham, graduate students at Southern Illinois University, for research assistance.

Financial support for the period during which this volume was prepared came from Southern Illinois University and the National Historical Publications and Records Commission.

JOHN Y. SIMON

March 31, 1982

Editorial Procedure

═══

1. *Editorial Insertions*

A. Words or letters in roman type within brackets represent editorial reconstruction of parts of manuscripts torn, mutilated, or illegible.

B. [. . .] or [— — —] within brackets represent lost material which cannot be reconstructed. The number of dots represents the approximate number of lost letters; dashes represent lost words.

C. Words in *italic* type within brackets represent material such as dates which were not part of the original manuscript.

D. Other material crossed out is indicated by ~~cancelled type~~.

E. Material raised in manuscript, as "4th," has been brought in line, as "4th."

2. *Symbols Used to Describe Manuscripts*

AD	Autograph Document
ADS	Autograph Document Signed
ADf	Autograph Draft
ADfS	Autograph Draft Signed
AES	Autograph Endorsement Signed
AL	Autograph Letter
ALS	Autograph Letter Signed
ANS	Autograph Note Signed
D	Document
DS	Document Signed
Df	Draft

DfS	Draft Signed
ES	Endorsement Signed
LS	Letter Signed

3. Military Terms and Abbreviations

Act.	Acting
Adjt.	Adjutant
AG	Adjutant General
AGO	Adjutant General's Office
Art.	Artillery
Asst.	Assistant
Bvt.	Brevet
Brig.	Brigadier
Capt.	Captain
Cav.	Cavalry
Col.	Colonel
Co.	Company
C.S.A.	Confederate States of America
Dept.	Department
Div.	Division
Gen.	General
Hd. Qrs.	Headquarters
Inf.	Infantry
Lt.	Lieutenant
Maj.	Major
Q. M.	Quartermaster
Regt.	Regiment or regimental
Sgt.	Sergeant
USMA	United States Military Academy, West Point, N.Y.
Vols.	Volunteers

4. Short Titles and Abbreviations

ABPC	*American Book-Prices Current* (New York, 1895–)
CG	*Congressional Globe* Numbers following represent the Congress, session, and page.
J. G. Cramer	Jesse Grant Cramer, ed., *Letters of Ulysses S.*

	Grant to his Father and his Youngest Sister, 1857–78 (New York and London, 1912)
DAB	*Dictionary of American Biography* (New York, 1928–36)
Garland	Hamlin Garland, *Ulysses S. Grant: His Life and Character* (New York, 1898)
HED	*House Executive Documents*
HMD	*House Miscellaneous Documents*
HRC	*House Reports of Committees* Numbers following *HED, HMD,* or *HRC* represent the number of the Congress, the session, and the document.
Ill. AG Repoi t	J. N. Reece, ed., *Report of the Adjutant General of the State of Illinois* (Springfield, 1900)
Johnson, Papers	LeRoy P. Graf and Ralph W. Haskins, eds., *The Papers of Andrew Johnson* (Knoxville, 1967–)
Lewis	Lloyd Lewis, *Captain Sam Grant* (Boston, 1950)
Lincoln, Works	Roy P. Basler, Marion Dolores Pratt, and Lloyd A. Dunlap, eds., *The Collected Works of Abraham Lincoln* (New Brunswick, 1953–55)
Memoirs	*Personal Memoirs of U. S. Grant* (New York, 1885–86)
O.R.	*The War of the Rebellion: A Compilation of the Official Records of the Union and Confederate Armies* (Washington, 1880–1901)
O.R. (Navy)	*Official Records of the Union and Confederate Navies in the War of the Rebellion* (Washington, 1894–1927) Roman numerals following *O.R.* or *O.R.* (Navy) represent the series and the volume.
PUSG	John Y. Simon, ed., *The Papers of Ulysses S. Grant* (Carbondale and Edwardsville, 1967–)
Richardson	Albert D. Richardson, *A Personal History of Ulysses S. Grant* (Hartford, Conn., 1868)
SED	*Senate Executive Documents*
SMD	*Senate Miscellaneous Documents*
SRC	*Senate Reports of Committees* Numbers following *SED, SMD,* or *SRC* represent the number of the Congress, the session, and the document.
USGA Newsletter	*Ulysses S. Grant Association Newsletter*

| Young | John Russell Young, *Around the World with General Grant* (New York, 1879) |

5. *Location Symbols*

CLU	University of California at Los Angeles, Los Angeles, Calif.
CoHi	Colorado State Historical Society, Denver, Colo.
CSmH	Henry E. Huntington Library, San Marino, Calif.
CSt	Stanford University, Stanford, Calif.
CtY	Yale University, New Haven, Conn.
CU-B	Bancroft Library, University of California, Berkeley, Calif.
DLC	Library of Congress, Washington, D.C. Numbers following DLC-USG represent the series and volume of military records in the USG papers.
DNA	National Archives, Washington, D.C. Additional numbers identify record groups.
IaHA	Iowa State Department of History and Archives, Des Moines, Iowa.
I-ar	Illinois State Archives, Springfield, Ill.
IC	Chicago Public Library, Chicago, Ill.
ICarbS	Southern Illinois University, Carbondale, Ill.
ICHi	Chicago Historical Society, Chicago, Ill.
ICN	Newberry Library, Chicago, Ill.
ICU	University of Chicago, Chicago, Ill.
IHi	Illinois State Historical Library, Springfield, Ill.
In	Indiana State Library, Indianapolis, Ind.
InFtwL	Lincoln National Life Foundation, Fort Wayne, Ind.
InHi	Indiana Historical Society, Indianapolis, Ind.
InNd	University of Notre Dame, Notre Dame, Ind.
InU	Indiana University, Bloomington, Ind.
KHi	Kansas State Historical Society, Topeka, Kan.
MdAN	United States Naval Academy Museum, Annapolis, Md.
MeB	Bowdoin College, Brunswick, Me.
MH	Harvard University, Cambridge, Mass.

MHi	Massachusetts Historical Society, Boston, Mass.
MiD	Detroit Public Library, Detroit, Mich.
MiU-C	William L. Clements Library, University of Michigan, Ann Arbor, Mich.
MoSHi	Missouri Historical Society, St. Louis, Mo.
NHi	New-York Historical Society, New York, N.Y.
NIC	Cornell University, Ithaca, N.Y.
NjP	Princeton University, Princeton, N.J.
NjR	Rutgers University, New Brunswick, N.J.
NN	New York Public Library, New York, N.Y.
NNP	Pierpont Morgan Library, New York, N.Y.
NRU	University of Rochester, Rochester, N.Y.
OClWHi	Western Reserve Historical Society, Cleveland, Ohio.
OFH	Rutherford B. Hayes Library, Fremont, Ohio.
OHi	Ohio Historical Society, Columbus, Ohio.
OrHi	Oregon Historical Society, Portland, Ore.
PCarlA	U.S. Army Military History Institute, Carlisle Barracks, Pa.
PHi	Historical Society of Pennsylvania, Philadelphia, Pa.
PPRF	Rosenbach Foundation, Philadelphia, Pa.
RPB	Brown University, Providence, R.I.
TxHR	Rice University, Houston, Tex.
USG 3	Maj. Gen. Ulysses S. Grant 3rd, Clinton, N.Y.
USMA	United States Military Academy Library, West Point, N.Y.
ViHi	Virginia Historical Society, Richmond, Va.
ViU	University of Virginia, Charlottesville, Va.
WHi	State Historical Society of Wisconsin, Madison, Wis.
Wy-Ar	Wyoming State Archives and Historical Department, Cheyenne, Wyo.
WyU	University of Wyoming, Laramie, Wyo.

Chronology

—————

JUNE 1. The battle of Cold Harbor, Va., started with U.S. forces making initial gains. USG planned to renew the assault the following day but postponed the attack due to delays in troop movements.

JUNE 3. U.S. forces made an unsuccessful second assault at Cold Harbor sustaining heavy casualties. "I regret this assault more than any one I have ever ordered," USG later remarked.

JUNE 3. USG directed that surplus troops in the West be used against Mobile.

JUNE 4. USG ordered Maj. Gen. George G. Meade to fire art. at Cold Harbor to keep C.S.A. forces awake.

JUNE 5. USG planned to move the Army of the Potomac across the James River to attack C.S.A. forces south of Richmond.

JUNE 5–7. USG corresponded with C.S.A. Gen. Robert E. Lee regarding wounded between the lines at Cold Harbor.

JUNE 7. USG sent Maj. Gen. Philip H. Sheridan on a cav. raid from Cold Harbor to destroy C.S.A. supply lines with instructions to connect with Maj. Gen. David Hunter advancing on Lynchburg, Va.

JUNE 8. President Abraham Lincoln nominated to run for a second term.

JUNE 9.   USG believed that the campaign in Va. would ultimately "settle down to a siege."

JUNE 11.   USG instructed Maj. Gen. Benjamin F. Butler about the movement of U.S. forces south of the James River.

JUNE 12.   USG began a movement to cross the James River.

JUNE 13.   USG arrived at the James River.

JUNE 14.   USG at Bermuda Hundred, Va.

JUNE 15.   USG decided to make City Point, Va., his hd. qrs. for operations against Petersburg, Va.

JUNE 15.   Maj. Gen. William F. Smith attacked and captured lightly held C.S.A. fortifications in front of Petersburg but inexplicably failed to exploit his advantage.

JUNE 16.   USG arrived near Petersburg, while U.S. forces assaulted C.S.A. lines with limited success.

JUNE 17.   U.S. forces under Butler failed to break the railroad between Petersburg and Richmond.

JUNE 18.   After another unsuccessful assault, USG suspended offensive operations and began the siege of Petersburg.

JUNE 19.   C.S.S. *Alabama* sunk by the U.S.S. *Kearsarge* off Cherbourg, France.

JUNE 19.   Sheridan returned from cav. raid without making a junction with Hunter.

JUNE 21.   Lincoln arrived at City Point and toured the front with USG.

JUNE 22.   USG sent cav. led by Brig. Gen. James H. Wilson to interdict supply lines at Burkeville, Va.

JUNE 22.   Lee repulsed an attempt to cut the Weldon Railroad as USG extended the siege lines west and south of Petersburg.

JUNE 23.   USG anticipated a protracted siege at Petersburg.

JUNE 24.   USG suggested the removal of Maj. Gen. William S. Rosecrans.

JUNE 24.   Sheridan's cav. repulsed an attack at St. Mary's Church, Va., while on the way to City Point.

JUNE 25.   Coalminers of 48th Pa. began a tunnel at Petersburg to undermine C.S.A. works. USG informed on July 4.

JUNE 27.   U.S. forces under Maj. Gen. William T. Sherman repulsed at the battle of Kennesaw Mountain, Ga.

JUNE 28.   USG planned to attack C.S.A. lines between Petersburg and Richmond.

JULY 1.   USG requested that Butler be relieved from field command and asked for a specific order on July 6. After talking with Butler on July 9, USG suspended the order the following day.

JULY 1.   Wilson returned with his cav. from Burkeville losing his art. and much of his equipment. Damage inflicted by the raiders on C.S.A. supply lines was quickly repaired.

JULY 2.   Sherman forced evacuation of C.S.A. positions at Kennesaw Mountain by a flanking movement.

JULY 2.   Maj. Gen. William F. Smith requested a leave of absence, complaining bitterly to USG about Butler.

JULY 3.   C.S.A. Lt. Gen. Jubal A. Early, continuing an advance in the Shenandoah Valley, arrived at Harpers Ferry, W. Va.

JULY 5.   USG ordered some cav. and a div. of the 6th Army Corps to Washington via Baltimore to counter Early's movement.

JULY 5.   USG concluded that C.S.A. lines at Petersburg were too strong to be taken by frontal assault.

JULY 7.   USG requested the relief of Maj. Gen. Franz Sigel because his "operations from the beginning of the war have been so unsuccessful . . ."

JULY 8.   USG asked Lee to allow Col. James F. Jaquess and James R. Gilmore to pass through C.S.A. lines on an unofficial peace mission sanctioned by Lincoln.

JULY 9.   USG ordered the remainder of the 6th Army Corps and the 19th Army Corps to Washington to defend against Early.

JULY 9.   Maj. Gen. Lewis Wallace defeated by Early in the battle of Monocacy, Md., but delayed the C.S.A. advance on Washington by one day.

JULY 11.   Early's forces skirmished with U.S. forces in the defenses of Washington.

JULY 12.   USG directed Maj. Gen. Horatio G. Wright to pursue Early as C.S.A. forces withdrew from Washington.

JULY 14.   USG ordered that the Shenandoah Valley be stripped of supplies "so that Crows flying over it for the balance of this season will have to carry their provender with them."

JULY 14.   C.S.A. Maj. Gen. Nathan B. Forrest checked at the battle of Tupelo or Harrisburg, Miss.

JULY 16.   USG warned Sherman that C.S.A. reinforcements might be sent to Ga. in light of the failure of the raid against Washington.

JULY 17.   C.S.A. Gen. Joseph E. Johnston replaced in command in Ga. by Gen. John B. Hood.

JULY 18.   USG wanted to establish one dept. to control all operations around Washington and in the Shenandoah Valley.

JULY 18.   Lincoln issued a call for 500,000 volunteers.

JULY 19.   USG relieved Maj. Gen. William F. Smith from command of the 18th Army Corps.

JULY 20.   Hood defeated at the battle of Peachtree Creek, Ga.

JULY 21.   USG decided to leave the 6th Army Corps and 19th Army Corps in the Shenandoah Valley for offensive operations.

JULY 22.   Maj. Gen. James B. McPherson killed during the battle of Atlanta as U.S. forces closed in on the city.

JULY 24.   Early won the second battle of Kernstown, Va., and again moved north through the Shenandoah Valley.

JULY 24.   Meade informed USG that he had little confidence that an assault on Maj. Gen. Ambrose E. Burnside's front would succeed after the explosion of the mine.

JULY 25.   USG planned a two-pronged offensive at Petersburg operating north of the James River to draw off C.S.A. forces from the area of the undermined line, south of the city.

JULY 27.   USG, at Deep Bottom, Va., oversaw the movement of Maj. Gen. Winfield S. Hancock north of the James River.

JULY 28.   USG again at Deep Bottom to observe Hancock's movements which had drawn substantial C.S.A. forces north of the river weakening C.S.A. lines south of Petersburg.

JULY 28.   Hood defeated in the battle of Ezra Church, Ga.

JULY 30.   USG witnessed the battle of the Crater, later calling it the "saddest affair I have witnessed in this war. Such opportunity for carrying fortifications I have never seen and do not expect again to have."

JULY 31.   USG conferred with Lincoln at Fort Monroe, Va., for five hours.

AUG. 1.   USG decided to send Sheridan to the Shenandoah Valley to command "all the troops in the field with instructions to put himself south of the enemy and follow him to the death. . . ."

AUG. 2.   USG, ill after the battle of the Crater, requested a court of inquiry.

AUG. 4.   USG went to Washington to arrange affairs in the Shenandoah Valley after Lincoln telegraphed on Aug. 3 that nothing would be accomplished there unless "you watch it every day, and hour, and force it."

AUG. 5.   USG at War Dept. in Washington.

AUG. 5.   U.S. Navy victory at the battle of Mobile Bay.

AUG. 7.   USG at Washington.

AUG. 8.   USG at Fort Monroe on his way to City Point.

AUG. 9.   USG informed Maj. Gen. Henry W. Halleck that "Every part of the yard occupied as my Hd Qrs is filled with splinters and fragments of shells," as C.S.A. agents exploded an ordnance boat being unloaded at the wharf at City Point.

Aug. 12.   USG warned Sheridan that C.S.A. reinforcements might have gone to Shenandoah Valley.

Aug. 13.   USG arranged to reinforce Sherman.

Aug. 13.   USG granted Burnside a leave of absence from command of the 9th Army Corps after the failure of the battle of the Crater. He decided on Sept. 1 not to allow Burnside to return to the field although never officially relieving him from command.

Aug. 14.   USG, at Strawberry Plains, Va., observed a demonstration led by Hancock.

Aug. 15.   USG made clear his determination to continue the siege at Petersburg despite numerous disappointments.

The Papers of Ulysses S. Grant
June 1–August 15, 1864

======

To Brig. Gen. Lorenzo Thomas

Cold Harbor Va. June 1st 1864

BRIG GEN L. THOMAS
ADJUTANT GENERAL U. S. A.
GENERAL,

In compliance with War Dept. General Orders No. 244 Series of 1863, I have the honor to report the following named Officers as composing my Staff and on duty with me as such during the past month—

Brig Gen John A. Rawlins Chief of Staff—
Lieut Col. T. S. Bowers Asst. Adjt. Genl.
Lieut Col. C. B. Comstock Aid-de-Camp—
Lieut Col. F. T. Dent Aid-de-Camp—
Lieut Col. Horace Porter Aid-de-Camp—
Lieut Col. O. E. Babcock Aid-de-Camp—
Lieut Col. Wm. L. Duff Asst. Inspector General—
Lieut Col. Wm R. Rowley Military Secretary—
Lieut Col Adam Badeau Military Secretary—
Capt E. S. Parker Asst. Adjt. Genl.
Capt Geo. K. Leet Asst. Adjt. Genl.
Capt. P. T. Hudson Aid-de-Camp—
Lieut Wm M. Dunn Jr. Addnl. Aid-de-Camp—
Capt. H. W. Janes Asst. Quarter Master—

Very Respectfully
Your Obt. Servt.
U. S. GRANT
Lieut Genl.

LS, DNA, RG 94, ACP 4754/1885. Subsequent staff reports, usually dated the first of each month, followed the same format and will not be printed.

To Brig. Gen. John J. Abercrombie

Near Haws Shop Va. June 1. 1864

BRIG GEN. J. J. ABERCROMBIE
COM'D'G U. S. FORCES, WHITE HOUSE VA

GENERAL: Capt G. H Mendell[1] of the Engineers, reports to you for the purpose of laying out proper fortifications for the ~~Depot~~ protection of our Depot at the White House. From the proximity of the enemy's position to the White House a dash upon our supplies there is possible at any time. The temptation to such a dash will be very great. You will therefore please use every man within your command who can be spared from other duties upon such works as Capt Mendell with your approval, may lay out. Stragglers who go to the rear may also be worked upon the fortifications, under guard until such time as it may be convenient to return them to their Command. The importance of the work to ~~the~~ be done at White House is such that I hope it will secure your immediate attention.

Gen Meade will be sending back forty pieces of Artillery to be shipped to Washington. Such of them as you may deem it advisable to retain for your fortifications you are authorized to retain

U S GRANT
Lt Gen

Copies, DLC-USG, V, 45, 59, 66; DNA, RG 108, Letters Sent. *O.R.*, I, xxxvi, part 3, 471–72.

On June 3, 1864, Brig. Gen. John J. Abercrombie, White House, wrote to Brig. Gen. John A. Rawlins. "We have a locomotive here and a construction corps under Major Wentz, of the Engineers, who says the road can be repaired to the Chickahominy in four days—Shall it be done? Genl. Ames had been already ordered forward when your despatch arrived—I did not intend keeping him longer than to-day—" LS, DNA, RG 108, Letters Received. *O.R.*, I, xxxvi, part 3, 563. On the same day, Rawlins wrote to Abercrombie. "Your communication of this day received—Let Maj Wentz commence at once to repair the rail road from White House to Chickahomony—" Copies, DLC-USG, V, 45, 59, 66; DNA, RG 108, Letters Sent. *O.R.*, I, xxxvi, part 3, 563.

On June 5, Abercrombie wrote to Rawlins. "The telegraph wire between this place and West Point and beyond has been tampered with. I inclose herewith telegrams from the operator at West Point; also communications from operator here. I have sent all my available cavalry force, 125 mounted men, to West Point." *Ibid.*, p. 634.

1. George H. Mendell of Pa., USMA 1852, served as a topographical engineer (1852–59) and at USMA (1859–63), then commanded the U.S. Engineer Battalion, Army of the Potomac. See *ibid.*, I, xxxvi, part 1, 317; *ibid.*, I, xl, part 1, 300–2.

To Julia Dent Grant

<del>May</del> June 1st 1864

Dear Julia,

There has been a very severe battle this afternoon and as I write, now 9 O'clock at night firing is still continued on some parts of the battle line. What the result of the days fighting has been I will know but little about before midnight and possibly not then. The rebels are making a desperate fight and I presume will continue to do so as long as they can get a respectable number of men to stand.

I send pay accounts for May to Washington by Col. Bowers, who starts in the morning, with directions to send you $800 00 of it. April pay I sent all to Jones in liquidation of my indebtedness.[1] In June I hope to pay all up.—I see by the papers dear little Nellie acquitted herself very handsomely at the Sanitary Fair.[2] I would like very much to see you and the children but cannot hope to do so until this Campaign is over. How long it will last is a problem. I can hardly hope to get through this month.—With the night booming of Artillery and musketry I do not feel much like writing so you must excuse a short letter this time. Dr. Sharp is with me apparently enjoying himself very much. Fred. has been suffering intensely for several days with rheumatism. He has to lay upon his back in the ambulance unable to turn himself. I think he will be well in a day or two. Orvil Grant is at the White House and will probably be here to morrow.[3]

My love to all. Kisses for yourself and the children.

Ulys.

ALS, DLC-USG.

1. See letter to Julia Dent Grant, April 27, 1864.

2. See letter to Ellen Wrenshall Grant, June 4, 1864.

3. Lt. Col. Frederick T. Dent noted in his diary, June 2–5, 1864, the presence of USG's brother Orvil at hd. qrs. Typescript, USGA. An account by Frank M. Pixley of his visit to USG's hd. qrs. with Orvil and three others, first published in the San Francisco *Bulletin*, was reprinted in the *Galena Weekly Gazette*, Sept. 27, 1864. See John Gibbon, *Personal Recollections of the Civil War* (New York, 1928; reprinted, Dayton, Ohio, 1978), p. 235.

To Maj. Gen. Henry W. Halleck

Bethsaida Church Va.
7 a m June 2. 1864

MAJ GEN HALLECK,
CHIEF OF STAFF,

Yesterday afternoon an attack was ordered to be made on our left at Cold Harbor by the 6th Corps and the troops under Smith, Warren, Burnside and Hancock being held in readiness to advance in their respective fronts. The attack was made with spirit about 5 P M continuing until after dark, resulting in our carrying the enemy's works on the right of the 6th Corps where we still hold them, and also the first line in front of Smith. The latter however were commanded by another line in rear which made those carried untenable. The enemy made repeated assaults on each of the Corps not [en]gaged in the main assault but were [r]epulsed with loss in Every instance,

Several hundred prisoners w[ere] taken but I cannot now say what number [nor] estimate either our or the enemy's Casualties.

During the night the Enemy made several assaults to regain what they had lost but failed—

U S GRANT
Lt Genl

Telegram received (at 8:30 P.M.), DNA, RG 107, Telegrams Collected (Bound); copies, *ibid.*, RG 108, Letters Sent; DLC-USG, V, 45, 59, 66. *O.R.*, I, xxxvi, part 1, 10–11; *ibid.*, I, xxxvi, part 3, 477. On June 2, 1864, 9:30 P.M., Maj. Gen. Henry W. Halleck telegraphed to USG. "Yours of 7 A M just recieved. I have nearly exhausted all my resources of volunteers to reinforce you; but if you can use them to advantage I can send you six or eight good regiments of hundred days militia. Many of them are anxious to go. Shall I send them?" ALS (telegram sent), DNA, RG 107, Telegrams Collected (Bound); telegram received, *ibid. O.R.*, I, xxxvi, part 3, 478. On June 4, 1:00 P.M., USG telegraphed to Halleck. "The one hundred (100) day men can be of no great service here, but if they can be just as well supplied at White House as elsewhere it might be well to put as many of them at that point as can be spared" Telegram received (on June 5, 10:10 A.M.), DNA, RG 107, Telegrams Collected (Bound); copies, *ibid.*, RG 108, Letters Sent; DLC-USG, V, 45, 59, 66. *O.R.*, I, xxxvi, part 3, 569. On the same day, 2:20 P.M., Halleck telegraphed to USG. "In the month of May we sent to the Army of the Potomac six thousand six hundred & eighty three cavalry horses, in addition to the cavalrymen remounted here. About a thousand more cavalry horses are being shipped to White House. Not hearing from you in regard to the Ohio militia, I am preparing ten regiments for the field & will send them as fast as transportation can be procured. The 5th Md. regt. vols. has been ordered from Fort Delaware. Genl Gillmore thinks that five thousand more men can safely be withdrawn from Dept of the South; Genl Hatch on the contrary is asking for reinforcements. Genl Crook at Lewisburg May 31st; expected to join Genl Hunter at Staunton in about six days. Genl Canby has sent forces to Memphis to protect Sherman's communications. I doubt if he will be able to do much on Mobile at present. Moreover, the movement would be too late to help Sherman. The latter is in possession of Alltona Pass and [is] moving against Marietta." ALS (telegram sent), DNA, RG 107, Telegrams Collected (Bound); telegram received, *ibid. O.R.*, I, xxxvi, part 3, 569; (incomplete) *ibid.*, I, xxxiv, part 4, 211.

On June 1, 10:15 P.M., Maj. Gen. George G. Meade wrote to USG. "What are your views about tomorrow—I think the attack should be renewed as soon as Hancock is within supporting distance, and should be made by Wright Smith & Hancock—I have heard nothing from Smith and do not believe he was much engaged this afternoon—He is aware of the telegraph from Wrights Hd. Qrs but does not report—Hancock has been urged to push forward, with despatch, & guides sent him—I think his advance will be at Coal Harbor early in the morning—say by 6. a m   Warren does not seem to have effected any thing in his front except repulsing attacks made on him—He should however be ordered to attack in conjunction with the others—Burnside I would hold ready to re-enforce Warren if necessary— . . . Hd Qrs to move at 7. a m to a point on the road to Coal Harbor & in rear of that place.—" ALS, DNA, RG 108, Letters Received. *O.R.*, I, xxxvi, part 3, 432–33. At 10:40 P.M., Lt. Col. Cyrus B. Comstock, "Camp near Via's house," twice wrote to Meade. "Lt. Gen. Grant desires me to say that he thinks the attack should be renewed tomorrow morning by all means, but not till Hancock is within supporting distance of Smith. Warren should attack in conjunction with Smith & Wright and Burnside be held in readiness to support Warren." "Lt. Gen. Grant desires that Gen. Lockwood be at once relieved from his command, ~~orders for him will be sent in the morning.~~ and directed to report to these H. Q. for orders." ALS, DNA, RG 94, War Records Office, Army of the Potomac. *O.R.*, I, xxxvi, part 3, 433. On June 2, Lt. Col. Theodore S. Bowers issued Special Orders No. 26. "Brig Gen. H. H. Lockwood is hereby relieved from duty with the 5th Corps Army of the Potomac, and will proceed to Baltimore and await further orders, reporting to the Adjutant General of the Army." Copies, DLC-USG, V, 57, 62, 66. *O.R.*, I, xxxvi, part 3, 494.

On June 1, 9:30 P.M., Maj. Gen. Horatio G. Wright wrote to Maj. Gen. Andrew A. Humphreys stating that C.S.A. forces had attacked that evening.

Ibid., p. 457. USG endorsed this letter. "General Hancock had better be advised
to get one division of his corps through to Wright before daylight, and the whole
corps as soon as possible." *Ibid.*

On June 2, 2:30 P.M., Halleck telegraphed to USG. "The telegraph line
from Gloucester to West Point north of York River has been cut, probably by
the country people. I think Genl. Smith should be directed to send a small cavalry
picket along the line for its protection." ALS (telegram sent), DNA, RG 107,
Telegrams Collected (Bound); telegram received, *ibid*. *O.R.*, I, xxxvi, part 3,
477. This telegram is not entered in USG's register of letters received.

To Maj. Gen. George G. Meade

June 2d/64 2 p. m.

MAJ. GEN. MEADE,
COMD.G A. P.
GENERAL,

In view of the want of preparation for an attack this evening,
and the heat and want of energy among the men from moving
during the night last night, I think it advisable to postpone assault
until early to-morrow morning. All changes of position already
ordered should be completed to day and a good nights rest given
the men preparatory to an assault at say 4.30 a. m. in the morning.

Very respectfully
U. S. GRANT
Lt. Gen.

ALS, DNA, RG 94, War Records Office, Army of the Potomac. *O.R.*, I, xxxvi,
part 3, 478.

On June 2, 1864, 10:25 P.M., Maj. Gen. George G. Meade wrote to USG.
"I send Maj. Roebling of Warren's Staff who will explain the position of affairs
on the right when he left—It would appear from Maj. R's statement that the
enemy at dark were in force in front both of Burnside & Warren—I do not believe they will remain in front of Burnside—I have however sent orders both to
Warren & Burnside that they must at all hazards attack the enemy tomorrow at
4.30 a m and if he is not in force in their front they must swing round to the left
& follow up & attack on Smiths right flank—In like manner should the enemy be
in great force in their front & check them, then our attacks here ought to prevail,
and we will swing by the right and move up on Warren's left. In order to insure
energy and harmony of action, I propose to place, with your approval, Burnside
under Warren's orders." ALS (incomplete), DNA, RG 108, Letters Received.
O.R., I, xxxvi, part 3, 478. On the same day, USG wrote to Meade. "From Maj.
Robelings account Ewel's Corps has put itself in a position where it should be

badly used up if it remains until morning. What you have directed is right, though I do not know whether it would be right to place Burnside under Warren, the latter being his junior, but I would direct him to advise with Warren and to act in concert with him." ALS, DNA, RG 94, War Records Office, Army of the Potomac. *O.R.*, I, xxxvi, part 3, 478–79.

To Maj. Gen. Henry W. Halleck

———

Head Q'rs Army U. S.
Coal Harbor Va.
June 3rd 2. P. M 1864

MAJ GEN H. W. HALLECK
CHIEF OF STAFF.

We assaulted at 4 30 A. M this morning driving the Enemy within his entrenchments at all points but without gaining any decisive advantage—Our troops now occupy a position close to the Enemy—some places within fifty yards—and are remaining. Our loss was not severe nor do I suppose the Enemy to have lost heavily. We captured over 300 prisoners mostly from Breckenridge

U. S. GRANT
Lt Genl

Telegram received (on June 4, 1864, 7:55 A.M.), DNA, RG 107, Telegrams Collected (Bound); copies, *ibid.*, RG 108, Letters Sent; DLC-USG, V, 45, 59, 66. *O.R.*, I, xxxvi, part 1, 11; *ibid.*, I, xxxvi, part 3, 524.

To Maj. Gen. Henry W. Halleck

———

Head Qrs Armies U S.
Coal Harbor Va.
June 3rd 3. P. M. 1864

MAJ GEN H W HALLECK
CHIEF OF STAFF.

In view of the time it would take to get orders to New Orleans and to transport troops from there here, I do not think it advisable to bring the 19th Corps to this field—Since Banks disaster too all the troops in the Trans Mississippi Division may be required there.

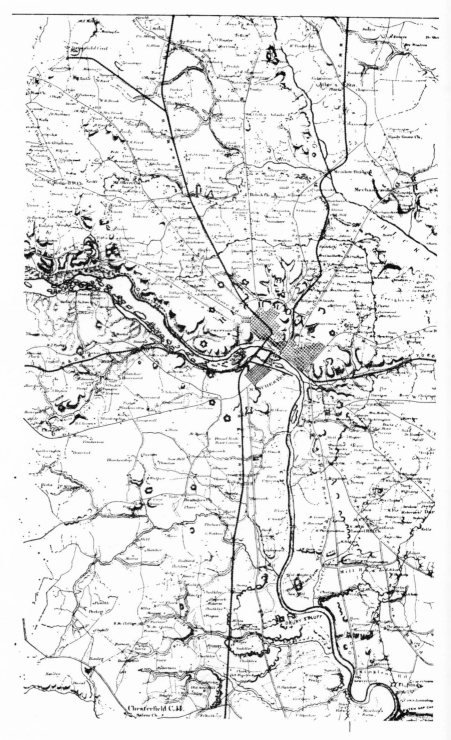

Cold Harbor, Richmond and Vicinity

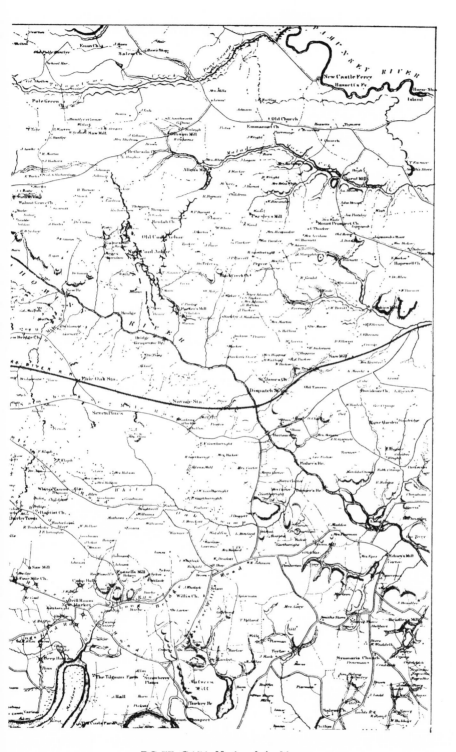

RG 77, G151, *National Archives*

If there are any surplus troops West they could be advantageously
used against Mobile as suggested in Sherman's despatch of May
30th.[1] Please so order and let Reynolds or Franklin command the
expedition.

The sixty 60 pontoon boats coming from New York with what
we have here and at Ft Monroe will be sufficient

U S. GRANT
Lt Gen'l

Telegram received (on June 4, 1864, 8:00 A.M.), DNA, RG 107, Telegrams
Collected (Bound); copies, *ibid.*, RG 108, Letters Sent; DLC-USG, V, 45, 59,
66. *O.R.*, I, xxxiv, part 4, 185; *ibid.*, I, xxxvi, part 3, 524. On May 29, 8:30
P.M., Secretary of War Edwin M. Stanton telegraphed to USG. "A telegram of
this morning from General Butler giving extracts from the Rebel papers as th to
the retreat of Banks contains the following suggestion which is submitted for
your directions. 'In view of this news, as the 19th Army Corps are disengaged,
I respectfully suggest that it be sent by water to land here, or at West Point in
reach of Gen. Grant. Gen. Weitzell who so well knows the military situation in
Louisiana concurs in the suggestion. It can be here in 14 days to reinforce army
depleted by the battles to be fought in the meantime.' " ALS (telegram sent),
DNA, RG 107, Telegrams Collected (Bound); telegram received (on May 30),
ibid., RG 108, Letters Received. *O.R.*, I, xxxiv, part 4, 103.

1. On May 30, 8:00 A.M., Maj. Gen. William T. Sherman telegraphed to
Maj. Gen. Henry W. Halleck. ". . . If Banks and Porter are all out of Red river,
instead of acting offensively on West Louisiana I advise that the same Command
that A J Smith took with him, reinforced by two or Three Thousand from
Memphis & Vicksburg be sent to Pascagoula to act against Mobile in Concert
with Farrigut according to the original plan of the campaign   In case this is
feasible I wish the necessary orders to go direct from the General-in-Chief to
Gen A. J. Smith giving him authority to make up his command to 10.000 at
Vicksburg & Memphis and at once proceed via Ponchatrain to Pascagoula   I
know that all of Polks army and all the garrisons of Alabama and Fla. are with
Johnston, as we have prisoners who have been for two years on local duties in
those states as well as from their active divisions viz Loring, French and Mau-
ray . . ." Telegram received (at 9:30 P.M.), DNA, RG 107, Telegrams Collected
(Bound); *ibid.*, RG 108, Letters Received. *O.R.*, I, xxxviii, part 4, 351.

To Maj. Gen. Henry W. Halleck

Cold Harbor June 3rd/64

MAJ GEN HALLECK WASHINGTON—

Please order the 16th Corps staff to report to Gen Washburne
for duty. The 16th Corps is now without a Commander, that por-

tion of it in the field being commanded by Gen Dodge and the remainder by Gen Washburne. It may be well to leave this Corps without a named commander until Sherman can be heard from, when he may recommended the union of that portion of the 16th and 17th in the field into one Corps, and the peace establishment of them, the troops in West Tennessee and below, into another

U. S. GRANT Lt. Genl—

Copies, DLC-USG, V, 45, 59, 66; DNA, RG 108, Letters Sent. *O.R.*, I, xxxviii, part 4, 392. See letter to Elihu B. Washburne, June 9, 1864.

To Maj. Gen. George G. Meade

Cold Harbor, ~~May~~ June 3d/64 12.30 p. m.

MAJ. GEN. MEADE,
COMD.G A. P.
GENERAL,

The opinion of Corps commanders not being sanguine of success in case an assault is ordered you may direct a suspension of further advance for the present. Hold our most advanced positions and strengthen them. Whilst on the defensive our lines may be contracted from the right if practicable. Reconnoissances should be made in front of every Corps and advances made to advantageous positions by regular approaches. To aid the expedition under Gen. Hunter it is necessary that we should detain all the Army now with Lee until the former gets well on his way to Lynchburg. To do this effectually it will be better to keep the enemy out of the intrenchments of Richmond than to have them go back there.

Wright & Hancock should be ready to assault in case the enemy should break through Gen. Smith's lines, and all should be ready to resist an assault.

Very respectfully
U. S. GRANT
Lt. Gen.

ALS, DNA, RG 94, War Records Office, Army of the Potomac. *O.R.*, I, xxxvi, part 3, 526.

On June 3, 1864, Maj. Gen. George G. Meade sent to USG a note received at 5:15 A.M., and messages at 5:30 A.M., 6:30 A.M., and 7:00 A.M. "Gen Barlow reports that he has enemys works with colors & guns   I am at Gen Wrights hd qrs" "Hancock reports Barlow could not hold the works carried but has retired a short distance & is about attacking again   Colors advancing & near the works. Heavy firing in Smiths front but no report of progress from either him or Wright" "I send dispatch from Hancock & reply. No reports from Wright & Smith . . . 'My first and second Divisions have both been engaged. The men are very close to the enemy under a crest but seem unable to carry it—Birney is occupying the advanced line of works vacated by 1st & 2nd Divisions in the morning to the assault—The Commanders of 1st & 2nd Divisions do not think they can use more troops than their own with any great certainty of success. I shall await your orders but express the opinion that if the first dash in an assault fails other attempts are not apt to succeed better.' . . . Your despatch recvd—You will make the attack and support it well so that in the event of being successful the advantage gained can be held   If unsuccessful report at once" ALS, DNA, RG 108, Letters Received. *O.R.*, I, xxxvi, part 3, 524–25. "Reports from Wright announce some progress   his advance occupies a line of the enemys pits   I presume their skirmish line—He reports the 18th corps having occupied the same line but retiring   His Wrights line is pushing on.—No report from Smith—I sent you one from Hancock reporting he was about attempting another assault written before my order to him to do so had reached him—I should be glad to have your views as to the continuance of these efforts if unsuccessful—" ALS, DNA, RG 94, War Records Office, Army of the Potomac. *O.R.*, I, xxxvi, part 3, 525. At 7:00 A.M., USG wrote to Meade. "The moment it becomes certain that an assault cannot succeed suspend the offensive. But when one does succeed push it vigorously & if necessary pile in troops at the successful point from wherever they can be taken,   I shall go to where you are in the course of one hour" Telegram received, DNA, RG 94, War Records Office, Army of the Potomac; copies, *ibid.*, RG 108, Letters Sent; DLC-USG, V, 45, 59, 66; Meade Papers, PHi. *O.R.*, I, xxxvi, part 3, 526.

At 5:45 P.M., Meade wrote to USG. "The telegrams you return are sent from here by me, so that you need not return them—Warren *was reinforced* by Birney & posted him on his left where he now is, forming connection between Smith & Warren—I have notified Warren there are no other troops to send him & that he & Burnside must contract their lines tonight.—Every thing is apparently quiet along the lines—We hold all our advanced positions & are entrenching   Tonight Hancock will establish batteries, and we will begin all along the lines digging up to the enemys works—I have sent out officers to each of the corps & to the hospitals to endeavor to form some estimate of the casualties today—" ALS, DNA, RG 108, Letters Received. *O.R.*, I, xxxvi, part 3, 526.

Also on June 3, USG wrote to Meade. "Might not two or more cohorns be well used in front of Barlow to-night?" ALS (misdated May 3), DNA, RG 94, War Records Office, Army of the Potomac. *O.R.*, I, xxxvi, part 3, 527. At 8:30 P.M., Meade wrote to USG. "The Coehorns have been in position and in use all the afternoon in Hancock's front." *Ibid.*

At 9:25 P.M., Meade wrote to USG. "Do you think it worth while to do any thing about the York river R. Rd in the way of bringing Locomotives & cars—If the weather continues good we can haul but if we have rain & are detained on the Chickahominy we shall be embarrassed with bad detestably bad roads"

ALS, DNA, RG 94, War Records Office, Army of the Potomac. *O.R.*, I, xxxvi, part 3, 527. USG endorsed this letter. "I think I will not order cars for the York River R. R. just yet. The wagons now at White House will give us supplies to about the 15th and before that I hope our base will be changed to the James River." AES, DNA, RG 94, War Records Office, Army of the Potomac. *O.R.*, I, xxxvi, part 3, 527.

To Maj. Gen. George G. Meade

Cold Harbor Va. June 4th/64 8.20 p. m.

MAJ. GEN. MEADE,
COMD.G A. P.
GENERAL,

If the firing this evening has been opened by the enemy without further attack, or if they attack and are repulsed, I think it will be well to retaliate by opening every battery that bears upon them at 12 or 1 to-night. It will have the effect to wake up the whole of the enemy's camp and keep them on the watch until day light

Respectfully &c
U. S. GRANT
Lt. Gen Com

ALS, DNA, RG 94, War Records Office, Army of the Potomac. *O.R.*, I, xxxvi, part 3, 570. On June 4, 1864, 8:30 P.M., Maj. Gen. George G. Meade wrote to USG. "I was about sending the accompanying despatch when your note arrived —I can order the batteries to be opened as you suggest, but whilst it keeps the enemy 'awake,' their reply which they will undoubtedly make, will keep our people awake, & in addition it will interfere with the approaches I have ordered to be made tonight.—" ALS, DNA, RG 94, War Records Office, Army of the Potomac. *O.R.*, I, xxxvi, part 3, 570. USG endorsed this letter. "It was only a desire to retaliate for annoyances that made me suggest opening our batteries to-night. If it is going to interfere with any operations you need not direct it." AES, DNA, RG 94, War Records Office, Army of the Potomac. *O.R.*, I, xxxvi, part 3, 570.

On the same day, Capt. Ely S. Parker issued Special Orders No. 27. "To prevent confusion and delay in the forwarding of supplies to the Army of the Potomac, all troops, posts and stations on the line over which such supplies at present or may hereafter pass, in consequence of any change in the position of the Army, are assigned to the command of Maj Gen Geo. G. Meade Commanding the Army of the Potomac, and will so report and receive orders without reference to the Territorial Department in which they may be or to which they may belong, until otherwise directed—" ADS, DLC-Benjamin F. Butler. *O.R.*, I, xxxvi, part 3, 569–70.

Also on June 4, Brig. Gen. Rufus Ingalls telegraphed to Brig. Gen. Montgomery C. Meigs. "Lt Gen Grant wishes to receive a Lot of Implements to be used by our Cavalry in the Destruction of Rail Roads. Gen Haupt had several Kinds at Alexandria Will you please have as many as can be procured sent by Express to Capt P P Pitkin at White House & inform me by Telegraph of what we may Expect" ALS (telegram sent—press), DNA, RG 107, Telegrams Collected (Bound); telegram received, *ibid.*

To Ellen Wrenshall Grant

————

Cold Harbor Va. June 4th 1864

MY DEAR LITTLE NELLY,

I received your pretty well written letter more than a week ago. You do not know how happy it made me feel to see how well my little girl not yet nine years old could write. I expect by the end of the year you and Buck will be able to speak German and then I will have to buy you those nice gold watches I promised. I see in the papers, and also from Mamas letter, that you have been representing "the Old Woman that lived in a Shoe" at the Fair! I know you must have enjoyed it very much. You must send me one of your photographs taken at the Fair.[1]

We have been fighting now for thirty days and have every prospect of still more fighting to do before we get into Richmond. When we do get there I shall go home to see you and Ma Fred, Buck and Jess. I expect Jess rides Little Rebel every day! I think when I go home I will get a little buggy to work Rebel in so that you and Jess can ride about the country during vacation. Tell Ma to let Fred learn French as soon as she thinks he is able to study it. It will be a great help to him when he goes to West Point. You must send this letter to Ma to read because I will not write to her to-day. Kiss Ma, Cousin Louisa[2] and all the young ladies for pa. Be a good little girl as you have always been, study your lessons and you will be contented and happy.

From
PAPA

ALS, ICHi.

1. A photograph of Ellen Grant as "The Old Woman in the Shoe" is repro-
duced in John Y. Simon, ed., *The Personal Memoirs of Julia Dent Grant* (New
York, 1975), following p. 170.
2. See letter to Louisa Boggs, April 24, 1864.

To Gen. Robert E. Lee

[*June 5, 1864*]

GEN R. E. LEE
COMD'G CONFEDERATE ARMY
GENERAL

It is reported to me that there are wounded men, probably of
both Armies, now lying exposed and suffering between the lines
occupied respectively by the two armies—Humanity would dictate
that some provision should be made to provide against such hard-
ships. I would propose therefore that hereafter when no battle is
raging, either party be authorized to send to any point between
the picket or skirmish line, unarmed men bearing litters, to pick up
their dead or wounded without being fired upon by the other party
—Any other method equally fair to both parties you may propose
for meeting the end designed will be accepted by me—

> I am Gen. Very Respectfully
> Your Obt Svt.
> U. S. GRANT Lt. Gen

Copies, DLC-USG, V, 45, 59, 66; DNA, RG 108, Letters Sent. *O.R.*, I, xxxvi,
part 3, 600. On June 5, 1864, Gen. Robert E. Lee wrote to USG. "I have the
honor to acknowledge the receipt of your letter of this date, proposing that hereafter, except in time of action, either party be at liberty to remove the dead and
wounded from between the lines. I fear that such an arrangement will lead to
misunderstanding and difficulty. I propose therefore instead, that when either
party desires to remove their dead or wounded, a flag of truce be sent as is customary. It will always afford me pleasure to comply with such a request, as far
as circumstances will permit." Copy, ICHi. *O.R.*, I, xxxvi, part 3, 600. On June
7, 11:00 A.M., USG telegraphed to Secretary of War Edwin M. Stanton. "The
subjoined correspondence [h]as just been exchanged between the commanders
of the two armies—" Copies (telegram sent), DNA, RG 107, Telegrams Collected (Unbound); telegram received, *ibid.*, Telegrams Collected (Bound). At
2:00 P.M. and 5:30 P.M., USG transmitted the remainder of the correspondence.

On June 5, 1:00 P.M., Maj. Gen. Winfield S. Hancock had written to Brig. Gen. Seth Williams asking that arrangements be made to move wounded men who had remained in front of the lines since June 3. *O.R.*, I, xxxvi, part 3, 603. Maj. Gen. George G. Meade endorsed this letter. "Respectfully referred to Lieutenant-General Grant. Is it possible to ask, under flag of truce, for permission to remove the wounded now lying between our lines, and which the enemy's sharpshooters prevent me bringing off? The wounded are lying in front of the Second, Sixth, and Eighteenth Corps." *Ibid.*, p. 604. USG also endorsed this letter. "A flag might be sent proposing to suspend firing where the wounded are, until each party get their own. I have no objection to such a course." *Ibid.* At 1:30 P.M., Meade wrote to USG. "Any communication by flag of truce will have to come from you, as the enemy do not recognize me as in command whilst you are present." ALS, DNA, RG 108, Letters Received. *O.R.*, I, xxxvi, part 3, 599.

To Maj. Gen. Henry W. Halleck

Cold Harbor
June 5th 1864 7 p m

MAJ GEN HALLECK
CHF OF STAFF

The object in sending troops to Mobile now would not be so much to assist Genl Sherman against Johnston as to secure for him a base of supplies after his work is done. Mobile also important to us and would be a great loss to the enemy. Let the one hundred day men, such of them as you have to spare, come on

U S GRANT
Lt Genl

Telegram received, DNA, RG 107, Telegrams Collected (Bound); copies, *ibid.*, RG 108, Letters Sent; DLC-USG, V, 45, 59, 66. *O.R.*, I, xxxvi, part 3, 599; *ibid.*, I, xxxix, part 2, 79. See telegram to Maj. Gen. Henry W. Halleck, June 3, 1864.

To Maj. Gen. Henry W. Halleck

Cold Harbor Va. June 5th 1864

MAJ. GEN. H. W. HALLECK,
CHIEF OF STAFF OF THE ARMY,
GENERAL,

A full survey of all the ground satisfies me that it would not be practicable to hold a line Northeast of Richmond that would protect the Fredericksburg rail-road to enable us to use it for supplying the Army. To do so would give us a long vulnerable line of road to protect, exhausting much of our strength in guarding it, and would leave open to the enemy all of his lines of communications on the South side of the James. My idea from the start has been to beat Lee's Army, if possible, North of Richmond, then after destroying his lines of communication North of the James river to transfer the Army to the South side and besiege Lee in Richmond, or follow him South if he should retreat.

I now find after more than thirty days of trial that the enemy deems it of the first importance to run no risks with the Armies they now have. They act purely on the defensive, behind breast works, or febly on the offensive immediately in front of them and where, in case of repulse, they can instantly retire behind them. Without a greater sacrifice of human life than I am willing to make all cannot be accomplished that I had designed outside of the City. I have therefore resolved upon the following plan. I will continue to hold substantially the ground now occupied by the Army of the Potomac, taking advantage of any favorable circumstance that may present itself, until the cavalry can be sent West to destroy the Va. Central rail-road from about Beaver Dam for some twenty-five or thirty miles West. When this is effected I will move the Army to the South side of James River either by crossing the Chickahominy and marching near to City Point, or by going to the mouth of the Chickahominy, on the North side, and crossing there. To provide for this last, and most probable, contingency six or more Ferry-boats of the largest size ought to be immediately provided.

Once on the South side of James river I can cut off all sources of supply to the enemy except what is furnished by the Canal. If Hunter succeeds in reaching Lynchburg that will be lost to him also. Should Hunter not succeed I will still make the effort to destroy the Canal by sending Cavalry up the South side of the river with a pontoon train to cross wherever they can.

The feeling of the two Armies now seems to be that the rebels can protect themselves only by strong intrenchments, whilst our Army is not only confidant of protecting itself, without intrenchments, but that it can beat and drive the enemy whenever and wherever he can be found without this this protection.

Very respectfully
U. S. GRANT
Lt. Gen.

ALS, deCoppet Collection, NjP. *O.R.*, I, xxxvi, part 1, 11–12; *ibid.*, I, xxxvi, part 3, 598–99. On June 7, 1864, Maj. Gen. Henry W. Halleck wrote to USG. "Your letter of the 5th by Lieut Col Babcock was recieved last evening. Genl Meigs has been advised of your wishes in regard to Ferry-boats. He will keep all he has or can procure in the vicinity of Fort Monroe subject to your orders. Many of the side-wheel boats in the Qr Mr. Dept will also answer all the purposes of Ferry-boats. The barges will also be excellent for teams and stores, and can be towed by the Tugs. Every thing will be sent forward as soon as you direct. They are now mostly engaged as transports to White House. Nothing has recently been heard of Genls Hunter & Crook. Sherman is still doing well, but some apprehension has been felt about Forrests movements to cut off his communications. Genl Canby has sent forces to Memphis to assist in driving Forrest out of that country. Nothing recently from Steele. I enclose a list of the troops forwarded from this Dept to the Army of the Potomac since the campaign opened—48.265 men. I shall send you a few regiments more, when all resources will be exhausted, till another draft is made." ALS, DNA, RG 108, Letters Sent (Press). *O.R.*, I, xxxvi, part 3, 665; *ibid.*, I, xxxvii, part 1, 601–2. The list enclosed is printed *ibid.*, I, xxxvi, part 3, 665–66.

To Maj. Gen. George G. Meade

———

Cold Harbor Va. June 5th/64

MAJ. GEN. MEADE,
COMD.G A. P.
GENERAL,

The object of the Cavalry expedition to Charlottesville & Gordonsville is to effectually break up the rail-road connection between Richmond and the Shenandoah Valley and Lynchburg. To secure this end they should go as far as Charlottesville and work upon the Lynchburg branch and main line to Staunton for several miles beyond the junction. This done they could work back this way to where the road is already destroyed or until driven off by a superior force.

It is desirable that every rail on the road destroyed should be so bent or twisted as to make it impossible to repair the road without supplying new rails. After the work is accomplished herin directed the Cavalry will rejoin the main Army keeping North of the Pamunky until the position of the Army is known to them. It may be found necessary to keep on the North side as far down as West Point.

Instructions will be sent to Gen. Hunter by the Cavalry expedition. He will be required to join his force to Gen. Sheridans and return with him to the Army of the Potom[ac.] If it is found practicable whilst the Cavalry is at the most Westerly point reached by it to detach a Brigade or more to go over to the James River and destroy the Canal it will be a service well repaying for three or four days detention.

Respectfully
U. S. GRANT
Lt. Gen.

ALS, DNA, RG 94, War Records Office, Army of the Potomac. *O.R.*, I, xxxvi, part 3, 599; *ibid.*, I, xxxvii, part 1, 593.

To Gen. Robert E. Lee

Hdqrs Armies of the U. S.
June 6th 1864

GEN R. E. LEE.
COMD'G ARMY NO. VA.
GENERAL,

Your communication of yesterdays date is received—I will send immediately as you propose, to collect the dead and wounded between the lines of the two armies, and will also instruct that you be allowed to do the same—

I propose that the time for doing this be between the hours of 12 M. and 3 P. M. to day—

I will direct all parties going out to bear a white flag and not to attempt to go beyond where we have dead or wounded and not beyond or on ground occupied by your troops—

Very Respectfully
U. S GRANT Lt. Gen

Copies, DLC-USG, V, 45, 59, 66; DNA, RG 108, Letters Sent. *O.R.*, I, xxxvi, part 3, 638. On June 6, 1864, Gen. Robert E. Lee wrote to USG. "I have the honor to acknowledge the receipt of your letter of this date, and regret to find that I did not make myself understood in my communication of yesterday. I intended to say that I could not consent to the burial of the dead and removal of the wounded between the armies in the way you proposed, but that when either party desires such permission, it shall be asked for by flag of truce in the usual way. Until I receive a proposition from you on the subject, to which I can exccede propriety. I have directed any parties you may send under white flags as mentioned in your letter to be turned back." Copy, ICHi. *O.R.*, I, xxxvi, part 3, 638.

On the same day, USG again wrote to Lee. "The knowledge that wounded men are now suffering from want of attention, between the two armies, compels me to ask a suspension of hostilities for sufficient time to collect them in, say two hours—Permit me to say that the hours you may fix upon for this, will be agreable to me and the same privilege will be extended to such parties as you may wish to send out, on the same duty, without further application—" Copies, DLC-USG, V, 45, 59, 66; DNA, RG 108, Letters Sent. *O.R.*, I, xxxvi, part 3, 638–39. On the same day, 7:00 P.M., Lee wrote to USG. "I regret that your letter of this date, asking a suspension of hostilities to enable you to remove your wounded from between the two armies, was received at so late an hour as to make it impossible to give the necessary directions so as to enable you to effect this purpose by daylight. ln order that the suffering of the wounded may not be

further protracted, I have ordered that any parties you may send out for the purpose, between the hours of 8 and 10 P. M. to day, shall not be molested, and will avail myself of the privilege extended to those from this Army, to collect any of its wounded that may remain upon the field. I will direct our skirmishers to be drawn close to our lines between the hours indicated, with the understanding that at the expiration of that time, they be allowed to resume their positions without molestation, and that during the interval, all military movements be suspended."
Copy, ICHi. *O.R.*, I, xxxvi, part 3, 639.

To Maj. Gen. Benjamin F. Butler

Cold Harbor Va. June 6th 1864

MAJ. GEN. B. F. BUTLER,
COMD.G DEPT. OF VA. & N. C.
GENERAL,

An expedition under Maj. Gen. Hunter is now on its way up the Shenandoah Valley and a large Cavalry force will leave here tomorrow, under Gen. Sheridan, to join him, for the purpose of utterly destroying the enemys lines of communication on the North side of James river. When this is done it is my intention to transfer all the force now with me to the South side. To do this I may be compelled to go to the mouth of the Chickahominy. I now send Col. Comstock of my Staff to you to see what preparations are necessary to secure the rapid crossing of the river and to learn if your position will be secure during the time the enemy would necessarily be able to spare a large force to operate with against you before reinforcements could reach you from me.

Col. Comstock will explain to you fully the situation here.

Very respectfully
U. S. GRANT
Lt. Gen.

ALS, DLC-Benjamin F. Butler. *O.R.*, I, xxxvi, part 3, 662; *ibid.*, I, xxxvii, part 1, 598–99.

To Maj. Gen. David Hunter

Head qrs Armies of the U. S.
Cold Harbor Va June 6th 1864.

MAJ GEN D. HUNTER
COMD'G DEPT WEST VA
GENERAL

General Sheridan leaves here tomorrow morning with instructions to proceed to Charlottesville Va, and to commence there the destruction of the Va. Cen. Rail road, destroying this way as much as possible. The complete destruction of this road and of the Canal on James River is of great importance to us   According to the instructions I sent to Gen Halleck for your guidance you were to proceed to Lynchburg and commence there. It would be of great value to us to get possession of Lynchburg for a single day. But that point is of so much importance to the enemy that in attempting to get it, such resistance may be met as to defeat your getting on to the road or canal at all. I see in looking over my letter to Gen Halleck on the subject of your instructions that it rather indicates that your route should be from Staunton via Charlottesville. If you have so understood it, you will be doing just what I want. The direction I would now give is that if this letter reaches you in the valley between Staunton and Lynchburg, you immediately turn east by the most practicable road until you strike the Lynchburg branch of the Va Central road. From there move Eastward along the line of the road, destroying it completely and thoroughly until you join Gen Sheridan. After the work laid out for Gen Sheridan and yourself is thoroughly done proceed to join the Army of the Potomac by the route laid out in Gen Sheridans instructions—

If any portion of your force, especially of your Cavalry, is needed back in your Dept. you are authorized to send it back—

If on receipt of this you should be near to Lynchburg and deem it practicable to reach that point, you will exercise your judgment about going there—

If you should be on the rail road between Charlottesville and

Lynchburg, it may be practicable to detach a cavalry force to de-stroy the Canal. Lose no opportunity to destroy the Canal—

Very Respectfully Your Obt Svt

U. S. GRANT Lt Gen

Copies, DLC-USG, V, 45, 59, 66; DNA, RG 108, Letters Sent; (misdated June 16, 1864) *ibid.*, Letters Received. *O.R.*, I, xxxvii, part 1, 598.

To Julia Dent Grant

Cold Harbor Va. June 6th 1864

DEAR JULIA,

The photographs of "the old woman who lived in a shoe" and little Jess are received. I also received yours and Jess' a few days before. They are all very fine. Gen. Rawlins asks me to get one of Missie's for him. She looks right cunning dressed as an old woman. This is likely to prove a very tedious job I have on hand but I feel very confidant of ultimate sucsess. The enemy keeps himself be-hind strong intrenchments all the time and seems determined to hold on to the last.—You ask me if I have received Cousin Louisa's letter? I have not received a letter from her since leaving Culpep-per. At that time I was very busy and neglected to answer and since forgot it until your letter reminded me of it. She asked me to recommend her brother who is a soldier at Indianapolis Ia. I in-tended to write to her that she did not probably understand what that position was and that I would not advise him to accept such a position. Further that likely a recommendation from me to Gover-nor Morton for his promotion might injure his prospects. Governor Morton I believe is one of the influential men who tried to have me removed from the command of the Dept. of the Ten. He complained to Jo Reynolds about some remarks I had made also and I replied that they were well founded and he, the Gov, must acknowledge it. I wish you would tell Cousin Louisa this and apologize for my not answering before. You need not tell her that you had picked her out for my second wife forgeting all about her having a husband already.

Kiss all the children for me. I wrote to Nelly the other day and told her to send the letter to you. I sent you $800. the other day. June pay I must send to pay my debts. I think that will about let me out. Kisses for yourself and love to all at your house. Fred. is just getting out again.

ULYS.

ALS, DLC-USG.

To Gen. Robert E. Lee

June 7th 1864—10:30. A M.

GENERAL R. E. LEE
COM'D'G ARMY NO. VA
GENERAL:

I regret that your note of 7. P. M. yesterday should have been received at the nearest Corps Headquarters to where it was delivered, after the hour you had given for the removal of the dead and wounded had expired. 10:45 p. m. was the hour at which it was received at Corp Headquarters and between 11 and 12 it reached my Hd. Quarters. As a consequence it was not understood by the troops of this army that there was a cessation of hostilities for the purpose of collecting the dead and wounded and none were collected. Two officers and six men of the 8th and 25th North Carolina Regts who were out in search of the bodies of officers of their respective Regiments were captured and brought into our lines owing to this want of understanding. I regret this, but will state that as soon as I learned the fact, directed that they should not be held as prisoners, but must be returned to their Commands. These officers and men having been carelessly brought through our lines to the rear, I have not determined whether they will be sent back the way they came or whether they will be sent by some other route.

Regretting that all my efforts for alleviating the sufferings of wounded men, left upon the ~~field~~ Battle-field have been rendered nugatory I remain Very Respectfully Your Obt Servt

U. S. GRANT

Lieut. Gen.

Copies, DLC-USG, V, 45, 59, 66; DNA, RG 108, Letters Sent. *O.R.*, I, xxxvi, part 3, 666. On June 7, 1864, 2:00 P.M., Gen. Robert E. Lee wrote to USG. "Your note of 10½ a. m. to-day has just been recieved. I regret that my letter to you of 7 P. M. yesterday should have been too late in reaching you to effect the removal of the wounded. I am willing, if you desire it, to devote the hours between 6 and 8 this afternoon to accomplish that object upon the same terms and conditions as set forth in my letter of 7 P. M yesterday. If this will answer your purpose and you will send parties from your lines at the hour designated, with white flags, I will direct that they be recognized, and be permitted to collect the dead and wounded. I will also notify the officers on my lines that they will be permitted at the same hour to collect any of our men that may be on the field.—I request you will notify me as soon as practicable if this arrangement is agreeable to you. Lieut. McAlister, Corpl. Martin and two privates of the 8th N. C. Regt. and Lieut. Hartman, Corpl. Kinlow, and Privates Bass and Grey were sent last night, between the hours of 8 and 10 P. M. for the purpose of recovering the body of Col. Murchison, and as they have not returned, I presume they are the men mentioned in your letter.—I request that they be returned to our lines." LS, PPRF. *O.R.*, I, xxxvi, part 3, 667. USG endorsed this letter. "Refered to Gen. G. G. Meade Comdg A. P.   I will notify Gen. Lee that hostilities will cease from 6 to 8 for the purposes mentioned. You may send the officers and men refered to as you deem best. Please return this." AES, PPRF. *O.R.*, I, xxxvi, part 3, 667. At 5:30 P.M., USG wrote to Lee. "Your note of this date is just received. It will be impossible for me to communicate the fact of the truce by the hour named by you, (6 P. M.) but I will avail myself of your offer at the earliest possible moment which ~~will~~ I hope will not be much after that hour. The officers and men taken last ~~night~~ evening, are the same mentioned in your note and will be returned" Copies, DLC-USG, V, 45, 59, 66; DNA, RG 108, Letters Sent. *O.R.*, I, xxxvi, part 3, 667; (misdated June 30) *ibid.*, I, xl, part 2, 519.

To Edwin M. Stanton

―――――――

Cold Harbor 3.05 P M June 7th *1864*.

HON. E. M. STANTON.
SECY. WAR.

All has been very quiet today   No casualties reported   My telegrams would be more frequent but for the fact that Mr Dana keeps you fully advised—Permit me to renew my recommendation of T. S. Bowers for the position of asst Adjt General in the Regular

Army to fill the vacancy created by the resignation of Col Buell[1] placing Bowers at the foot of the List of Majors?

U. S. GRANT
Lt Gen

Telegram received (on June 8, 1864, 8:50 A.M.), DNA, RG 107, Telegrams Collected (Bound); copies, *ibid.*, RG 108, Letters Sent; DLC-USG, V, 45, 59, 66. *O.R.*, I, xxxvi, part 3, 665.

On June 7, 12:30 P.M., Maj. Gen. Benjamin F. Butler telegraphed to both USG and Secretary of War Edwin M. Stanton. "All quiet on my lines. Richmond paper of June 7th gives intelligence of a fight at Mount Crawford between Genl Hunter & Gen W E. Jones in which Hunter was victorious and Jones Rebel Commander was killed   Staunton was afterwards occupied by the Union forces Fight was on Sunday"   ALS (telegram sent), DNA, RG 94, War Records Office, Army of the Potomac; telegram received, *ibid.*; *ibid.*, RG 107, Telegrams Collected (Unbound). *O.R.*, I, xxxvi, part 3, 691.

1. Don Carlos Buell, who spent more than a year awaiting orders, refused to serve under either Maj. Gen. Edward R. S. Canby or Maj. Gen. William T. Sherman. *Memoirs*, II, 121. After being mustered out of service as maj. gen. of vols., he resigned as col., asst. adjt. gen., in the regular army, on June 1. Theodore S. Bowers was later appointed maj., asst. adjt. gen., as of Jan. 6, 1865.

To Brig. Gen. John J. Abercrombie

Cold Harbor, Va June 7, 1864

BRIG GEN. J. J. ABERCROMBIE
COMDG U. S. FORCES
WHITE HOUSE VA
GENERAL

Capt. Parker, Asst Adj Gen. goes to White House this morning for the purpose of ascertaining certainly the time when cars can commence moving and the probable time it would take thereafter to remove all the iron from the York river R. R. from the Chickahominy back to White House and place it on board of steamers. I shall not want to use the railroad at all for supplying the army, but will destroy it so that the enemy cannot use the iron for the purpose of relaying other roads

Very Respectfully
U S GRANT, Lt Gen

Copies, DLC-USG, V, 45, 59, 66; DNA, RG 108, Letters Sent. *O.R.*, I, xxxvi, part 3, 690. See *ibid.*, p. 691. Also on June 7, 1864, Brig. Gen. John A. Rawlins wrote to Brig. Gen. John J. Abercrombie. "Please direct Maj Wentz to to commence immediately the removal of the rail from the Richmond and York. Railroad, beginning at or as near the bridge over the Chickahominy river as possible, taking the rails to White House and from there ship them to Washington." Copies, DLC-USG, V, 45, 59.

On June 9, Rawlins wrote to Abercrombie. "Direct all organized troops arriving at the White House from and after to-day to proceed without debarking from transports they may be on to City Point or Bermuda Hundreds and there report to Maj. Gen. B. F. Butler Commanding" Copies, *ibid.*, V, 45, 59, 66; DNA, RG 108, Letters Sent. *O.R.*, I, xxxvi, part 3, 716. On the same day, Abercrombie wrote to USG. "Yours of this date in relation to debarkation of organized troops is received. I have three regiments here of 100-days' militia from Ohio. They arrived here before receipt of your letter. Shall I send them by water? These regiments were landed here before receipt of your order. The engineer constructor, Major Wentz, informs me the road cannot be taken up and shipped before Sunday a. m., June 12. The medical director says all the sick can be got away in twenty-four hours." *Ibid.*, p. 717.

On June 12, Abercrombie twice wrote to Rawlins. "Having received intelligence of the presence of a considerable force of guerrillas, say 60 or upwards, at or near King William Court-House, I dispatched about 100 of the First Rhode Island Cavalry, under Captain Capron, to ascertain the facts in relation thereto. He returned last night, and makes the accompanying report. Before sending out again, I have thought it proper to ascertain first whether there would be sufficient time to do so; the distance from here is between 8 and 9 miles." "I have the honor to make the following statement for the information of the General-in-Chief in reference to the time the different departments will require for abandoning this depot. The railroad iron and stock is now shipped; the road as far as West Point destroyed. The medical director will be prepared to move to-day by noon, unless more wounded are sent here from the front. Captain Strang, in charge of depot of repairs, will be ready in five hours. Captain Pitkin, in charge of water transportation, will be ready in twenty-four hours after receiving orders to remove. Captain Schaff, ordnance officer, can be ready in two hours. Captain Wiley, assistant commissary of subsistence, will require eight hours." *Ibid.*, pp. 767–68. The enclosure in the first letter is *ibid.*, p. 768. On the same day, Lt. Col. Theodore S. Bowers issued Special Orders No. 34. "Brig Gen J. J. Abercrombie U. S. Vols, is hereby relieved from ~~duty~~ command at White House Va, and will proceed to Washington D. C. and report to the Adjutant General of the Army for order. Maj Gen G. G. Meade Comd'g army of the Potomac will assign Brig Gen Geo W Getty U. S. Vols, to the command of the garrison at White House, Va." Copies, DLC-USG, V, 57, 62, 66. *O.R.*, I, xxxvi, part 3, 758. On the same day, noon, Brig. Gen. Seth Williams wrote to Abercrombie ordering him to remain at White House until relieved. *Ibid.*, pp. 768–69.

To Julia Dent Grant

———

June 7th/64

DEAR JULIA,

I wrote to you last night but having had my hair cut to-day and remembering that you asked me to send you a lock I now write again to send it. I have nothing to add. To-day has been the quietest since leaving Culpepper. There has been no fighting except a little Artillery ~~skirmish~~ firing and some skirmishing driving the enemy's pickets south of the Chickahominy at two of the bridges below our main line. War will get to be so common with me if this thing continues much longer that I will not be able to sleep after a while unless there is an occational gun shot near me during the night.

Love and kisses for you and the children.

ULYS.

ALS, DLC-USG.

To Maj. Gen. George G. Meade

———

June 8th/64 7.40 p. m.

MAJ. GEN. G. G. MEADE
COMD.G A. P.
GENERAL,

To prepare for the withdrawel of the Army from its present position, which will take place in a few days, a direct line from the present right to left should be marked out and partially fortified. Such a line can be occupied by the two Divisions of the 5th Corps, now loose, and a sufficient number from other Corps, when the movement takes place, to perfectly cover such a withdrawel. ~~perfectly.~~

Gen. Barnard[1] has been looking to-day with the view of location such a line and will direct your Chief Eng. in the work to be done.

Very respectfully

U. S. GRANT

Lt. Gen

ALS, DNA, RG 94, War Records Office, Army of the Potomac. *O.R.*, I, xxxvi, part 3, 695.

On June 7, 1864, 2:30 P.M., Maj. Gen. Gouverneur K. Warren wrote to Maj. Gen. Andrew A. Humphreys reporting preparations to cross the Chickahominy River. *Ibid.*, p. 675. USG endorsed this letter. "It is not desirable that General Warren should cross the river, but hold the crossing to prevent the enemy coming to this side." *Ibid.*

1. On May 31, 11:00 P.M., Maj. Gen. Henry W. Halleck telegraphed to USG. "I know of no one who has a more thorough knowledge of all the passes of the Chickahominy & of the approaches to Richmon than Brig Genl J. G. Barnard. Although I do not agree with Genl Barnard in all his opinions on the strategy of the campaign, I think he is a man of very great military ability, and that the information which he can give you will be very valuable. His mind is clear & judgement excellent. Of course if you do not want him you will order him back to Washington." ALS (telegram sent), DNA, RG 107, Telegrams Collected (Bound); telegram received, *ibid.* Printed as sent at 9:30 P.M. in *O.R.*, I, xxxvi, part 3, 375–76. On June 5, Capt. Ely S. Parker issued Special Orders No. 28. "Brig Gen J. G. Barnard U. S. Vols. having reported for duty ~~for~~ to the Lieut Gen. Comd'g, is hereby announced as Chief Engineer of the armies in the Field and will be respected and obeyed accordingly—" Copies, DLC-USG, V, 57, 62, 66. *O.R.*, I, xxxvi, part 3, 600. On June 6, Brig. Gen. John G. Barnard, Cold Harbor, wrote to USG. "It is quite probable that the present campaign may result in heavy siege work, and your own experience at Vicksburg must have shown you the need of a sufficient number of Engineer Officers. Every Corps should have an Engineer Officer at HeadQuarters &, so far as practicable, every Division. I would recommend that all the Engineer Officers not now in the field, fit for field duty, & whom it may be possible to spare from the duties on which they are engaged, be ordered to the Army of the Potomac. Brig. Gen Woodbury (Lt. Col. of Engineers) now commanding at Key West, would from his ability & knowledge of this country be a great acquisition The only objection in his case & that of some others would be the want of rank in the present meritorious & capable Chief Engineer of the Army of the Potomac, Major Duane I noticed the great value of Cohorn mortars in the trenches of this position—Whether needed here or not, similar circumstances may arise elsewhere & I mention them under the impression that, if needed the Ordnance Depart' may not be able to furnish them at short notice In view of possible siege operations it would be well to collect a siege train at Fort Monroe." ALS, DNA, RG 108, Letters Received. *O.R.*, I, xxxvi, part 3, 637–38. On June 9, Lt. Col. Theodore S. Bowers issued Special Orders No. 31. "While the Army of the Potomac continues to operate separate and independent of other armies, Brig Gen J. G. Barnard. Chief Engineer of the Armies in the field will report to and receive orders from Maj. Gen. Geo. G. Meade, Commanding same." Copies, DLC-USG, V, 57, 62, 66.

O.R., I, xxxvi, part 3, 710. On June 11, 3:00 P.M., Secretary of War Edwin M. Stanton telegraphed to Asst. Secretary of War Charles A. Dana. "I hope General Grant will not put too much confidence in, Barnard. I have no confidence in his judgment on practical military affairs and believe that he is ~~no small~~ degree in large degree responsible for McClellans blunders. He was sent down by General Halleck for General Grant to use as an Engineer if he needed ~~it~~ him but if ~~he is~~ trusted too far it may lead to deplorable results. He will never be ready never has enough and all that he undertakes will be in danger of failure ~~from prope~~ for want of proper comprehension of practical purposes. If General Grant trusts to his own judgment we are safe, but trust in Barnard is dangerous." ALS (telegram sent), DLC-Edwin M. Stanton.

To Elihu B. Washburne

Col. Harbor Va. June 9th/64

Hon E. B. Washburn
Dear Sir:

Your two letters enclosing orders published by Maj. Gen Washburn have been received. I highly approve the course he is taking and am glad to see that Gen. Slocum is pursuing a similar course about Vicksburg.—I directed some days ago that the 16th Corps Staff should report to your brother.[1] I recommended however that no Commander be named for the 16th Corps until Sherman is heard from to know whether he would not prefer the consolidation of that portion of the 16th & 17th Corps, in the field, into one Corps, and that serving in garrison from these two Corps into another. It makes but little difference however about this for as soon as this Campaign is over it is probable there will be a reconstruction of Departments and commands.

Every thing is progressing favorably but slowly. All the fight, except defensive and behind breast works, is taken out of Lee's army. Unless my next move brings on a battle the balance of the campaign will settle down to a siege.

All here are well and desire to be remembered to you. When Congress adjourns, come down and see us.

Yours Truly
U. S. Grant
Lt. Gen.

ALS, IHi.

1. See letter to Maj. Gen. Henry W. Halleck, June 3, 1864.

To Maj. Gen. Henry W. Halleck

Hd Qrs Armies U. S.
Cold Harbor Va
June 10th 1864 4 p m

[M]AJ GEN H W HALLECK
CHF OF STAFF

Please order Capt. [Mc]Alister her[e] if he can be spar[ed] from Wes[t] Point[1]   Also or[der] the Saw Mill a[t] Fort Monroe to saw all th[e] two inch lumber they can, [a]nd place it on board barges subject to [my] ord[ers][2]—The Cohorn Mortars on transports leave where they are[3]—[We will] no[t] wan[t] them now—

U. S. GRANT
Lt. Gen.

Telegram received (on June 11, 1864, 1:45 A.M.), DNA, RG 107, Telegrams Collected (Bound); copies, *ibid.*, Telegrams Received in Cipher; *ibid.*, RG 108, Letters Sent; DLC-USG, V, 45, 59, 66. *O.R.*, I, xxxvi, part 3, 722.

On June 9, 7:30 A.M., USG had telegraphed to Maj. Gen. Henry W. Halleck. "[All re-en]forcements sen[t hereafter please] send to City Point—" Telegram received (on June 10), DNA, RG 107, Telegrams Collected (Bound); copies, *ibid.*, RG 108, Letters Sent; DLC-USG, V, 45, 59, 66. Printed as received at 3:00 A.M. in *O.R.*, I, xxxvi, part 3, 709.

1. Miles D. McAlester of Mich., USMA 1856, held the rank of capt., Corps of Engineers, from March 3, 1863, and bvt. lt. col. as of July 1, 1862, for service in the Peninsular campaign. After serving at Vicksburg during the final two weeks of the siege, he went to USMA as principal asst. professor of engineering until his assignment, as of July 15, 1864, as chief engineer, Military Div. of West Miss.

2. See *ibid.*, p. 756.

3. On June 9, 3:30 P.M., Halleck telegraphed to USG. "Genl Meade has asked for twenty two cohorn mortars. This requisition cannot be filled without taking a part of those on transports for Col. Abbott, as ordered by you. Shall these be taken & sent to Genl Meade?" ALS (telegram sent), DNA, RG 107, Telegrams Collected (Bound); telegram received, *ibid. O.R.*, I, xxxvi, part 3, 709.

To Maj. Gen. Henry W. Halleck

———

Hd Qrs Armies [U. S.]
June 11th 1864

MAJ GENL H W HALLECK
CHF OF STAFF

Richmond papers of this morning announce the junction of
Crook an[d] Av[er]ill with Hunter, at Staunton on the [8]th
inst. A portion of their forces are on the Greenville and Middle-
brook road. Five hundred Cavalry mad[e] a demonstration [on]
W[ay]nes[boro] and w[ere] repulsed [by] Imboden[1] On the 9th
a[d]vanced again, but [were] driven back burning the Railroad as
they retired

U S GRANT
Lt Genl

Telegram received (on June 12, 1864, 11:00 A.M.), DNA, RG 107, Telegrams
Collected (Bound); copies, *ibid.*, RG 108, Letters Sent; DLC-USG, V, 45, 59,
66. *O.R.*, I, xxxvii, part 1, 624.

1. John D. Imboden, born in Va. in 1823, a lawyer-politician of Staunton
before the Civil War, entered C.S.A. service as capt. of an art. co. and was appointed brig. gen. as of Jan. 28, 1863. For the skirmish at Waynesboro, Va.,
June 10, 1864, see *ibid.*, I, xxxvii, part 1, 96.

To Maj. Gen. Benjamin F. Butler

———

Cold Harbor Va. June 11th/64

MAJ. GEN. B. F. BUTLER,
COMD.G DEPT. OF VA. & N. C.
GENERAL,

The movement to transfer this Army to the South side of James
River will commence after dark to-morrow night. Col. Comstock,
of my Staff, was sent specially to ascertain what was necessary to
make your position secure in the interval ~~that~~ during which the
enemy might use most of his force against you, and also to ascertain
what point on the river we should reach to effect a crossing if it

should not be practicable to reach this side of the river at Bermuda Hundred. Col. Comstock has not yet returnd[1] so that I cannot make instructions as definite as I would wish, but the time between this and Sunday[2] night being so short in which to get word to you I must do the best I can. Col. Dent goes to make arrangements for Gun boats and transportation to send up the Chickahominy to take to you the 18th Corps. This Corps will leave its position in the trenches as early in the evening to-morrow as possible and make a forced march to Cole's Landing or Ferry where it should reach by 10 a. m. the following morning. This Corps numbers now 15300 men. They take with them neither wagons nor Artilery these latter marching with the balance of the Army to the James River.

The remainder of the Army will cross the Chickahominy at Long Bridge and at Jones' and strike the river at the most practicable crossing below City Point.

I directed several days ago that all reinforcements for the Army should be sent to you. I am not advised of the number that may have gone but suppose you have received from six to ten thousand. Gen. Smith will also reach you as soon as the enemy could going by the way of Richmond. The balance of the force will not be more than one day behind, unless detained by the whole of Lee's Army in which case you will be strong enough.

I wish you to direct the proper staff officers, your Chief Eng. and Chief Q. M. to commence at once the collection of all the means in their reach for crossing the Army on its arrival. If there is a point below City Point where a pontoon bridge can be thrown have it laid.

Expecting the arrival of the 18th Corps by Monday night if you deem it practicable from the force you now have to seize and hold Petersburg you may prepare to start on the arrival of troops to hold your present lines. I do not want Petersburg visited however unless it is held nor an attempt to take it unless you feel a reasonable degree of confidance of success. If you should go there I think troops should take nothing with them except what they carry, depending upon supplies being sent after the place was secured.

If Col. Dent should not succeed in securing the requisite amount of transportation for the 18th Corps before reaching you please have the balance supplied.

> I am Gen. Very resptly
> your obt. svt.
> U. S. GRANT
> Lt. Gen. Com

P. S. On reflection I will send the 18th Corps by way of White House. The distance which they will have to march will be enough shorter to enable them to reach you about the same time and the uncertainty of navigation on the Chickahominy will be avoided.

> U. S. G.

ALS, deCoppet Collection, NjP. *O.R.*, I, xxxvi, part 3, 754–55.

1. On June 9, 1864, 7:30 P.M., Lt. Col. Cyrus B. Comstock telegraphed to USG. "Will start back early in the morning   Gen Gillmore with 2000 men started today to demonstrate on Petersburg while Kautz with 1500 cavalry was to go around, enter Petersburg if practicable and destroy rail road bridge and to go south on the rail road   Gillmore reconnoitred the enemys works & has returned finding them strong   Kautz has not yet been heard from"   Telegram received (on June 10), DNA, RG 108, Letters Received. *O.R.*, I, xxxvi, part 3, 709. On June 12, USG wrote to Maj. Gen. Benjamin F. Butler. "Go on with the corduroy suggested by Col Comstock. A Staff officer is on the way with letter of instructions to you, but did not leave here until last night. Your Chief Engr. will understand the corduroy meant." Copies, DLC-USG, V, 45, 59, 66; DNA, RG 108, Letters Sent. *O.R.*, I, xxxvi, part 3, 769.

2. June 12.

To Maj. Gen. George G. Meade

Cold Harbor Va. June 11th/64

MAJ. GEN. G. G. MEADE,
COMD.G A. P.
GEN.

Col. Comstock who visited the James River for the purpose of ascertaining the best point below Bermuda Hundred to which to march the Army has not yet returned. It is now getting so late however that all preparations may be made for the move, to-morrow night, without waiting longer.

The movement will be made as heretofore agreed upon: that is, the 18th Corps make a rapid march with the Infantry alone, their wagons and Artillery accompanying the balance of the Army, to Coles Landing or Ferry, and there embark for City Point, loosing no time for rest until they reach the latter point. The 5th Corps will seize Long Bridge and move out on the Long Bridge Road to its junction with Quaker Road, or until stoped by the enemy. The other three Corps will follow in such order as you may direct, one of them crossing at Long Bridge and two at Jones Bridge. After the crossing is effected the most practica[ble] roads will be taken to reach about Fort Powhatan. Of course this is supposing the enemy makes no opposition to our advance.—The 5th Corps, after securing the passage of the balance of the Army will join, or follow in rear of, the Corps which crosses the same bridge with themselves.

The wagon trains should be kept well East of the troops and if a crossing can be found, or made, lower down than Jones' they should take it.

very respectfully

U. S. GRANT

Lt. Gen.

P. S. In view of the long march to reach Coles Landing, and the uncertainty of being able to embark so large a number of men there, the direction of the 18th Corps may be changed to White House. They should be directed to load up transports and start them as fast as loaded without waiting for the whole Corps, or even whole Divisions, to go together.

U. S. G.

ALS, DNA, RG 94, War Records Office, Army of the Potomac. *O.R.*, I, xxxvi, part 3, 745–46.

On June 10, 1864, Brig. Gen. Rufus Ingalls wrote to Brig. Gen. Seth Williams concerning boats to move the 18th Army Corps to Bermuda Hundred. *Ibid.*, p. 724. At 11:00 P.M., Maj. Gen. George G. Meade endorsed this letter. "Respectfully forwarded. I agree with General Ingalls in the suggestion that Lieutenant-Colonel Biggs be directed to prepare the necessary transportation. In regard to the suggestion that the command should be embarked at the White House, as it is only contemplated embarking infantry, I should think the shorter water route, from Cole's Ferry to Bermuda Hundred, would cause the operation to be greatly hastened, although the facilities may not be so good for embarking the troops." *Ibid.*, p. 725.

To Col. Herman Biggs

Cold Harbor, Va. June 12. 1864

COL BRIGGS
CHIEF QUARTER MASTER 18TH A C.

Lt. Col. Dent of my staff has gone to Fortress Monroe and Bermuda Hundreds to make or rather communicate the necessary orders for securing the crossing of the army over James River at Fort Powhattan. Special instructions however ~~will~~ were not ~~be~~ given to send Ferry boats, Pontons &c that may yet be at Fort Monroe. This will be understood ~~however~~ no doubt by Gen Butler from the instructions that have gone to him, but to expedite, I now direct that you you forward up the James river all these things within your charge, and request the Engineer Officer at Fort Monroe for me to send all the ponton bridge material he may have on hand.

Send also all the lumber you can, particularly the 2 inch plank

This will not be construed to interfere with sending the amount of transportation to the White House heretofore called for

Respectfully &c
U. S. GRANT
Lt Gen'l

Copies, DLC-USG, V, 45, 59, 66; DNA, RG 108, Letters Sent. *O.R.*, I, xxxvi, part 3, 769. A variant copy is in DNA, RG 94, War Records Office, Army of the Potomac. Herman Biggs of N. Y., USMA 1856, was serving as 2nd lt. and asst. professor of geography, history, and ethics at USMA when the Civil War began. As lt. col. and chief q. m., Dept. of Va. and N. C., Biggs served under Maj. Gen. Benjamin F. Butler.

To Maj. Gen. Henry W. Halleck

Hd Qrs Wilcox Landing
5 30 P M June 13, 186[4]

MAJ. GEN. HALLECK,
CHF OF STAFF.

The advance of our troops has just reached this place   Will commence crossing the James tomorrow. Wilson's Cavalry & Warren's Corps moved from Long Bridge to White Oak Swamp to cover the crossing of the balance of the army. No fighting has been reported except a little Cavalry skirmishing.

Smith's Corps went round by water & will commence arriving at City Point tonight.[1]

U S GRANT
Lt. Genl

Telegram received, DNA, RG 107, Telegrams Collected (Bound); (undated) *ibid.*, Telegrams Collected (Unbound); copies (entered as sent at 4:30 P.M.), *ibid.*, RG 108, Letters Sent; DLC-USG, V, 45, 59. Printed as sent at 4:30 P.M. in *O.R.*, I, xl, part 1, 12; *ibid.*, I, xl, part 2, 3.

1. On June 13, 1864, Brig. Gen. John A. Rawlins wrote to Maj. Gen. William F. Smith. "Send forward your troops, to Bermuda Hundred, as fast as they embark, without waiting for Divisions. The object being, to get them to Bermuda Hundred at the earliest possible moment." Copies, DLC-USG, V, 45, 59; DNA, RG 94, War Records Office, Dept. of Va. and N. C., Army of the James; *ibid.*, RG 108, Letters Sent. *O.R.*, I, xl, part 2, 17.

To Maj. Gen. Benjamin F. Butler

Hd qrs &c Clark House, 2 miles West
of Charles City C. H. Va. June, 13th 1864, 4-20 P. M.

MAJ GEN B. F. BUTLER.
BERMUDA HUNDRED,

Head of column has just reached this place. Will be at Fort Powhatton to commence crossing by 10-a. m. to-morrow. Communicate with me if Infantry can be transferred rapidly from Wil-

cox's Wharf. If so please direct Quartermasters to make all necessary preparations

U S. GRANT
Lieut Genl.

Copies, DLC-USG, V, 45, 59; DNA, RG 108, Letters Sent. *O.R.*, I, xl, part 2,
12. On June 13, 1864, 7:30 P.M., Lt. Col. Orville E. Babcock, sent by USG with
this letter, wrote to Maj. Gen. Benjamin F. Butler quoting the message in full.
ALS, DNA, RG 107, Telegrams Collected (Unbound). Also on June 13, Butler
wrote to USG. "Major Babcock has reported to me with your despatch—Owing
to the burning of the wharves, it may take a little time to be ready to transfer
troops from Wilcox Wharf to Windmill Point, which is directly opposite, but I
have ordered barges, landing material and water transportation down there—
You will then land about fourteen miles from Petersburg—There were this morning, but about two thousand men in Petersburg, partly militia—I can by three
o'clock to morrow, have three thousand well mounted Cavalry ready to cooperate with you against Petersburg—Gen Weitzel is at Fort Powhattan and will
have ~~two~~ a bridges ready there, I think by ten A. M—to morrow. Gen Benham's
pontoon train will also be at Fort Powhattan to night—I should be very happy to
meet you at my Head Quarters" LS, *ibid.*, RG 108, Letters Received. *O.R.*, I,
xl, part 2, 12. On the same day, Brig. Gen. John A. Rawlins wrote to Butler.
"You will please turn over to such Officers of the Quartermasters and Engineer
Departments as Maj Gen Geo G Meade Comd'g Army of the Potomac may
designate all the Ferry Boats and other transportation available, including Ponton boats and bridging material, you have at your command, to be used in crossing the Army to the south side of the James River This is not intended to interfere with any bridge you may have laid absolutely necessary for your operations.
Also immediately cause the boats you have loaded with stone to be sunk so as to
obstruct navigation at a point in the James River above where our Gunboats run,
but within reach of their protection that they may prevent the enemy's removing
them should he attempt to do so" Copies, DLC-USG, V, 45, 59, 67; (incomplete) DNA, RG 94, War Records Office, Dept. of Va. and N. C.; *ibid.*, RG 108,
Letters Sent. *O.R.*, I, xl, part 2, 12–13.

On Dec. 22, Bvt. Maj. Gen. John G. Barnard wrote to Lt. Col. Theodore S.
Bowers recommending bvt. promotions for engineer officers involved in laying
the pontoon bridge over the James River in June. ALS, DNA, RG 94, ACP, B78
CB 1865. On Feb. 3, 1865, Maj. Gen. George G. Meade endorsed a variant copy
of this letter. "Respectfully returned to Head Quarters Armies of the U. S. Brig.
Genl. Benham, Major Luby, Captain Livingston, Maj. Chester Cap't Clapp and
Cap't Templeton, are all officers belonging to the Engineer Brigade attached to
this army, and would have been recommended by me for promotion, when others
were so recommended, if in my judgement, their services had entitled them to
this distinction. I did not recommend these officers because, although I most
cheerfully acknowledge, they have performed their duties in a most creditable
and satisfactory manner, yet the character of these duties has not, in my opinion,
been such as to justify promotion. Until the throwing of the bridge across the
James, these officers were serving in Washington, and since the construction of
that bridge, they have been at City Point. In the construction of this bridge, the
approaches, and considerable portions at each end were laid before the arrival of

these officers—but even had they executed the whole, the building of a bridge, without opposition from an enemy, is not such services, as to entitle officers to promotion. Whilst therefore, I do not desire to to detract from the meretorious services of these officers, I cannot recommend their promotion, for if I did, it would compel my recommending every officer of this army, who has done his duty in the campaign, which has not been the rule governing my action, and from which I cannot consistently depart. At the same time, it is not my intention to object to the promotion of Brig. Genl. Benham. From all I can learn, Genl. Benham's services, prior to my assuming command, entitle his claims to consideration, and I now only refer to the service performed by him under my immediate directions." ES, *ibid.* On Feb. 4, USG endorsed the letter. "Respectfully forwarded to the Adjutant General of the Army. and attention invited to the endorsement within of Maj. Gen. G. G. Meade, Com'd'g Army Potomac, which endorsement I approve." ES, *ibid.*

On March 21, Meade wrote to Bowers. "Some time since, a letter of Bvt. Maj. Genl. J. G. Barnard recommending Brig Genl. H. G. Benham for promotion, was referred to me. On returning this communication, I endorsed on it, the principle which had governed me in making nominations for Brevets, and on which I had not considered the services of Genl. Benham & certain of his staff officers, as justifying me in presenting their names.—Mere meritorious & faithful services in connection with military operations do not entitle officers in, my judgement to promotion by Brevet, which should be confined to distinguished good conduct & gallantry in the field & in the presence of the enemy.—I find however that this rule does not govern the War Dept in the appointments that have been made—numerous officers of this army of different staff departments, precisely in the same category as Brig Genl Benham, besides many officers in the Departments at Washington & elsewhere, having been brevetted for 'faithful & meritorious services'—I learn also that an application has been made for the promotion of Brig Genl Benham, by my predecessor in command of this army, for distinguished services in the presence of the enemy at Chancellorville & elsewhere.—Under these circumstances, fearing my action, may operate to the injustice of Genl Benham, by excluding him from a promotion given to others, who have no greater claims, but were more fortunate in the superiors thro' whom their claims were presented to the Dept—I have thought it my duty to state that, the failure to adopt as a rule, the principle enunciated by me, entitles Brig. Genl. Benham & those officers of the staff recommended with him, to the promotion asked for them.—Brig. Genl. Benham has been most earnest & faithful in the discharge of all the duties assigned to him—He has moreover designed and introduced into the service—a light shovel for pickets, which is universally approved, and is really a very valuable suggestion—and in view of all these facts I desire to withdraw any objection to his promotion, and to recommend the same.—This communication is forwarded for the information & action of the Lt. Genl Comdg as the letter of Brvt Maj. Genl. Barnard was referred to me by his order.—" ALS, *ibid.,* B447 CB 1864. *O.R.,* I, xlvi, part 3, 63. On March 27, USG endorsed this letter. "Respectfully forwarded with the recommendation that Brig Gen. H W Benham be brevetted as Major General" ES, DNA, RG 94, ACP, B447 CB 1864. On March 22, Brig. Gen. Henry W. Benham wrote to Bowers. "I have this day received from Col. Ruggles. the copy of a letter of General Meade to yourself for Lieut General Grant, in which he recommends my promotion alluding at the same time to more dangerous services in the field, under his predecessor—for which as I have only recently been informed, that predecessor—Genl Hooker;—had forwarded to the Departments some months ago—a strong and decided recommendation for promotion—As I understood Genl Barnard, he— Gen Hooker confirmed that fact in a personal interview with Genl Barnard but a short time since. As to the principal of these services under General Hooker, I may say that I believe they were the successful laying and removal of the ponton bridges, during the Chancellorville campaign—in which 14 bridges were laid and removed—by my brigade on the Rappahannock, between the 29th of April and the 7th of May 1863.—with the most entire success, and of these fully one half were constructed under my own personal supervision, the greater portion of them under fire,—As the most successful of which I would take leave to refer to the three laid under my eye at Franklins crossing, upon the morning of the 29th of April—where by the precautions taken by my directions, of which Genl Sharp (on General Grant's staff) is at least one personal witness, now here— although there was severe firing and some of our men wounded—and my own horse shot under me—not a man of all our forces there was killed. I have referred to this affair especially in case the Lieut General should consider the letter of Genl Meade favorably, and desire the date of any special service under Gen H   I also enclose copy of my letter to Gen Humphreys in relation to the picket shovel—with his endorsement—to which some remarks and notes are added.—& of the date July 28, 1864" LS, *ibid.*

On May 31, Benham wrote to USG. "I desire to lay before you a matter which, whatever others may think of it, I know you will feel that any soldier would be excused in bringing to your notice—and in asking your aid and action in the case   I find in the brevet appointment as Major General of Volunteers recently conferred upon me—that it is stated it is given for 'faithful and meritorious services during the war'—as though I had not had the opportunity of commanding or doing effective service in any of its battles—for which battle services as you are aware if effective—I believe it is the invariable rule—to refer in a brevet commission to the bravery or gallant conduct of the officer—which cannot but add greatly to the value of the compliment given—to any one with a true soldiers feelings—Though the duties, which for the most part I have performed with the Engineer Brigade, for the past two years, have not been so much those of *battle* service, yet I feel that I have been at other times greatly exposed in battle during this war, of which fortunately there is the written record from some of my different commanding officers—which I would now respectfully submit to you herewith—I think I may ask of you that the terms of that appointment might be changed to such as will bear some testimony to my having done such service in battle. And I feel I may be excused for stating to you briefly—some of the occasions on which I have been on duty and exposed under the fire of the enemy—in confirmation of the statements in these letters   At Corricks Ford where Gen Garnett fell and I was in sole command—I was one of the few (some 6 or 8 only) mounted persons on that field and perhaps as much exposed as any other in the position I held between the Infantry & the Artillery during all the contest. At Carnifex Ferry—I led the leading brigade and was in advance of it (to avoid masked batteries) when the fire of musketry & artillery burst out, as my leading Lt. Colonel—stated 'heavier than in any of 12 pitched battles he had seen in Europe'—and I did not leave that position for 200 yards during the action—And beside other exposure under fire when I commanded in the rout of Floyd in November, '61 I was afterwards—*as the General present*

Commanding at the bombardment [o]f Fort Pulaski—as I passed each day back and forth between the batteries under constant & very accurate artillery fire that was poured upon myself and Staff, the captured commander admitte̶d̶ing to me that he fired on single men in passing between these batteries—And again even with this Army and my present duties—I have had the opportunity of sharing with my men the dangers of their *unarmed labor under fire*—During the Chancellorsville fights, I personally superintended the laying of seven bridges—and nearly all of these under the fire of the enemy, having my horse shot under me at one time—at another a Captain of Regular Engineers, (Cross—) and many others killed & wounded—*within a few yards* of my position—And even later in our last fight, on the 2nd of April when I brought up my men to the support of Gen. Parke before Petersburg—I was for hours exposed in the same fort—and in nearly the position where Gen Potter was so severely—supposed for so long to have been mortally wounded—I do not mention or refer to these things in any boastful way, far be it from me when so many others have been so much more exposed, the contrary—I only regret, that I had not been permitted to serve the country in its recent struggle—more often in its most dangerous hours of trial— as so many others of our great and good Generals have done—But I have felt—I might refer to these cases—in connection with the statements of Genls Morris, McClellan & Hooker here enclosed—to show that in any acknowledgement of my efforts from the War Department I might be justified in expecting—that some of their commendations in reference to my services in battle should be referred to." LS, *ibid.*, RG 108, Letters Received.

On Sept. 17, 1866, Benham wrote to USG. "As reports continue to reach the officers of Engineers here that efforts are still being made for the sanction of the promotions by selection for the increased rank constituted in the corps by the late law of Congress—I have felt I might properly send to you a copy of a letter to an Engineer officer here, from Senator Wilson—who I beleive drew up— and was principally instrumental in carrying that law through Congress—a law, that, by a published letter from yourself General, appeared to have your sanction also—Not knowing whether a former letter of mine upon this subject has reached your notice I feel you will not object to the consideration of this enclosed letter—which is respectfully offered—with the belief that I have, that it is your earnest wish to carry out all laws in their true intent and meaning—which laws I think are only best explained by those who draw them up and pass them. While at the same time I am unwilling to beleive that the rumored action on this subject of promoting others over me, can have your sanction to such injustice to myself—After as I beleive the most ample evidence can shew my long continued faithful and efficient service in my own Corps' duties both in peace and war—as well as other and effective service, in every way I was permitted, in command of troops on several occasions in the field. And in view of— this I must feel that you will not, that you cannot permit the injustice of my being overslaughed—if your action can prevent it." ALS, *ibid.*, RG 94, ACP, B447 CB 1864. On Sept. 19, USG endorsed this letter. "Respectfully refered to the Sec. of War." AES, *ibid.* On Nov. 26, USG wrote to Secretary of War Edwin M. Stanton. "I have the honor to recommend that Bvt. Brig. Gen. H. W. Benham be breveted Maj. Gen. from March 13th 1865, in accordanc[e] with the rule that has been generally adopted, that of breveting officers of the regular Army to the highest grade held by them in the Volunteer service either by brevet or otherwise." ALS, *ibid.*

On March 20, 1875, Benham wrote to USG asking that he not be retired. LS, *ibid*. Benham retired in 1882.

To Maj. Gen. George G. Meade

Charles City C. H. Va June 13th *1864.*

MAJ. GEN. MEADE,
COMD.G A. P.
GENERAL,

I think it will be advisabl to send the Cavalry, supported by a Division of Infantry, at an early hour in the morning to Hill Carters to see if that point cannot be secured for our crossing. This can be done at the same time with the reconnoisance at Ft. Powhatan and we can afterwards determine which to use.

I will direct Gen. Butler to turn over to the Engineers, and Quartermasters you designate all tran[s]portation bridging &c. to be used under their direction until the Army is crossed.

The Army of the Potomac will be put into camp at the nearest suitable place on the South side of James River to where they cross until further orders.

Very respectfully
U. S. GRANT
Lt. Gen.

P. S. Direct the reconnoisance to ascertain if Malvern Hill is held by the enemy and if they can, in what force.

U. S. G.

ALS, DNA, RG 94, War Records Office, Army of the Potomac. *O.R.*, I, xl, part 2, 3.

To Maj. Gen. Henry W. Halleck

———

Burmuda Hundred
June 14th 1864. 1 30 p m

Maj Gen H. W. Halleck
Chf of Staff

Our forces will commence crossing James River to day. The Enemy show no signs of yet having brought troops to south side of Richmond.

I will have Petersburg secured if possible before they get there in much force. Our movement from Cold Harbor to the James River has been made with great celerity, and so far, without loss or accident.

U. S. Grant
Lt. Genl.

Telegram received (on June 15, 1864, 2:00 a.m.), DNA, RG 107, Telegrams Collected (Bound); copies, *ibid.*, RG 108, Letters Sent; DLC-USG, V, 45, 59, 67; Mr. and Mrs. Philip D. Sang, River Forest, Ill.; (facsimile) IHi. *O.R.*, I, xl, part 1, 12; *ibid.*, I, xl, part 2, 18–19. On June 15, 7:00 a.m., President Abraham Lincoln telegraphed to USG. "I have just recd. your despatch of 1 P. M. yesterday—I begin to see it. You will succeed—God bless you all" Telegram received (on June 16), DNA, RG 108, Letters Received; copy, *ibid.*, RG 107, Telegrams Collected (Bound). *O.R.*, I, xl, part 2, 47. Lincoln, *Works*, VII, 393.

To Maj. Gen. Benjamin F. Butler

———

Charles City C. H. Va. June 14th *1864*. 8. p. m.
Maj. Gen. B. F. Butler,
Comd.g Dept. of Va. & N. C.
General,

The Cavalry Commander, Gen. Wilson, reports that Ewells and Hills Corps have taken up the line from Malvern Hill to White-oak Swamp. I enclose you the evidence he has of this,[1] in addition to our Cavalry having encountered Infantry on this line. This looks favorable for the success of your attack on Petersburg to-night.

Gen. Hancock's Corps, numbering about 28,000 men, will be

all over to the South side of the James River, at Windmill Point, before daylight, and will march in the morning directly for Petersburg, with directions however to halt at the point on that road nearest City Point unless he receives further orders. If the forces going into Petersburg find reinforcements necessary by sending back to Gen. Hancock he will push forward.

The rations of the 2d Corps, Hancock's, will be out to-morrow evening. It will be impossible to supply him from here earlyer than that. To have this Corps ready for service you will please direct your Commissary to send down by boat, to Windmill Point, to-night, sixty thousand rations to issue to them. Without this precaution the services of this Corps cannot be had for an imergency to-morrow.

Please direct one of the Army Gunboats to move down to Fort Powhattan at once to remain there until the crossing of the Army is completed. If you can communicate with Admiral Lee I would be pleased if you would request him also to send a Gunboat to remain in same way.

Very respectfully
U. S. Grant
Lt. Gen.

ALS, DLC-Benjamin F. Butler. *O.R.*, I, xl, part 2, 36.
  On June 14, 1864, Lt. Col. Charles E. Fuller, q. m., telegraphed to Maj. Gen. Benjamin F. Butler. "Lt. Genl Grant and a number of officers have left here for point of Rocks in the Tug boat Com Dupont—They have no horses with them." ALS (telegram sent), DNA, RG 107, Telegrams Collected (Unbound).

  1. *O.R.*, I, xl, part 2, 34–35.

To Maj. Gen. George G. Meade

Headqrs. Armies of the United States
Wilcox's Wharf, Va June 14. 1863[4]. 9½ a m

Maj. Gen. Meade
Com'd'g Army Potomac

There are three boats here for immediate use in crossing troops and the officer in charge reports several others in the vicinity of

Fort. Powhattan.

Expedition in crossing is what is wanted, and to secure this you can cross from different points or all from one place as you deem best. One Corps should remain on this side until the Artillery and wagons are well over.

U. S. GRANT
Lieut General.

Copies, DLC-USG, V, 45, 59, 67; DNA, RG 108, Letters Sent; Meade Papers, PHi. *O.R.*, I, xl, part 2, 19. On June 14, 1864, Brig. Gen. John A. Rawlins wrote to Maj. Gen. George G. Meade. "The moment the Corduroy approaches opposite Fort Powhattan are finished to the river, have the ponton bridge laid, and the river closed against the passage of boats until all your troops and trains are crossed to the south side. Direct boats arriving with troops to debark them below the bridge, from where they will march to their place of destination. When you have completed the crossing of your army, have the ponton boats, bridging, &c., taken to City Point." LS, DNA, RG 94, War Records Office, Army of the Potomac. *O.R.*, I, xl, part 2, 19.

To Maj. Gen. Benjamin F. Butler

———

By Telegraph from Bermuda Hundred
Dated June 15th *1864.*

To MAJ. GEN. BUTLER,

Have just arrived. Will make Hd Qrs. at City Point. Have you any news from Petersburg? No rations arrived yet for Hancock. I started him however this morning on the road to Petersburg with directions to stop at Harrisons Creek unless he should receive other orders. Rations must now be sent for him by wagons as soon as possible to H. Creek. 30.000 will do but double that will be better. I await answer.

U. S GRANT
Lt Gen

ALS (telegram sent), DNA, RG 107, Telegrams Collected (Unbound); telegram received, *ibid.*, RG 393, Dept. of Va. and N. C., Telegrams Received. *O.R.*, I, xl, part 2, 72. Col. John W. Shaffer, chief of staff for Maj. Gen. Benjamin F. Butler, endorsed this telegram. "I ansered. Genl Butler at look out   Will forward Despatch to him   Rations was sent down River to Hancock. Will forward ~~other~~ more to him at once by land. Nothing heard here from Smith"   AES,

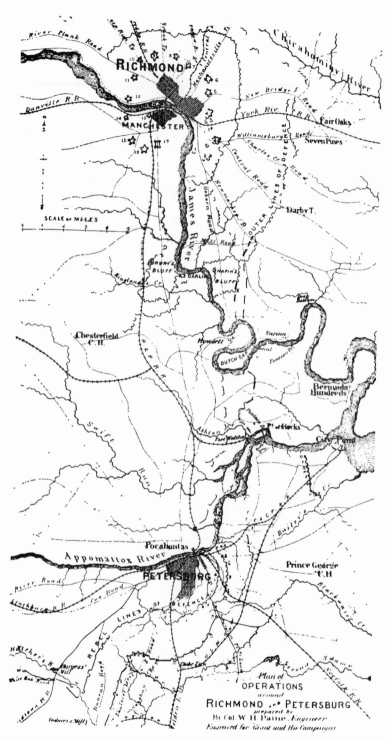

Area of Operations around Richmond and Petersburg

Prepared by Bvt. Col. William H. Paine for Henry Coppée, Grant and his Campaigns: A Military Biography (*New York, 1866*), *between pp. 388–89*

DNA, RG 393, Dept. of Va. and N. C., Telegrams Received. *O.R.*, I, xl, part 2, 72. The ALS (telegram sent) is in DNA, RG 107, Telegrams Collected (Unbound). On June 15, 1864, USG telegraphed to Shaffer. "Say to Gen. Butler as fast as Gen. Meade's Army crosses the river they will march up to Harrison's Creek. One of the Pontoon bridges has been laid and in use since 1 a. m. this morning. Nothing however is crossing yet but wagons and Artillery nor will not until they are all over unless there should be a necessity." ALS (telegram sent), *ibid. O.R.*, I, xl, part 2, 72.

An undated telegram from Butler to USG may have been sent on June 15. "My signal officer reports that a column of about 2500 cavalry was seen at 9.30 a m on turnpike opposite R. R. Junction going toward Petersburg" Copy, DLC-Benjamin F. Butler.

To Maj. Gen. Benjamin F. Butler and Maj. Gen. William F. Smith

Hdqrs Armies of the U. S.
City Point Va. June 15th 3.30 P. M 1864

MAJ GEN BUTLER OR SMITH

The 2nd Corps 28,000 strong was directed to march this morning on the direct road from Wind-Mill Point to Petersburg stopping at Harrisons creek in the absence of further orders. I have not yet heard a word of the result of the expedition against Petersburg, but still hearing firing in that direction and seeing indications of the enemy moving from the north to the south side of the James river, I have sent back orders to hurry up this Corps, If you require it send back to Gen Hancock under cover to Gen Gibbon with directions for him to read, and it the corps will push forward with all speed.

Respectfully &c
U. S. GRANT Lt. Gen

Copies, DLC-USG, V, 45, 59, 67; DNA, RG 108, Letters Sent. *O.R.*, I, xl, part 2, 73.

On June 15, 1864, 3:30 P.M., Lt. Col. Frederick T. Dent telegraphed to Maj. Gen. Benjamin F. Butler. "Lt Gen Grant wishes to know if you have heard from Gen Smith" ALS (telegram sent), DNA, RG 107, Telegrams Collected (Unbound); telegram received (at 3:40 P.M.), *ibid.*, RG 94, War Records Office, Army of the Potomac. Printed as sent at 3:40 P.M. in *O.R.*, I, xl, part 2, 73. On the same day, Butler drafted his reply at the foot of the telegram received. "I have not two ~~Gentlem~~ of my Staff have gone with a Squadron of Cavalry to

Communicate with him   will telegraph at once. at on hearing"   ADfS, DNA, RG 94, War Records Office, Army of the Potomac. *O.R.*, I, xl, part 2, 73.

At 3:12 P.M., 5:00 P.M., and 5:20 P.M., Butler telegraphed to USG. "I have been watching the progress upon Petersburg at the lookout. There has been pretty sharp fighting and I could see the enemy withdrawing on one part of the line and our forces advancing, but further I could not see. Smith must have at least Fifteen thousand (15000) men with him besides cavalry and four (4) batteries of artillery. I cannot concieve of any more force being needed but if Hancock advances to Harrisons creek if I understand the place being the creek that enters into the Appomattox above Port Walthall he will be within one mile of Smiths point of attack and can afford aid. Nothing has passed down the railroad since morning nor nothing last night that my lookout could determine.   so up to this there are no reinforcements save those that have gone from my front if any, but they have not been seen to go down the turnpike which our lookout commands   The signal officer on the right of our line reports that a cloud of dust has been along the road during an hour and a half between Chaffins farm and Richmond indicating the march of a body of troops there, they apparently taking the course to the river. The signal officer further reports that there is a long line of smoke at the North East indicating as he says 'the burning of much powder,' or, it may be brush. Later he reports that a part of the troops and trains have crossed the river and are coming in this direction"   LS (telegram sent), DNA, RG 94, War Records Office, Dept. of Va. and N. C.; telegram received, *ibid.*, RG 108, Letters Received. *O.R.*, I, xl, part 2, 73–74. "A civilian is just in from the Gen Smith's line and reports that the 22nd U. S. Colored Troops carried the rifle pits near Beasley's House at about 12 M, and that the troops were advancing—He left at 3½ o'clock, but brought no despatch from Gen Smith—From my signal tower on the left fighting is seen going on in the direction of due South which would bring it at the point where Gen Kautz should be making his demonstration on the Norfolk road both artillery & infantry firing—The rebel line of battle can be seen from the signal station—A battery is also reported as opening upon our troops in the interior of the town—From the right signal station a six horse team is seen taking a siege gun across Chapins Bluff—"   LS (telegram sent), DNA, RG 94, War Records Office, Army of the Potomac; telegram received, *ibid.*, RG 108, Letters Received. *O.R.*, I, xl, part 2, 74. "The lookout at the signal station on the right, just reports that clouds of dust are seen on the north side of the James seeming to be caused by two brigades of Infantry and about two hundred wagons and ambulances crossing Chpins Farm." LS (telegram sent), DNA, RG 107, Telegrams Collected (Unbound); telegram received, *ibid.*, RG 108, Letters Received. *O.R.*, I, xl, part 2, 74. At 7:00 P.M., Butler transmitted to USG a signal of 6:20 P.M. "River Bk. Spring Hill Sig. Sta. June 15th 1864. 6.20 P. M CAPT. NORTON   A train of eleven (11) cars loaded with troops has just passed towards Petersburg. (Sgd) SERGT. GARRETT Sig. Corps"   Signal received, DNA, RG 94, War Records Office, Army of the Potomac. On the same day, Col. John W. Shaffer forwarded to USG a telegram of 6:35 P.M. from Capt. Lemuel B. Norton, chief signal officer, to Shaffer. "I have the honor to state that the Signal Officer at Gen. Terry's Head Qrs. reports that at 6 P. M. he observed one (1) regiment of Infantry crossing Chapin's Bluff and another at 6.20 P. M, with wagons looking like pontons. . . . P. S. The Sig. Offr. at the Tower reports that he sees nothing of Hancock's troops unless his is the force *still* engaged in a line due South from the Tower. The battery on the outskirts of Petersburg has ceased firing." Telegram received, *ibid.*, RG 107, Telegrams Collected (Unbound). *O.R.*, I, xl, part 2, 78.

To Maj. Gen. Benjamin F. Butler

————

8:15 p. m. Hd Qrs. Armies of the U. S.
City Pt. Va. June 15th/64

MAJ. GEN. BUTLER,
COMD.G DEPT. OF N. C. & VA,
GEN.

Your dispatc[h] received. Order Hancock up as you suggest.

I have ordered Gen. Meade to cross another Army Corps and to direct them to march all night towards Petersburg. This order was sent about 3 p. m.   I think they will be up with Gen. Smith by 10 a m to-morrow

Respectfully
U. S. GRANT
Lt. Gen.

ALS, DNA, RG 107, Telegrams Collected (Unbound). *O.R.*, I, xl, part 2, 75. On June 15, 1864, 7:15 P.M., Maj. Gen. Benjamin F. Butler telegraphed to USG. "In your despatch you informed me that Hancock had been ordered to Harrisons Creek. If you will look upon the map compiled in the Bureau of the Topographical Engineers, Washington 1861 with additions and corrections by Captain H L Abbot you will see that Harrisons Creek runs into the Appomattox across the City Point railroad about four (4) miles from Petersburg—That is the only Harrisons Creek I know. My messenger returning from General Smith says that General Hancocks Corps is at Baileys Creek about five (5) or six (6) miles in t[he] rear [of] the position on H[ar]ri[s]ons Creek. I have ordered the wagon trains with the rations out there under an escort of two squadrons of Cavalry, and with your leave I will order Hancocks Corps to advance to Smith whom I have just heard has not been able yet to carry the interior line of the enemys works. I would desire Hancock to move up in view of the possible reinforcements of the enemy during the night. The boat that brings this to City Point will wait answer" LS (telegram sent), DNA, RG 94, War Records Office, Army of the Potomac; telegram received, *ibid.*, RG 108, Letters Received. *O.R.*, I, xl, part 2, 75. At 8:00 P.M., Butler telegraphed to USG a signal of 6:50 P.M. "No troops are visible. Hancoks seems to be driving them slowly. The fight has been raging with great violence for half an hour near Harrison's Creek   A train of fourteen (14) cars loaded with troops just passed towards Petersburg,   They also appear to be sending troops on the Roads west of Petersburg,   Another train of twenty two (22) cars has just passed towards Petersburg loaded with troops." Telegram received, DNA, RG 108, Letters Received. *O.R.*, I, xl, part 2, 79.

At 8:45 P.M. and 11:40 P.M., Butler telegraphed to USG. "General Smiths aid reports to me that at 7.25 General Smith carried the line of defences near Jordans, before which General Gillmore paused, and is pushing forward for the river. These are believed to be the only line of defences to Petersburg. At least they were so ten (10) days ago   I have sent a note to General Hancock in the following words. MAJ GENL HANCOCK   General Smith has carried the outer line of works, and the only defensive line of Petersburg. They are crowding down troops from Richmond. General Grant supposes that you will move out and aid General Smith. Please move up at once to the aid of Smith and put the Appomattox between you and Lee's Army. This is important. I have already forwarded you the same suggestion by Major Ludlow. Provisions are on the way to you. More will be started during the night. I will see you supplied. I can send you, if needed, a couple of batteries of artillery. BENJ F BUTLER Maj Genl Comg While writing the above have recieved your despatch and have added to General Hancocks despatch the following words: 'General Grant directs me to order you up.'" "Lieut Davenport acting as my Secretary has just returned from Gen Smith's front—He holds a line of from two miles to the left of the Jordan Point Road to the Appomattox, five miles in all—I have sent him back word to again push on to the Appomattox.—Gen Hancock's corps has [probably] joined him ere [th]is—They were about five miles from him at half past nine and were advancing—Gen Smith has captured thirteen guns and two hundred and sixty prisoners —We have reason to believe that the enemy in this front has been reinforced, and we have made every disposition to hold our own here—The colored troops fought gallantly taking five guns" LS (telegrams sent), DNA, RG 94, War Records Office, Army of the Potomac; telegrams received, DNA, RG 108, Letters Received. Incomplete in *O.R.*, I, xl, part 2, 74–75.

To Maj. Gen. John Gibbon

City Point June 15th 1864

MAJ GEN GIBBON

Some of my staff who came up from Ft Powhattan report not having seen the 2nd Corps marching as they passed. Orders were sent for the Corps to march early this morning, and Gen Hancock reported that the orders were sent at 6 a. m—Use all haste in getting up. Smith carried the outer works at Petersburg to day and may ~~want~~ need your assistance—This order is intended for the whole 2nd corps and is directed to you supposing you to have the advance. Communicate it to all the Div. Commanders and to Gen. Hancock and push forward as rapidly as possible—Com.y Stores are now

being loaded in wagons here for you and will reach you some time
to night on the road—

U. S. GRANT
Lt Gen

Copies, DLC-USG, V, 45, 59, 67; DNA, RG 108, Letters Sent. Printed as received at 5:25 P.M. in *O.R.*, I, xl, part 2, 63. John Gibbon, born in Pa. in 1827,
raised in N. C., USMA 1847, was appointed brig. gen. as of May 2, 1862, severely wounded at Gettysburg, and promoted to maj. gen. as of June 7, 1864.
Commanding the 2nd Div., 2nd Army Corps, Gibbon arrived at Petersburg
during the night of June 15–16. *Ibid.*, I, xl, part 1, 366. See John Gibbon, *Personal Recollections of the Civil War* (New York, 1928; reprinted, Dayton, Ohio,
1978), pp. 243–44.

To Maj. Gen. Winfield S. Hancock

———

Headqrs Armies of the U. S.
City Point Va June 15th/64 8.30 P. M.

MAJ GEN HANCOCK
COMD'G 2ND A. C.
GEN,

If requested by Gen Butler or Smith to move up to where Smith
now is do so. The enemy are now seen to be reinforcing Petersburg
by rail and by troops marching. So far however but two regiments
and eleven car loads have been reported. Your rations have gone up.
Hope they have reached you by this time. Gen Butler says he understands you have halted at a creek short of the one (Harrisons
Creek) to which you were to go—

Respectfully &c
U. S. GRANT Lt Gen.

P. S. If Petersburg is not captured tonight it will be advisable
that you and Smith take up a defensive position and maintain it
until all the forces are up. It was hoped to be able to ~~capture~~ carry
Petersburg before the Enemy could reinforce their garrison—

U. S. GRANT Lt Gen

Copy, DLC-USG, V, 67. Incomplete *ibid.*, 45, 59; DNA, RG 108, Letters Sent.
Printed as received at 11:12 P.M. and incomplete in *O.R.*, I, xl, part 2, 60.

On June 15, 1864, Maj. Gen. Winfield S. Hancock wrote to Maj. Gen. Benjamin F. Butler. "My leading Divn connected with Gen Smith about 5 o c P M I now have two Divns in line. they [are n]ow formed on his left I have another Divn to place in reserve as soon as it arrives, it having found difficulty in finding its way on account of the darkness. The night iss of that nature in my having arrived at this point after dark I can deter[m]ine little about the features of the country, and I cannot tell what the morning will bring forth But I think we cover all of the commandg points in front of Petersburg. I am now at the 'Bryant house' but am going to move to the vicinity of Gen Smiths' Head Qrs in a short time. I will be glad if the provisions arrive early in the morning. I am much oblige[d] for your offer of Artilery, and if my reserve Artiley does not come up I may apply to you for some, but at present I think I have enough to place in position as I know the country at present, I received a communica[tion] from Gen Grant this afternoon but have not had time to reply to it. You will oblige me by sending a copy of this communication to him. Gen Smith and myself have examined the country but cannot determine the exact position of the enemy." ALS, DNA, RG 109, Copies of Miscellaneous Correspondence. *O.R.*, I, xl, part 2, 60–61. On June 16, 9:30 A.M., Butler telegraphed this message to USG. Telegram received, DNA, RG 108, Letters Received. *O.R.*, I, xl, part 2, 61.

On June 15, 4:45 P.M., Maj. Gen. George G. Meade signaled to USG. "The following received from Wilson. Col Chapman at 9.45 from Haxalls reports the Enemy occupying Malvern Hills with Cavalry in force. Prisoner from Picketts Division who was taken at his home says he left his Division this morning on its way to Drury's Bluff & that all the infantry are moving that way. The main train is now crossing the bridge—before its arrival I opened the bridge for an hour or so, not requiring it, & passed through the rear of Smith's command & our depot fleet.—I propose to make our depot at City Point—" Copies, DNA, RG 108, Letters Received; (misdated June 10, 2:00 P.M.) *ibid.*, RG 94, War Records Office, Army of the Potomac; *ibid.*, RG 393, Army of the Potomac, Letters Sent; (2) Meade Papers, PHi; DLC-Andrew Johnson. *O.R.*, I, xl, part 2, 49. On June 15, Brig. Gen. John A. Rawlins wrote to Meade. "Judging from indications the Lt. Gen is of the opinion that the enemy are crossing from the north to the south side of the James. He therefore wishes you to cross another Corps as rapidly as possible and send it forward to its position. A night march may be necessary to be enable them to reach their position." LS, DNA, RG 94, War Records Office, Army of the Potomac. *O.R.*, I, xl, part 2, 49. At 10:30 P.M., Meade wrote to Rawlins. "I have the honor to enclose for the information of the Lt. Genl. Comd. an order just issued for the movement of this army.—At the present moment, the 9th Corps, artillery & trains have crossed the river, and will move promptly to the front.—I expect by 12 a M tomorrow the whole of the 5th Corps will be across & in motion for the front.—It will probably take till day light of the 17th before the whole supply train will have crossed, and during that day & night the Cavalry & 6th Corps should be over, and the bridge taken up.—Every effort will be made to push the troops to the front I send a despatch just received from Genl. Wilson—it confirms my view that the enemy took first a position from White Oak Swamp to Malvern Hill, and on discerning our movement, probably Hancocks crossing, at once commenced moving to the South Side—They undoubtedly have a bridge above Drurys bluff, which with their rail roads will give them an advantage—I will hurry up the troops all I can consistently with securing our long train which I do not like to leave outside of our entrenched line.—

I shall leave here about 9 or 10 tomorrow & will proceed at once to the vicinity of Burnsides position . . . Burnside will move all night.—" ALS, DNA, RG 108, Letters Received. *O.R.*, I, xl, part 2, 49. The enclosures are *ibid.*, pp. 50–51, 71.

To Julia Dent Grant

City Point Va. June 15th/64

DEAR JULIA,

Since Sunday[1] we have been engaged in one of the most perilous movements ever executed by a large army, that of withdrawing from the front of an enemy and moving past his flank crossing two rivers over which the enemy has bridges and rail-roads whilst we have bridges to improvise. So far it has been eminently successful and I hope will prove so to the end. About one half my troops are now on the South side of James River. A few days now will enable me to form a judgement of the work before me. It will be hard and may be tedious however.

I am in excellent health and feel no doubt about holding the enemy in much greater alarm than I ever felt in my life. They are now on a strain that no people ever endured for any great length of time. As soon as I get a little settled I will write Buck and Missy. each a letter in answer to theirs and will write to Cousin Louisa who I have received another short letter from enclosing Buck's. I want the children to write to me often. It improves them very much. I forgot that I had received a letter from Fred. since I wrote to him. I will answer his first.

Give my love to all at home. Did you receive the draft for $800 00? It is all I can send you until the end of July.—Kisses for you and the children.

ULYS.

ALS, DLC-USG.

1. June 12, 1864.

To Maj. Gen. Ambrose E. Burnside

———

Near Petersburg June 16th *1864*. 10.30 *o'clock*, A. M.
MAJ. GEN. BURNSIDE
COMD.G 9TH A. C.
GENERAL,

Mass your Corps on the left of the 2d Corps in such position as Gen Barnard Chief Eng. may direct and prepare as soon as possible either for attack or defence. From appearances the enemy are massing heavily on our left and may attack this afternoon. If they do not we want to prepare to improve the advantage gained by Smith last night.

U. S. GRANT
Lt. Gen

ALS, DNA, RG 94, War Records Office, Army of the Potomac. *O.R.*, I, xl, part 2, 97.

To Maj. Gen. Benjamin F. Butler

———

1.15 p. m.
City Point Va. June 16th 1864.
MAJ. GEN. BUTLER. COMD.G DEPT. VA & N. C.

Whilst the body of the troops are engaged at Petersburg I do not think it advisable to make an attack on the center of the enemy's line. Their troops are now moving from Richmond to Petersburg and at any time enough could be stopped oposite you to hold their strong works. It would detain a force from going to Petersburg but would attract attention to a point where we may want to make a reel attack some days hence.

I have been up to-day and examined the work done by our troops. The advantages gained are important.

U. S. GRANT
[Lt. Gen.]

ALS (telegram sent), DNA, RG 107, Telegrams Collected (Unbound); telegram received, *ibid.*, RG 393, Dept. of Va. and N. C., Telegrams Received. *O.R.*, I, xl, part 2, 98.

On June 16, 1864, 7:45 A.M., Maj. Gen. Benjamin F. Butler telegraphed to USG. "The enemy have evacuated our front. I have ordered out Fosters Division to make a reconnesance They Enemy have all gone to Petersburg. Hokes Division has come from the army of Northern Va. and gone to Petersburg—will try to reach the railroad." LS (telegram sent), DNA, RG 94, War Records Office, Army of the Potomac; telegram received (datelined 7:00 A.M.), *ibid.*, RG 108, Letters Received. *O.R.*, I, xl, part 2, 97. At 8:00 A.M., Butler transmitted to USG a signal message. "The signal officer at Genl. Terry's Hd Qrs. reports at 7.30 A M that rebel troops were still crossing chaffins farm." Telegram received, DNA, RG 107, Telegrams Collected (Unbound); *ibid.*, RG 108, Letters Received. At 8:00 A.M. and 12:50 P.M., Butler telegraphed to USG. "The news from Smith continues to improve. Hancock joined him at 1 o clock A M and formed on Smiths left. The Conflict was renewed at 4 30. this morning. Smith has taken 17. ~~pieces~~ guns. 9. by white and eight by colored troops, who assaulted and carried their advanced works Smith says they behaved admirably and he is not a partial witness—This is the concurrent testimony of all As the enemy have evacuated our front I would respectfully suggest whether the steamers at Wilcox Wharf might not take the troops of one of the Corps to Bermuda. Then in Conjunction with the troops of this line we could I think advance on the Rail road and isolate Petersburgh and as only a part of Lee's army has passed down cut it in two and hold it cut. Our line would be a short one and we could protect our Flanks—At least we should hold an opening from which to envelope Richmond on the South Side and save marching The suggestion is a crude one and is most respectfully submitted" ALS (telegram sent), DNA, RG 94, War Records Office, Army of the Potomac; telegram received, *ibid.*, RG 108, Letters Received. *O.R.*, I, xl, part 2, 98. "Gen Turner is now at Port Walthal Junction with 530 men all them tried soldiers he has, tearing up the Petersburgh R Road Gen Terry has moved out on the Turnpike and and is endeavoring to strike the Railroad there I have ordered Kautz Cavalry in as I am very much in need of them to feel the Enemy on the Right" ALS (telegram sent), DNA, RG 393, Dept. of Va. and N. C., Telegrams Sent (Press); telegram received, *ibid.*, RG 108, Letters Received. *O.R.*, I, xl, part 2, 98.

To Maj. Gen. Benjamin F. Butler

4.10 p m.
City Pt. Va. June 16/64

Maj. Gen. Butler
Comd. Dept. of Va & N. C.
Gen.

Your dispatches received and I have notified Gen. Meade of

contents. Whilst at Petersburg this morning I directed troops to be in readiness to make an assault to carry the remainder of the enemy's works South of the Appomattix at 6 p. m. this evening. Gen. Meade is on the field in person and has been directed to make the assault if there is any chance of success.—Two Divisions of Wrights Corps were directed to get aboard vessels and come directly to City Point. They will probably arrive about six this evening. If you w̶i̶l̶l̶ still hold your present advantage when they reach here I will send them to you. Now if it is possible we should hold a position in advance of your present line. Can you not turn the enemys works to face the other way and occupy their line. Let me know if you are compelled to return to your old lines.

Very respectfully
your obt. svt
U. S. GRANT
Lt. Gen

ALS (telegram sent), deCoppet Collection, NjP; telegram received, DNA, RG 393, Dept. of Va. and N. C., Telegrams Received. *O.R.*, I, xl, part 2, 99. On June 16, 1864, 3:15 P.M., Maj. Gen. Benjamin F. Butler wrote to USG. "I have just recieved the enclosed despatch from Genl Terry. It would seem that if this is true that the evacuation of our front was a mistake or blunder of the enemy I have very reliable information that Gen Pickett is upon our right. Our forces are now engaged. I have order Terry Back to our lines as quickly as possible, holding the Enemy in check" ALS, DNA, RG 108, Letters Received. *O.R.*, I, xl, part 2, 98–99. The enclosure is *ibid.*, pp. 106–7.

On the same day, 3:50 P.M. and 5:30 P.M., Butler telegraphed to USG. "I have the honor to report that five vessels prepared for obstructions have been sunk under the direction of Gen Weitzel at places pointed out by the Senior officer of the Navy—A requisition has been made by the Navy for another which has been ordered to be filled with stones for the purpose" "Despatch recieved I have examine[d] an intelligent deserter & prisoners. The evacuation was an Enormous blunder. Beauregard ordered out his troops and Longstreets Corps was to occupy their places but Lonstreet did not get up. I have improved the opportunity to destroy some three miles of the rail road. I will order my picket line to hold if possible the line of the A̶r̶m̶y̶s̶ W̶ Enemies Works But as the line is so much longer than my old line I cannot hold it with my present force. If we can hold on till Wrights two Divisions come up we may then hold it. Heavy skirmishing is now going on" ALS (telegrams sent), DNA, RG 107, Telegrams Collected (Unbound); telegrams received, *ibid.*, RG 108, Letters Received. *O.R.*, I, xl, part 2, 99. At 6:45 P.M., USG telegraphed to Butler. "Your dispatch received. Wright is every moment expected to arrive and has been ordered to report to you. He lands at Point of Rocks There are two or three more regiments of colored troops between the Pontoon bridge and Smiths command. You can take them at once" Telegram received, DNA, RG 393, Dept. of Va. and N. C., Telegrams Received; copies, *ibid.*, RG 107, Telegrams Collected (Unbound); *ibid.*, RG 108, Letters Sent; DLC-USG, V, 45, 59, 67. *O.R.*, I, xl, part 2, 100.

At 7:35 P.M., Butler transmitted to USG a message of 7:10 P.M. from Act. Rear Admiral S. Phillips Lee. "Large bodies of troops, estimated by the gun-boats at from 40,000 to 50,000, seen passing Deep Bottom from Malvern Hill toward Richmond this afternoon," *Ibid.* USG endorsed this message. "Forwarded to General Meade for information. This would show the enemy not yet on south side of James River in great force." *Ibid.*

At 10:00 P.M., USG telegraphed to Butler. "What news from the front?" Telegram received, DNA, RG 393, Dept. of Va. and N. C., Telegrams Received. *O.R.*, I, xl, part 2, 100. At 10:45 P.M., Butler telegraphed to USG. "The exact state of affairs in my front is this. At day break this morning ~~my~~ the enemies line was evacuated by the troops defending it to go to Petersburgh from orders from Beauregard, but to leave a picket line which should amuse us till Earlys division should take their place. By a blunder the pickets were withdrawn on a part of the line   This was endeavored to be corrected about 9 o Clock; but our pickets discovered the fact early in the morning and I ordered an advance along the whole line. This flanked the remaining pickets and all are driven or captured The railroad being thus open we moved upon it at once and after throwing out a brigade toward our right to observe the enemy in the direction of Richmond we commenced upon the R Road and have torn up the track for nearly three miles piling up the ties burning them with the rails laid over them and in some places digging down the embankments   About two o clock the enemy appeared in force on our right and drove in our pickets forcing us back to their line of entrenchments and near the James back to Ware Bottom Church. If we hold what we have now we can turn their line at any time after Wrights Corps which I have not yet heard of comes up. I shall have three regiments on picket after I withdraw five Regiment the whole eight being left out ~~there~~ on that line to be sure and hold it but as it leaves too large a force being nearly one half of my best men to fight on a picket line and endangers the safety of my principal line I with draw the five Regts.   Specially as they have been working & fighting all day. My right is within two miles of the Turnpike over which Lee must march as the rail road is gone and within one mile of the gun-boats   we are dropping shells upon it at intervals [of] once in three minutes which is the firing you hear"   ALS (telegram sent), DNA, RG 94, War Records Office, Army of the Potomac; telegram received, *ibid.*, RG 108, Letters Received. Printed as received at midnight in *O.R.*, I, xl, part 2, 101.

To Maj. Gen. Winfield S. Hancock

———

Headqrs Armies of the U. S.
Near Petersburg June 16th/64 10.30 A. M.

MAJ GEN HANCOCK
COMDG 2ND A. C.
GENERAL,

Push the reconnoissance in your front carefully to ascertain if an advance can be made, and at what point, ~~best~~ at about 6 P. M. to day. Make all preparations for such an advance, but do not make it without further orders. This is not to be understood however as an order preventing you from taking advantage of any weakness shown by the enemy.

Gen Burnside has been directed to mass his Corps on your left in position to be designated, or to aid, if the enemy should come out and attack. In the absence of Gen Meade and myself, you will take general control of all the troops now in position about Petersburg. Orders have gone to Gen Meade to come up in person and I think he may be looked for at about 5 P. M.

Respy &c U. S. GRANT Lt. Gen.

Copies, DLC-USG, V, 45, 59, 67; DNA, RG 108, Letters Sent. *O.R.*, I, xl, part 2, 90–91. On June 16, 1864, 10:30 A.M., Maj. Gen. Winfield S. Hancock wrote to USG. "The commander of the picket in front of General Birney's division reports a column of the enemy about a mile long, moving to our left. General Burnside is here at my headquarters, and his troops are close at hand. I also enclose a report of a signal officer on the same subject." LS, DNA, RG 108, Letters Received. *O.R.*, I, xl, part 2, 91. The enclosure is *ibid.*

To Maj. Gen. George G. Meade

———

Near Petersburg June 16th *1864*,
10.15 *o'clock*, A. M.

MAJ. GEN. MEADE
COMD.G A. P.
GEN

Gen. Smith carried very strongly located and well constructed works forming the left of the enemys defences of Petersburg taking some prisoners and sixteen pieces of Artillery. The enemy still hold their right works and are massing heavily in that direction. Hurry Warren up by the nearest road to reach the Jerusalem plank road about three miles out from Petersburg. As soon as you receive this and can give the necessary directions start yourself, by steamer, and get here to take command in person. Leave your Hd Qrs. train to follow by land. Put Wright in charge of all left behind with directions to get the trains over as rapidly as possible to be followed by the Cavalry the Cavalry to cut in as soon as the last wagon gets within his, Wrights, lines.

U. S. Grant
Lt. Gen

ALS, DNA, RG 94, War Records Office, Army of the Potomac. *O.R.*, I, xl, part 2, 86. On June 16, 1864, 3:00 P.M., Maj. Gen. George G. Meade wrote to USG. "Genl. Butler has sent a despatch reporting that his troops have advanced to the Richmond R. Rd. & the pike without opposition—This is most remarkable in my judgement & indicates the abandonment of Richmond & the holding of Petersburgh with the roads to Lynchburgh & Weldon, thus preventing our forcing them out of Richmond by holding the Peters & the Danville road—Barnard & Comstock have just come in from an examination of the lines. The latter is of opinion an attack can be made to advantage—the former is also of opinion an attack is practicable,   I have therefore, ordered one for 6 o'clock.—" ALS, DNA, RG 108, Letters Received. *O.R.*, I, xl, part 2, 86.

To Maj. Gen. George G. Meade

City Pt. Va. June 16th 8.35 p m *1864*

Maj. Gen. Meade,
Comd.g A. P.
General,

No part of the 5th Corps has yet arrived. Gen. Butler has not reported the withdrawel of his troops from their advanced position. —It was not my intention to take Wright from you for any longer time than the imergency lasted. I think now he had better go to Bermuda Hundred for to-night under any circumstances. It gives him but a short march his steamers landing up the Appomattox near to where he is wanted, and to-morrow, if all is quiet he will be near where Smith is and the change can be made.

very respectfully

U. S. GRANT

Lt. Gen.

ALS, DNA, RG 94, War Records Office, Army of the Potomac. *O.R.*, I, xl, part 2, 87. On June 16, 1864, Lt. Col. Theodore S. Bowers issued Special Orders No. 35. "The 6th Army Corps will proceed to Point of Rocks landing, on the Appomattox, where it will disembark and report to Maj. Gen. B. F. Butler Com'dg &c, for orders. Steamers of to great draught to go up the Appomattox will debark the troops at Bermuda Hundreds" Copies, DLC-USG, V, 57, 62, 67. *O.R.*, I, xl, part 2, 88.

To Maj. Gen. George G. Meade

[*June 16, 1864, 10:30* P.M.]

The result of your operations this evening not yet being fully determined and not knowing appearances in front of you, I cannot give positive directions how far or how hard you should push in the morning—I will leave this to your judgment, knowing that you will push any advantage that may be gained to night—If you do not require Smith further than to hold his present line, you may direct him to move all the troops he has, except enough for that, to Bermuda Hundred in the morning and as soon as the other Division of Wrights Corps arrives, put it in Smith's place and order his remaining Divisions up to join him—I have no further news from Butler but have sent for information—I understand however that besides the R Rd. destroyed our troops leveled much of the enemy's line fronting us—I had previously asked the question if they could not be turned to face the other way so that we might occupy them —I will go out in the morning to see you, after hearing from Genl. Butler—

U S GRANT

Lt. Genl.

Copy, Meade Papers, PHi. *O.R.*, I, xl, part 2, 87. On June 17, 1864, 6:00 A.M., Maj. Gen. George G. Meade wrote to USG. "The attack was made at 6 p. m.

yesterday, as ordered, on the whole of the front of the Second Corps and by that corps. Birney made considerable progress, taking some of the advanced works of the enemy and one of their main works of their first line. About 8 p. m. I directed Burnside to form a strong column of attack to move from Barlow's left. This column was organized and the attack made about 4 a. m. Burnside carried the enemy's works, capturing 2 guns, 400 prisoners, and, he reports, two redoubts. This advantage will be pushed. There has been continuous fighting all along the line since the attack commenced at 6 p. m. yesterday. Advantage was taken of the fine moonlight to press the enemy all night. The loss has not been great. A rough estimate would make it under 2000 killed & wounded—I regret to say many valuable officers are among this number—Col Kelly comd. Irish brigade Lt Col McCreary 146. [*145*] Pa Vols are reported killed—Col Egan 40th N Y. Lt. Col. McGee 69. N. Y. Col Hopgood 5th N. H. wounded.—The 5th Corps reached the ground about 11. P. M & will be placed in position this morning—Two brigades of the 18th were taken to support & take part in the attack of the 2d Corps—I can not ascertain from prisoners that any considerable part of Lee's army is in our front—They report Hokes command, Bushrod Johnston Division, Wise legion & some say Longstreet or a part of his corps are present.—Their men are tired, and the attacks have not been made with the vigor & force which characterized our fighting in the Wilderness—if they had been I think we should have been more successfull—I will continue to press.—" ALS (incomplete), DNA, RG 108, Letters Received. *O.R.*, I, xl, part 2, 117. On the same day, Meade wrote to USG. "In addition to the report made this morning I have to state that the 9th Corps captured Two redoubts with an advanced work around a house—Four guns—450 prisoners and Three ~~rebel~~ colors ~~& a captured also~~ Maj. Genl. Burnside reports that Genl. Potter in his attack was materially aided by a co-operative attack made by Barlows division 2d Corps.—The existing situation is that Burnside is preparing to renew the attack & Warren is taking position to cover our left flank, placing one division in line of battle and holding the balance of his corps to meet any attack on our left flank which I anticipate from the enemy so soon as Lee's army gets up;—it being the only point of our position assailable—I am holding the 18th corps ready to relieve them so soon as sufficient of the 6 corps get up to take their place—I would suggest this is a good oppertunity to transfer from the 18th those troops belonging to the 9th & Ferrero to the 18th as my supply train will be to day near Bailys' creek where it will be measurably protected by the army & with Wilson & the dismounted men guarded from any cavalry attack—I think the bridge will be taken up by nighfall & all the army up by daylight tomorrow morning.—I have reason to believe that 2000 will cover our casualties up to this moment including some 200 men captur[ed] from Barlow in one of his efforts to dislodge the enemy. The 9th Corps deserve great credit for their attack this morning, as they were marching *all yesterday* & *the night before* & had no rest *last night* being formed preparatory to attacking.—" ALS, DNA, RG 108, Letters Received. *O.R.*, I, xl, part 2, 117–18. See letter to Maj. Gen. George G. Meade, June 17, 1864.

To Maj. Gen. William F. Smith

———

Headqrs Armies of the U. S.
Near Petersburg June 16th/64 10.30 A. M.

MAJ GEN W. F. SMITH
COMD'G 18TH A. C.
GENERAL,

Push the reconnoissance in your front with the view of ascertaining the best point and manner of advancing this evening at 6 P. M. if such an advance should be ~~made~~ ordered. Make all preliminary preparations for such an advance ~~if ordered~~ and at same time hold all your forces not necessary for holding your present line, ready to reinforce the left in case of an attack from that direction. In the absence of myself and Gen Meade, Gen Hancock by virtue of seniority will have the general command of all the troops now in position about Petersburg—

Respy &c
U. S. GRANT Lt Gen.

Copies, DLC-USG, V, 45, 59, 67; DNA, RG 108, Letters Sent. *O.R.*, I, xl, part 2, 112.

To Maj. Gen. Henry W. Halleck

———

City Point Va
11 a m June 17 64

MAJOR GENL H W HALLECK
CHF OF STAFF

The 9th Corps this morning carried two more redoubts forming part of the defence[s] of Petersburg capturing four hundred & fifty (450) Prisoners and four (4) guns—Our successes are being foll[o]w[e]d [up]   Our [forces] dr[ew] out from within fifty yards of the enemys entrenchments at Cold Harbor made a flank m[o]vement of an average of about fifty five miles march crossing the Chickahominy and James River—the latter two thousand feet wide and Eighty four feet deep at point of crossing and surprised the enemys rear at Petersburg, this was done with out the loss of a wagon or piece of artillery and only about one hundred and fifty (150) stragglers picked up by the enemy.

In covering this move Warrens Corps and Wilsons Cavalry had frequent skirmishing with the Enemy each losing from fifty to sixty killed and wounded but inflicting an equal if not greater loss upon the enemy—The 18th Corps, Smith's were transferred from White House to Bermuda Hundred by water moved out near to Petersburg the night of their arrival and surprised or rather captured the very strong works north east of Petersburg before sufficient force could be got in them by the enemy to hold them. He was joined the night following this capture, by the 2nd Corps which in turn captured more of the enemys redoubts further south and this corps was followed by the 9th with the result above stated.

All the troops are now up except two Divisions covering the wagon trains and they will be up tonight. The enemy in their endeavors to re-enforce Petersburg abandoned their entrenchments in front of Bermuda Hundreds. They no doubt expected troops from north of the James River to take their place before we discovered it. Butler took advantage of this and moved a force at once upon the Railroad and plank road between Richmond and Petersburg which I hope to retain possession of.

Too much credit cannot be given the troops and their commanders for the energy and fortitude displayed the last five days. Day and night has been all the same no delays being allowed on any account

U. S. GRANT

Lt Genl

Telegram received (on June 18, 1864, 7:30 A.M.), DNA, RG 107, Telegrams Collected (Bound); copies, *ibid.*, RG 108, Letters Sent; DLC-USG, V, 45, 59, 67. *O.R.*, I, xl, part 1, 12–13; *ibid.*, I, xl, part 2, 115–16. On June 15, Maj. Gen. Henry W. Halleck wrote to USG. "I enclose herewith a list of regts & detachments forwarded to the Army of the Potomac from May 1st to date, making in all 55,178. This is exclusive of those sent to Genl Butler. I do not know the amount of its losses, but I presume that these reenforcements will make that army as strong as at the beginning of the campaign. You will have learned from telegrams forwarded and official & semi-official statements by the press, that Genl

Sherman is progressing favorably, that Genl Burbridge has defeated & scattered Morgans robber band in Kentucky, but that the expedition sent out by Genl Washburne, about 9,000 strong, under Genl Sturgis against Forrest was defeated at Guntown, Miss. with great loss. We have as yet no details & only vague reports of the disaster. The rebels having blockaded the Miss. River at Greenfield [*Greenville*], Miss., Genl Canby sent Genl A. J. Smith to attack & disperse these blockading forces. I have not heard of the result. It is understood that as soon as he accomplishes this object he is to go to Memphis, organize a proper force and move against Forrest. It was fortunate that we wrung some forces out of Genl Rosecrans to send to Memphis, otherwise that place would have been seriously endangered by Sturgis' defeat. I think it probable that Forrest will now move into middle Tennessee to cut Sherman's communications & capture some of his depôts. I shall, therefore, order a portion of Genl Burbridge's forces to Nashville & Huntsville, if it prove true that Morgan is virtually disposed of, and the rumor of a second invasion of Kentucky proves, as I think it will, unfounded. We are getting the new troops out of Illinois, Iowa & Wisconsin as fast as possible. I dont think they will prove efficient or be of much use before the expiration of their term of service ~~expires~~. I have uniformly opposed these short enlistments as money utterly thrown away. I have no news directly from Genl Hunter as late as that recieved from your Head Qu'rs. & rebel newspapers. Where he is, and what he intends to do at the present time is merely conjecture. When last heard from he was moving on Lynchburg; but if it be true that Breckenridge has moved with a superior force by Orange Court House on his communications he will hardly be able to reach your army & may be obliged to fall back to Western Va. If, however, Sheridan opens communication with him, the problem may be changed. In ignorance of what instructions he may have recently r[ecei]ved from you I have simply sent him the purport of your telegrams, without any orders, leaving him to act as circumstances may arise or as you may have directed. I learn from Genl Sigel that he (Hunter) has ordered reenforcements from West Virginia, but Breckenridge may prevent their reaching him. On the whole, I feel, since your last change of base, some apprehension for his safety. But this is one of the usual contingencies of every [c]ampaign where forces move on seperate and distant lines. As nearly all our resources for supplying the losses of our armies in the field are now exhausted, I have urged the resort to a new draft. I think one will be ordered as soon as Congress ~~will~~ repeals the three hundred dollar commutation clause. So long as that exists we cannot get *men*, although a draft would bring some *money* into the treasury. I will write you in a day or two on some other matters of importance now under examination in the Executive Bureaus." LS, DNA, RG 108, Letters Sent (Press). *O.R.*, I, xl, part 2, 47–48. The enclosure is *ibid.*, p. 48.

To Maj. Gen. Henry W. Halleck

City Pt Va
1 P m June 17. [*1864*]

Maj. Gen Halleck.
Chf of Staff—

Gen Butler learns that Lee has sent Dole's & Kershaw's[1] brigade & Gordon's[2] Division to Lynchburg—They started Monday[3] & Tuesday—

It will probably be too late to get word to Gen Hunter but he will likely get word through his large Cavalry force—Such a force as he has should never be surprised or find difficulty in making their way to a place of safety if attacked by a superior force. The only apprehension I have for Gen Hunter is that he may get out of ammunition.

U. S. Grant Lt [Gen]

Telegram received (on June 18, 1864, 9:00 A.M.), DNA, RG 107, Telegrams Collected (Bound); copies, *ibid.*, RG 108, Letters Sent; DLC-USG, V, 45, 59, 67. *O.R.*, I, xxxvii, part 1, 644–45; *ibid.*, I, xl, part 2, 116. On June 17, 3:00 P.M., Maj. Gen. Henry W. Halleck telegraphed to USG. "A German Engineer officer who left Lees Army June seventh says that Pickett's division about six thousand Infantry & Breckenridge's division about seven thousand Infantry, passed through Gordonsville in cars on the Sixth & Seventh against Hunter. He did not see their cavalry or artillery. He estimates entire force left under Lee & Beauregard from sixty to seventy five thousand, exclusive of Home guards (militia) in Richmond. He says that all damage to Rail Roads has been repaired and cars run from Richmond to Charlottesville & Staunton. Lee's army well supplied with provisions, but ammunition of inferior quality & much complained of. Many of this man's statements are verified by others." ALS (telegram sent), DNA, RG 107, Telegrams Collected (Bound); telegram received, *ibid. O.R.*, I, xxxvii, part 1, 644; *ibid.*, I, xl, part 2, 116.

1. Joseph B. Kershaw, born in S. C. in 1822, a lawyer-politician before the Civil War, served as col., 1st S. C., before being confirmed as brig. gen. on Feb. 13, 1862. Appointed maj. gen. as of May 18, 1864, he commanded a div., 1st Corps, which was in Petersburg on June 18. *Ibid.*, p. 667.
2. John B. Gordon, born in Ga. in 1832, entered the Civil War as capt. of the Raccoon Roughs and rose to maj. gen. As commander of a div., 2nd Corps, he reached Lynchburg, Va., before the U.S. Army arrived. John B. Gordon, *Reminiscences of the Civil War* (New York, 1903), p. 300.
3. June 13.

To Maj. Gen. Benjamin F. Butler

———

Tel Office Bermuda Hundred
June 17th/64 9.15 a m

MAJ. GEN. BUTLER,

I have sent a Staff Officer to communicate with you and to go out on your line and report what you think can be done with reinforcements and how many will be needed. It seems to me important that we should hold our advantage gained yesterday and maintain a position commanding the road between Petersburg and Richmond. With such advantage it seems to me we can always force a heavy Column between the two cities and force the enemy to abandon one or the other. I remain here for an Answer

U. S. GRANT
Lt. Gen

ALS (telegram sent), DNA, RG 107, Telegrams Collected (Unbound); telegram received (at 9:40 P.M.), DNA, RG 393, Dept. of Va. and N. C., Telegrams Received. *O.R.*, I, xl, part 2, 140–41. On June 17, 1864, 6:30 A.M., Maj. Gen. Benjamin F. Butler had telegraphed to USG. "There has been no change during the night. I have reinforced my picket line b[e]tween [whi]ch and the enemy there has been [so]me slight skirmishing. I have rec[ei]ved one negro regiment [and am] now awaiting the coming up [of] Gen W[r]ights Corps about 2000 only of which, have arrived. The enemy are reported in considerable numbers on our right   If you desire I ~~will endeavor to drive the~~ when Gen Wrig[h]t[s] troops get up and are refreshed by a little rest, I will endeavor to drive the enemy back on the rail road or turnpike—" ALS (telegram sent), DNA, RG 94, War Records Office, Army of the Potomac; telegram received (datelined 6:40 A.M.), DNA, RG 108, Letters Received. Printed as received at 6:45 A.M. in *O.R.*, I, xl, part 2, 140.

To Maj. Gen. Benjamin F. Butler

———

June 17th/64 10:20 a. m.

MAJ. GEN. BUTLER,

I will get Smith's Corps to you as rapidly as possible. In the mean time Wright will remain, only withdrawing as Smith takes his place. In the 9th Corps, there is one Division of Colored troops which I think I will transfer to your command and transfer the old ~~Getty~~ 9th Corps Division (Getty) ~~to~~ back. Burnside was ~~expected~~ led to expect the return of this Div. to him long ago but to this time I have declined sending it on the ground that the exigencies of service would not admit of the change.

I think Brooks[1] had better be assigned to the Command of the 10th Corps at once.

~~U.~~ S.

The telegraph will be working to my Hd Qrs. in a short time. Send next dispatch there.

U. S. GRANT

Lt. Gen

ALS (telegram sent), DNA, RG 107, Telegrams Collected (Unbound); telegram received (at 11:13 A.M.), *ibid.*, RG 393, Dept. of Va. and N. C., Telegrams Received. *O.R.*, I, xl, part 2, 141. On June 17, 1864, 10:10 A.M., Maj. Gen. Benjamin F. Butler telegraphed to USG. "Lt. Col Babcock and General Wietzel have just gone to get the material for the information caled for in your despatch Against the force at present designed for this point by Lee i e Longstreets (Earleys) Corps either Wrights or Smiths Corps will be sufficient preferably Smiths as he and his officers know the ground   Lee has sent Doles & Kershaws brigades—Gordons Division to Lynch burgh   they started Monday and Tuesday. There is nothing new in Peters burgh save Hokes Division Clingmans brigade and Johnsons Division—I learn that Johnson waggon train was ordered by Lee to Chester in event of accidents to Peters burgh thus indicating & intention of swing round on the upper James—I am trying the Rail Road this mong. again near Port Walthal Junction   Will telegraph immediately on the return of Babcock & Weitzel" ALS (telegram sent), DNA, RG 107, Telegrams Collected (Unbound); telegram received, *ibid.*, RG 108, Letters Received. *O.R.*, I, xl, part 2, 141. At noon, Lt. Col. Orville E. Babcock telegraphed to Brig. Gen. John A. Rawlins. "I have examined the ground in front of General Butler. I agree with General Weitzel, that an advance should be made to drive them back and build some works in our advance. I will bring you full information." *Ibid.*, p. 142.

1. William T. H. Brooks, born in Ohio in 1821, USMA 1841, served in the Mexican War and held the rank of capt. on the eve of the Civil War. Appointed brig. gen. as of Sept. 28, 1861, he was nominated as maj. gen. on Dec. 23, 1863, but the nomination was withdrawn on March 23, 1864. He commanded the 1st Div., 18th Army Corps, before his assignment to command the 10th Army Corps on June 17. He resigned as of July 14. See letter to Brig. Gen. William T. H. Brooks, July 6, 1864.

To Maj. Gen. Benjamin F. Butler

By Telegraph from City Pt
Dated June. 17 *1864.*

To MAJ GENL BUTLER

If you have no objections to withdrawing your order relieving
Genl Gilmore I will relieve him at his own request   the way the
matter now stands it is a severe punishment to Genl Gilmore even
if a Court of Enquiry should hereafter acquit him   I think the
course here suggested advisable & would be pleased if you agree
to it though I do not order or insist upon it

U S. GRANT,
Lt Genl

Telegram received, DNA, RG 393, Dept. of Va. and N. C., Telegrams Received;
copies, *ibid.*, RG 108, Letters Sent; DLC-USG, V, 45, 59, 67. *O.R.*, I, xxxvi,
part 2, 286; *ibid.*, I, xl, part 2, 142. On June 17, 1864, 2:35 P.M., Maj. Gen.
Benjamin F. Butler telegraphed to USG. "I can have no objection to the course
you suggest in relation to relieving General Gilmore as I have no personal feeling
in the matter. Perhaps it would be better that the order should be dated on the
date of my order in consequence of other arrangement of command depending
upon Genl Gilmores being relieved   I have in accordance with your suggestion
and the necessities of the service assigned Gen Brooks to the command of the
troops of the 10th Army Corps serving in this department. It would have been
done before but I was unwilling to take him away when he was ~~from~~ winning
Laurels from before Petersburgh   ~~You will see Having~~ As the 18th Corps is
coming back that objection is now removed"   ALS (telegram sent), DNA, RG
94, War Records Office, Army of the Potomac; telegram received (at 3:30 P.M.),
ibid., RG 108, Letters Received. *O.R.*, I, xl, part 2, 142. On the same day, Butler
wrote to USG. "I send you the withdrawal of so much of my special order as
relieves Major-General Gillmore, according to your request, to take date as of
the day of its issue, upon the supposition that it is to be operative and simultaneous with yours, relieving him at his request." *Ibid.*, I, xxxvi, part 2, 286. The
enclosure is *ibid.*, p. 287.

On June 14, Butler wrote to USG. "I have the honor to inclose the report of
General Gillmore of his operations on Petersburg, with my indorsement thereon;
also a copy of a note to my chief of staff received in reply, also the reply furnished
him [Gillmore] by me at his request, and a copy of my special order of this date,
being the action taken upon the whole subject. I need not say to you how un-
pleasant and painful this whole matter has been, and the necessity of taking the
action I have, which seemed to me imperative. The whole matter will be investigated by a competent court of inquiry. Not taking into account the loss of valuable lives in other engagements in the war, a more disastrous defeat has not been
sustained by the American arms than this has been to the success of the opera-

tions on the south side of the James. Had the movement been a success, as it easily might have been, Petersburg would have been in our possession, as all subsequent and prior information shows it might and ought to have been, the whole railroad destroyed effectually, the line of the Appomattox secured, and the enemy's defensive works in our front rendered useless. I also inclose a copy of the Richmond Sentinel with the account of the Petersburg Express of the affair. It will be seen by that account that the enemy never discovered that Generals Gillmore and Hinks with the real attacking column came against them at all. They describe the movements of the real column of attack simply 'as feints to deceive our forces' while the real movement for the surprise and capture of the city was on the Jerusalem plank road coming to Petersburg from a southerly direction. On the two first roads (*i. e.*, the City Point road and the Prince George Court-House road, upon which was General Gillmore's column) the enemy appeared in considerable numbers as early as 7 o'clock, and this skirmishing was kept up for some time. I also inclose a copy of the map furnished General Gillmore, with a sketch of the line of fortifications, and an indication of his and General Hinks' position and General Kautz's attack. I inclose official copies of General Hinks' and General Kautz's reports of the same movement without indorsement, as they have been sufficiently commented upon in my reply to General Gillmore, furnished at his request." *Ibid.*, pp. 282–83.

On June 16, Lt. Col. Theodore S. Bowers issued Special Orders No. 35. "Maj Gen Q. A. Gillmore U. S. V. under orders from Gen. Butler to proceed to Fortress Monroe, has permission to remain at City Point until the General Commanding examines the papers relating to his case" Copies, DLC-USG, V, 57, 62, 67. *O.R.*, I, xl, part 2, 88. On June 17, Bowers issued Special Orders No. 36. "Maj Gen Q. A. Gillmore U. S. V. is at his own request hereby relieved from command of the 10th Army Corps serving in the Department of Virginia and North Carolina, to take effect and date from June 14th inst. and will proceed to Washington D. C. and report to the Adjutant General of the Army for orders. His personal Staff has permission to accompany him" Copies, DLC-USG, V, 57, 62, 67; DNA, RG 94, Letters Received, 599A 1864. *O.R.*, I, xxxvi, part 2, 287; *ibid.*, I, xl, part 2, 120. Documents pertaining to the controversy are printed *ibid.*, I, xxxvi, part 2, 273–96. Some time between June 19 and June 23, USG endorsed to Secretary of War Edwin M. Stanton a group of documents sent by Butler bearing on the matter. Copy, DLC-USG, V, 58.

On June 21, Lt. Col. Martin P. Buffum, Point Lookout, telegraphed to Butler. "Genl Gillmore is here to see prisoners from Petersburg I refused permission—He has telegraphed Washington to see them—" Telegram received, DNA, RG 108, Letters Received. Printed as received at 2:00 P.M. in *O.R.*, I, xl, part 2, 302. On the same day, Butler transmitted this message to USG. "What action shall I take if any in this matter—Gen Gilmore refuses to demand a Court of Inquiry & yet is preparing his Case—" Telegram received, DNA, RG 108, Letters Received. *O.R.*, I, xl, part 2, 302. On the same day, 3:15 P.M., Bowers telegraphed to Maj. Gen. Quincy A. Gillmore. "You will proceed at once to Washington in obeydiance to your order." ALS (telegram sent), DNA, RG 94, War Records Office, Dept. of the Cumberland; telegram received, *ibid.*, RG 107, Telegrams Collected (Bound); *ibid.*, Telegrams Collected (Unbound). *O.R.*, I, xl, part 2, 293. See telegram to Maj. Gen. Henry W. Halleck, July 8, 1864, 6:00 P.M.

To Maj. Gen. Benjamin F. Butler

By Telegraph from City. Pt 6.45 [P.M.]
Dated June 17 *1864.*

To MAJ GENL BUTLER

Your dispatch was recd some miles out on the Petersburg Road hence the delay in answering—Smith has been ordered to join to-night—You need not send Wright back till I direct—if possible the Enemy should be driven back and the Elevated point occupied by you this morning fortified & held—if Wright is no longer required you can relieve him tomorrow.

U S GRANT
Lt Genl

Telegram received, DNA, RG 393, Dept. of Va. and N. C., Telegrams Received; copies, *ibid.*, RG 108, Letters Sent; DLC-USG, V, 45, 59, 67. *O.R.*, I, xl, part 2, 143; (incomplete) *ibid.*, p. 151. On June 17, 1864, 4:40 P.M., Maj. Gen. Benjamin F. Butler telegraphed to USG. "I should be quite willing to make the exchange your note suggests getting the Colored troops and giving up the division to Genl Burnside but there is one difficulty   There is no such Division now as Getty['s] Division the troops composing it having been differently assigned Some I believe to be in North Carolina but of that I am not sure. And my adjutant general office in the field gives me no information   Smith sends word that he desires to get back with the 18th Corps and will relieve Wright   I ~~have~~ will send him word that as soon as he will send up Martindales Division I will send down one of Wright but this will interfere with the moving out if to be done tonight" ALS (telegram sent), DNA, RG 107, Telegrams Collected (Unbound); telegram received, *ibid.*, RG 108, Letters Received. *O.R.*, I, xl, part 2, 142–43.

At 5:15 P.M., Butler telegraphed to USG. "The Enemy have formed in line of battle and driven in our picket line in front of our centre and advanced up to their former line   Shall we attack them in force   Our artillery will open at once upon their line" ALS (telegram sent), DNA, RG 107, Telegrams Collected (Unbound); telegram received, *ibid.*, RG 108, Letters Received. *O.R.*, I, xl, part 2, 143; (incomplete) *ibid.*, p. 151. On the same day, Lt. Col. Theodore S. Bowers telegraphed to Butler. "Gen Grant is at the front, in vicinity of Gen Meade's Headqrs   Have sent your dispatches to him" ALS (telegram sent), DNA, RG 107, Telegrams Collected (Unbound); telegram received (at 6:00 P.M.), *ibid.*, RG 393, Dept. of Va. and N. C., Telegrams Received. *O.R.*, I, xl, part 2, 143.

At 9:00 P.M., Butler telegraphed to USG. "I have ordered a regiment of 100 day men (155th Ohio) to garrison City Point and relieve the Colored troops there. Also another to Spring Hill to relieve the Colored troops there. I design to concentrate the Colored troops—I have also garrisoned Wilsons Wharf & Fort

Powhatan ~~the~~ with the Ohio troops" ALS (telegram sent), DNA, RG 94, War Records Office, Army of the Potomac; telegram received (at 9:05 P.M.), *ibid.*, RG 108, Letters Received. *O.R.*, I, xl, part 2, 141.

At 9:45 P.M. and 10:45 P.M., USG telegraphed to Butler. "Has anything been done this evening towards reoccupying the ground held this morning? I was in hopes after gaining the Railroad you would be able to fortify a position that would command it & render it useless to the enemy if this is yet within your power I want it done." "The following dispatch just received. from Genl Meade & in consequence the order relieving Smith has been suspended, he may probably be sent to you tomorrow—" Telegrams received (the first at 10:45 P.M.), DNA, RG 393, Dept. of Va. and N. C., Telegrams Received; copies, *ibid.*, RG 108, Letters Sent; DLC-USG, V, 45, 59, 67. *O.R.*, I, xl, part 2, 143–44. The enclosure was datelined 9:00 P.M. "General Burnside made, about 3 p. m., an attack with Willcox's division, which succeeded in gaining a position in advance of the works taken this morning by Potter. This evening at 8 p. m. a third attack was made by Ledlie, of Burnside's corps, which resulted in carrying a line of intrenchments, which prisoners taken in it say is the enemy's main and last line at that place, and that there is nothing behind it to Petersburg. General Warren immediately sent in two divisions to support and hold Burnside's acquisition. I have sent orders to Burnside and Warren to continue operations if anything decisive is likely to result, if not, to hold on till daylight, when, if the theory that the enemy's main line has been penetrated is confirmed, I will assault vigorously with the Fifth, Ninth, and Second Corps. In view of this contingency I shall only relieve Smith in part with one division of the Sixth Corps and defer relieving the balance of his force till the result of to-morrow's attack. I have received no detailed report from Burnside, and cannot, therefore, report casualties or prisoners." *Ibid.*, p. 118.

At 11:30 P.M., Butler telegraphed to USG. "I am sorry to say nothing has been done or even a vigorous attempt made. I gave the following orders at the times indicated & after waiting a long time I sent out one of my Aides to learn why they were not executed & received the following reply which is sent for the information of the Lieut. Genl 'Genl Terrys Hd Qrs 10.20 P M June 17th 1864 Maj Genl BUTLER, After conference with Genl Terry and Col Abbot & after examining the best survey of the localities I am of opinion that while we may carry the line in front of Battery No 4 now occupied by the enemy it is doubtful whether we can hold it. the advance position of the enemy take their lines in flanks & their position we can hardly hope to get tonight. A successful assault will therefore probably be finally repulsed whether or not this risk should be undertaken depends much on whether the movement is offensive or defensive if the latter my judgement is against it. If the former & it can be instantly followed up by an adequate force, I should advise that the risk be undertaken. My troops are still held in readiness to move. My own opinion that this advanced position should be taken & held only when we are prepared to take & hold the whole line on the right & left to the two rivers. Please instruct me as to what you desire in the matter H. G. WRIGHT Maj-Genl Comdg' 'Genl WRIGHT It is impossible to get on if orders are not obeyed sd B F BUTLER' 'From Genl Butler's Hd Qrs 7.12 P M 17th To Genl TERRY I desire the most strenuous efforts made to retake the line which we held this morning. it is most important. B F BUTLER Maj Genl' 'Genl Butlers Hd Qrs 7.15 P M. 17th To Gen WRIGHT, I have sent Genl Terry orders to make the most strenuous efforts to retake the picket line of this morning   it is important. Please aid him with your whole force   B F. BUTLER Maj Genl' "   ALS (telegram sent— incomplete), DNA, RG 107, Telegrams Collected (Unbound); *ibid.*, RG 393, Dept. of Va. and N. C., Telegrams Sent; telegram received, *ibid.*, RG 108, Letters Received. Incomplete in *O.R.*, I, xl, part 2, 144.

To Maj. Gen. George G. Meade

Armies of the U States

June 1[7] *1864.*

MAJ. GEN MEADE,

COMD.G A. P.

GENERAL,

Reliev[e] the 18th Corps from the trenches as soon as possible and direct it when relieved to return to Bermuda Hundred.

The two Divisions of Gen. Wright's Corps now with Gen Butler will be directed to return to you as soon as relieved unless the report of Gen. Witzel[1] & Col. Babcock now out on a reconnoisance on Gen. Butler's front should demonstrate the practicability of an advance there and the necessity of a greater force than would be left after Wrights withdrawel. It will be determined to-night probably whether it will be necessary to retain Wright or not and orders given him directly from my Hd Qrs. notifying you of what they may be.

Gen. Smith should be got back to Bermuda Hundred during the night.

Respy

U. S. GRANT

Lt. Gen.

ALS, DNA, RG 94, War Records Office, Army of the Potomac. *O.R.*, I, xl, part 2, 118. See letter to Maj. Gen. George G. Meade, June 16, 1864.

1. Godfrey Weitzel, born in Ohio in 1835, USMA 1855, served in the Corps of Engineers and at USMA as professor of engineering before the Civil War. After his appointment as brig. gen. as of Aug. 29, 1862, he commanded troops in the Dept. of the Gulf and led a div. in the siege of Port Hudson. In the Va. campaign of 1864, he commanded the 2nd Div., 18th Army Corps, and served as chief engineer, Dept. of Va. and N. C.

To Maj. Gen. George G. Meade

———

Headquarters Armies of the United States
City Point Va June 17th 1864 10 P. M.

MAJ. GEN. MEADE
COMDG A. P.
GENERAL

Your note brought by Capt Mason[1] just received   The news is good and I hope your efforts in the morning will improve it. You have done right in suspending the order in part relieving Smith from your front and you are authorized to suspend it all if you deem it ~~available~~ advisable to do so   If Smith has been drawn out of the line and not yet moved away it will give you his whole force for an attack or support as you may deem most advisable

Respy Your obt svt
U. S. GRANT Lieut. Gen.

Copies, DLC-USG, V, 45, 59, 67; DNA, RG 108, Letters Sent; Meade Papers, PHi. *O.R.*, I, xl, part 2, 119. See telegram to Maj. Gen. Benjamin F. Butler, June 17, 1864.

1. Addison G. Mason of Pa. served as 1st lt. and adjt., 5th Pa. Reserves, then was appointed capt. and aide as of April 25, 1863.

To Maj. Gen. Benjamin F. Butler

———

By Telegraph from City Point 1. a. m.
Dated June 18 *1864.*

To GENL BUTLER

Your despatch just recd   as you were unable to make the attack at the time first ordered you will suspend the attack you have ordered to be made bowes this is day [*between this and daylight*] but hold all your Troops in readiness to take advantage of any weakening of the Enemy in your front that may be caused by their with-

drawal of Troops to reinforce Petersburg against an attack that will
be made there by Meade in the morning

U. S. GRANT
Lt Genl

Telegram received, DNA, RG 393, Dept. of Va. and N. C., Telegrams Received;
copies, *ibid.*, RG 108, Letters Sent; DLC-USG, V, 45, 59, 67. *O.R.*, I, xl, part 2,
197. On June 18, 1864, 12:15 A.M., Maj. Gen. Benjamin F. Butler telegraphed
to USG. "I have directed the attack to be made betwixt this and day break—and
if the line is got to intrench and hold it" ALS (telegram sent), DNA, RG 107,
Telegrams Collected (Unbound); telegram received (marked as sent at 12:20
A.M., received at 12:30 A.M.), *ibid.*, RG 108, Letters Received. *O.R.*, I, xl, part
2, 197.

To Maj. Gen. Benjamin F. Butler

———

By Telegraph from City Point 8.15 a m
Dated [June] 18 *1864.*

To MAJ GEN BUTLER

Send two (2) of the Army Gunboats if they can be spared ~~if they~~,
& one if two cannot go up the Pamunky to White House to remain
& guard the river from West Point up until the garrison is removed.
A small garrison was left at White House to cover the return of
Sheridan & Hunter & to hold the Railroad bridge for them to cross
on.

U. S. GRANT
Lt Genl.

Telegram received, DNA, RG 393, Dept. of Va. and N. C., Telegrams Received;
copies, *ibid.*, RG 108, Letters Sent; DLC-USG, V, 45, 59, 67. *O.R.*, I, xxxvi,
part 3, 777; *ibid.*, I, xl, part 2, 197. On June 18, 1864, 9:40 A.M., Maj. Gen.
Benjamin F. Butler telegraphed to USG. "Despatch concerning the sending of
Army Gunboats to the Pam[un]ky [r]ec[eived. I] had sent Graham with the
Jesup & Chamberlain down the river to protect transports from the light guns at
Wilcoxs Wharf   Will send down the River an order that the two best boats go
at once upon the Pamunkey." ALS (telegram sent), DNA, RG 94, War Records
Office, Army of the Potomac; telegram received, *ibid.*, RG 108, Letters Received.
O.R., I, xxxvi, part 3, 777; *ibid.*, I, xl, part 2, 198.

On June 15, Brig. Gen. John J. Abercrombie, White House, Va., wrote to
Brig. Gen. Seth Williams concerning guerrilla activity nearby. *Ibid.*, I, xxxvi,

part 3, 776. On June 17, Maj. Gen. George G. Meade endorsed this letter. "Re-spcfy. referred to the Lt Genl. Comd. I am not apprised what arrangements have been made for preventing the obstruction of the navigation of the Pamun-key—the only trouble I can anticipate with Genl Abercrombie—If none have been made I would suggest Admiral Lee's detaching two or three gun boats to prevent the enemy from interrupting communications at Cumberland bar & other points below—" AES, DNA, RG 108, Letters Received. *O.R.*, I, xxxvi, part 3, 776–77.

To Maj. Gen. Benjamin F. Butler

By Telegraph from City Point
Dated June. 18 *1864.*

To MAJ GEN BUTLER

If you can dispense with Wright, direct him to join Gen Meade with his Command, so that the balance of the 18th Corps can be returned to you   Before starting in this campaign I directed a siege train to be put afloat subject to my orders   I understand that it came to Ft Monroe some time since & was under the impression that it had come up here. Do you know anything about it? Col Abbot was in command.[1]

U. S. GRANT.
Lt Genl

Telegram received, DNA, RG 393, Dept. of Va. and N. C., Telegrams Received; copies, *ibid.*, RG 108, Letters Sent; DLC-USG, V, 45, 59, 67. *O.R.*, I, xl, part 2, 198. On June 19, 1864, 12:10 A.M., Maj. Gen. Benjamin F. Butler telegraphed to USG. "I have ordered one division of Wrights Corps to march to Genl Meade at Daylight tomorrow morning—The other to march as soon as the troops of the 18th Corps come in. Col. Abbot siege train was afloat at Washington the last I heard of it. I have sent for him to get information—will forward it as soon as received" ALS (telegram sent), DNA, RG 107, Telegrams Collected (Un-bound); telegram received (misdated June 18), *ibid.*, RG 108, Letters Received. *O.R.*, I, xl, part 2, 221.

1. Henry L. Abbot of Mass., USMA 1854, served as a topographical engi-neer before and during the early part of the Civil War. Appointed col., 1st Conn. Art., as of Jan. 19, 1863, he organized the siege art. for the Va. campaign of 1864 and commanded that of Butler. On June 19, 1:30 A.M., Abbot wrote to Col. John W. Shaffer, chief of staff for Butler. "My train is afloat at Washington Arsenal in Charge of Capt. S. P. Hatfield 1st Conn Arty. Gen. Hunt knows all details of its composition—" ALS, DNA, RG 107, Telegrams Collected (Un-bound). Butler then telegraphed this message to USG. AES, *ibid.* On June 19,

10:00 A.M., USG telegraphed to Maj. Gen. Henry W. Halleck. "Please order ~~the~~ Col. Abbott's siege train forward"   Telegram received (at 5:50 P.M.), *ibid.*, Telegrams Collected (Bound); copies, *ibid.*, RG 108, Letters Sent; DLC-USG, V, 45, 59, 67. *O.R.*, I, xl, part 2, 207. On June 20, Halleck telegraphed to USG. "The last of the siege train has just started, the coehorn mortars included." ALS (telegram sent), DNA, RG 107, Telegrams Collected (Bound). *O.R.*, I, xl, part 2, 230.

To Maj. Gen. George G. Meade

By Telegraph from Grants hd qrs 10 P M
Dated June 18th *1864.*

To MAJ GENL MEADE

I am perfectly satisfied that all has been done that could be done and that the assaults today were called for by all the appearances and information that could be obtained   Now we will rest the men and use the shade for their protection u[ntil] a new vein can be [s]truck   As soon as Wilsons Cavalry [i]s rested we must try & cut the Enemys lines of communication   In view of a temporary blockade of the river being possible I think it advisable that supplies in depot should be kept up to full twenty 20 days besides ten 10 days in wagons & haversacks   If nothing occurs to prevent I shall be absent tomorrow from ten 10 A. M. to about three 3 P. M. up the river near the Naval Fleeet

U. S. GRANT
Lt Gen[er]al

Telegram received, DNA, RG 94, War Records Office, Army of the Potomac; copies, *ibid.*, RG 108, Letters Sent; DLC-USG, V, 45, 59, 67; Meade Papers, PHi. *O.R.*, I, xl, part 2, 157.

On June 18, 1864, 5:30 A.M., Maj. Gen. George G. Meade wrote to USG. "On advancing this morning the enemys w[orks] of yesterday were fou[n]d [e]vacuated—Prisoners & deserters report that the enemy fell back about 2 A M. to a shorter line, said to envelop the R. R. bridge & to be about one mile from Petersburgh—My lines are advancing & will continue to do so till the enemy is found & felt—further movements will depend on the developments of the morning—Ledlie was forced back last night from the advanced position he had taken —his command suffered quite severely in his attack—The men require rest & it is probable unless some favorable chance presents itself, that we shall not do more than envelop the enemy I have made every effort to open telegraphic communication with you & hope this morning to succeed.—" ALS, DNA, RG 108, Letters Received. *O.R.*, I, xl, part 2, 156.

At 9:00 A.M. and 6:00 P.M., Lt. Col. Cyrus B. Comstock telegraphed to USG. "Burnside has been moving to right to connect with Hancock. Have not yet heard that connection is complete, but an attack is ordered. . . . Gen Burnside wishes to know if Wright & Warren have attacked" ALS (undated telegram sent), DNA, RG 107, Telegrams Collected (Unbound). *O.R.*, I, xl, part 2, 155. "Birney made an assault an hour ago—vigorous with nine brigades but was repulsed with considerable loss. The attack is reported to have been well made and the troops still in good condition. Burnside is about attacking or has done so, but nothing has been heard from him yet.—nor any heavy firing." ALS (telegram sent), DNA, RG 94, War Records Office, Army of the Potomac. *O.R.*, I, xl, part 2, 155–56.

At 4:25 P.M., USG wrote to Meade. "How do matters stand with you now?" Copy, DLC-USG, V, 67. Cancellation marks through this message indicate that it may not have been sent.

At 6:30 P.M., Meade telegraphed to USG. "No report from the front since Comstocks report—Birney & Martindale (6 & 18th) are quiet—Warren & Burnside are still advancing & I have yet hopes that a successful assault may be made —I fear however from indications that Beauregard has been reinforced by Lee Birneys attack was formidable nine brigades in columns of regiments—men behaved well & yet they could not carry the lines—I will report as soon as matters are settled" ALS (telegram sent), DNA, RG 94, War Records Office, Army of the Potomac; telegram received, *ibid.*, RG 108, Letters Received. *O.R.*, I, xl, part 2, 156. At 6:50 P.M., USG wrote to Meade. "I think after the present assault, unless a decided advantage presents itself, our men should have rest, protecting themselves as well as possible. If this assault does not carry we will try to gain advantages without assaulting fortifications" Copies, DLC-USG, V, 45, 59, 67; DNA, RG 108, Letters Sent; (misdated June 13) Meade Papers, PHi. *O.R.*, I, xl, part 2, 156.

At 9:50 P.M., Meade telegraphed to USG. "I advised you of the withdrawl of the enemy this morning from the position occupied last night—I immediately ordered an advance of the whole line, which in a short time found the enemy in force in an interior line about one mile from Petersburgh—Having taken numerous prisoners, all of whom agreed in the statement that there was no force in our front but Beauregards composed of 3 Divisions Ransoms (or Clingmans) Bushrod Johnstons, & Hokes—I determined to endeavor to force them across the Appomatox I accordingly directed strong columns of assault to be advanced at 12 m by Warren Burnside, Birney & Martindale the latter commanding two divisions of the 18th & one of the 6th corps—This attack was made punctually by Martindale with success, he occupying the enemys line & taking some Forty prisoners—Birney who assaulted in Gibbons front (his left) was unsuccessful Warren was not quite ready & Burnside whose movements were some what connected with Warren delayed also—About 2 p. m Warren & Burnside commenced advancing & made considerable progress without coming in contact with the enemys main line About 4 p m Birney made a vigorous assault with nine brigades in columns of regiments, but was not able to carry the enemys line Martindale also failed in an attempt to advance—Both these officers reported the enemy in very strong force with heavy reserves masked in rear from which

I inferred that Lee has reinforced Beauregard.—These assaults were all well made & I feel satisfied that all that men could do under the circumstan[ces] was done   I directed Birney & Martindale to secure their acquired ground & entrench their positions—At 7. P M Wilcox of the 9th Corps assaulted but with no better success than the others—Warrens assault about the same time was also without result.—This terminated operations on our part—Our advanced lines are held & will be entrenched—The result of the last three days operations has been the driving the enemy from two lines of entrenchments—the capture of 4 guns 4 colors & about 500 prisoners—Our losses particularly today have been severe tho not more so, tha[n] would be expected from the numbers engaged—It is a source of great regret that I am not able to report more success but I believe every effort to command it has been made—" ALS (telegram sent), DNA, RG 94, War Records Office, Army of the Potomac; telegram received (at 10:00 P.M.), *ibid.*, RG 108, Letters Received. *O.R.*, I, xl, part 2, 156–57. The operator noted on Meade's copy: "This msg was delayed by break in wire"

At 10:00 P.M., Meade telegraphed to USG. "I am informed by Genl. Hunt that the siege train which was ordered before leaving the Rapidan altho afloat at Washington has not been brought to the James—I think it proper to advise you of this fact as in case you contemplated using them it would take some time to procure them." ALS (telegram sent), DNA, RG 94, War Records Office, Army of the Potomac; telegram received, *ibid.*, RG 108, Letters Received. *O.R.*, I, xl, part 2, 158.

To Maj. Gen. Benjamin F. Butler

By Telegraph from City Point, 6.20. P. M.
Dated June 19 *1864.*

To MAJ GEN BUTLER

I have directed Gen Meade to require Gen Benham to turn over to Gen Weitzel such bridge material as he may call for. The call may be made direct on Gen Benham. Unless otherwise directed send a brigade, of not less than two thousand men tomorrow night to seize hold & fortify the most commanding & defensible ground that can be found North of James river, & so near the river that with the protection of the Gunboats & their own strength they can always get back to Bermuda Hundred if attacked by superior numbers. Connect the two (2 banks of the river by a pontoon bridge running from Jones Neck, to Deep bottom, of course the point held must be near Deep bottom. Habitually a passage way for vessels will be left in the bridge but have at hand the means to close the gap whenever it is necessary to use it.

U. S. GRANT.
Lt Gen U. S. A.

Telegram received (at 7:30 P.M.), DNA, RG 393, Dept. of Va. and N. C., Telegrams Received; copies, *ibid.*, RG 108, Letters Sent; DLC-USG, V, 45, 59, 67. *O.R.*, I, xl, part 2, 222. On June 19, 1864, 8:10 P.M., Maj. Gen. Benjamin F. Butler telegraphed to USG. "Despatch relating to the movement of a brigade near Deep Bottom recieved   Dispositions are being made to that end and the order executed" ALS (telegram sent), DNA, RG 107, Telegrams Collected (Unbound); telegram received (datelined 7:10 P.M.), *ibid.*, RG 108, Letters Received. *O.R.*, I, xl, part 2, 222.

Also on June 19, USG telegraphed to Butler. "Shall I go over to Bermuda Hundred or will you meet me at the wharf here? I am ready now at any time" Telegram received, DNA, RG 393, Dept. of Va. and N. C., Telegrams Received.

At 9:20 P.M., Lt. Col. Adam Badeau telegraphed to Maj. Gen. George G. Meade. "Lieut Gen Grant understands that Gen Hunt wants some 30 pound parrot guns. If you will inform Gen Grant, how many are wanted he will send them out tonight." ALS (telegram sent), *ibid.*, RG 107, Telegrams Collected (Unbound); copy, DLC-USG, V, 67. At 9:35 P.M., Brig. Gen. Henry J. Hunt telegraphed to Badeau. "Despatch to Genl Meade respecting 30-pounder Parrotts received. If four or six of the guns with a hundred rounds of Ammunition each are sent up they can be placed in a servicable position. ~~If men~~ gunners who have used them can be sent with them it would be well." ALS (telegram sent), DNA, RG 107, Telegrams Collected (Unbound). At 10:40 P.M., USG telegraphed to Butler. "Gen Hunt, Chief of Art. A. P. reports that if he had some 30 pound parrott guns, he could do excellent service with them. I understand they would give him control of the rail roads bridge. If you have such a battery, I wish you would send it out." Copies, DLC-USG, V, 45, 59, 67; DNA, RG 108, Letters Sent. *O.R.*, I, xl, part 2, 223. On June 20, 8:25 A.M., Butler telegraphed to USG. "Two thirty pounder parrots can be spared from our line and ~~will~~ can be sent at once to Gen Hunt   There is another in the works at City point which is at present useless   There is a four and a half inch Rodman Gun at Fort Powhatan a point not to be attacked at present. ~~Benj~~ We shall need some of these long range guns for our work at Deep Bottom   Please suggest which shall be sent" ALS (telegram sent), DNA, RG 94, War Records Office, Army of the Potomac. Printed as received at 8:30 A.M. in *O.R.*, I, xl, part 2, 256. At 9:25 A.M., Lt. Col. Cyrus B. Comstock wrote to Butler. "Lieutenant-General Grant wishes you to send the three 30-pounder Parrotts spoken of in your telegram, if you can spare them. They will only be needed for a few days." *Ibid.* At 9:30 A.M. (sent at 9:45 A.M.), Meade telegraphed to Badeau. "Gen'l Hunt asked you last evening for six thirty pounders—Are they coming and when may we expect them?" Copy, Meade Papers, PHi. *O.R.*, I, xl, part 2, 232. At 10:30 A.M., Badeau telegraphed to Meade. "Lieut Gen Grant ordered the 30 pounders to be sent out to you at once. There are however only three (3) or four (4.)   The Gunners were ordered with them." ALS (telegram sent), DNA, RG 107, Telegrams Collected (Unbound); telegram received, *ibid.*, RG 94, War Records Office, Army of the Potomac. *O.R.*, I, xl, part 2, 232.

To Maj. Gen. George G. Meade

By Telegraph from City Point
Dated June 19 *1864.*

To MAJ GEN MEADE

I notified Gen Butler on the 17th that it was my intention to transfer Gettys old Div. back to the 9th Corps and—give him in place of it the colored Division commanded by Ferrero   Genl Butler expressed no objection to the change so far as it could be made but said that the division had been broken up long ago and that Part of it is now in North Carolina   He said however he would ascertain what regiments were here of the old organization and report to me so they might be transferred   Tell Burnside to send me a list of the regiments he wants and I will transfer such of them as are here—

U. S. GRANT
Lieut Genl

Telegram received, DNA, RG 94, War Records Office, Army of the Potomac; copies (2), *ibid.*; *ibid.*, RG 108, Letters Sent; DLC-USG, V, 45, 59, 67; (2) Meade Papers, PHi. *O.R.*, I, xl, part 2, 208. On June 19, 1864, 7:00 A.M. and 10:00 A.M., Maj. Gen. George G. Meade telegraphed to USG. "*Martindale &* *Ferero* are both here,   can I make the exchange you promised Burnside & will you issue the orders.—" ALS (telegram sent), DNA, RG 94, War Records Office, Army of the Potomac; telegram received, *ibid.*, RG 108, Letters Received. *O.R.*, I, xl, part 2, 207. "What do you say to my proposal about exchanging Ferero for Martindale—Burnside seems anxious to get his old troops back & now would be an excellent time for the exchange if it is to be done.—" ALS (telegram sent), DNA, RG 94, War Records Office, Army of the Potomac; copies, *ibid.*, RG 393, Army of the Potomac, Letters Sent; DLC-Andrew Johnson; Meade Papers, PHi. *O.R.*, I, xl, part 2, 208. On the same day, Brig. Gen. John A. Rawlins telegraphed to Meade. "Gen Grant has gone up the river—Will answer your dispatch relative to exchange of troops upon his return—" Telegram received, DNA, RG 107, Telegrams Collected (Unbound); copy, DLC-USG, V, 67.

At 8:30 A.M., Meade telegraphed to USG. "The close proximity of our assaulting columns to the enemys line & their being compelled to retire has necessarily left a number of dead & wounded between our lines & those of the enemy— Have you any objection to my asking for a flag of truce for an hour or two to remove the wounded & bury the dead.—" ALS (telegram sent), DNA, RG 94, War Records Office, Army of the Potomac; telegram received, *ibid.*, RG 108, Letters Received. *O.R.*, I, xl, part 2, 207. On the same day, USG telegraphed to Meade. "I have no objection to any arrangement you may make for the recovery

of the dead & wounded between the lines"   Telegram received (at 9:40 A.M.),
DNA, RG 94, War Records Office, Army of the Potomac; copies, DLC-USG, V,
67; (2) Meade Papers, PHi. *O.R.*, I, xl, part 2, 208.

On June 20, 7:30 A.M. (sent at 8:00 A.M.), Meade telegraphed to USG.
"The following has been received from General Burnside in relation to the trans-
fer of Getty's old Division back to the 9th Corps." Telegram sent, DNA, RG 94,
War Records Office, Army of the Potomac; copies, *ibid.*, RG 393, Army of the
Potomac, Letters Sent; (2) Meade Papers, PHi; DLC-Andrew Johnson. *O.R.*, I,
xl, part 2, 231. The enclosure is *ibid.*, p. 252.

To Maj. Gen. George G. Meade

By Telegraph from City Point [*6:15* P.M.]
Dated June 19 *1864.*

To MAJOR GEN MEADE
I have directed Major Gen Butler to throw a small force, One
Brigade, across the river from Jones Neck to Deep Bottom and to
fortify and hold that point connecting the two shores by a Pontoon
Bridge. This will be done tomorrow night. I wish you would direct
General Benham to turn over as many Pontoons and such other
Bridge Matterial as General Wright [*Weitzel*] may call for to ac-
complish this

U. S. GRANT
Lieut Genl

Telegram received (at 6:30 P.M.), DNA, RG 94, War Records Office, Army of
the Potomac; copies, *ibid.*, RG 108, Letters Sent; DLC-USG, V, 45, 59, 67; (2)
Meade Papers, PHi. *O.R.*, I, xl, part 2, 209. On June 19, 1864, 8:00 P.M. and
9:00 P.M. (both sent at 9:10 P.M.), Maj. Gen. George G. Meade telegraphed
to USG. "Your despatch directing that a ponton bridge be laid across the James
River from Jones N Neck to Deep Bottom has been received and General Benham
has been directed to furnish the necessary bridging material on the requisition
of Mjr General Butler or any officer designated by him—General Wright has
rejoined this Army and will at once relive the troops yet here under the command
of Brig General Martindale belonging to the 18th Corps" "The party sent
from these Head Quarters to construct the telegraph line from Fort Powhatan
to Swans' Point opposite Jamestown Island has returned, having performed the
service assigned it. The Sergeant in charge of the party reports that in returning
he found that the line had been cut in several places in the vicinity of Swans'
Point—The line was thoroughly repaired. ~~And it is feared that unless it is
guarded it cannot be kept in working order~~" Telegrams sent, DNA, RG 94,
War Records Office, Army of the Potomac; telegrams received (marked as sent
at 9:00 P.M.), *ibid.*, RG 108, Letters Received. *O.R.*, I, xl, part 2, 210.

To Maj. Gen. George G. Meade

City Point June 19th/64 6.30 P. M,

MAJ GEN MEADE

Gen Sheridan having returned without forming a junction with Gen Hunter, another diversion may become necessary for the protection of the latter. I wish therefore you would direct him to remain at White House and await further orders. His horses require rest which they can get as well at White House as here. His stock of ammunition ought to be replenished at the same time ~~the~~ his orders go to him. Two Army Gunboats were sent from here yesterday to keep the river clear from West Point to White House

U. S. GRANT Lt. Gen.

Copies, DLC-USG, V, 45, 59, 67; DNA, RG 108, Letters Sent; (2) Meade Papers, PHi. *O.R.*, I, xxxvi, part 3, 779; *ibid.*, I, xxxvii, part 1, 651; *ibid.*, I, xl, part 2, 209. On June 19, 1864, 8:30 P.M. (sent at 9:10 P.M.) and 10:00 P.M. (sent at 10:35 P.M.), Maj. Gen. George G. Meade telegraphed to USG. "Your despatch directing that General Sheridan remain at the White House until further orders has been received, and the necessary ~~orders~~ instructions have been given for the ~~renewa~~ renewal of his ammunition." Copy (telegram sent), DNA, RG 94, War Records Office, Army of the Potomac; telegram received, *ibid.*, RG 108, Letters Received. *O.R.*, I, xxxvi, part 3, 779; *ibid.*, I, xl, part 2, 210. "The Richmond Examiner of yesterday says Hunter on Thursday last was at Forest Depot on the Va. & Tenee. R. Rd. destroying that road—Forest Depot is supposed to be where the R. Rd crosses Forest Creek some 8 or 10 miles south west from Lynch burgh & appears to be on the road from Lexington—I will send you the paper tomorrow if you have not seen it.—Genl Beauregard in reply to my application to remove the dead & wounded declines, on the ground that he sees no occasion from recent operations for such a request but will be willing to accede to it after a general battle.—I have reason to believe there are but few wounded not brought off, but some dead of both armies unburied—The casualties for the 16. 17 & 18th will amount to about 7000 in all.—" ALS (telegram sent), DNA, RG 94, War Records Office, Army of the Potomac; telegram received, *ibid.*, RG 108, Letters Received. *O.R.*, I, xxxvii, part 1, 651; *ibid.*, I, xl, part 2, 210–11.

To Julia Dent Grant

City Point Va. June 19th *1864.*

DEAR JULIA,

I send you three steoriscopic views taken at Mattaponix [*Massa-*

ponax] Church, near Spotsylvania Court House. Brady[1] is along with the Army and is taking a great many views and will send you a copy of each. To see them you will want a Sterioscope. Send to Covington for Buck's or buy one.

I received a letter from you just after I had mailed one and now forget the questions you asked.—I received two copies of Miss. Photograph

There has been some very hard fighting here the last four days, but now I hope it is over.

There are no buildings here to live in and no place for you and the children to stay or I might send for you. I will however send down to Fortress Monroe and if a suitable place can be found there for you you and the children may spend their vacation there where I can see you occationally. If you do come wont Cousin Louisa come with you? I will ascertain about this as soon as possible.

Did I tell you that my horse rail-road stock paid 5 per cent the last quarter? This makes that $5.000 investment pay over $100 00 per month.

Love and kisses for you and the children and love to Aunt Fanny and your father.

ULYS.

ALS, DLC-USG.

1. For one of the Mathew B. Brady photographs, see *PUSG*, 10, 392. On Oct. 29, 1864, Col. Lafayette C. Baker, New York City, wrote to Asst. Secretary of War Charles A. Dana. "I have just come into possession of certain facts in relation to a plan arranged and devised by a number of prominent Wall Street Brokers, for procuring information from the Army of the Potomac, as to the success or defeat of General Grant's intended movements on Richmond. Some time last spring 'Mr Brady' the well known Daugareotyphist of New York, made application to Mr Stanton for a pass to visit the Army of the Potomac, for the purpose of taking views of Battle scenes &c,—The request of Mr Brady was refused at the War Department, he Brady then applied to the President, who also refused to grant his request, A few days afterwards Mrs Brady wrote a letter to Mrs. General Grant, asking Mrs Grant to use her influence with the General to procure the desired pass,—This letter obtained the wished for result, *viz*, the procuring of the pass from General Grant, Brady went to the Army and by his gratuitous offers to take the pictures of prominent Army Officers for the Illustrated papers in this City, placed himself on the most intimate terms with these officers, The Brokers referred to, having learned Brady's position in the Army, and knowing that he (Brady) possessed Genl. Grant's confidence, at once selected him as a medium through which they proposed to obtain the

information desired. It was understood by the Brokers referred to, that immediately preceeding or during any important movement or battle, that no telegrams could be sent from the Army without General Grant's approval or endorsement, (Brady then being with the Army of the Potomac) is to write and forward a telegram, purporting to be addressed to one of his (Brady's) Artists in this City, asking the Artist or employee to come to the Army at once to assist: This or some similarly worded telegram, is to be taken by Brady to Genl. Grant for his endorsement, but to be held and forwarded at a moment when the success or defeat of our Army will materially affect the Stock and Gold market, Inasmuch as Brady has obtained the unlimited confidence of General Grant (as he alledges,) I have deemed it proper to communicate these facts to the Department, in order that the General may know how he is being deceived by one to whom to whom he has granted various priveledges and favors. The facts and circumstances herein stated have been obtained from one of the principal (supposed) actors in the scheme, and can be relied upon as being strictly true," LS, DNA, RG 108, Letters Received. On Oct. 31, Dana endorsed this letter. "Confidentially referred to Lieutenant General U. S. Grant." ES, *ibid.*

To Edwin M. Stanton

Headquarters Armies of the United States
City Point, Va. June 20. 1864.

HON. EDWIN M STANTON
SECRETARY OF WAR,
WASHINGTON, D. C.

I have the honor to transmit herewith copy of telegram from Maj. Gen. G. K. Warren commanding 5th Corps to Maj. Gen. G. G. Meade, Com'd'g Army of the Potomac, and by him telegraphed to me with his approval and recommendation; also, a copy of my order appointing Col Joshua L Chamberlain a Brigadier General of Volunteers to rank as such from the 18th inst, subject to the approval of the President. This is done in pursuance of your telegram of date May 15th, and I respectfully request the sanction of my action by the President, and that the name of Col. Chamberlain be sent to the Senate for confirmation.

I have the honor to be, Sir,
Very Respectfully
Your Ob't. Serv't.
U. S. GRANT
Lieutenant General

LS, DLC-Ainsworth L. Spofford. On June 19, 1864, Maj. Gen. Gouverneur K. Warren telegraphed to Maj. Gen. George G. Meade. "Col. J. L. Chamberlain of the 20th Maine regt. commanding the 1st Brigade of the 1st Division was mortally wounded it is thought in the assaults on the enemy yesterday The ball having passed through the pelvis and bladder He has been recommended for promotion for gallant and efficient conduct on previous occasions and yesterday led his brigade against the enemy under a most destructive fire He expresses the wish that he may receive the recognition of his service by promotion before he died for the gratification of his family & friends & I beg that if possible it may be done. He has been sent to City Point." Telegram received, DNA, RG 94, War Records Office, Army of the Potomac. *O.R.*, I, xl, part 2, 216–17. On the same day, 7:00 P.M., Meade endorsed the telegram. "The above telegram is transmitted to the Lt. Genl. Comd. with the earnest recommendation that Col Chamberlins wish be gratified—" AES (telegram sent), DNA, RG 94, War Records Office, Army of the Potomac; telegram received, *ibid.*, RG 108, Letters Received. *O.R.*, I, xl, part 2, 217. Although the *O.R.* prints the Warren telegram as sent at 9:16 P.M., this is the time when it was transmitted to USG. On June 20, Lt. Col. Theodore S. Bowers issued Special Orders No. 39. "Colonel *Joshua L. Chamberlain.* 20th Regiment Maine Infantry Volunteers, is, for meritorious and efficient services on the field of battle, and especially for gallant conduct in leading his Brigade against the enemy at Petersburg, Va., on the 18th inst., (in which he was dangerously wounded,) hereby, in pursuance of authority of the Secretary of War, appointed *Brigadier General* of United States Volunteers, to rank as such from the 18th day of June, 1864, subject to the approval of the President" DS (by USG), DLC-Ainsworth L. Spofford; DNA, RG 94, ACP, C411 CB 1866. *O.R.*, I, xl, part 2, 236. On the same day, USG telegraphed the text of the order to Capt. George K. Leet for delivery to Col. Joshua L. Chamberlain, presumably because of the expectation of his death. Telegram received, DNA, RG 107, Telegrams Collected (Bound). Chamberlain, however, recovered.

To Edwin M. Stanton

City Point Va. June 20th *1864.*

HON. E. M. STANTON,
SEC. OF WAR,
SIR;

Permit me to intercede in behalf of Capt. G. A. Williams, 1st U. S. Inf.y, who has been dismissed the service, without trial, and ask a revocation of the order so dismissing him. Capt. Williams served under me in the West, a portion of the time commanding the 1st Infantry as a Regiment of Heavy Artillery and part of the time as Col. of a Volunteer regiment. His services attracted my attention to such an extent that I recommended him for a Brigadier

Generalcy. Becoming disabled for active field duty, by reason of a rupture, I sent him to Memphis, and, at my suggestion, he was appointed Provost Marshal.

If anything can be proven against Capt. Williams I will not attempt to shield him. But I do know him to be a most active and efficient officer, well qualified for the command of a Division at least, and all that I do know of him too leads me to believe him to be an officer of great purity of character. If he is not so I have been grossly deceived.

Hoping that full justice may be done Capt. Williams, I remain,

your obt. svt.

U. S. GRANT

Lt. Gen.

ALS, DNA, RG 94, Letters Received, 688W 1864.
On May 20, 1864, Maj. Gen. Cadwallader C. Washburn, Memphis, wrote to USG. "Some ten days ago I received a dispatch of which the enclosed is a copy, from the War Dept. Satisfied that great injustice was likely to be done to a meritorious Officer, I immediately sent a dispatch asking him to suspend the order until Capt. Williams could be heard. Since then I have heard nothing either in answer to my telegram, nor of the dispatches that were promised in the telegram from Col. Hardee: Capt. Williams was a perfect stranger to me when I came here. I have watched his course closely and a sense of justice compels me to say that he is one of the few Provost Marshalls that I have known that has discharged his duty with unswerving fidelity and ability. His place cannot be made good. The charge in regard to his mismanagement of the Military Prison, I believe does him great injustice. The Prison is a very unfit one and no doubt some abuses have grown up. The immense business of Capt. Williams prevents him from attending to all the details of his Office. I have had all abuses corrected as far as possible and shall prevent their reccurrence. Waiting for an answer to my dispatch to the War Dept. I have not relieved Capt Williams. I believe that you will agree with me and interpose to prevent injustice being done. him. He deserves promotion and not censure unless I am grossly deceived." LS, *ibid.*, RG 108, Letters Received. Washburn enclosed a telegram of May 7, 4:30 P.M., from Col. James A. Hardie to Washburn. "The attention of the Secy of War has been called to the Shameful condition of the Military Prison at Memphis, Tenn. He directs that Capt Geo A. Williams 1st U. S. Infantry, the commanding officer at the prison, be informed that he stands dismissed from the Service of the U. S. for flagrant neglect of his duty as Comdt of the prison. The Secy of War further directs, that you make an immediate inspection in every Dept of the prison, remedy neglect and abuses, establish order and discipline, and while providing for the Security of prisoners, See that they are not made the object of improper treatment, or inauthorized Severity. Report your action in this case. A copy of the inspection report will be sent you by mail with more definite instructions." Telegram received, *ibid.*

On June 14, Lt. Col. William L. Duff, Washington, wrote to U.S. Representative Elihu B. Washburne. "Capt Geo Williams of the 1st U. S. Infantry has shewn me a letter from your Brother Maj Gen Washburn and has proved to me by that and what he has told me that he is a very badly used man—In the estimation of Genl Grant Genl Rawlins and all of the staff that know Capt Williams he is known to be a gentleman above reproach and one of the most brave & gallant soldiers of the army and without a doubt in conjunction with Capt Phillips & Lieut Robinett & others of His Regt the saviour of Corinth when attacked by Price & Vandorn in 1862   Anything you can do for him to set him right and get him reinstated in his position ~~and~~ will be done for a worthy object and I have told him that in cases of that sort you will do all that can be done for him" ALS, DLC-Elihu B. Washburne. For a report exonerating Capt. George A. Williams, see *O.R.*, II, vii, 404–8.

To Maj. Gen. Benjamin F. Butler

By Telegraph from City Point.
Dated June 20 *1864.*

To Maj Gen Butler.

I shall start a Cavalry expedition tomorrow night or the following morning, to cut the enemys lines of communications south, & want all of Kautz force that you do not require to accompany it. Gen Wilson will take with him all of the Cavy under Gen Meade's command present, except a few hundred for Provost duty. Please direct Gen Kautz to report to Gen Wilson tomorrow for this service.

U. S. Grant
Lt Genl.

Telegram received (at 3:08 P.M., June 20, 1864), DNA, RG 393, Dept. of Va. and N. C., Telegrams Received; copies, *ibid.*, RG 108, Letters Sent; DLC-USG, V, 45, 59, 67. *O.R.*, I, xl, part 2, 257. At 3:30 P.M., Maj. Gen. Benjamin F. Butler telegraphed to USG. "Orders have been issued to Gen Kautz to report to Genl Wilson, with four Regiments of Cavalry and two peices of Artillery prepared to start on an expedition to cut the lines of communication South. My signal officer reports a regiment of Rebel Cavalry passing the turnpike North toward Richmond" ALS (telegram sent), DNA, RG 94, War Records Office, Army of the Potomac; telegram received, *ibid.*, RG 108, Letters Received. *O.R.*, I, xl, part 2, 257.

At 10:40 A.M., Lt. Col. Theodore S. Bowers had telegraphed to Butler. "Gen Meade has authorized a certain amount of mess stores and vegetables to come forward to his Army, and has an Officer of his Staff at Washington to regulate shipments. These stores are stopped at Fortress Monroe. Direct the Commanding Officer at Fortress Monroe to allow all vessels and persons having Gen

Meades pass to come to City Point without detention or interference—" Copies, DLC-USG, V, 45, 59, 67; DNA, RG 108, Letters Sent. *O.R.*, I, xl, part 2, 256. On June 21, Bowers telegraphed to the commanding officer, Fort Monroe. "It is reported to these Head Quarters that Vessels and persons that have permits from Genl. Meade or his Provost Marshal General to come to to the Army of the Potomac are detained by you at Fortress Monroe—Immediately upon the receipt of this order, you will notify all such Vessels and persons that they can come forward and hereafter you will respect and obey all passes issued by Genl. Meade or by his order for Vessels and their Cargoe's, and for persons to come to his Army, Acknowledge the receipt of this order." Telegram received, DNA, RG 107, Telegrams Collected (Unbound); (press) *ibid.*, Telegrams Collected (Bound); *ibid.*, RG 393, Dept. of Va. and N. C., Telegrams Received; copies, *ibid.*, RG 108, Letters Sent; DLC-USG, V, 45, 59, 67. On June 22, Bowers issued Special Orders No. 41. "The passes and permits of the Lieut Genl. Commanding, of Maj Gen B. F. Butler Comd'g Department of Virginia and North Carolina, and of Maj Gen G. G. Meade Commanding Army of the Potomac, given by themselves respectively, or by their order, for persons, vessels, property and supplies of all kinds to pass and be passed from Washington D. C. or Baltimore Md. to their respective Headquarters, City Point and Bermuda Hundred Va, and intermediate points, and from their respective Head quarters, City Point, Bermuda Hundred and intermediate points to Washington and Baltimore, will be respected and obeyed by all Military Authorities Provosts Marshals and Guards. Any disregard of these passes or permits or interference with the subjects of them will be an offense subjecting the guilty party to summary punishment— City Point, Va, will be the Depot of supplies for the Army of the Potomac and for such purposes is hereby transferred from the Command of Maj Gen B. F. Butler to the command of Maj Gen G. G. Meade Commanding Army of the Potomac, who will immediately designate a garrison under a proper officer to releive the present garrison, which, when releived will report to Maj Gen Butler for orders. Bermuda Hundred Va. will be the Depot of supplies for the army in the Field of the Department of Virginia and North Carolina—" Copies, *ibid.*, V, 57, 62, 67; (2—incomplete) Meade Papers, PHi. *O.R.*, I, xl, part 2, 305. At 10:50 P.M., Brig. Gen. Seth Williams telegraphed to Bowers. "General Meade desires that you will present his compliments to Lieutenant General Grant and a inquire whether he can delay relieving the garrison at City Point until the arrival of the troops from the White House, which may be expected within two or three days" ALS (telegram sent), DNA, RG 94, War Records Office, Army of the Potomac; copy, *ibid.*, RG 393, Army of the Potomac, Letters Sent. On June 24, 7:15 A.M. (sent at 8:05 A.M.), Williams telegraphed to Bowers. "N̶ Did you receive my despatch of 22d asking for General Meade whether he could delay releiving the garrison at City Point until the arrival of the troops expected there from the White House, and which should reach that place by d̶ tomorrow. General Meade directs me to add that it will embarrass him to detach at this time a g̶a̶r̶r̶ garrison for City Point from the troops here a̶t̶ ̶t̶h̶i̶s̶ ̶t̶i̶m̶e̶. If it is thought advisable the Engineer troops a̶t̶ ̶C̶i̶t̶y̶ ̶P̶o̶i̶n̶t̶ under General Benham can be assigned temporarily to garrison duty at City Point" ALS (telegram sent), *ibid.*, RG 94, War Records Office, Army of the Potomac; copy, *ibid.*, RG 393, Army of the Potomac, Letters Sent. *O.R.*, I, xl, part 2, 373. On the same day, Bowers telegraphed to Williams. "I presume there is no objection to the present garrison remaining at City Point until the troops from White House arrive Gen Grant is now on his way to your HdQrs & can give you definite information" Telegram received, DNA, RG 94, War Records Office, Army of the Potomac. *O.R.*, I, xl, part 2, 373.

On June 20, 3:00 P.M., Butler telegraphed to USG. "Genl. Weitzel has just returned from a careful reconnoisance of the position at Deep Bottom. He reports the problem as of the most difficult solution and not capable of a thoroughly satisfactory one. The best position would bring the bridge under close artillery fire from commanding positions, and the work itself would be under this fire. He does not feel justified to decide what to recommend, and suggests that Col. Comstock be sent over ~~to morrow morning to ride over~~ and look at the position with him, or for such others ~~ord~~ instructions as we may be favored with" LS (telegram sent), DNA, RG 94, War Records Office, Army of the Potomac; telegram received, *ibid.*, RG 108, Letters Received. Printed as sent at 2:45 P.M. in *O.R.*, I, xl, part 2, 257. On the same day, USG telegraphed to Butler. "Neither Col Comstock or Gen Barnard are here to accompany Gen Weitzel on a reconnoissance over the river. I think Genl Weitzel had better give the problem the best solution he can & after occupying the North bank of the river we can occupy also the ground commanding the fortifications & bridge or can make any change that may be necessary." Telegram received (at 3:25 P.M.), DNA, RG 393, Dept. of Va. and N. C., Telegrams Received; copies, *ibid.*, RG 108, Letters Sent; DLC-USG, V, 45, 59, 67. Printed as sent at 3:25 P.M. in *O.R.*, I, xl, part 2, 257.

Also on June 20, Butler telegraphed to USG a message received at 4:00 P.M. from Sgt. Baird, Signal Corps, "River Bank Spring Hill Sta." "A train of cars from the direction of Richmond came to within 300 yards of port Waltham station & went back immediately   Two (2) wagon trains one of 29 & another of thirty (30) wagons have just passed down the pike towards Petersburg" ALS (telegram sent), DNA, RG 107, Telegrams Collected (Unbound); telegram received, *ibid.*, RG 108, Letters Received.

To Maj. Gen. Benjamin F. Butler

By Telegraph from City Point. June 20, 64. 5.25 P. M.

Genl Butler

I have determined to try to envelope Petersburg so as to have the left of the Army of the Potomac rest on the Appomattox above the City.

This will make offensive operations from between the two Rivers impracticable until we are fortified in the new position taken up. To release as many of Genl Meades command as possible you will extend your left so as to release the entire 6th Corps, the right of the Army of the Potomac. Reduce the force kept between the two rivers to the lowest number necessary to hold it & ½ put all the balance except the force sent north of the James, South of the Appomattox & between the Pontoon Bridge and the present left of the 6th [Corps]

Make this change as soon as practicable and so as to relieve the 6th Corps by 12 M. tomorrow if you can

U. S. GRANT
Lt. Genl.

Telegram received, DNA, RG 393, Dept. of Va. and N. C., Telegrams Received; copies, *ibid.*, RG 94, War Records Office, Dept. of Va. and N. C., Army of the James, Unentered Papers; *ibid.*, RG 108, Letters Sent; DLC-USG, V, 45, 59, 67. Printed as sent at 6:45 P.M., June 20, 1864, in *O.R.*, I, xl, part 2, 258.

To Maj. Gen. Benjamin F. Butler

By Telegraph from City Point.
Dated June 20 *1864.*

To MAJ GEN BUTLER

I have directed white House, to be broken up as a military Post. You may direct the abandonment of Yorktown by the military. Let the garrison leave there as soon as practicable after the troops from White House pass, the troops brought from Yorktown you may dispose of as you deem best. As soon as all the troops are out of York river, direct the Army Gunboats to return here.

U. S. GRANT.
Lt Genl.

Telegram received (at 5:50 P.M.), DNA, RG 393, Dept. of Va. and N. C., Telegrams Received; copies, *ibid.*, RG 108, Letters Sent; DLC-USG, V, 45, 59, 67. *O.R.*, I, xl, part 2, 258.

To Maj. Gen. George G. Meade

City Point, June 20th/64

MAJ GEN MEADE

As soon as Wilson's Cavalry is rested sufficiently they should

make a raid upon the enemys rail roads. My view is that the road
to Weldon should be crossed as near Petersburg as possible and
the first strike made for the Lynchburg & Petersburg road thence
to the Danville road upon which all the damags possible should be
done. Kautz can be thrown upon your left while Wilson is gone

U. S. GRANT Lt. Gen.

Telegram, copies, DLC-USG, V, 45, 59, 67; DNA, RG 108, Letters Sent; (2)
Meade Papers, PHi; (marked as sent at 9:30 A.M.) Alcorn Collection, WyU.
O.R., I, xl, part 2, 232. On June 20, 1864, 10:00 A.M., Maj. Gen. George G.
Meade telegraphed to USG. "Wilson was directed to report the moment he was
ready for service—To day is his third day of rest—Your despatch has been sent
to him to show him the importance of being ready—Where do you suppose the
enemys cavalry to be? and do you not think that with the knowledge of Sheridans
withdrawal Hampton will be drawn in to Richmond ready to be thrown on any
raiding party reported—It has occurred to me that with Hunters position as
known Sheridan would be more likely to communicate with him & assist him by
going from here up the South bank of the James, than from the White house   In
that case Wilson could join him & make his force such that he could not be
stopped—If a bridge is thrown over at Deep Bottom Sheridan could cross there.—
I make these suggestions for what they are worth.—I proposed riding down to
the Point to see you if you remained at home today but have had no reply to my
enquiry.—" ALS (telegram sent), DNA, RG 94, War Records Office, Army of
the Potomac; telegram received, *ibid.*, RG 108, Letters Received. *O.R.*, I, xxxvi,
part 3, 781; *ibid.*, I, xl, part 2, 232. At 10:00 A.M., Lt. Col. Orville E. Babcock
telegraphed to Meade. "The Lieut Genl says he shall not go away from here to
day"   ALS (telegram sent), DNA, RG 107, Telegrams Collected (Unbound);
telegram received (at 10:30 A.M.), *ibid.*, RG 94, War Records Office, Army of
the Potomac. Printed as sent at 10:30 A.M. in *O.R.*, I, xl, part 2, 233. On the
same day, USG telegraphed to Meade. "Immediately on receipt of your dispatch
saying that you would come down today if I was going to remain in I directed a
dispatch to be sent back saying I would be at home. I would like very much to
see you down." Telegram received (at noon), DNA, RG 94, War Records Office,
Army of the Potomac; copies, *ibid.*, RG 108, Letters Sent; DLC-USG, V, 45, 59,
67; (2) Meade Papers, PHi. *O.R.*, I, xl, part 2, 233.

To Maj. Gen. George G. Meade

By Telegraph from City Point 5 40 P M
Dated June 20 *1864.*

To GEN MEADE
To give you another Army Corps foot loose I will order Gen Butler

to extend his lines so as to cover the ground now occupied by the 6th Corps

I will direct this to be done between this & 12 M tomorrow. With the use of guns that will probably reach here tomorrow with the seige train I think Butlers left will be able to destroy the Railroad bridge & possibly silence the [e]nemy guns on the north side of the Appomattox   As you extend to the left I think [i]t will be adviseable to do it by rapid movement & with as heavy force as possible

U S GRANT

Lt Gen

Telegram received, DNA, RG 94, War Records Office, Army of the Potomac; copies, *ibid.*, RG 108, Letters Sent; DLC-USG, V, 45, 59, 67; (2) Meade Papers, PHi. *O.R.*, I, xl, part 2, 233. On June 20, 1864, 6:30 P.M. and 8:00 P.M., Maj. Gen. George G. Meade telegraphed to USG. "Warren now holds to the Jerusalem plank road.—Tonight I shall withdraw the 2d. corps, the 9th holding between the 5th & 6th, and will mass the 2d. on the left & rear of the 5th then when the 6th is relieved as you propose I will move both corps 2d. & 6th to the left and endeavor to stretch to the Appomatox. A deserter in today belongs to McLaws Division Longstreets corps—He says the corps came to our front on the 18th last day of our fight, and that the corps is on the enemys right.—Sheridan's last despatch by Maj. Forsyth was dated the 18th at Walkertown on the Mattapony— This place is only Ten miles from White house—I dont know where Sheridan could be this morning because even if he had gone to West Point, on the 19th as he indicated he would have learned of the White House being still occupied & would have returned there—In case he ~~had~~ was not on the way this morning he will certainly hear the guns & hurry up—so that Abercrombie ought to be all right—" "Maj. Genl. Wright informs me that Maj. Genl. Smith has applied again for Genl. Neill to be transferred to the 18th Corps. & Genl. Wright is willing the transfer should be made—Under these circumstances I would be glad if you would allow the transfer." ALS (telegrams sent), DNA, RG 94, War Records Office, Army of the Potomac; telegrams received, *ibid.*, RG 108, Letters Received. *O.R.*, I, xl, part 2, 233, 234. The first is also *ibid.*, I, xxxvi, part 3, 782–83. See *ibid.*, I, xl, part 2, 270.

At 10:20 A.M., Brig. Gen. John J. Abercrombie telegraphed to USG. "We were attacked early this morning by a large force of cavalry infantry and artillery   The fight still going on   Gen Sheridan has not arrived" Telegram received, DNA, RG 94, War Records Office, Dept. of Va. and N. C., Army of the James, Unentered Papers; *ibid.*, RG 107, Telegrams Collected (Unbound); *ibid.*, RG 108, Letters Received. USG endorsed this telegram to Meade. "The above dispatch just received." AES, *ibid.* At 6:00 P.M., USG telegraphed to Abercrombie. "Your dispatch of 10.20 A. M. received. Hold out at all hazards. Two Gunboats were sent from here yesterday and must now be at White House. Gen Sheridan is also near you if not yet arrived." Copies, DLC-USG, V, 45, 59, 67; DNA, RG 108, Letters Sent. *O.R.*, I, xxxvi, part 3, 785.

To Maj. Gen. George G. Meade

City Point, June 20th *1864.*

MAJ. GEN. MEADE,
COMD.G A. P.
GENERAL,

In view of the location of Gen. Hunter as reported in the Rebel papers, and the fact that General Sheridan cannot carry supplies with him from the White House to make an efective raid against the Enemy's Communications, North of the James, you may direct his immediate return to the Army of the Potomac. The manner of returning, and route, is left to you. Direct the commanding officer at White House to break up that post and send his Veteran Reserve troops to Washington ~~and~~ bringing all the balance here, to City Point. This latter to take place on the departure of Gen. Sheridan.

Very respectfully
U. S. GRANT
Lt. Gen

ALS, DNA, RG 94, War Records Office, Army of the Potomac. *O.R.*, I, xxxvi, part 3, 781–82; *ibid.*, I, xxxvii, part 1, 653; *ibid.*, I, xl, part 2, 231. On June 20, 1864, 9:00 A.M., Maj. Gen. George G. Meade telegraphed to USG. "No reports indicating any thing but quiet along the lines have been this morning received.— Maj. Forsyth 8th Ills. Cav. arrived last night with despatches from Genl. Sheridan—the duplicate of those sent by telegraph from Yorktown.—Maj. Forsyth has been directed to await the orders of the Lt. Genl. Comdg.—Orders have been sent to Genl. Sheridan to await further instructions at the White House.—Your attention was called last evening to the reported position of Genl. Hunter Ten miles South West of Lynchburgh   This renders the probability of his reaching the White House very remote & it becomes a question how long that post should be retained after Sheridan leaves it   It will be maintained, so far as my orders, until otherwise instructed. I propose tonight to hold my present lines with the 6th 9. & 5th corps & keep the 2d in reserve. I have reason to believe from prisoners & contrabands that Beauregard has been re-inforced by 2 divisions of Hills corps Wilcox's & Andersons and possibly others.—The enemy line is continued as far beyond my left flank as I have been able to reconnoitre, and they are busily occupied strengthening it.—~~No~~ I do not propose making any movement today— If you will be at home this morning, I will ride down to see you.—" ALS (telegram sent), DNA, RG 94, War Records Office, Army of the Potomac; telegram received, *ibid.*, RG 108, Letters Received. *O.R.*, I, xxxvi, part 3, 780–81; *ibid.*, I, xl, part 2, 231.

To Maj. Gen. George G. Meade

City Point Va. June 20th *1864*.

MAJ. GEN. MEADE,
COMD.G A. P.
GENERAL,

Lieut. E. P. Brooks with Thirty soldiers, all volunteers for the service, are now equiped and ready to start on an expedition to destroy distant rail-road bridges. I think it advisable that the party should not start until a more formidable expedition is going out. They could accompany such an expedition until it was deemed safe to strike out independently. The party, if successful, will not probably attempt to reach here ~~until~~ except through some Military post further south, likely New Bern. Will you please instruct Gen. Wilson to let Lt. Brooks and party accompany him until the proper time for cutting loose.

Very respectfully
U. S. GRANT
Lt. Gen.

ALS, DNA, RG 393, Army of the Potomac, Cav. Corps, 3rd Div., Letters Received. *O.R.*, I, xl, part 2, 234. On June 12, 1864, 1st Lt. Edward P. Brooks, 6th Wis., wrote to USG. "After some hesitation I have made up my mind to do an exceedingly unmilitary act by addressing you directly relative to a matter which has always seemed to me to be of great importance to this army while operating against Richmond. I propose that thirty determined men can make a raid into the South-Western portion of this State ~~out~~ the results of which will be equal to any demonstration of the sort ever made by our army here. My plan is as follows:—As the army now lays I would cross the James River at Goochland C. H. & proceeding over south via Scottsville, destroy the junction of the Danville & Richmond & the Virginia & Tennesse Railroads at Burkesville. And if possible go still farther south & demolish the R. R. bridge over the Roanoke River at Roanoke Station at its junction with the Little Roanoke. This could be accomplished in three days by travelling a distance of one hundred & twenty miles at the farthest. With thirty men whom I could select from Western Infantry Regts in my Brigade—well mounted—I would promise to effect all this & join this army or that under Maj. Gen. Hunter in one week. The great difficulty to my mind would be the crossing of the James. I do not apprehend that there is any force of consequences guarding the Burkesville Junction & I think it safe to calculate that the Roanoke crossing is unprotected—Hoping that you will appreciate the motive which prompts this intrusion as arising from a desire to serve you & my country" ALS, DNA, RG 108, Letters Received. Brooks enclosed a list of men for his expedition, and they were assigned for duty on June 18 by Special Orders No. 37, Armies of the U.S. Copies, DLC-USG, V, 57, 62, 67.

To Julia Dent Grant

City Point, Va. June 20th *1864*.

DEAR JULIA,

I spoke to Gen. Butler about the opportunity of you staying at Fortress Monroe during the vacation of the children and he says for you to go and stay with Mrs. Butler who will be delighted at having company. Mrs. Butler is almost alone and has a large house. You and Mrs. B. could keep house to-gether or rather let Mrs. Butler keep house and share expenses. There are other houses in the fort but the difficulty would be want of furnature.—If you were at Fortress Monroe you could occationaly come to City Point when the Dispatch steamer is coming up and go back with it. I would keep Fred & Buck with me most of the time, and Jess too some times. I leave it entirely with you whether to come or not.

All well. Kisses for yourself and the children. If Louisa Boggs will come and spend the Summer with you bring her along also.

ULYS.

ALS, DLC-USG.

To Maj. Gen. Benjamin F. Butler

By Telegraph from City Point
Dated June 21 *1864*.

To MAJ GEN BUTLER.

The President is here. Tomorrow he will go up the river to see Admiral Lee & requests you to join him. I will go along, starting from here at eight 8 a m on the boat brought by the President and

will touch at Bermuda Hundred for you. Would go to the wharf on
Appomattox but the Pilot probably does not know the river

U. S. GRANT.

Lt Genl

Telegram received (at 10:30 P.M.), DNA, RG 393, Dept. of Va. and N. C.,
Telegrams Received; copies, *ibid.*, RG 108, Letters Sent; DLC-USG, V, 45, 59,
67. Printed as sent at 10:50 A.M. in *O.R.*, I, xl, part 2, 287. On June 21, 1864,
9:30 A.M., Lt. Col. Orville E. Babcock telegraphed to Maj. Gen. Benjamin F.
Butler. "The President desires you to notify Admiral Lee, that he will visit him
tomorrow leaving here at 8 a. m." ALS (telegram sent), DNA, RG 107, Telegrams Collected (Unbound). Printed as received at 10:45 A.M. in *O.R.*, I, xl,
part 2, 288.

On June 21, 1st Lt. Charles F. Cross telegraphed to Capt. Lemuel B. Norton.
"The enemies vessels are rounding Dutch Gap" Telegram received, DNA, RG
107, Telegrams Collected (Unbound). Butler endorsed this telegram to USG.
"The ~~batter~~ Guns heard are the rebels from the Howlet House Battery shelling
my camp. I have ordered the ~~Howlet~~ Battery on the bank to open upon it—"
AES, *ibid.* Butler also transmitted to USG another telegram of June 21 from
Cross to Norton. "The Navy are slowly moving down stream   4 of their vessels
are in Devils Neck" Telegram received, *ibid.* On June 23, Act. Rear Admiral
S. Phillips Lee wrote to USG. "In the engagement day before yesterday with the
rebel battery at Howlett's in which their iron clads, out of view in a reach above,
participated, we silenced one (1) of the guns at Howletts, but expended a good
deal of our heavy and expensive ammunition. One of the monitors was injured
by a 10 inch solid shot from the battery at Howlett's—The XV inch gun has a
short life so far as it has been proved, and it is difficult to replace it in the turret
of a monitor. We have to fire it at extreme elevation to reach Howlett's battery
which increases the strain on the gun and breaks its long screws. As it was arranged yesterday between Asst. Secretary Fox and yourself to increase the obstructions already placed by the army in Trent's reach so that two (2) iron-clads
would be sufficient here for the present, leaving the Navy Department to withdraw the other two (2)—one of which is now under orders for sea—for more
pressing service else where, I respectfully suggest that the cheapest and most
convenient control of rebel battery at Howletts, of Trents reach and its obstructions and of Dutch Gap would be by mounting a few heavy guns at the lower
end of the reach. This would allow the iron-clads to drop round the point—withdrawing a few hundred yards—where they could keep their hatches off in hot
weather—whence they could in a few minutes return, and engage the rebel iron
clads, should they appear in the upper part of the reach or intefere with the obstructions. Our Naval resources would thus be reserved for their iron-clads, and
not exhausted on their earthworks—" LS, *ibid.*, RG 108, Letters Received;
(press) DLC-S. Phillips Lee. *O.R.*, I, xl, part 2, 335; *O.R.* (Navy), I, x, 184.

On June 21, 6:45 A.M., Butler telegraphed to USG. "My Brigade under
Brig Genl R. S. Foster made a successful lodgement on the North Bank of the
James at Deep Bottom without opposition and are entrenching making good
progress." ALS (telegram sent), DNA, RG 94, War Records Office, Dept. of
Va. and N. C., Army of the James, Unentered Papers; telegram received (at
8:00 A.M.), *ibid.*, RG 108, Letters Received. *O.R.*, I, xl, part 2, 286. On the

same day, Butler telegraphed to USG a message of 2:10 P.M. from Brig. Gen. Robert S. Foster reporting C.S.A. movements in his front. Telegram received, DNA, RG 108, Letters Received. Printed as sent at 2:00 P.M. in *O.R.*, I, xl, part 2, 298.

At 11:00 A.M., USG telegraphed to Butler. "Please furnish me a statement approximate one at least of the number of troops sent south of the appomattox under instructions of yesterday & the number left for the defense of Entrenchment in front of Bermuda Hundred." Telegram received (at 11:30 A.M.), DNA, RG 393, Dept. of Va. and N. C., Army of the James, Telegrams Received; copies, *ibid.*, RG 108, Letters Sent; DLC-USG, V, 45, 59, 67. Printed as sent at 11:30 A.M. in *O.R.*, I, xl, part 2, 288. At 3:00 P.M., Butler telegraphed to USG. "I have sent with Genl Smith South of Appomattox 15000 Infantry 8 Batteries of Artillery Gen Kautz has also gone with two thousand five hundred effective Cavaly one Battery of horse Artillery I have on line 7000 old troops 2000 on the north bank of the James I have 2600 Ohio men (100 days) 1800 of which are a working party on the north Side Remainder on fatigue & detail duty This is approximate only as. the troops were reorganized yesterday. and ~~only returning left~~ returns are not yet in" ALS (telegram sent), DNA, RG 94, War Records Office, Army of the Potomac; telegram received, *ibid.*, RG 108, Letters Received. *O.R.*, I, xl, part 2, 288.

At 8:20 P.M. and 8:30 P.M., Butler telegraphed to USG. "I have reliable information that the Rail road is not yet repaired" "I have reliable information that the Rail road between Petersburgh & Richmond is not yet repaired" ALS (telegrams sent), DNA, RG 393, Dept. of Va. and N. C., Telegrams Sent (Press). The second, also an ALS (telegram sent), *ibid.*, RG 107, Telegrams Collected (Unbound), apparently the revision actually sent, is in *O.R.*, I, xl, part 2, 288.

To Maj. Gen. Benjamin F. Butler

City Point Va June 21st *1864.*

MAJ. GEN. B. F. BUTLER,
COMD.G DEPT. of N. C. & VA.
GENERAL,

Your communication of this date in reference to the transfer of Colored Troops from the Dept. of the Gulf to this Dept. is received. I have not got with me in the field returns to show how the troops in the Dept. of the Gulf are distributed, but I will forward your communications to Washington with instructions to send as many of the Colored troops here as can be spared.

I am aware that the command of the Colored troops in the Dept.

of the Gulf has been in bad hands and will so state in my indors-ment of your paper, suggesting a change.

Since the advent of Gen. Canby it is probable a very great change will be made in the location of troops on the Miss. I will ascertain however as soon as possible.

> I am Gen. very respectfully
> your obt. svt.
> U. S. GRANT
> Lt. Gen.

ALS, DLC-Benjamin F. Butler. On June 21, 1864, Maj. Gen. Benjamin F. But-ler, Point of Rocks, Va., wrote to USG. "I am informed by Brig Genl Wietzal that there are now at Baton Rouge some 30 regiments of Negro infantry prob-ably averaging 500 that they have been there for a year simply garrisoning that place. I know Baton Rouge very well. with its fortifications 3000 determined men can hold it against 15. Certain it is that 1500 men under the lamented Wil-liams held it against 8000 under Breckenridge. I am informed from various sources and [b]elieve that for some cause and I think so far as my experiance [h]as gone want of attention to hygenic principles the negro soldiers there are dying at a very great rate of mortality   The negro soldiers in this [d]epartment are by far the [h]ealthiest troops I have. With [t]he exception of casualties in [b]attle the sick are not one & [a] half pr cent. Not in the [l]imits of this note but more at [l]ength I am convinced I could explain the causes of this mortality in Louisiana which has been made the subject of parade in rebel newspapers and of alarm to the friends of the black man. In view of this the need of troops and specially those as well adapted for siege operations as the negro are I suggest that as many as could be spared from the Department of the Gulf and that would be just as many as ~~could be spared from the Department of the Gulf~~ are ordered away be sent for to come into this department   I think that 10 or 15000 of ef-fective men could be got in this manner, and the change of the sea air upon their health in the saving of the men would actually pay for the transportation   Par-don these suggestions if out of place but my familiarity with the Department of the Gulf has given me means of knowledge upon this subject which I supposed might not be readily within the reach of the Lieut Genl Comd'g and therefore have taken leave to make these suggestions   If it should be thought best to adopt them I have a staff [o]fficer who commanded a regiment at Port Hudson and served two years in the Department of the Gulf whom I could recommend as a very competant and efficient person to take charge of the transportation of these negro troops to Fortress Monroe." Copy, DNA, RG 393, Dept. of Va. and N. C., Telegrams Sent (Press). *O.R.*, I, xl, part 2, 287. On June 24, USG en-dorsed this letter. "Respy. forwarded   A letter forwarded asks for such of the troops as can be spared from the Department of the Gulf, black and white." Copy, DLC-USG, V, 58. *O.R.*, I, xl, part 2, 287. See letter to Maj. Gen. Henry W. Halleck, June 23, 1864.

To Maj. Gen. George G. Meade

By Telegraph from City Point 10 a m
Dated June 21st *1864.*

To MAJ GEN MEADE

Looking at the position of our troops as marked on the map by Gen Barnard & Col Comstock it looks to me as if a concentration of Artillery about your present left would hold the enemy within his present line whilst you take up a position crossing the Jerusalem road. When you get there in force I do not see how the enemy can hold his present line. You certainly will have it in reverse—Would it not be will have the 5th & 9th Corps hold a threatening attitude when you move to the left & be prepared to advance on to & occupy the Enemys present line the moment he weakens it. I do not give this as an order knowing that you are better posted on the topography of the country over which you have to operate than I am. but to suggest attention to what seems to me from the map, proper

U S GRANT
Lt Gen

Telegram received, DNA, RG 94, War Records Office, Army of the Potomac; copies, *ibid.*, RG 108, Letters Sent; DLC-USG, V, *45, 59, 67;* (2) Meade Papers, PHi. *O.R.*, I, xl, part 2, 268. On June 21, 1864, 11:00 A.M., Maj. Gen. George G. Meade telegraphed to USG. "Telegram 10. a m received. I do not fully understand your views—Can you not send Barnard & Comstock here to explain them—I shall be most glad to carry them out whenever I fully understand what it is you propose to do." ALS (telegram sent), DNA, RG 94, War Records Office, Army of the Potomac; telegram received (at 11:15 A.M.), *ibid.*, RG 108, Letters Received. *O.R.*, I, xl, part 2, 268.

To Maj. Gen. George G. Meade

By Telegraph from City Point 10 15 a m
Dated June 21 *1864.*

To MAJ GEN MEADE

The only word I would sent Hunter would be verbal & simply let him know where we are & tell him to save his army in the way he thinks best either by getting back into own Dept or by joining us. If we had the enemy driven north of the Appomatox I think he would have no difficulty in joining us by taking a wide swee[p] south

U S GRANT
Lt Gen

Telegram received, DNA, RG 94, War Records Office, Army of the Potomac; copies, *ibid.*, RG 108, Letters Sent; *ibid.*, RG 393, Army of the Potomac, Cav. Corps, 3rd Div., Letters Received; DLC-USG, V, 45, 59, 67; (2) Meade Papers, PHi. *O.R.*, I, xxxvii, part 1, 657; *ibid.*, I, xl, part 2, 268. On June 21, 1864, 9:00 A.M., Maj. Gen. George G. Meade telegraphed to USG. "All is quiet this morning—The 2d. corps is moving to take position on the left of the 5th the 5th extending as far as the Jerusalem plank road—At this point I find the enemy occupy their old line of works, which being on a radius of three miles from Petersburgh will make the line to hold from the Plank road to the river above considerably longer than to the river below—There is no doubt Lee will throw his whole force over except sufficient to hold in check the force at Bermuda Hundreds. Wilson will be ordered to leave at 2. A M tomorrow & directed to proceed as rapidly as possible to the junction of the Lynchburgh & Danville roads & do them as much damage as possible to both these roads—Hampton being yesterday at the White house will releive Wilson of any apprehension of being disturbed & I trust Sheridan will keep Hampton occupied—I dont think Sheridan will have much chance of getting to the Deep bottom bridge in the face of Hampton unless he is able to give him a severe & serious defeat.—Wilson will be instructed when at the Junction to endeavor to communicate with Hunter near Lynchburgh—the Junction is about half way between this point & Lynchburgh—If Sheridan were here there would be no doubt I think of he & Wilson going to Lynchburgh   Do you wish to send any instructions to Hunter by Wilson.—" ALS (telegram sent), DNA, RG 94, War Records Office, Army of the Potomac; telegram received, *ibid.*, RG 108, Letters Received. *O.R.*, I, xxxvi, part 3, 786–87; *ibid.*, I, xl, part 2, 267.

At 3:00 P.M., Meade telegraphed to USG. "Birney is slowly getting into position—I have a Petersburgh paper of today.—It reports Hunter fighting at Lynchburgh on Saturday last & says he was repulsed in his attempts to carry the works around the city—a general battle it said was expected to come off the next day—:... I will send the paper by Genl. Barnard.—" ALS (telegram sent), DNA, RG 94, War Records Office, Army of the Potomac; telegram received, *ibid.*, RG 108, Letters Received. *O.R.*, I, xl, part 2, 269–70.

To Maj. Gen. George G. Meade

By Telegraph from City Point [*11:30* A.M.]
Dated June 21 *1864.*

To MAJ GEN MEADE

Your dispatch of 11 *15* just recvd. Genl Barnard was on his way
to Petersburg when it came. My desire is that Petersburg be en-
veloped as far as possible without attacking fortifications & the way
the positions the 2 armies is marked it looks as if the front of the
enemy can be swept from about Warrens left or left center thereby
giving our troops the position desired without exposure unless the
enemy exposes himself equally   I do not know that the threatening attitude recommended for the troops left to hold ground already ours will be so adviseable as to hold our front with a thin line
and form as large reserves from each corps as possible ready to
move to the front or to the left to support the troops moving in that
direction as circumstances may require. I am satisfied that you will
adopt the best c[our]se to accomplish the work that is [to be] done
& only give this as being suggested by the map without having the
personal knowledge of the ground that you have. A paper has just
reached me sent by Admiral Lee found in a bottle floating in the
river & picked up by the Navy. I will telegraph you a copy[1]

U S GRANT
Lt Gen

Telegram received (at 11:50 A.M.), DNA, RG 94, War Records Office, Army
of the Potomac; copies, *ibid.*, RG 108, Letters Sent; DLC-USG, V, 45, 59, 67;
(2) Meade Papers, PHi. *O.R.*, I, xl, part 2, 268–69. On June 21, 1864, 1:00
P.M., Maj. Gen. George G. Meade telegraphed to USG. "Telegram 11.30 received—Gen. Barnard has arived—He explains that he proposes to occupy certain ground from which the enemys works on the Jerusalem road can be enfiladed
& our attack on these works thus materially aided—I am now going to the front
to see that this is immediately done, if not already in progress of execution.—I
have no report from Birney tho' I hear firing.—Wright at 9.20 reported one division from Bermuda Hundreds, but says it is impracticacle to relieve his front
line two divisions till after dark they are so close to the enemy & exposed to such
fire of artillery & infantry—" ALS (telegram sent), DNA, RG 94, War Records
Office, Army of the Potomac; telegram received, *ibid.*, RG 108, Letters Received.
O.R., I, xl, part 2, 269.

At 12:40 P.M., USG telegraphed to Meade. "The President is here & will ride out to the front with me leaving here about 3 P. M   we will go to the house where Smith had his Hd Qrs the first day you arrived." Telegrams received (3), DNA, RG 94, War Records Office, Army of the Potomac; copies, *ibid.*, RG 108, Letters Sent; DLC-USG, V, 45, 59, 67; (2) Meade Papers, PHi. Printed as sent at 11:40 P.M. in *O.R.*, I, xl, part 2, 269.

On the same day, Meade wrote a letter to Brig. Gen. John A. Rawlins which he may have decided not to send or withdrew after consultation with USG. "I find myself, most reluctantly and with great pain, compelled to ask the Lieut Genl Com'd'g to relieve from duty with this army, Maj Genl G. K. Warren, Com'd'g 5th Corps. The Lieut Genl Comdg is well aware, from numerous conversations of my opinion of Genl Warren, and of the efforts I have made to *place* and *sustain* that officer in his present Command; but I regret to say that since his accession to command—General Warren whilst he has fully shewn all the good qualities I had given him credit for, has developed a serious defect against which I have vainly struggled in the hope that time and other causes would remove, but which circumstances now lead me to believe is incorigible and is a matter of constitutional organization. No officer in this Army exceeds Genl Warren in personal gallantry, in activity, in zeal and sleepless energy, nor in devotion to his duties—The defect with Genl Warren consists in too great reliance on his own judgment, and in an apparent impossibility on his part to yield his judgment so as to promptly execute orders, where these orders should happen not to receive his sanction or be in accordance with his views—To illustrate this point I will refer 1st to the well known case of Mine Run—where on Genl Warren's judgment, an attack on the enemy was planned, and orders given directing it to be made at a specified hour.—When the hour arrived, owing to a change in the condition of affairs as they were supposed to exist—Genl Warren assumed the responsibility of suspending his positive orders and referring to his Com'd'g Genl. for additional instructions, causing such delay and loss of time as virtually produced an entire suspension of operations and the withdrawal of the Army—Again at Spottsylvania Court House, on the morning of the 12th when Hancock was so severely pressed, under the instructions of the Lieut Genl Com'd'g, I sent a clear and positive order to Genl Warren directing him to attack immediately—Genl Warren led me to believe my order would be executed— His command he had previously told me was within fifty yards of the enemy, and it only required a run of that distance to bring them in contact. After waiting for a considerable time, more than an hour, I ascertained from Genl Warren's despatches not only that no attack had been made, but that his judgment was opposed to making any. A peremptory order was then sent to him to make it—directing him on its failure to immediately withdraw from his front and take his troops to the position of the 6th Corps where they could be made available—My complaint here is not against Genl Warren's judgement, because so far as such matters could be judged in advance, his opportunities were much better than mine.—but I maintain Genl Warren had no right to delay executing his orders under any circumstances, and that if he did think himself justified in so doing he should have advised me promptly of what his views were, saying such is my opinion, but I shall proceed to attack unless otherwise ordered—Such is my opinion of Genl Warren's judgment that in nine cases out of ten, I would have yielded my judgment—possibly in this case, where the attack was intended as much for a threat and to occupy the enemy, as for other objects—I might still have reiterated ~~my~~ my order, for there are occasions where doubtful attacks are

rendered of the highest importance for their bearing and influence at other points
—The last case which I shall refer to occurred at this point on the 18th instant—
On the night of the 17th Genl Warren had one division in position and the others
of his Corps massed in rear—During the night of the 17th orders were sent to
him to attack with his Corps at 4. A. M. the next day—On advancing the next
day, the enemy had evacuated their lines—Genl Warren was then ordered to
advance promptly against the enemy and develop his position—The enemy having assumed a line some one mile nearer Petersburg, about 10. A. M. Corps
Commanders were called on to report at what hour they would be ready to assault—All responded that they were then ready except Genl Warren who said he
could not tell when he would be ready—A positive and peremptory order was
then issued, directing an assault at 12. M.—Genl Warren acknowledged it, but
said he could not be ready by 12. M.—but would be by 1. P. M. also he thought
his right could be moved forward at 12—Genl Warren was then authorized on
moving his right forward at 12. to suspend his attack till 1. At 2. P. M a despatch
was received from Genl Warren stating he had been ready to attack since 1.
P. M, but not hearing any thing going on, on his right he had not attacked—
furthermore proposing a simultaneous attack should be made at 3. P. M. and
stating if the others were not ready he could attack alone—To this a reply was
sent that he was considered under orders since 11. to attack, that the designated
hour 12. had been postponed in his case until 1: that his acknowledgment of
being ready at 1. but waiting till 2 to ask for further orders, had produced
astonishment—the peremptory order to attack was reiterated and he was told he
would be held responsible for any further delay—The attack was soon after made,
but during the delay Birney's attack had failed and the enemy were able to reinforce Warren's and Burnside's fronts, and their attacks also failed. I do not
charge Gen Warren with intentional and willful disobedience of orders, or with
any designs of embarrassing my plans, but I maintain that the fact of his failure
to obey the orders sent him was a serious misfortune, and that this failure resulted from his assuming to judge that because the attack ordered at 12. was
expected to be simultaneous, and he was not ready then that he was relieved from
the order, not withstanding the order postponing the hour in his case explicitly
told him he was to attack at 1. or as soon as ready. I have endeavored to shew
what I consider a defect in Genl Warren's character—viz: an assumption of
responsibility where no discretion is left him by his orders—This defect has been
a source of serious embarrassment to me, but my appreciation of Genl Warren's
good qualities, and my strong personal regard for him have been such, that I
have forborne to notice it, and have hoped that Genl Warren would see himself
the necessity of trying to correct it—As however in an interview on the 19th
Genl Warren exhibited so much temper and bad feeling forgetting the respect
due to me as his superior officer and his senior in years—and ignoring every thing
but his own sense of injury, because I told him in despaches on the 18th that my
construction of my own orders was different from his—I no longer feel called to
exercise any further patience—indeed as I stated before I am forced to conclude
that this defect in Genl Warren is not controllable by him, and that he cannot
execute an order without modifying it, unless it is predicated on his suggestions
and even then as at Mine Run he will fail to execute if he thinks proper—Such a
defect strikes at the root of all Military subordination, and it is entirely out of
the question that I can command this Army, if each Corps Commander is to
exercise a similar independence of action—I think the favor I have shewn Genl

Warren, the confidence I have had in his judgment and the reliance placed on him have served perhaps to lead him into this error, but I hoped the gravity of his error at Mine Run would have called his attention to the danger he was in. The Lieut Genl Com'd'g, is aware that he authorized the relieving of Genl Warren at Spottsylvania, but that I resisted hoping I should be able to overcome the difficulty. I now acknowledge my inability to do so and ask that he be at once relieved from command—If he could be assigned to some independent and separate command he would do very well, for he is full of resources, of great coolness and firmness—It is only the difficulty he labors under of yielding his judgment to that of his superior officer, which impairs his efficiency." Copy, Meade Papers, PHi.

1. On June 17, "A Union Man in Bondage" placed a note in a bottle. "If this should fall into the hands of a Union man, this is to let the northern people know that the Loyal League of the city of Richmond are ready to come to a starting point to help the Union forces to capture the city of Richmond. There is 300 and 50 of us left Richmond to try to get to the lines of the north if it please God to aid us in the undertaking, but the Southerners watch us very sharply. We have been in the swamps for two weeks now. The rebels are very weak and Gen Grant can take Richmond with half of his Army. The rebels have placed 50 torpedoes in the river ready to blow up the Union Gunboats—Please take warning in time—" Copies, DLC-USG, V, 45, 59, 67; DNA, RG 108, Letters Sent. *O.R.*, I, xl, part 2, 161. Between June 21 and June 23, USG endorsed this letter. "Respectfully forwarded to the Secretary of War" Copy, DLC-USG, V, 58.

To Maj. Gen. Benjamin F. Butler

By Telegraph from City Pt
Dated June 22 *1864.*

To MAJ GENL BUTLER

Nothing from Meade since ten a. m—at 10 all was quiet & the line of investment being extended   Our Cavalry left at 2 a m in an exped to destroy the Danvile R R & to Communicate with Genl Hunter

U. S. GRANT
Lt Gnl

Telegram received, DNA, RG 393, Dept. of Va. and N. C., Telegrams Received. *O.R.*, I, xl, part 2, 320.
On June 22, 1864, USG telegraphed to Maj. Gen. Benjamin F. Butler. "The siege train is now arriving & it will be necessary to place Col Abbot in charge of it   Please direct him to report to me in person   A portion of his regt will be required to take care of the train" Telegram received, DNA, RG 393, Dept. of Va. and N. C., Telegrams Received; copies, *ibid.*, RG 108, Letters Sent; DLC-

USG, V, 45, 59, 67. *O.R.*, I, xl, part 2, 320. At 6:50 P.M., Butler telegraphed
to USG. "Gen Smith asks of me two batteries of Rifled guns and two thirty
pounder parrots or 4½ in guns with ammunition. I have sent him a battery of
Rifled 10s. Three of my thirty Pounders are with Meade out of six which are all
I have. Smith has four 20s out of 9. already. As Meades Seige Train has got up
will you direct that he turn over to Smith the three 30 pdr and ammunition"
ALS (telegram sent), DNA, RG 94, War Records Office, Army of the Potomac;
telegram received, *ibid.*, RG 108, Letters Received. *O.R.*, I, xl, part 2, 321. At
8:15 P.M., Brig. Gen. John A. Rawlins telegraphed to Butler. "The three (3)
thirty pounder parat guns and ammunition will be ordered turned over to Gen
Smith from these Headquarters" Telegram received, DNA, RG 107, Telegrams
Collected (Unbound). *O.R.*, I, xl, part 2, 321. On the same day, USG telegraphed to Butler. "Please direct Col. Abbat to get four (4) of the 30 pd Parrott
siege guns of the siege train just arrived to Gen Smith, as soon as possible."
Telegram received (at 11:15 P.M.), DNA, RG 393, Dept. of Va. and N. C.,
Telegrams Received; copies, *ibid.*, RG 108, Letters Sent; DLC-USG, V, 45, 59,
67. Printed as sent at 11:15 P.M. in *O.R.*, I, xl, part 2, 321. See letter to Maj.
Gen. William F. Smith, June 23, 1864.

At 7:20 P.M., Butler telegraphed to USG. "A Prisoner belonging to the 48th
N. C. Cook's brigade ~~he th~~ Heth's division of a. P. Hills Corps was captured by
General Foster today at Grovers House on the north side of the James He states
that his brigade consisting of the 48th 27th 46th & 15th N. C. numbering about
a thousand men left their breast works five miles in front of Richmond last night
on a scout Some Cavalry had preceeded them by several days that they moved
there from before us near Petersburg on the south side of the Appomattox yesterday about twelve (12) leaving Longstreets corps in our front. His brigade
crossed the James on a pontoon bridge below the Bluff. He further states that
the remainder of Hill's corps was distributed some in Petersburg & some upon
the other side of the Appomattox. That it was currently rumored in Camp that
Ewell had gone up the Valley to meet Hunter. He also states that the rear line
his brigades being the last withdrew from my front yesterday about 12 & that
none but the front line remain. My signal officer reports that at two P. m. a train
of twenty five freight cars five (5) of them loaded with troops passed Port
~~Walthare~~ Waltham Junction. This is the first train that has crossed since the
tearing up of the track" Telegram received, DNA, RG 108, Letters Received;
copy, *ibid.*, RG 94, War Records Office, Army of the Potomac. *O.R.*, I, xl, part 2,
320.

Also on June 22, Rawlins telegaphed to Butler. "Your troops garrison this
place, and will until relieved by Gen Meade" Telegram received, DNA, RG
107, Telegrams Collected (Unbound).

To Maj. Gen. George G. Meade

City Point Va June 22d/64
Gen.

The enclosed is the only thing tangible I have seen of the report put in circulation after the "Battle of the Wilderness. Your are aware they have been corrected so far as any impression that may have been made by them with the Authorities in Washington is concerned.—If you see fit to forward the enclosed to Mr. Clark you are at liberty to do so. It is but just to you that this contradiction should be made public. and also that Capt. C. mintioned by Mr. Clark should be made to give his authority for his statements.

yours U. S. GRANT

ALS, Meade Papers, PHi. *O.R.*, I, xl, part 2, 304–5. USG enclosed a letter of June 14, 1864, from Isaac P. Clark, Boston, to USG. "A Capt Carruth of 1st Mass Rgt Vol—returned home, reports. That at the Battle of the Wilderness— Genl. Meade, advised that the Army fall back again, as being impossible to advance, but that you would not permit it. Not believing that the Gallant Meade volunteered any such advice, I have taken the liberty of informing you of the report—which if untrue you will not require, even, laurels, forced upon you, at the discredit of the hero of Gettysburg." ALS, Meade Papers, PHi. *O.R.*, I, xl, part 2, 305. On June 22, USG endorsed this letter. "Gen. Meade on no occation advised or counsiled falling back towards, much less across, the Rapidann. There has been no word or act of his from the begining of this Campaign which indicated even a belief on his part that such a step would ever become necessary Such rumors as you speak of are entirely idle and without the shadow of foundation." AES, Meade Papers, PHi.

At 9:40 A.M., USG telegraphed to Maj. Gen. George G. Meade. "What success have you met with in extending the investment of Petersburg" Copies, DLC-USG, V, 45, 59, 67; DNA, RG 108, Letters Sent. *O.R.*, I, xl, part 2, 303. At 10:30 A.M., Meade telegraphed to USG. "Birneys left was attacked last evening which required him to throw it back & take a position in rear of the line of circumvallation—He is moving up this morning & Wright is moving on his left—As yet all is apparently quiet—" ALS (telegram sent), DNA, RG 94, War Records Office, Army of the Potomac; telegram received (at 10:00 A.M.), *ibid.*, RG 108, Letters Received. *O.R.*, I, xl, part 2, 303.

At 6:00 P.M. and 9:00 P.M., Meade telegraphed to USG. "Birney advanced this morning his left to envelop the enemy—Wright advanced on his left by a road that separated him somewhat from Birney—Wright soon found the enemys skirmishers & reported them in considerable force—Fearing Birneys left would be exposed Barlow was ordered to move back so as to make connection with Wright—While doing this he was vigorously attacked & thrown into some confusion—At the same time Gibbon on the plank road Birneys right, was very warmly attacked & forced back from his first line losing I regret to say 4 guns Order was soon restored, but in view of these facts I directed the withdrawal of Wright so as to make a secure connection with Birney—At this time all is quiet— It is reported but I fear not reliable that Gibbon has retaken his rifle pits & guns —I have ordered Birney & Wright at 7. P. M to make a vigorous attack & try to drive the enemy back   Prisoners report the whole of A. P. Hills corps with others in our front—They say they marched out of their breastworks or fortifications advancing nearly a mile—We have taken prisoners from each of the divisions of

Hills corps—The morale of the men is not so good as I would like it, but I deem it of the utmost consequence to take the offensive—Scouts on our left report Wilson at Reams Station on the Weldon Road at 10 a m today—They say he burned the station & did other damage but on retiring was attacked by cavalry & infantry—I hope to send you after dark some favorable news   A prisoner who states he was on Provost guard at Petersburgh reports the arrival there day before yesterday of troops from Johnstons army—"   "Our line advanced at 7. P M and have since been engaged—One the left & the center the enemy have been pressed back considerably—On the right no advantage was gained—Our lines are now secure and the effect of the advance has been good—I have ordered a general advance at daylight & will try to push the enemy back to his works— I regret to say there is no confirmation of the report of the recapture of our guns It is believed the enemy drew them off—We have taken about 110 prisoners probably lost as many—Our casualties are I think light—"   ALS (telegrams sent), DNA, RG 94, War Records Office, Army of the Potomac; telegrams received, *ibid.*, RG 108, Letters Received. *O.R.*, I, xl, part 2, 304.

To Maj. Gen. William F. Smith

City Point June 22nd/64 10.45 a. m.

Maj Gen Smith Comd'g 18th A. C.

General,

In glancing at your position yesterday it looked to me as if, with the commanding positions on the high grounds about the house, where Wright had his Hdqrs, there is no necessity for keeping more than picket guards in the bottom lands in front. If this is so, it would leave a large ~~portion~~ part of your force from under fire, and leave them ready to assist any place where they might be required. It would enable you to hold a greater length of line, and move the whole of the A. P. to the left. Please give me your views on this matter.

U. S. Grant Lt. Gen.

Telegram, copies, DLC-USG, V, 45, 59, 67; DNA, RG 108, Letters Sent. *O.R.*, I, xl, part 2, 327–28.

To Julia Dent Grant

———

City Point, Va. June 22d *1864.*

DEAR JULIA,

This will be the last letter I shall write you until I receive an answer to the one in which I gave you permission to come to Ft. Monroe to spend the Summer. I feel certain you will come and probably you will have started before this reaches you.

Our work progresses here slowly and I feel will progress securely until Richmond finally falls. The task is a big one and has to be performed by some one.

Kisses for yourself and the children.

ULYS.

ALS, DLC-USG.

To Maj. Gen. Henry W. Halleck

———

City Point 9 a m
June 23d 1864

MAJ GENL H W HALLECK
CHF OF STAFF

Yesterday and this morning have been consumed in [e]xtending our lines to the left to envelope Petersburg. The 2nd & 6th Corps are now west of the Jerusalem plank road. Yesterday in moving to this position the two corps became separated. the enemy pushed out between them and caus[e]d some confusion on the left of the 2nd Corps and captured four pieces of artillery

Order was soon restored and the enemy pushed back. This morning no enemy is found on our left. This will be pushed forward until the enemy is found. The Petersburg papers of yesterday states that Hunter has been routed and already three thousand of his men have been captured

U S GRANT
Lt Genl

Telegram received (at 7:00 P.M.), DNA, RG 107, Telegrams Collected (Bound); copies, *ibid.*, RG 108, Letters Sent; DLC-USG, V, 45, 59, 67. *O.R.*, I, xl, part 2, 330.

On June 23, 1864, 1:30 P.M., USG telegraphed to Maj. Gen. Henry W. Halleck. "Please order Genl De Trobriand [to] report to Genl Meade for duty, [a]nd Genl L C Hunt to Genl Dix   Hunt is here—" Telegram received (on June 24, 5:30 A.M.), DNA, RG 107, Telegrams Collected (Bound); *ibid.*, RG 94, Letters Received, 610A 1864; copies, *ibid.*, RG 108, Letters Sent; DLC-USG, V, 45, 59, 67. *O.R.*, I, xl, part 2, 331. On June 2, Brig. Gen. Lewis C. Hunt, Fort Leavenworth, Kan., had telegraphed to USG. "I have finished my inspection tour & am ready for a Command any where   Can you give me a good Brigade in the Army of the Potomac   Answer at St Louis Lindell House" Telegram received, DNA, RG 107, Telegrams Collected (Unbound). On June 5, USG telegraphed to Hunt, St. Louis. "Report to Gen Meade for duty" Copies, DLC-USG, V, 45, 59, 66; DNA, RG 108, Letters Sent. See telegram to Maj. Gen. Henry W. Halleck, June 28, 1864.

To Maj. Gen. Henry W. Halleck

City Point, Va. June 23d *1864*.

MAJ. GEN. H. W. HALLECK
CHIEF OF STAFF OF THE ARMY,
GENERAL,

The siege of Richmond bids fare to be tedious, and in consequence of the very extended lines we must have, a much larger force will be necessary than would be required in ordinary sieges against the same force that now opposes us. With my present force I feel perfectly safe against Lee's Army, and acting defensively would still feel so against Lee and Johnston combined. But we want to act offensively. In my opinion to do this, effectively we should concentrate our whole energy against the two principal Armies of the enemy. In other words nothing should be attempted except in Georgia and here, that is not directly in co-operation with these moves. West of the Miss. I would not attempt any thing until the rebellion East of the it is entirely subdued. I would then direct Canby to leave Smith unmolested where he is; to make no move except such as is necessary to protect what he now holds. All the troops he can spare should be sent here at once. In my opinion the white troops of the 19th Corps can all come together, with many of the colored troops.

I wish you would place this matter before the Sec. of War and urge that no offensive operations West of the Miss. be allowed to commence until matters here are settled. Send the 19th Corps and such other troops as you can, from the Dept. of the Gulf, to me.

> Very respectfully
> your obt. svt.
> U. S. GRANT
> Lt. Gen.

ALS, Schoff Collection, MiU-C. *O.R.*, I, xxxiv, part 4, 514–15; *ibid.*, I, xl, part 2, 330–31. On June 26, 1864, 11:30 A.M., Maj. Gen. Henry W. Halleck telegraphed to USG. "I have telegraphed instructions to Genl Canby in accordance with your note, and sent copies by special messengers." ALS (telegram sent), DNA, RG 107, Telegrams Collected (Bound); telegram received, *ibid.* See *O.R.*, I, xxxiv, part 4, 528.

To Maj. Gen. Benjamin F. Butler

> By Telegraph from City Point [4:0Q P.M.]
> Dated June 23 1864.

To MAJ GEN BUTLER

Give Gen Smith as many reinforcements as you can & instruct him to relieve as much of Burnsides as he can, at least one di'n front, so as to enable Meade to extend & protect his left. Meade is now to the Welden Railroad. If possible I would like Burnside relieved between this & morning.

> U. S. GRANT
> Lt Genl

Telegram received (at 4:23 P.M.), DNA, RG 393, Dept. of Va. and N. C., Telegrams Received; copies, *ibid.*, RG 108, Letters Sent; DLC-USG, V, 45, 59, 67. *O.R.*, I, xl, part 2, 362. On June 23, 1864, 4:35 P.M., Maj. Gen. Benjamin F. Butler telegraphed to USG. "Despatch in regard to reinforcing Smith recieved—It shall be done—Orders will go out immediately. The troops will be moved at once. I will send Turners Division which will leave me four thousand (4000) old troops on this line—" LS (telegram sent), DNA, RG 107, Telegrams Collected (Unbound); telegram received, *ibid.*, RG 108, Letters Received. Printed as received at 5:03 P.M. in *O.R.*, I, xl, part 2, 362.

At 3:40 P.M., Butler telegraphed to USG. "A Party of N. Carolina troops have cut the telegraph line we are endeavoring to Establish to James town Island I have sent down a small cavalry squad who report all that part of the Country near Branden & Surry Court House filled with deserters—stragglers from the Army of Potomac. Might not General Patrick ~~take~~ send a company or two Cavalry to gather them up   I have sent fifty Cavalry to clean out the gurrillas at Surry C. H. and to warn the inhabitants there that is not respected their houses will be burnt and some of them get hanged" ALS (telegram sent), DNA, RG 107, Telegrams Collected (Unbound); telegram received, *ibid.*, RG 108, Letters Received. Printed as received at 4:30 P.M. in *O.R.*, I, xl, part 2, 362. On the same day, Butler telegraphed to USG. "I have the honor to forward the following portion of a deserters statement made this evening. 'John Conroy 14th Va regt Huntons brigades states that he saw a Richmond paper of today & that it stated that Early now commanding Ewells Corps had a fight yesterday with Maj Gen Hunter 12 Miles from Lynchburg, & that Hunter was retreating & endeavoring to join Gen Averill's forces" LS (telegram sent), DNA, RG 107, Telegrams Collected (Unbound); telegram received, *ibid.*, RG 108, Letters Received.

At 6:20 P.M. and 8:30 P.M., Butler telegraphed to USG. "I take leave to send you my memo. of the present organisation of the Armies on this line with their positions   I believe it nearly accurate   It is from an examination of the prisoners deserters and refugees from almost every Brigade   I have a few cigars which I think pretty good   Will you try them" ALS (telegram sent), *ibid.*, RG 393, Dept. of Va. and N. C., Telegrams Sent (Press). "Two Brigades of Turners division had passed the Ponton bridge at 8 o clock   I think I can promise you an advance by Smith taking the hill in his front in the moring" ALS (telegram sent), *ibid.*, RG 94, War Records Office, Army of the Potomac. *O.R.*, I, xl, part 2, 363.

Also on June 23, Brig. Gen. Godfrey Weitzel telegraphed to USG. "Foster has been re-inforced by one brigade, which is now entrenching on the down stream side of Four Mile Creek. That second bridge from Jones Neck to the lower side of the creek was laid last night. That point is now I think, for good, in our possession, and I suppose some picket firing is going on. I will telegraph at once to Foster." ALS (telegram sent), DNA, RG 94, War Records Office, Dept. of Va. and N. C., Army of the James, Unentered Papers. *O.R.*, I, xl, part 2, 362.

On June 24, 8:15 A.M., Butler telegraphed to USG. "The signal officer reports. River Bank Spring Hill Signal Station 8.15 A M. Fifteen (15) cars loaded with troops just passed the Junction towards Richmond and fifteen wagons down the turnpike towards Petersburg" Copy, DNA, RG 107, Telegrams Collected (Unbound). See *O.R.*, I, xl, part 2, 397; telegram to Maj. Gen. Benjamin F. Butler, June 25, 1864. Also on June 24, Butler forwarded to USG a signal message of 10:30 A.M. reporting skirmishing on his picket line. Copy, DNA, RG 107, Telegrams Collected (Unbound). See *O.R.*, I, xl, part 2, 398.

To Maj. Gen. George G. Meade

By Telegraph from City Point
Dated June 23 *1864.*

To MAJ GEN MEADE

I wish you would send two (2) Companies of Engineers to Smiths front to establish Mortar batteries   if you are not using the Co-horns with the A. P please send them also   our siege train has not yet arrived   on the 19th I received a despatch from Washington saying that the last vessel having this train on board of sailed that afternoon   I have sent Comstock to look it up and hurry it up—

U. S. GRANT
Lieut Genl

Telegram received, DNA, RG 94, War Records Office, Army of the Potomac; copies, *ibid.*, RG 108, Letters Sent; DLC-USG, V, 45, 59, 67; (2) Meade Papers, PHi. *O.R.*, I, xl, part 2, 331. On June 24, 1864, 7:00 A.M., Maj. Gen. George G. Meade telegraphed to USG. "Your despatch of yesterday in relation to cohorns just received.—Genl. Hunt has six mortars at City Point which he designed for the 18th corps when it was a part of this army   I have directed him to turn them over to Maj. Genl. Smith—My Engineer troops are actively employed and can not well be spared—besides I understand the mortars are furnished with beds & there is n[o]thing whatever to be done but to smooth a level place to set them in—"   ALS (telegram sent), DNA, RG 94, War Records Office, Army of the Potomac; telegram received, *ibid.*, RG 108, Letters Received. *O.R.*, I, xl, part 2, 373. See telegram to Maj. Gen. George G. Meade, June 24, 1864.

On June 23, 7:30 A.M., 8:00 A.M., and 2:00 P.M. (sent at 2:45 P.M.), Meade telegraphed to USG. "The lines of the 6 & 2d corps were advanced at daylight   The 6 corps found no enemy in their front.—The 2d corps found none on their left but met a strong skirmish line on the right centre & right—This has been forced back & the right of the corps occupies the line, which was occupied yesterday—The whole line is advancing & swinging on the right of the 2d corps which is close up to the main line of the enemy on the Jerusalem plank road—I shall continue to advance & develop the enemys position, but the process will be long & tedious arising 1st from the nature of the country which is a densely wooded thicket, but principally from the necessity of keeping a close connection—the omission to do which yesterday enabled the enemy to penetrate between the 6th & 2d corps taking the latter in reverse & producing much confusion & disorder   the reestablishing order taking more time than would have been consumed, if the connection had never been broken—Prisoners taken this morning report the enemy falling back last night to what line they do not know—the presumption is to their fortifications; but I must watch my left flank carefully, as the more we envelop the enemy, the farther advanced the left is & until we hold to the river, my centre & rear is greatly exposed. I have retained from Wilsons command a small force of cavalry to watch the left.—Burnside reports an attack about 11 P M yesterday, which he repulsed   His picket line he says was at one point driven in but quickly re-established—I am not able to judge of the practicability of holding to the river above till more information of the line held by the enemy is known but from present appearances I infer we shall have to extend our right corps 5th & 9th more to the left & across the Jerusalem plank road to enable me to hold to the river—I will keep you advised of any thing occurring—" "Petersburgh paper of the 22d inst has the following—'A despatch from Lynchburgh of Monday states that the Reserve forces were ordered to Liberty to take charge of the prisoners captured from Hunter—It is no longer a retreat but a rout a stampede in which the vandals are vainly endeavoring to escape the just vengeance due their crimes—The Sentinel says a report was current in Richmond on Monday night that three thousand of Hunters men had been captured'—The paper will be sent to you—Nothing new since last despatch from the lines.—" "There is nothing new—The 6 & 2d corps are endeavoring to get into position, but the character of the ground & the difficulty of ensuring co-operation has delayed the movement—Signal officers report the enemy moving to our left—possibly to attack Wright—possibly to occupy their works in anticipation of his advance—Wrights skirmishers have reached the Wldon R. Rd—Contrabands report the cars returning this A. M Wilson having destroyed the road at Reems Station—It is also reported that Lee's division of Cavalry have gone after him—I have ordered the small cavalry force with me to endeavor to destroy still more of the road & should Wright secure a position on it, I will set infantry at the same work—I am a little anxious about my left, we are so extended, it gives the enemy a chance to mass at that point & I have no re-inforcements to send—If attacked by superior force Wright will have to withdraw doubling on Birney who will reinforce him as his line can be vacated by Wrights movement—I forward a plan of operations suggested by Warren with my reply thereto.—" ALS (telegrams sent), DNA, RG 94, War Records Office, Army of the Potomac; telegrams received, DNA, RG 108, Letters Received. *O.R.,* I, xl, part 2, 331–33. The enclosures in the last telegram are printed *ibid.,* p. 333.

To Maj. Gen. George G. Meade

By Telegraph from City Point 3.30 [P.M.]
Dated June 23 *1864.*

To MAJ GEN MEADE

Gen Butler can spare several thousand more troops for Smith as soon as fortifications North of the James are a little stronger which will enable Smith to extend over a greater front & give you troops to move to the left. I will ~~him~~ direct him to send what he can at once & to order Smith to relieve Smiths [*Burnside's*] right Div   I would not think of moving the whole of your Command with less than ten days rations & then it would ~~to~~ be to turn the enemys right—Cross the Appomattox & force a connection with Butler between Richmond & Petersburg   I have directed the 19th Corps to be sent here but it will take 20 days to bring them   By keeping the little Cavalry you have well on the watch at the left I think you will have timely notice to save it if attacked

U S GRANT

Lt Gen

Telegram received, DNA, RG 94, War Records Office, Army of the Potomac; copies, *ibid.*, RG 108, Letters Sent; DLC-USG, V, 45, 59, 67; (2) Meade Papers, PHi. *O.R.*, I, xl, part 2, 333–34.

On June 23, 1864, 4:00 P.M. and 5:00 P.M., USG telegraphed to Maj. Gen. George G. Meade. "I have directed Gen Butler to try to relieve Burnside of at least one division front of his line between this & morning"   "A Div will start this evening to increase Smiths force & enable him to relieve at least a Div front of Burnside   you can make your arrangements accordingly"   Telegrams received, DNA, RG 94, War Records Office, Army of the Potomac; copies, *ibid.*, RG 108, Letters Sent; DLC-USG, V, 45, 59, 67; (2) Meade Papers, PHi. *O.R.*, I, xl, part 2, 334.

At 9:00 P.M., Meade telegraphed to USG. "Whilst the 6th corps was moving into position, signal officers reported the movement of a heavy column of the enemy to our left—I immediately notified Genl. Wright, and directed him if the enemy threatened him to take the initiative, and attack him unless the movement of the enemy should be such as to endanger his flank—About 4 P M Genl. Wright reported the appearance of the enemy on his left having driven in his advance guard & a working party on the R. Rd—I immediately reiterated my orders to him to act at once & promptly—Instead of taking either of these courses, he permitted the enemy to move at will until he became alarmed not only for his left but his rear, and called for reenforcements—I again urged him to attack at all hazards and received for reply there was no time to form columns—I ordered an attack in line, but darkness was the excuse—As Genl. Wrights position & line is faulty, and as he can give me no information of the enemy, except he believes him in great force on his flank, I have autherised him to with draw to the position occupied last night, which is better fitted for maneuvering [to-m]orrow.—I can not understand there has been any thing but heavy skirmishing—I think you had better come up here tomorrow if convenient.—" ALS (telegram sent), DNA, RG 94, War Records Office, Army of the Potomac; telegram received (on June 24, 3:15 A.M.), *ibid.*, RG 108, Letters Received. *O.R.*, I, xl, part 2, 334. On June 24, 8:00 A.M., Meade telegraphed to USG. "May I expect you at the front this morning—I deem it of importance to ~~you tha~~ have an interview with you—"   ALS (telegram sent), DNA, RG 94, War Records Office, Army of the Potomac; copies, *ibid.*, RG 393, Army of the Potomac, Letters Sent; (2) Meade Papers, PHi; DLC-Andrew Johnson. *O.R.*, I, xl, part 2, 373. At 8:00 A.M., USG telegraphed to Meade. "I leave here at once for your Head quarters"   ALS (telegram sent), Connecticut State Library, Hartford, Conn. At 10:50 A.M., USG telegraphed to Meade. "Will I meet you at your Hd Qrs or elswhere on the line? I want to go to the left before going back even if I should meet you before." ALS (telegram sent), DNA, RG 107, Telegrams Collected (Unbound). At 11:00 A.M., Meade telegraphed to USG. "I am awaiting you at my Hd. Qrs which are on the Jerusalem plank road on the left hand side just beyond the Jones House or about a mile from the line of battle on that road   I send Maj. Riddle A. D C. who will guide you here." ALS (telegram sent), *ibid.*, RG 94, War Records Office, Army of the Potomac; copies, *ibid.*, RG 393, Army of the Potomac, Letters Sent; (2) Meade Papers, PHi; DLC-Andrew Johnson. *O.R.*, I, xl, part 2, 374.

To Maj. Gen. William F. Smith

June 23rd 1864

MAJ GEN W. F. SMITH
COMD'G 18TH CORPS

Gen Halleck telegraphed on the 19th that the last of the seige train had left Washington. Seeing some of Gen Butlers artillery on boat, I supposed it was the seige train. Comstock has gone to hurry it up. As soon as received it will be forwarded   Two companies of Engineers will be sent you in the morning.

U. S GRANT Lt Gen

Telegram, copies, DLC-USG, V, 45, 59, 67; DNA, RG 108, Letters Sent. *O.R.*, I, xl, part 2, 369. On June 22, 1864, Lt. Col. Cyrus B. Comstock telegraphed to Maj. Gen. William F. Smith. "Lieut Gen Grant directs me to say that Gen Butler has sent 4 seige guns and that if you will telegraph what you need others will be sent you from the seige train so soon as possible"   Telegram received, DNA, RG 94, War Records Office, Dept. of Va. and N. C., Army of the James, Unentered Papers. *O.R.*, I, xl, part 2, 328. See telegram to Maj. Gen. Benjamin F. Butler, June 22, 1864. At 8:00 P.M. and 8:20 P.M., Smith telegraphed to Comstock. "Since the receipt of your despatch Gen'l Butler telegraphs me that he has asked from your H'd Qr's. that seige guns be sent me from the seige train, which he says has just arrived. I have but 3 30 lb guns in position & they are needed to keep the Battery quiet on the other side of the Appomattox." "Four 8 inch Mortars Could be used with great advantage on my front." Telegrams received (the second at 10:20 P.M.), DNA, RG 107, Telegrams Collected (Unbound). On June 23, Smith telegraphed to Comstock. "I have as yet heard nothing of the Heavy guns. I have been shelling the town & R. R. bridge slowly all day but the guns are too small to effect any serious result." Telegram received, *ibid.* On the same day, Lt. Col. Orville E. Babcock telegraphed to Smith. "Comstock has gone to Fort Monroe to hunt up and hurry along the heavy guns" Telegram received, *ibid.*, RG 94, War Records Office, Army of the Potomac; (dated June 24) *ibid.* On June 23, Comstock telegraphed to Smith, care of Brig. Gen. Seth Williams. "Telegrams received. Colonel Abbot has been directed to send you the 8-inch mortars as soon as they arrive." *O.R.*, I, xl, part 2, 369. On the same day, Williams wrote to Comstock. "Your dispatch for General Smith has been received and will be at once forwarded. Our telegraph line from City Point runs it is believed within a short distance of Genl. Smith's present Headquarters and if operators are sent to him he will be enabled to have telegraphic communication with you. All the operators we have are indispensably necessary at these Headquarters and with the several Corps, and we have no more field wire than is required for this Army. Should you have occasion to send dispatches to General Smith, as matters now are, it will save time to send your dispatches to General Burnside's Headquarters, or to the Point of Rocks if there is an office at that place." Copy, DLC-Andrew Johnson. *O.R.*, I, xl, part 2, 370.

On June 24, Smith wrote to Brig. Gen. John A. Rawlins. "My wagons & men with proper requisitions went to City Point today for Coehorn mortars— The depot ordnance officer refused to issue without approval of Lt. Edie—Will you please give orders to issue as my wagons are at City Point also for the issue of Spencer Rifles & Sharps Carbines" ALS, DNA, RG 108, Letters Received. *O.R.*, I, xl, part 2, 401.

Also on June 24, Smith twice telegraphed to USG. "I have the honor to en[c]lose to you a rebel newspaper that came [t]hrough our picket line without my knowl[e]dge, but as it contains important news from Genl. Hunters command, I take the liberty of forwarding it to you direct" LS (telegram sent), DNA, RG 393, 18th Army Corps, Telegrams Sent (Press). "I have made all arrangements to take the hill in front of my left which will save me from much annoyance if I succeed. I think I can do it without serious loss—the time appointed is 7 P. M. But learning that you are on the field, I have judged best to defer to your judgment" Copies, *ibid.*; *ibid.*, RG 107, Telegrams Collected (Unbound). *O.R.*, I, xl, part 2, 400. At 7:35 P.M., Smith telegraphed to USG. "Finding that Genl Turner had only 2800 men & that his preparations were not as complete as I wished owing to unforseen difficulties & for ~~that~~ reasons besides that I think good, I have postponed the attack" Copy, DNA, RG 107, Telegrams Collected (Unbound). At 10:00 P.M., Smith telegraphed to Rawlins. "Private Patrick Lee of the 27th S. C. Regt., a deserter from the enemy, has just ~~been brought~~ come in He states that most of his regt. were captured this morning in the chge. in front of the 18th A. C., and that Genl. Beauregard is in command and has about thirty thousand (30 000) troops." Copy, *ibid.* On June 25, Smith telegraphed to USG. "In giving Genl Turner notice that I should not make the attack until I had seen or heard from you he misunderstood me & suspended his preparations. When I arrived on the ground I found that it would be too dark for my artillery to be effective in cleaning the rifle pits & in addition to that Gen Turner had but 2800. in place of 3500 men as I supposed & it took all my reserves to fill his first line after his assaulting column was out & as that left me weak I determined under all the Circumstances to postpone the affair, rather than run risk of a failure when I think there is no necessity for one" ALS (telegram sent), *ibid.*; telegram received, *ibid.*, RG 108, Letters Received. *O.R.*, I, xl, part 2, 426.

On June 26, Smith telegraphed to USG. "There was a good deal of firing yesterday on my front but I have succeeded in almost entirely quieting the rebel batteries that were acting on me. This morning I am firing one 30 pound shot into the city every fifteen minutes & practising to get the ranges with the 8 inch mortars. The small ones are not yet ready to open but will be soon. The enemy are doing a little mortar firing this morning but not doing much damage I believe." ALS (telegram sent—undated), DNA, RG 107, Telegrams Collected (Unbound); telegram received, *ibid.*, RG 108, Letters Received. On the same day, Smith telegraphed to Rawlins. "A. Deserter from the 20th G.A infantry has just come in, He States that Longstreets Corps is on this front & Genl Beauregard in Petersburg & A. Strong force Extending to Druries Bluff." Copy, *ibid.*, RG 94, War Records Office, Dept. of Va. and N. C., Army of the James, Unentered Papers. *O.R.*, I, xl, part 2, 458.

Also on June 26, Smith telegraphed to Rawlins, sending a copy to Maj. Gen. Benjamin F. Butler. "The ill health of Brig. Gen. Hinks, Comd'g Colored Division, will compel him to give up his duties for a while, if not permanently and I am left without a proper officer to command a Division, the value of which will depend upon the ability with which it is ledt. The second in command, Brig Genl. Wild, is entirely unfitted for the command & besides is in arrest at present, for insubordination. Gen Hinks Division now numb[ers] in the field return of today five thousand men nearly—of this there are four regiments, three of dismounted cavalry & one of infantry, yet undrilled in loading their muskets, numbering in all about twenty two hundred men, & Genl. Hinks reports them unfitted, by reason of ignorance of drills, for service in the field. I would therefore respectfully recommend that these men be sent back to some point where they can be instructed and aid in holding entrenched lines or positions which will have to be held wherever the main army may be. taking out these regimen[ts] which I dare not trust in any responsible position, will leave to Genl. Hinks about Twenty Eight hundred men. [I] understand that Genl. Ferrero Comd'g Di[v] of co[lore]d troops [in the Ninth Corps, has abou]t four thousand men. I have therefore respectfully to suggest that the two Divisions be consolidated under the command of Genl. Ferrero, known to be an excellent Division Commander, and that the consolidated Division be assigned to the 9th, or 18th. Corps, as the Genl. in-chief may judge best for the interest of the service. There is also in this command, one light Battery with colored Cannoneers—which is expensive and wor[se] than worthless, which I respectfully recommended be broken up—the men transferred to the Infantry. The Captain of the Battery is well recommended to me & it might be judged good to allow him to fill up his Battery from volunteers from the Heavy Artillery in this corps. I deem the Subject of this letter, one of such importance, as to require the immediate attention of the Lt. Genl. Comdg." ALS (telegram sent), DNA, RG 393, 18th Army Corps, Telegrams Sent (Press); telegram received, *ibid.*, RG 108, Letters Received. Misdated June 18 in *O.R.*, I, xl, part 2, 202–3. On June 26, 11:00 P.M., Butler telegraphed to Smith, sending a copy to Rawlins. "I have the honor to acknowledge the receipt of of your telegram a copy of which you have forwarded directly to the Lt General as I am informed in regard to colored troops—T͟h͟e From some of its propositions I dissent—your field ration of the twenty third (23) inst gives seven thousand eight hundred & fifty two colored troops for duty in this despatch you say you have now nearly five thousand 5000 what has become of nearly three thousand (3000) of these troops in three (3) days— As to Choates colored battery it has been well drilled highly spoken of I know its commander is a good officer and he has expressed confidence in his men—In your dispatch of the twenty third (23d) upon the authority of your chief of Artillery you reported the colored battery inefficient but as that officer is of that class who do not trust any colored troops and has since proved his own inefficiency by deliberately riding into the enemys lines in a fit of aberration or other delerium as I am informed & been captured by them, I am not inclined to base much official action on his judgement—It can hardly be true in fact that the three (3) regiments of colored cavalry and one (1) of infantry are yet undrilled in loading their muskets as one of these regiments was in the charge for which you have publicly so highly completer the colored troops and took the works they were ordered to do—If these are not to be depended upon you have few colored or other troops that can be—Much as I value Genl Hinks services and I yield to no man in my appreciation of them I should hardly advise the disorganization of his division because of his loss   If however the Lt General chooses to carry out a suggestion made by him some days since giving to Genl Burnside the troops of the ninth army corps which are now in this department in the eighteenth 18th corps and giving us General Ferreros division instead as you seem to desire this change for the purpose of consolidating the colored troops I will not object— Supposing however until now that this was against your wish I have objected but will now withdraw it and allow the change to be made so far as it rests with me—As you are entrenching before Petersburgh as you suggest you will find the good troops to hold entrenchments   I will forward a copy of this note to the Chief of Staff of the Commanding General so that he may have our views before him at the same time although as a rule I would not send forward such communications without an interchange of views—" ALS (telegram sent—incomplete), DNA, RG 107, Telegrams Collected (Unbound); copy, *ibid.*, RG 108, Letters Received. *O.R.*, I, xl, part 2, 458–59. On June 28, Smith telegraphed to Rawlins. "The Maj. Genl: Comd'g Dept: Va. & N. C. having done me the honor to forward to ~~you~~ me a copy of his Endorsement on a letter to you of the 26th inst, with reference to the Colored Troops, I deem it due to myself, and the interests of the Service, which I was honestly endeavouring to promote, to forward for the information of the Lieut Genl: Comdg, communications upon the subject, from Brig: Genl. Hinks, Comd'g Colored Div, and Capt. Choate Comd'g Colored Battery, with a brief statement of my own. My 'field return' of the 23rd inst had in it a Clerical Error, in which one of Genl: Hinks' Brigade was twi[ce] counted, which will account for th[e] discrepancy men[tion]ed. In my letter to you, I made the assertion therein contained, giving no authority, & therefore taking the responsibility as to the correctness of the Statement, upon myself,   Therefore the Maj Genl: Comd'g. Dept. Va & N. C. had no warrant for his assertion, that my statement was based upon that of my Chief of Arty. With reference to Captn Elder, I have to remark that he had been hard at work night & day since my arrival here & from the best information that I can gather, his aberration was due to his exposure during the entire day, to the extreme heat of the sun. The accompanying papers will show to the Lt. Genl: Comdg my authority for the statement I have made. That testimony may be corroborated by my own observations on the field of Battle. I would particularly call attention to the statement of Genl: Hinks with reference to the 5th Mass: Colored Cavly. (dismounted) & the part of the action ~~of~~ in which that regiment was engaged. I did not propose in my letter to entirely break up the Two Whit[e] Divisions of the 18th Corps or to have white regiments transferred from [a corps w]here [they] were well contented, to a Corps where they had no associations & to which, as I learn, have expressed no disposition to go. But if the reorganization which I have proposed to the Lt Genl, should be adopted, & that reorganization should carry with it the disorganization of the two White Divisions of this Corps, I would rest satisfied thinking the Genl, in chief judged it best for the interests of the Service—"

LS (telegram sent), DNA, RG 393, 18th Army Corps, Telegrams Sent (Press). *O.R.*, I, xl, part 2, 489. An undated telegram from Smith to Rawlins was probably sent on June 29. "The Documents I sent you yesterday in reference to colored troops, were sent to you direct by mistake—will you please send them back to me that I may send them through Genl. Butler" Copy, DNA, RG 107, Telegrams Collected (Unbound). On July 3, Smith telegraphed to Rawlins. "Have you received my communications ~~from~~ through Genl. Butler, concerning the condition of negro troops & Battery" ALS (telegram sent), *ibid. O.R.*, I, xl, part 2, 618.

On July 5, 11:20 A.M., Butler telegraphed to USG. "Brig Gen E W Hinks was ordered by me to report for duty in command at Point Look Out because his wounds unfitted him for service in the field Gen Hinks was taken from that Post to come into the field hoping to be able to go through He is admirably fitted for that position. This order was made while that Post was in my command, and Genl Hinks started for his post. But since I am informed ~~Brig Genl Barnes~~ that Post has been annexed to the dept of Washington I desire therefore an order from the Lt General assingng Genl Hinks—to that duty—relieving Col. Draper of the 36th U S Colored who is now detained from his regiment in that Command and is a Valuable officer I believe it to be in contemplation to assign Brig Gen James Barnes to point Look Out but Gen Barnes is an educated able bodied officer ~~whose is much~~ whose services are much needed in the field" ALS (telegram sent), DNA, RG 94, War Records Office, Dept. of Va. and N. C., Army of the James, Unentered Papers; copy, *ibid.*, RG 393, Dept. of Va. and N. C., Telegrams Sent. *O.R.*, I, xl, part 3, 18. See *ibid.*, I, xl, part 2, 459–60, 540, 577, 639. On the same day, Lt. Col. Theodore S. Bowers issued Special Orders No. 49. "Brig Gen E. W. Hineks U. S. Vols is hereby assigned to the command of Point Lookout Md and will relieve Col Draper 36th Regiment U. S. Colored Troops now on duty there," Copies, DLC-USG, V, 57, 62, 67; (2) DNA, RG 107, Telegrams Collected (Bound). *O.R.*, I, xl, part 3, 6. On the same day, Smith wrote to Rawlins. "Have you received the letter from me inclosing the statements of Brig. Gen. E. W. Hinks and Captain Choate with reference to the condition of the colored troops of this corps? The division is now commanded by a colonel, who is reported to me by General Hinks as being inefficient. I am extremely anxious the general should take some steps to make this organization as effective as possible. While I think them capable of being made excellent infantry soldiers, they particularly need intelligent, brave, energetic, and resolute officers. I think unless care is taken to give them officers of this class the experiment will prove a failure. If the general is not entirely satisfied regarding the correctness of the report as to the condition of these troops I would respectfully suggest that a commission be appointed to examine into and report upon their necessities in order to render them effective at once." *Ibid.*, pp. 26–27.

On July 7, 12:40 P.M., Col. Edward D. Townsend telegraphed to USG. "General Order two hundred fourteen (214) of June twenty first (21st) adds that portion of Maryland between the Patuxent, the Cheasapeake, and Potomac including Point-Lookout to Department of Washington Previous to your Special Order of July fifth (5th) the Secretary of War had assigned General Barnes to command at Point-Lookout. He has now ordered General Hinks to report for temporary duty here—Please acknowledge receipt" ALS (telegram sent), DNA, RG 107, Telegrams Collected (Unbound); telegram received, *ibid. O.R.*, I, xxxvii, part 2, 99. On the same day, USG telegraphed to Townsend. "Dispatch of twelve forty (12 40) p. m. this date relative to orders for General Hinks to report to Washington for duty received." Telegram received (on July 8, 12:30 A.M.), DNA, RG 94, Letters Received, 658A 1864; *ibid.*, RG 107, Telegrams Collected (Bound); copies, *ibid.*, RG 108, Letters Sent; DLC-USG, V, 45, 59, 67.

On July 8, Smith twice telegraphed to Rawlins, the first time at 1:55 P.M. "Have some documents forwarded by me through General Butler's headquarters, with reference to the colored troops, been received at your headquarters?" "More than one week since I had the honor to forward certain papers for the consideration of the lieutenant-general commanding the armies of the United States. These papers had reference to the condition of the negro troops, and I deemed the suggestions of importance to the service. I have, therefore, respectfully to request that the major-general commanding the Department of Virginia and North Carolina may be called upon to forward those papers, which were sent to the headquarters of the armies through the headquarters of the department." *O.R.*, I, xl, part 3, 87–88.

On June 21, Smith had forwarded to Rawlins copies of his acrimonious correspondence with Butler and asked to be relieved. *Ibid.*, I, xl, part 2, 301. The enclosures are *ibid.*, pp. 299–301. See telegram to Maj. Gen. William F. Smith, July 2, 1864.

To Elihu B. Washburne

City Point Va. June 23d *1864*.

HON. E. B. WASH~~INGTON~~BURN,

DEAR SIR.

In answer to your letter of a few days ago asking what "S" stands for in my name I can only state *nothing*. It was a mistake made by Senator Morris of Ohio when application was first made for my appointment as Cadet to West Point. My mother's family name is Simpson and having a brother of that name Mr. Morris, who knew both of us as children, got the matter confounded and sent in the application for Cadetship for Ulysses S. Grant. I tried on entering West Point to correct this mistake but failing, after I received my Diploma and Commission, with the "S" inserted, adopted it and have so signed my name ever since.

Every thing ~~is~~ progresses here slowly. The dispatches given by the Sec. of War contains all the news.

Yours Truly

U. S. GRANT

ALS, NHi.

To Maj. Gen. Henry W. Halleck

———

City Point 9 a m
June 24th 1864

MAJ GEN H W HALLECK
CHF OF STAFF

No special change [or] news to report for yesterday   The enemy shew himself in large force on our left in the evening and Meade
ordered him attacked   Failing in getting the attack made before
dark he then ordered the left corps back to the position which they
had just left—This was taken without being followed [u]p by
enemy

U. S. GRANT
Lt Genl

Telegram received, DNA, RG 107, Telegrams Collected (Bound); copies, *ibid.*,
RG 108, Letters Sent; DLC-USG, V, 45, 59, 67. *O.R.*, I, xl, part 1, 13–14; *ibid.*,
I, xl, part 2, 372.

To Maj. Gen. Henry W. Halleck

———

Hd Qrs Army Potomac
2 30 p m June 24th 1864

MAJ GEN H W HALLECK
CHF OF STAFF

I find the affair of the 22nd was much worse than I had heretofore learned. Our losses (nearly all captures) was not far from
two thousand, and [f]our pieces of artillery. The affair was a stampede and surprise to both parties and ought to have been turned in
our favor.

Richmond paper of yesterday states that Hunter at last accounts was at Salem retiring by the route taken by Averill last fall.
Our cavalry [(s]mall detachment) is now on the Weldon road
destroying it.

Wilson with Seven thousand Cavalry started the night of the

22nd   Richmond paper announces that he struck the South side road in Dinwiddie

This morning about 7 a m the enemy attempted an assault [on] Genl W F Smiths front—Prisoners [sa]y in three lines.   none but the skirmish line reached our advance and most of them were captured

U. S. GRANT
Lt Genl

Telegram received (on June 25, 1864, 7:40 A.M.), DNA, RG 107, Telegrams Collected (Bound). *O.R.*, I, xl, part 1, 14; *ibid.*, I, xl, part 2, 372–73.

To Maj. Gen. Henry W. Halleck

City Point, Va., June 24th 1864.

MAJ. GEN. H. W. HALLECK,
CHIEF OF STAFF OF THE ARMY,
GENERAL:

Your letter stating that Gens. Rosecrans and Curtis are calling for more troops is received. I am satisfied you would hear the same call if they were stationed in Maine. The fact is the two Depts. should be merged into one and some officer, who does not govern so largely through a secret police system as Rosecrans does, put in command. I do think the best interests of the service demands that Rosecrans should be removed and some one else placed in that command. It makes but little difference who you assign it would be an improvement. I had suspected wrong management on the Miss. river but believed Washburne and Slocum would purify matters, so far as their commands and their powers go. Have they not done so?

You ask if the resignation of Gen. Crocker should be accepted, and if he is qualified for the command of New Mexico. Crocker and Sheridan, I think, were the best Division Commanders I have ever known. Either of them are qualified for any command. I would say by all means retain Gen. Crocker in the service and send him to

New Mexico. The only available Maj. Gen. I can think of to take the Dept. of the Mo., if the President will consent to the change, and I hope he will, is N. J. T. Dana.[1]

> Very respectfully
> Your Obt. Svt.
> U. S. GRANT
> Lt. Gen.

LS, Schoff Collection, MiU-C. *O.R.*, I, xxxiv, part 4, 527. On June 22, 1864, Maj. Gen. Henry W. Halleck wrote to USG. "I enclose herewith a copy of Genl Sherman's report of operations, just recieved. Genl Stahl is organizing a column of all available forces in West Virginia to protect an ammunition train for Genl Hunter. If the enemy's forces in the valley in Hunter's rear should prove as numerous as reported, it will hardly be possible to get through. Nothing has been heard here directly from Genl Hunter since he sent Stahl back and our scouts have not been able to [p]as[s] the rebel [lines. General St]ahl [is] acting under verbal instructions of Hunter and may be able to communicate with him as he advances. Difficulties in Kentucky seem to have subsided for the present. Genls Rosecrans & Curtis are continually calling for more troops in their Depts, the President & members of congress being flooded with stampeding telegrams. They want twenty thousand men to oppose two thousand guerrillas. Brig Genl M. M. Crocker has tendered his resignation on account of ill-health, but his friends are urging that it be *not* accepted & that he be sent to New Mexico or Arizona. The Secty is willing to do this, if in you[r] opinion Genl C. should be retained in service & is compete[n]t for a frontier command like the one suggested. He desires your opinion on this matter as early as convenient. Reports to Staff Depts indicate stupendous frauds in Genl Banks' command, at Vicksburg and on the Miss river generally. Genl Canby proposes a very general change of commanders, and for this purpose nearly all general officers not in virtual command have been sent to him." LS, DNA, RG 108, Letters Sent (Press). *O.R.*, I, xxxvii, part 1, 660; *ibid.*, I, xl, part 2, 303; (incomplete) *ibid.*, I, xxxiv, part 4, 504–5. See telegram to Maj. Gen. Henry W. Halleck, June 25, 1864.

On June 27, Halleck wrote to USG. "Your note of the 24th is recieved & has been submitted to the Secty of War. As both the Secty and myself strongly opposed the appointment of Genl Rosecrans to the Dept of Mo. it is not probable that we can effect any change at the present time. Genl Crocker's resignation has not been accepted, & he has been ordered to New Mexico for the benefit of his health. I hear no complaints of Genl Washburne at Memphis or of Genl Slocum at Vicksburg. I believe it was partly through them that the frauds to which I referred were developped. Many of these frauds seen to have their source in Agents of the Treasy Dept and to be connected with trade licenses and the leasing & stocking of abandoned plantations. Cotton trading & speculation seem to be the main levers of corruption & fraud on the Miss. both in the army & navy. I hope congress will enable us to make a draft soon. Unless the commutation clause is repealed we can get no men, and our armies are melting away at a frightful rate. We must have some means of keeping up the supply or we go to the wall." ALS, DNA, RG 108, Letters Sent (Press). *O.R.*, I, xxxiv, part 4, 568.

On July 1, 10:30 A.M., Asst. Secretary of War Charles A. Dana telegraphed to President Abraham Lincoln. ". . . I have in the most informal way communicated to Gen Grant the substance of what you said respecting Rosecrans & Curtis. He thinks the most useful way to employ Rosecrans would be to station him at some convenient point on the northern frontier with the duty of detecting & exposing rebel conspiracies in Canada" Telegram received (at 8:00 P.M.), DLC-Edwin M. Stanton. *O.R.*, I, xl, part 1, 28.

1. Napoleon J. T. Dana of Maine, USMA 1842, served in the Mexican War and resigned as of March 1, 1855, to become a banker in St. Paul, Minn. Appointed col., 1st Minn., as of Oct. 2, 1861, and brig. gen. as of Feb. 3, 1862, he served in Va. until severely wounded at Antietam. Appointed maj. gen. as of Nov. 29, 1862, he commanded briefly in Texas after his recovery, and on Aug. 17, 1864, was assigned command of the District of Vicksburg.

To Maj. Gen. George G. Meade

By Telegraph from City Point 10 15 P M
Dated June 24th *1864.*

To MAJ. GENERAL MEADE

If you can spare Col Burton[1] I wish you would send him to report to Gen Smith to take charge of the portion of the siege train now on its way out to him. The whole of the siege train is now up. Such portions of it as you think can be used advantageously on your front will be sent to you at any time

U. S GRANT
Lieut Gnl

Telegram received, DNA, RG 94, War Records Office, Army of the Potomac; copies, *ibid.*, RG 108, Letters Sent; DLC-USG, V, 45, 59, 67; (2) Meade Papers, PHi. *O.R.*, I, xl, part 2, 374. On June 24, 1864, 11:00 P.M., Maj. Gen. George G. Meade telegraphed to USG. "Your despatch of 10.15 received. I can use a portion of the siege train and shall require Col Burton to take charge of it now that Col. Abbott for whom I applied in April last, & who I understood would be sent with the train, is now with Genl Butler & can be given to Genl Smith—I am also informed that Genl. Smith has a competent officer Col. Gibson under his immediate command who is available for this duty; I have therefore less hesitation in asking to retaining Col. Burton for my own purposes." ALS (telegram sent), DNA, RG 94, War Records Office, Army of the Potomac; telegram received, *ibid.*, RG 108, Letters Received. *O.R.*, I, xl, part 2, 375.

On the same day, Maj. Gen. William F. Smith telegraphed to Brig. Gen. John A. Rawlins. "In my opinion it is highly important to have an Artillery officer of great experience & high attainments in charge of all the Artillery in my line. I have no one to fill this position. Understanding that the reserve artillery of the A. P. is broken up, I would respectfully ask that Col. Burton be ordered to report to me at once, if consistent with the interests of the service" LS (telegram sent), DNA, RG 107, Telegrams Collected (Unbound). *O.R.*, I, xl, part 2, 400. On June 25, Smith telegraphed to Rawlins. "I have the honor to request that Lt Daniel T. Wells 8th U S Inf.y may be detailed to act as Commissary of Musters for the 18th Army Corps. Capt Cogswell Commanding the Regiment informs me that Lt Wells can be spared." ALS (telegram sent), DNA, RG 107, Telegrams Collected (Unbound); telegram received, *ibid.*, RG 108, Letters Received. On the same day, Smith telegraphed to Lt. Col. Theodore S. Bowers. "It is highly important that I should have a commissary of musters before muster day. Many of my officers have not been mustered owing to the fact that the Division officers are volunteers & their musters have to be countersigned by a Regular Corps Commissary. I have applied for several, but have as yet received no reply. I also repeat my request for Col. Burton as Chief of Artillery. I am importunate in my request, as I consider an efficient Staff necessary to the welfare & success of my ~~mr~~ command & the operations before me." Copies, *ibid.*, RG 107, Telegrams Collected (Unbound); *ibid.*, RG 393, 18th Army Corps, Telegrams Sent (Press). *O.R.*, I, xl, part 2, 426–27. Also on June 25, Bowers wrote to Smith. "General Meade has been asked if he can spare Colonel Burton. He says he cannot. Colonel Piper, of the Tenth New York Artillery, is with you. Can you not take him?" *Ibid.*, p. 427. On the same day, Smith twice telegraphed to Bowers. "Col. Piper has been necessarily placed in command of a Brigade. I gave him up as chief of artillery for this purpose as I thought it for the best." "If I can have a Brigade Commander, I can take Col. Piper as chief artillery   I have had to reorganize & break up Brigades to get them out of the hands of incompetent commanders & have now one Brigade without a suitable one. Should Col. Piper be taken away his Brigade would be left in the hands of a very incompetent officer & I can not supply his place" ALS (telegrams sent), DNA, RG 107, Telegrams Collected (Unbound). On the same day, Rawlins telegraphed to Smith. "Gen Meade Says he requires the Services of Col Burton. The Lieutenant of the 8th infantry you wish as commissary of musters will be detailed at once if you know of an officer fitted to perform the duties you desired Col Burton assigned to Please Send his name & He will be ordered to You if His Services Can possibly be Spared" Telegram received, *ibid.*, RG 393, 24th Army Corps, Telegrams Received (Unarranged); copy, *ibid.*, RG 94, War Records Office, Dept. of the Cumberland. *O.R.*, I, xl, part 2, 427. On June 26, Rawlins telegraphed to Meade, sending a copy to Smith. "You will please order Col Burton of the artillery to report at once to Maj Gen W F Smith to take charge of the artillery on his Line temporarily   Gen. Smith has no officer available for that duty without detaching a Brigade Commander" Telegrams received (2), DNA, RG 94, War Records Office, Army of the Potomac; copies, *ibid.*, RG 108, Letters Sent; DLC-USG, V, 45, 59, 67; (2) Meade Papers, PHi. *O.R.*, I, xl, part 2, 430. See *ibid.*, p. 435. See also telegram to Maj. Gen. George G. Meade, June 27, 1864.

On June 25, 2:00 P.M., Col. Henry L. Abbot telegraphed to USG. "Gen Smith directs me to ask authority to send four (4) more eight inch Mortars and three (3) more 30 pdr Parrotts to his front. I await instructions here." ALS (telegram sent), DNA, RG 107, Telegrams Collected (Unbound). *O.R.*, I, xl, part 2, 421. On the same day, Bowers telegraphed to Abbot. "Furnish the additional guns and mortars asked for by Gen. Smith. It is desired that he have all the guns and mortars that he can use to advantage" ALS (telegram sent),

DNA, RG 107, Telegrams Collected (Unbound). *O.R.*, I, xl, part 2, 421.

Also on June 25, Lt. Col. Cyrus B. Comstock wrote to Abbot. "The general desires that you send Burnside 7,000 sand-bags if you have them. Please inform me how many you have, by bearer. If you have no transportation arrange it as you best can or call on General Ingalls here." *Ibid.*, p. 422. On the same day, Abbot wrote to Comstock. "I made requisition for 25,000 sand-bags—5,000 for each gun, excluding the 100-pounders. How many were actually obtained I cannot say without seeing my ordnance officer, who is now at Broadway Landing. I have no transportation for them. I would suggest that you direct General Ingalls to send transportation to the Broadway Landing (one mile below the pontoon bridge), and let the wagon-master carry an order for Capt. S. P. Hatfield, ordnance officer of siege train, to issue the required number of bags to General Burnside. I think this plan would save much time. These bags, I hope, will be replaced, as I find I shall be obliged to supply them for my embrasures. Several times to-day I have been much inconvenienced by having no telegraphic communication with Broadway Landing. The wire crosses the river there to General Butler's headquarters so that an operator is all that is needed. I shall move my headquarters there on Monday, and I shall need a very large detail of orderlies if the operator cannot be supplied. My guns are now in position from the James River to Petersburg and I receive many telegrams which require prompt attention. If you can help me to an operator it will be of very great assistance." *Ibid.*, pp. 422–23.

1. Henry S. Burton, born in N. Y., appointed from Vt., USMA 1839, was appointed maj., 3rd Art., as of May 14, 1861, and col., 5th Art., as of Aug. 11, 1863. He commanded the art. reserve, Army of the Potomac (Jan.–May, 1864) and served as inspector of art. (May–June) before his assignment to command the art. of the 18th Army Corps.

To Edwin M. Stanton

City Point Va
10 30 p m June 25 1864

HON EDWIN M STANTON
SECY OF WAR

I will feel obliged to you if you will order Genl Rosecrans to release Dr J A Barrett a citizen prisoner lately confined in St Louis on bonds whilst awaiting trial or to give him an immediate trial— The Doctor is a Copperhead but I have no idea that he has done anything more than that class of people are constantly doing and not so much. He was a neighbor of mine—a clever man, & ha[s] a practice in the neighborhood which it will be very inconvenient to other people than himself to have interrupted—

U S GRANT Lt. Genl

Telegram received (on June 26, 1864, 12:25 A.M.), DNA, RG 107, Telegrams Collected (Bound); copies, *ibid.*, Telegrams Received in Cipher; *ibid.*, RG 108, Letters Sent; DLC-USG, V, 45, 59, 67. *O.R.*, II, vii, 411. On June 26, Col. James A. Hardie telegraphed to USG. "I am directed to say that the Secretary of War has directed Genl Rosecrans to release Dr. J. A. Barrett on his parole and bond in accordance with your request as conveyed per telegram June 25th." ALS (telegram sent), DNA, RG 107, Telegrams Collected (Bound); copy, *ibid.*, Telegrams Collected (Unbound). Dr. James A. Barrett, accused of disloyal activity in the Order of American Knights, was released from jail at USG's request despite the protests of Maj. Gen. William S. Rosecrans. *O.R.*, II, vii, 245, 340, 417, 447, 448; Lincoln, *Works*, VII, 436.

To Maj. Gen. Henry W. Halleck

City Point 11 30 a m
June 25th 1864

MAJ GEN H W. HALLECK
CHF [O]F STAFF

Richmond papers o[f] yesterday state that Hunter at last accounts was at Fincastle

There will be no use in Stahel[1] attempting to reach him.

All quiet here. Sheridan is now crossing the road where the Army crossed. Yesterday evening Greggs[2] Division had a very severe fight with the Enemy between Charles City C H & Long Bridge. I do not know the result but understand officially that we saved all the wagon trains which seemed to be the object of the attack. The loss was said to be heavy on both sides the Enemy coming in close canister range

The same Richmond Paper announces that Wilson reached Burkesville. I shall try to give the army a few days rest which they now stand much in need of

U S. GRANT
Lt Genl

Telegram received (at 2:20 P.M.), DNA, RG 107, Telegrams Collected (Bound); copies, *ibid.*, RG 108, Letters Sent; DLC-USG, V, 45, 59, 67. *O.R.*, I, xxxvi, part 3, 792; *ibid.*, xxxvii, part 1, 673; *ibid.*, I, xl, part 1, 14; *ibid.*, I, xl, part 2, 402.

On June 19, 1864, 12:40 P.M., Maj. Gen. Henry W. Halleck telegraphed to USG. "Telegrams from West Va state that the cavalry sent out with despatches to Genl Hunter find the enemy in possession of Staunton & Lexington in Hunter's rear, and have returned without being able to reach him or ascertain his whereabouts. I hardly think it possible that Genl Stahl who was sent back for ammunition can return to him even if he knew where Hunter is. He, however will make the attempt, hopeless as it appears. If the enemys force, as reported, is superior to Hunters, his only escape will be into West Va, or, by crossing the James & reaching you on the south side. The latter is very possible for cavalry but extremely perilous for infantry. It is hardly possible to get any communication to him from this side." ALS (telegram sent), DNA, RG 107, Telegrams Collected (Bound); telegram received, *ibid.* *O.R.*, I, xxxvii, part 1, 650–51.

On June 24, 11:30 A.M., Halleck telegraphed to USG. "As stated in my former despatch Major Genl Stahel was sent back by Genl Hunter to collect troops & escort to him a train of ammunition   Genl Stahel is nearly ready to start, but has no information as to where he can find Genl Hunter. Should your information be such that you deem Genl Stahel's expedition too perilous to be undertaken, please telegraph to that effect; otherwise he will proceed the best he can up the Shenandoah Valley." ALS (telegram sent), DNA, RG 107, Telegrams Collected (Bound); telegram received, *ibid.* *O.R.*, I, xxxvii, part 1, 670.

On June 24, 4:50 P.M., Lt. Col. Theodore S. Bowers wrote to Brig. Gen. John A. Rawlins. "Col. Smith of Gen. Sheridans Command has just arrived here. to see Gen. Grant. He reports that Sheridans Comand and wagon trains has arrived at Wilcoxs Wharf   The enemy appear and are reported to be in great force on the opposite side of Herring creek. Hampton's force crossed by Saint Mary's Church last night towards Westover, and the negroes say that it was about three fu hours in passing. Yesterday one Brigade of the enemy's Cavalry made an attack for the purpose of getting into the wagon train, but were repulsed. This morning the advance guard of the train was attacked, but were the enemy was driven back until they took up the position on the opposite side of Herring's Creek. The enemy is supposed to be in force at Phillips. Gen. Sheridan desires to know whether he had better crossd push through with his train—Whether we have any force on the north side of the river to assist him if necessary. Whether it is deemed safe to try to risk the train to come up to Harrisons landing, or whether   Gen Ingalls is of opinion that the Command can would better drop down in the neck where the army crossed, and where the train could be easily protected, and ferried over at Dotard's [*Douthat's*] and at the point where the ponton was laid. Please give directions. The officer is waiting"   ALS, DNA, RG 94, War Records Office, Army of the Potomac. *O.R.*, I, xxxvi, part 3, 790–91; *ibid.*, I, xl, part 2, 374. On the same day, USG wrote to Bowers. "Direct General Sheridan to drop down to where the army crossed James River, and General Ingalls to furnish transportation to cross his command." *Ibid.*

On June 25, Maj. Gen. George G. Meade wrote to Bowers. "The accompanying copies of communications from the Chf Qtr Master and Chf Com'y of this Army are respectfully referred for the consideration of the Lieut: Genl Comdg in connection with so much of the telegram's from Major Genl Sheridan,

Comd'g the Cav'y Corps, dated June 20 & 23rd as represents, in substance, that his movements from the White house after the return from his recent expedition were delayed in consequence of his finding an insufficiency of supplies at that place.—" Copy, Meade Papers, PHi. *O.R.*, I, xl, part 2, 402. The enclosure is *ibid.* On July 5, Maj. Gen. Philip H. Sheridan wrote to Bowers reporting his movements on June 20–23, especially as they concerned an absence of supplies at White House. *Ibid.*, I, xl, part 3, 14. See also *ibid.*, I, xl, part 2, 255, 562.

1. Julius Stahel (Számvald), born in Hungary in 1825, fought in the Hungarian Revolution and left the country in 1849, came to New York City in 1856, and was on the staff of the *New York Illustrated News* before the Civil War. Appointed col., 8th N. Y., as of Aug. 11, 1861, brig. gen. as of Nov. 12, and maj. gen. as of March 14, 1863, he commanded a cav. div. under Maj. Gen. David Hunter, who doubted his competence.

2. David M. Gregg, born into a prominent family in Pa. in 1833, USMA 1855, served in the 1st Dragoons on the Pacific Coast before the Civil War. Appointed col., 8th Pa. Cav., as of Jan. 24, 1862, and brig. gen. as of Nov. 29, he served in the Army of the Potomac and won special distinction at Gettysburg. Commanding the 2nd Cav. Div., Army of the Potomac, in the engagement at St. Mary's Church, June 24, 1864, he had 329 casualties but was credited by Maj. Gen. Philip H. Sheridan with preventing the loss of the supply train. *Ibid.*, I, xxxvi, part 1, 187, 799.

To Maj. Gen. Benjamin F. Butler

By Telegraph from City Point 1 P. M

Dated June 25 *1864.*

To MAJ GEN BUTLER

Can you send a thousand or fifteen hundred Infy to Hothards [*Douthat's*] wharf, before daylight. Sheridan has been attacked this evening & with great difficulty & with heavy loss of men, has saved his train so far. He expects another attack at daylight & wold be much assisted if some Infy. could reach him in time

U. S GRANT.

Lt G

Telegram received, DNA, RG 393, Dept. of Va. and N. C., Telegrams Received; copies (sent on June 25, 1864, 1:00 A.M.), *ibid.*, RG 108, Letters Sent; DLC-USG, V, 45, 59, 67. *O.R.*, I, xxxvi, part 3, 792; *ibid.*, I, xl, part 2, 419. At 2:55 A.M., Maj. Gen. Benjamin F. Butler telegraphed to USG. "Have ordered two regiments from my line to march to wharf at point of Rocks. Have ordered up transpertation to ~~go~~ take them to Doutharts wharf—Will you send down ~~to~~ and get ready a boat or boats at Cit[y] Point in case mine have not steam up or are unready—Cannot Sheridan fall back to Wilsons wharf about four Miles   he will there have the cover of our work and 1500 men to assist him—There are also two Gunboats there to aid him   A boat from City point can reach Wilsons wharf in an hour & fifteen minutes . . . Your telegram reached me at 2 35 A. M." ALS (telegram sent), DNA, RG 94, War Records Office, Army of the Potomac. Incomplete in *O.R.*, I, xxxvi, part 3, 792; *ibid.*, I, xl, part 2, 419. At 3:15 A.M., Butler telegraphed to USG. "Will Gen Grant please tell me exactly where Sheridan is that I may ~~send~~ be able to give directions to the officer in charge of my men" ALS (telegram sent), DNA, RG 94, War Records Office, Army of the Potomac. *O.R.*, I, xxxvi, part 3, 793; *ibid.*, I, xl, part 2, 419. On the same day, USG telegraphed to Butler. "The Charles City Court House, is the place where our troops are, & the enemy Confronting them. The wagons & one (1) division of cavalry have come through to Wilcoxs wharf—but have been moving during the night to Charles City. Court House." Telegram received, DNA, RG 393, Dept. of Va. and N. C., Telegrams Received; copies, *ibid.*, RG 108, Letters Sent; DLC-USG, V, 45, 59, 67. *O.R.*, I, xxxvi, part 3, 793; *ibid.*, I, xl, part 2, 419. At 9:45 (probably A.M.), Butler telegraphed to USG. "My three Regiments sent to Sheridan have returned   He thinks he can hold without them. Two substittutes from the 7th N. Hampshire deserted to the Enemy to day from Picket" ALS (telegram sent), DNA, RG 107, Telegrams Collected (Unbound). *O.R.*, I, xl, part 2, 420.

On June 25, Butler forwarded to USG, adding a postscript, a message of 6:00 A.M. from Lt. Alfred G. Simons, Spring Hill Signal Station, to Capt. Lemuel B. Norton. ". . . Twenty (20) cars just passed the Junction towards Richmond. They were loaded with troops. . . . Fifteen others cars passed yesterday loaded with troop in same direction" LS (telegram sent), DNA, RG 107, Telegrams Collected (Unbound). At 3:50 P.M., Butler forwarded to USG a message from Norton. "The Signal Officer on the tower reports 'heavy firing near Petersburg at a point S 15° W from the tower. It extends for a mile along our lines.' " LS (telegram sent), *ibid.*, RG 94, War Records Office, Dept. of Va. and N. C., Army of the James, Unentered Papers.

At 7:20 P.M., Butler telegraphed to USG. "The following has been rec'd from N. Carolina & is sent for the information of the Comd'g General—'Head Qr's Dist of N. Carolina   Newberne June 23/64   GENERAL   The expedition towards Kinston made to amuse the enemy towards Goldsboro while more important work was to be performed below has returned. The commander of this portion of the forces has reported the capture of a large number of prisoners and horses. Col Folk, the commander of the rebel forces at Kinston is among the prisoners. I hope to report good things from below very soon. The news from Kinston has just been sent to me by the officer who was in command but who has not yet reported fully. The train is just leaving for Morehead where the steamer is waiting   (signed) I. N. PALMER   Brig Genl' " Copy (telegram sent), *ibid.*, Army of the Potomac; telegram received (at 7:10 P.M.), *ibid.*, RG 108, Letters Received. *O.R.*, I, xl, part 2, 420.

At 9:00 P.M., USG telegraphed to Butler. "It was Genl Smiths intentions to carry an advanced point in front last night but finding he had fewr men than that he thought was postponed. If he can secure this advance tomorrow night I would like it to be done" Telegram received (at 9:15 P.M.), DNA, RG 393, Dept. of Va. and N. C., Telegrams Received. *O.R.*, I, xl, part 2, 421.

To Maj. Gen. Henry W. Halleck

Hd Qrs City Point
4 p m June 26th 1864

MAJ GENL H W HALLECK
CHF OF STAFF

All is quiet and our men resting—

Sheridan is crossing the river near Fort Powhattan unmolested by the enemy

Greggs loss was much less than I was led to suppose by the verbal report first received—

Sheridan says he thinks two hundred and twenty five (225) killed wounded and missing will cover it, whilst he thinks the enemys killed and wounded is much greater—This is Greggs loss between the Chickahominy and James River not counting losses in previous engagements

Nothing heard from Wilson since he left Burkesville—

If it is possible I wish pay masters could be sent here to pay troops—The officers particularly are suffering

U S GRANT
Lt Genl

Telegram received (at 6:00 P.M.), DNA, RG 107, Telegrams Collected (Bound); (in cipher) *ibid.*, Telegrams Collected (Unbound); copies (sent at 3:00 P.M.), *ibid.*, RG 108, Letters Sent; DLC-USG, V, 45, 59, 67; (incomplete) DNA, RG 108, Letters Received. *O.R.*, I, xxxvi, part 3, 793–94; *ibid.*, I, xl, part 1, 14–15; *ibid.*, I, xl, part 2, 430. On June 28, 1864, Maj. Gen. Henry W. Halleck wrote to USG. "I am informed that the delay in paying the Army of the Potomac has resulted from the failure of the Treasury Dept to furnish the money. Not only are the requisitions for May & June unfilled, but some eighteen millions for April is behind. The Pay master Genl has made a special requisition of two millions to pay officers in Army of the Potomac who require it for their current expenses, and that the moment the money is recieved Pay masters will be sent to the army with it. Sherman has found the rebel intrenchments in front of Marietta stronger than he expected. His assaulting columns were driven back with a loss of about three thousand." ALS, DNA, RG 108, Letters Sent (Press). *O.R.*, I, xl, part 2, 476–77.

To Maj. Gen. Benjamin F. Butler

Dated June 26 *1864.*

To GENL BUTLER

I think it will advisable to put up 2 or 4 guns of Heavy Calibre on your shore Battery to Command Howletts Battery and the Reach above the obstruction   this will enable the monitors to drop down out of range of the land Batteries   is desirable that they should not lay habitually under fire But should be where in a few minutes they Can run up to engage the Enemys I Iron Clads or land Batteries if necessary.

U. S. GRANT
Lt Genl

Telegram received, DNA, RG 393, Dept. of Va. and N. C., Telegrams Received; copies (dated June 25, 1864), *ibid.*, RG 108, Letters Sent; DLC-USG, V, 45, 59, 67. Dated June 26 in *O.R.*, I, xl, part 2, 450. On June 26, 10:40 A.M., Maj. Gen. Benjamin F. Butler telegraphed to USG. "In addition to the shore battery which you saw 4.20 pounder & one 30 pounder Parrot works are already in progress for Mounting two one hundred pounders one six inch Sawyer and two 16 inch Mortars which will see not only the Howlet house battery and the obstructions but the the reach above Farrars Island and the reach above Dutch Gap where the rebel iron clads take shelter" ALS (telegram sent), DNA, RG 94, War Records Office, Dept. of Va. and N. C., Army of the James, Unentered Papers; telegram received, *ibid.*, RG 108, Letters Received. *O.R.*, I, xl, part 2, 450.

At 7:45 A.M., Butler had telegraphed to USG. "Gen Smith had telegraph informed me that he intended to attack that advanced position last night. I heard sharp firing and supposed he might have done so   Upon reciept of your telegram I inquired as to the possibilit result of his attack and recieved the folowing telegram which I give verbatim although I suppose it must contain a blunder of the operator. GEN BUTLER. I thought it best to defer the attack indefinitely. On a second reconnoisance of the enemy's position and view of the small forces at Genl Turners disposal last night (June 24) and reconnoisances to day have developed the enemies lines so strong that the loss of Could life would not be worth the hill (*sic*)   WILLIAM F SMITH   In view of this opinions of General Smith do you think it advisable to make the attempt. If so I will go over in the course of the day and arrange the attack for tonight as suggested" ALS (telegram sent), DNA, RG 107, Telegrams Collected (Unbound); (incomplete) *ibid.*, RG 393, Dept. of Va. and N. C., Telegrams Sent (Press); telegram received, *ibid.*, RG 108, Letters Received. *O.R.*, I, xl, part 2, 449. At 8:15 A.M., USG telegraphed to Butler. "It was on Gen. Smiths report that I ordered the advance, I did last night. I would not now insist on it against his judgement without knowing more about the ground & the feasability of carrying it than I do." Telegram received, DNA, RG 393, Dept. of Va. and N. C., Telegrams Received; copies, *ibid.*, RG 108, Letters Sent; DLC-USG, V, 45, 59, 67. Printed as received at 8:40 A.M. in *O.R.*, I, xl, part 2, 449.

To Maj. Gen. Benjamin F. Butler

By Telegraph from City Pt
4 30 [P.M.] *Dated* June 26 *1864.*

To GENL BUTLER

the force passing James River is probably the f̶ enemys cavalry which was after Sheridan. The latter is all safe and no doubt the e̶n̶e̶y̶ enemy have abandoned all i̶n̶t̶e̶ Idea further molesting him. If reenforcements should become s̶o̶ a̶b̶s̶l̶ absolutey essential to s̶e̶n̶d̶ y̶o̶u̶r̶ l̶i̶n̶e̶s̶ hold your lines the troop north of the river may be brought in, not however until the necessity arises

U. S. GRANT
Lt Genl

Telegram received, DNA, RG 393, Dept. of Va. and N. C., Telegrams Received; copies, *ibid.*, RG 108, Letters Sent; DLC-USG, V, 45, 59, 67. *O.R.*, I, xl, part 2, 451. On June 26, 1864, 4:45 P.M., Maj. Gen. Benjamin F. Butler telegraphed to USG. "Reported from Lookout that the Column of the enemy reported this morning a̶s̶ p̶a̶s̶s̶i̶g̶ occupied 4½ hours in passing (four hours and a half)" ALS (telegram sent), DNA, RG 94, War Records Office, Dept. of Va. and N. C., Army of the James, Unentered Papers. *O.R.*, I, xl, part 2, 451.

At 11:40 A.M., Butler forwarded a signal message of 11:00 A.M. from 1st Lt. Charles F. Cross to Capt. Lemuel B. Norton. "Lt Bruyn reports that Cavalry & wagons have been seen crossing the r̶i̶v̶e̶t̶ river at Cox's Ferry towards the west for an hour & are still passing" Copy, DNA, RG 107, Telegrams Collected (Unbound). *O.R.*, I, xl, part 2, 452. Also on June 26, Butler telegraphed to USG a message from Brig. Gen. William T. H. Brooks. "Signal officer at water battery reports that cavalry and wagons have been for an hour and are still crossing from east to west at Cox's Ferry." *Ibid.*, p. 454. On the same day, Lt. Col. Cyrus B. Comstock telegraphed to Butler. "Lieutenant-General Grant desires me to ask where Cox's Ferry, referred to in your telegram of to-day, is. It does not appear on our map." *Ibid.*, p. 450. At 3:00 P.M., Butler telegraphed to Comstock. "Cox Ferry is in the bend of the Rever next above Farrars Island as it bends to the south at the mouth of V̶i̶n̶e̶y̶ C̶ Procters Creek" ALS (telegram sent), DNA, RG 107, Telegrams Collected (Unbound). *O.R.*, I, xl, part 2, 450.

Also on June 26, Lt. Col. Theodore S. Bowers telegraphed to Butler. "Please send by messenger as soon as practicable a statement of your effective force opperating from the James river." ALS (telegram sent), DNA, RG 107, Telegrams Collected (Unbound). *O.R.*, I, xl, part 2, 451. At 7:15 P.M., Butler telegraphed to Bowers. "Pardon me it is probably my stupidity   you say in your despatch your effective force operating from the James River—Do you intend the forces on my line from the Appomattox to the James or those on the Richmond side of the James at Deep Bottom or both   I shall be obliged for the explanation"   ALS (telegram sent), DNA, RG 107, Telegrams Collected (Unbound). *O.R.*, I, xl, part 2, 451. On the same day, Bowers telegraphed to Butler. "I intended to ask for the effective strength of the Army in the field with you, ~~to~~ which includes the troops on both sides of the river, belonging to the 10th and 18th Corps, and all others located on the line of ~~the~~ present ~~campaign~~ opperations this side of Fortress Monroe. Please excuse ~~the~~ my failure to make the dispatch intelligible." ALS (telegram sent), DNA, RG 107, Telegrams Collected (Unbound). *O.R.*, I, xl, part 2, 451. On June 27, Maj. Robert S. Davis telegraphed to Bowers. "In answer to your telegraph to Gen Butler I would state that the ~~a~~ effective force of this command at present is Infantry 30,430 of which 4501 is Ohio new. Dismounted Cavalry 2,463. Cavalry 4,080. Artillery 1,916   these Amts including Officers Total 38,889" ALS (telegram sent), DNA, RG 107, Telegrams Collected (Unbound).

On June 26, Bowers twice telegraphed to Col. John W. Shaffer, chief of staff for Butler. "Gen Meade has found it impracticable to detail a force from his front as a garrison to relieve your troops, here. The garrison from White House which was detained at Wilcox Landing to aid Sheridan is expected tomorrow. As soon as it arrives the present garrison will be relieved. Will notify you of their arrival." Telegram received, *ibid.*, RG 393, Dept. of Va. and N. C., Telegrams Received. *O.R.*, I, xl, part 2, 450. "The Garrison from White House has just arrived and will soon relieve your troops here" ALS (telegram sent), DNA, RG 107, Telegrams Collected (Unbound).

To Maj. Gen. George G. Meade

By Telegraph from City Point
Dated June 26th *1864.*

To MAJ GEN. MEADE

After Greggs loss Genl Sheridan sent an officer to me with a verbal statement of his situation   I immediately sent the garrison from here to his relief and also all the men that could be well spared from Bermuda Hundred & Wrote him a note telling him what to do in case of another attack   It was then after one 1 oclock at night and you and your troops being distant I did not think it worth while to bother you particularly as all that could be done for the relief of Sheridan had to be done from here or bermuda   Sheridan is now safe & in as comfortable a place as he can be for recruiting his men & horses   You can send him such orders as you deem best. I think he should be got up liesurely to your left where he can rest and at the same time add strength to your position   Whilst this excessively hot and dry weather lasts we will give the men all the rest we can—I have ordered out all the guns and other articles called for by gen Hunt

U. S. GRANT

Lt. Genl

Telegram received (at 10:30 A.M.), DNA, RG 94, War Records Office, Army of the Potomac; copies, *ibid.*, RG 108, Letters Sent; DLC-USG, V, 45, 59, 67; (2) Meade Papers, PHi. Printed as sent at 10:30 A.M. in *O.R.*, I, xxxvi, part 3, 794; *ibid.*, I, xl, part 2, 431. On June 26, 1864, Lt. Col. Orville E. Babcock telegraphed to Maj. Gen. George G. Meade. "Maj Genl Sheridan is now at these Head Qr if you wish to send him any I instructions." ALS (telegram sent), DNA, RG 107, Telegrams Collected (Unbound); telegram received, *ibid.*, RG 94, War Records Office, Army of the Potomac. *O.R.*, I, xxxvi, part 3, 794; *ibid.*, I, xl, part 2, 432.

On the same day, USG telegraphed to Meade. "Is there any news from the front for yesterday & last night? I am obliged in the absence of Mr. Dana to send one or two despatches each day to Washington & want to give the actual state of affairs as nearly as possible—" Telegram received (at 9:00 A.M.), DNA, RG 94, War Records Office, Army of the Potomac; copies (2), Meade Papers, PHi; (dated June 25) DNA, RG 108, Letters Sent; DLC-USG, V, 45, 59, 67. Dated June 26 in *O.R.*, I, xl, part 2, 430. At 9:00 A.M., Meade telegraphed to USG. "No report was made yesterday as all was quiet along the lines except occasional exchange of shots at those portions of the lines most advanced—About 10 a m reports were received of a movement of the enemy down the Weldon R. Rd—Measures were immediately taken to assume either the offensive or defensive should the enemy develop any force   The cavalry were thrown well out to the left & the pickets of the 6th & 2d corps advanced up to the enemy— Towards afternoon I became satisfied the movement of the enemy was simply a covering force to a working party to repair the damages done to the road—The cavaly went as far as Ream's Station finding there a small force of local cavalry engaged in trying to repair the road—they were easily driven off. The distance of the road from our lines—the extreme heat of the weather & my desire to give the men some rest, operated to prevent my sending a force to interrupt the enemy, as it would have been without practical result unless I had maintained my position on the road—I can easily secure possession of the road so soon as I can get force enough to maintain myself there, which will be done if any extension of the force now on the lines from the Gregory to the Page house can be effected—I understood you would enquire into the amt of Genl. Smiths force & ascertain if he could securely hold more than he does now.—Last night a 10. p. m a noisy attack was made on Burnsides front, on a working party engaged in strengthening his skirmish line   There were but few casualties on our side & no part of our line was disturbed—. Genl. Burnside having expressed the opinion he could successfully advance against the enemy by opening trenches, I have directed him to be furnished with engineer officers & troops & the necessary ordnance & materials from the siege train.—I have no report from Genl Sheridan but such as you received when last here, and as you sent him orders direct, I presume his movements & progress are known to you.—" ALS (telegram sent), DNA, RG 94, War Records Office, Army of the Potomac; telegram received, *ibid.*, RG 108, Letters Received. *O.R.*, I, xl, part 2, 431; (incomplete) *ibid.*, I, xxxvi, part 3, 794.

To Maj. Gen. Henry W. Halleck

City Point 3.30 p m
June 27th 1864.

MAJ GENL H W HALLECK
CHF OF STAFF

All is quiet here now except from our own guns which fire into the bridge at Petersburg from a distance of 2000 yards.

Petersburg papers of the 25th state that Hunter is striking for Jackson river Depot about forty miles north of Salem and says that if he reaches Covington which they suppose he will do with most of his forces but with loss of material he will be safe   The same paper accuses Hunter of destroying a great amount of private property and stealing a large number of wagons, horses and cattle—

The same paper also states that Wilson destroyed a train of cars loaded with cotton and furniture, burned the depot buildings &c at Burkesville and destroyed some of the track and was still pushing south. All the Railroads [le]ading into Richmond are now destroyed and some of them badly

U S GRANT
Lt Genl

Telegram received (at 7:00 P.M.), DNA, RG 107, Telegrams Collected (Bound); copies, *ibid.*, RG 108, Letters Sent; DLC-USG, V, 45, 59, 67. Printed (as entered in USG's letterbooks) as sent at 3:00 P.M. in *O.R.*, I, xl, part 1, 15; *ibid.*, I, xl, part 2, 461–62; (as sent at 3:30 P.M.) *ibid.*, I, xxxvii, part 1, 677.

To Maj. Gen. George G. Meade

By Telegraph from City Point 9 30 a m
Dated June 27 *1864.*

To MAJ GEN MEADE

The enemys Cavalry, or at least Rebel troops supposed to be the Cavalry that engaged Sheridan were seen to cross James River yesterday. It is highly probable that this Cavalry will take position to try to prevent operations by us on the Weldon road. You can give Sheridan such directions as you deem best under the circumstances

U S GRANT
L Gen

Telegram received, DNA, RG 94, War Records Office, Army of the Potomac; copies, *ibid.*, RG 108, Letters Sent; DLC-USG, V, 45, 59, 67; (2) Meade Papers, PHi. *O.R.*, I, xl, part 2, 462. On June 27, 1864, 7:00 A.M. (sent at 8:35 A.M.), Maj. Gen. George G. Meade telegraphed to USG. "Nothing important occurred yesterday on the the the lines of this Army—A working party of the 9th Corps were annoyed during the night by frequent discharges of artillery & infantry—No casualties reported. Col Burton who was employed in ~~charg~~ placing mortar & siege batteries for Genl. Burnside has been transferred to the 18th corps to the great inconvenience of Genl. Burnside ~~& the m~~ & his operations.—. A heavy column of Cavalry was seen this morning moving along the Weldon R. Rd.— undoubtedly with a view to meet Sheridan's force or perhaps to attempt to annoy our rear.—To secure the rear of this army & prevent annoyances from Cavalry raids—the enemy's cavalry must either be occupied, or a force must be stationed on our left & rear.—" ALS (telegram sent), DNA, RG 94, War Records Office, Army of the Potomac; copies, *ibid.*, RG 393, Army of the Potomac, Letters Sent; (2) Meade Papers, PHi. *O.R.*, I, xl, part 2, 462. At 10:00 A.M., Meade telegraphed to USG. "Despatch of 9.30. a m received.—I have already notified you, the enemyes cavalry have been seen passing to our left & rear by the Weldon R. Rd.—I have no doubt their object is to interpose between Wilson & Sheridan to attack either as opportunity offers & in the mean time to make a dash into our rear if practicable   Orders were yesterday sent to Sheridan after crossing the river to move up the Jerusalem plank road & take post on the left of the Army— These orders will be renewed today & he will be notified of the existing condition of affairs & the position of this army—The following disposition of troops have been made to meet any Cavalry attack until the arrival of Sheridan—The 6th corps will hold the Jerusalem plank road. Genl. Gibbons Division will be sent to the Norfolk Pike to its crossing of the Black water—Genl. Ferrero will be sent to Prince Georges C. H, and Col. Gould in command of dismounted cavalry is at Old C. H. Each of these commanders will be directed to watch the roads between their relative positions & co-operate with each other.—The withdrawal of two divisions will render it necessary to hasten Sheridans movements." ALS (telegram sent—misdated June 25), DNA, RG 94, War Records Office, Army of the Potomac; telegram received (dated June 27), *ibid.*, RG 108, Letters Received. *O.R.*, I, xl, part 2, 462–63.

To Maj. Gen. George G. Meade

By Telegraph from City Point
Dated June 27 1864.

To MAJ GEN MEADE

Have you had any information through rebel sources of the whereabouts of Wilson since he reached Burkesville—I will send you by a staff officer this evening or in the morning what I propose to do as soon as the troops are in condition for more active service—To what extent did the Cavalry succeed in destroying the Weldon road the other day   if Wilson finds his return cut off he will be apt to go out by Newbern or if it is found that Hamptons Cavalry has gone south Sheridan will have to be put on his track

U S GRANT
Lt Gen

Telegram received (at 6:00 P.M.), DNA, RG 94, War Records Office, Army of the Potomac; copies, *ibid.*, RG 108, Letters Sent; DLC-USG, V, 45, 59, 67; (2) Meade Papers, PHi. Printed as sent at 6:00 P.M. in *O.R.*, I, xl, part 2, 463. On June 28, 1864, 8:00 A.M., Maj. Gen. George G. Meade telegraphed to USG. "Your despatch of yesterday P. M owing to the interruption of telegraphic communication was not recieved by me till late last night. I have heard nothing from Genl. Wilson or of him since his departure—except the reports of contrabands that the roads out of Petersburgh had been cut. Unusual quiet prevailed along the lines yesterday—No indications of the movement of the enemys cavalry to our left or rear could be ascertained ~~yesterday~~—Reconnoitring parties both of cavalry & infantry reached the vicinity of the Weldon road, driving in the enemys pickets to the road—No indications of any repairs to the road, but it was ascertained from negros & others, that wagon trains were passing between Petersburgh & a point beyond Reams station where Wilson cut the Rail Road.—The order directing Brig Genl. Hunt, to superintend the siege operations of the 18th Corps & requiring Col Abbott in charge of siege train to report to Genl. Hunt, has been received—and a copy furnished Genl. Hunt.—Maj. Genl. Hancock has reported for duty and assumed command of the 2d. Corps." ALS (telegram sent), DNA, RG 94, War Records Office, Army of the Potomac; telegram received, *ibid.*, RG 108, Letters Received. *O.R.*, I, xl, part 2, 477.

On June 27, Lt. Col. Theodore S. Bowers issued Special Orders No. 42, a copy of which was telegraphed to Meade. "Special order No 242—In all siege operations about Petersburg south of the Appomatox Brig. Gen. H. J. Hunt Chf. of Arty. of the Army of the Potomac will have general charge & will be obeyed & respected accordingly—Col H. J. Abbott in charge of siege train will report to Gen Hunt for orders" Telegram received (at 8:30 P.M.), DNA, RG 94, War Records Office, Army of the Potomac; copies (2), Meade Papers, PHi; DLC-Henry J. Hunt. Designated Special Orders No. 43 in *O.R.*, I, xl, part 2, 464. On June 28, Asst. Secretary of War Charles A. Dana telegraphed to USG. "If you could put Lt Col Porter in charge of the ordnance business of the combined armies it would greatly facilitate the ~~operations~~ working of the department here and would also, as I think, be of great advantage to the military operations. At present there is ~~much~~ some confusion and inefficiency in that branch of the service in the different armies operating against Richmond. I am expecting to start for Head Quarters every day, but am detained by accumulated business." ALS (telegram sent), DNA, RG 107, Telegrams Collected (Bound); telegram received, *ibid.*, Telegrams Collected (Unbound). Dana arrived at City Point on July 1. *O.R.*, I, xl, part 1, 28.

To Maj. Gen. Henry W. Halleck

City Point 10 a m
June 28th 1864

MAJ GEN H W HALLECK
CHF OF STAFF

Please telegraph Sherman that he can move his army independent of the desire which he has expressed of detaining all of Johnstons force where it is.

I think Lee now would only be weakened by reenforcements. He has force enough to act defensively behind his entrenchments and any addition would only consume supplies which he must find it difficult to transport. Every road leading from Richmond is now destroyed and the Danville road so badly I hope, as to take a long time for its repair.

The Weldon road we can keep destroying. Is Foster doing anything? I see from the Petersburg papers that Sam Jones[1] has called upon the citizens far and near to rally to Augusta Ga to protect that place from a formidable raid which he now knows threatens it. I do not know the geography of the S. C. coast but it seems to me that Foster has a force to do the enemy great injury in the present hollow condition of the interior of the South.

Has A J Smith started yet after Forrest? I am afraid Sherman will have difficulty with his communications if Forrest is not kept busy.

U S GRANT
Lt Genl

Telegram received (at 12:15 P.M.), DNA, RG 107, Telegrams Collected (Bound); copies, *ibid.*, RG 108, Letters Sent; DLC-USG, V, 45, 59, 67. *O.R.*, I, xl, part 2, 475. Also on June 28, 1864, USG telegraphed to Maj. Gen. Henry W. Halleck. "Has any order been made ordering Genl L. C Hunt to report to Genl Dix and Genl DeTrobrian to the field? Genl. H M Judah who has been so often off duty since the beginning of the war now applies for orders. I think he should be ordered before the retiring board" Telegram received (at 1:00 P.M.), DNA, RG 107, Telegrams Collected (Bound); (undated) *ibid.*, Telegrams Collected (Unbound); copies, *ibid.*, RG 108, Letters Sent; DLC-USG, V, 45, 59, 67. *O.R.*, I, xl, part 2, 476. At 3:00 P.M., Halleck telegraphed to USG. "Orders respecting Genls Hunt & De Tobriand were issued on the 24th. I have heard nothing of Smith A. J. since he landed, and presume that he is in the interior. Genl Foster was at last accounts intending to make an expedition, but the navy was not ready to cooperate. Perhaps he has started by this time, but there can be no foundation for the panic at Augusta." ALS (telegram sent), DNA, RG 107, Telegrams Collected (Bound); telegram received, *ibid.*; *ibid.*, Telegrams Collected (Unbound). *O.R.*, I, xl, part 2, 476.

On June 29, USG telegraphed to Halleck. "Please detail first Lieut C S. Tripler 96th N Y Vols as Aide de Camp to Brig Gen L C Hunt" Telegram received (at 11:00 A.M.), DNA, RG 107, Telegrams Collected (Bound); (undated) *ibid.*, Telegrams Collected (Unbound).

1. Samuel Jones of Va., USMA 1841, resigned as of Aug. 27, 1861, and rose to C.S.A. maj. gen. On April 20, 1864, he assumed command of the Dept. of S. C., Ga., and Fla. For rumors of an attack on Augusta, Ga., see *O.R.*, I, xxxv, part 2, 524–27.

To Maj. Gen. Henry W. Halleck

———

Head Qrs U. S. Armies 7.30 P. M
Via City Point
June 28th 1864.

MAJ GEN H. W. HALLECK
CHIEF OF STAFF.

The latest southern papers (Petersburg 27th) give favorable news from Wilson. At latest accounts he seemed to have destroyed three locomotives and a corresponding number of cars. One train loaded with cotton and furniture, the others with provisions &c. Having mailed the papers to you I give no further particulars. All is quiet here now and men resting, but it will not be long before I have news for you.

I wish you would put Gen Hunter in a good place to rest and as soon as possible start him for Charlottesville to destroy the Rail Road there effectually. If he could get on the canal also it would be a great help

U. S. GRANT
Lt Genl

Telegram received (at 9:40 P.M.), DNA, RG 107, Telegrams Collected (Bound); copies, *ibid.*, RG 108, Letters Sent; DLC-USG, V, 45, 59, 67. *O.R.*, I, xxxvii, part 1, 683; *ibid.*, I, xl, part 2, 476.

On June 28, 1864, Maj. Gen. David Hunter reported to Brig. Gen. Lorenzo Thomas, sending a copy to USG, that his expedition had been successful but he had thought it best to withdraw in the face of C.S.A. reinforcements. ALS (telegram sent), DNA, RG 107, Telegrams Collected (Unbound); copy, DLC-Robert T. Lincoln. *O.R.*, I, xxxvii, part 1, 683–84. See *Memoirs*, II, 304.

To Maj. Gen. George G. Meade

By Telegraph from City Point
Dated June 28 *1864.*

To GEN MEADE

I have seen a Petersburg paper of the 27th which says that Wilson was south of Burkesville about ten miles on friday I think it was

He had destroyed 3 trains One loaded with Cotton & furniture the others with stores &c. They seemed to anticipate his reaching their roads south of Danville & cutting Richmond off from the south west for sometime   I will go out in the morning

Will you meet me at Burnsides say at 10 a m

U S GRANT Lt Gen

Telegram received (at 7:10 P.M.), DNA, RG 94, War Records Office, Army of the Potomac; copies, *ibid.*, RG 108, Letters Sent; DLC-USG, V, 45, 59, 67; (2) Meade Papers, PHi. *O.R.*, I, xl, part 2, 478. On June 28, 1864, 8:00 P.M., Maj. Gen. George G. Meade telegraphed to USG. "Telegram received—I will be at Burnsides tomorrow by 10. a m—Nothing new—all quiet—men improving with the rest & change of temperature.—" ALS (telegram sent), DNA, RG 94, War Records Office, Army of the Potomac; copies, *ibid.*, RG 393, Army of the Potomac, Letters Sent; (2) Meade Papers, PHi. *O.R.*, I, xl, part 2, 478. On June 29, 11:30 A.M., Meade telegraphed to USG. "I have been here since 10. a m—Do you propose to come out here—" ALS (telegram sent), DNA, RG 94, War Records Office, Army of the Potomac; telegram received, *ibid.*, RG 107, Telegrams Collected (Unbound). *O.R.*, I, xl, part 2, 492. At the foot of the telegram, Lt. Col. Theodore S. Bowers wrote a reply in the name of Brig. Gen. John A. Rawlins. "Gen. Grant left here at 8 o'clock this morning for Gen. Burnsides' Headquarters to meet you. He should be there shortly." ADf, DNA, RG 107, Telegrams Collected (Unbound).

On June 28, Col. John W. Shaffer, chief of staff for Maj. Gen. Benjamin F. Butler, telegraphed to Rawlins. "Genl Butler desires to to know if the Lieut General will See him to day. And if So what time will Suit him to have Genl Butler go [dow]n" ALS (telegram sent), *ibid.* On the same day, Rawlins telegraphed to Shaffer. "Gen Grant will be at home all day. Gen Butler can see him at any time he desires." LS (telegram sent), *ibid.*; telegram received, *ibid.*, RG 393, Dept. of Va. and N. C., Telegrams Received. Printed as sent at 1:20 P.M. in *O.R.*, I, xl, part 2, 484. Also on June 28, Butler forwarded to USG a message of 1:30 P.M. from Lt. Alfred G. Simons to Capt. Lemuel B. Norton. "A large Cavalry force moving towards Petersburg." Copy, DNA, RG 107, Telegrams Collected (Unbound). *O.R.*, I, xl, part 2, 485.

On June 29, Rawlins telegraphed to Meade a message of the same day from Samuel H. Beckwith, U.S. Military Telegraph. "Three hundred 300 dollar clause repealed by house yesterday probably pass Senate today authorizes President to call troops one two or three years" Telegram received, DNA, RG 94, War Records Office, Army of the Potomac.

To Maj. Gen. George G. Meade

City Point, Va, June 28th *1864*

MAJ. GEN. G. G. MEADE
COMD.G A. P.
GENERAL,

I am now having a reconnoisance made to determine the practicability of forcing in between Petersburg and Richmond either by the North bank of Swift Creek or between Swift Creek and the Appomattox. If this proves practicable I will take for the execution of it the three left Corps of your command, leaving the 18th Corps, the Cavalry and one Corps of the A. P. on the South side to defend what we now hold and to be used as circumstances may require.

If this move is made you will want to use all the roads you can from your position to the crossing of the Appomattox. It will be desirable to make a night march, without attracting the attention of the enemy, and to attack before they can reinforce. The details however can be made after thise adoption of the plan.

If it should not prove practicable to operate with an Army as here indicated it is likely that we will adopt the plan of taking the whole of the A. P. with ten days rations, and move round the enemys right until the Appomattox is reached. and We could then move on Petersburg from above, or cross, as circumstances may prove to be most advantageous, and come down between the two rivers. In either case all that can now be done will be to acquire all the knowledge that can be gained of the routes that will have to be traveled in the execution of either of these plans.

> I am Gen. very respectfully
> your obt. svt.
> U. S. GRANT
> Lt. Gen.

ALS, deCoppet Collection, NjP. *O.R.*, I, xl, part 2, 477–78.

To Maj. Gen. George G. Meade

City Point, Va. June 28th *1864*

MAJ. GEN. G. G. MEADE,
COMD.G A. P.
GEN.

The communication of Gen. Hancock enclosing a newspaper article and asking for an investigation of the conduct of the 2d Corps, and its Commander, in the affair of the 15th inst. with your endorsment, is received. No investigation can now be had without great prejudice to the service, nor do I think an investigation necessary at any time. The reputation of the 2d Corps, and its Commander, is so high both with the public and in the Army that an investigation could not add to it. It cannot be tarnished by newspaper articlers or scriblers. No official dispatch has ever been sent from these Hd Qrs. which, by any construction, could cast blame on the 2d Corps, or its Commander, for the part they have played in this Campaign. ~~The dispatches sent directly to the Sec. of War however are sent by the Asst. Sec. and are not seen or read at Hd Qrs. except as they are seen in the prints of the day.~~

I am very much mistaken if you were not informed of the contemplated movement against Petersburg as soon as I returned to Wilcox Landing, from Bermuda Hundred, and that the object of getting the 2d Corps up without waiting for the supply train to come up to issue rations to them, was that they might be on hand if required. I arranged to have rations sent down from Bermuda Hundred to issue as the troops crossed. Finding they did not arrive I then directed that the Corps should march without them and arranged that the rations should be sent in wagons from Bermuda Hundred to meet them on the road.

This is not said in any spirit of fault finding for any delay, for there was no fault to be found in what was done either by the 2d Corps, its Commander or the Commander of the A. P. The only delay that I know of was an hour or two arising from the report that the provisions which had been ordered down by water had arrived and details from the different Divisions that had already crossed had come to the river to draw them. This was after the order had been given to march without them but I believe before the troops had received the order. ~~It had no practical bearing because the 2d Corps could not have reached Petersburg before dark and as it was not reached its destination during the night.—This is in answer to what may not have been intended, but is, a answer in the latter part of your endorsement to the last paragraph of your endorsement which implies censure for not negligence on my part in not fully advising you.~~

ADf, IHi. *O.R.*, I, xl, part 1, 315. On June 26, 1864, Maj. Gen. Winfield S. Hancock wrote to Brig. Gen. Seth Williams protesting newspaper accounts which blamed his corps for the failure to take Petersburg on June 15. Copy, DNA, RG 393, 2nd Army Corps, Letters Sent. *O.R.*, I, xl, part 1, 313–14. On June 27, Maj. Gen. George G. Meade endorsed this letter to USG. "Respectfully forwarded for the action of the lieutenant-general commanding, inasmuch as the occurrences to which Major-General Hancock refers took place on the evening of the 15th and morning of the 16th before my arrival on the field and assumption of the command of the Eighteenth Corps agreeably to the instructions of the lieutenant-general commanding. Had Major-General Hancock and myself been apprised in time of the contemplated movement against Petersburg, and the necessity of his co-operation, I am of the opinion he could have been pushed much earlier to the scene of operations, but as matters occurred and with our knowledge of them I do not see how any censure can be attached to General Hancock and his corps." *Ibid.*, p. 315.

To Maj. Gen. George G. Meade

By Telegraph from City Point
Dated June 30th [*29*] *1864.*

To MAJ GEN MEADE

The showing is against us by Kautz's despatch but with Wright at Ream's station Wilson south of the enemy & Sheridan marching in that direction you have done all possible and it will be queer if the count does not turn in our favor—I am very much in hopes that the enemy will be struck in the rear most disagreeably to him and that his road in the meantime will be destroyed effectually as far as our troops occupy the line of it—I see nothing you can do beyond what you ~~what~~ have done—~~The~~ If the enemy should follow Wright & Sheridan with infantry of course we will follow him with infantry —All that I see beyond what you have already done is to follow up the same principle you have started upon—Follow up ~~&~~ a force of the enemy with a larger one

U S GRANT
Lt Gen

Telegram received (at 12:30 A.M.), DNA, RG 393, Army of the Potomac, Cav. Corps, Letters Received; copies (2), Meade Papers, PHi; (dated June 29, 1864) DNA, RG 108, Letters Sent; DLC-USG, V, 45, 59, 67. Dated June 30, 12:30 A.M., in *O.R.*, I, xl, part 2, 516. On June 29, 10:30 P.M., Maj. Gen. George G. Meade telegraphed to USG. "A despatch of 7.30 P. M from Genl. Wright reports his arrival at Reams station without meeting the enemy or hearing of Genl. Wilson—except from citizens who say he was fighting the enemys cavalry successfully till about 4. P. M when they were reinforced by infantry & Wilson forced back.—Since Wrights despatch was received the accompanying despatch has been received from Kautz—it shows a very unfortunate state of affairs and makes me anxious for Wilson.—Kautz has been directed to communicate with

Wright & endeavor to ascertain the whereabouts of Wilson—Wright is ordered
to remain at Reams & in conjunction with Sheridan, whom I hope will join
Wright tonight and Kautz endeavor to ascertain Wilsons position & extricate
him from his difficult position.—When Wilson is secure I shall withdraw Wright
& the cavalry & get the latter into condition for further operations" ALS (telegram sent), DNA, RG 94, War Records Office, Army of the Potomac; telegram
received, *ibid.*, RG 108, Letters Received. *O.R.*, I, xl, part 2, 492. The enclosure
is *ibid.*, p. 512.

On June 30, 9:00 A.M., Meade telegraphed to USG. "I send you the statement of a prisoner taken last night which is somewhat confirmed by Genl. Kautz
—I fear that Wilson is in a very precarious condition & that his command is
pretty much scattered.—Wright is still at Reams a despatch from him of 7.30
A. M—says he can hear nothing of Wilson or the enemy—He is pushing out his
parties in all directions & in the mean time is destroying the road in the vicinity
of his command—Nothing has been heard of Sheridan—He received his orders at
4. P M yesterday & was moving at 5. P M when my staff officer left him. He
ought to have been at Reams by day light, but had not reached there at 7.30—
The instructions to Wright & himself are the same as reported last night viz to
endeavor to extricate Wilson & to fall on the enemy, if he can be found—I do not
care to move Wright any farther than he is now till Sheridan arrives & ascertains
something definite.—I fear there is no doubt Wilson has lost all his artillery &
trains & that his command is greatly broken & dispersed." ALS (telegram sent),
DNA, RG 94, War Records Office, Army of the Potomac; telegram received,
ibid., RG 108, Letters Received. *O.R.*, I, xl, part 2, 516–17. The enclosure is
ibid., p. 517. At 9:20 A.M., Meade telegraphed to USG. "Genl. Kautz has sent
his command back to Bermuda Hundreds to refit & get supplies. I beg to suggest, orders be sent to Genl. Butler requiring Genl. Kautz to return at the earliest practicable moment, to report to Genl. Sheridan—The enemy have the whole
of their cavalry south of the Appomatox & with the loss of Wilson & his own
losses Sheridan will be weak—& will require all the cavalry we can get together,
else I fear we shall have trouble with the enemys cavalry in our rear.—" ALS
(telegram sent), DNA, RG 94, War Records Office, Army of the Potomac; copies,
ibid., RG 393, Army of the Potomac, Letters Sent; (2) Meade Papers, PHi.
O.R., I, xl, part 2, 518.

At 10:20 A.M., USG telegraphed to Maj. Gen. Benjamin F. Butler. "Please
send Kautz back to our left to report to Sheridan, as soon as possible. It will take
all our [cavalr]ly to extricate Wilson from his present perilous position" Telegram received, DNA, RG 393, Dept. of Va. and N. C., Telegrams Received.
O.R., I, xl, part 2, 531. At 10:45 A.M., Butler telegraphed to USG. "Gen Kautz
has not yet reported to me I suppose him to be with Wilson If Kautz does
report to me I will send him at once I have not heard from him since he left."
ALS (telegram sent), DNA, RG 107, Telegrams Collected (Unbound); copy,
ibid., RG 393, Dept. of Va. and N. C., Telegrams Sent (Press). *O.R.*, I, xl,
part 2, 531. On the same day, 11:00 A.M., Butler telegraphed to USG. "Since my
last dispatch I have heard of Gen Kautz by report that he is coming to Bermuda
I have sent an order by telegraph to Smith to send Kautz back if he is near him.
Also an order by Maj Ludlow my inspector of Cavalry ~~te~~ to Kautz to report at
once to Sheridan" ALS (telegram sent), DNA, RG 107, Telegrams Collected
(Unbound); copy, *ibid.*, RG 393, Dept. of Va. and N. C., Telegrams Sent. *O.R.*,
I, xl, part 2, 531.

Also on June 30, USG sent Brig. Gen. August V. Kautz a telegram received at 11:00 A.M. "You will report to Gen Meade who will give you such orders as he may deem best" Telegram received, DNA, RG 94, War Records Office, Dept. of Va. and N. C., Army of the James, Unentered Papers; *ibid.*, RG 107, Telegrams Collected (Unbound). *O.R.*, I, xl, part 2, 540. On the same day, noon, Kautz telegraphed to USG. "I have just received an order to return and assist Genl. Sheridan in extricating Genl. Wilson. I have just come from Genl. Mead's Hd. Qrs, and explained the whole position to him, & he is satisfied that all has been done that can be done. My command is in no condition to do anything. The main cause of our route was the worn out condition of the men, men and horses have had nothing to eat for forty eight hours, and they are exhausted from loss of sleep. If Wilson cannot extricate himself we can do nothing more for him. I advised Genl. Mead to send a force down the Plank road as far as towards Jerusalem, for when I was cut off from him it was his intention to go that back and cross the railroad in the vicinity of Jarrats Station and the Notoway at Allens, Peters or Jerusalem Bridges. I hope the order will be recinded, my command has reached Spring Hill & has been halted there" ALS (telegram sent), DNA, RG 107, Telegrams Collected (Unbound); telegram received, *ibid.*, RG 108, Letters Received. *O.R.*, I, xl, part 2, 540.

At noon, USG telegraphed to Meade. "Orders have been sent to Kautz to remain with Sheridan or to report to him if he has left" Telegram received, DNA, RG 94, War Records Office, Army of the Potomac; *ibid.*, Dept. of the Cumberland. *O.R.*, I, xl, part 2, 518. On the same day, USG sent Meade a telegram received at 1:20 P.M. "The following has been sent to Brig Gen Kautz You will give him such orders as you may be deemed necessary taking into consideration the condition of his Command" Telegram received, DNA, RG 94, War Records Office, Army of the Potomac; *ibid.*, Dept. of the Cumberland; copies (2), Meade Papers, PHi. *O.R.*, I, xl, part 2, 518.

At 10:00 P.M., Meade telegraphed to USG. "Nothing additional has been heard of or from Wilson—Sheridan did not reach Reams station till late this afternoon—On consultation with Genl. Wright, they concluded nothing could be done to aid Wilson & Wright started to return. So soon as this was reported, I sent orders & halted Wright on the Plank road some 5 miles from the left of the army & sent instructions to Sheridan to move at early daylight tomorrow in the direction Wilson was supposed to have taken & endeavor to obtain some information of about him or the enemy—and to call on Wright for support who would remain in his present position till he Sheridan returned—From all the information that has been gathered from citizens & contrabands, there is every reason to believe the enemys infantry returned last night to Petersburgh leaving the pursuit of Wilson to the cavalry." ALS (telegram sent), DNA, RG 94, War Records Office, Army of the Potomac; telegram received, *ibid.*, RG 108, Letters Received. *O.R.*, I, xl, part 2, 518.

On July 1, 9:00 A.M., Meade telegraphed to USG. "Nothing reliable from or of Wilson There is a report from some of the escaped men that he was obliged to surrender, but I can not trace it to any reliable source.—I forward you a despatch received this a. m from Maj. Genl. Sheridan with my reply thereto.— I can not understand how Genl. Sheridan at Windmill Pt. could be Forty eight hours without forage & have directed an investigation to ascertain upon whom the responsibility rests. As to the fatigue of his animals I presume the enemy can not be in much better condition & Hampton must have made a forced march from the White House via Richmond. The heavy firing between midnight & day break this morning was Burnside trying to silence a battery of the enemy, who were shelling the 10th corps on his right—All the rest of the lines quiet." ALS (telegram sent), DNA, RG 393, Army of the Potomac, Miscellaneous Letters Received; telegram received, *ibid.*, RG 108, Letters Received. *O.R.*, I, xl, part 2, 560. The enclosures are *ibid.*, pp. 573–74.

To Julia Dent Grant

City Point July *1864*.

DEAR JULIA,

Your letter of the 26th & 27th of last month has just reached me. It is the first line from you for about ten days. I have not written to you for a long time because I expected you would start on as soon as you received my letter. I think on reflection it will be better for you to remain where you are. You would be lonesom shut up in Fortress Monroe and there is no place here where you could stay for a single night. I hope too this siege will not last a great while longer and then I will go where you are.—Why not make the same arrangement for the childrens schooling you did before? They could not be at a better place than with Louisa Boggs. You could then see them when you wished except whilst it might be convenient for you to be with me. Of course you cannot be where I am and have the children with you so long as the War lasts.—The lock of hair was sent for you.

If Lewis wants the place back[1] you can let him have it for what I paid adding if you choose whatever you may have paid out in repairs. I care nothing about this however. Lewis is a generous man and I would not for the world be otherwise than generous towards him.

I received your letter with one from Mrs. Barrett enclosed. I immediately asked the Sec. of War to order the Drs. release and received a prompt reply that the order was given.[2] If he is not released Gen. Rosecrans has not complied with orders. I remain very well and full of hope and confidance.—I will now write to you twice each week, not long letters but long enough to let you know that I think of you. I will be too glad when all is settled and I can have a settled and quiet home. How have Buck and Missy progressed with their German? I think you had better put rascal Jess to board in a German family until he learns to speak the language. What does he say to the arrangement?—I am sorry you have allowed Jess' pony to get lost. You had better offer a reward of $20 00 for him. I think your fathers an unsafe place to keep any thing however.—I am glad Mrs. White charges you with being the cause of her husbands arrest. It serves you right after your interceeding for the release of such an old rascall.[3]—My love to Aunt Fanny, your father, Emma, Anna and the balance. Kisses for yourself and the children. The Staff are all well except Rawlins and he is as well as he ever will be. We have not had a rain here for more than a month and with our enormous wagon train the roads have become so worn into dust that it is suffocating to move about. The weather too has been intolerably warm.

ULYS.

A very fine Sewing Machine was voted to you at the Philadelphia Fair. They have asked me where it should be sent. I directed it to be sent to Mr. Ford. You probably will get it a few days after you receive this.

ALS, DLC-USG. Although the letter is not dated precisely, the discussion of the visit to Fort Monroe appears to place it between USG's letters of June 22 and July 7, 1864, probably closer to the latter.

1. USG retained ownership of Wish-ton-wish, the house built by his brother-in-law Lewis Dent. *The Courier-Journal* (Louisville), Feb. 24, 1873.
2. See telegram to Edwin M. Stanton, June 25, 1864.
3. On June 10, Julia Dent Grant wrote to Maj. Gen. William S. Rosecrans asking the release of Joseph W. White, "a servant of mine . . ." and his sons. ALS, Rosecrans Papers, CLU.

To Maj. Gen. Henry W. Halleck

———

Grant's Hd Qrs July 1 1864

MAJ. GENL HALLECK
CHIEF OF STAFF

The Enemys Cavalry finding that Sheridan was secure where he was Crossing the James River left him and interposed themselves on the Weldon Road between Wilson and his return. Kautz with his & a portion of Wilsons succeeded in passing the Enemy and getting in but with the loss of his artillery and wagons   Wilson with most of his Command was Cut off and is supposed to have gone back South. Immediately on receipt of news that Wilson was returning Meade sent Wrights Corps to Reams Station to aid him. Sherid[an] was also ordered to join him. Wright and Sheridan are both now out and the latter with orders to push on until he learns reliably from Wilson. Our artillery is now so located that it plays Easily on the Bridges in Petersburg. They were hit a number of times yesterday by Smiths guns   A Small Steamer lying at the Petersburg Wharf was also hit and burned

U. S GRANT
Lt. Genl.

Telegram received (at 4:00 P.M.), DNA, RG 107, Telegrams Collected (Bound); copies, *ibid.*, RG 108, Letters Sent; DLC-USG, V, 45, 59, 67. *O.R.*, I, xl, part 1, 15; *ibid.*, I, xl, part 2, 557–58.

To Maj. Gen. Henry W. Halleck

———

Head Qrs Army U. S.
City Point
July 1st 1864 5 P. M.

MAJ GEN H. W. HALLECK
CHIEF OF STAFF.

Senators Lane and Wilson and Congressman Wilder apply to have Gen'l Blunt ordered to report to Gen Canby. Please say to them if Gen'l Canby applies for Gen'l Blunt he can have him, I cannot however order an officer with rank above all subordinates in Gen'l Canbys Military Division without first knowing his pleasure in the matter

U. S. GRANT
Lt Genl

Telegram received (on July 2, 1864, 11:30 A.M.), DNA, RG 107, Telegrams Collected (Bound); copies, *ibid.*, RG 108, Letters Sent; DLC-USG, V, 45, 59, 67. *O.R.*, I, xli, part 2, 3. On July 1, U.S. Senator James H. Lane of Kan., U.S. Representative Abel C. Wilder of Kan., and U.S. Senator Henry Wilson of Mass. telegraphed to USG. "We earnistly ~~request~~ recommend & requist an order for Maj Genl Blunt to report for duty to Maj Genl Canby—" Telegram received, DNA, RG 107, Telegrams Collected (Bound); *ibid.*, RG 108, Letters Received.

Also on July 1, 10:00 A.M., USG telegraphed to Maj. Gen. Henry W. Halleck. "I understand many of the hundred days men express a willingness to reenlist for the long term. I think it advisable that an order should be published authorizing such of them as wish to ~~r~~eenlist in the old regiments giving them the benefit of the bounties offered and Crediting the State to which they belong with the number so reenlisting" Telegram received (at 9:00 P.M.), *ibid.*, RG 107, Telegrams Collected (Bound); copies, *ibid.*, RG 108, Letters Sent; DLC-USG, V, 45, 59, 67. *O.R.*, III, iv, 466–67.

To Maj. Gen. Henry W. Halleck

———

Hd Qrs Armies
City Point 11 30 p m
July 1st 1864

MAJ GEN H W HALLECK
CHF OF STAFF

You need not send any artillery beyond the three Batteries already started[1]

Ewells Corps has returned here but I have no evidence of Breckenridge having returned

Hunter ought to get back on the Baltimore & Ohio Railroad as soon as possible[2]—Operating from there he will have the enemy in front of him

U S GRANT
Lt Genl

Telegram received (on July 2, 1864, 9:00 A.M.), DNA, RG 107, Telegrams Collected (Bound); copies, *ibid.*, RG 108, Letters Sent; DLC-USG, V, 45, 59, 67. *O.R.*, I, xxxvii, part 2, 3; *ibid.*, I, xl, part 2, 558. On July 1, 1:30 P.M., Maj. Gen. Henry W. Halleck telegraphed to USG. "On the 28th I telegraphed to Genl Hunter granting his request to visit Washington, and directing him in the mean time to telegraph to you about his operations. Since then I have heard nothing of him, the line west of Harper's Ferry having been broken by rebil raids. I telegraphed him to day that you wished to consult with him at your Head Qrs. As you are aware, all batteries here were dismounted & put in the forts to replace in part the heavy regiments, and their horses sent to the front. I have remounted three & sent them forward & will remount five more, by taking horses from Qr Mr's teams. This leaves very little in the forts except militia who are not sufficiently instructed to work the guns. There are conflicting reports about the rebel forces in the Shenandoah valley. Some say that Beckenridge & Pickett are following the cavalry which has just made a raid on the B & O Rail Road, while others say they are not in the valley at all. It certainly would be good policy for them, while Hunter's army is on the Kanawha, to destroy the B & O Rail Road & make a raid in Maryland & Penn. Sigel has very little besides militia at Harper's Ferry and on the Rail Road, and by sending away the artillery we shall have nothing left here with which to reinforce him." ALS (telegram sent), DNA, RG 107, Telegrams Collected (Bound); telegram received, *ibid.*; (at 10:00 P.M.) *ibid.*, RG 108, Letters Received. *O.R.*, I, xxxvii, part 2, 4; *ibid.*, I, xl, part 2, 558.

1. On June 28, USG wrote to Maj. Gen. Ambrose E. Burnside. "Did you want any artillery, except Benjamin's battery, ordered you from Washington?" *Ibid.*, p. 482. On the same day, Burnside wrote to USG. "In addition to Benjamin's battery I should like Gittings' battery, of the Third Artillery, and Allen's and Buckley's (Rhode Island) batteries, unless by so doing it would bring up too much field artillery. These have all been sent to Washington. If we are to continue our operations here guns of heavier caliber will also be required, but these have been promised by General Hunt." *Ibid.* Also on June 28, USG telegraphed to Halleck. "Please order here Benjamins Battery and also Gettings of the 3rd Artillery if it can be spared" Telegram received (at 2:10 P.M.), DNA, RG 107, Telegrams Collected (Bound); copies, *ibid.*, RG 94, Letters Received, 618A 1864; *ibid.*, RG 108, Letters Sent; DLC-USG, V, 45, 59, 67. On June 29, USG telegraphed to Halleck. "I have just been examening our front around Petersburg in person and find that more field artillery can be used advantageous[ly.] Please send Tafts Batter[y] 20 pdr Parrotts and four or Six other Batteries if they can be spared. This is in addition to the two Batteries heretofore ordered" Telegram received (at 6:30 P.M.), DNA, RG 107, Telegrams Collected (Bound). *O.R.*, I, xl, part 2, 491.

2. On June 29, 10:30 A.M., Halleck telegraphed to USG. "Genl Hunter has applied for and obtained leave to come to Washington for consultation in respect to future operations. I have directed him to telegraph in the meantime directly to you such information as he may have. I only know that he has reached his supplies on Loup creek near Gauley." ALS (telegram sent), DNA, RG 107, Telegrams Collected (Bound); telegram received, *ibid.*; *ibid.*, Telegrams Collected (Unbound). *O.R.*, I, xxxvii, part 1, 688. At 9:00 P.M., USG telegraphed to Halleck. "Please send Gen Hunter here immediately on his arrival in Wash-

ington—Probably on consultation I can better direct future movements for him after such consultation—" Telegram received, DNA, RG 107, Telegrams Collected (Bound); copy, DLC-USG, V, 67. *O.R.,* I, xxxvii, part 1, 689.

To Maj. Gen. Henry W. Halleck

City Point, Va. July 1st *1864.*

MAJ. GEN H. W. HALLECK,
CHIEF OF STAFF OF THE ARM[Y]
GENERAL,

Mr. Dana Asst. Sec. of War, has just returned. He inform[s] me that he called attention to the necessity of sending Gen. Butler to another field of duty. Whilst I have no diff[i]culty with Gen. Butler, finding him always cle[ar] in his conception of orders, and prompt to obey, yet there is a want of knowledge how to execute, and particularly a prejudice against him, as a commander, that operates against his usefulness. I have feared that it might become necessary to separate him and Gen. Smith. The latter is really one of the most efficient officers in service, readiest in expedients an[d] most skilful in the management of troops in action. I would dislike removing him from his present command unless it was to increas[e] it, but as I say, may have it to do yet if Gen. Butler remains.

As an administrative officer Gen. Butler has no superior. In taking charge of a Dept.mt where there are no great battles to be fought, but a dissatisfied element to controll no one could manage it better than he. If a command could be cut out such as Mr Dana proposed, namely Ky. Ill. & Ia. or if the Depts. of the Mo. Kansas and the states of Ill. & Ia. could be merged together and Gen. Butler put over it I believe the good of the service would be subserved.

I regret the necessity of asking for a change in commander here, but Gen. Butler not being a soldier by education or experience, is in the hands of his subordinates in the execution of all operations Military. I would feel strengthened with Smith, Franklin or J. J. Reynolds commanding the right wing of this Army. At the same time, as I have here stated, Gen. Butler has always been prompt in his obedience to orders, with me, and clear in his understanding of them. I would not therefore be willing to recommend his retirement.

I send this by Mail for consideration but will telegraph if I think it absolutely necessary to make a change.

> I am General, very respectf.
> your obt. svt.
> U. S. GRANT
> Lt. Gen

ALS, Schoff Collection, MiU-C. *O.R.*, I, xl, part 2, 558–59. On July 3, 1864, Maj. Gen. Henry W. Halleck wrote to USG. "Private. . . . Your note of the 1st. inst in relation to Genl. Butler is just received. I will, as you propose, await further advices from you before I submit the matter officially to the Secty of War and the President. It was foreseen from the first that you would eventually find it necessary to relieve Genl. B. on account of his total unfitness to command in the field, and his generally quarrelsome character. *What shall be done with him*, has therefore already been, as I am informed; a matter of consultation. To send him to Kentucky would probably cause an insurrection in that state, and an immediate call for large reenforcements. Moreover, he would probably greatly embarras Sherman, or if he did not attempt to supersede him, by using against him all his talent at political intrigue and his facilities for newspaper abuse. If you send him to Missouri, nearly the same thing will occur there. Although it might not be objectionable to have a free fight between him and Rosecrans, the Government would be seriously embarrassed by the local difficulties, and calls for reinforcements likely to follow. Inveterate as is Rosecran's habit of continually calling for more troops, Butler differs only in demanding instead of *calling*. As things now stand in the west, I think we can keep the peace; but if Butler be thrown in as a disturbing element, I anticipate very serious results. Why not leave Genl Butler in the local command of his Dept, including N. C. Norfolk, Fort Monroe, Yorktown, &c, and make a new army corps of the part of the 18th under Smith? This would leave B. under your immediate control, and at the same time would relieve you of his presence in the field. Moreover, it would save the necessity of organizing a new Dept. If he must be relieved entirely, I think it would be best to make a new Dept. for him in New England. I make these remarks merely as suggestions. Whatever you may finally determine on, I will try to have done. As Genl. B. claims to rank me, I shall give him no orders wherever he may go, without the special direction of yourself or the Secty of War." Copy, DNA, RG 108, Letters Sent. *O.R.*, I, xl, part 2, 598.

To Maj. Gen. George G. Meade

City Point, July 2d 1st/64

MAJ. GEN. MEADE,

Will it not be well to send orders for Sheridan to return now that Wilson is heard from? I regret the disater but the work done by Wilson and his Cavalry is of great importance. I understand from Kautz discreption that it will take the enemy several weeks to repair the damages done the Southside and Danville roads.

U. S. GRANT
Lt. Gen.

ALS (telegram sent), CSmH; telegram received (on July 1, 1864, 5:45 P.M.), DNA, RG 94, War Records Office, Army of the Potomac. *O.R.*, I, xl, part 2, 560. At 5:00 P.M., Maj. Gen. George G. Meade had telegraphed to USG. "One of Col Sharpes scouts is just in, who left Wilsons command this morning at 7: oclock on the road from Suffolk to Prince Georges C H—Wilson having yesterday succeeded in crossing the Blackwater. The scout thinks he has most of his men with him altho he was obliged to abandon all property & many of the men are dismounted. He will be in by night.—" ALS (telegram sent), DNA, RG 393, Army of the Potomac, Miscellaneous Letters Received; telegram received, *ibid.*, RG 108, Letters Received. *O.R.*, I, xl, part 2, 560. At 6:00 P.M., Meade telegraphed to USG. "Sheridans orders require him to return so soon as any definite intelligence of Wilson's command was received—and he has been notified of Wilson's safe return.—" ALS (telegram sent), DNA, RG 393, Army of the Potomac, Miscellaneous Letters Received; copies, *ibid.*, Letters Sent; (2) Meade Papers, PHi. *O.R.*, I, xl, part 2, 561.

At 10:20 A.M., Maj. Gen. Winfield S. Hancock telegraphed to Brig. Gen. Seth Williams. "I send you 3 Mississipp[i] deserters from Hills Corps they say that they understood this morning that Ewells Corps arrived yesterday & that part of it was marching to their right outside of their defences they place the troops in their intrenchments from their left to the right as follows Beauregard Longstreat Hill A. P." Telegram received, DNA, RG 393, Army of the Potomac, Telegrams Received. *O.R.*, I, xl, part 2, 566. At 10:50 A.M., Meade transmitted this telegram to USG. AES, DNA, RG 393, Army of the Potomac, Telegrams Received.

At 10:00 P.M., Meade telegraphed to USG. "Genl. Wilson having returned orders have been given to Genl. Sheridan to withdraw to Prince Georges C. H. and there to re-organise the cavalry and prepare them for further service—He is directed to detach one brigade to picket on the left flank of the army The 6th Corps is directed to resume its former position & Genl. Ferero's division will be sent to take post on the Norfolk or Baxter road where it crosses the Blackwater Swamp.—The enemy have been passing in considerable force to day into Petersburgh on a road just South of the Weldon R. Rd—this is probably the force sent to support the cavalry when Wilson was attacked, with perhaps re-inforcements sent out when Wrights movement was reported.—It seems to be pretty well ascertained, that supplies are brought on the Weldon road to Stony creek depot & wagoned from thence to Petersburgh—if the cavalry was in better condition this might be stopped—The mere occupation of the Weldon R. Rd. will not do it, as by making more of a detour they can reach the part of the road where the trains stop, by using roads nearer the Appomatox;—and then moving across to the Weldon Road.—" ALS (telegram sent), *ibid.*, Miscellaneous Letters Received; telegram received, *ibid.*, RG 108, Letters Received. *O.R.*, I, xl, part 2, 561. On July 2, 10:00 A.M., Meade telegraphed to USG. "Sheridan's cavalry being unserviceable there is no occasion for Genl. Kautz coming here & I have accordingly so advised him at Bermuda Hundred.—" ALS (telegram sent), DNA, RG 393, Army of the Potomac, Miscellaneous Letters Received; copies, *ibid.*, Letters Sent; (2) Meade Papers, PHi. *O.R.*, I, xl, part 2, 582. On July 12, 10:50 A.M., Maj. Gen. Benjamin F. Butler telegraphed to USG. "On Kautz' Expedition Elder's Batty lost all its guns and equipments—The enclosed requisitions are to remount it—My own belief is, that a Batty should never be remounted where it loses its guns without an investigation and I therefore forward the requisitions to the Lieut Gen Comdg for his judgment—This, is probably all right, but we lose guns too easily when there is no penalty attached to the loss except to get new ones—" LS (telegram sent), DNA, RG 393, Dept. of Va. and N. C., Telegrams Sent (Press). *O.R.*, I, xl, part 3, 200.

On July 1, USG telegraphed to Meade. "Where is the heavy firing now going on. Is it an attack made by the enemy" Telegram received (at 10:27 P.M.), DNA, RG 94, War Records Office, Army of the Potomac; copies (2), Meade Papers, PHi. *O.R.*, I, xl, part 2, 562. At 10:30 P.M., Meade telegraphed to USG. "The firing is apparently on Burnsides front—He has made no report—Warren says it is on his right will report as soon as I am advised of what has occurred." ALS (telegram sent), DNA, RG 393, Army of the Potomac, Miscellaneous Letters Received; copies, *ibid.*, Letters Sent; (2) Meade Papers, PHi. *O.R.*, I, xl, part 2, 562.

To Maj. Gen. George G. Meade

City Point July 2d *1864*

MAJ. GEN. MEADE,

I have directed Gen. Butler to have Kent, the Tribune Correspondent, arrested and sent to these Hd Qrs. As soon as he arrives I will send him to your Provost Marshal Gen for such disposition as you deem fit to make of him. If you desire it I will order him away from the Army not to return either before or after sending him to you.

U. S. GRANT
Lt. Gen.

ALS (telegram sent), DNA, RG 107, Telegrams Collected (Unbound); telegram received (at 10:00 A.M.), *ibid.*, RG 94, War Records Office, Army of the Potomac. *O.R.*, I, xl, part 2, 583. On July 1, 1864, 1:00 P.M., Maj. Gen. Winfield S. Hancock wrote to Brig. Gen. Seth Williams. "An article in the New York Tribune of the 27th instant, purporting to have been written at the headquarters of General Butler, has just been shown to me. I inclose it for the examination of the major-general commanding the army. I have marked the paragraphs to which I desire to call his attention, and request that he may take measures to discover the author of the false and injurious statements referred to, and that the author thereof may be punished in such a manner that the fact will be likely to have as great a circulation as the slanders which he has uttered." *Ibid.*, p. 567. On the same day, Maj. Gen. George G. Meade endorsed this letter. "Respectfully forwarded for the action of the lieutenant-general commanding. It is understood the correspondent referred to is named Kent, and is within the control of the major-general commanding the Department of Virginia and North Carolina. I respectfully request he be directed either to order him out of the lines of the army, or to turn him over to the provost-marshal-general of this army. His article is full of malicious falsehoods, and he should be severely punished for it." *Ibid.* In a lengthy account of the assault on Petersburg, correspondent William H. Kent noted: "Gen. Smith, finding that Gen. Hancock would not cooperate in the attempt to take the city early in the morning, was compelled to abandon what subsequent events prove would have been a successful movement, and to act independently as to minor details. . . ." *New York Tribune*, June 27, 1864. On July 2, 10:30 A.M., Meade telegraphed to USG. "The exclusion of Mr. Kent from the armies around Richmond will ~~be~~ in my judgment answer all purposes— I proposed his being turned over to the Prov. Mar. Genl. A. P. in order to bring him before a military commission for trial on the charge of publishing false intelligence for a malicious purpose—but this is probably attaching more importance to the individual than he deserves.—" ALS (telegram sent), DNA, RG 393, Army of the Potomac, Miscellaneous Letters Received; telegram received, *ibid.*, RG 108, Letters Received. *O.R.*, I, xl, part 2, 583.

Also on July 2, USG telegraphed to Maj. Gen. Benjamin F. Butler. "A correspondent named Kent, understood to be with your command, has published in the N. Y. Tribune of the 27th an article false and slanderous upon a portion of the Army now in the field. You will please direct his arrest and have him sent to these Hd Qrs." ALS (telegram sent), DNA, RG 107, Telegrams Collected (Unbound); telegram received (at 11:00 A.M.), DLC-Benjamin F. Butler. *O.R.*, I, xl, part 2, 593. On the same day, Brig. Gen. Godfrey Weitzel, act. chief of staff for Butler, telegraphed to USG. "Dispatch rec'd. It will be done at once. Genl Kautz's Adjutant Genl has just returned with 600 men more of his command." ALS (telegram sent), DNA, RG 94, War Records Office, Dept. of Va. and N. C., Army of the James, Unentered Papers; copy, *ibid.*, RG 393, Dept. of Va. and N. C., Telegrams Sent. On the same day, Weitzel telegraphed to USG. "Mr. Kent has gone North. I will show your dispatch to Genl Butler when he returns." ALS (telegram sent), *ibid.*, RG 107, Telegrams Collected (Unbound); copy, *ibid.*, RG 393, Dept. of Va. and N. C., Telegrams Sent. *O.R.*, I, xl, part 2, 593. On the same day, USG telegraphed to Weitzel. "Please ~~r~~ dirct the Provost Mar. to notify Mr Kent that his pass to ~~vist~~ visit this army is revoked and that he will not be permitted to return" Telegram received, DLC-Benjamin F. Butler. On the same day, USG telegraphed to Meade. "On enquiry Mr. Kent is found to have gone North. I have directed notice to be sent to him that his pass to visit this Army is revoked and that he will not be allowed to return." ALS (telegram sent), DNA, RG 107, Telegrams Collected (Unbound); telegram received (at 11:45 A.M.), *ibid.*, RG 393, Army of the Potomac, Telegrams Received. *O.R.*, I, xl, part 2, 583. For an inaccurate account, see *Butler's Book* (Boston, 1892), pp. 700–1.

On July 1 or 2, USG telegraphed to Meade. "Please direct your Provost Marshal to ascertain if the Correspondent Swinton is within our lines and if so to expell him." ALS (telegram sent), DNA, RG 109, Copies of Miscellaneous Correspondence; telegram received (dated July 1), *ibid.*, RG 94, War Records Office, Army of the Potomac; copies (2), Meade Papers, PHi. Dated July 1 in *O.R.*, I, xl, part 2, 559. Endorsements (dated July 1) are *ibid.*, pp. 559–60. On July 2, 9:00 A.M., Meade telegraphed to USG. "I have nothing new to report this morning—Your order in regard to Mr. Swinton registered correspondent of the N. Y. Times was sent to the Prov. Mar. Genl. who returned for answer that Mr. Swinton was not now with this army, it being understood he was in Washington to which place a notice has been sent him, that his pass is annulled and that he will not be permitted to return.—" ALS (telegram sent), DNA, RG 393, Army of the Potomac, Miscellaneous Letters Received; telegram received, *ibid.*, RG 108, Letters Received. *O.R.*, I, xl, part 2, 582. See J. Cutler Andrews, *The North Reports the Civil War* (Pittsburgh, 1955), pp. 595–96; *O.R.*, I, xl, part 3, 40–41.

On Sept. 27, Kent wrote to President Abraham Lincoln. "In July last, my Pass as Army Correspondent of the N. Y. Tribune was revoked by order of Lt. Gen. Grant, at the request, I believe of Maj. Gen. Meade. I am not conscious of and certainly did not intend to write aught but what was true and proper for publication. Since that time the order relating to Mr. Wm. Swinton of the N. Y. Times who was sent from the Army at the same time has been rescinded by Gen. Meade. In behalf of the Tribune and myself I have respectfully to ask that similar action be taken in my case." ALS, DLC-Robert T. Lincoln. On the same day, Lincoln endorsed this letter. "Respectfully referred to Lieutenant General Grant for his consideration and decision." ES, *ibid.* Lincoln, *Works*, VIII, 26. On Oct. 7, Hancock endorsed this letter. ". . . When I saw the article, which was by mere accident I observed statements therein which were false and exceedingly injurious to myself and the troops I had the honor to command. The Author purported to be from Gen'l Butler's Army and initials only were given. I addressed a letter to Major General Meade asking that measures might be taken to ascertain the name of the correspondent and to have him held responsible for the injury done. It was intended and it was my wish that the matter should be investigated in the a formal manner in order that the correspondent should be made to show his authority if he had any,—but it was found that he had left the Army. Lt Genl Grant then ordered that he be not permitted to return. If the correspondent did not know with what he had been charged he could readily have ascertained it by inquiry, at an earlier date,—then it would not have been too late for him to have repaired the injury he had done. The article was apparently written in the interest of Genl Smith's command of General Butler's Army, against myself and my command. As to the falsity of the paragraph referred to I have the most conclusive evidence.—a letter written voluntarily to me by General Smith, denying the facts alleged, and stating that he had only delayed writing thus long hoping to have Mr. Kent deny the article, but that as he, Mr K., had left the Army he wrote me the letter in question, as the next best means of repairing the injury done. This newspaper Article originate in the advance on Petersburg by General Grant." ES, *ibid*. On the same day, Meade endorsed this letter. "Respectfully returned—the fore going statement of Maj. Genl Hancock accords with my recollection of the case—No permit has been given by me to Mr. Swinton.—" AES, *ibid*. On Oct. 10, USG endorsed this letter. "Respectfully returned to His Ex. The President, and attention invited to the endorsements hereon of Gens. Hancock and Meade. The most liberal facilities are afforded to newspaper correspondents, but they cannot be permitted to misrepresent facts to the injury of the service. When they so offend their pass to accompany the army is with drawn, and they are excluded from its lines. In this case there appears to have been a deliberate attempt to injure one of the best Generals and Corps in the service. I cannot therefore consent to Mr. Kent's return to this army" ES, *ibid*.

To Maj. Gen. George G. Meade

By Telegraph from City Point 2 P. M
Dated July 2 *1864*.

To GEN GEO G MEADE

Please detail One hundred & fifty men as an additional guard for the General Herd of Cattle now numbering some 3000 and being grazed or directed to be grazed on the James River near Coggins point. Direct the detail to report to Capt W R Murphy[1] C S in charge of herd. It would be a further protection to locate the camp for the dismounted Cavalry at Coggins point while waiting to be mounted if it can be done without inconvenience

U S GRANT
Lt Gen

Telegram received, DNA, RG 393, Army of the Potomac, Telegrams Received; copies, *ibid*., RG 107, Telegrams Collected (Unbound); *ibid*., RG 108, Letters Sent; DLC-USG, V, 45, 59, 67; (2) Meade Papers, PHi. *O.R*., I, xl, part 2, 583. On July 2, 1864, 4:30 P.M., Maj. Gen. George G. Meade telegraphed to USG. "Your telegram of 2. P. M received   A detail of 150 men has been ordered to report to Capt. Murphy C. S. in charge of cattle herd at or near Coggins Point— and Maj. Genl. Sheridan in command of dismounted Cavalry has been advised of your wishes in regard to the location of the camp of that part of his command." ALS (telegram sent), DNA, RG 393, Army of the Potomac, Miscellaneous Letters Received; copy, *ibid*., Letters Sent. At 5:20 P.M., Meade telegraphed to USG. "I have directed General Sheridan to furnish an additional guard of one hundred and fifty (150) men for the general cattle herd at Coggins Point, and also to locate the camp for the dismounted cavalry at or near that place ~~as directed in your dispatch of this date~~. if it can be done without inconvenience." Telegram sent, *ibid.*, Miscellaneous Letters Received; *ibid.*, Letters Sent.

1. William R. Murphy of Pa., appointed capt. and commissary as of Sept. 10, 1862.

To Maj. Gen. William F. Smith

City Point July 2d 1864

Maj. Gen. Smith,

Your application for leave of absence has just come to me. Unless it is absolutely necessary that you should leave at this time I would much prefer not having you go. It will not be necessary for you to expose yourself in the hot sun and if it should become necessary I can temporarily attach Humphreys to relieve you of such duty.

U S Grant
Lt Gen.

AL (telegram sent), DNA, RG 107, Telegrams Collected (Unbound). *O.R.*, I, xl, part 2, 594. On June 30, 1864, Maj. Gen. William F. Smith wrote to Brig. Gen. John A. Rawlins. "I have the honor to forward a Certificate from the Medical Director of this Corps, and to ask that I may have a leave of absence of twenty days. I have been unable for some time, to do any duty which exposed me to the heat of the Sun, and, as this position is one requiring constant attention, I beg leave to ask that I may be relieved as soon as possible, and some one placed in Command, who can keep the saddle, if necessary, during the heat of the day. As General Butler has informed me that he has left for Fort Monroe, I send this direct, being temporarily in Command of the troops of this Dept. in this vicinity." LS, DNA, RG 108, Letters Received. *O.R.*, I, xl, part 2, 538. Smith enclosed a statement of June 30 of Surgeon George Suckley. ALS, DNA, RG 108, Letters Received. On July 2, Smith wrote to Rawlins. "If there is to be no reorganization soon I will take advantage of the Generals permission & go away for a few days as this hot weather is *one* too many for me." ALS, *ibid.*, RG 107, Telegrams Collected (Unbound). *O.R.*, I, xl, part 2, 594. On the same day, Smith wrote to USG. "In acknowledging your dispatch, with reference to my leave, I ~~deem~~ consider it due to you who have been so kind to me, and to myself who have never had any thing but the warmest wish for your success, and for the prosperous termination of this war, to render some explanation. One of my troubles (that of my head) has three times driven me from a southern climate, and I really feel quite helpless here, unable to go out at all during the heat of the day, even to visit my lines, and therefore I do not do the duty of a corps commander as I think it should be done. I have, during this war, held my health & my life at the service of the country, when I thought I was doing any good, & as I stand now unfortuna[tely] & as I think, I can say with the clearest conscience from no fault of my own, I have deemed that some other with more ambitions, & no hostilities, could better serve the country here in my place, therefore I was in no wise called upon to risk a permanent disability, by remaining here. I wish to say to you, unofficially, that from the time I joined the Dept. of Va, until the campaign terminated disgracefully, I gave to the work the utmost energies of mind & body. Then I wanted to be where I could be useful & thinking the more troops there were in this Dep[t.] the more blunders & murders would be committed, I went gladly to the A of P with the most hearty good will & intentions. In look[ing] back over the [snee]rs & the false charges & the snubbing I have recd there, I only wonder General, at my own moderation   I then [ca]m[e back] here thinking that your presence here, would prevent blunders, & that I could once more be useful here. Two letters have been written to me which I think any gentleman would be ashamed to acknowledge as emanating from him, & for which there was not even the shadow of an excuse. This has induced me to believe, that some one else would be of far more service here than I am here, and as my only ambition is to be of service, I determined to present the just plea of my health, to remove one of the obstacles to harmony in this army, & that, General, if you will look closely into the campaign, you will find to have been be one of the causes of want of the success where you needed & expected it. In conclusion, General, I am willing to do any thing & endure anything which will be of service to the country, or yourself. Now I am with the personal, & I want simply to call your attention to the fact, that no man, since the Revolution, has had the tithe of the responsibility which now sits on your shoulders & to ask you, how you can place a man in command of two army corps, who is as helpless as a child on the field of battle, & as visionary as an opium eater in council, & that, too, when you have such men as Franklin & Wright availa[ble to] help you, to make you famous for all time & our country great & free beyond all other nations of the world. Think of it, my dear General, & let your good sense, & not your heart decide questions of this kind." ALS, DNA, RG 393, 18th Army Corps, Telegrams Sent (Press). *O.R.*, I, xl, part 2, 595. On the same day, 9:45 P.M., Smith telegraphed to Rawlins. "There is a good deal of reorganization to be done in this command & therefore I dare not take advantage of the General's kindness & must stick it out as long as possible & hope for a change of weather. Please mention this to Genl Grant. As soon as the order is out I shall come down & have a talk with you on what I consider a question of vital moment to the Country & in these questions personal hostility I don't think ever interferes with my judgement" ALS (telegram sent), DNA, RG 107, Telegrams Collected (Unbound). *O.R.*, I, xl, part 2, 595–96.

On June 30, Smith telegraphed to Rawlins. "The thirty pounders [o]n the river got the ranges of the [b]ridges very nicely yesterday & today have been doing good service [i]n hitting—They have not yet injured them so seriously as to break them down, though they have hit them several times   They have in addition to this [b]urnt the steamer lying at [P]ocahontas bridge. [T]he mortars on river bank have [d]one good service in aiding to [si]lence artillry fire." Copy (telegram sent), DNA, RG 393, 18th Army Corps, Telegrams Sent (Press); *ibid.*, RG 107, Telegrams Collected (Unbound); telegram received (at 9:10 P.M.), *ibid.*, RG 108, Letters Received. *O.R.*, I, xl, part 2, 537. On the same day,

Smith telegraphed to Rawlins. "I understood from Genl. Grant yesterday that he wished me to try to take the Enemy's lines in front of my left. I have made Every preparation to make the attack at 5 P. M. today. Are there any changes in our lines that will cause this attack to be postponed." Copy (undated), DNA, RG 107, Telegrams Collected (Unbound). On the same day, Rawlins wrote to Smith. "No change has been made in our lines requiring the postponement of your attack. You will therefore make it at the time you have ordered." *O.R.*, I, xl, part 2, 537. On the same day, Smith telegraphed to Rawlins. "The Brigade Commander who was to lead in the assault to night, in place of forming his men under [c]over, concealed, as he was directed, has [ma]de his formation in the open ground to the left of the position indicated. This brought in so sharp a fire from the [E]nemy as to detained Genl Turner in the [fo]rmation of the rest of his column—[gi]ving time to the Enemy to throw in reinforcements into the portion of the line we wished to take, which movement we could see—As our great hope of success depended upon taking the Enemy by surprise, as our only chance of doing that had gone with the long delay, I ordered a withdrawal of the troops to their original position—I have as yet no return of casualities but the loss [is sligh]t" ALS (telegram sent), DNA, RG 393, 18th Army Corps, Telegrams Sent (Press); *ibid.*, RG 107, Telegrams Collected (Unbound); telegram received, *ibid.*, RG 108, Letters Received. *O.R.*, I, xl, part 2, 538.

On July 1, Smith telegraphed to Rawlins. "Quite a conflagration was observed last night in Petersburg, probably caused by our shells. General Weitzel telegraphs me as follows this morning, and I think he is correct in his supposition: 'Eight car-loads of troops, apparently dressed in blue uniforms, have just passed to Petersburg. Is it not possible that these are our men to be put there to prevent the shelling of the city?' " *Ibid.*, p. 580.

On July 2, Lt. Col. Cyrus B. Comstock telegraphed to Smith. "Lieut Gen Grant wishes me to ask where & what is the artillery firing" Telegram received, DNA, RG 393, 24th Army Corps, Telegrams Received (Unarranged). On the same day, Smith telegraphed to Comstock. "The enemy opened upon my batteries near the river from their batteries on the opposite side & I am replying. The firing is entirely confined to this." Telegram received, *ibid.*, RG 94, War Records Office, Dept. of Va. and N. C., Army of the James, Unentered Papers. *O.R.*, I, xl, part 2, 596.

On July 5, Smith wrote to USG. "I am very anxious to show you a portion of my line which can only be seen in the morning about daylight, or in the evening after sunset. If your duties will permit, will you ride up this evening and spend the night with me, or to-morrow afternoon and go with me in the evening?" *Ibid.*, I, xl, part 3, 26. On the same day, USG wrote to Smith. "I will be at your Hd. Qrs. and visit your lines with you tomorrow evening," Copy, DLC-USG, V, 67. Cancellation marks indicate this message may not have been sent. On July 7, Smith wrote to Rawlins. "Will you suggest to the Lt Gen'l, to have all regular approaches at the salient discontinued, & have them begun at other places in the line to prevent attracting attention, until he has examined the ground & made up his mind for himself." Copy, DNA, RG 94, War Records Office, Dept. of Va. and N. C., Army of the James, Unentered Papers. *O.R.*, I, xl, part 3, 70.

On July 6, Smith twice wrote to Rawlins. "My Artillery succeeded this afternoon in blowing up a small magazine or limber chest in the enemys works on my left." "Will you have the Kindness to hurry up those two Batteries that have come for me, My reports show an increase of enemies artillery in my front. If you have a 100 lb Parrott lying idle & it meets ~~with~~ the approbation of the Lieut Gen'l, would it not be well to send it to me." Copies, DNA, RG 94, War Records Office, Army of the James, Unentered Papers. *O.R.*, I, xl, part 3, 57. See *ibid.*, p. 60. On the same day, Lt. Col. Orville E. Babcock telegraphed to Smith. "A party Composed of Senators Wade, Wilkenson Chandler & Sprague with some others will go out on the morning train at ten (10) A. M. The Lieut Gen desires you to have two (2) Carriages and five or six Saddle horses at the Cars to meet them to take them around" Telegram received, DNA, RG 393, 24th Army Corps, Telegrams Received (Unarranged).

On July 7, Smith telegraphed to Rawlins. "Is there any objection to my visiting City Point this evening Genl Franklin will be there ~~& is to lame to ride here~~." Copy, *ibid.*, RG 107, Telegrams Collected (Unbound). *O.R.*, I, xl, part 3, 70. See *ibid.*, p. 86.

On July 8, Smith twice telegraphed to Rawlins, the second time at 7:15 P.M. "Is it not possible to send me some troops to releive a portion of my line My troops are so exhausted it is very difficult to make them work." Telegram received (at 9:15 A.M.), DNA, RG 94, War Records Office, Dept. of Va. and N. C., Army of the James, Unentered Papers. *O.R.*, I, xl, part 3, 88. "The enemy opened quite heavily with artillery upon my lines about two hours since, after which their Infantry mounted the parapet of their rifle pits & delivered a volley but upon receiving a volley from my lines they again retired." Telegram received, DNA, RG 94, War Records Office, Dept. of Va. and N. C., Army of the James, Unentered Papers; *ibid.*, RG 108, Letters Received. *O.R.*, I, xl, part 3, 88. On the same day, USG telegraphed to Maj. Gen. Benjamin F. Butler. "Is it not practicable for you to send a Brigade of Troops from the Peninsula between the Appomattox & James to Genl Smith his line is so long & exposed that it is necessary to relieve the men in the trenches" Telegram received, DLC-Benjamin F. Butler; copies, DLC-USG, V, 45, 59, 67; DNA, RG 108, Letters Sent. *O.R.*, I, xl, part 3, 81. On the following day, Butler responded directly to Smith, not failing to include a rebuke for not following the chain of command. *Ibid.*, p. 118. On July 8, Rawlins telegraphed to Smith. "There will probably be no movements for a week or ten days, and you have permission to use this time to visit New York. Communicate this to Gen Butler with whom the Lt. Gen has spoken." Telegram received, DNA, RG 107, Telegrams Collected (Unbound); copies, *ibid.*, RG 108, Letters Sent; DLC-USG, V, 45, 59, 67. *O.R.*, I, xl, part 3, 88. On July 9, USG wrote to Smith. "Gen. Ord can be assigned to the command of your Corps during your absence if you think it advisable" Copies, DLC-USG, V, 45, 59, 67; DNA, RG 108, Letters Sent. *O.R.*, I, xl, part 3, 118. On the same day, Smith wrote to USG. "I think Genl Martindale perfectly competent to the Command & he knows the situation perfectly which Genl Ord would have to learn. It would seem to be a want of confidence considering the shortness of time that I am to be absent & I think Genl Martindale would feel hurt by it." ALS, DNA, RG 94, War Records Office, Dept. of Va. and N. C., Army of the James, Unentered Papers. *O.R.*, I, xl, part 3, 118. Brig. Gen. John H. Martindale assumed temporary command of the 18th Army Corps; Maj. Gen. Edward O. C. Ord replaced him on July 21. *Ibid.*, p. 361. See telegram to Maj. Gen. Henry W. Halleck, July 10, 1864.

To Maj. Gen. Henry W. Halleck

Genl Grant Hd Qrs
5 P. M. July 3, 1864

MAJ GENL HALLECK
CHIEF OF STAFF

You can direct Sigel in answer to his dispatch of 10.30 A. M of today better than I can. Earlys corps is now here[1]   There are no troops that can now be threatening Hunters Dept, except the remnant of the force W. E. Jones[2] had and possibly Breckenridge   If there is any thing threatening any portion of his Department however you need not send him here

U. S. GRANT
Lt. Genl.

Telegram received (at 8:15 P.M.), DNA, RG 107, Telegrams Collected (Bound); copies, *ibid.*, RG 108, Letters Sent; DLC-USG, V, 45, 59, 67. *O.R.*, I, xxxvii, part 2, 15. On July 3, 1864, 4:00 P.M., Maj. Gen. Henry W. Halleck telegraphed to USG. "Genl Sigel reports that Early Breckenridge & Jackson, with Moseby's guerrillas, are said to be moving from Staunton down the Shenandoah valley. I ordered Genl Hunter up to the line of the Rail-road, but he has replied to none of my telegrams, and has made no report of his operations or present condition. Sigel has been ordered to telegraph directly to him, to inform him of the condition of affairs & to ask for instructions. It is possible that Hunter is marching by Beverly & Moorefield or Romney, which would account for his not answering dispatches. The three principal officers on the line of the road are Sigel, Stahl, and Max Weber. You can therefore judge what probability there is of a good defence, if the enemy should attack the line in force." ALS (telegram sent), DNA, RG 107, Telegrams Collected (Bound); telegram received, *ibid.*; (at 6:40 P.M.) *ibid.*, RG 108, Letters Received. *O.R.*, I, xxxvii, part 2, 15. Halleck was probably responsible for the transmission to USG of a telegram of 10:30 A.M. from Maj. Gen. Franz Sigel to Brig. Gen. Lorenzo Thomas. "Gen Hunter informed today that Gen. Sullivan's Division is ordered here but that it could not arrive here before four or six days. I have here two regiments of Ohio Guards and one battery. At *Lee-town* there are two old regts of Infantry and five pieces of artillery, and about one thousand dismounted Cavalry armed here. Our mounted Cavalry consists of detachments to the number of 1800 men. The Cavalry is in front with the exception of a reserve near Martinsburg. I have taken command of all these troops and will concentrate them at a proper point in case of emergency. In view of the expected movement of Sullivan I will defend Martinsburg with all our power in case of an attack and hold communication with Cumberland if you do not wish me to hold communication with Harpers Ferry. In this case I must evacuate Martinsburg and concentrate our force at Charlestown. Please answer immediately." Telegram received (at 2:30 P.M.), DNA, RG 108,

Letters Received. At 8:00 P.M., USG telegraphed to Halleck. "Since telegraphing you today I have made enquiries to ascertain the grounds upon which Earlys (Ewells Corps) had returned to our front. I find no Prisoners have been taken from it since its reported return—Deserters however from other Commands state that it returned about five or six days ago" Telegram received (at 8:50 P.M.), *ibid.*, RG 107, Telegrams Collected (Bound); copies, *ibid.*, RG 108, Letters Sent; DLC-USG, V, 45 (misdated June 3), 59, 67. *O.R.*, I, xxxvii, part 2, 15.

Also on July 3, USG telegraphed to Maj. Gen. George G. Meade. "Gen Sigel telegraphs that Early, Breckenridge, Jackson and Mosby are reported to be moving down the Shenandoah Valley. Is it not certain that Early has returned to your front." Copies, DLC-USG, V, 45, 59, 67; DNA, RG 108, Letters Sent; (2) Meade Papers, PHi. *O.R.*, I, xxxvii, part 2, 16; *ibid.*, I, xl, part 2, 599. At 7:00 P.M., Meade telegraphed to USG. "The only information I have as to Ewell's corps was derived from deserters, who said it had returned from Lynchburgh. No prisoners have been taken from any of the divisions of that corps or any other information obtained than above—It is not It was never reported as in our front but only that it had returned from Lynchburgh.—" ALS (telegram sent), DNA, RG 393, Army of the Potomac, Miscellaneous Letters Received; copies, *ibid.*, Letters Sent; (2–1 misdated June 3) Meade Papers, PHi. *O.R.*, I, xxxvii, part 2, 16; *ibid.*, I, xl, part 2, 600.

1. Jubal A. Early, born in Va., USMA 1837, resigned from the U.S. Army and embarked upon a career as a Va. Whig lawyer-politician interrupted by service in the Mexican War. An opponent of secession, he nonetheless immediately embraced the southern cause and advanced in rank to lt. gen. and corps commander as of May 30, 1864, and replaced Lt. Gen. Richard S. Ewell in command of the 2nd Corps, Army of Northern Va. Ordered to the Shenandoah Valley on June 12, Early repulsed Maj. Gen. David Hunter at Lynchburg (June 18) then moved northward, reaching Harpers Ferry on July 3.

2. William E. "Grumble" Jones of Va., USMA 1848, resigned as 1st lt., Mounted Rifles, as of Jan. 26, 1857, and became a Va. farmer. As capt., Washington Mounted Rifles, col., 1st and 7th Va. Cav., and brig. gen. as of Sept. 19, 1862, he acquired a reputation as an outstanding cav. officer before his death, June 5, 1864, at the engagement of Piedmont, Va.

To Maj. Gen. George G. Meade

By Telegraph from City Point 10 30 P M.
Dated July 3d *1864.*

To MAJOR GEN MEADE

Do you think it possible by a bold and decisive attack to break through the enemys centre, say in Warrens front somewhere? If this is determined on we would want full preparations made in advance so there should be no balk—Roads would have to be made to bring the troops up [rapid]ly, batteries constructed so as to bring the greatest amou[nt] of Artillery to bear possible on the points of attack and all to the right of the attack strengthened to be held by the smallest number of men—I have felt unwilling to give the troops any violent exercise until we get rain to settle the dust, and now even if we should get rain all operations except preparations will have to be deferred until the Cavalry is again fit for service.

I send this to get your views on the subject—If it is not attempted we will have to give you an Army sufficient to meet most of Lees forces and march around Petersburg and come in from above—This probably could not be done before the arrival of the 19th Corps.

U S GRANT
Lt Genl

Telegram received, DNA, RG 94, War Records Office, Army of the Potomac; copies, *ibid.*, RG 108, Letters Sent; DLC-USG, V, 45, 59, 67; (2) Meade Papers, PHi. Printed as sent on July 3, 1864, at 10:30 A.M., in *O.R.*, I, xl, part 2, 599; (incomplete) *ibid.*, p. 603. At noon, Maj. Gen. George G. Meade telegraphed to USG. "Your despatch received. before replying it will be necessary I should see both Warren & Burnside to obtain information. I am now under the impression that the former does not consider an advance in his front practicable but the latter some days ago was of the opinion that he could in his front break through the enemys line—I will advise you as soon as possible of my views fully—" ALS (telegram sent), DNA, RG 393, Army of the Potomac, Miscellaneous Letters Received; telegram received, *ibid.*, RG 108, Letters Received. *O.R.*, I, xl, part 2, 599.

At 10:00 A.M., Meade telegraphed to USG. "I have nothing particular to report from the lines of this army during the past 24 hours.—Maj. Genl. Burnside has made progress in the construction of his siege batteries, one of which will be completed by tonight—He has met with difficulty in his mining operations owing to the presence of water & quicksands—He expresses himself confident of being able to overcome all these obstacles & shortly finish the mine.—Maj. Genl. Warren continues to strengthen his front & is about placing in position a battery of heavy guns.—There has been no Change in the lines of Genls. Hancock & Wright.—The cavalry ordered to Prince Georges C. H.—finding that position destitute of water, has gone to Jordans Pt on the James to recuperate—A deserter yesterday reported the troops that were seen to pass into Petersburgh the day before as Mahone's Division, which had been sent to support the cavalry in the attack on Wilson—I understand a late Richmond paper claims the capture of 1600 prisoners & 10 guns from Wilson.—No report has been recieved from Genl. Wilson since his return.—" ALS (telegram sent), DNA, RG 393, Army of the Potomac, Miscellaneous Letters Received; telegram received, *ibid.*, RG 108, Letters Received. *O.R.*, I, xl, part 2, 598–99.

Also on July 3, USG telegraphed to Meade and to Maj. Gen. Benjamin F.

Butler the text of a telegram of July 3 from Maj. Gen. William T. Sherman, Marietta, Ga., to Maj. Gen. Henry W. Halleck reporting his advance. Telegram received, DNA, RG 94, War Records Office, Dept. of Va. and N. C., Army of the James, Unentered Papers; *ibid.*, RG 393, 24th Army Corps, Telegrams Received (Unarranged). See *O.R.*, I, xxxviii, part 5, 29.

To Maj. Gen. Henry W. Halleck

City Point 4 p m
July 4th 1864

MAJ GEN H W HALLECK
CHF OF STAFF

A deserter who came in this morning reports that Ewells Corps has not returned here but is off in the valley with the intention of going into Maryland and Washington City. They now have the report that he already has Arlington Heights and expects to take the City soon. Of course the soldiers know nothing about this force further than that it is away from here and north somewhere. Under the circumstances, I think it advisable to hold all of the forces you can about Washington Baltimore, Cumberland and Harpers Ferry ready to concentrate against any advance of the enemy.

Except from the despatches forwarded from Washington in the last two days I have learned nothing which indicated an intention on part of the rebels to attempt any northern movement.

If Genl Hunter is in striking distance there ought to be veteran force enough to meet anything the enemy have and if once put to flight he ought to be followed as long as possible.

This report of Ewells Corps being north is only the report of a deserter and we have similar authority for it being here and on the right of Lees Army. We know however that it does not occupy this position

U S. GRANT
Lt Genl

Telegram received (on July 5, 1864), DNA, RG 107, Telegrams Collected (Bound); copies, *ibid.*, RG 108, Letters Sent; DLC-USG, V, 45, 59, 67. *O.R.*, I, xxxvii, part 2, 33; *ibid.*, I, xl, part 2, 618.

To Maj. Gen. Henry W. Halleck

Hd Qrs City Point Va.
12 midnight July 5. 1864.

MAJ. GEN HALLECK.
CHF OF STAFF.

Your dispatch of 12 30 p m recd. I have ordered to Washington the dismounted Cavalry & one Divn of Infantry which will be followed by the balance of the Corps if necessary. We want now to crush out & destroy any force the enemy dares send north. Force enough can be spared from here to do it. I think now there is no doubt but Ewell's Corps is away from here—[1]

U. S. GRANT
Lt Gen

Telegram received (on July 6, 1864, 2:30 P.M.), DNA, RG 107, Telegrams Collected (Bound); copies, *ibid.*, Telegrams Collected (Unbound); (incomplete) *ibid.*, RG 94, Letters Received, 685A 1864; *ibid.*, RG 108, Letters Sent; (incomplete) *ibid.*, RG 393, Dept. of Washington, Telegrams Received; DLC-USG, V, 45, 59, 67. Entered as sent at 11:50 P.M. in USG's letterbooks and *O.R.*, I, xxxvii, part 2, 60; *ibid.*, I, xl, part 3, 4. On July 5, 12:30 P.M., Maj. Gen. Henry W. Halleck telegraphed to USG. "There has been no telegraphic communication with Harpers Ferry since yesterday a little after noon, but we learn through the railroad company that Sigel had reached Maryland Heights and withdrawn all troops from south of the river, destroying the bridges. We can learn nothing whatever of Hunter. The enemy has destroyed bridges from Harpers Ferry to Patterson's Creek where Kelly succeeded in driving them back. The line from the Monocacy to to Harpers Ferry has been cut & the reinforcements sent from here fell back to the Monocacy. Genl Howe has been sent there with about twenty-eight hundred men to force his way to Harper's Ferry. We have nothing reliable in regard to enemy's force. Some accounts, probably very exaggerated, state it to be between twenty & thirty thousand. If one half that number, we cannot meet it in the field till Hunter's troops arrive. As you are aware we have almost nothing in Baltimore or Washington except militia, and considerable alarm has been created by sending troops from these places to reinforce Harper's Ferry. You probably have a large dismounted cavalry force, & I would advise that it be sent here immediately. It can be remounted by impressing horses in the parts of Maryland likely to be overrun by the enemy. All the dismounted fragments here were armed as infantry & sent to Harper's Ferry." ALS (telegram sent), DNA, RG 107, Telegrams Collected (Bound); telegram received, *ibid.*; *ibid.*, Telegrams Collected (Unbound); *ibid.*, RG 108, Letters Received. Printed as sent at 1:00 P.M. in *O.R.*, I, xxxvii, part 2, 59; *ibid.*, I, xl, part 3, 3.

At 12:30 P.M., USG telegraphed to Halleck. "If the enemy cross into Maryland or Pennsylvania I can send an army corps from here to meet them or cut off their return South. If required direct the Qr Mr Genl to send transportation" Telegram received (at 6:45 P.M.), DNA, RG 107, Telegrams Collected (Bound); *ibid.*, Telegrams Collected (Unbound); copies, *ibid.*, RG 108, Letters Sent; DLC-USG, V, 45, 59, 67. *O.R.*, I, xxxvii, part 2, 58; *ibid.*, I, xl, part 3, 3.

At 4:30 P.M. and 10:30 P.M., Halleck telegraphed to USG. "Genl Hunter has just been heard from at Parkersburg. Thirteen hundred of his men are coming forward to reinforce Genl Kelley at Cumberland & New Creek." "All available water transportation is now at Fort Monroe & in James River. Genl Meigs recommends that it all be placed under Genl Ingalls, as by a divided command there is conflict of orders. As Hunter's force is now coming within reach, I think your operations should not be interferred with by sending troops here. If Washington or Baltimore should be so seriously threatened as to require your aid, I will inform you in time. Although [m]ost of our forces are not of a character suitable for the field—Invalids & Militia—yet I have no apprehensions at present about the safety of Washington, Baltimore, Harpers Ferry or Cumberland. These points cover our supplies, & raids between cannot effect any damage that cannot soon be repaired. If, however, you can send us your dismounted cavalry, we can use it to advantage, & perhaps soon return it remounted." ALS (telegrams sent), DNA, RG 107, Telegrams Collected (Bound); telegrams received, *ibid.*; *ibid.*, Telegrams Collected (Unbound); (second misdated July 6) *ibid.*, RG 108, Letters Received. *O.R.*, I, xxxvii, part 2, 59; *ibid.*, I, xl, part 3, 4.

1. Also on July 5, Maj. Gen. Benjamin F. Butler telegraphed to USG. "From the best infomation I can get from Deserters and prisoners I am inclined to the opinion that Earlys Corps with Imboden Mosby and Breckenridge are making a raid up the Valley near Harpers Ferry—or Martinsburg   I think this may be reasonably relied on"   ALS (telegram sent), DNA, RG 94, War Records Office, Dept. of Va. and N. C., Army of the James, Unentered Papers; copy, *ibid.*, RG 393, Dept. of Va. and N. C., Telegrams Sent. *O.R.*, I, xl, part 3, 18.

To Maj. Gen. George G. Meade

By Telegraph from City Point
Dated July 6th [5] *1864.*

To MAJ. GEN MEADE

Sigel has fallen back to Md. heights destroying the bridges at that point   Some of Hunter's forces have arrived at Pattersons Creek where they drove the enemy   Other despatches are coming through which when deciphered I will inform you of if they contain any thing of importance   Among them is the announcement of the sinking of the Alabama by our Navy Semmes however escap-

ing[1] Vessels will be ready for the troops ordered from here between now and two 2 P. M. tomorrow. No Artillery will be sent

U. S. GRANT
Lieut Genl

Telegram received (on July 6, 1864, 12:30 A.M.), DNA, RG 94, War Records
Office, Army of the Potomac; copies, *ibid.*, RG 108, Letters Sent; DLC-USG, V,
45, 59, 67; (2—misdated July 6) Meade Papers, PHi. *O.R.*, I, xxxvii, part 2,
60; *ibid.*, I, xl, part 3, 6. Earlier on July 5, USG telegraphed to Maj. Gen.
George G. Meade. "The enemy have got to the B & O road and have destroyed
the railroad bridge from Pattersons Creek to Harpers Ferry   Send in one (1)
good Division of your troops & all the dismounted Cavalry to be forwarded at
once   I will not send an army Corps until more is learned   I will order the
Q. M. here to have transportation ready." Telegram received (misdated July
6, received at 12:20 A.M.), DNA, RG 94, War Records Office, Army of the
Potomac; copies, *ibid.*, RG 108, Letters Sent; DLC-USG, V, 45, 59, 67; (2—
misdated July 6) Meade Papers, PHi. *O.R.*, I, xxxvii, part 2, 60; *ibid.*, I, xl, part
3, 6. At 1:00 P.M., Meade telegraphed to USG. "The following information obtained from two deserters who came in this morning is sent to you for what it is
worth.—'They state it to be currently reported at Richmond & in Petersburgh
that Early in command of two Divisions of Ewells Corps with Breckenridges
command & other forces was making an invasion of Maryland with a view of
capturing Washington supposed to be defenceless—It was understood Early
would reach Winchester by the 3d inst'—" ALS (telegram sent), DNA, RG
393, Army of the Potomac, Miscellaneous Letters Received; copies, *ibid.*, Letters
Sent; (2) Meade Papers, PHi. *O.R.*, I, xxxvii, part 2, 60; *ibid.*, I, xl, part 3, 5.
On July 6, 1:30 A.M., Meade telegraphed to USG. "Your two despatches received. I have ordered a strong Division of the 6th Corps to report to city Point
as soon as possible and directed Gen Sheridan to report to Gen Ingalls the number of dismounted Cavy. of his Command at once"   Telegram received, DNA,
RG 108, Letters Received; copies, *ibid.*, RG 393, Army of the Potomac, Miscellaneous Letters Received; *ibid.*, Letters Sent. *O.R.*, I, xl, part 3, 32. On the same
day, Brig. Gen. John A. Rawlins telegraphed to Meade. "Please direct the troops
ordered to Washington to proceed via of Baltimore and from Baltimore to Report by telegraph to Maj. Genl Halleck chief of staff of the Army for orders."
ALS (telegram sent), DNA, RG 107, Telegrams Collected (Unbound); telegram received (at 9:46 A.M.), *ibid.*, RG 94, War Records Office, Army of the
Potomac. Printed as sent at 9:40 A.M. in *O.R.*, I, xl, part 3, 32.

1. Raphael Semmes, born in Md. in 1809, served in the U.S. Navy from
1826 until he resigned as commander as of Feb. 15, 1861. In command of the
C.S.S. *Sumter*, then of the C.S.S. *Alabama*, Semmes captured eighty-two mer-
chantmen valued at more than $6,000,000. On June 19, 1864, off Cherbourg,
the *Alabama* was sunk by the U.S.S. *Kearsarge*. Picked up by an English yacht,
Semmes went to England.

To Maj. Gen. George G. Meade

City Point July 5th 1864

MAJ. GEN. MEADE,

My Eng. officers make the same report of the lack of practicability of assault any where along our present front that you do. At present we are doing very well all the roads are cut and the enemy are living now on half rations. This I presume is certain as well as the further fact that discontent is begining to prevail. I believe the enemy are preparing to make an effort to establish themselves on the North bank of the river below with the view of blockading or it may be only a force going to the North side of James river to cover foraging parties whilst they collect and get out all they can between the James & Chickahominy. It may be necessary to march Wright over there to prevent this but I will not do so until more is known about what the enemy are doing. The best we can do now is to strengthen our present line on Burnside's and Warren's front and advance by gradual approaches as you propose. As soon as the Cavalry is in working order we will make another raid supporting the Cavalry as far as the Welden road with Infantry. The troops in North Carolina started out to cut the Welden road but as near as I can learn turned back on the report that the enemy were reinforcing

U. S. GRANT Lt G[en]

ALS, deCoppet Collection, NjP. *O.R.*, I, xl, part 3, 5. On July 4, 1864, 10:00 A.M. and noon, Maj. Gen. George G. Meade telegraphed to USG. "Every thing was quiet along my lines yesterday and last night, except the usual picket & artillery practice in front of the 9th corps which does not seem to result in any casualties. Report of scouting parties of the cavalry on my left would seem to indicate the presence of the enemy's cavalry & one report states infantry at *Rowanty* Swamp—Stony Creek & Dinwiddie C H—These are undoubtedly precautions taken to meet any cavalry raids on our part, or attempts to interrupt the communications heretofore reported as existing between Petersburgh & the R. Rd. below Stony Creek Depot.—Maj. Genl. Sheridan reports his command at Jordan's point & old C H. & expresses the opinion it will require 15 days to get his animals into a serviceable condition." "After examination & conference with Corps Comdrs. I am satisfied an immediate assault on the enemys line in my front is impracticable—The enemy now occupy the line held by him on the 18th inst ultimo, which I vainly endeavored to dislodge him from—Not having suc-

ceeded then; when he had only occupied this line some Twelve hours I can not
expect to do it now that he has been two weeks strengthening & adding to it—
The only plan to dislodge the enemy from this line is by a regular approach—
Maj. Genl. Burnside is now running a gallery to a mine to be constructed under
a battery on this line which Genl. B thinks when exploded will enable him by a
formidable assault to carry the line of works—I have directed the Chief of
Artilr. & of Engrs. to examine into this point & to make all the necessay preliminary arrangements for the establishment of batteries bearing on the point of
attack—opening roads & preparing places of arms for the assembling of the supporting columns—Should this attack be made, which under existing circumstances
I deem the most practicable it will be necessary to withdraw the 2d & 6 corps to
take part in it and the left of the 5th corps will have to be thrown back for self
protection—A line for this purpose will be prepared in advance, but this will
require the giving up the Jerusalem plank road. With your present numbers &
existing condition of affairs I am of the opinion active operations against the
enemy in his present position the most advisable, as it leaves our communications
open & intact—The movement on the enemys right flank as suggested is liable to
the objection of separating your forces with the enemy between the two parts—
with having to abandon the communications of this army & the danger after
crossing the Appomatox that the enemy may be found strongly posted behind
Swift run—requiring further flank movements, more time, further separation
from a base & more hazard in re-opening communications—our experience since
crossing the Rapidann having proved the facility with which the enemy can interpose to check an onward movement—If we had the force to extend around
the south side of the Appomatox, I should prefer doing so and employing the
cavalry to destroy the enemys communications—It will take Genl Burnside over
a week to complete his mine—& Genl Sheridan two weeks to get his animals into
a serviceable condition—" ALS (telegrams sent), DNA, RG 393, Army of the
Potomac, Miscellaneous Letters Received; telegrams received, *ibid.*, RG 108,
Letters Received. *O.R.*, I, xl, part 2, 619–20. Also on July 4, Meade forwarded
to USG a signal officer's report of troop and railroad movements near Petersburg.
Ibid., p. 621.

On July 4, 10:40 P.M., Maj. Gen. Benjamin F. Butler telegraphed to USG.
"Gen. Smith telegraphed me this ~~morning~~ afternoon that six Regt's of Infantry,
22 Army wagons and 26 Ambulances passed over the turnpike toward Richmond,
and also a train of cars loaded with troops and a Battery—A deserter from
Foster's front at Deep Bottom reports that Cook and Kirkland's Brigades of
Heth's Division of Hills Corps have left there and that there is now in front of
Foster—Davis Brigade of Heth's Division and Lane's and Conner's Brigades of
Wilcox Division of Hill's Corps with one Regt from Gracie's Brigade—These
troops have gone there within two days—Another deserter just in reports that
Pick[et]t's Division is being withdrawn from our front, their place to be sup-
plied by Batt'ns of reserve militia who are to hold our lines, while Pickett's
Division is to cross the Appomattox—He also reports Gen Early present in person but does not know of his division—He states that his officers say that there
is to be a flank movement ~~against~~ This may possibly be a movement against
Meade's left—The troops that Smith reports going up may be the reserves to take
the place of ~~Petersburg~~ Pickett's veteran troops that are to cross the appomattox
—I have thought the man's story of sufficient consequence to send him to you
for examination in ~~I~~ addition to this synopsis ofh his information—He reports

also, felling the trees by the enemy in our front which would show that they do not mean a movement upon us—By careful questioning you may be able to make something more out of him—It is quite possible that an attack, which will probably be a feint, will be made on Foster, while a real attack will be made on Meades left, and this may be the flank movement spoken of—" LS (telegram sent), DNA, RG 94, War Records Office, Dept. of Va. and N. C., Army of the James, Unentered Papers; copy, *ibid.*, RG 393, Dept. of Va. and N. C., Telegrams Sent. *O.R.*, I, xl, part 2, 633. On the same day, USG transmitted this telegram to Meade. Telegram received (on July 5, 1:45 A.M.), DNA, RG 94, War Records Office, Army of the Potomac.

On July 5, 10:00 A.M. and 10:30 P.M., Meade telegraphed to USG. "The usual quiet along the lines of this army prevailed yesterday & last night, disturbed only by the usual artillery & musketry practice in front of the 9th corps, which occurred at 2 a m this morning—Genl. Burnside reports the enemy as having established a mortar battery in his front from which they occasionally shell his lines—He reports the casualties during the last ten days as amounting to 480 in all—An examination of the proposed point of attack in front of Burnsides line made by the Chief Engineer of this army has resulted in a less favorable report than was anticipated—a written report will be forwarded In the mean time a critical examination of the lines of both the 5th & 9th corps has been ordered to ascertain the practicability of making an immediate attack & for selecting the most suitable point in the event of regular approaches being decided upon.—" "Richmond papers of the 4th inst state—'It was believed to be satisfactorily ascertained that Warren's army corps had been thrown across to the north bank of the James river near Deep Bottom—The Yankees have removed the obstructions recently sunk by them in Trents reach.'—The above may account for the sending troops from Petersburgh towards Richmond.—I will send the paper tomorrow—" ALS (telegrams sent), *ibid.*, RG 393, Army of the Potomac, Miscellaneous Letters Received; telegrams received, *ibid.*, RG 108, Letters Received. *O.R.*, I, xl, part 3, 4–5. At 8:30 P.M., Meade telegraphed to USG. "B. S. Snider private 64 N. Y. Vols, has endeavored to pass the picket line of this army presenting a pass signed in your name—Is this pass genuine? If so to prevent delay in future please advise me when such passes are given.—" ALS (telegram sent), DNA, RG 393, Army of the Potomac, Miscellaneous Letters Received; copy, *ibid.*, Letters Sent.

To J. Russell Jones

City Point July 5th *1864.*

DEAR JONES,

I wish you to keep what funds I have, collect the interest on the Bonds and retain the gold so collected as a special deposit. I also send herewith $500 00 more and will continue to send as I can save from my pay. At any time you see any little investment for me with the funds on hand make it without hesitation. You are also authorized to run me in debt as far as you can borrow on the Bonds besides.

You people up North now must be of good cheer. Recollect that we have the bulk of the Rebel Army in two grand Armies both besieged and both conscious that they cannot stand a single battle outside their fortifications with the Armies confronting them. The last man in the Confederacy is now in the Army. They are becoming discouraged, their men deserting, dying and being killed and captured every day. We loose to but can replace our losses. If the rebellion is not perfectly and thoroughly crushed it will be the fault and through the weakness of the people North. Be of good cheer and rest assured that all will come out right.

Yours Truly
U. S. GRANT

ALS, ICHi.

To Maj. Gen. Henry W. Halleck

Hd Qrs City Point 10 a m
July 6th 1864

MAJ GENL H W HALLECK
CHF OF STAFF

Please obtain an order assigning the troops of the Dept of North Carolina and Virginia serving in the field to the command of Maj Gen W F Smith and order Genl Butler to his Head Quarters Fortress Monroe[1]

One Division of troops besides the dismounted cavalry will sail from here for Baltimore during the day—They are directed to report their arrival in Baltimore to you by telegraph

U S GRANT
Lt Genl

Telegram received (at 7:00 P.M.), DNA, RG 107, Telegrams Collected (Bound); *ibid.*, Telegrams Collected (Unbound); copies, *ibid.*, RG 108, Letters Sent; DLC-

USG, V, 45, 59, 67; (incomplete) USG 3. *O.R.*, I, xl, part 3, 31. On July 6, 1864, 1:30 P.M., 4:30 P.M., and twice at 10:00 P.M., Maj. Gen. Henry W. Halleck telegraphed to USG. "Genl Howe has reached Harper's Ferry with his command. Sigel is expecting an attack to day. Most of Hunter's forces have reached Parkersburg & are coming forward. It is believed that Ewell's corps under Early is in the valley. It is reported that Sigel abandoned a large amount of public stores at Martinsburg without making any defence. As that place was without fortifications & only a mere out post it is difficult to understand why the stores were taken from the Depot at Harpers Ferry. Genl Hunter says that Sigel had sufficient forces to defend the Railroad, if he had used them properly." ALS (telegram sent), DNA, RG 107, Telegrams Collected (Bound); telegram received, *ibid.*; (marked as sent at 2:00 P.M., received on July 7) *ibid.*, RG 108, Letters Received. Printed as sent at 2:00 P.M. in *O.R.*, I, xxxvii, part 2, 79. "Please give me an estimate of number of dismounted cavalry sent, in order that I may provide remounts. They should bring their equipments with them. It appears that Genl Sigel had no scouts out to give notice of enemy's approach, & he seems to guess at their numbers, estimating them from seven to over twenty thousand. Other estimates are from twenty to thirty thousand. I think there is no further doubt about Ewell's corps. Probably also Breckenridge, Imboden Jackson and Moseby. If so the invasion is of a pretty formidable character. I have hurried Genl Hunter forward, but get no reply from him. I fear that the Railroad is so much injured that his advance will be slow. Can you send a good Major Genl to command in the field till Hunter arrives? I think Genl Augur should not leave Washington." ALS (telegram sent), DNA, RG 107, Telegrams Collected (Bound); telegram received, *ibid.*; (marked as sent at 5:00 P.M., received on July 7) *ibid.*, RG 108, Letters Received. Printed as sent at 5:00 P.M. in *O.R.*, I, xxxvii, part 2, 79; *ibid.*, I, xl, part 3, 31–32. "The artillery prepared to send to you have been sent to Harper's Ferry. Moreover they were not drilled at Heavy Artillery. One regiment of the latter is almost indispensable to mix in with militia, who can scarcely fire a gun. Sigel has been removed from Harper's Ferry & Howe sent to take his place till Hunter arrives. Nothing heard from the latter to day. Of Couch, Ord & Gillmore, I think the latter the best, & have sent for him to-night. Early & Breckenridge [ar]e unquestionably in this raid, which is probably larger than we first supposed. Their special object [i]s not yet develloped." ALS (telegram sent), DNA, RG 107, Telegrams Collected (Bound); telegram received, *ibid.*; (dated July 7) *ibid.*, Telegrams Collected (Unbound); (marked as sent at 10:00 P.M., July 7) *ibid.*, RG 108, Letters Received. Printed as sent at 10:00 P.M., July 7, in *O.R.*, I, xxxvii, part 2, 98; *ibid.*, I, xl, part 3, 60. "Genl Augur is of opinion that one regiment of heavy artillery should be returned to Washington, to be distributed among the hundred day militia in the forts, as the latter are not sufficiently instructed in the use of heavy batteries." ALS (telegram sent), DNA, RG 107, Telegrams Collected (Bound); telegram received, *ibid.*; (in cipher) *ibid.*, Telegrams Collected (Unbound); *ibid.*, RG 108, Letters Received. *O.R.*, I, xxxvii, part 2, 80; *ibid.*, I, xl, part 3, 32. See telegram to Maj. Gen. Henry W. Halleck, July 7, 1864.

1. See telegram to Maj. Gen. Henry W. Halleck, July 10, 1864, 1:30 P.M.

To Maj. Gen. Henry W. Halleck

City Point Va
July 6th 1864—3 p m

MAJ GEN H W HALLECK
CHF OF STAFF

A part of the force directed by me to go north is already off, and the whole of it will be in course of an hour or two.

It will probably be as well to let it go now and return it as soon as you deem it perfectly safe to do so—I think there is no doubt but Earlys Corps is near the Baltimore & Ohio Road, and if it can be caught and broken up it will be highly desirable to do so. It is important to our success here that another raid should be made up the Shenandoah Valley and stores destroyed and communications broken again—

U S GRANT
Lt Gen'l

Telegram received (on July 7, 1864), DNA, RG 107, Telegrams Collected (Bound); (in cipher) *ibid.*, Telegrams Collected (Unbound); copies, *ibid.*, RG 108, Letters Sent; DLC-USG, V, 45, 59, 67. *O.R.*, I, xxxvii, part 2, 79; *ibid.*, I, xl, part 3, 31.

To Maj. Gen. George G. Meade

By Telegraph from City Point
Dated July 6th *1864.*

To GEN MEADE

I have no doubt but that the force have sent to Washington will prove sufficient & not only that but that they will speedily return the Cavalry fully mounted & equipped—Hunter has got a portion of his forces up to the enemy and is concentrating the balance as rapidly as possible

If they succeed in nearly annihilating Ewell Breckenridge &c Hunter will be able to move through to Charlottesville & utterly destroy the Railroad & Canals without the help of the troops sent from here

U S GRANT

Lt Gen

Telegram received (at 11:30 A.M.), DNA, RG 94, War Records Office, Army of the Potomac; copies, *ibid.*, RG 108, Letters Sent; DLC-USG, V, 45, 59, 67; (2) Meade Papers, PHi. *O.R.*, I, xxxvii, part 2, 80; (printed as sent at 11:30 A.M.) *ibid.*, I, xl, part 3, 33. On July 6, 1864, 10:30 A.M., Maj. Gen. George G. Meade telegraphed to USG. "Genl Wright reports the division sent to Washington will amount to nearly 5000 men—Genl. Sheridan reports over 2500 dismounted men equipped & some 1500 dismounted & unequipped He has been directed to send them all to Washington, as they can be equipped more readily there than here & be put to some service at once—This will make nearly 9000 men sent from this army which I trust will meet the exigency as I should be reluctant to spare any more.—Every thing was quiet yesterday & last night with the exception of Genl Burnside who opened a battery on what he believed to be a working party of the enemy, during the night.—" ALS (telegram sent), DNA, RG 393, Army of the Potomac, Miscellaneous Letters Received; telegram received, *ibid.*, RG 108, Letters Received. *O.R.*, I, xl, part 3, 32–33. On the same day, USG telegraphed to Meade. "The troops going to Washington need not take teams Ambulances or Ammunition except what they carry in boxes I expect them back here so soon that there is no necessity of transporting the teams back and forth besides there is now in Washington about 600 teams ready for issue if necessary" Telegram received (at 11:35 A.M.), DNA, RG 94, War Records Office, Army of the Potomac; copies, *ibid.*, RG 108, Letters Sent; DLC-USG, V, 45, 59, 67; (2) Meade Papers, PHi. *O.R.*, I, xxxvii, part 2, 80; (printed as sent at 11:35 A.M.) *ibid.*, I, xl, part 3, 33. At 2:10 P.M., Meade telegraphed to Lt. Col. Theodore S. Bowers. "Just before this Army left Brandy Station the Lt Genl Commanding Verbally instructed me to move with One Hundred & fifty (150) rounds of Small arm ammunition per man fifty round to be carried on the persons & One Hundred (100) rounds in the Wagons & for the transportation of small arm ammunition five Wagons were allowed for Every one thousand men —special orders Number forty four of June 28th 1864 from your Head Quarters provides three (3) Wagons Only for Every one thousand (1,000) men for the transportation of Small arm ammunition It is estimated that one thousand (1000) rounds of small arm ammunition Weigh about One Hundred pounds & under the allowance of 3 Wagons per one thousand (1000) men each Wagon would have to Carry about thirty three Hundred (3,300) pounds besides The forage for the team—It is respectfully submitted that With this Weight the Wagons would be Considerably overloaded & I have therefore the honor to request that I may be informed whether in reducing the allowance of transportation for small arm ammunition The Lt Gen designed also to reduce in proper the amount of ammunition to be Carried—Heretofore when 3 Wagons have been allowed for such ammunition sixty (60) rounds per man only have been Carried in the Wagons" Telegram received, DNA, RG 108, Letters Received. *O.R.*, I, xl, part 3, 33–34. For Special Orders No. 44, June 28, see *ibid.*, I, xl, part 1, 40–41. On the same day, USG telegraphed to Meade. "The number of rounds of small arm ammunition will be reduced in proportion to the reduction of transportation" Telegram received, DNA, RG 94, War Records Office, Army of the Potomac; copies, DLC-USG, V, 67; (2) Meade Papers, PHi. *O.R.*, I, xl, part 3, 34.

On July 4, Bowers had issued Special Orders No. 48, which had been telegraphed to Meade and to Maj. Gen. Benjamin F. Butler. "Brig. Gen. M. R. Patrick, U. S. Vols Provost Marshal General of the Army of the Potomac, is announced as Provost Marshal General of the Armies operating against Richmond, including their lines of Communication with Washington and Baltimore, and will be obeyed and respected accordingly." ALS (telegram sent), DNA, RG 107, Telegrams Collected (Unbound); telegrams received, *ibid.*; (2) *ibid.*, RG 94, War Records Office, Army of the Potomac. *O.R.*, I, xl, part 2, 622. On July 6, 11:00 A.M., Meade telegraphed to USG. "Genl. Patrick has gone to City Point today to see about the additional duties recently assigned to him—I trust it may not be considered necessary for him to remove his Hd. Qrs from here—there—I consider it o̶f̶ essential, that the Prov. Mar. Genl. of this army, whose duties are so intimately connected with its police & discipline, should be permanently at these Hd. Qrs and with the telegraph & deputies I see no reason for the separation of Genl. Patrick.—In the case of the Chief Qr. Mst., his transfer was at my suggestion because I clearly foresaw his duties would require it—It has resulted practically in his complete separation so far as I have any authority or control, and in the selection of a deputy who is in reality the Chief Qr. Mst—Such an arrangement would not in my judgement be convenient in the cases of other staff departments, and I sincerely trust it will not be deemed necessary—" ALS (telegram sent), DNA, RG 393, Army of the Potomac, Miscellaneous Letters Received; *ibid.*, Letters Sent. *O.R.*, I, xl, part 3, 35. On the same day, USG telegraphed to Meade. "Gen. Patrick need not move from your Hd Qrs at least a̶t̶ l̶e̶a̶s̶t̶ not until I see you & give furth[er] orders in the matter. I should visit the front at least every other day but the heat & dust makes it a days work to go up there & back without seeing anything on the lines whilst up there." Telegram received (at 2:40 P.M.), DNA, RG 94, War Records Office, Army of the Potomac; copies, *ibid.*, RG 108, Letters Sent; DLC-USG, V, 45, 59, 67; (2) Meade Papers, PHi. *O.R.*, I, xl, part 3, 35.

At 9:00 P.M., Meade telegraphed to USG. "A Deserter just in reports that day before yesterday an officer of his regiment said he saw on the bulletin board at Richmond a dispatch reporting the defeat of Sherman at Atalanta & his retreat. The same Deserter says he left a Richmond paper of today at the Picket line which announced the capture of Harpers Ferry by Early—I have sent for the paper & will forward it when I get it." ALS (telegram sent), DNA, RG 393, Army of the Potomac, Miscellaneous Letters Received; copies, *ibid.*, Letters Sent; Meade Papers, PHi. *O.R.*, I, xl, part 3, 34. On the same day, USG telegraphed to Meade. "I have rcd a despatch from Harper's Ferry direct dated 12 m. today & no special alarm is felt for the safety of that place. The enemy are crossing however at Antietam ford. This part of the deserter's story is therefore premature and I have no doubt but the other is. I expect it will be ascertained that Johnston retreated to inside his works, at Atlanta, & Sherman has failed in an attack on that place." Telegram received (dated July), DNA, RG 94, War Records Office, Army of the Potomac; copies (2), Meade Papers, PHi. *O.R.*, I, xl, part 3, 34. See *ibid.*, I, xxxvii, part 1, 177. At 10:15 P.M., Meade telegraphed to USG. "I am glad to hear the satisfactory news from Harpers Ferry—I attached no importance to the deserters story in either particular, but as he made the statement, I

thought you ought to be apprised of it.—" ALS (telegram sent), DNA, RG
393, Army of the Potomac, Miscellaneous Letters Received; copies, *ibid.*, Letters
Sent; Meade Papers, PHi. *O.R.*, I, xl, part 3, 34. On July 7, USG telegraphed
to Meade. "I have word from Sherman to 7 P M last evening he is near the
Chattahoochee & has not attempted to cross. This shows the report of the deserter that he had been beaten at Atlanta is without foundation" Telegram
received, DNA, RG 94, War Records Office, Army of the Potomac; copy, *ibid.*,
RG 108, Letters Sent; DLC-USG, V, 45, 59, 67; (2) Meade Papers, PHi. *O.R.*,
I, xl, part 3, 61.

To Brig. Gen. William T. H. Brooks

City Point July 6th 1864

GEN. W. T. H BROOKS
COM'DG 10TH A. C.

Your Letter was received and would have been answered but
that I expected to see you soon and would explain. There has been
a misunderstanding about what I said on the subject of recommendation for promotion   I directed that you should be assigned to
the command of the 10th Corps because you were the senior Officer
with the Army under Gen. Butler and I thought further that you
should have an opportunity of getting back rank which you had before held. I may have stated, what was the fact, that there was no
use of making recommendations for promotion to the rank of Maj.
General whilst Congress was in session because there was no vacancy in the number which the Senate were willing to confirm. The
law allows a Maj. Gen. to each Division and the present limit as I
understand it is an arbitrary one given by the Senate

U. S. GRANT Lt. Genl.

Copies, DLC-USG, V, 45, 59, 67; DNA, RG 108, Letters Sent. *O.R.*, I, xl, part
3, 56. On July 6, 1864, Brig. Gen. William T. H. Brooks telegraphed to Brig.
Gen. John A. Rawlins. "Will you do me the favor to ask the General if he has
received a letter from me within the last ten days—The letter did not require an
answer, but I would like very much to know if it was receivd" ALS (telegram
sent), DNA, RG 107, Telegrams Collected (Unbound). *O.R.*, I, xl, part 3, 55.
On the same day, Brooks telegraphed to USG. "Dispatch received—Sorry to have
troubled you, on such erroneous impressions—" ALS (telegram sent), DNA,
RG 107, Telegrams Collected (Unbound). *O.R.*, I, xl, part 3, 56. Brooks, whose
nomination as maj. gen. was withdrawn on March 23, submitted his resignation

on July 7. ALS, DNA, RG 94, ACP, B1046 CB 1863. On July 10, Brooks wrote to Rawlins. "Will you do me the favor to ask the General if he has acted on the paper handed to him yesterday by Gen Butler—if not—will he not please ~~forward it at once~~ act on it soon" ALS, *ibid.*, War Records Office, Dept. of Va. and N. C., Army of the James, Unentered Papers. *O.R.*, I, xl, part 3, 139. Also on July 10, Maj. Gen. Benjamin F. Butler wrote to Brooks that USG planned to recommend him for maj. gen., but Brooks did not receive the message. *Ibid.*, pp. 139, 172. On July 11, Rawlins telegraphed to Brooks. "No paper was handed the Lt Genl by Genl Butler, that he has any recollection of—" Telegram received, DNA, RG 94, War Records Office, Dept. of Va. and N. C., Army of the James, Unentered Papers. *O.R.*, I, xl, part 3, 171. On the same day, USG endorsed the resignation. "Approved and respectfully forwarded. Gen. Brooks is usually regarded as a very efficient officer but I have heretofore found to retain officers who become dissatisfied and tender their resignations always proves bad for the service. I recommend therefore early action on this." AES, DNA, RG 94, ACP, B1046 CB 1863. On July 14, Secretary of War Edwin M. Stanton accepted the resignation. AES, *ibid.* On July 11, 3:00 P.M., USG telegraphed to Maj. Gen. Henry W. Halleck. "Gen W. T. H. Brooks has tendered his risignation which I approve. If Gen Ord is not already assigned to duty I wish to have him assigned to the command of the 10th Corps and ordered to it as soon as he can be spared" Telegram received (on July 12, 9:00 A.M.), DNA, RG 107, Telegrams Collected (Bound); *ibid.*, Telegrams Collected (Unbound); copies, *ibid.*, RG 108, Letters Sent; DLC-USG, V, 45, 59, 67. *O.R.*, I, xxxvii, part 2, 192; *ibid.*, I, xl, part 3, 144. Maj. Gen. Edward O. C. Ord was detained for the defense of Washington and when he returned to the armies near Richmond was assigned to command the 18th Army Corps. See telegram to Maj. Gen. William F. Smith, July 2, 1864. On July 17, Brooks telegraphed to Rawlins. "I have notice by telegraph that ~~notice of~~ acceptance of my resignation was ~~sent~~ mailed on 14th has it been received at your Hd Qrs—" ALS (telegram sent), DNA, RG 94, War Records Office, Dept. of Va. and N. C., Army of the James, Unentered Papers. *O.R.*, I, xl, part 3, 308. On the following day, Brooks relinquished command of the 10th Army Corps to Brig. Gen. Alfred H. Terry. *Ibid.*, p. 330.

To Gen. Robert E. Lee

Headqrs. Armies of the U. S.
July 7th 1864

GEN R. E. LEE
COMD'G CONFED. ARMY
GENERAL,

Mrs Sackett the wife of Col Wm Sackett,[1] who was wounded on the 11th of June near Trevillian Station Va, is here in deep distress, and feeling great anxiety to learn the fate of her husband.

Col Sackett was left at a house some two and a half miles from the station, in charge of Surgeon Ray U. S. Vols.[2]

If you can let me know the fate and present whereabouts of Col Sackett, you will alleviate the anxiety of his wife and family. I will add that it always has, and always will, afford me pleasure to releive the minds of persons in the South, having friends North, Either by forwarding open letters to them or by ascertaining where they are, their condition &c.—

Mrs Sackett is very desirous that I should ask you for permission to visit her husband if he is still alive. She would not Expect to go through Richmond but would start from Alexandria, by private conveyance, if authorized to do so.

> I have the honor to be
> with great respect
> Your Obt. Svt.
> U. S. Grant
> Lt. Gen.

Copies, DLC-USG, V, 45, 59, 67; DNA, RG 108, Letters Sent. *O.R.*, I, xl, part 3, 60.

On July 1, 1864, 10:00 P.M., Maj. Gen. George G. Meade had telegraphed to USG. "I have received a letter from Mrs. Wadsworth the widow of Genl. Wadsworth, enclosing one for Genl. R. E. Lee asking the return of certain articles found on the General's person.—As I do not feel authorised to send a flag of truce, without your sanction during your presence in the field, the subject is respectfully referred to you." ALS (telegram sent), DNA, RG 393, Army of the Potomac, Miscellaneous Letters Received; telegram received, *ibid.*, RG 108, Letters Received. *O.R.*, I, xl, part 2, 561. On the same day, USG telegraphed to Meade. "I do not think it a fit time just now to send Mrs Wadsworth Communication through but the first time a flag is being sent for any other purpose it can go" Telegram received, DNA, RG 94, War Records Office, Army of the Potomac; copies (2), Meade Papers, PHi. *O.R.*, I, xl, part 2, 561.

On July 7, USG telegraphed to Meade. "I shall send a flag of truce through to Gen Lee this evening   If you will forward Mrs. Wadsworths letter here I will send it along—" Telegram received (at 12:20 P.M.), DNA, RG 94, War Records Office, Army of the Potomac; copies, *ibid.*, RG 108, Letters Sent; DLC-USG, V, 45, 59, 67; (2) Meade Papers, PHi. At 1:00 P.M., Meade telegraphed to USG. "The letter of Mrs. Wadsworth's letter for General Lee will at once be transmitted to you" Copy (telegram sent), DNA, RG 393, Army of the Potomac, Miscellaneous Letters Received; copy, *ibid.*, Letters Sent. On the same day, USG twice telegraphed to Maj. Gen. Benjamin F. Butler. "Col Porter of my staff is just leaving here with letters to send through by Flag of Truce including a letter from me to Gen Lee. Please have them forwarded through such part of the line as you deem most advisable. Please send a horse to Pt of Rocks for Col Porter." Telegram received (at 6:10 P.M.), DLC-Benjamin F. Butler; copies, DLC-USG, V, 45, 59, 67; DNA, RG 108, Letters Sent. "Can you inform me where Col Cole 2d Colored Cavy now is—His brother is here & desires to see him." Telegram received (at 6:10 P.M.), DLC-Benjamin F. Butler; copy, DLC-USG, V, 67. On the same day, Capt. Alfred F. Puffer, aide to Butler, telegraphed to USG. "Gen Butler is ~~absent from Hdqr~~ out on the line. 2d U. S. Cols Cavly. is about a mile to the right of Gen. Smith's Hdqrs. The horse will be waiting for Col. Porter" ALS (telegram sent), DNA, RG 94, War Records Office, Dept. of Va. and N. C., Army of the James, Unentered Papers; copy, *ibid.*, RG 393, Dept. of Va. and N. C., Telegrams Sent. On July 10, Gen. Robert E. Lee wrote to USG. "Your letters with reference to Mrs. Wadsworth and Mrs. Sackett are received. I have directed inquiries to be made for the effects of the late General Wadsworth, and if they can be found will take great pleasure in restoring them to his widow. I have also taken measures to ascertain the condition, and whereabouts of Colonel Sackett, and the information you ask shall be conveyed to you as soon as it can be ascertained. I regret, however, that it is not in my power to permit Mrs. Sackett to visit her husband at this time. The reasons that induce me to withhold my consent are applicable to the route she proposes to take, as indicated by you." *O.R.*, I, xl, part 3, 125.

1. Col. William H. Sackett, 9th N. Y. Cav., died on June 14 of wounds received three days earlier at the battle of Trevilian Station, Va.
2. Probably Asst. Surgeon Robert Rae, 1st N. Y. Dragoons, captured at the battle of Trevilian Station.

To Maj. Gen. Henry W. Halleck

H'd Qrs City Pt V[a.]
July 7. [*1864.*]

MAJ. GEN HALLECK
CHF STAFF.

The number of dismounted Cavalry sent from here reaches nearly 3.000 men: the whole force sent about 9.000   Will it not answer your purposes to retain the artillery you were preparing to send here, to distribute among the one hundred day men instead of sending back a regt of Heavy artly?

It breaks up a brigade to send [one] of th[es]e large regts now.

The dismounted Cavy took with them such arms & accoutrements as they had but they were not completely armed.

Won't Gen Couch[1] do well to command until Hunter reaches?

All of Sigel's operations from the beginning of the war have been so unsuccessful that I think it advisable to relieve him from all duty, at least until present troubles are over.

I do not feel certain at any time that he will not after abandoning stores, artillery & trains, make a successful retreat to some safe place.

U. S. GRANT
Lt. Genl.

Telegram received (at 9:00 P.M.), DNA, RG 107, Telegrams Collected (Bound); copies, *ibid.*, RG 108, Letters Sent; DLC-USG, V, 45, 59, 67. *O.R.*, I, xxxvii, part 2, 98; *ibid.*, I, xl, part 3, 59. The last two sentences were entered in USG's letterbooks as a separate telegram. See telegram to Maj. Gen. Henry W. Halleck, July 6, 1864.

1. Darius N. Couch, born in N. Y., USMA 1846, resigned from the U.S. Army as of April 30, 1855, to become a merchant in New York City (1855–57) and a manufacturer in Mass. (1858–61). Entering the Civil War as col., 7th Mass., he was appointed brig. gen. to rank from May 17, 1861, and maj. gen. to rank from July 4, 1862. Health problems and dissatisfaction with the course of the war led him to request reassignment from the Army of the Potomac, and he commanded the Dept. of the Susquehanna from June 11, 1863, until Dec. 1, 1864.

To Maj. Gen. George G. Meade

———

By Telegraph from City Point
Dated July 7, 11 P. M. *1864.*

To MAJOR GEN MEADE

In making regular approaches would it not be well to avoid making any at the salient where Gen Barnard[1] gave it as his opinion that a successful assault could be made if one could be made at all—

U S GRANT
Lt Gen

Telegram received, DNA, RG 94, War Records Office, Army of the Potomac; copies, *ibid.*, RG 108, Letters Sent; DLC-USG, V, 45, 59, 67; (2) Meade Papers, PHi. *O.R.*, I, xl, part 3, 62. On July 7, 1864, 11:20 P.M., Maj. Gen. George G. Meade telegraphed to USG. "Genl. Barnard never communicated any opinion to me—I presume however you & he refer to the salient on the Jerusalem plank road. If so this is the best point for a regular approach—indeed it is essential it should be taken, before a lodgment in any other part of the line, if made, could be main-

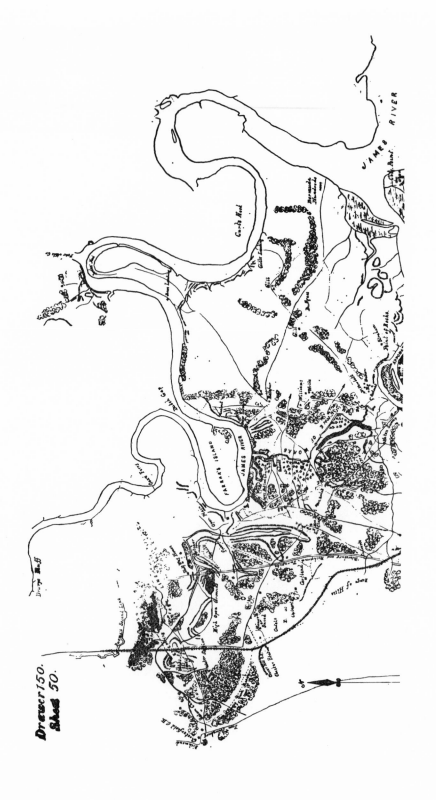

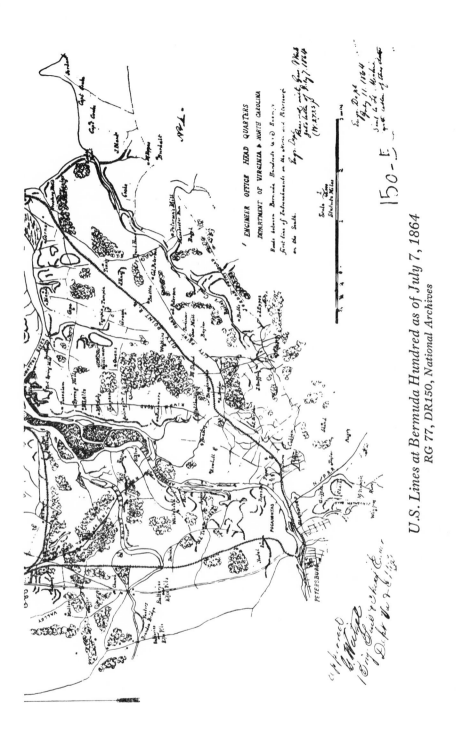

U.S. Lines at Bermuda Hundred as of July 7, 1864
RG 77, DR150, National Archives

tained—I will send you tomorrow early a report with a sketch.—" ALS (telegram sent), DNA, RG 393, Army of the Potomac, Miscellaneous Letters Received; telegram received, *ibid.*, RG 108, Letters Received. *O.R.*, I, xl, part 3, 62. On the same day, Meade wrote to USG. "I transmit herewith the report of the Chief of Artilley & the Actg. Chief Engineer made in pursuance of an order to reconnoiter the enemys position in front of the lines of this army. You will see from the accompanying sketh, that the point, where the mine now being dug by Maj. Genl. Burnside, is to be exploded, is ~~rev~~ taken ~~in~~ somewhat in reverse by the guns in the salient of the work near the Gregory house on the plank road—It therefore becomes necessary to effect a lodgement in this salient before the mine can be exploded—In order to obtain troops to relieve those in the trenches & also to have a reserve, it is proposed in case regular approaches are made to occupy the line of redoubts & breastworks as indicated on the sketch—This will effectually cover the left flank of the army & leave at least a corps in reserve. These redoubts are in process of construction, and the materials for regular approaches being collected, but no work as yet undertaken beyond the running of the gallery for the mine—Further operations will be dependant on your orders.—It is proper I should advise you that in my judgement the operations proposed will be slow & tedious— that we shall perhaps have to take several lines before reaching the Appomatox— that then we shall have this river to cross & subsequently Swift run—all of which would be turned & avoided, should regular approaches be successfully made from the Bermuda Hundred front—Please advise me at your earliest convenience, if you desire the operations commenced here, against the salient on the Plank road.—" ALS, DNA, RG 108, Letters Received. *O.R.*, I, xl, part 3, 61. The enclosure is *ibid.*, I, xl, part 1, 285.

At 9:30 A.M., Meade had telegraphed to USG. "I have nothing of importance to report during the last 24 hours. A mortar battery of 8. in pieces has been established on the front of the 9th corps—and redoubts for the protection of the left flank of the trenches & the army have been commenced on the line of the 5th corps—also the preparation of materials for the regular approaches, about to be made.—" ALS (telegram sent), DNA, RG 393, Army of the Potomac, Miscellaneous Letters Received; telegram received, *ibid.*, RG 108, Letters Received. *O.R.*, I, xl, part 3, 60–61.

On the same day, Brig. Gen. John A. Rawlins telegraphed to Meade. "Battery F 5th U S Arty Capt Martin Comdg was intended for the 18th Army Corps & orders to so report have been given it." Telegram received, DNA, RG 94, War Records Office, Army of the Potomac; copies, *ibid.*, RG 108, Letters Sent; DLC-USG, V, 45, 59, 67. The text was also included in Special Orders No. 51, July 7. Copies, DLC-USG, V, 57, 62, 67. *O.R.*, I, xl, part 3, 60.

Also on July 7, 8:00 A.M., Asst. Secretary of War Charles A. Dana telegraphed to Secretary of War Edwin M. Stanton that Meade's bad temper, bad judgment, and criticism of Brig. Gen. James H. Wilson had brought USG to the brink of a decision to relieve Meade and replace him with Maj. Gen. Winfield S. Hancock. Telegram received, DLC-Edwin M. Stanton. *O.R.*, I, xl, part 1, 35–36.

1. On July 5, Col. Edward D. Townsend telegraphed to USG. "The Secretary of War directs that Brigadier General J. G. Barnard be relieved from his present duties and ordered to report in person without delay to the Chief of Engineers in this City. Please acknowledge receipt" ALS (telegram sent), DNA,

RG 107, Telegrams Collected (Unbound); telegrams received (2), *ibid.*; *ibid.*, RG 108, Letters Received. Printed as sent on July 4 in *O.R.*, I, xl, part 2, 619. On the same day, 11:00 P.M., USG telegraphed to Townsend. "Despatch directing Brig Gen J G Barnard to be ordered to report to Chief Engineer received. Orders will sent to Genl Barnard accordingly" Telegram received (on July 6, 7:00 P.M.), DNA, RG 94, Letters Received, 652A 1864; *ibid.*, RG 107, Telegrams Collected (Bound); *ibid.*, Telegrams Collected (Unbound); copies, *ibid.*, Telegrams Received in Cipher; *ibid.*, RG 108, Letters Sent; DLC-USG, V, 45, 59, 67. See telegram to Maj. Gen. Henry W. Halleck, July 20, 1864.

To Julia Dent Grant

City Point, Va. July 7th *1864.*

DEAR JULIA,

I received two letters from you this evening, written after you had received mine stating that you could come to Fortress Monroe to spend the Summer. I am satisfied it is best you should not come. It would be expensive to furnish a house there and difficult supplying it afterwards. The camp life we are leading you would not be able to be where I am often and then only to come up and go immediately back, with an express boat that might be running at the time.

I wrote to you in my last why not make the same arrangement for the children as last year? Permanency is a great thing for children at school and you could not have a better home for them than with Louisa Boggs. If they were with her I should always feel easy for you to leave them for two or three months to stay with me if I was where you could possibly be with me. I want the children to prossecute their studies, and especially in languages. Speaking languages is a much greater accomplishment than the little parapharnalias of society such as music, dancing &c. I would have no objection to music being added to Nellies studies but with the boys I would never have it occupy one day of their time, or thought.

If you think it advisable to go some place where you can keep the children with you, and where they will be at a good school, I will not object. But I cannot settle for you where such a place would be, probably the City of St. Louis would be as good as any other, for the present. Love and Kisses for yourself and the children. How much I wish I could see you all.

ULYS.

ALS, DLC-USG.

To Gen. Robert E. Lee

———

Headqrs &c

City Point Va. July 8th 1864

GEN R. E. LEE,
COMD'G CONFED. FORCES
NEAR PETERSBURG, VA.
GENERAL,

I would request that Col. Jas. F. Jaquess[1] 73 Ills. Vol. Infantry and J. R. Gillmore Esq,[2] be allowed to meet Col Robt. Ould, Commissioner for the exchange of Prisoners at such place between the lines of the two Armies as you may designate—The object of the meeting is legitimate with the duties of Col Ould as Commissioner

If not consistent for you to grant the request here asked, I would beg that this be referred to President Davis for his action—

Requesting as early an answer to this communication as you may find it convenient to make,

I subscribe myself

Very Respectfully

Your Obt. Svt.

U. S. GRANT

Lt. Gen. U. S. A.

Copies, DLC-USG, V, 45, 59, 67; DNA, RG 108, Letters Sent; USG 3. *O.R.*, I, xl, part 3, 74–75; *ibid.*, II, vii, 447; *O.R.* (Navy), II, iii, 1190–91. On July 6, 1864, President Abraham Lincoln may have written to USG. "Will General Grant allow J. R. Gillmore and friend to pass our lines, with ordinary baggage, and go South?" Lincoln, *Works*, VII, 429. On July 8, Capt. Ely S. Parker wrote to Maj. Gen. Benjamin F. Butler. "The Lieut Genl. Comd'g sends herewith a letter addressed to Gen. R. E. Lee &c, and desires that you will send the same by Flag of Truce as early as possible." ALS, DLC-Benjamin F. Butler. On the same day, 8:10 P.M., Butler telegraphed to USG. "Your letter to Gen Lee was received by me and duly forwarded, being received by Lieut Bowling of the 9th Va Infty at about 7.30 P. M.—who promised that it should at once be forwarded to Gen Lee—" LS (telegram sent), DNA, RG 107, Telegrams Collected (Unbound). *O.R.*, I, xl, part 3, 81. On July 10, Gen. Robert E. Lee wrote to USG. "I have the honor to acknowledge the receipt of your letter of the 8th instant, requesting that an interview take place between Col. James F. Jaquess and J. R. Gilmore, esq., and Col. Robert Ould, commissioner for the exchange of prisoners. I will submit the communication to the Secretary of War and you will be duly informed of his decision. Should the proposition be acceded to, the time and place most convenient for the meeting will be made known to you." *Ibid.*, II, vii, 452. See telegram to Maj. Gen. Benjamin F. Butler, July 11, 1864. On July 12, 6:45 P.M. and 7:05 P.M., Butler telegraphed to USG. "I have the honor to enclose a package received by Flag of Truce, in the manner shown by the enclosed note to Gen Brooks, together with a Richmond paper of this morning—Col Jaquess and Mr Gilmore are here, awaiting any answer if it concerns them—I have received no answer from my Flag of this morning—The bearer will await an answer from you if you do not choose to send it by telegraph—" "Since writing my first communication I have received the enclosed from Deep Bottom which I take it covers the whole matter in question, and have returned the following answer. BRIG GEN FOSTER Comdg Deep Bottom   Please inform Mr Ould that Col Jaquess and Mr. Gillmore will meet him at the time & place proposed—one o'clock Thursday the 14th at Buffin's house between Deep Bottom and Chapin's Farm—" LS (telegrams sent), DNA, RG 393, Dept. of Va. and N. C., Telegrams Sent (Press). *O.R.*, I, xl, part 3, 201, 202. See *ibid.*, pp. 201–2. On the same day, USG telegraphed to Butler. "The Communications from Gen Lee, & Col Ould, the latter of which you have seen, are both on the same subject. Your action in the matter is satisfactory." Telegram received (at 10:25 P.M.), DLC-Benjamin F. Butler; copies, DLC-USG, V, 45, 59, 67; (2) USG 3; DNA, RG 108, Letters Sent. *O.R.*, I, xl, part 3, 201. On July 19, 10:00 P.M., Butler telegraphed to USG. "The commissioners, Jaquess and Gilmore, have returned. Were received by Davis, but the only terms were independence or fight. They go to Washington tomorrow. I send you the Richmond papers, by which you will learn that you died Saturday." *Ibid.*, p. 340.

1. James F. Jaquess, born near Evansville, Ind., Nov. 18, 1819, graduated from Indiana Asbury University in 1845, passed the bar in 1846, and entered the Methodist ministry in 1847. In 1848, he became president of Illinois Female Academy in Jacksonville, Ill., and, in 1854, moved to Quincy, Ill., as president of Quincy College. He was appointed chaplain, 6th Ill. Cav., as of Aug. 28, 1861, and col., 73rd Ill., as of Aug. 2, 1862. In the spring of 1863, Jaquess believed that he could convince C.S.A. President Jefferson Davis to end the war. With the assistance of James R. Gilmore, he secured a leave of absence to go to Richmond in July although Lincoln would not give the mission official sanction. Unable to see Davis, he returned to his regt. in time to participate in the battle of Chattanooga. In 1864, Jaquess's idea to meet with Davis was revived by Gilmore.

See Edward C. Kirkland, *The Peacemakers of 1864* (New York, 1927), pp. 87–96; Lincoln, *Works*, VI, 225, 236, 329; VII, 429, 461.

2. Gilmore, born in Boston, Sept. 10, 1822, established a shipping and cotton business in New York City. He retired in 1857, becoming a prolific writer. A friend of Horace Greeley, he traveled to Tenn. in spring, 1863, to sound out Maj. Gen. William S. Rosecrans about running against Lincoln. Gilmore met Jaquess, and at Rosecrans's request, presented the idea of a peace mission to Lincoln, in the process converting to an admirer of Lincoln. Gilmore persuaded Lincoln in 1864 to sanction another attempt to meet unofficially with Davis. For the failure of the mission, see Kirkland, pp. 93–96.

To Maj. Gen. Henry W. Halleck

Gen Grants Hd Qrs
July 8th 1864—6 p m

MAJ GEN H W HALLECK
CHF OF STAFF

I would feel much greater confidence when Genl Ord commanded than when Genl Gillmore did—The former I know to be skillful in the management of troops, and brave and prompt—the latter I do not know so much about—

I do not wish however to change any order that may have been made—

U. S. GRANT
Lt Gen

Telegram received (on July 9, 1864, 7:45 A.M.), DNA, RG 107, Telegrams Collected (Bound); copies, *ibid.*, RG 108, Letters Sent; DLC-USG, V, 45, 59, 67. *O.R.*, I, xxxvii, part 2, 119. On July 8, 8:30 A.M., USG telegraphed to Maj. Gen. Henry W. Halleck. "Genl Ord is here in good health. I can send him to take Gen Sigels place at once. Shall I send him—Please answer" Telegram received (at 1:30 P.M.), DNA, RG 107, Telegrams Collected (Bound); copies, *ibid.*, RG 108, Letters Sent; DLC-USG, V, 45, 59, 67. *O.R.*, I, xxxvii, part 2, 118. See telegram to Maj. Gen. Henry W. Halleck, July 6, 1864. On July 9, Capt. Ely S. Parker issued Special Orders No. 52 sending Maj. Gen. Edward O. C. Ord to Washington to report to Halleck. Copies, DLC-USG, V, 57, 62, 67. *O.R.*, I, xxxvii, part 2, 136; *ibid.*, I, xl, part 3, 93. On July 8, 7:00 P.M., USG telegraphed to Halleck. "Two Battalion of the Ninth 9 New York Heavy Artillery are now with the Division of troops sent to Baltimore. Order them to Washington. The third Battalion will be sent direct to Washington at once—" Telegram received (marked as sent at 6:30 P.M., received on July 9, 7:40 A.M.),

DNA, RG 107, Telegrams Collected (Bound); copies, *ibid.*, RG 108, Letters Sent; DLC-USG, V, 45, 59, 67. *O.R.*, I, xxxvii, part 2, 119.

At 2:30 P.M. and 10:30 P.M., Halleck telegraphed to USG. "Genl Canby telegraphs from New Orleans July 2d that over six thousand men would embark that day and would reach Fort Monroe from the 8th to the 10th. Six thousand more would be ready as soon as transports arrived, & that the whole number to be sent will be twenty thousand. Ricketts division arrived at Baltimore & sent forward to the Monocacy. Dismounted cavalry oreded here for remounts, but none yet arrived. Genl Sheridan says 2496 of those sent are sick. If so, we shall have but five hundred for the field. Hunter's army moves so slow & the Railroad is so broken up that I fear he will be too late to give us much aid. Enemy around Maryland Heights, at Hagerstown, Boonsboro, & Middletown, and threatening Frederick. Also guerrillas at Brookville threatening Washington & Baltimore Road. There has been considerable alarm in Washington, Baltimore & Pennsylvania." "Latest dispatches state that heavy column of enemy have crossed the Monocacy & is moving on Urbana. Sigel & Couch say that scouts, prisoners & country people confirm ~~his~~ previous reports of enemy's force, that is, some twenty or thirty thousand. Until more forces arrive we have nothing to meet that number in the field, and the militia are not reliable even to hold the fortifications of Washington & Baltimore. It is the impression that one third of Lee's entire force is with Early & Breckinridge, & that Ransom has some three or four thousand cavalry. None of the cavalry sent up by you has arrived, nor do we get any thing from Hunter. Troops sent from James River should come here, not to Baltimore, where they cannot be supplied or equipped. If you propose to cut off this raid, and not merely to secure our depots, we must have more forces here. Indeed, if the enemy's strength is as great as represented it is doubtful if the militia can hold all of our defences. I do not think that we can expect much from Hunter. He is too far off & moves too slowly. I think therefore that very considerable reinforcements should be sent directly to this place." ALS (telegrams sent), DNA, RG 107, Telegrams Collected (Bound); telegrams received, *ibid.*; (incomplete) *ibid.*, Telegrams Collected (Unbound); *ibid.*, RG 108, Letters Received. *O.R.*, I, xxxvii, part 2, 119–20. The first is *ibid.*, I, xl, part 3, 72.

To Maj. Gen. George G. Meade

City Point July 8th/64 [*11:30* A.M.]

MAJ. GEN. MEADE,

Col. Comstock is going out this morning and will explain to you my idea. If the approaches are made it will be with the view of ultimately making an assault on the enemy's lines, but I have always hoped to go through in Butler's front so as to carry the North bank of Swift Creek. This however cannot be done until the 19th

Corps arrives without giving up to much ground that we have already fought for. This would make no difference except in case of failure to get through to Swift Creek. The advantages of commencing our regular approaches on your front now would simply be that we would be that far advanced if we were compelled at last to advance in that way, and it would tend to divert the enemy from the proposed advance in Butler's front. We ought by all means to cut the Weldon road so as to make it useless to the enemy. I think Wright's two Divisions should take the place of Hancock's Corps and the latter should report support the Cavalry whilst it destroys the road down as far as Hicksford. The preparation for this I think should be made at once so as to start from your left by the night of the 10th.

U. S. GRANT
Lt Gen.

ALS (telegram sent), PPRF; telegram received, DNA, RG 94, War Records Office, Army of the Potomac. *O.R.*, I, xl, part 3, 72–73. On July 8, 1864, 10:15 A.M., Maj. Gen. George G. Meade telegraphed to USG. "There was considerable artillery & musketry firing in front of the 9. corps last night—principally the enemy who seem to suspect the operations there—Maj. Genl. Burnsides reports that the enemys mortars are beginning to annoy him.—The work on the redoubts to the left & rear of the 5th corps is progressing rapidly.—The signal officers report a train of cars, with materials as going out of Petersburgh this morning on the Weldon R. Rd—towards Reams station and there is no doubt from the report of deserters & refugees that the enemy are repairing this road, their working parties protected by their cavalry force with infantry supports.—" ALS (telegram sent), DNA, RG 393, Army of the Potomac, Miscellaneous Letters Received; telegram received, *ibid.*, RG 108, Letters Received. *O.R.*, I, xl, part 3, 72.

At noon, Meade telegraphed to USG. "The order sending sutlers to the rear issued by me before crossing the Rapidann, has never been rescinded. The objection to permitting them to come to the front is the necessity either of allowing them the use of govt. wagons to bring their goods from City Point, or else permitting them to bring their own wagons, thus increasing the animals to be fed & the number of wagons using the roads some 3 or 400—Another objection is the uncertainty of our position & the difficulty of getting rid of them in the event of a sudden movement.—Situated as I am I neither feel that I have the full authority to act in this matter nor the proper information to enable me to act advisedly, without a reference to you—I would therefore be glad to have your idea upon this point—There are many articles, only to be procured from the sutlers, which are necessary to the mens comfort, and which they are now in want of & I think it would be well to let the sutlers come if it is practicable.—" ALS (telegram sent), DNA, RG 393, Army of the Potomac, Miscellaneous Letters Received; telegram received, *ibid.*, RG 108, Letters Received. *O.R.*, I, xl, part 3, 73. On the same day, USG telegraphed to Meade. "You are authorized to exercise your own judgement about allowing sutlers with the army & the manner of getting their goods to the front" Telegram received, DNA, RG 94, War Records Office, Army of the Potomac; copies, *ibid.*, RG 108, Letters Sent; DLC-USG, V, 45, 59, 67; (2) Meade Papers, PHi. *O.R.*, I, xl, part 3, 73.

At 5:50 P.M., Meade telegraphed to USG. "Burnside & Warren report the enemy opening their batteries on them, also on Smiths—front—some little musketry with Burnside—The object not known.—" ALS (telegram sent), DNA, RG 393, Army of the Potomac, Miscellaneous Letters Received; telegram received, *ibid.*, RG 108, Letters Received. *O.R.*, I, xl, part 3, 74.

Also on July 8, Brig. Gen. John A. Rawlins telegraphed to Meade. "Several days since the Lt Gen Comdg telegraphed to Washington to have sent here for the 9th A C two Batteries by name particularly designated neither of which has arrived so far as any information has been recvd here. You will therefore assign the 3rd Maine Battery to the 9th A C in lieu of those telegraphed for" Telegram received, DNA, RG 94, War Records Office, Army of the Potomac; copies, *ibid.*, RG 108, Letters Sent; DLC-USG, V, 45, 59, 67; (2) Meade Papers, PHi. *O.R.*, I, xl, part 3, 74. On the same day, USG telegraphed to Meade. "Was there any Heavy Artillery Regiment in the Division sent North under Gen Ricketts. If not, one will have to be sent to Washington without delay. There are no troops in the trenches about Washington who know any thing about Artillery, and I have now received two dispatches to return one of the Heavy Artillery regiments—" Telegram received (at 5:10 P.M., incomplete), DNA, RG 94, War Records Office, Army of the Potomac; copies, *ibid.*, RG 108, Letters Sent; DLC-USG, V, 45, 59, 67; (2) Meade Papers, PHi. Printed as sent at 5:10 P.M. in *O.R.*, I, xl, part 3, 73. At 6:00 P.M., Meade telegraphed to USG. "Two battalions of the 9th New York heavy Artillery accompanied Ricketts' Division—The remaining battalion will at once be ordered to Washington—This regiment is probably as familiar with Artillery as any we have." Copies, DNA, RG 393, Army of the Potomac, Miscellaneous Letters Received; *ibid.*, Letters Sent; Meade Papers, PHi. *O.R.*, I, xl, part 3, 74.

To Gideon Welles

City Point Va. July 9th *1864*.

HON. G. WELLES,
SEC. OF THE NAVY,
DEAR SIR;

Your letter of the 30th ultimo, with one from your son of same date, is but this moment received.

The first duty for your son is to report to the regiment to which he has been appointed and be mustered into service. If he will report to me on his arrival here I will take great pleasure in advising him what to do, and also in assigning him to the class of duties he is desirous of performing.

> With great respect,
> your obt. svt.
> U. S. GRANT
> Lt. Gen.

ALS, Connecticut Historical Society, Hartford, Conn. Thomas G. Welles, eighteen-year-old son of Secretary of the Navy Gideon Welles, who had resigned from the U.S. Naval Academy, was appointed 2nd lt., 1st Conn. Cav., as of July 11, 1864, apparently with an understanding that he would serve as a staff officer. Howard K. Beale, ed., *Diary of Gideon Welles* (New York, 1960), II, 71, 82; John Niven, *Gideon Welles: Lincoln's Secretary of the Navy* (New York, 1973), pp. 441, 461.

To Brig. Gen. Montgomery C. Meigs

City Point July 9th 1864 [*9* A.M.]

GEN. M. C. MEIGS Q. M. GEN. WASHINGTON.

I can see no earthly object in opening the M. & C. rail-road. Dont know where the troops are to come from to guard it if it was open. Who makes the requisition for rolling stock and material for it? To supply Shermans army we now have two roads as far as the Ten. river. Working the M. & C. road would give us three roads to the same point after which all supplies ~~would~~ from the three roads would have to pass over a single road. Unless there is some object in view that I do not see I would not approve putting any work on that road.

> U. S. GRANT
> Lt. Gen.

ALS (telegram sent), PPRF; telegram received, DNA, RG 92, Office of Military Railroads, Letters Received; (at 2:00 P.M.) *ibid.*, RG 107, Telegrams Collected (Bound); *ibid.*, Telegrams Collected (Unbound). On July 8, 1864, Brig. Gen. Montgomery C. Meigs telegraphed to USG. "Requisitions are made for rolling stock & materials to open in great haste, seventy five (75) miles & perhaps more of the Memphis & Charleston Rail-Road from Memphis. I thought you directed as much as possible of the iron of these roads to be taken up & the rolling stock sent to Tennessee & Georgia. We have lately lost a number of Rail-road trains in Georgia & Tennessee—& find it difficult to provide Engines & cars—The monthly pay roll of the Rail-Road Service in the Division of the Mississippi under Gen Sherman now Exceeds five hundred thousand dollars. Materials & stock also cost heavily   Shall the attempt be made to furnish rolling stock materials for reopening this portion of the Memphis & Charleston Rail-Road? This Department will of course be governed by your decision"   ALS (telegram sent), *ibid.*, RG 92, Miscellaneous Telegrams Sent (Press); *ibid.*, RG 107, Telegrams Collected (Unbound); telegram received, *ibid.*; *ibid.*, RG 108, Letters Received. On July 9, Col. Charles Thomas, deputy q. m. gen., wrote to USG transmitting a copy of Meigs's telegram. LS, *ibid.*, RG 92, Miscellaneous Letters Sent (Press); *ibid.*, RG 108, Letters Received. See *O.R.*, I, xxxix, part 2, 208.

To Maj. Gen. Henry W. Halleck

(Cipher)   City Point July 9th/64
MAJ. GEN. HALLECK, WASHINGTON
    If you think ~~them~~ it necessary order the 19th Corps as it arrives at Fortress Monroe to Washington. About the 18th or 20th is the time I should like to have a large force here, but if the rebel force now North can be captured or destroyed I would willingly postpone aggressive operations to destroy them and could send in a~~l~~ddition to the 19th Corps the balance of the 6th Corps.
                                                                         U. S. GRANT
                                                                         Lt. Gen.

ALS (telegram sent), OClWHi; telegram received (marked as sent at noon, received at 7:30 P.M.), DNA, RG 107, Telegrams Collected (Bound); *ibid.*, Telegrams Collected (Unbound). *O.R.*, I, xxxvii, part 2, 133; *ibid.*, I, xl, part 3, 92. On July 9, 1864, 12:30 P.M., Maj. Gen. Henry W. Halleck telegraphed to USG. "If Genl Canby's troops arrive in time, I respectfully suggest that they be sent here without disembarking at Fort Monroe. Only one division of Hunter's army has passed cumberland; his advance is at Cherry Run. Low water in the Ohio river is given as the cause of delay. Rhode's division is said to be with Breckenridge. No important change reported since my telegram of last evening." ALS (telegram sent), DNA, RG 107, Telegrams Collected (Bound); telegram received, *ibid.*; *ibid.*, Telegrams Collected (Unbound); (marked as sent at 1:00 P.M.), *ibid.*, RG 108, Letters Received. Printed as sent at 1:00 P.M. in *O.R.*, I, xxxvii, part 2, 133; *ibid.*, I, xl, part 3, 91–92. On the same day, USG telegraphed to the commanding officer, Fort Monroe. "Please inform me by telegraph of the arrival of the first transport of the advance of the nineteenth (19th) Army Corps from New Orleans"   Telegram received (at 6:00 P.M.), DNA, RG 94, War Records Office, Dept. of Va. and N. C., Army of the James,

Unentered Papers; copies, *ibid.*, RG 108, Letters Sent; DLC-USG, V, 45, 59, 67. *O.R.*, I, xxxvii, part 2, 136; *ibid.*, I, xl, part 3, 119.

To Maj. Gen. Henry W. Halleck

City Point Va.
July 9th 1864 5 30 P M 1864

MAJ GEN H. W. HALLECK
CHIEF OF STAFF.

I have ordered the remainder of the 6th Corps to Washington—On account of scarcity of transportation I do not send wagons or Artillery but they will follow if you say it is wanted. I think most of the three thousand (3000) Cavalry sent are fit for duty—They certainly must have reached Baltimore with the other troops   If the 19th Corps reaches Ft Monroe in time you can take it also if you deem it advisable

U. S. GRANT
Lt Genl

Telegram received (on July 10, 1864, 1:30 P.M.), DNA, RG 107, Telegrams Collected (Bound); *ibid.*, Telegrams Collected (Unbound); copies, *ibid.*, RG 108, Letters Sent; DLC-USG, V, 45, 59, 67. *O.R.*, I, xxxvii, part 2, 134; *ibid.*, I, xl, part 3, 92. On July 9, 1864, 11:00 P.M., Maj. Gen. Henry W. Halleck telegraphed to USG. "As arrival of 19th corps is very uncertain, I think remainder of 6th corps should be sent to this place. I have ordered all troops from the north to be stopt at Baltimore for defence of that city"   ALS (telegram sent), DNA, RG 107, Telegrams Collected (Bound); telegram received, *ibid.*; *ibid.*, Telegrams Collected (Unbound); *ibid.*, RG 108, Letters Received. *O.R.*, I, xxxvii, part 2, 135; *ibid.*, I, xl, part 3, 93.

To Maj. Gen. Henry W. Halleck

(Cipher)   City Point Va. July 9th *1864*
MAJ. GEN. HALLECK, WASHINGTON,

Force enough to defeat all that Early has with him should get in his rear, South of him, and follow him up sharply, leaving him to go North,—defending, depots, towns &c., with small garrisons

and the Militia. If the President thinks it advisabl[e] that I should
go to Washington in person I can start in an hour after receiving
notice leaving everything here on the defensive.

U. S. GRANT

Lt. Gen.

ALS (telegram sent), IHi; telegram received (sent at 6:00 P.M., received July
10, 1864, 1:05 P.M.), DNA, RG 107, Telegrams Collected (Bound). *O.R.*, I,
xxxvii, part 2, 134; *ibid.*, I, xl, part 3, 92. On July 10, 2:00 P.M., President
Abraham Lincoln telegraphed to USG. "Your despatch to Gen. Halleck, refering
to what I may think in the present emergency, is shown me—Gen. Halleck says
we have absolutely no force here fit to go to the field. He thinks that with the
hundred day-men, and invalids we have here, we ~~may possibly~~ ~~but not certainly~~
can defend Washngington, and scarcely Baltimore. Besides these, there are about
eight thousand not very reliable, under Howe at Harper's Ferry, with Hunter
approaching that point very slowly, with what number I suppose you know better than I. Wallace with some odds and ends, and part of what came up with
Ricketts, was so badly beaten yesterday at Monocacy, that what is left ~~of it~~ can
attempt no more than to defend Baltimore. What we shall get in from Penn. &
N. Y. will scarcely be worth counting, I fear. Now what I think is that you
should provide to retain your hold where you are certainly, and bring the rest
with you personally, and make a vigorous effort to destroy the enemie's force in
this vicinity. I think there is really a fair chance to do ~~it~~. this if the movement
is prompt. This is what I think, upon your suggestion, and is not an order"   ALS
(telegram sent), DNA, RG 107, Telegrams Collected (Bound); telegram received (marked as sent at 2:30 P.M.), *ibid.*, RG 108, Letters Received. *O.R.*, I,
xxxvii, part 2, 155; *ibid.*, I, xl, part 3, 121. Lincoln, *Works*, VII, 437. See telegram to Abraham Lincoln, July 10, 1864. On July 9, 9:00 P.M., Maj. Gen.
Henry W. Halleck telegraphed to USG. "A despatch, not signed by Genl L.
Wallace, but approved by him, to the newspaper press, states that they had a
severe battle to day near Monocacy bridge & that our troops were defeated and
are now retreating on the Baltimore road. Knowing the character of the source
you can judge of its reliability. Nothing further from Hunter. I do not deem it
safe to withdraw any forces from Harpers Ferry till he forms a junction. Please
inform me what forces besides Ricketts division have been sent to Baltimore, in
order that I may know the means of defence to arrive at that place." ALS (telegram sent), DNA, RG 107, Telegrams Collected (Bound); telegram received,
ibid.; *ibid.*, RG 108, Letters Received. Printed as received on July 10, 11:20
A.M. in *O.R.*, I, xxxvii, part 2, 134–35; *ibid.*, I, xl, part 3, 93.

On July 10, 3:30 P.M., Halleck telegraphed to USG. "Your telegram of 6
P M yesterday is recieved. Whether you had better come here or remain there,
is a question upon which I cannot advise. What you say about getting into Early's
rear is perfectly correct, but unfortunately we have no forces here for the field.
All such forces were sent to you long ago. What we have here are raw militia,
Invalids, convalescents from the hospitals, a few dismounted batteries, & the dismounted & disorganized cavalry sent up from James River. With these we expect
to defend our immense depots of stores & the line of entrenchments around the
city; but what can we do with such forces in the field against a column of twenty

thousand veterans? One half of the men cannot march at all. The only men fit for the field was Ricketts division, which has been defeated and badly cut up under Wallace. If the remains can hold Baltimore till we can reinforce it, I shall be satisfied. I sent invalid troops from here this morning to assist them. I can draw nothing from Harpers Ferry till Hunter effects his junction. When Hunter's army gets within reach & the Sixth corps arrives, what you propose can probably be done. Sullivan's division has reached Hedgeville & Crook's is passing Cumberland. How strong these are, & where the remainder of Hunter's army is, I cannot ascertain. Rumour says that it has lost almost everything, & is badly cut up. Only one battalion of heavy artillery has reached here. The other two went with Ricketts & what is left of them is probably retreating on Baltimore. We are impressing horses to remount the cavalry. It arrives destitute of every thing, there is necessary delay in preparing it for service." ALS (telegram sent), DNA, RG 107, Telegrams Collected (Bound); telegram received, *ibid.*; *ibid.*, RG 108, Letters Received. *O.R.*, I, xxxvii, part 2, 157; *ibid.*, I, xl, part 3, 123.

To Maj. Gen. Henry W. Halleck

(Cipher).   City Point July 9th/64 7. p. m.
MAJ. GEN. HALLECK, WASHINGTON,

After the dismounted Cavalry had left here I learned accidentally that it was composed of detachments from all regiments. My order was worded to send the dismounted Cavalry but I never intended that detachments should be sent but that organized regiments should go. If I had thought of the matter I would have ordered so many regiments to be dismounted and their horses turned over to the detachments and sendt them back to their regiments.

U. S. GRANT
Lt. Gen

ALS (telegram sent), OClWHi; telegram received (on July 10, 1864, 1:20 P.M.), DNA, RG 107, Telegrams Collected (Bound); *ibid.*, RG 108, Letters Received. *O.R.*, I, xxxvii, part 2, 134; *ibid.*, I, xl, part 3, 92–93.

To Maj. Gen. George G. Meade

By Telegraph from City Point
Dated July 9 *1864.*

To MAJ GEN MEADE

I have just recvd a despatch from Gen Canby of the Second inst

He would send twenty thousand men. The first Division six thousand strong he thought would reach Fort Monroe by the 8th or tenth and the remainder would follow as fast as transportation could [b]e provided   Under these circumstances I think it may be as well to defer the raid ordered yesterday until these troops arrive when we will make a Combined movement of Infantry & Cavalry that will enable the latter to get off in good order & remain absent until they have perfected the work of destruction on the roads south

U S GRANT
Lieut Gen

Telegram received, DNA, RG 94, War Records Office, Army of the Potomac; copies, *ibid.*, RG 108, Letters Sent; DLC-USG, V, 45, 59, 67; (2) Meade Papers, PHi. *O.R.*, I, xl, part 3, 94. On July 9, 1864, 10:00 A.M. and 11:00 A.M., Maj. Gen. George G. Meade telegraphed to USG. "I have nothing of importance to report as occurring along the lines during the past 24 hours—About 5. P. M yesterday the enemy opened his batteries all along our front & kept up a canonading for some half hour—In front of the 9th Corps there was some musketry but not of any great extent, the enemy firing from his breastworks—The object of this demonstration is unknown—possibly an assault may have been designed but abandoned at the last moment.—About the same time or a little later, a force of the enemy estimated at Two regts of infantry, a battery of artillery & a couple of squadrons of Cavalry were seen to pass out of the enemys works & move down the Halifax road. A deserter came in last night, who left Welden yesterday morning—He reports the road nearly repaired, there being only a small break at Ream's Sta. around which passengers have to walk. He states the enemy have but small forces at Welden Goldsboro' & Raleigh—No depot at Stony Creek, tho he heard supplies had been forwarded to that point & wagoned from thence to Petersburgh—He reports Hamptons Cavalry at Stony Creek & guarding the road from thence to Reams Station—Saw no infantry as far as he went viz Reams Sta. When the passengers got out here to walk he took to the woods & came into our lines.—" "I saw Col Comstock last evening when your telegram was received.— Your orders in relation to making regular approaches & sending the 2d Corps & Cavalry to destroy the Welden road, shall be executed as promptly as possible— Some little delay will be necessary to enable me to complete the line of redoubts, which are necessary to protect the left flank of the army after the departure of the 2d Corps.—This delay will however be advantageous because the Cavalry are not yet in condition for very active service—In reply to an enquiry when he would be ready, Genl Sheridan telegraphs—'My Command is recruiting rapidly but is not fit for hard work yet if required for active service at once I can turn out about nine thousand men.'—Every days delay will strengthen Sheridan—The engineers say the redoubts will be ready by the 12th   this will enable Hancock & Sheridan to get off on the 13th—How far do you think the infantry support should go?.—The whole distance 40 miles or only part of the way?" ALS (telegrams sent), DNA, RG 393, Army of the Potomac, Miscellaneous Letters Received; telegrams received, *ibid.*, RG 108, Letters Received. *O.R.*, I, xl, part 3, 93–95.

To Maj. Gen. George G. Meade

By Telegraph from City Point
Dated July 9 *1864.*

To Maj Gen Meade

Send in the balance of the 6 Corps to be forwarded to Washington they need not take their artillery or wagons with them   the rebels have crossed the Monocacy & Hallack gives it as his opinion that one third of Lees army is with him   they are now Calling urgently for troops & I am in hopes ~~that~~ with Wright the enemy will not be allowed to get back

U S Grant
Lt Gen

Telegram received (at 5:40 P.M.), DNA, RG 94, War Records Office, Army of the Potomac; copies, *ibid.*, RG 108, Letters Sent; DLC-USG, V, 45, 59, 67; (2) Meade Papers, PHi. *O.R.*, I, xl, part 3, 95. On July 9, 1864, 8:00 P.M. and 9:00 P.M., Maj. Gen. George G. Meade telegraphed to USG. "An accident has delayed the receipt of your telegram of 6. p. m till this moment—The 6th Corps has been ordered & will proceed at once to City Point—" "The 2d Connecticut Heavy Artillery belongs to the 6th Corps—Genl Hunt desires its services to take charge of the siege guns it being drilled in this duty—Can I retain it—" ALS (telegrams sent), DNA, RG 393, Army of the Potomac, Miscellaneous Letters Received; copies, *ibid.*, Letters Sent; Meade Papers, PHi. *O.R.*, I, xl, part 3, 95. On the same day, USG telegraphed to Meade. "You can retain the 2nd Conn Heavy Arty regt" Telegram received (at 9:30 P.M.), DNA, RG 94, War Records Office, Army of the Potomac; copies, DLC-USG, V, 67; (2) Meade Papers, PHi. *O.R.*, I, xl, part 3, 95.

At 9:20 P.M., USG telegraphed to Meade. "Have you any evidence in the last three 3 days that Longstreets Corps is still here. I am afraid that it too may have gone—" Telegram received, DNA, RG 94, War Records Office, Army of the Potomac; copies, *ibid.*, RG 108, Letters Sent; DLC-USG, V, 45, 59, 67; (2)

Meade Papers, PHi. *O.R.*, I, xxxvii, part 2, 135; *ibid.*, I, xl, part 3, 95. At 9:30 P.M., Meade telegraphed to USG. "I telegraphed you at 3.50 P. M this day the account of two contrabands, who represented themselves as servants to officers on the staff of Lt. Genl—Anderson now commanding Longstreets corps—They asserted positively that all three of the divisions of this corps were in our front occupying the centre of their line Beauregard on the left & A. P. Hill on the right —I have no doubt Longstreets corps is here." ALS (telegram sent), DNA, RG 393, Army of the Potomac, Miscellaneous Letters Received; copies, *ibid.*, Letters Sent; (2) Meade Papers, PHi. *O.R.*, I, xxxvii, part 2, 135–36; *ibid.*, I, xl, part 3, 96.

To Abraham Lincoln

City Point, Va, July 10th 10.30 [P.M.] *1864*

A. LINCOLN PRESIDENT,

I have sent from here a whole Corps commanded by an excellent officer, besides over 3000 other troops. ~~The~~ One Division of the 19th Corps 6000 strong is now on its way to ~~w~~Washington one steamer loaded with these troops having passed Fortress Monroe to-day.[1] They will probably reach Washington to-morrow night. This force under Wright will be able to compete with the whole force with Ewell. Before more troops can be sent from here Hunter will be able to join Wright in rear of the enemy with at least 10,000 men besides a force sufficient to hold Maryland Heights. I think on reflection it would have a bad effect for me to leave here and with Ord at Baltimore and Hunter and Wright with the forces following the enemy up could do no good. I have great faith that the enemy will never be able to get back with much of his force.

U. S. GRANT
Lt. Gen.

ALS (telegram sent), OClWHi; telegram received (on July 11, 1864, 7:00 A.M.), DLC-Robert T. Lincoln; DNA, RG 107, Telegrams Collected (Bound); *ibid.*, Telegrams Collected (Unbound). *O.R.*, I, xxxvii, part 2, 155–56; *ibid.*, I, xl, part 3, 122. See telegram to Maj. Gen. Henry W. Halleck, July 9, 1864. On July 11, 8:00 A.M., President Abraham Lincoln telegraphed to USG. "Yours of 10.30 P. M. yesterday received, and very satisfactory. The enemy will learn ~~that~~ of Wright's arrival, and then the difficulty will be to unite Wright and Hunter, South of the enemy before he will recross the Potomaac. Some firing between Rockville and here now." ALS (telegram sent), DNA, RG 107, Telegrams Collected (Bound); telegram received (on July 12), *ibid.*, RG 108, Letters Received. *O.R.*, I, xxxvii, part 2, 191; *ibid.*, I, xl, part 3, 143. Lincoln, *Works*, VII, 438.

1. On July 10, 1:00 P.M., Col. John W. Shaffer, chief of staff for Maj. Gen. Benjamin F. Butler, telegraphed to Brig. Gen. John A. Rawlins. "Steamer Cresent has just arrived with Troops from New Orleans and have been ordered to Washington. She left on 3d and Says six other Steamers w̶i̶l̶l̶ would leave on 4th Shall they all be ordered to Washington" ALS (telegram sent), DNA, RG 107, Telegrams Collected (Unbound). Printed as addressed to USG and incomplete in *O.R.*, I, xl, part 3, 142. On the same day, USG telegraphed to Shaffer. "Yes order them all to Washington" Telegram received, DNA, RG 94, War Records Office, Dept. of Va. and N. C., Army of the James, Unentered Papers; (press) *ibid.*, RG 107, Telegrams Collected (Bound); copy, DLC-USG, V, 67. *O.R.*, I, xl, part 3, 142. On July 11, Rawlins telegraphed to Shaffer. "How Many vessels with the 19th Corps from New-Orleans, have passed Fort Monroe for Washington up to this time—Please keep these HeadQuarters advised of the vessels as they pass that the Lieut general commanding may be informed of the probable time they will reach Washington" ALS (telegram sent), DNA, RG 107, Telegrams Collected (Unbound); telegram received, *ibid.*, RG 94, War Records Office, Dept. of Va. and N. C., Army of the James, Unentered Papers. *O.R.*, I, xl, part 3, 173. At 11:10 A.M., Shaffer telegraphed to Rawlins. "The 'Cresent' is the only B̶o̶a̶t̶ Vessel that has reached here from New Orleans I will notify you of the arrival of Each Vessels as soon as they get here and will push them forward to Washington without delay. I think there will be several here today" ALS (telegram sent), DNA, RG 107, Telegrams Collected (Unbound).

To Maj. Gen. Henry W. Halleck

(Cipher)   City Point Va. July 10th/64 12.30 p. m.
MAJ. GEN. HALLECK, WASHINGTON,

I have sent no troops to Baltimore except Ricketts Div. and the dismounted Cavalry. Two Divisions, the balance of the 6th Corps, are now on their way to Washington the advance having sailed at 10 a. m. the remainder embarking and starting as fast as the steamers are loaded. I have sent Ord to Washington. I would give more for him as a commander in the field than most of the Generals now n̶o̶w̶ in Maryland. Probably it will be well to send him to Baltimore to command and hold the place forcing into service for the purpose, if necessary all Citizens capable of bearing arms. He should also have discretion to move out against the enemy. All other force it looks to me should be collected in rear of the enemy, about Edwards Ferry, and follow him up and cut off retreat if possible. All losses sustained by loyal Citizens can be paid back to them by contributions collected from rebel sympathizers after the enemy is got rid of.

U. S. GRANT
Lt. Gen.

ALS (telegram sent), OClWHi; telegram received (at 9:00 P.M.), DNA, RG 107, Telegrams Collected (Bound). *O.R.*, I, xxxvii, part 2, 156; *ibid.*, I, xl, part 3, 122. On July 10, 1864, 1:00 P.M., USG wrote a telegram to Maj. Gen. Henry W. Halleck, subsequently marked "*ordered* not sent." "Has Hunter got all his force with him at Cumberland and East of there? His dispatch does not make it clear to me whether only one Division has reached Cumberland and the advance or whether his whole command had got as far as Cumberland and one Division was in advance of that place." ADfS, OClWHi. At 12:30 A.M., Halleck telegraphed to USG. "Despatch just recieved from Genl Wallace who admits a serious defeat at Monocacy Junction to-day. He is in full retreat on Baltimore with, he says, his column demoralized,   A part of Ricketts division is covering his retreat. He estimates the enemy's force at twenty thousand." ALS (telegram sent), DNA, RG 107, Telegrams Collected (Bound); telegram received, *ibid.*; *ibid.*, Telegrams Collected (Unbound); *ibid.*, RG 108, Letters Received. *O.R.*, I, xxxvii, part 2, 156. See *ibid.*, p. 145.

To Maj. Gen. Henry W. Halleck

(Cipher)   City Point Va. July 10th/64 [*1:30* P.M.]
MAJ. GEN. HALLECK, WASHINGTON

Gen. Order No. 225 of July 7th/64 would take ~~Gen.~~ the 18th Corps from the Dept. of Va. and N. C. and leave it a separate command, thus giving a third Army in the field, as the 10th Corps is also serving here. I would not desire this change made but simply Gen. Smith assigned to the Command of the 18th Corps, and if there is no objection to a Brig. Gen. holding such a position, Gen. W. T. H. Brooks to the command of the 10th Corps, leaving both these Corps in the Dept. as before, ~~Official~~ Hd Qrs. of which is at Ft. Monroe. When the 19th Corps arrives I will add it too to the same Dept. ~~and~~

U. S. ~~GRANT~~
~~Lt. Gen.~~

and.

I will take the liberty of suspending this order until I hear again. I will ask to have Gen. Franklin assigned to the active command in the field under Gen. Butlers orders as soon as he is fit for duty.

U. S. GRANT
Lt. Gen.

ALS (telegram sent), OClWHi; telegram received (at 8:40 P.M.), DNA, RG 107, Telegrams Collected (Bound); (incomplete) *ibid.*, Telegrams Collected (Unbound). *O.R.*, I, xl, part 3, 122–23. See telegram to Maj. Gen. Henry W. Halleck, July 6, 1864. Presumably on July 7, 1864, Maj. Gen. Henry W. Halleck drafted General Orders No. 225. "The troops of the Department of North Carolina and Virginia serving with the Army of the Potomac in the field under Major-General Smith will constitute the Eighteenth Army Corps, and Maj. Gen. William F. Smith is assigned by the President to the command of the corps. Maj. Gen. B. F. Butler will command the remainder of the troops in that department, having his headquarters at Fort Monroe." *O.R.*, I, xl, part 3, 59. After consultation with President Abraham Lincoln, the orders remained the same, except that the phrase "By order of the President" appeared at the end, and the phrase "by the President" disappeared from the body. *Ibid.*, p. 69.

On July 9, Brig. Gen. Godfrey Weitzel, chief of staff for Maj. Gen. Benjamin F. Butler, telegraphed to Lt. Col. Cyrus B. Comstock. "Has Genl Grant gone to the front today or is he at his Head Qrs." ALS (telegram sent), DNA, RG 94, War Records Office, Dept. of Va. and N. C., Army of the James, Unentered Papers. *O.R.*, I, xl, part 3, 114. On the same day, Butler telegraphed to "Senior Staff Officer at Headquarters." "Has General Grant gone to the front?" *Ibid.* On the same day, Comstock wrote to Butler. "Lt. Gen. Grant desires me to say that he will be at his Hd City Point during the day." ALS, DNA, RG 94, War Records Office, Dept. of Va. and N. C., Army of the James, Unentered Papers. *O.R.*, I, xl, part 3, 114.

Also on July 9, Butler wrote to his wife. "I have only time to say I am well and that you may see me sooner than you think. The mail is closing and I am just up." *Private and Official Correspondence of Gen. Benjamin F. Butler . . .* (n. p., 1917), IV, 478. On July 10, Butler wrote to his wife. "I wrote you a very mysterious epistle yesterday because I was in doubt myself. I had just received an order from Washington (which may the Rebels take), appointing Smith to the command of the troops serving under him, and the remainder of the troops in the department to be under the Command of Maj. Gen'l. Butler, headqrs. Fortress Monroe. Immediately after breakfast I went to Gen. Grant, as I had seen him the night before and was treated by him with the utmost cordiality, and had a confidential conference. I could not tell why this order should come out and he not have mentioned it then. He received me with cordial greeting. As soon as possible after the usual compliments, and the staff had retired, I showed him the order, and told him I did not understand it. He says, 'Oh,—I did not mean you should have seen that order. It is a mistake. I suppressed all the copies that were transmitted through me. How did you get this?' 'Some friend in the War Department, fearing perhaps I should not see it, forwarded me one direct,' said I. 'Well,' said he, 'I don't want this at all. I want Smith to report to you—

you to have the full command. I was going to add the 19th corps to your department, and I shall when it comes here from Washington. I will telegraph now.' He then telegraphed that he had suspended the order, and that he desired that Gen. Franklin be ordered to report to me for active duty in the field as soon as he was able to take the saddle, and so the order has gone up. This was the work of Halleck upon the application of Smith, but it has failed, and I have gained by it. From Grant's suspension of the order, and saying that he proposed to have the 19th corps added to my command, he has vindicated me and my military operations in a way it would not have been done but for these people—whom God and his humble instrument will take care of before we get through. So you see I shall not come to Fortress Monroe as soon as you thought and I hoped. But the mail closes. Read this to Shaffer." *Ibid.*, pp. 481–82.

In his article, "Grant's Liquor Drinking," Washington correspondent Henry Van Ness Boynton printed a letter of June 30, 1864, from Brig. Gen. John A. Rawlins to Maj. Gen. William F. Smith. "Your kind note of this date in regard to the General while at your headquarters yesterday is received. I am thankful to you for your friendly forethought, and the interest manifested in his behalf. Yet 'tis only what one knowing your friendship for him might have expected. Being thus timely advised of the slippery ground he is on, I shall not fail to use my utmost endeavors to stay him from falling. Your application for a leave of absence will be presented to the General for his favorable consideration. I can assure you, however, he will be loath to part with you from the field even for a few days." *New York Sun*, Jan. 23, 1887. Boynton also printed a letter of July 30 from Smith to U.S. Senator Solomon Foot of Vt. "I am extremely anxious that my friends in my native State should not think that the reason of Gen. Grant's relieving me from duty was brought about by any misconduct of mine, and, therefore, I write to put you in possession of such facts in the case as I am aware of, and think will throw light upon the subject. About the very last of June, or the first of July, Gens. Grant and Butler came to my headquarters, and shortly after their arrival Gen. Grant turned to Gen. Butler, and said: 'That drink of whiskey I took has done me good;' and then, directly afterward, asked me for a drink. My servant opened a bottle for him, and he drank of it, when the bottle was corked and put away. I was aware at this time, that Gen. Grant had within six months pledged himself to drink nothing intoxicating, but did not feel it would better matters to decline to give it upon his request in Gen. Butler's presence. After the lapse of an hour or less, the General asked for another drink, which he took. Shortly after, his voice showed plainly that the liquor had affected him, and after a little time he left. I went to see him upon his horse, and as soon as I returned to my tent, I said to a staff officer of mine, who had witnessed his departure: 'Gen. Grant has gone away drunk. Gen. Butler has seen it, and will never fail to use the weapon which has been put into his hands.' Two or three days after that, I applied for a leave of absence for the benefit of my health, and Gen. Grant sent word to me not to go, if it were possible to stay, and I replied in a private note warranted by our former relations, a copy of which note I will send you in a few days. The next day Assistant Secretary of War, Mr. Dana, came to tell me that he had been sent by Gen. Grant to say what it becomes necessary to repeat in view of subsequent events, to wit: That he, Gen. G., had written a letter the day before to ask that Gen. Butler might be relieved from that department, and I placed in command of it, giving as a reason that he could not trust Gen. Butler with the command of troops in the movements about to be made, and saying also that, next to Gen. Sherman, he had more confidence in my ability than in that of any General in the field. The order from Washington, dated July 7, sent Gen. Butler to Fort Monroe, and placed me in command of the troops then under me and Gen. Grant. He would make the changes necessary to give me the troops in the field belonging to that department. I had only asked that I should not be commanded in battle by a man that could not give an order on the field, and I had recommended Gen. Franklin or Gen. Wright for the command of the department. I was at the headquarters of Gen. Grant on Sunday, July 15, and there saw Gen. B., but had no conversation with him. After Gen. B. had left, I had a confidential conversation with Gen. Grant about changes he was going to make. In this connection, it is proper to state that our personal relations were of the most friendly character. He had listened to and acted upon the suggestions made by me upon more than one important occasion. I then thought and still think, whatever Gen. Butler's letter writers may say to the contrary, that he knew that any suggestion I might make for his consideration would be dictated solely by an intense desire to put down this rebellion, and not from any personal considerations, personal to myself, and that no personal friendship had stood in the way of what I considered my duty with regard to military management—a course not likely to be pursued by any man ambitious of advancement. In this confidential conversation with Gen. Grant I tried to show him the blunders of the late campaign of the Army of the Potomac, and the terrible waste of life that had resulted from what I had considered a want of generalship in its present commander. Among other instances, I referred to the fearful slaughter at Cold Harbor on the 3d of June. Gen. Grant went into the discussion, defending Gen. Meade stoutly, but finally acknowledged, to use his own words, 'that there had been a butchery at Cold Harbor, but that he had said nothing about it because it could do no good.' Not a word was said as to my right to criticise Gen. Meade then, and I left without a suspicion that Gen. Grant had taken it in any other way than it was meant, and I do not think he did misunderstand me. On my return from a short leave of absence on the 19th of July, Gen. Grant sent for me to report to him, and then told me that he 'could not relieve Gen. Butler,' and that as I had so severely criticised Gen. Meade, he had determined to relieve me from the command of the Eighteenth Corps and order me to New York city, to await orders. The next morning the General gave some other reasons, such as an article in the *Tribune* reflecting on Gen. Hancock, which I had nothing in the world to do with, and two letters, which I had written before the campaign began, to two of Gen. Grant's most devoted friends, urging upon them to try and prevent him from making the campaign he has just made. These letters, sent to Gen. Grant's nearest friends and intended for his eye, necessarily sprang from an earnest desire to serve the man upon whom the country had been depending, and these warnings ought to have been my highest justification in his opinion, and indeed would have been, but that it has become necessary to make out a case against me. All these matters, moreover, were known to the General before he asked that I might be put in command of the Department of Virginia and North Carolina, and therefore they formed no excuse for relieving me from the command I held. I also submit to you that if it had been proven to him that I was unfitted for the command I then held, that that in no wise changed the case with reference to Gen. Butler and his competency, and did not furnish a reason why he should not go where the President had ordered him at the request of Gen. Grant: and that as Gen. Grant did, immediately after an interview with Gen. B., suspend the order and announce his intention of relieving me from duty there, other reasons must be sought, different from any assigned, for this sudden change of views and action. Since I have been in New York, I have heard from two different sources (one being from Gen. Grant's headquarters, and one a staff officer of a General on intimate official relations with Gen. B.) that Gen. Butler went to Gen. Grant and threatened to expose his intoxication if the order was not revoked. I also learned that Gen. B. had threatened to make public something that would prevent the President's reëlection. Gen. Grant told me (when I asked him about Gen. Butler's threat of crushing me) that he had heard that Gen. B. had made some threat with reference to the Chicago Convention, which he (B.) said he 'had in his breeches pocket,' but Gen. G. was not clear in expressing what the threat was. I refer to this simply because I feel convinced that the change was not made for any of the reasons that have been assigned: and whether Gen. Butler has threatened Gen. Grant with his opposition to Mr. Lincoln at the coming election or has appealed to any political aspirations which Gen. Grant may entertain, I do not know: but one thing is certain. I was not guilty of any acts of insubordination between my appointment and my suspension, for I was absent all those days on leave from Gen. Grant. I only hope that this long story will not tire you, and that it will convince you that I have done nothing to deserve a loss of the confidence which was reposed in me. . . . P. S.—I have not referred to the state of things existing at headquarters when I left, and to the fact that Gen. Grant was then in the habit of getting liquor in a surreptitious manner, because it was not relevant to my case; but if you think at any time the matter may be of importance to the country, I will give it to you. Should you wish to write to me, please address, care of S. E. Lyon, Jauncey court, 39 Wall street, New York." *Ibid.* See letter to Maj. Gen. John A. McClernand, June 6, 1863. Smith later stated that his letter to Foot was found among his papers after his death and published without Smith's "knowledge or consent." William Farrar Smith, *From Chattanooga to Petersburg Under Generals Grant and Butler* (Boston and New York, 1893), p. 52. Foot died in 1866, the letter was first printed in 1887, and it was printed with a letter from Rawlins to Smith, circumstances which throw doubt on Smith's account and the authenticity of the text as well. Smith also printed an 1893 letter from former Brig. Gen. Isaac J. Wistar which included an explanation of Smith's removal given by Asst. Secretary of War John Tucker that USG had been drinking heavily on July 9 when Butler induced him to change his mind. *Ibid.*, p. 193. Rawlins, unlikely to minimize USG's drinking, wrote to his wife on June 29 that USG had consumed "a glass of liquor." James Harrison Wilson, *The Life of John A. Rawlins* (New York, 1916), p. 239. William D. Mallam, "The Grant-Butler Relationship," *Mississippi Valley Historical Review,* XLI, 2 (Sept., 1954), pp. 262–63, rejected Smith's contentions about his removal, pointing to the explanation given by USG to Halleck and mentioning USG's disenchantment with Smith. See telegram to Maj. Gen. Henry W. Halleck, May 21, 1864. In his book, Smith quoted from a letter to him of unspecified date from Maj. Gen. James H. Wilson which reported USG as stating on July 19, 1864: "No man in the army, not General Smith himself, regrets it [*the removal*] more than I do; for no man appreciates the general's great abilities better than I do, or is more anxious to use them in this war." *From Chattanooga to Petersburg . . . ,* p. 48. Bruce Catton, however, argues that Smith's removal was based upon USG's realization that Smith's disruptive criticism extended beyond Butler to Maj. Gen. George G. Meade and USG himself. *Grant Takes Command* (Boston and Toronto, 1969), pp. 326–35. Comstock wrote of Smith and Butler in his diary on July 2. "Went up to Smiths H. Q. He is in trouble with Butler, Butler having reprimanded him for delay & then written a letter of reply to Smith's reproving him for taking offense at a friendly letter. I think neither could get on well with any one, much less with each other." DLC-Cyrus B. Comstock. On July 17, Comstock wrote, "Some time ago Smith criticisd in his ex cathedra way, this campaign as having been a succession of useless slaughters. The general heard of it and told me he did not know which to do, relieve him or talk to him. Subsequently Smith carried the works here at Petersburg & though they were scarcely defended at all, the general was greatly pleased. Since, Smith has constantly been talking against Meade, wishes Franklin to take his place—and last a few nights ago just before going on an unnecessary & improper leave of ten days, insisted on the generals making the change he wished & finally asked the general in the most offensive way, if he expected he was ever going to do any thing with that man (Meade) in command. The Smith has declared he will not serve with Butler—if & as Butler is to stay for the present Smith will probably be shelved. Gen. had proposed to put Franklin in Butlers place—but he has now recomnded F. for general command at Washington. F. says he does not wish command of A. of P. though he knows Smith has urged it:" *Ibid.* On July 19, Rawlins wrote to his wife. "General Grant to-day relieved Major General William F. Smith from command and duty in this army, because of his spirit of criticism of all military movements and men, and his failure to get along with any one he is placed under, and his disposition to scatter the seeds of discontent throughout the army. . . ." Wilson, *Rawlins*, p. 247. Smith's removal created much gossip in the Army of the Potomac, and Brig. Gen. Marsena R. Patrick heard one day that Smith had been removed because of his criticism of Meade and USG, and on another day that Butler had blackmailed USG. David S. Sparks, ed., *Inside Lincoln's Army* . . . (New York and London, 1964), pp. 401–2, 415.

On July 11, 10:30 A.M., Asst. Secretary of War Charles A. Dana telegraphed to Rawlins. "Please send back to the War Dept any letters that may come for me—There was a tremendous excitement here yesterday but all is comparatively calm this morning—The defences of Washington have not yet been attacked though Genl McDowell McCook went out to take command on the Tenallytown road last evening where the rebels were reported as reported as approaching in force—With Gilmore Couch Wallace McCook and Sigel we only need Milroy McClernand Rosecrans and Kilby Smith to make us safe—If the General could spare Butler for the Chief Supreme Command all danger danger would certainly cease—Especially as Hunter is at hand—Dont forget that the last named commander has beaten even Sigel in retreating not having stopped his flight till he reached the Ohio River—although it was certain all the time that the enemy would come down the Valley—I see that the General has backed down on Butler but I hope that he will fix it so that that military lawyer will not be able to ruin the end of the campaign as he has ruined and foiled the beginning— Nullifying all its vast cost and awful bloodshed—We were all wrong at City Point about the tenth Corps—that has never been assigned to Butlers command and was only temporarily under his orders when it was sent into his dept and he was Senior to Gilmore—When Butler was sent to Fort Munroe it was for Genl Grant to dispose of the tenth as he chose—The white troops of the tenth and eighteenth Corps ought to be consolidated and new Corps made out of their blacks and the blacks of the nineteenth—Dont let any one but the General see this" Telegram received, USG 3; DNA, RG 107, Telegrams Collected (Unbound).

On July 19, Capt. Ely S. Parker issued Special Orders No. 62. "All troops of the 19th Army Corps arriving at this point will report to Maj. Gen. B. F. Butler comd'g. Dept of Va & N. C. at Bermuda Hundred for orders. Subject to the approval of the President Maj. Gen. W. F. Smith is hereby relieved from the Command of the 18th Army Corps and will proceed to New York City and await further orders. His personal Staff will accompany him. The Corps Staff of the 18th Army Corps will report to Brig Gen J. H. Martindale temporarily comd'g for duty." Copies, DLC-USG, V, 57, 62, 67. *O.R.*, I, xl, part 3, 334.

To Maj. Gen. George G. Meade

By Telegraph from City Point
Dated July 10 *1864.*

To MAJ. GEN MEADE & ALL CORPS COMDRS—
A telegram of the 9th from Baltimore 11 30 a. m states that the operator at Menocacy reports severe fighting near that point The advance of the enemy being within three fourths (¾) of a mile of Monocacy on the road from Frederick to Georgetown   Another telegram at one P. M. from a point thirty (30) miles east of Monocacy states that the reports from Monocacy by the last train that left that place were that, a battle was then in progress   Later advices report that our troops under Gen Wallace were driven back— The rebel troops are estimated ~~of~~ at from 15 to 20.000. strong under Breckenridge Brad. Johnson[1] & McCausland[2]   Telegrams of today report our forces still retreating towards Baltimore. A part of Ricketts Division are covering the retreat   Hunter on the 9th reports himself at Cumberland and says his advance division was then on Cherry Run—He is moving forward as rapidly as possible —Sherman has effected lodgments across the Chattahoochee at two points viz. The mouth of Seps [*Soap*] Creek & at Roswells   He will make these points secure before crossing his main Army—

U. S. GRANT
Lt. Genl

Telegrams received (2—at 2:05 P.M.), DNA, RG 94, War Records Office, Army of the Potomac; (incomplete) *ibid.*, RG 393, 24th Army Corps, Telegrams Received (Unarranged); copies (2), Meade Papers, PHi. *O.R.*, I, xl, part 3, 123–24. On July 9, 1864, John W. Garrett, president of the Baltimore and Ohio Railroad, Camden Station, Baltimore, telegraphed to President Abraham Lincoln and to Secretary of War Edwin M. Stanton news of the battle of Monocacy, Md., in both cases sending copies to USG. Telegrams received, DNA, RG 108, Letters Received; (1) *ibid.*, RG 107, Telegrams Collected (Unbound). *O.R.*, I, xxxvii, part 2, 138–39.

1. Bradley T. Johnson, born in 1829 in Frederick, Md., graduated from Princeton (1849) and returned to Frederick to become a Democratic lawyer-politician. After initial service as maj., lt. col., then col., 1st Md., Johnson often commanded brigades but only received appointment as brig. gen. as of June 28, 1864, to replace William E. Jones commanding cav., and he led this command in the 1864 campaign of Lt. Gen. Jubal A. Early.

2. John McCausland, born in St. Louis in 1836, graduated from Virginia Military Institute in 1857, where he remained as an asst. professor of mathematics until the Civil War. First commissioned col., 36th Va., he escaped from Fort Donelson with a brigade which he commanded in West Va. Appointed brig. gen. as of May 18, 1864, he was given a cav. command, which he led at the battle of Monocacy, July 9. On July 30, he burned Chambersburg, Pa., in retaliation for U.S. destruction in the Shenandoah Valley.

To Maj. Gen. George G. Meade

By Telegraph from City Point 11 40 p m
Dated July 10th *1864.*

To GENL MEADE

Not receiving a reply from Gen Lee to communications sent on the 8th I begin to believe it possible that he may have gone on the Maryland Campaign taking with him considerable reinforcements from the Army in your front   I think it adviseable to make a recconnoisance around towards the Weldon road pushing out skirmishers to make the enemy develope himself and to ascertain if this be the fact. Sheridan might get up three thousand (3000) of his best Cavalry to move with such a recconnoisance. The object would be solely to ascertain if the enemy still occupies his position in full force & if that can be ascertained without going to the Weldon road either by swinging round a heavy line of skirmishers from Hancocks front to drive ~~th~~ in the enemys advance pickets & make him develope behind his works. ~~or get~~ Or if it is certainly known by deserters who have Come in within the last 24 hours that no movement has taken place it will be satisfactory

U S GRANT
Lt Gen

Telegram received, DNA, RG 94, War Records Office, Army of the Potomac; copies, *ibid.*, RG 108, Letters Sent; DLC-USG, V, 45, 59, 67; (2) Meade Papers, PHi. *O.R.*, I, xxxvii, part 2, 157; *ibid.*, I, xl, part 3, 124. On July 10, 1864, midnight, Maj. Gen. George G. Meade telegraphed to USG. "No movements have been reported by deserters, on the contrary they all agree in stating Hills—Longstreets & Bearegards forces to be in our front—A negro woman came in to night who lives near the Welden R. Rd. who says she heard the soldiers say, that yesterday Genl. Lee made it known he would grant a 30 days furlough to any soldier who would capture a yankee soldier—I think this plausible as he undoubtedly desires to know what detachments if any you are making.—Last night the 6th Corps when leaving made a great deal of noise beating marches blowing calls & making bonfires of their camps—This attracted the attention of the enemy & this morning at daylight they advanced on a portion of the 2d Corps pickets crying out the Yankees are gone—Our pickets received them with a brisk fire driving them back, when all was quieted & has remained so during the day. The reconnaissance you suggest can be made—I see no advantage in swinging round the left of the 2d. Corps as I am satisfied it will only result in confronting the enemy in his works, but the Corps with the cavalry can be sent on to the Welden road, which will I have no doubt develop a force of the enemy, and perhaps bring some out of the Petersburgh lines It will take tomorrow however to get the cavalry up here—There have been several deserters in today, some coming in as late as 10 a m up to which time there had been, no change in Hills or Longstreets Corps—they knew nothing of Beauregards Corps. Unless otherwise directed I shall send the 2d. Corps to the Weldon Road, as soon as I can get a brigade of cavalry up here to go with it.—I have just learned that two men from the 48th Missi. Mahones Div. Hills Corps, have been captured by our men, they having come into the trenches to exchange papers—These men say they have heard nothing of any recent movement of any part of their army & that Hill & Longstreet are in our front. I have a scout out who expects to get into Petersburgh, but I do not look for his return before tomorrow night.—" ALS (telegram sent), DNA, RG 393, Army of the Potomac, Miscellaneous Letters Received; telegram received, *ibid.*, RG 108, Letters Received. *O.R.*, I, xxxvii, part 2, 158; *ibid.*, I, xl, part 3, 124–25. See telegram to Maj. Gen. George G. Meade, July 11, 1864.

On July 10, 11:30 A.M., Meade had telegraphed to USG. "Above despatch sent for your information—Pickets & signal officers report the passage this a m of several trains confirming the above statement of the negroes that the enemy is running off his rolling stock for security—The report of Wilcox's division going to Chaffins bluff would account for the troops seen going some days since from Petersburgh—I am of the opinion the estimate of Earlys forces is too low I should think he had in the valley nearly 25,000 men—" ALS (telegram sent), DNA, RG 94, War Records Office, Army of the Potomac. *O.R.*, I, xl, part 3, 128–29. The enclosure is *ibid.*, pp. 127–28.

To Maj. Gen. Benjamin F. Butler

By Telegraph from City Pt
Dated July 11 1864.

To MAJ GENL BUTLER

Hills Corps was moved from its position at 5 p m yesterday—
Citizens say to Go north   has your scouts or man from the observatory discovered any movement of Troops between Petersburg
& Richmond—please make an effort to ascertain about this—I am
not willing to let Mr Gilmore & Col Jaques go through our Lines
until I know the object of their going[1]

U. S. GRANT
Lt Genl.

Telegram received, DLC-Benjamin F. Butler; copies, DLC-USG, V, 45, 59, 67;
DNA, RG 108, Letters Sent. *O.R.*, I, xl, part 3, 169. On July 11, 1864, 4:20
P.M., Maj. Gen. Benjamin F. Butler telegraphed to USG. "I have caused the matter in relation to the moving of Hill's Corps to be investigated—I cannot hear of
any movement of any troops either over the turnpike or railroad or over Chapin's
Farm—It is certain that none have been moved by daylight and that none have
been moved at night, over the railroad, because we can hear them—They might
go over the turnpike at night without our hearing them—Five Deserters Are
just in from our front, from Pickett's Division but they have heard nothing of
any movement of any troops—I will take every pains to keep you informed upon
this and kindred subjects—" LS (telegram sent), DNA, RG 94, War Records
Office, Dept. of Va. and N. C., Army of the James, Unentered Papers; telegram
received, *ibid.*, RG 108, Letters Received. *O.R.*, I, xl, part 3, 169.
    Earlier on July 11, USG telegraphed to Butler. "Have you ~~heard~~ had any
recent information from Wilcoxs Division   it did Cross the James River only
this month & was said to have gone to Chapins Bluff   I would like to know if
it is still there" Telegram received, DLC-Benjamin F. Butler; DLC-USG, V,
45, 59, 67; DNA, RG 108, Letters Sent. *O.R.*, I, xl, part 3, 168. At 12:15 P.M.,
Butler telegraphed to USG. "Wilcox Division of Hill's Corps consists of Scales',
Lane's, McGowan's (now Conner's) and Thomas' Brigades   We have deserters
this morning from Thomas' Brigade which is on their right and rear from the
Junction to Swift Creek—They report Scales Brigade holding the line from
Swift Creek to the Appomattox—McGowan's (Conner's) and Lane's Brigades
are in our front opposite Deep Bottom—We had deserters from them yesterday—
Allowing 300 men to a Regt the Division has 5,700 men—Thomas Brigade is
very small—about eight hundred men—McGowan's (Conner) is reported not
over a thousand men—Lane not over twelve hundred—probably not over a thousand—Of Scales' Brigade we have no accurate information—Calling it twelve
hundred strong and the division has forty two hundred men—We have no accurate information as to Lee's whereabouts—Some say he is at Petersburg and

some at Richmond—I am inclined to think he is not at either place—" LS (telegram sent), DNA, RG 94, War Records Office, Dept. of Va. and N. C., Army of the James, Unentered Papers; telegram received, *ibid.*, RG 108, Letters Received. *O.R.*, I, xl, part 3, 168.

Also on July 11, Butler telegraphed to USG a signal message of 3:40 P.M. from Lt. Alfred G. Simons, Spring Hill, to Capt. Lemuel B. Norton. "A train of seven (7) passenger and two (2) freight cars loaded with troops has just passed the Junction towards Richmond." LS (telegram sent), DNA, RG 107, Telegrams Collected (Unbound). *O.R.*, I, xl, part 3, 169. See *ibid.*, p. 199.

1. At 12:25 P.M., Butler had telegraphed to USG. "Col Jaquess and Mr Gillmore, are here and are of course desirous to go forward on their mission—If you desire them to go and will trust to me to get them through the lines, I think I can accomplish it—The means I should adopt would be to send to ask Ould to meet Maj Mulford at Port Walthall   They will explain to you if you desire it, or will inform me, before they go, the subject of their mission—" LS (telegram sent), DNA, RG 94, War Records Office, Dept. of Va. and N. C., Army of the James, Unentered Papers; telegram received, *ibid.*, RG 108, Letters Received. *O.R.*, I, xl, part 3, 168–69. On the same day, USG telegraphed to Butler. "I have seen and heard Mr Gillmore and Col Jaques. You may effect an interview between them and commissioner Ould & Permit them to pass through our lines if they will be recd by the other party" Telegram received, DLC-Benjamin F. Butler; copies, DLC-USG, V, 45, 59, 67; DNA, RG 108, Letters Sent; USG 3. *O.R.*, I, xl, part 3, 169. See letter to Gen. Robert E. Lee, July 8, 1864.

To Maj. Gen. George G. Meade

By Telegraph from City Point
Dated July 11th *1864.*

To MAJ GEN MEADE

Your dispatch of 12 just received   it would seem to quiet all apprehension about Lee or any considerable portion of his force being gone & therefore obviates the necessity of making any demonstration. Unless necessary I would prefer being quiet until we make a real move so will take what you report as being sufficent evidence of Lee & his forces being still in our front   there is great alarm felt in Washington. Wallace has been whipped at Monocacy bridge & driven back in great confusion   he had with him a part of Ricketts Division   I have sent Ord up there to Command Baltimore & to press into service every able bodied man to defend the place   asked that Wright be sent with his 2 Divisions and the one Division of the 19th Corps a portion of which passed Fort Monroe about noon today to form a junction with Hunter who must be at Harpers Ferry by tonight & for them then to follow up in the enemys rear altogether everything looks favorable to me but I want to avoid the possibility of Lee getting off with a great part of his force without taking advantage of it. I think you had better order Sheridan to get ready for service as soon as possible but with the assurance that his troops will not be used until it is necessary.

U S GRANT
Lt. Gen

Telegram received (at 1:30 A.M.), DNA, RG 94, War Records Office, Army of the Potomac; copies (dated July 10, 1864), *ibid.*, RG 108, Letters Sent; DLC-USG, V, 45, 59, 67; (2—dated July 11), Meade Papers, PHi. Dated July 10 in *O.R.*, I, xxxvii, part 2, 158–59; (dated July 11) *ibid.*, I, xl, part 3, 144. On July 11, 1864, 11:00 A.M., Maj. Gen. George G. Meade telegraphed to USG. "Nothing of importance occurred on the lines of this army during the past 24 hours not previously reported. The redoubts to cover the left flank will be completed today & the contraction of the line, made by their occupation will be effected either tonight or tomorrow—This contraction will leave the 2d Corps free, the lines being held by the 5th Corps & Ferero's division.—A negro came in this morning who lives near Dr. Gurley's house & He reports the enemy having an earthwork whe[re] the road from Gurleys house crosses the R. Rd. Infantry in it does not know of any guns.—Says the infantry pickets extend along the R. Rd. about ½ a mile below Aikens house, which is below Gurleys—there the ~~infan~~ Cavalry pickets extend to Reams Station & beyond.—At Ream's reports Cavalry in considerable force—Trains are reported as passing up & down the road.—Contents unknown." ALS (telegram sent), DNA, RG 393, Army of the Potomac, Miscellaneous Letters Received; telegram received, *ibid.*, RG 108, Letters Received. *O.R.*, I, xl, part 3, 144.

To Maj. Gen. George G. Meade

By Telegraph from City Point
Dated July 11th *1864.*

To MAJ GEN MEADE

Wilcox[1] division crossed the pontoon bridge at Drurys bluff about the 2d or 3d and took station at Chapins bluff where I think it still remains—Deserters come in daily on Butlers front all saying they belong to Picketts Div—There is no other force between Swift

Creek & Howells [*Howlett's*] House—All the prisoners captured in
Maryland say they belong to Breckenridge Command but they may
belong to McCauslins Johnsons & Imbodens brigade & Ransoms
Cavalry²—All under Breckenridge whilst the Div he brought from
West Va may still be here

U S Grant
Lt Gen

Telegram received (at noon), DNA, RG 94, War Records Office, Army of the
Potomac; copies, *ibid.*, RG 108, Letters Sent; DLC-USG, V, 45, 59, 67; (2)
Meade Papers, PHi. *O.R.*, I, xl, part 3, 145. On July 11, 1864, John C. Babcock,
office of the provost marshal, Army of the Potomac, wrote to Maj. Gen. Andrew
A. Humphreys. "A deserter from the 61st Va. Mahone's Division came into our
lines last night between twelve (12) & 1 oclock   he brings important information. Wilcoxs entire Division went to Chaffins Bluff or farm about a week ago &
is there now to the best of informants belief. Heth's Div. was under marching
orders yesterday with two days cooked rations. They were expected to move at
four P. m.   informant being on picket Could not say whether they had moved
or not. Wilcoxs Div went to Chaffins bluff to relieve Heth's   the latter Div returning to our front took a position on the right of Mahones extending nearly to
the lead works   this was about the 4th inst. Informant has heard of no other
movements   Saw some men from the Div. Commanded by Breckridge two days
ago that were visiting in his Division   He understands Breckenridge is to be
in Butlers front   General Early is absent with only Ransoms Gordons, & Rhodes
Division according to informants belief. The rest of his force he has taken from
the valley. 'Note' Early has certainly one brigade McCauslands that was under
Breckenridge in the valley but it has never been in our front   Also B T. Johnson Maryland Line was under Breckenridge at Coal Harbor,   we think informants statement correct otherwise the force in front of Butler must be very
small   Gen Ewell is in Richmond on the retired list, Phisically unable to do
field duty   Informant heard the maj of his regiment make this statement a few
days since. No troops are being recd. via the Weldon R. R.   of this informant is
positive though he states a very few furloughed men and & convalescents may be
returning that way"   Telegram received, DNA, RG 108, Letters Received. *O.R.*,
I, xl, part 3, 145. On the same day, 11:15 a.m., Maj. Gen. George G. Meade
telegraphed this message to USG, adding his own message. "Above forwarded
for your information,   This is the first intelligence of the return of Breckridge
& is not relied on   Have you any information of Wilcox being at Chapins farm
or what troops are in front of Butler. Up to yesterday I was under the belief Wilcox was in my front"   Telegram received, DNA, RG 108, Letters Received.
O.R., I, xl, part 3, 145.

1. Cadmus M. Wilcox, born in N. C. in 1824, raised in Tenn., USMA 1846,
USG's groomsman, asst. instructor of inf. tactics at USMA (1852–57), resigned
from the U.S. Army as of June 8, 1861. Entering the Civil War as col., 9th
Ala., Wilcox was appointed brig. gen. as of Oct. 21, 1861, and maj. gen. as of
Aug. 3, 1863, and served in the eastern theatre of war. On July 10, 1864, his
div., 3rd Army Corps, reported 5,581 officers and men present. *Ibid.*, p. 762.

2. Robert Ransom, Jr., born in N. C. in 1828, USMA 1850, served in the U.S. Army in the cav. until he resigned as of May 24, 1861. After service as col., 1st N. C. Cav., he was appointed brig. gen. as of March 1, 1862, and maj. gen. as of May 26, 1863. On June 13, 1864, he was relieved of command of the Dept. of Richmond and assigned to command all cav. in the Dept. of Western Va. under Maj. Gen. John C. Breckinridge. *Ibid.*, I, xl, part 2, 646.

To Maj. Gen. George G. Meade

By Telegraph from City Point Va
Dated July 11 *1864.*

To MAJ GEN MEADE

If Hills Corps has gone we must find out where it has gone & take advantage of its absence. If your Cavalry does not succeed in ascertaining today where it has gone I think it will be adviseable to get up all the well mounted men of One Division of Sheridans Cavalry tonight & push it out until definite information is obtained   If they have gone to Washn we will try to carry Petersburg before detaching further from this Army. The best way to accomplish this will probably be by turning the enemys right with Hancocks & Warrens Corps & Sheridans Cavalry with heavy columns of assault from Burnsides & Smiths Corps on one well chosen point in the front of one or the other of these Corps probably about the Hare House

U S GRANT
Lt Gen

Telegram received, DNA, RG 94, War Records Office, Army of the Potomac; copies, *ibid.*, RG 108, Letters Sent; DLC-USG, V, 45, 59, 67; (2) Meade Papers, PHi. *O.R.*, I, xxxvii, part 2, 192; *ibid.*, I, xl, part 3, 147. On July 11, 1864, 11:00 A.M., John C. Babcock, office of the provost marshal, Army of the Potomac, wrote to Maj. Gen. Andrew A. Humphreys. "A deserter from 8th Alabama Mahones Division just received from Col. Bryan Comdg detachment Cavalry Corps—He states that Hills entire Corps left the front yesterday at five (5) oclock P. M. Informant was in town when they moved having a pass from General Saunders Commanding his brigade to purchase mess stores. Came out of Petersburg about 8 P. M. & found his Corps had moved toward the Weldon R. R. with McIntosh battalion of artillery   Could not find where or which way they went after they reached the Railroad—Was told in Petersburg that the Corps was moving Citizens thought to Pennsylvania—Informant thinks they have gone south down the Railroad—about two (2) or three (3) oclock this a. m. he saw a train of 20 or more box cars going into Petersburg also another about the same length at Four (4) or 5 oclock—The Cars were all Closed & no soldiers to be seen on them—thought they run heavy as though they were loaded—That Longstreets Corps & Beauregards forces had Closed up the space left by the removal of Hills Corps—Informant saw the old line Hill had occupied filled up again by Longstreets Corps and the Washington artillery moved into the works vacated by McIntoshs battalion—That there are no double lines now or any reserves—Informant Came out of the City along the line nearly all the way—He says it is the same in length as before—" Telegram received, DNA, RG 108, Letters Received. *O.R.*, I, xl, part 3, 146. At noon, Maj. Gen. George G. Meade telegraphed this message to USG, adding his own message. "Following just received—It confirms the Intelligence sent at 10.30 from another deserter—There appears no doubt that Hills Corps or a portion of it moved last Evening but there is nothing to Indicate the direction taken. It may prove a movement on our left flank due to the withdrawal of the Sixth (6th) Corps—I have directed the Cavalry on our left to push out Scouts in all directions—" Telegram received, DNA, RG 108, Letters Received. *O.R.*, I, xl, part 3, 146. At 1:30 P.M. and 10:30 P.M., Meade telegraphed to USG. "I have questioned the last deserter from Mahones Div. Hills Corps—He tells a straight story, that he left his Div. yesterday at 7 a m. on a pass into Petersburgh—that on his return at 7. P. m the Div. was gone bag & bagage—hospitals & all—that he understood they moved up to the R. Rd. which he took advantage of, by going to the R. Rd. outside the works & following down the R. Rd. till he got out some 3 or 4 miles when he slipped across & came into our lines—He says he could hear nothing of his Division along the R Rd & saw no stragglers—He says Heths division left at the same time, and that he heard in Petersburgh a report that Hills Corps was going to Penna. Per contra the signal officer on the Jordan House reports two trains filled with troops & having artillery, as passing into Petersburgh from Richmond at 4. a m this morning.—I think there is no doubt Hill has moved, but in what direction is as yet uncertain. It may be on our left flank, or it may be to join Early.—" "No further information has been obtained of the enemys movements since last despatch—All efforts of our scouts to get through the enemys pickets on the rail-road have failed, and the cavalry I have here is so miserable they have done nothing.—I have no doubt Hills two ~~Corps~~ Divisions that were in my front yesterday moved last night and as nothing has been heard or seen of them on our left flank I conclude they have been sent to re-inforce Early.—Intelligence of Earlys success, combined with the knowledge of the departure of the 6th Corps together with a confidence in the strength of his lines & his capability to hold them with a diminished force, has doutless induced Lee to send Hill in hopes of thus transferring the seat of operations to Maryland & Penna,—by drawing the greater portion of your army there to defend Washn. & Baltre—I have ordered a division of Cavalry here & expect it will be up during the night—I have also drawn the 2d Corps from the line it held & by daylight tomorrow will have it massed ready for a movement in any direction that may be desired.—I am a little doubtful of sending the Cavalry Division alone, as all the information I have obtained places all of Hamptons Cavalry South of the Appomatox, at Stony Creek Reames & Dinwiddie C. H. evidently posted in anticipation of another raid on our part. There are two negroes out in the enemys lines who are expected back during the night with some definite information—I shall not give any orders to

Hancock or the Cavalry tonight but await the arrival of the latter & more definite information or your instructions.—. . . I should have mentioned as confirming Hills movement that heavy clouds of dust were observed to day on a road leading N. W from Petersburgh on the N. side & that the following intercepted rebel message was read by our signal officers.—'To L. H. B—Are you going this P. M & at what time? When will H be ready? Answer Roux.' There is said to be an officer of the name of Roux on Lees staff. I had commenced the erection of batteries & other preparations for seige operations on Warrens front, but if there is any probability of his being moved the guns & materials would have first to be sent to the rear.—Also Burnside should have some time to prepare to cover his left flank—He has been ordered to make his arrangements." ALS (telegrams sent), DNA, RG 393, Army of the Potomac, Miscellaneous Letters Received; telegrams received, *ibid.*, RG 108, Letters Received. *O.R.*, I, xl, part 3, 147–48.

At 2:00 P.M., Capt. Benjamin F. Fisher telegraphed to Humphreys. "The station north of the City Point Railroad in front of Fort Cliftons reports a large Column of dust rising in front of the 18th Corps & south west of Petersburg— He fails to indicate the Cause of it though I suppose they were unable to tell There is much travelling upon the P & R road in both directions by horsemen ambulances & Wagons. The following rebel messages taken—To Gen Brent— One (1) Gunboat above & one below the pontoon   signed W. S. L. Cobur—To L. H. B.   are you going this P. M. and at what time. When shall H. be ready answer   signed—Rowe" Telegram received, DNA, RG 108, Letters Received. *O.R.*, I, xl, part 3, 146. On the same day, Meade telegraphed this message to USG, adding his own message. "Just received & forwarded—" Telegram received, DNA, RG 108, Letters Received. *O.R.*, I, xl, part 3, 146.

To Col. Edward D. Townsend

(Cipher)   City Point, July 12th/64 10. p. m
Col. E. D. Townsend, A. A. Gen. Washington
Dispatch announcing Gen. Orders No 228 of July 11th received.

I have made strenuous efforts to discover if any troops besides Ewells Corps has left here. I beleive none others have left. I now have Infantry and Cavalry out near Reams Station where the enemy are found intrenched. The night of the 9th a deserter from Hills Corps come in who stated that he left his corps in the morning on a pass to go into Petersburg. Returning in the evening he found the Corps gone. Other deserters since in state that this Corps has not moved.

U. S. Grant
Lt. Gen

ALS (telegram sent), OClWHi; telegram received (on July 13, 1864, 1:30 P.M.), DNA, RG 94, Letters Received, 703A 1864; *ibid.*, RG 107, Telegrams Collected (Bound). *O.R.*, I, xxxvii, part 2, 222; *ibid.*, I, xl, part 3, 175–76. On July 12, Col. Edward D. Townsend, AGO, telegraphed to USG. "General Orders No. two hundred twenty-eight (228) of July eleventh (11th) is as follows. First. MajorGeneral E. O. C. Ord is assigned by the President to the command of the (8th) (eighth Army Corps and of all troops in the Middle Department. Second MajorGeneral Gillmore is assigned to the temporary command of the part of the (19th) nineteenth Corps in the Department of Washington. . . . Please acknowledge receipt." ALS (telegram sent), DNA, RG 107, Telegrams Collected (Unbound); telegram received, *ibid.*, RG 94, War Records Office, Dept. of Va. and N. C., Army of the James, Unentered Papers; *ibid.*, RG 108, Letters Received. See *O.R.*, I, xxxvii, part 2, 210, 214.

To Maj. Gen. Henry W. Halleck

Cipher   City Point July 12th/64 11.45 p. m
MAJ. GEN. HALLECK WASHINGTON

Give orders assigning Maj. Gen. H. G. Wright to supreme command of all troops moving out against the enemy regardless of the rank of other commanders. He should get out side of the trenches with all the force he possibly can and should push him to the last moment supplying himself from the country. This will not place Gen. Wright over Gen. Augur who commands the defenses but will place him of such of his troops and commanders as may be sent out side. The 6th Corps has all reached Washington [&] Baltimore and two Divisions of the 19th Corps must reach there during to-morrow, besides the 3000 dismounted Cavalry sent from here This with Hunter's force must be sufficient to guard all our fortifications and leave an abundant force to go out side. To this time reinforcements have been sent from here as fast as transportation could be provided and then Hospital steamers have been used at that. Longstreet's Corps is here deserters being received from it within the last day.[1]

U. S. ~~GRANT~~
~~Lt. Gen~~

Ord should move out from Baltimore cautiously the moment it

becomes evident the enemy have left his front, or so weakened it as
to enable him to do so.

U. S. GRANT

Lt. Gen.

ALS (telegram sent), OClWHi; telegram received (datelined 12:00 P.M., received on July 13, 1864, 1:20 P.M.), DNA, RG 107, Telegrams Collected
(Bound). *O.R.*, I, xxxvii, part 2, 222–23; *ibid.*, I, xl, part 3, 176. On July 11,
noon, Maj. Gen. Henry W. Halleck telegraphed to USG. "Genl Wright has just
arrived & a part of his corps will soon be in. He will take position, until ready
for the field, near Fort Sumner, on the Potomac above Chain Bridge. We can
give him transportation, but very little or no artillery. Please send up his batteries as nearly ready for the field as possible. Enemy close to our lines on Rockville road, skirmishing with our cavalry & pickets. His cavalry advance is pretty
strong, with artillery and infantry behind, but how much not ascertained. Accounts from Wallace indicate that he was badly cut up. Militia ordered from
New York to Baltimore delayed by the Governor for some reason not explained.
Pennsylvania will do nothing to help us. The President has seen your telegram
about putting Ord in Wallace's place at Baltimore, but has given me no orders
on the subject." ALS (telegram sent), DNA, RG 107, Telegrams Collected
(Bound); telegram received, *ibid.*; (incomplete) *ibid.*, Telegrams Collected
(Unbound); (2) *ibid.*, RG 108, Letters Received. *O.R.*, I, xxxvii, part 2, 192;
ibid., I, xl, part 3, 143.

1. On July 12, 11:30 A.M., President Abraham Lincoln telegraphed to USG.
"Vague rumors have been ~~reaching~~ reaching us for two or three days that Longstreet's corps is also on its way this vicinity. Look out for it's absence from your
front." ALS (telegram sent), DNA, RG 107, Telegrams Collected (Bound);
telegram received, *ibid.*, Telegrams Collected (Unbound); *ibid.*, RG 108, Letters
Received. *O.R.*, I, xxxvii, part 2, 221; *ibid.*, I, xl, part 3, 175. Lincoln, *Works*,
VII, 438. See telegram to Maj. Gen. Henry W. Halleck, July 13, 1864.

To Maj. Gen. Benjamin F. Butler

By Telegraph from City Pt.
Dated July 12 *1864.*

To MAJ GEN BUTLER.

Have you heard whether the enemy have yet run cars from
Richmond North, to Gordonsville,   If you have any scouts who
can go out & ascertain certainly I would be glad to have them go.

U. S. GRANT

Lt Genl

Telegram received, DLC-Benjamin F. Butler; copies, DLC-USG, V, 45, 59, 67; DNA, RG 108, Letters Sent. *O.R.*, I, xl, part 3, 200. On July 12, 1864, 11:10 A.M., Maj. Gen. Benjamin F. Butler telegraphed to USG. "I examined a deserter on Saturday who gave me a very intelligent and graphic account of Hunter's proceedings near Lynchburg, which he received in a letter from his family which came to him via Gordonsville Junction—He had no doubt that the road was open upon inquiring of him particularly upon that subject   Further information will be obtained and forwarded—" LS (telegram sent), DNA, RG 107, Telegrams Collected (Unbound); copy (undated), *ibid.*, RG 393, Dept. of Va. and N. C., Telegrams Sent. *O.R.*, I, xl, part 3, 200. On the same day, Butler telegraphed to USG. "The ~~Va~~ Virginia Central Road is running as far at least as Gordens ville will send a refugee with particulars" ALS (telegram sent), DNA, RG 107, Telegrams Collected (Unbound); copy (undated), *ibid.*, RG 393, Dept. of Va. and N. C., Telegrams Sent. Printed as sent at 12:10 P.M. in *O.R.*, I, xl, part 3, 201.

At 9:30 A.M., Butler telegraphed to USG. "This report respectfully forwarded for the information of Lt Genl Comdig. Is there any news from Maryland that can be communitecated without detriment to the public Service" ALS (telegram sent), DNA, RG 94, War Records Office, Dept. of Va. and N. C., Army of the James, Unentered Papers; copy, *ibid.*, RG 393, Dept. of Va. and N. C., Telegrams Sent. *O.R.*, I, xl, part 3, 199. The enclosure is *ibid.* At noon, Lt. Col. Cyrus B. Comstock wrote to Brig. Gen. Godfrey Weitzel. "Nothing has been heard from Baltimore since the report of Wallace's defeat at Monocacy and retreat toward Baltimore. There seems to be little apprehension in ~~Batimore~~ Washington & it is thought there that the enemy will recross the Potomac on hearing of Wrights arrival. Some of them are reported in a dispatch just received as passing between Rockville & Washington." ALS, DNA, RG 94, War Records Office, Dept. of Va. and N. C., Army of the James, Unentered Papers. *O.R.*, I, xl, part 3, 200.

To Maj. Gen. George G. Meade

July 12—[*1864*]

The last news I have had from Maryland was to the evening of the 10th., at that time Wallace had been beaten at Monocacy, & was retreating towards Baltimore in disorder.

I got a despatch from the President, dated yesterday, but it gave no news of the invasion. Butler sent last night a party of 50 men across from Deep Bottom to Dutch Gap   at 2.30 this morning they crossed to "Cox's Wharf" & captured an officer & 12 men, burned a mill, shop & dwelling & captured a quantity of small arms, a galvanic battery, two boxes of powder & a torpedo—returned without casualty.[1]

U. S. Grant—

Copies (2), Meade Papers, PHi. Printed as received at 10:30 a.m. in *O.R.*, I, xl, part 3, 178–79.

1. On July 12, 1864, Maj. Gen. Benjamin F. Butler telegraphed to USG a message of 9:30 a.m. from Brig. Gen. Robert S. Foster reporting the raid. Telegram received, DNA, RG 108, Letters Received. *O.R.*, I, xl, part 3, 205.

To Maj. Gen. George G. Meade

City Point July 12th/64 8.20 P. M.

Maj Gen Meade

The present move is not intended as any thing more than a reconnoissance to determine the position and designs of the enemy, and especially to determine if A. P. Hills Corps has left its position in our front. I would not permit any attack against the enemy, in an entrenched position. It may be advisable even to direct your troops to start back tonight. What is the distance from Gregg and his Infantry supports ~~from~~ and the other two Divisions of the 2nd Corps. Unless near enough to be readily supported, I would certainly direct their return tonight—

U. S. Grant Lt. Genl.

Telegram, copies, DLC-USG, V, 45, 59, 67; DNA, RG 108, Letters Sent; (2) Meade Papers, PHi. *O.R.*, I, xl, part 3, 180. On July 12, 1864, 9:30 p.m., Maj. Gen. George G. Meade telegraphed to USG. "Your directions have been received & the necessary orders sent to Hancock & Gregg—Hancocks two divisions are at the Williams House, in front of the left of Warrens line—with pickets on the line he picketed before we contracted our lines—His third division is supporting Gregg & is down the plank road 3 miles from the Williams House & 4 miles from Reams Stn. in good supporting distance   The last report from Gregg—6.40 P. M he had with drawn from Reams Stn. & intended to move down the plank road to Procters tavern to feel the enemy in that direction & ascertain if they had infantry there—He reported to Hancock that he did not require the Division sent him.—Hancock has been instructed to with draw the division sent to Gregg to night & tomorrow after daylight to with draw his corps within the line held by the 5th corps & ready to support that corps—Gregg is ordered to take a position on the plank road in front of our left and to picket strongly in front of the left of the infantry & round in his own front.—" ALS (telegram sent), DNA, RG 393,

Army of the Potomac, Miscellaneous Letters Received; telegram received, *ibid.*, RG 108, Letters Received. *O.R.*, I, xl, part 3, 180.

At 7:00 A.M., Meade had telegraphed to USG. "I send two despatches containing the latest information from scouts & deserters—They change the whole face of affairs & would indicate a movement on our left flank—A negro at work yesterday afternoon near the R. Rd. asserting positively that he saw troops passing South—It may be that they are preparing to meet another attempt on our part to destroy the road or they may themselves be endeavoring to get in our rear —As soon as our Cavalry is up I will send out to feel for the Enemy—" ALS (telegram sent), DNA, RG 393, Army of the Potomac, Miscellaneous Letters Received; telegram received, *ibid.*, RG 108, Letters Received. *O.R.*, I, xl, part 3, 176–77. The enclosures are *ibid.*, pp. 177–78. On July 13, 4:45 P.M., Maj. Gen. Andrew A. Humphreys telegraphed to Lt. Col. Cyrus B. Comstock forwarding the same report of deserters. *Ibid.*, pp. 208–9. On July 12, Meade telegraphed to USG. "The following just received—This looks as if the troops saw yesterday morning down the Rail Road were the infantry guards on the road And the body now mentioned are the relieved returning—Gregg has come up with his division & has been ordered to reconnoitre towards Reams Station & Proctors Tavern—I hope he will get some information" Telegram received, DNA, RG 108, Letters Received; copies, *ibid.*, RG 393, Army of the Potomac, Telegrams Sent; (2) Meade Papers, PHi. Printed as sent at 8:30 A.M. in *O.R.*, I, xl, part 3, 178. The enclosure is *ibid.* At 10:45 A.M., Meade telegraphed to USG. "I send you the latest information received—It shows how conflicting is the information we receive & how accurately the enemy is posted in our affairs—Mahones Division of Hills Corps has now been positively placed in our front—on our left & rear & on its way to Pa." ALS (telegram sent), DNA, RG 393, Army of the Potomac, Miscellaneous Letters Received; telegram received, *ibid.*, RG 108, Letters Received. *O.R.*, I, xl, part 3, 179. The enclosure is *ibid.* At 4:30 P.M., 7:30 P.M., and 9:00 P.M., Meade telegraphed to USG. "The latest intelligence from Gregg at 2. p. m he had met the enemys cavalry both on the Reams Stn. road & also on the plank road near Procters tavern.—I have moved my Hd. Qrs to the Prince Georges C. H road about half a mile west of Burchards [*Birchett's*] & near the 5th Corps Hospitals—" ALS (telegram sent), DNA, RG 393, Army of the Potomac, Miscellaneous Letters Received; copies, *ibid.*, Telegrams Sent; (2) Meade Papers, PHi. *O.R.*, I, xl, part 3, 179. "Gregg reports encountering the enemy in force cavalry & infantry behind earth works at Reams Station—No report from the force sent down the plank road—Hancock has sent a division to support Gregg & holds the balance of his corps ready to move—I have no doubt that by tonight the enemy will have all of Hamptons cavalry at the scene of action supported by one or more divisions of infantry With the superiority of cavalry it will require all of Hancocks Corps, and if the enemy are strongly posted & reinforce from Petersburgh, it may be difficult for him to dislodge them—It becomes a question whether under existing circumstances it is judicious to make the attempt now, or whether we had better wait till all of Sheridans cavalry can be brought to he[r]e & some of our absent troops return—I should like to have your views on this" ALS (telegram sent), DNA, RG 393, Army of the Potomac, Miscellaneous Letters Received; telegram received, *ibid.*, RG 108, Letters Received. *O.R.*, I, xl, part 3, 180. "This despatch just received is forwarded—It confirms my idea that the enemy will reinforce the force at Reams & not allow themselves to be dislodged without making all the resistance possible—" ALS (telegram sent), DNA, RG 94, War Records Office, Army of the Potomac. *O.R.*, I, xl, part 3, 185. The enclosure is *ibid.*

To Julia Dent Grant

City Point Va.
July 12th 1864

DEAR JULIA,

Again I write you without having change in our situation to note. We are doing very well the Army with all the facilities given by the James River being abundantly supplied. The enemy we think is not so supplied and must come out of their fortifications to attack us after a while.

I have neglected to say anything about Fred in my last letters. He was compelled to leave here on account of health about two weeks ago. The fact is Fred is broken down. He has no disease endangering life, but between rheumatism, phistulo [*fistula*] and other ailings I do not think he will ever do much active duty. Bowers & Rowley[1] have gone off sick, and Duff too, and Badeau is now laying quite unwell. Porter,[2] Babcock & Hudson have all been sick. The fact is I am the only one at Head Quarters who has not had a days sickness since the campaign commenced.—I wrote to you that you could make your own arrangement for the balance of the time the war may last. I want the children to be at good schools and do not like the idea of frequent changes.—Fred must commence French and the other children must continue their German.

Love and kisses for yourself and the children. Love to all the rest.

ULYS.

ALS, DLC-USG.

1. Lt. Col. William R. Rowley eventually resigned as of Aug. 30, 1864, and was replaced as private secretary to USG by Ely S. Parker, who advanced to the rank of lt. col. *O.R.*, I, xlii, part 2, 592.

2. On July 12, Parker issued Special Orders No. 55. "Lt Col. Horace Porter A. D. C. will proceed without delay to Harrisburg Pa. on business specially entrusted to him by the Lt. Genl. comd'g. Upon the execution of his orders he will

rejoin these Headquarters." Copies, DLC-USG, V, 57, 62, 67. The family of Lt. Col. Horace Porter lived in Harrisburg, Pa.

To Isaac N. Morris

City Point Va. July 12th *1864*

HON. I. N. MORRIS,

DEAR SIR:

Your letter in relation to Mr. Crapsy is just received. At the time of Mr. Crapsys expulsion from the lines of the Army I spoke to Gen. Meade on the subject telling him of my acquaintance with this family, but like yourself declining to allow personal concidera-tions to interfere with public duties. Gen. Meade however said that he did not care to humiliate the young man but was satisfied with the publication of his order, as a warning to others, without the execution of it. He did suspend the order as I understand but before the Provost Marshal received the notice Mr. Crapsey was gone in the manner prescribed.

I never saw the article which gave the offence. It charged Gen. Meade however with advising our withdrawal to the North side of the Rapidann after the battle in the Wilderness whereas Gen. Meade has not shown to this day the slightest weakening or desire to stop short of complete triumph over the rebellion.

I received a letter from Mr. Crapsey some time since asking to be allowed to return to the Army. Courtisy to Gen. Meade de-manded that before doing so I should submit the matter to him, which I did a day or two after the receipt of the application. Gen. M. expressed his entire willingness for his return. In the mean time I had lost Mr. C's letter and not having noticed his address could not send him the pass. I now enclose it herewith. All are well here and feeling the usual degree of confidance in our success.

Yours Truly

U. S. GRANT

ALS, ICarbS. For the expulsion of correspondent Edward Crapsey, Philadelphia *Inquirer*, from the Army of the Potomac, see J. Cutler Andrews, *The North Re-*

ports the Civil War (Pittsburgh, 1955), pp. 546–48. See also letter to Isaac N. Morris, Aug. 10, 1864. On July 12, 1864, USG wrote a pass. "Pass Mr Edward Crapsey from the North to the Armies now operating against Richmond." Copy, Morris Family Papers, IHi.

To Charles A. Dana

City Point
2 30 p m July 13 1864

Hon C A Dana
Asst Secy War

Deserters are coming in daily giving the position of every division of the Rebel Army—Some are in to day from Longstreets giving the position of two 2 of his [d]ivisions, and the third, we know to be in front of Butler, and have received probably fifty 50 deserters from [it in] the last week—

Boldness is all that is wanted to [drive the] enemy out of Maryland in confusion

I hope and believe Wright is the man to assume that.—The advance of two divisions of the 19th Corps passed Ft Monroe yesterday, and I hope the whole of them will reach Washington within the twenty four hours[1]

U S Grant
Lt Genl

Telegram received (on July 14, 1864, 1:00 A.M.), DNA, RG 107, Telegrams Collected (Bound); copies, *ibid.*, Telegrams Received in Cipher; *ibid.*, RG 108, Letters Sent; DLC-USG, V, 45, 59, 67. *O.R.*, I, xxxvii, part 2, 259; *ibid.*, I, xl, part 3, 207. On July 11, 10:00 P.M., Asst. Secretary of War Charles A. Dana telegraphed to USG. "A body of about 150 rebel Cavalry attacked Gunpowder Bridge at about four thirty a. m. today, drove off the guards at each end, which consisted of some 70 Ohio National Guards, destroyed a considerable part of the bridge and captured and destroyed two trains of cars, one going north, the other south. Gen Franklin was captured and the other officers on the train; Gen W. F Smiths name is not mentioned but we conclude that he was among them   A gunboat reached the scene after it was all over   Gen Wallace reports a large force of the enemy near Baltimore this morning but seems to have had no fighting since his defeat on the Monocacy on saturday, as to his losses there we have no specific figures but I estimate them at from two to four hundred. We have positive information that Early Breckenridge and Imboden dined together at

Rockville at three P. M. sunday   In front of Washington Lowells Cavalry had
some pretty sharp skirmishing yesterday on the Tenleytown road; his pickets
were driven in & major Fry who commanded them reports that the enemy was
there in great force with infantry and artillery. Nothing has occurred there today to demonstrate the presence of any such force and the skirmishing has borne
away to the right in front of Fort Stevens   Col Hardee who was at Fort Reno
about noon reports that the rebels had one rifle gun bearing upon that work   He
saw also a train of wagons (or artillery) which he judged to be about a mile in
length and a column of infantry of a rather straggling character moving in the
direction of Fort Stevens   The Country has constantly been filled with clouds of
dust which are believed to have been raised by bodies of cavalry   today the
pickets are very active in front of Fort Stevens, but they are composed mostly
of hundred day men—and the cannon of the Fort have also been used though not
a gun has been fired at the Fort   A few of our men have been wounded. The
Telegraph Operator there reports a considerable number of Camp Fires burning
in front   He says between Baltimore and Washington wire not yet been inter-
fered with—Five boat-loads of Gen Wrights troops have arrived and one of the
19th Corps   Gen Wright and his troops have gone to Fort Stevens—All the
Convalescents from the hospitals have been collected and organized & sent to the
trenches also   QM Gen Meigs moved out this afternoon in Command of about
1500 armed employees of the Qr. Mrs. Department—Gen Meigs has also furnished guards to relieve the Veteran Reserve guarding the depot in this city and
Alexandria and they have likewise gone to the front   Gen Auger has drawn
from fortifications on the south side all the men that in his judgement could possibly be spared from there. Gen Gillmore has arrived in town and will take the
Chief Command of the troops as soon as they are able to move out of the Defences   I find that Gen Halleck has great Confidence in this officer   I should
also state that Gen McCook is in Command at Fort Stevens   Gen Auger has
been very actively engaged in getting these miscellanious troops to the front
His precise position in relation to Gen Gillmore I do not understand but will ascertain and inform you in the morning   Gen Ord went over to Baltimore this
P M at 4.30 to take command of the troops in the field—Gen Wallace being directed to make his Hd Qrs in the city   Washington & Baltimore are in a state of
great excitement, both Cities are filled with country people fleeing from the
enemy—The damage to private property done by the invaders is almost beyond
Calculation—mills workshops & Factories have been destroyed—from 25 to 50
miles of the Balt. & O. R. R. have been torn up, Governor Bradfords house was
burned this morning and it is reported that the house of old Mr. Blair & the P. M.
General near this City were also burned today. No news from Hunter. The force
of the enemy is everywhere stated at from 20 to 30.000   the idea of cutting off
their retreat would seem to be futile for there are plenty of fords & ferries now in
their control where they can cross the Potomac & get off in spite of all our efforts
to intercept them, long before our forces can be so concentrated as to be able to
strike an effective blow"   Telegram received, DNA, RG 108, Letters Received;
(incomplete) *ibid.*, RG 107, Telegrams Collected (Unbound). *O.R.*, I, xxxvii,
part 2, 192–94.

On July 12, 11:30 A.M. and noon, Dana telegraphed to USG. "No attack,
either on this city or Baltimore—General McCook has been passing artillery all
night from Forts Reno and Massachusetts, which remain within his command,
General Wright having relieved him at Fort Stevens   He telegraphs this morn-

ing that he is about to drive the rebel skirmishers away from his front, after which the artillery will cease—Nothing can possibly be done here towards pursuing or cutting off the enemy for want of a Commander   Gen Auger Commands the defenses of Washington with McCook and a lot of Brigadier Generals under him, but he is not allowed to go outside—Wright Commands his own Corps— Gen Gillmore has been assigned to the temporary Command of those troops of the 19th Corps in the City of Washington—Gen Ord to Command the 8th Corps and all other troops in the Middle Department leaving Wallace to command the City alone   But there is no head to the whole and it seems indispensable that you should at once appoint one—Hunter will be the ranking officer if he ever gets up but he will not do; indeed the Secy of War directs me to tell you, in his judgement Hunter, ought instantly to be relieved, having proven himself far more incompetent than even Sigel: He also directs me to say that advice or suggestions from you will not be sufficient   Gen Halleck will not give orders except as he receives them—The President will give none, and until you direct positively and explicitly what is to be done everything will go on in the deplorable and fatal way in which it has gone on for the past week"   "We have reports from many quarters that Longstreets Corps is coming down the valley   The secessionists here and in Baltimore have told it confidentially to their friends for several days past   It has been reported that the Corps was at Gordonsville on its way north on the fourth instant   An officer of Earlys, wounded and Captured by Gen Wallace on sunday, who has since died positively affirmed that they were on their way   General Couch reports this morning that his scouts in the valley state that they are rapidly advancing   It is possible that the inactivity of the rebels in this vicinity is because they are waiting for reinforcements   Three more transports with troops, have arrived here this morning—I think they were all from City Point but have sent to ascertain"   Telegrams received (the second on July 13), DNA, RG 108, Letters Received; *ibid.*, RG 107, Telegrams Collected (Unbound). *O.R.*, I, xxxvii, part 2, 223–24. At 9:00 P.M., Dana telegraphed to Brig. Gen. John A. Rawlins. "The rebels struck the Balto & O. R. R. just beyond Bladensburg at about 8 P. m Destroying bridges and tearing up the track—The force there which is reported to be encamped upon the road this evening is said to Number about 1500 cavalry with a battery of artillery—Of course this ends for a the time being all railroad communication between Washington and the North   It would be difficult to give you an idea how little we know respecting this force which has been before Washington now for nearly three (3) days—It is still undetermined how much infantry there is in it or whether there is more than one battery of Artillery—The only man I have found who has been able to state anything positively with sense and intelligence is Col Lowell commanding Augurs cavalry who knows that McCausland is here with a brigade of the fourth virginia mounted regiments and one Battery   Some infantry has been seen and Doctor Barnes tells me that he witnessed a little fight on the Seventh Street road at about six P. M. between a part of the Vermont Battery and about 800 rebels on foot in which the latter were severely punished—This is the largest body of rebel infantry that I have been able clearly to locate—There are all sorts of reports respecting heavy columns seen moving in the distance with enormous wagon trains but I am unable to arrive at any certainty on the subject   I visited a considerable part of the lines this afternoon on the left and I found Genl Wrights Corps was in reserve—The General himself was in the city attending to the debarkation of his troops—General McCook is in Command of Fort Stevens which by the way is the same as Fort Massachusetts   He told me that the mass of the enemys infantry was withdrawn from his front   He had captured this morning two (2) prisoners from Rhodes Division who informed him that they had been encamped about two miles off in the direction of Rockville but that their Division was under orders to march this morning at daylight—where they did not know A few rebel skirmishers still remained MackCook told me in a house about twelve hundred yards distant and another body of them in a wood about three thousand yards distant—He was firing thirty pound Parrotts at the house—Br Gen Harden who if possible is a bigger fool than McCook notwithstanding his inferior rank was also firing thirty pound Parrotts from Fort Reno at the same sharpshooters— I think Harden had a hundred pounder which he discharged occasionally   I was glad to notice that the fifteen inch mortars had not yet been brought into use—A vigorous artillery fire was also kept up from Fort Slocum at the woods in which McCooks second body of rebel sharpshooters were established—General Hardin was also positive that the rebels had constructed a work thirty five hundred yards distant in his front but I think that it exists nowhere but in his imagination—No reconnoissance had been undertaken from our lines—nor had any skirmishers been pushed forward to any considerable distance—Indeed until Wright reached the scene yesterday evening McCook had had no skirmishers out at all but had allowed the rebel sharpshooters to get up near line and pick the men off at the embrasures of the fort—Along this part of the lines there was no general commander—no real knowledge of what was in the front—nothing but wild imagination and stupidity—From what I can hear the same system reigns throughout the whole length of the lines—and I do not exaggerate in the least when I say that such a lamentable want of intelligence energy and purpose was never before seen in any command—I cannot learn that Augur has personally visited any part of the lines—and I sure that he knows as little respecting them as I did before I went out—Indeed the Secretary has very sharply reprimanded him for his want of attention to his duties—Halleck seems to be about as well informed as Augur and I judge that he contributes quite as much as the latter to the prevailing confusion & inefficiency   The testimony of those best informed says that Hallecks mind has been seriously impaired by the excessive use of liquor and that as general thing it is regularly muddled after dinner every day—Of the sixth corps 9216 men are reported as having arrived since 5 P. M yesterday—Of the 19th Corps none have come on except a single ship load which I reported last night— We have no news from any part of the country later than three (8) P. M. today when the wires were cut between here and Baltimore   Up to that time nothing had been recd from Sherman nor anything from Ord beyond the fact of his assuming command—The militia of N York and Penna Cannot be got towards the seat of action in any considerable numbers before saturday or monday next—The reports of the approach of Longstreets Corps given in my last despatch to Genl Grant still continue though we have no new evidences of their truth—The fact however that the rebels still remain between Washington and Baltimore and have even moved further towards our right seems to indicate a reliance from upon reinforcements from some quarter   The only troops here that can be counted upon for real fighting outside of the fortifications are Wrights two divisions and the eight hundred men of the 19th Corps—The dismounted cavalry sent up from the Army of the Potomac are generally worthless   The detachments being for

the most part without their field officers—Of course you will understand that
this despatch is intended for your eye and that of the General alone" Telegram
received, USG 3; DNA, RG 107, Telegrams Collected (Unbound).

At 10:00 P.M., Maj. Gen. Edward O. C. Ord, Baltimore, telegraphed to
USG. "R Road bridge at gunpowder only slightly damaged   can be repaired in
three days.   rebel cavalry between Beltsville and ~~Washington~~ Laurel have torn
up the R. Road—~~Laurel~~ guard at Laurel and Anapolis Junction have fallen back
—the latter to Annapolis by order—York R Road cut—I have no reliable cavalry
and the rebels under Gilmor and Bradley Johnson have raided in the last few
days to within five miles of this city—the citizens temporarily armed I can not
send out as they stampede   I want two or three field Batteries or Seige Howitzers
—and ammunition for them—have but few guns mounted   have in conjunction
with the governor called for (10000) ten thousand militia to complete and man
works—Genl Ricketts division reduced to 2488—aggregate—Averells Cavalry
(4000) four thousand reported to have b[een] in Frederick on the 10th"   ALS
(telegram sent), *ibid.*; telegram received (on July 13), *ibid.*, RG 108, Letters
Received. *O.R.*, I, xxxvii, part 2, 247–48. On July 13, Col. John W. Shaffer,
chief of staff for Maj. Gen. Benjamin F. Butler, wrote to Rawlins. "From passengers from Baltimore I gather the following: Hunter is at Martinsburg. We
hold Hagerstown. The force of enemy operating around Baltimore is principally
cavalry, said to be about 8,000. There is said to be 15,000 rebels at Silver Spring,
within seven miles of Washington. I can't learn that the rebels have shown any
disposition to attack our works, either at Baltimore or at Washington. I would
say that there is no earthly danger of the rebels getting into either city, but they
will do much damage around them, and get large supplies, but it won't hurt any
to stir the natives up in that neighborhood. The Baltimore paper puts the entire
rebel force at 45,000, and says that Longstreet is at Gordonsville advancing with
another column. Telegraphic communication between Washington and Baltimore cut. I can't see anything like reasonable ground for believing that Longstreet is at Gordonsville, or that the enemy are so numerous as estimated above.
I will let you know should I get any further information." *Ibid.*, pp. 258–59. On
the same day, Lt. Col. Cyrus B. Comstock wrote to Brig. Gen. Godfrey Weitzel.
"Rebels have cut Philadelphia R. R north of Baltimore capturing two trains of
passengers, Gen. Franklin among other officers. Have destroyed much private
property outside of Washington and have been firing at one of the forts with
artillery but at last reports had made no attack. They are on the Rockville side
of the city. Latest despatch was 11 a. m. yesterday. Nothing official from Hunter"   ALS, DNA, RG 94, War Records Office, Dept. of Va. and N. C., Army of
the James, Unentered Papers. *O.R.*, I, xl, part 3, 218.

1. On July 12, 4:35 P.M., Brig. Gen. William H. Emory, Fort Monroe,
telegraphed to USG. "I have reached here with the advance of the two Divisions
of the 19th Army Corps, and received orders to go to Washington, and shall
start tonight. It will be one week before the rear of the column gets here. Col.
Schaffer will continue to report the ships, with the number of troops as they arrive." Copy, DNA, RG 393, 19th Army Corps, Letters Sent. *O.R.*, I, xxxvii, part
2, 243; *ibid.*, I, xl, part 3, 206. At 11:00 A.M., 4:15 P.M., and 5:20 P.M., Shaffer
telegraphed to Rawlins. "The Steamer 'Clinton' with 800 men and Steamer
'Corinthian' with 300 men just arrived from New Orleans and will proceed at
once to Washington" "Steamer St Marys has just arrived from New Orleans—

with 675 men & gone to Washington" "Creole from New Orleans with 600 and Mississippi with 1000 men have arrived and started for Washington" ALS (telegrams sent), DNA, RG 107, Telegrams Collected (Unbound).

To Maj. Gen. Henry W. Halleck

City Point. Va July 13, 12. m *1864*

Maj Genl Halleck
Chief of Staff
Washington D. C.

Summary of evidence gathered from deserters, scouts & Cavalry reconnoissance by Gregg on our left show that none of Hills or Longstreets Corps have left our front 2 brigades (Lane's[1] & McGowans[2]) of Willcox Div Hills Corps are on north side of James in Fosters[3] front, 2 brig. (Thomas[4] & Scales[5]), same divisn same Corps are between Walthall and Appommottox.

Pickets Div in Butlers immediate front and deserters say Davis[6] brig of Heath[7] Div Hills Corps is in reserve in rear of Pickett.[8]

Gregg ascertained by reconnoissance, that Fitz Lees[9] Div & Bowen[10] Brig Cavalry are at Reoms Station entrenched, and the Citizens say some infantry though he found no other evidence of infantry.

Mahones[11] Division Hills Longstreets Corps is in front of 5th Corps.[12] Evidence of this seems positiv[e.] Deserters from Mohones Div (Florida Regimts) say that Heaths division has returned to its old position in reserve

Its movement seems to have been made down the Rail Road fearing Wright was moving in that direction but finding it did not it has returned[13] Progress of Works good as could be expected under such hot sun. Very little picket firing yesterday

U S Grant
Lt Genl U S A

Copy (telegram sent), OCIWHi; telegram received (on July 14, 1864, 12:15 A.M.), DNA, RG 107, Telegrams Collected (Bound). *O.R.*, I, xxxvii, part 2,

257; *ibid.*, I, xl, part 3, 207. On July 12, 11:45 P.M., Maj. Gen. Henry W. Halleck telegraphed to USG. "At the request of Genl Canby Genl Reynolds was appointed to command of the 19th corps. I presume, however, that he will command only what remains on the Miss. Genl Gillmore is appointed temporary commander of the portion that may arrive here. Genl Ord has been appointed to command the 8th corps & troops in the middle Dept in place of [G]enl Wallace. I think the matter of a permanent commander of the 10th corps should be delayed till present difficulties are over. The order respecting Genl Butler & the 18th corps was made precisely to carry out your views as expressed in your letter & telegram. If not satisfactory please make for the Adjt Genl a draft of one that will embrace exactly what you desire. Only about half of the 6th corps has landed & only one transport of the 19th corps. Till more arrive & are organized nothing can be done in the field. I think, however, that Washington is now pretty safe, unless the forces in some part of the entrenchments, and they are by no means reliable being made up of all kinds of fragments, should give way, before they can be reinforced from other points. A line thirty seven miles in length is very difficult to guard at all points with an inferior force. The forces in our front seem to be those previously named. Prisoners & citizens say that parts of Hills & Longstreets corps are expected. If this be true the enemy in your front must be very weak indeed. Nothing heard of Hunter. The breaking of the wires to Baltimore & Harrisburg has cut off all communication with him & with Genl Howe at Harpers Ferry. It seems to be the impression here that the enemy is massing his forces to attack us tomorrow. The boldness of his movements would indicate that he is stronger than we supposed." ALS (telegram sent), DNA, RG 107, Telegrams Collected (Bound); telegram received, *ibid.*; *ibid.*, RG 108, Letters Received. *O.R.*, I, xxxvii, part 2, 221–22; *ibid.*, I, xl, part 3, 175. On July 13, 3:00 P.M. and 4:00 P.M., Halleck telegraphed to USG. "There was some skirmishing in front of the works last evening by the 6th corps in which our loss is reported about three hundred. A few men in the trenches were picked off by rebel sharpshooters. The enemy fell back during the night on the Rockville road, and Genl Wright moves out to-day on River road towards Edward's Ferry. He numbers only about ten thousand effective, & the 19th corps only Six hundred & fifty. Genl Emory with thirteen hundred more is just arriving & another vessel aground down the river has eleven hundred. It is believed that the enemy will make for Edward's Ferry and Wright is directed on that point. He may be able to attack their rear, but is too weak to fight their main body. It is possible that this retreat has resulted from Hunter's approach, but we hear nothing of him. It is to be regretted that the 19th corps arrives too late to assist the 6th. The most reliable estimates we can get of the enemy's force it numbers from 23 to 25 thousand exclusive of cavalry. They state that a part of Hill's corps, is coming to reinforce them, & that without them they would have captured Washington if the 6th corps had not arrived." ALS (telegram sent), DNA, RG 107, Telegrams Collected (Bound); telegram received, *ibid.*; (incomplete) *ibid.*, Telegrams Collected (Unbound); *ibid.*, RG 108, Letters Received. *O.R.*, I, xxxvii, part 2, 257–58. "Your telegram of 12 P. M yesterday is just recieved. Genl Wright had already been assigned to the command of the troops to go to the field. I have telegraphed to Genl Ord as you directed. He reports Rickett's Division to be reduced to an aggregate of 2488. The only other force he has is five hundred colored, two hundred sailors, three thousand militia & a body of armed citizens. The remains of Ricketts division are the only forces that can take the field. I telegraphed you this morning the number of available troops here for the field, & also the most reliable estimate of enemy's strength. Nothing whatever about Hunter." ALS (telegram sent), DNA, RG 107, Telegrams Collected (Bound); telegram received, *ibid.*; *ibid.*, Telegrams Collected (Unbound); *ibid.*, RG 108, Letters Received. *O.R.*, I, xxxvii, part 2, 258; *ibid.*, I, xl, part 3, 207.

1. James H. Lane, born in Va. in 1833, graduated from Virginia Military Institute (1854) and the University of Virginia (1857), then taught at VMI and other schools before the Civil War. Entering the war as maj., 1st N. C., he was appointed brig. gen. as of Nov. 1, 1862.

2. Samuel McGowan, born in S. C. in 1819, graduated from South Carolina College (1841) and became a lawyer-politician in Abbeville, S. C. As col., 14th S. C., he served in the brigade of Brig. Gen. Maxcy Gregg, whom he succeeded in command with the rank of brig. gen. as of Feb. 20, 1863.

3. Robert S. Foster, born in Ind. in 1834, worked in a store before becoming capt., 11th Ind., as of April 22, 1861, rising to col., 13th Ind., as of April 30, 1862. Appointed brig. gen. as of June 12, 1863, he commanded a brigade near Charleston, S. C., under Maj. Gen. Quincy A. Gillmore and later served as chief of staff for Gillmore in the Army of the James. In June, 1864, he led a brigade which seized Deep Bottom, Va.

4. Edward L. Thomas, born in Ga. in 1825, graduated from Emory College, served in the Mexican War, and was a Ga. planter before the Civil War. Col., 35th Ga., and brig. gen. as of Nov. 1, 1862, he served throughout the war in the Army of Northern Va., and commanded a brigade in Wilcox's div. in July, 1864.

5. Alfred M. Scales, born in N. C. in 1827, educated at the University of North Carolina, was a lawyer-politician in N. C. and U.S. Representative (1857–59). He enlisted as a private in the Civil War and rose to col., 13th N. C., before appointed brig. gen. as of June 13, 1863. Still recovering from a severe wound received at Gettysburg, Scales commanded a brigade in Wilcox's div. in July, 1864.

6. Joseph R. Davis, born in Woodville, Miss., in 1825, educated at Miami University, was a lawyer-politician in Miss. before entering C.S.A. service as capt. He later served on the staff of his uncle, Jefferson Davis, which raised charges of nepotism concerning his appointment as brig. gen. as of Sept. 15, 1862. USG accurately described his position in July, 1864.

7. Henry Heth, born in Va. in 1825, USMA 1847, resigned from the U.S. Army as of April 25, 1861. Appointed C.S.A. brig. gen. as of Jan. 6, 1862, and maj. gen. as of Oct. 10, his div. took heavy losses at Gettysburg, and Heth won little reputation as a soldier. His previous acquaintance with USG is discussed in James L. Morrison, ed., *The Memoirs of Henry Heth* (Westport, Conn., 1974), pp. 111–12, 113–14, 198.

8. On July 13, 1864, 10:30 A.M., Maj. Gen. Benjamin F. Butler telegraphed to USG. "We have in front of us here, from Walthall Junction to the Appomattox Thomas' and Scales' Brigades of Wilcox' Division of Hill's Corps and in front of Gen. Foster upon the North side of the James are Lane's and McGowan's (now Conner's) Brig of the same division & Corps making the whole of Wilcox Division present here   In the rear of Picketts Division which is in my immediate front a deserter states Davis Brigade of Heth's Division of Hill's Corps to be stationed acting as a reserve Brigade—From all the information I can get I do not

believe for a moment that any of Hill's Corps have gone North"   LS (telegram
sent), DNA, RG 94, War Records Office, Dept. of Va. and N. C., Army of the
James, Unentered Papers; copy, *ibid. O.R.*, I, xl, part 3, 217. On the same day,
Butler transmitted to USG a signal message of 4:00 P.M. "Ten (10) cars partly
loaded with troops and two pieces of artillery just passed the Railroad Junction
towards Petersburg—"   Copies, DNA, RG 107, Telegrams Collected (Unbound); *ibid.*, RG 393, Dept. of Va. and N. C., Telegrams Sent. *O.R.*, I, xl, part
3, 218.

9. Fitzhugh Lee, born in Va. in 1835, USMA 1856, nephew of Robert E.
Lee, resigned from the U.S. Army as of May 21, 1861. Appointed C.S.A. brig.
gen. as of July 25, 1862, he commanded a brigade of cav. which won a victory at
Kelly's Ford (March 17, 1863) and performed ably at Chancellorsville. Promoted maj. gen. as of Aug. 3, his div. was at Ream's Station when USG wrote.

10. A garbled reference to Thomas L. Rosser, born in Va. in 1836, USMA
1861, who commanded the 5th Va. Cav., before appointment as brig. gen. as of
Sept. 28, 1863.

11. William Mahone, born in Va. in 1826, graduated from Virginia Military Institute (1847), and was active in engineering work with Va. railroads
before the Civil War. As col., 6th Va., he commanded the Norfolk district, and
later a brigade in the Army of Northern Va. although he was not nominated as
brig. gen. until Feb. 11, 1864.

12. On July 13, 10:30 A.M., Maj. Gen. George G. Meade telegraphed to
USG. "I have nothing particular to report beyond what was contained in special
despatches, of the transactions during the past 24. hours.—Greggs cavalry was
withdrawn last night to Lee's mills—from whence he pickets towards Reams Stn.
& along the R. Rd to the left of the army—I deem it proper to retain him there
for the present w as he obtained undoubted evidence from prisoners that Fitz
Lee's division & Rosser's brigade of Cavalry were at the station.—He could hear
nothing of infantry beyond the reports of citizens who stated that Hills Corps
was at the station supporting the cavalry—This probably meant Heths division
which from other sources we had reason to believe was on the R. Rd. guarding
it & supporting the cavalry   There appears to be no doubt that up to noon
yesterday & even later Mahone's division of Hills corps was in front of the 5th
corps.—The preparation of batteries in front of the 5th corps & 9th corps & the
running of the gallery for the mine, made good progress yesterday notwith-
standig the excessive heat—The engineers have established a depot at a convenient point and are collecting gabions & other material for operations   The
heavy guns will soon be put in position in front of the 5th Corps, and an effort
made to silence the fire of the batteries in the salient on the plank road—In the
mean time the enemy is busily employed strengthening his line, and can be seen
preparing another one in rear of the one now occupied.—" ALS (telegram sent),
DNA, RG 393, Army of the Potomac, Miscellaneous Letters Received; telegram
received, *ibid.*, RG 108, Letters Received. *O.R.*, I, xl, part 3, 208. At 11:00 A.M.,
Meade telegraphed to USG. "I propose with your permission visiting you at City
Point today unless you are going to be away from your Hd. Qrs—"   ALS (telegram sent), DNA, RG 393, Army of the Potomac, Miscellaneous Letters Received; copy, *ibid.*, Letters Sent. The start of a reply exists in USG's letterbook.
"I shall remain"   Copy, DLC-USG, V, 67.

13. At 11:30 A.M., Meade wrote to USG. "The above dispatch forwarded
for your information. It proves Hill's two divisions are still in our front. It con-

firms the movement of Heth previously reported, and is in conformity with Gregg's report that he could find no infantry at Reams'. I now think the enemy having heard of Wright's movement sent Heth to Reams' to meet an attack on the road, which not being made, he was brought back; or he may have gone to guard returning trains." *O.R.*, I, xl, part 3, 210. The enclosure contained the information USG reported to Halleck. *Ibid.*, pp. 209–10.

To Maj. Gen. Benjamin F. Butler

By Telegraph from City Pt
Dated July 13 *1864.*

To GEN BUTLER.

Please inform Capt Smith,[1] of the Navy, that the rebels have placed a battery at Wilcox landing & request him to send a gun boat or two down to dislodge them. The difficulty in landing troops there I presume will render it useless to send any down but if you think a speedy landing can be effected & can spare the troops you may send down a regt. I think no greater force necessary. They would be under the protection of Gunboats if the enemy were found superior to them. If any troops are sent, instruct them to destroy as much of the crops as they can but to keep out of the houses.

U. S. GRANT. Lt Genl

Telegram received (at 7:20 P.M.), DLC-Benjamin F. Butler; copies, DLC-USG, V, 45, 59, 67; DNA, RG 108, Letters Sent. *O.R.*, I, xl, part 3, 217. On July 13, 1864, 7:50 P.M., Brig. Gen. Godfrey Weitzel telegraphed to USG. "Gen Butler is absent out on the line. He has already directed Gen. Graham to dislodge the Rebels at Wilcox landing I have no doubt it will be done—In view of this fact do you wish me to communicate [yo]ur dispatch to Capt Smith" ALS (telegram sent), DNA, RG 107, Telegrams Collected (Unbound); copy, *ibid.*, RG 393, Dept. of Va. and N. C., Telegrams Sent. *O.R.*, I, xl, part 3, 217. On the same day, USG telegraphed to Weitzel. "It is not necessary—A Gun Boat has been sent from here" Telegram received, DLC-Benjamin F. Butler; copy, DNA, RG 94, War Records Office, Dept. of Va. and N. C., Army of the James, Unentered Papers. *O.R.*, I, xl, part 3, 218. On the same day, Maj. Gen. Benjamin F. Butler transmitted to USG a message from Brig. Gen. Charles K. Graham reporting that the C.S.A. battery had gone. Telegram received, DNA, RG 107, Telegrams Collected (Unbound); copy, *ibid.*, RG 393, Dept. of Va. and N. C., Telegrams Sent. *O.R.*, I, xl, part 3, 221.

1. Melancton Smith, born in New York City in 1810, entered the U.S. Navy in 1826, was promoted to capt. as of July 16, 1862, and commanded the U.S.S.

Mississippi in Rear Admiral David G. Farragut's Mississippi River campaign. On June 21, 1864, he was assigned to command the U.S.S. *Onondaga* on the James River, and on July 14 commanded gunboats fired upon by a C.S.A. battery near Malvern Hill. *O.R.* (Navy), I, x, 175, 268–69.

To Maj. Gen. Edward O. C. Ord

City Point July 13th/64.

MAJ. GEN. ORD, BALTIMORE,

I have ordered four batteries to you. They are now embarking. I will send ~~Col. Comstock~~ Babcock ~~to you~~ an Engineer officer for temporary duty with you. Send him back as soon as his services can be dispensed with.

U. S. GRANT
Lt. Gen.

ALS (telegram sent), CtY; telegram received (marked as sent at 5:00 P.M.), Ord Papers, CU-B; DNA, RG 393, Middle Dept. and 8th Army Corps, Telegrams Received (Press). *O.R.*, I, xxxvii, part 2, 294. On July 13, 1864, Capt. Ely S. Parker wrote to Col. Charles H. Tompkins, art. brigade, 6th Army Corps. "You will please take four of Your Batteries (2 Batteries of rifled guns and 2 Batteries of Smooth bore guns) and proceed without delay to Baltimore Md. reporting to Maj Gen E. O. C. Ord Com'd'g, Middle Department for duty. You will accompanny the Batteries in person." Copies, DLC-USG, V, 45, 59, 67; DNA, RG 108, Letters Sent. *O.R.*, I, xxxvii, part 2, 294. On the same day, Brig. Gen. John A. Rawlins telegraphed to Brig. Gen. Seth Williams. "Please order Capt Turnbull of the Engineer Corps, to report in person immediately to these Head quarters for temporary assignment to duty at Baltimore. It is desirable that he should leave here for Baltimore thi[s] evening. Hence the request for the order in Gen'l Meades absence" Copies, DLC-USG, V, 45, 59, 67; DNA, RG 108, Letters Sent. *O.R.*, I, xxxvii, part 2, 294. On July 15, 1:30 P.M., Capt. Charles N. Turnbull, Baltimore, telegraphed to USG. "I find Gen[l] Ord has gone to Washington. Sha[ll] I follow him up or return to the Army of the Potomac." ALS (telegram sent), DNA, RG 107, Telegrams Collected (Unbound). On the same day, USG telegraphed to Turnbull. "You were sent to Baltimore to lay out and complete its defences, and more esspecially to connect the works allready constructed by lines of rifle pits. You will not leave Baltimore until all this work has been laid out then if Your services are no longer required there, You will return and report to Gen. Meade for further duty." Copies, DLC-USG, V, 45, 59, 67; DNA, RG 108, Letters Sent. *O.R.*, I, xxxvii, part 2, 346.

On July 14, 2:00 P.M., USG telegraphed to Ord. "Push out all the force you can and make the enemy develope himself if in your front. If gone follow with as much strength as you can having proper regard for the safety of the City." ALS (telegram sent), OClWHi; telegram received, Ord Papers, CU-B; DNA,

RG 107, Telegrams Collected (Unbound). Printed as received July 15, 7:20
A.M., in *O.R.*, I, xxxvii, part 2, 322. On the same day, Ord telegraphed to USG.
"The rebels have disappeared from between here and Washington. The four
Batteries ~~(4) four~~ will not be wanted—I am ordered to Washington with my
force. Leave to-day." ALS (telegram sent), DNA, RG 107, Telegrams Collected
(Unbound). *O.R.*, I, xxxvii, part 2, 322.

On July 15, 3:00 P.M., USG telegraphed to Ord. "Four 4 Batteries of the
6th Corps, Maj Tompkins Commanding, left here yesterday morning for Baltimore. Please order them to return at once to this place without debarking" Telegram received (on July 16, 3:15 P.M.), DNA, RG 107, Telegrams Collected
(Bound); *ibid.*, Telegrams Collected (Unbound); copies, *ibid.*, RG 94, Letters
Received, 765A 1864; *ibid.*, RG 108, Letters Sent; DLC-USG, V, 45, 59, 67.
Printed as received July 16, 3:00 P.M., in *O.R.*, I, xl, part 3, 256.

To Maj. Gen. Henry W. Halleck

(Cipher)   City Point Va. July 14th *1864*
MAJ. GEN. HALLECK, WASHINGTON,

For the last few days I have made every effort to ascertain
whether the enemy have further detached to send North. He shows
every where as strong a front as he has done from the start and
deserters constantly coming in locate every Division of Longstreet's
& Hill's Corps and Beaurigards forces   If any detachments have
been made it has been Brigades and not Divisions and I have no
evidence of even this having been done. I received a communication
from Lee dated the 10th showing his presence at that time but I
received one dated the 13th from Beaurigard ~~date~~ in answer to one
directed to Lee. This I do not understand. It seems to me that by
promptly pushing the enemy he can be driven from Maryland with
great loss. Now however it will be necessary to hold force enough
in the City to hold the enemy at bay if he should attack, until reinforcements can be got. I have sent Ord four batteries from here and
will direct him to push out and at least develope the enemy in his
front and drive him if he can. Not being able to communicate with
all the commanders it will be hard to get anything like uninimity of
action but if they will push boldly from all quarters the enemy will
certainly be destroyed.

If I find further detachments have been sent from here I will make a determined push to obtain a firm foothold that will ultimately secure Richmond, and be easily held, and detach all I can.

U. S. Grant

Lt. Gen.

ALS (telegram sent), CSmH; telegram received (sent at 2:00 P.M.), DNA, RG 107, Telegrams Collected (Bound). Printed as received July 15, 1864, 6:50 A.M., in *O.R.*, I, xxxvii, part 2, 301; *ibid.*, I, xl, part 3, 223.

On July 15, 12:30 P.M. and 6:00 P.M., Maj. Gen. Henry W. Halleck telegraphed to USG. "Yours of 2 P M yesterday is just recieved. citizens of Maryland who had intercourse with the enemy in our front say that rebel officers attributed their retreat to their disappointment in the expected cooperation of Genl Hill's corps; that they could hear nothing of him & could wait no longer lest Hunter should come up. Wright's advance reached Poolsville last night & had a smart cavalry skirmish. As the enemy's main body have nearly twenty four hours the start Wright can at best only reach their rear guard. The 19th corps, about 4,000 men, have landed in fragments destitute of every thing, but as soon as supplied have been sent forward. They will reach the vicinity of Edwards Ferry to-day. Ord's command from Baltimore arrived during the night, & has gone forward this morning. It is nearly 5,000. Some of Howe's forces were reported on the Monocacy yesterday & may join Wright this morning. We hear nothing directly from Hunter. Rail road men say Sullivan's command was at Harper's Ferry yesterday. Genl Kelley telegraphs from Cumberland that when Hunter left he said he intended to strike the enemy's flank, but where or how, he does not state. Message after message has been sent to him, but no reply has been recieved. All your instructions have been communicated to Genl Wright & he will do his best to carry them out; but from the late hour in which forces fit to take the field have reached here he will hardly be able to do the enemy much injury. He is directed to pursue him south, till further instructions are recieved from you. While writing the above yours of 8 P. M. is recieved. I will telegraph to Fort Monroe to send no more of the 19th corps here than the fragments of Emory's divisions still behind. The story about an intended raid on Point Lookout is without foundation. No enemy passed Bladensburg. Rail road communication to Philadelphia will be reopened to-morrow. B & O railroad is reported nearly repaired from west to Harpers Ferry." "From the most reliable information we have been able to collect, ~~makes~~ the raiding force in Maryland consisted of, 1st Early's corps, reorganized in three divisions, under Rhodes, Gordon & Ramseur (Johnsons old), reenforced in Virginia by conscripts & convalescents to about 12,000. 2d Breckenridge's corps (a new one), consisting of two divisions reenforced by all rebel troops at Staunton, Charlottsville, Lynchburg & in the valley, to about 12,000. 3d The cavalry of McClauseland, Ransom, Imboden, Bradley Johnston, Gillmore & Moseby. Ransom seems to have had principal command. Its force is estimated by good observers from 4 to 6 thousand. All dismounted men have been remounted on stolen horses. The artillery & trains have also been supplied with fresh animals. They have between 20 & 30 pieces of artillery. Some, however, who pretend to have counted them, say they number much higher. Many estimate the entire force at from thirty to forty thousand. The mass of evidence would make it a little less than the former number. Their loss at Monocacy & near Silver Spring was considerable, but they say they have made it up by volunteers & conscripts. Their captures have not been valuable except in horses. The foregoing is formed from the most reliable data I can obtain, and is about the lowest estimate. Some estimates are unquestionably very exaggerated. I give the organizations ~~in detail~~ in order that you may compare them with data which you have." ALS (telegrams sent), DNA, RG 107, Telegrams Collected (Bound); telegrams received, *ibid.*; *ibid.*, RG 108, Letters Received. *O.R.*, I, xxxvii, part 2, 329–31. On the same day, USG telegraphed to the commanding officer, Fort Monroe. "Turn all Steamers arriving from the south with troops to City Point." Telegram received (press), DNA, RG 107, Telegrams Collected (Bound); copies, *ibid.*, RG 108, Letters Sent; DLC-USG, V, 45, 59, 67. *O.R.*, I, xxxvii, part 2, 333.

To Maj. Gen. Henry W. Halleck

City Point 8 p m
July 14th 1864

MAJ GEN H W HALLECK
CHF OF STAFF

Dispatch from Mr Dana just received indicates the enemy leaving Maryland—If so instructions ought to be sent to Fort Monroe directing the 19th Corps as they reach there to be [se]nt here—Genl Ord telegraphs a rumor in Baltimore that the enemy have sent to Point Lookout to rescue prisoners there[1]   This can hardly be possible in view of the narrow outlet through which they would have to go through in passing Washington with them—I call your attention to the rumor however that you may direct the proper steps if such a thing should be possible—I think it well to notify the Navy Dept of this that they may [pr]event the possibility of an attempt to cross [the P]otomac in boats

U S GRANT

Telegram received, DNA, RG 107, Telegrams Collected (Bound); *ibid.*, Telegrams Collected (Unbound); copies (sent at 3:00 P.M.), *ibid.*, RG 108, Letters Sent; DLC-USG, V, 45, 59, (sent at 8:00 P.M.) 67. Printed as sent at 3:00 P.M., received on July 15, 1864, 7:30 A.M., in *O.R.*, I, xxxvii, part 2, 301; *ibid.*, I, xl, part 3, 224.

1. On July 13, Maj. Gen. Edward O. C. Ord telegraphed to USG. "One of the Staff here has recieved information which he deems reliable that a force of rebel cavalry crossed the Rail Road to Washington—between Laurel and Beltsville with instructions to go to Point Lookout and release the rebels confined

there—Precautions would do no harm—a rebel force is reported south of the R Road near the places named" ALS (telegram sent), DNA, RG 107, Telegrams Collected (Unbound); telegram received (on July 14), *ibid.*, RG 108, Letters Received. *O.R.*, I, xxxvii, part 2, 293.

To Maj. Gen. Henry W. Halleck

City Point, Va, July 14th *1864*

MAJ. GEN. H. W. HALLECK,
CHIEF OF STAFF OF THE ARMY,
GENERAL,

It would seem from dispatches just received from Mr. Dana, Asst. Sec. of War, that the enemy are leaving Maryland.[1] If so Hunter should follow ~~them~~ him as rapidly as the jaded condition of his men and horses will admit. The 6th & 19th Corps should be got here without any delay so that they may be used before the return of the troops sent into the valley by the enemy. Hunter moving up the valley will either hold a large force of the enemy or he will be enabled to reach Gordonsville & Charlottesville. The utter destruction of the road at, and between, these two points will be of immense value to us.

I do not intend this as an order to bring Wright back whilst he is in pursuit of the enemy with any prospect of punishing him, but to secure his return at the earliest possible moment after he ceases to be absolutely necessary where he is.[2]

Col. Comstock who takes this can explain to you fully the situation here. The enemy have the Weldon road completed but are very cautious about bringing cars through on it. I shall endeavor to have it badly destroyed, and for a long distance, within a few days. I understand from a refugee that they have twenty-five miles of track yet to lay to complete the Danville road.

If the enemy has left Maryland, as I suppose he has, he should have upon his heels, veterans, Militiamen, men on horseback and everything that can be got to follow, to eat out Virginia clear and

clean as far as they go, so that Crows flying over it for the balance
of this season will have to carry their provender with them.

> I am Gen. very respectfully
> your obt. svt.
> U. S. GRANT
> Lt. Gen.

ALS, IHi. *O.R.*, I, xxxvii, part 2, 300–1; *ibid.*, I, xl, part 3, 223.

1. On July 13, 1864, 10:00 A.M., 1:15 P.M., and 9:00 P.M. (marked as
sent at 11:00 P.M.), Asst. Secretary of War Charles A. Dana telegraphed to USG.
"The enemy have disappeared along the entire line—McCook reports that the
enemy's pickets in front of Fort Stevens were changed in the night from infantry
to cavalry and that the cavalry departed just before daybreak—Gen Augur reports to Halleck that he has Wrights corps all ready to move in pursuit—should
Halleck so order—cavalry will be sent both in the direction of Baltimore and on
the Rockville road to ascertain which route they have taken—Montgomery Blairs
house was burned by them last night but the house of old Mr Blair still stands—
The amount of damage to the R R between here and Baltimore is not yet ascertained—a neighbor of Mr Blairs who made the his way through from Silver
Springs to the city last night says that the rebel force which has been in that
neighborhood was all of cavalry & did not exceed three hundred in number—We
have a report from Point Lookout that a U. S. Steamer passed that point early
this morning coming in this direction with fifteen hundred troops of the 19th
Corps   These will probably arrive here about 6.30 P. M." Telegram received
(July 14), DNA, RG 108, Letters Received. *O.R.*, I, xxxvii, part 2, 259. "It is
now pretty certain that the rebels have retreated by way of Rockville toward
Edwards Ferry. McCook reports that both Early & Breckinridge ~~retreated~~ moved
out ~~in the night toward Leesburg~~ in the night leaving Rockville at 3 a. m. with
200 waggons & a drove of 2000 cattle. ~~90~~ Ninety wounded rebel soldiers & 11
officers were found this morning in Mr. Blair's house at Silver Spring. McCook
reports that some wounded are also left on the ground in front of Fort Stevens.
Wright with Lowell's cavalry is moving in pursuit by the river road. No news
from Hunter. Our loss by the siege is about 300 killed & wounded. Wright says
his skirmish of last evening was with men of Rode's division. Col. McCallum
sent out to examine the Baltimore & Ohio railroad reports it unhurt." ALS (telegram sent—misdated July 12), DNA, RG 107, Telegrams Collected (Bound);
telegram received (July 14), *ibid.*, RG 108, Letters Received. *O.R.*, I, xxxvii,
part 2, 260. "Since my dispatch of last evening to General Rawlins there have
debarked here of the Sixth Corps 1689 men, and of the Nineteenth Corps 3560
men. As you will remember eight hundred men of the Nineteenth Corps were
landed on Monday. General Emory has also reported in person, and says that
the remainder of two divisions of his Corps is close at hand. The head of General
Wright's column passed Fort Reno at five P. M. moving out on the Rockville
road. His force consists of his own two Divisions, and of the troops of the Nineteenth Corps, in all about ~~sixten~~ fifteen thousand men. Colonel Lowell's cavalry,
which is serving with him, amounts to about seven hundred and fifty men.
Wright will move on with all practicable energy, but as yet his command is

inferior in numbers to the enemy. Orders were sent to General Ord at 4.10 P M. to move to Washington as soon as he was satisfied that the enemy left his front, bringing his troops by rail. General Halleck informed him that all the Evidence went to Show that the enemy was moving off by Edward's Ferry, and that it was not probable that any important force remained near Baltimore. Wright has been assigned to the chief command according to your orders. Of Hunter we know nothing. Lowell attacked McCausland, who covers the rear of Early's column at ~~Poolesville~~ Rockville, at about 5 P M. Lowell charged them with four Companies of his Regiment and a body of dismounted men but found them too strong to break through He lost about thirty killed and wounded, and brought away some fifty prisoners beside killing and wounding a number of the enemy. His retreat was favored by the dust which covered his flanks and prevented McCausland from seeing his weakness. The railroad between here and Baltimore proves to be totally unharmed and trains will be running on it tomorrow morning. The telegraph between here & Philadelphia is working tonight. The night is bright, and favorable for marching." LS (telegram sent), DNA, RG 107, Telegrams Collected (Bound); telegram received, *ibid.*, Telegrams Collected (Unbound); (marked as sent at 11:00 P.M., received July 14) *ibid.*, RG 108, Letters Received. *O.R.*, I, xxxvii, part 2, 259–60. On July 13, 11:00 P.M., Dana telegraphed to Brig. Gen. John A. Rawlins. "Previous to the receipt of the Generals order a considerable excitement prevailed with reference to the movement to be made Halleck strenuously opposed sending Wright out and the President was unwilling to take any responsibility—Senators Wade & Chandler were nearly frantic at the impossibility of getting anything done but found the President unwilling to overrule the obstenate prudence of Gen Halleck The Generals order however settled the question though I am not absolutely certain that it had not been determined to send Wright out before the order arrived I have omitted to mention in my former despatches that Maj Gen Doubleday was assigned to the command of the miscellaneous militia of the Dist. who were ordered to garrison the forts on the other side of the Eastern Branch but I believe neither the General nor his troops even got into position Immediately on the approach of the rebs. to the Balt. & O. R R Admiral Goldsboro took command at Fort Lincoln having under him a squad of Sailors marines and imployees of the Navy which position he still holds—A number of Brigadier Generals nominated to the Senate for confirmation were not acted upon—Among them were Ferero Shepard Whipple Gillem DeRussey & Wilson—DeRussey & Wilson have been reappointed with their original rank; the others expire by constitutional limitation" Telegram received, USG 3.

2. On July 15, 10:30 P.M., Lt. Col. Cyrus B. Comstock telegraphed to USG. "Gen Halleck thinks Hunters command very badly cut up by the Lynchburg expedition and that it does not now exceed twelve thousand effective men of all arms (12000). It is now at Harpers ferry or between there and Leesburg. Wright with ten thousand men should be between ~~Edwards~~ Whites ferry and Leesburg. Ricketts and what has arrived of the 19th Corps are between Wright and Washington. orders for Wright & the 19th corps to ~~return and~~ comply with your letter will be issued as soon as Gen. Halleck receives an answer to his telegram to you of today. It will take three or four days for Wright to get back. Gen Halleck does not understand your letter sent by me as an order for Wrights recall and awaits positive orders. He thinks on Wrights return the enemy ~~will~~ may come back. Wrights orders now are to follow enemy till recalled." ALS

(telegram sent—misdated June 15, 10:00 P.M.), DNA, RG 107, Telegrams
Collected (Bound); telegram received, *ibid.*; *ibid.*, RG 108, Letters Received.
O.R., I, xxxvii, part 2, 331; *ibid.*, I, xl, part 3, 253.

To Maj. Gen. Benjamin F. Butler

City Point July 14th/64

MAJ. GEN. BUTLER,

I received this morning a communication from Beaurigard,
of date the 13th, in answer to mine of the 8th inst. addressed to
Gen. Lee. On the 10th Gen. Lee answered one of the day before
but not answering the other himself I fear he may have gone North
taking more force with him. Have you any information of Lee's
presence about Petersburg later than the 10th obtained from deserters or refugees?

U. S. GRANT
Lt. Gen.

ALS (telegram sent), OClWHi; telegram received, DLC-Benjamin F. Butler.
O.R., I, xxxvii, part 2, 302; *ibid.*, I, xl, part 3, 245. On July 14, 1864, 3:30 P.M.,
Maj. Gen. Benjamin F. Butler telegraphed to USG. "I have made all investigation possible since receiving your telegram and I can learn nothing of Lee's
where abouts—Day before yesterday Pickett refused receiving any communication unless sent from Gen Grant to Gen Lee—When he returned the letter to you
yesterday a note was forwarded to me that my communication would be received,
but the answer of Ould obviated the necessity of sending—The communication
about Jaquess and Gilmore evidently went before the War Dept at Richmond
which may account for the delay of that without the necessity of supposing Lee
absent—I will keep endeavoring to hear advise you of anything more upon this
subject" LS (telegram sent), DNA, RG 94, War Records Office, Dept. of Va.
and N. C., Army of the James, Unentered Papers; telegram received, *ibid.*, RG
108, Letters Received. *O.R.*, I, xxxvii, part 2, 302; *ibid.*, I, xl, part 3, 245.

On the same day, Butler wrote to USG. "Assuming that this position in the
peninsula of Bermuda Hundreds will not be abandoned at least during the war
whatever may be the necessatiess of operations or the results of movements elsewhere, and specially in view of operations on the south side of Richmond, I take
leave to suggest to the Commanding General the propriety of constructing a
railroad from the landing at Bermuda Hundreds to our front. The route is very
practicable and I will have it run out. Whenever we advance the road can be
easily carried forward and make a junction with the Petersburg road. There is
iron enough for the purpose at Norfolk and Fortress Monroe, and while we are
remaining here the road might be easily built by a force detailed from the
Hundred days men, the timber for ties being directly along the road. I observe

that owing to the contraction of space for wharf room at City Point between the ravine and the Appomattox it is impossible to get wharfage enough there to land all the supplies so that large sums are being expended for demurrage, although the vessels lay six (6) or seven (7) deep along the whole extent of wharf. The wharves at Bermuda Hundred need not be more than Fifty (50) feet in width to get the deepest water and the entire expense of putting them in order and constructing the railroad, to the United States, would be saved by one weeks necessary demurrage as it exists at present   Of course in this I mean no criticism upon General Ingalls who seems to be doing the best he can in the space he occupies   I am aware of the cost of labor for loading and unloading stores from vessels, but as we advance I trust we shall be able to obtain that labor at a cheap rate—We should have had a surplus of it here if Kautz and Wilsons return had not been interrupted with the negroes they were bringing in with them   It is quite possible that hereafter, at some central point it may be necessary to make a depot for the recruitment and disciplining of negro troops in the necessity of garrisoning the southern country—For that purpose I know no better point than this—Healthy, easily defended, good water, plenty of wood and easy of access, a garrison which should control Richmond Petersburg, and all the country east of the Chowan river, and therefore Norfolk Portsmouth and Suffolk, might be most conveniently located here. Besides there will be land enough here for the safe location of a large colony of freedmen   Indeed, if the war should proceed further south and last any time, I do not see why this would not be as convenient a location as any for prisoners with the negroes on hand to guard them. I venture to submit these suggestions to the attention of the Commanding General." LS, DNA, RG 108, Letters Received. *O.R.*, I, xl, part 3, 246–47.

Also on July 14, Butler wrote to USG. "I know how difficult it is for gentlemen in high positions to get the exact opinions and thoughts of friends or foes. For myself, I am always glad to do so. From the feeling of grateful recognition of your kindness to me I send you the inclosed letter. It was never intended for your eye, and was written by a devoted and warm-hearted officer of mine and a sincere friend and admirer of yours. He is a good politician, and I know sincerely and truly wishes the success of yourself, and therein the success of the country. He gives these things, as he sees them, for my guidance. I cannot presume to have a solemn talk with you, but I think you should get the ideas of my friend, and with the exception of the manner of their expression many of them are my own; therefore pardon the expression; they are those of a warm-hearted, rough Western man, and are honest and true convictions. Permit me here to say that I desire to serve you, not in this only but in all things. My future is not in the army; yours is. Our paths can never cross, therefore amid all the selfishness of life I can see no reason why I cannot always subscribe myself as I do now, Most truly, your friend," *Ibid.*, p. 247.

To Maj. Gen. George G. Meade

———

City Point July 14th 1864

Maj. Gen. Meade,

There is no chance now of getting any more horses for the Cavalry for at least two weeks. This will be to long a time to wait before making another raid upon the enemy's communications. You may notify Sheridan to get ready at the earlyest practicable day. I will order Kautz to report to him with his available Cavalry.[1] The Cavalry will require a fair start with Infantry supports after which they should go on extending their raid upon the roads into North Carolinga as far as Welden. I do not think they should attempt to return immediately here but should get back to the James River below or might even find it better to go into Suffolk and work their way up slowly to the Army. A pontoon train will be necessary to carry out this programe.

U. S. Grant
Lt. Gen.

ALS (telegram sent), OClWHi; telegram received (at 10:00 A.M.), DNA, RG 94, War Records Office, Army of the Potomac. *O.R.*, I, xl, part 3, 224. See following telegram.

1. On July 14, 1864, USG telegraphed to Maj. Gen. Benjamin F. Butler. "I shall have an effort made by the 16th to cut the Rail Roads again this time far to the South—please direct Kautz to report to Sheridan in person tomorow for directions & to accompany the expedition with all of his force that can be spared—sheridan has or will receive his instructions by morning" Telegram received, DNA, RG 107, Telegrams Collected (Unbound); copies, *ibid.*, RG 108, Letters Sent; DLC-USG, V, 45, 59, 67. *O.R.*, I, xl, part 3, 246.

To Maj. Gen. George G. Meade

———

City Point Va July 14th, 1864

Maj Gen Meade

Please direct your Engineer Officers to demolish all works built by the enemy and now in rear of our lines. Of course this will not include any turned to face the enemy and now used by us, nor will it be well perhaps to destroy those in full view of the enemy. If you will send your Engineer Officers to direct what works should be leveled in rear of the 18th Corps I will order Gen Martindale[1] to destroy them.

U. S. GRANT
Lt. Gen

Telegram, copies, DLC-USG, V, 45, 59, 67; DNA, RG 108, Letters Sent; Meade Papers, PHi; ViU. Printed as sent at 12:30 P.M. in *O.R.*, I, xl, part 3, 224. On July 14, 1864, 2:00 P.M., Maj. Gen. George G. Meade telegraphed to USG. "Your despatches in relation to proposed raid & the destruction of enemy's works have been received—Orders have been sent to Sheridan to prepare his command & report when they will be ready.—Two divisions of the 2d. Corps will be put this afternoon on the work of levelling the enemys old works." ALS (telegram sent), DNA, RG 393, Army of the Potomac, Miscellaneous Letters Received; telegram received, *ibid.*, RG 108, Letters Received. *O.R.*, I, xl, part 3, 224–25. On the same day, USG telegraphed to Maj. Gen. Benjamin F. Butler. "I have directed such of the rebel works around Petersburg as are in our rear & not used by us by us to be leveled. Gen Weitzel being unwell I have directed Gen Meade to send his Engr officers to designate those in rear of the 18th Corps to be leveled & gle Gen Martindale to have them so leveled." Telegram received, DLC-Benjamin F. Butler; copies, DLC-USG, V, 45, 59, 67; DNA, RG 108, Letters Sent. *O.R.*, I, xl, part 3, 246. Also on July 14, USG telegraphed to Brig. Gen. John H. Martindale. "I have directed Gen Meade to destroy, by leveling, such of the works captured from the enemy as are of no use for our defense, in the rear of his line, and to send his Engineer to point out such in rear of the 18th Corps as should be leveled. Please order such work as the Engineer Officers may designate to be executed" Copies, DLC-USG, V, 45, 59, 67; DNA, RG 108, Letters Sent. *O.R.*, I, xl, part 3, 249.

1. John H. Martindale, born in N. Y. in 1815, USMA 1835, went on leave after graduation and resigned from the U.S. Army as of March 10, 1836, then pursued a career in law. Appointed brig. gen. as of Aug. 9, 1861, he served in the Peninsular campaign, then as military governor of D. C. until May, 1864, when he joined the Army of the James. Briefly in command of the 18th Army Corps (July 7–22), his ill health led to a leave of absence followed by resignation.

To Maj. Gen. George G. Meade

———

City Point July 14th/64

MAJ. GEN. MEADE,

If Sheridan succeeds in getting to Welden, or near there, I did not suppose he would be able to get to the Danville road. If he could however, and could follow the road up to Danville and south of it making the destruction of both roads sufficient to last for a month or two it would be a good thing. In starting out such parties a wide discretion must be given to commanding officers. I see from Atlanta papers that they look upon the loss of that place as probable but congratulate themselves that Sherman could not stay a month if he had it. Intimation seems strong that Johnston will fall back to Macon, where he thin[k]s he will not be followed for some time, and detach largely to join Lee's Army to drive us back when they can fall upon Sherman with an overwhelmning force. To cut both roads far south therefore will be a great help to us.

I think Sheridan should simply be informed fully of the importance of complete and extended destruction of the enemy's roads and be left to execute it in his own way and with discretion to return in his own time, with authority even to go into New Bern if he deems safety requiring it.

The object of an Infantry force is to give him a fair start beyond reach of the enemy's Infantry. If a Corps can get on the rail-road between the rebel Cavalry and Infantry that would be sufficient. they might remain one day, destroying road if not engaged with the enemy and then return moving well to the East in doing so.

U. S. GRANT
Lt.

ALS (telegram sent), Forbes Magazine Collection, New York, N. Y. Printed as received at 7:20 P.M. in *O.R.*, I, xl, part 3, 225. On July 14, 1864, 5:30 P.M., Maj. Gen. George G. Meade telegraphed to USG. "Genl. Sheridan reports he can have 9000 men ready to start on the 16th—What force of Infantry should accompany him & how far do you think the Infantry ought to go—Do you propose Sheridan should attempt the destruction of any other road than the Weldon, or do you desire the Danville & Lynchburgh also both cut?—" ALS (telegram sent), DNA, RG 393, Army of the Potomac, Miscellaneous Letters Received; telegram received, *ibid.*, RG 108, Letters Received. *O.R.*, I, xl, part 3, 225.

Also on July 14, Meade forwarded to USG two reports of information from deserters, the first at 10:30 A.M. *Ibid.*, pp. 226–27.

To Maj. Gen. George G. Meade

[*July 14, 1864*]

The Enemy are leaving Maryland it is supposed by Edwards ferry—Wright is following, but I presume the Enemy will get off, without punishment,   Hunter may hit him but, I doubt it.—The Baltimore road was not injured, and trains were expected to be running to day.—Telegraphic communication was open yesterday with Philadelphia,   it is rumored that Franklin who was captured with the train at Gunpowder bridge afterwards escaped—I have no confirmation of the report however.—

U. S. GRANT.

Telegram, copies (2), Meade Papers, PHi. Printed as received at 11:00 P.M. in *O.R.*, I, xl, part 3, 225–26. On July 14, 1864, USG sent an identical telegram to Maj. Gen. Benjamin F. Butler. Telegram received, DLC-Benjamin F. Butler.

To Edwin M. Stanton

City Point July 15th/64 [*3:00 P.M.*]

HON. E. M. STANTON, SEC. OF WAR,

I regret to learn that Brig. Gen. Edward Ferrero was not confirmed by the Senate. I hope he will be immediately reappointed with his former rank. He deserves great credit on this Campaigned for the manner in which he protected our immense wagon train with a Division of undisciplined Colored troops and detachments of dismounted Cavalry, without organization. He did his work of guarding the trains and disciplined his troops at the same time so that they come through to the James River better prepared to go into battle than if they had been at a quiet school of instruction during the same time. If Ferrero is taken from his Div. I do not know how he is to be replaced.

U. S. GRANT
Lt. Gen

ALS (telegram sent), OClWHi; telegram received (on July 16, 1864, 3:00 P.M.), DNA, RG 107, Telegrams Collected (Bound). *O.R.*, I, xl, part 3, 252. On July 16, 8:55 P.M., Col. James A. Hardie telegraphed to USG. "The Secretary of War directs me to inform you that he has re-appointed General Ferrero to be Brigadier General of Vols to rank May 6 1863, his old date." ALS (telegram sent), DNA, RG 107, Telegrams Collected (Bound); telegram received, *ibid.*, Telegrams Collected (Unbound); *ibid.*, RG 108, Letters Received. *O.R.*, I, xl, part 3, 292. On July 17, USG transmitted this message to Maj. Gen. George G. Meade. "The following has this day been received   Please Communicate same to Gen Ferrero"   Telegram received (undated), DNA, RG 94, War Records Office, Army of the Potomac; copy, Meade Papers, PHi. *O.R.*, I, xl, part 3, 292.

To Charles A. Dana

City Point, Va, July 15th/64

C. A. DANA, ASST. SEC. OF WAR,

I am sorry to see such a disposition to condemn a brave old soldier as Gen. Hunter is known to be without a hearing. He is known to have advanced into the enemys country, towards their Main Army, inflicting a much greater damage upon them than they have inflicted upon us, with double his force, and moving directly away from our Main Army. Hunter acted too in a country where we had no friends whilst the enemy have only operated in territory where to say the least ~~half~~ many of the ~~population~~ inhabitants ~~were~~ are their friends. If Gen. Hunter has made war upon the newspapers in West Va probably he has done right. In horswhiping a soldier he has laid himself subject to trial but nine chances out of ten he has only acted on the spur of the moment under great provocation. I fail to see yet that Gen. Hunter has not acted with great promptness and great success. Even the enemy give him great ~~gre~~ credit for courage and congratulate themselves that he will give them a chance of getting even with him.

U. S. GRANT
Lt. Gen,

ALS (telegram sent), OClWHi; telegram received (sent at 8:00 P.M.), DNA, RG 107, Telegrams Collected (Bound). *O.R.*, I, xxxvii, part 2, 332–33. On July 15, 1864, 10:45 A.M., 11:30 A.M., and 4:00 P.M., Asst. Secretary of War

Charles A. Dana telegraphed to USG. "General Ords command has not yet started from here; The night having been consumed in the effort of getting together wagons, knapsacks, haversacks &c I presume they will get off before noon Mr. Garrett, President of the B. & O. RailRoad reports that trains from the West are now running to Martinsburg Sullivan has arrived at Harpers Ferry. Hunters precise whereabouts is not yet known but Garret understands that he is moving with his forces to get East of the Blue Ridge to cut off the enemy Hunter appears to have been engaged in a pretty active campaign against the news papers in West Virginia—We also have Semi-Official reports of his having horsewhipped a soldier with his own hands It is reported that the rebels have carried 1700 recruits away with them from Md. Baldy Smith arrived in New York yesterday—No news from Wright this morning." "Our latest advices indicate that the head of the retreating rebel column has reached Ashbys gap Wright is not yet at Edwards Ferry—The enemy will doubtless escape with all his plunder and recruits leaving us nothing but the deepest shame that has yet befallen us" "Walter McClellan from N. Orleans with 860 men 19th Corps arrived here 12 30 P m A rail road agent who left Sandy Hook This morning reports Hunters forces a going to reach Harpers Ferry wednesday evening and were till this morning crossing river to Pleasant Valley, although footsore & badly used up One regiment remains at Martinsburg and a detachment at Daffield [*Duffield's*] Crook is with the main column A Signal Officer says Enemy crossed large wagon train at Nolans Ferry yesterday morning followed by the mass of their Cavalry and artillery Another Signal Officer at Sugar-loaf Mountain says, they Crossed 400 wagons at Whites Ford the miles below mouth of the Monocacy yesterday morning moving in direction of Snickers Gap, They were still Crossing at 11 A. M. according to this officers—Gen Halleck thinks main body have gone through Snickers & but a small portion through Ashbys Gap—Halleck estimates the force they have had before Washington at 28000 to 30,000 as follows Earlys Corps 3 Divisions, Rhodes, Gordons, Ramseys [*Ramseur's*] 12000 Breckenridges Corps; 2 Divisions 12000—Cavalry and Artillery 4000 to 6000 with thirty Cannon—Halleck thinks they have goodt 5 or 6000 excellent horses and 2000 poor Cattle—mostly Cows—Ord is ordered to you No news from Wright" Telegrams received, DNA, RG 108, Letters Received. *O.R.*, I, xxxvii, part 2, 331–32. On the same day, 10:00 P.M., Dana telegraphed to Brig. Gen. John A. Rawlins. "We have no report from Wright since this morning, nor from the troops of the 19th Corps nor Ricketts & Kenleys since they passed Fort Reno Mr Ashley M. C. from Ohio tells me confidentially that in an interview the other day with Gen Butler that officer showed him the order directing him to repair to Ft Monroe and said he would be damnd if he paid any attention to it: He did not receive orders from Staff Officers Mr Ashley tells me also that he found a good deal of discontented and mutinous spirit amongst staff officers in the Army of the Potomac—a good deal of McClellanism, he says, was manifested especially by officers of pretty high rank He tells me also that Gen Meade is universally disliked by officers of every sort" Telegram received, USG 3. Printed as sent by Maj. Thomas T. Eckert in *O.R.*, I, xxxvii, part 2, 331. On the same day, Dana wrote to Rawlins. "I have telegraphed you during the last week some things which might perhaps have been better said in a letter, but it seemed important that you should know the interior truth of some matters at once. I can only say that however severe some of my expressions may have seemed, they have been rather too weakly colered to do justice to the truth. You will find that the responsibility for this whole disgraceful affair will be put upon the general's shoulders. You did know the truth, but there are not many who will ever know it as we do, and the inaction of the general toward those who are really guilty will only confirm the opinion which will be made to prevail that it is his fault. In the first place, it will be said, he is the commander in chief, & is bound to provide for the whole field of operations. In the second place it was by his order & request that both Washington & Baltimore have been stripped of troops, so that when the enemy arrived there was no body but militia to defend either. In the third place, it was he who sent Hunter to Lynchburg leaving the valley open for Early. Fourthly, he does nothing to call Hunter to account for retreating to the Ohio river whence he could not possibly get his troops up to interfere with Early's movement. And fifthly he does not send troops enough to Washington till it is too late to do any thing more than begin a useless pursuit of an enemy whose escape with all his plunder we are impotent to prevent. These are some of the things which are already beginning to be said & which will be said more & more. I must also tell you that I hear from friends of the general & of the cause the decided opinion that the campaign is already a failure and that we are worse off, in a worse position & weaker, than we were the day you left Culpepper. Seventy thousand men have been killed & wounded, they say, to produce this nett result. It is vain to suggest that the failure was caused by Butler's total incompetency to make the best use of the troops under his command which landed at City Point on May 5, or that at least 20.000 men have been slaughtered by Meade's blind, unconsidered, fragmentary assaults at Cold Harbor and Petersburg, assaults even more deficient in all the elements of generalship than Burnside's infamous massacre at Fredericksburg. I say it is vain to say these things, for the answer is instant,—'But Grant is the commander, and he neither removes Butler nor Meade,—he is satisfied with their conduct, and adopts it for his own.—' That is true & there is no answer to it. I suppose he will also adopt Halleck's conduct and give that the benefit of his prelating approval, and so on till the end. The black & revolting dis honor of this siege of Washington with all its circumstances of poltroonery & stupidity, is yet too fresh & its brand is too stinging for one to have a cool judgment regarding its probable consequences; but, as far as I can now see, they are very likely to be the defeat of Mr Lincoln & the election of Gen. McClellan to the Presidency, not to mention a thousand other things almost as fatal to the country, which will come in the same concatenation. Possibly Sherman may have the good fortune to end the war in Georgia. God grant it!—for otherwise I fear it will have to be ended by a younger, more earnest, more manly & less self complacent race of men than the mental dwarfs & moral cowards who have the control of it at present. And who can assure us that the nation will escape the awful dangers which now menace it at every side. . . . P. S. You may show this Wilson." ALS, USG 3.

On July 14, 10:15 A.M., 11:00 A.M., and 10:00 P.M., Dana telegraphed to USG. "No news from Hunter, nor do we know where he is. At our last advices he was yet at Parkersburg. Mr Garrett president B & O. railroad telegraphs this morning that Sullivan reported himself at Martinsburg on the 11th but that Pillar bridge & two culverts were destroyed near there rendering it impossible for him to move in this dir farther. Aveill's division 3000 strong reached Parkersburg on the 12th. 1500 infantry & 700 cavalry left that place on the 10th & 11th. & on the 12th the Q. M. at Parkersburg stated there were 2500 infantry between that place & Gallipolis. No report whatever respecting Crook & his division. No report from Howe's force on Maryland heights. Monocacy bridge not very badly damaged." ALS (telegram sent), DNA, RG 107, Telegrams Collected (Bound); telegram received (marked as sent at 1:20 P.M.), *ibid.,* RG 108, Letters Received. Printed as sent at 2:00 P.M. in *O.R.,* I, xxxvii, part 2, 302–3. "the rebels carried Franklin from the railroad around to randalls town, where he escaped and was secreted till last night in a house 4 miles from Baltimore pike a cavalry company went out last evening to bring him in. Several naval officers and 2 army Lieutents are reported as plated [*captured*] with him   I hear nothing about baldy Smith"   Telegram received, DNA, RG 107, Telegrams Collected (Unbound). *O.R.,* I, xxxvii, part 2, 302. "No additional troops of the 19th Army Corps have arrived today—The total number debarked is 4400 while Emorys division alone exceeds Six Thousand   Several organizations are still incomplete   The men are pretty badly worn out by their Sea voyage and will dwindle greatly on a march   Gen Ord with Ricketts Division 2488 strong and Kenleys brigade of the 8th Corps 1500 strong has arrived here and by the order of the Secy of War moves out immediately to Wright the necessary transportation being furnished by Gen Auger   Ricketts leaves about a thousand men detached as guards of railroads & elswhere whom he expects to rejoin him—This makes his loss in the Campaign about fourteen hundred of whom about six hundred were taken prisoners by the Rebels on the Monocacy   Gen Gillmore having become disabled Gen Ord is assigned to the Command of the troops of the 19th Corps and Kenleys Brigade together   Nothing more from Hunter   Col Chipman has been sent from the Dep. to hunt him up   Augers Cavalry on the South side of the river captured (5) five men from McCauslands rear-guard who say that their command crossed the Potomac at Muddy Branch yesterday morning having moved from their camp in front of Washington about 3 P M Tuesday—Breckenridge moved immediately after them   A farmer who witnessed the skirmish between the Vermont Brigade and Rhodes div. men on tuesday evening says that at that time Breckenridges command was already out of sight on its way to the Potomac   There seems to be no doubt that Early has got the main body of his Command across the river with his plunder, what that is, it is impossible to say precisely   General McCook has reported one herd of Cattle as containing two thousand head and the number of horses & mules taken from Maryland is also reported by various parties at about about 5000, this however is probably somewhat exaggerated—Our total losses by the seige amount 500 killed and wounded —The Ir-rigulars in the fortifications here have been withdrawn—Brevet-Major-General Meigs marched his Division of Qr. Mrs. clerks and employees into town this morning & Admiral Goldsboro has also returned to smoke his pipe on his own door-step   Major General Doubleday I learn is still at his post as commander of the Defences east of the East Branch but is without troops"   Telegram received (on July 15), DNA, RG 108, Letters Received. *O.R.,* I, xxxvii, part 2, 303.

To Maj. Gen. Henry W. Halleck

Headquarters Armies of the United States
City Point, Va. July 15th 1864.

Maj Genl H. W. Halleck.
Chief of Staff of the army.
General;

In view of the possible recurrence of the late raid into Maryland, I would suggest the following precautions to be taken.

First, there should be an immediate call for all the troops we are likely to require.

Second; Washington City, Baltimore, and Harpers Ferry should be designated as schools of instruction, and all troops raised east of the state of Ohio, should be sent to one of these three places as fast as raised. Nashville Decatur and Stevenson, should also be named as schools of instruction and all troops raised in Ohio and west of it, should be sent to these. By doing this we always have the benifit of our increased force and they in turn improve more rapidly by contact with veteran troops. To supply Sherman, all the rolling stock that can possibly be got to him should be sent. An effort ought to be made to transfer a large portion of the stores now at Nashville, to Chattanooga. This might be facilitated by withdrawing for a while the rolling stock from the Nashville and Reynoldsburg road, and a large part of the stock from the Ky. roads.

There is every indication now, judging from the tone of the southern press, that unless Johnson is reinforced Atlanta will not be defended. They seem to calculate largely upon driving out Sherman by keeping his lines of communication cut. If he can supply himself once with Ordnance and Quartermasters stores, and partially with Subsistence, he will find no difficulty in staying until a permanant line can be opened with the south coast. The road from Chattanooga to Atlanta will be much more easily defended, than that North of the Tennessee. With the supplies above indicated at Chattanooga, with say sixty days provision there, I think there will be no doubt but the country will supply the balance. Sherman will, once in Atlanta, devote himself to collecting the resources of the country. He will take everything the people have, and will then issue from the stores so collected to rich and poor alike. As he will take all thier stock, they will have no use for grain further than is necessary for bread.

If the enemy do not detach from here against Sherman, they will in case Atlanta falls bring most of Johnsons Army here, with the expectation of driving us out, and then unite against Sherman. The will fail if they attempt this programme. My greatest fear is, of their sending troops to Johnston first.

Sherman ought to be notified of the possibility of a Corps going from here and should be prepared to take up a good defensive position in case one is sent, one which he can hold against such increase.

If Hunter cannot get to Gordonsville & Charlottesville to cut the rail-road he should make all the valleys south of the B. & O. road a desert as high up as possible. I do not mean that houses should be burned but every particle of provisions and stock should be removed and the people notified to move out.

> I am Gen very respectfully
> your obt svt.
> U. S. GRANT
> Lt. Gen.

Incomplete facsimile, Parke-Bernet Sale, March 23, 1938; copies, DLC-USG, V, 45, 59, 67; DNA, RG 108, Letters Sent; *ibid.*, Letters Received. *O.R.*, I, xxxvii, part 2, 328–29; *ibid.*, I, xxxviii, part 5, 143–44; *ibid.*, I, xl, part 3, 252–53.

To Maj. Gen. George G. Meade

City Point, Va July 15th 1864.

MAJ. GEN MEADE.

A dispatch just received from Gen Butler states that a deserter is just in who says that two Divisions of Longstreets Corps went south leaving their place in line last Friday.[1] Please ask your Provost Marshall if he has not evidence to the contrary of this statement. I have a Richmond paper of the 14th which gives the capture from Gregg at 33 men and two officers

U S GRANT
Lt Gen.

Telegram, copies, DLC-USG, V, 45, 59, 67; DNA, RG 108, Letters Sent; (misdated July 14) Meade Papers, PHi; (undated) *ibid.* Printed as sent on July 15, 1864, 11:00 A.M., in *O.R.*, I, xl, part 3, 254. On July 15, 1864, Maj. Gen. Andrew A. Humphreys telegraphed to USG. "Gen Meade is on the line of works. There is no evidence in the Provost Marshals Dept of any part of Longstreets Corps having left Lees army,   all the Evidence Concerning it is that fields & Kershaws Divisions are on this side the river between Hill & Beauregard— Picketts Div. on the north side of the Appomattox"   Telegram received, DNA, RG 108, Letters Sent; copies, *ibid.*, RG 393, Army of the Potomac, Letters Sent; Meade Papers, PHi. Printed as sent at noon in *O.R.*, I, xl, part 3, 254–55. On the same day, Humphreys telegraphed to Brig. Gen. John A. Rawlins. "Respectfully forwarded—The deserter Informed me that he received the information about the intended movement of Hokes Division from the sick & others of the Division unable to march who had been sent to Petersburg—He met them outside the town where Pies Cakes &c are sold to the soldiers." Telegram received, DNA, RG 108, Letters Received. *O.R.*, I, xl, part 3, 257. The enclosed report is *ibid.*, pp. 256–57. Another such telegram from Humphreys to Rawlins is *ibid.*, p. 255.

At 10:00 A.M., Maj. Gen. George G. Meade had telegraphed to USG. "Comparative quiet prevailed along the lines yesterday—Some musketry & cannonading on Genl. Burnsides front by the enemy during the night. Last evening several deserters came in to the 5th corps, who stated that if three rockets were sent up, to indicate they had been well received a large number would come in— After taking necessary precautions to guard against foul play the three rockets were sent up, but without any result.—The siege works, batteries & mine in front of the 5th & 9th corps are making good progress.—Two divisions of the 2d. corps are employed levelling the enemys old works in our rear.—Your telegram of yesterday in reference to the projected cavalry raid, has been sent to Genl. Sheridan, as his general instructions, and his views called for as to the disposition of the infantry force sent to support him.—I send per orderly a Richmond paper of the 14th inst, in which they claim taking 93 prisoners & two commissioned officers from Gregs in the recent reconnaissance of Reams Stn. No such report has been made by Gregg, but I have called for information." ALS (telegram sent), DNA, RG 393, Army of the Potomac, Miscellaneous Letters Received; telegram received, *ibid.*, RG 108, Letters Received. *O.R.*, I, xl, part 3, 254.

1. July 8. On July 15, 9:45 A.M., Maj. Gen. Benjamin F. Butler telegraphed to USG. "I am inclined to think that 2 Divisions of Longstreets Corps have gone from Petersburgh and our front. There has been a change of Pickets in our front. A deserter from Haygoods Brigade Hoke's Division formerly of Longstreets Corps but latterly of Beauregards forces says that it is so that they left last friday or Saturday—But I do not think they have gone to Maryland. It is

rumored among secesh in Norfolk that Lee is sending troops South." ALS (telegram sent), DNA, RG 94, War Records Office, Dept. of Va. and N. C., Army of the James, Unentered Papers; telegram received, *ibid.*, RG 108, Letters Received. Printed as received at 10:00 A.M. in *O.R.*, I, xl, part 3, 268. On the same day, USG telegraphed to Butler. "If you have a regt of hundred day men out of the line that Can possibly be spared I wish you would send it to City Point to aid in guard duty over public stores. There is but one small regiment here for that duty & it is not sufficient with the extent of wharf & quantity of stores." Telegram received, DNA, RG 393, Dept. of Va. and N. C., Telegrams Received; copies, *ibid.*, RG 108, Letters Sent; DLC-USG, V, 45, 59, 67. *O.R.*, I, xl, part 3, 269. At 6:15 P.M., Butler telegraphed to USG. "A Regiment will be sent as desired tomorrow   It is now certain that Lee is in Petersburgh—Picket is still in my front   Will send to-days Richmond papers" ALS (telegram sent), DNA, RG 107, Telegrams Collected (Unbound); copy, *ibid.*, RG 393, Dept. of Va. and N. C., Telegrams Sent. *O.R.*, I, xl, part 3, 269.

To Maj. Gen. George G. Meade

City Point. Va. July, 15th 1864. [8. p. m.][1]

MAJ. GEN. MEADE.

Your dispatch of 6 p. m. just this moment received. Since ordering the Cavalry raid we have found that the enemy have left Maryland and I have sent a Staff Officer to hasten the return of the 6th & 19th Corps. With these we can cover the Weldon road or make an Infantry movement which will obviate the necessity of a raid. Under these circumstances you may suspend Sheridans orders for the present

U. S. GRANT
Lieut Gen'l.

Telegram, copies, DLC-USG, V, 45, 59, 67; DNA, RG 108, Letters Sent; (2) Meade Papers, PHi. *O.R.*, I, xl, part 3, 256. On July 15, 1864, 6:00 P.M., Maj. Gen. George G. Meade telegraphed to USG. "Genl. Sheridan is here—He fears that unless the Infantry accompany him to Welden, that his return will be so obstructed, as to force him to Newbern, from whence he could only return by water which would take a very long time. He proposes the joint expedition keeping together the whole time—I think myself this is the surest & safest, course, but the question arises whether you can spare the 2d. Corps for so long a period say Ten days—or whether you deem it judicious to send any less force of infantry than the whole corps—Your views on these points are respectfully requested.—Genl Sheridan will await here your reply." ALS (telegram sent),

DNA, RG 393, Army of the Potomac, Miscellaneous Letters Received; telegram received, *ibid.*, RG 108, Letters Received. *O.R.*, I, xl, part 3, 255–56.

1. Brackets appear in USG's letterbook.

To Maj. Gen. George G. Meade

City Point Va. July 15th *1864*.

MAJ. GEN. G. G. MEADE,
COMD.G A. P.
GENERAL,

It is necessary that a Maj. Gen. should be appointed to the Command of the 10th Corps. I have been thinking of naming Maj. Gen. Humphreys for the place but did not wish to do so without first informing you and hearing whether you feel now as you did some time back about sparing him from his present position. Another thing too I want the Gen. to understand before nominating him for this Command. The 10th Corps as it now stands, that part of it serving in the Dept. of Va. & N. C. is very small, and composed entirely of White troops. In the Dept. however there are a large number of Colored troops many of whom are liable at any time to fall into the 10th either for service or permanently. If the Corps should be united as it was in the Dept. of the South then too it will be composed largely of Colored troops. I do not suppose this would make any difference with Gen. Humphrey's performance of his duties, but it might have something to do with his preference for the Command.

I am Gen. very respectfully
your obt. svt.
U. S. GRANT
Lt. Gen. Com

ALS, Humphreys Papers, PHi. *O.R.*, I, xl, part 3, 253–54. On July 15, 1864, 4:00 P.M., Maj. Gen. George G. Meade telegraphed to USG. "Your note in reference to Tenth Corps was received and referred to General Humphreys while I was on the lines. The general will take the matter into consideration, and by the time I return to my headquarters I will advise you of his decision." *Ibid.*, p. 255. On the same day, Maj. Gen. Andrew A. Humphreys wrote to USG. "You have placed me under a double obligation to you. First by proposing to place me in command of a Corps, and secondly by your considerate kindness in letting me know fully the circumstances connected with it that might occasion my preference for the duty I am already engaged upon. I confess that while I have the kindliest feelings for the negro race and gladly see anything done that promises to ameliorate their condition, yet as they are not my own people, nor my own race, I could not feel towards negro troops as I have always felt towards the troops I have commanded, that their character, their reputation, their honor was a part of mine, that the two were so intimately connected that they could not be separated. Feeling thus I would prefer not to command such troops, although I trust that my preferences could never interfere with the performance of duty." ADfS and ALS, Humphreys Papers, PHi. On July 16, USG telegraphed to Meade. "Six or seven days ago I asked to have Gen. Ord assigned to command of the 10th A. C. but before my dispatch was received in Washington they had assigned him to the command of 8th Corps and all troops in the Middle Dept. I now receive a dispatch saying that he is ordered here and probably it is to command the 10th Corps   If so Gen. Humphreys will not be changed from his present place at present." Copies, DLC-USG, V, 45, 59, 67; DNA, RG 108, Letters Sent; (2) Meade Papers, PHi. Printed as received at 9:40 A.M. in *O.R.*, I, xl, part 3, 276. On the same day, Humphreys wrote to USG. "I had written you in reply to your communication of yesterday to Genl. Meade and had sent the note, ~~when but recalled it upon~~ when the receipt of your telegram of this morning rendering it unnecessary ~~I~~ it was recalled. ~~it~~. But I cannot allow the occasion to pass without expressing my appreciation of the double obligation ~~to you~~ under which you have placed me, first by proposing to ~~place~~ give me ~~in~~ the command of a Corps, and secondly by your considerate kindness in letting me know fully ~~all~~ the circumstances connected with ~~it~~ that command that might occasion my preference for the duty I am already engaged upon." ADfS, Humphreys Papers, PHi. See Henry H. Humphreys, *Andrew Atkinson Humphreys: A Biography* (Philadelphia, 1924), p. 241.

To Maj. Gen. Henry W. Halleck

(Cipher)   City Point Va July 16th 4.40 p. m. *1864*
MAJ. GEN. HALLECK, WASHINGTON,

There can be no use in Wright following the enemy with the latter a day a ahead after he has passed entirely beyond, (south of,) all our communications. I want if possible to get the 6th & 19th Corps here to use them before the enemy can get Early back. With Hunter in the Shenandoah Valley and always between the enemy and Washington force enough can always be had to check an invasion until reinforcements can go from here. This does not prevent Hunter from following the enemy even to Gordonsville & Charlottesville if he can do it with his own force and such other improvised troops as he can get. But he should be cautious not to allow himself squeezed out to one side so as to make it necessary to fall back into Western Va. to save his Army. If he does have to fall back it should be in front of the enemy and with his force always between the latter and the main crossings of the Potomac. I do not think there is now any further danger of an attempt to invade Maryland. The position of the enemy in the West and here is such as to demand all the force they can get to-gether to save vital points to them. This last attempt brought to the field so many troops that they cannot concieve the possibility of succeeding in capturing any important point with a force of 30 or even 50,000 men whilst the main union army is within thirty hours of the Capitol. As soon as the rebel Army is known to have passed Hunter's forces recall Wright and send him back here with all dispatch and also send the 19th Corps. If the enemy have any notion of returning the fact will be developed before Wright can start back.

U. S. GRANT Lt. Gen.

ALS (telegram sent), PPRF; telegram received (marked as sent at 5:00 P.M., received on July 17, 1864, 6:30 A.M.), DNA, RG 107, Telegrams Collected (Bound). *O.R.*, I, xxxvii, part 2, 350; *ibid.*, I, xl, part 3, 275–76. On July 17, 3:00 P.M., Maj. Gen. Henry W. Halleck telegraphed to USG. "Your instructions in regard to the return of 6th & 19th corps, & the pursuit by Genl Hunter, have been transmitted to the latter & to Genl Wright. Genl Hunter reports only about twelve thousand men for the field; and says, 'I do not think the present force on the B & O. R. R. more than one third sufficient for its defence.' You will remember that the hundred days men in West Virginia, at Washington & at Baltimore begin to go out in about two weeks, and that neither of the northern states furnished a single man, under the President's call, to defend Washington or Baltimore. Moreover, the regiments of the Reserve or Invalid corps called from the west to the defence of these places must soon be returned to replace the hundred days men now guarding depots & camps of prisoners of war. Despatches recieved yesterday indicate preparations for an insurrection in Louisville & other parts of Kentucky. I ordered to Louisville two regiments from Nashville, which Genl Miller says is about one half of his force. Genl Burbridge has been directed to give his particular attention to Louisville." ALS (telegram sent), DNA, RG 107, Telegrams Collected (Bound); telegram received, *ibid.*; (incomplete) *ibid.*, Telegrams Collected (Unbound); (datelined 2:00 P.M.) *ibid.*, RG 108, Letters Received. *O.R.*, I, xxxvii, part 2, 361; *ibid.*, I, xl, part 3, 289–90.

On July 17, noon, Halleck telegraphed to Maj. Gen. David Hunter transmitting orders based upon USG's telegrams of July 14, 15, and 16. *Ibid.*, I, xxxvii, part 2, 366. On Dec. 6, Hunter wrote to USG. "I inclose you one of the telegrams received from General Halleck on the 17th of July, referred to in my last note. You can very readily imagine that the reception of such a dispatch, after I had been working hard, night and day, for two months, would have a very depressing tendency. When I relieved Sigel I found his command very much disorganized and demoralized, from his recent defeat at New Market, and the three generals with it, Sigel, Stahel, and Sullivan, not worth one cent; in fact, very much in my way. I supposed, however, that you were busily engaged with Lee, and that it was important that I should try and create a diversion in your favor, so I dashed on toward Lynchburg, and should certainly have taken it, if it had not been for the stupidity and conceit of that fellow Averell, who unfortunately joined me at Staunton, and of whom I unfortunately had at the time a very high opinion, and trusted him when I should not have done so. As for occupying all the gaps, so as to prevent the enemy getting between me and Washington, it was a perfect impossibility; I supposed you were fighting Lee before Richmond, and that it was all important that I should push on. I was not informed that I had any thing to do with the defense of Washington, and supposed General Halleck had made ample provision for this purpose. I hope, general, you will do me the justice to say that I have done my whole duty, and I beg that you will give me a command of some kind. If I am not deemed worthy of a corps, give me a division, a brigade, or a regiment. I have tried to do my whole duty, and if I have failed, I am much mortified." *Ibid.*, pp. 366–67.

To Maj. Gen. William T. Sherman

(Cipher)   City Point, Va, July, 146th[1] *1864*
MAJ. GEN. W. T. SHERMAN, CHATTAHOOCHE GA.

The attempted invation of Maryland having failed ~~in~~ to ~~giving~~ give the enemy a firm foothold North they are now returning with possibly 25 000 troops. All the men they have here beyond a sufficiency to hold their strong fortifications will be an element of weakness by eating up their supplies. It is not improbable therefore that you will find in the next fortnight reinforcements in your front to the number indicated above. I advise therefore that if you get Atlanta ~~that~~ you set about destroying rail-roads as far to the East and South of you as possible. Collect all the stores of the country for your own use and select a point that you can hold until help can be had. I shall make a desperate effort to get a position here which will hold the enemy without the necessity of so many men. If successful I can detach from here for other enterprises looking as much to your assistance as anything els.

U. S. Grant

Lt. Gen.

ALS (telegram sent), NNP; telegram received (datelined 10:00 A.M.), DNA, RG 107, Telegrams Collected (Bound). *O.R.*, I, xxxviii, part 5, 149. On July 17, 1864, 11:25 A.M., President Abraham Lincoln telegraphed to USG. "In your despatch of yesterday to Gen. Sherman, I find the following, towit: 'I shall make a desparate effort to get a position here which will hold the enemy without the necessity of so many men.' Pressed as we are by lapse of time, I am glad to hear you say this; and yet I do hope you may find a way that the effort shall not be desperate in the sense of great loss of life." ALS (telegram sent), DNA, RG 107, Telegrams Collected (Bound); telegram received, *ibid.*, RG 108, Letters Received. *O.R.*, I, xl, part 3, 289. Lincoln, *Works*, VII, 444.

On June 18, Maj. Gen. William T. Sherman had written to USG. "I have no doubt you want me to write you occasionally letters not purely official, but which will admit of a little more latitude than such documents possess. I have daily sent to Halleck, telegraphs which I asked him to repeat to you and which he says he has, done. You therefore know where we are and what we have done. If our movemt has been slower than you calculated I can explain the reasons though I know you believe me too earnest, and impatient to be behind time. My first movemt against Johnston was really fine, and now I believe I would have disposed of him at one blow if McPherson had crushed Resacca as he might have done, for then it was garrisonned only by a small Brigade, but Mc was a little over Cautious lest Johnston still at Dalton might move against him alone, but the truth was I got all of McPhersons Army 23,000, 18 miles to Johnstons Rear before he knew they had left Huntsville. With that single exception McPherson has done very well. Schofield also does as well as I could ask with his small force. Our Cavalry is dwindling away, we cannot get full forage and have to graise so that the Cavalry is always unable to attempt anything. Garrard is over Cautious and I think Stoneman is lazy. The former has 4300, & the latter about 2500. Each has had fine chances of Cutting in but were easily checked by the appearance of an Enemy. My Chief source of trouble is with the Army of the Cumberland which is dreadfully slow. A fresh furrow in a plowed field will stop the whole column, and all begin to intrench. I have again and again tried to impress on Thomas that we must assail & not defend. We are the offensive, & yet it seems the whole Army of the Cumberland is so habituated to be on the defensive that from its Commander down to the lowest private I cannot get it out of their heads. I came out without tents and ordered all to do likewise yet Thomas has a HeadQuarter Camp on the style of Halleck at Corinth, every aid, & orderly with a wall tent, and a Baggage train big enough for a Division. He promised to send it all back but the truth is every body there is allowed to do as he pleases, and they still think and act as though the Railroad and all its facilities were theirs. This slowness has cost me the loss of two splendid opportunities which never recur in War. At Dallas there was a delay of four hours to get ready to advance, when we first met Johnstons head of Column, and that four hours enabled him to throw up works to cover the head of his column and he extended the work about as fast as we deployed. Also here, I broke one of his Lines, and had we followed it up as I ordered at day light there was nothing between us & the Railroad back of Marietta. I ordered Thomas to move at day light and when I got to the point at half past nine I found Stanley & Wood quarrelling which should *not* lead. I'm afraid I swore, and said what I should not, but I got them started, but instead of reaching the Atlanta Road back of Marietta which is Johnstons centre, we only got to a creek to the south of it, by night, and now a heavy Rain stops us, and gives times to fortify a new Line. Still I have all the high and commanding ground but the *one* peak near Marietta which I can traverse   We have had an immense quantity of Rain, from June 2nd to 14th, and now it is raining as though it had no intention ever to stop. The enemys cavalry sweeps all round us and is now to my rear somewhere. The wires are broken very often but I have strong guards along the Road which make prompt repairs. Thus far our supplies of food have been good, and forage moderate, and we have fond growing wheat, rye oats &c. You may go on with the full assurance that I will continue to press Johnston as fast as I can over come the natural obstacles and inspire motion into a large, ponderous and slow (by habit) Army. Of course it cannot keep up with my thoughts & wishes but no impulse can be given it that I will not guide." ALS, CSmH. *O.R.,* I, xxxviii, part 4, 507–8.

On July 12, Sherman, "near Chattahoochee, Geo," wrote to USG. "I have written you but once since the opening of the Campaign, but I report by telegraph to Halleck daily and he furnishes you Copy. My progress was slower than I Calculated from two chief Causes, an uninterrupted Rain from June 2, to about the 22nd, and the peculiar sub-Mountainous Character of the Country from the Etowah to the Chattahoochee. But we have overcome all opposition and whipped Johnston in every fight when we were on any thing like fair terms, and I think the Army feels that way, that we can whip the Enemy in any thing, like a fair fight—but he has uniformly taken shelter behind parallels of strong profile, made in advance for him by Negros & Militia. I regarded an assault on the 27 of June necessary for two good reasons. 1st because the Enemy as well as my own Army had sittled down into the belief that flanking alone was my Game, and 2nd that on that day & ground, had the assault succeeded I could have broken Johnstons Centre and pushed his Army back in confusion and with great loss to his bridges over the Chattahoochee. We lost nothing in morale by the assault for I followed it up on the extreme right & compelled him to quit the very strong lines of Kenesaw, Smyrna Camp, and the Chattahoochee in quick succession. My Railroad & telegraph are now up, and we are rapidly accumulating stores in Marietta & Alatoona that will make us less timid about the Road to our Rear. We have been wonderfully supplied in provisions & ammunition, not a day has a regimt been without bread and essentials. Forage has been the hardest & we have cleaned the Country in a breadth of thirty miles of grain & grass. Now the Corn is getting a size which makes a good fodder and the Railroad has brought in grain to the extent of four pounds per animal per day. I have now fulfilled the first part of the Grand plan   Our Lines are up to the Chattahoochee & the Enemy is beyond —Morgan failed in his Kentucky Raid, and we have kept Forest employed in Mississippi. The defeat of Sturgis was unfortunate, still he kept Forest away from us, and now A. J. Smith is out with a force amply sufficient to whip him. I hear of Slocum at Jackson Miss. and Canby telegraphs me of a trip from Baton Rouge, & another against Mobile, so that I am well satisfied that all my people are well employed. At this momt I have Stoneman down the Chattahoochee with orders if possible to cross & strike the West Point Road, and Rousseau left Decatur the 8th inst with about 3000 Cavalry & no wagons, with orders to make a bold push for the Railroad between Montgomery & West Point & break it good, to return to the Tennessee if possible, but if headed off to make for Pensacola. The Momt I got Johnston to the Chattahoochee I sent Schofield, to a ford above and he effected a crossing without the loss of a man, & has two pontoon bridges. About the same time Garrards Cavalry crossed still above at Roswell factory and has been relieved by Dodge's Corps, so that I now cover the Chattahoochee & have two good crossings well secured. By tonight I will have a third. As soon as I hear from Stoneman, I will shift all of McPherson to Rosswell, & cross Thomas about 3 miles above the Railroad bridge & move against Atlanta, my Left well to the East to get possession of the Augusta Road, about Decatur, or Stone Mountain. I think all will be ready in three days. I will have nearly 100 000 men. I feel certain we have killed & crippled for Johnston, as many as we have sent to the Rear.   have sent back about 6 or 7000 prisoners—taken 11 Guns of Johnston & about 10 in Rome,—have destroyed immense iron, cotton & wool mills and have possession of all the nitre country. My operations have been rather cautious than bold, but on the whole I trust are satisfactory to you. *All* of Polks Corps is still here, & also Hardees & Hoods, & the Georgia Militia under G. W. Smith. Let us persevere & trust to the Fortunes of War, leaving statesmen to work out the solution." ALS, DNA, RG 108, Letters Received. *O.R.*, I, xxxviii, part 5, 123–24.

1. Dateline not in USG's hand.

To Lt. Col. Charles E. Fuller

City Point July 16th 1864

COL. C. E. FULLER A. Q. M.
BERMUDA HUNDRED

My Brother-in-law, who is now a prisoner in the south, is named John C. Dent. He was captured some place on the Miss. River not far from Vicksburg, and is now, or was when I last heard from him, at Columbia S. C. He is a citizen, never connected with the army since the breaking out of the War and I regret to say not a loyal man, otherwise I should have interested myself long ago for his exchange

U. S. GRANT Lt. Gen.

Copies, DLC-USG, V, 45, 59, 67; DNA, RG 108, Letters Sent. On July 16, 1864, Lt. Col. Charles E. Fuller, chief q. m., 10th and 18th Army Corps, Bermuda Hundred, telegraphed to USG. "Will you please give me the name, whereabouts and date of capture of your brother in law who is a prisoner. Major Mulford goes up to day & will try and arrange his exchange." ALS (telegram sent), *ibid.*, RG 107, Telegrams Collected (Unbound).

To Abraham Lincoln

City Point, Va., July 17th, 1864

HIS EXCELLENCY, A. LINCOLN
PRESIDENT OF THE UNITED STATES.
SIR:

Maj. J. H. Hammond, A. A. Gen. I have known from almost the first commencement of the War. He is one of the most industrious, indefatigable and bravest men I have ever seen in action. He has been engaged in command of the Draft Rendezvous at Louisville, Ky. and has been more or lest instrumental in bringing into the service three regiments of Colored troops in that state.[1] Maj. Hammond is now willing, and I suppose anxious, to take command of that kind of troops now in Ky. or to take them anywhere their services may be required. I do not hesitate to most cordially recommend him for such command with the rank of Brig. Gen. expressly given to command colored troops.

I believe Maj. Hammond would bring a Brigade or Division of Colored troops or any other troops into a state of discipline and drill as quick as any officer of my acquaintance. There is no officer I would sooner trust with them in action, and especially would I recommend him as a watchful vigilant officer in command of an outpost.

I sincerely hope this appointment can and will be made.

I have the honor,
Very respectfully,
Your obt. svt.
U. S. GRANT, Lt. Gen.

The Month at Goodspeed's, III, 6 (Feb., 1932), 171. On July 19, 1864, President Abraham Lincoln endorsed this letter. "I submit this high recommendation by Gen. Grant of Maj. Hammond, to the special consideration of the Sec. of War." AES (facsimile), *ibid.*, p. 172. Lincoln, *Works*, VII, 452.

John H. Hammond of N. Y., who entered the Civil War as private, 5th Calif., rose to the position of adjt. and chief of staff for Maj. Gen. William T. Sherman with the rank of maj. On Dec. 12, 1863, Maj. Gen. John A. Logan, Bridgeport, Ala., who had succeeded to command of Sherman's 15th Army Corps, wrote to USG. "I have the honor to forward through Gen Sherman, a letter from Genl Blair, recommending Lt. Col J. H Hammond Asst. Adjt Genl and chief of Staff of the Corps, for Brig Genl of Vols. I heartily endorse Gen Blairs letter, and add that while I fully appreciate Col Hammonds energy and industry in the Office, I consider him better fitted for the leadership of troops. Although a Staff Officer, he has established an excellent reputation for ability in action. He has enterprise, zeal in the cause, and personal bravery, and great perseverance. Genl Sherman knows what his services have been during the past two years, and I forward these recommendations earnestly hoping that they will go before the President with such endorsements from him and you as will secure Col Hammonds appointment. Should he be appointed and ordered to report to me, I will put him in command of any cavalry or mounted infantry that may be under my orders." LS, DNA, RG 94, ACP, H436 CB 1865. On Dec. 23, USG endorsed this letter to Secretary of War Edwin M. Stanton. "The recommendation of Gen. Sherman, in favor of Lieut. Col. Hammond, for promotion in the Cavalry service of the United States, in case of the organization of new Cavalry Regiments in the regular Army, is heartily endorsed by me. I know Col. Hammond to be an active and intelligent officer, peculiarly calculated for the Cavalry service both in his tastes and natural qualifications. For the command of a Cavalry regiment, or any force likely to come within the Command of a Colonel, I deem Col. Hammond so well qualified that I will be pleased to see this transfer made of his services, and feel no doubt but that with the opportunity to do so he will win further promotion." AES, *ibid*. No action resulted then or in response to USG's letter of July 17, 1864.

1. On Jan. 18, 1864, Maj. Robert Williams, AGO, wrote to USG. "The General-in-Chief directs, that you at once select some suitable Officer, belonging to your command and direct him to proceed without delay to Louisville, Kentucky, and assume command of the Depot for Drafted men at that place—and report your action to this Office. The officer selected should not be less in rank than Lieut Colonel" LS, *ibid*., RG 393, Military Div. of the Miss., Letters Received. On Feb. 6, USG telegraphed to Brig. Gen. Lorenzo Thomas. "Lt Col J. H. Hammonds A. A. G. Vols has been directed to proceed to Louisville Ky & assume command of Depot for drafted men at that place." Telegram received, *ibid*., RG 94, Letters Received, 182M 1864; *ibid*., RG 107, Telegrams Collected (Bound); copies, *ibid*., RG 393, Military Div. of the Miss., Hd. Qrs. Correspondence; DLC-USG, V, 40, 94. See *O.R.*, I, lii, part 1, 515. On Feb. 23, 11:39 A.M., Col. Edward D. Townsend, AGO, telegraphed to USG. "Please cause to be detailed two officers and four men from each of the Kentu[cky] regiments under your command, to report to Lieut. Col J. H. Hammond, Commanding Draft Rendezvous at Lo[uis]ville Kentucky, for duty conducting r[e]cruits to regiments—" LS (telegram sent), DNA, RG 107, Telegrams Collected (Unbound); copies, *ibid*., RG 393, Military Div. of the Miss., Hd. Qrs. Correspondence; DLC-USG, V, 40, 94. On Feb. 14, USG endorsed a letter from Hammond regarding the formation of a cav. regt. from 15th Army Corps veterans who were not expected to reenlist in the inf. "Respectfully forwarded to Head Quarters of the Army without special recommendation. Col Hammond I know well and believe he would make one of our best Cavalry commanders. I think too, that many volunteers might be obtained for the Cavalry service who would not otherwise re-enlist. I doubt however the propriety of raising more Cavalry regiments. I believe if we had but one half of our Cavalry force (on paper) we would have more Cavalry-men on horseback." Copies, *ibid*., V, 39; DNA, RG 393, Military Div. of the Miss., Endorsements.

To Maj. Gen. Henry W. Halleck

Head Qrs Army Potomac
July 17th 1. P. M 1864

MAJ GEN H. W. HALLECK
CHIEF OF STAFF.

If Early stops in the Valley or before returning to Richmond, with the view of going north again, I do not believe he will go to Maryland but will attempt to go through Western Virginia to Ohio possibly taking Pittsburgh by the way.

I think Pennsylvania and Ohio particularly ought to have their citizens organized for a sudden emergency. With the great number of discharged veterans now in the north this class of troops will be of great service in repelling invasion or at least checking it.

I think I will order back to Washington all regiments whose term of service will expire before the 20th of August,[1] this will give quite a force around which to rally new troops

U. S. GRANT
Lt Gen'l.

Telegram received (at 1:40 P.M.), DNA, RG 107, Telegrams Collected (Bound); *ibid.*, Telegrams Collected (Unbound); copies, *ibid.*, RG 108, Letters Sent; DLC-USG, V, 45, 59, 67. *O.R.*, I, xxxvii, part 2, 361; *ibid.*, I, xl, part 3, 289.

1. On July 18, 1864, Capt. Ely S. Parker issued Special Orders No. 61. "All Regiments now with the Armies operating from the James river, whose term of service expire before the 25th of August 1864. will be sent, without delay to Washington D. C. Also one Regiment of heavy Artillery will be sent to Washington D. C. from the Army of the Potomac. Army Commanders will attend to the prompt execution of this order." Copies, DLC-USG, V, 57, 62, 67. *O.R.*, I, xl, part 3, 313. At 9:50 P.M., Maj. Gen. George G. Meade telegraphed to USG. "Do you intend to include cavalry regiments in Special Order No. 61 and if so shall they not leave their horses & equippments.—" ALS (telegram sent), DNA, RG 393, Army of the Potomac, Miscellaneous Letters Received; copy, *ibid.*, Letters Sent. Printed as sent at 9:30 P.M. in *O.R.*, I, xl, part 3, 314. At 11:00 P.M., Brig. Gen. John A. Rawlins telegraphed to Meade. "The cavalry regiments are included but they must leave their horses & equipments here   The 100 days men you need not send" Telegrams received (2), DNA, RG 94, War Records Office, Army of the Potomac; copies (2), Meade Papers, PHi. *O.R.*, I, xl, part 3, 314. On the same day, Maj. Gen. Benjamin F. Butler telegraphed to Rawlins. "Does Special Order No. 61 from your head quarters of this date include one hundred days regiments?" Telegram received, DNA, RG 94, War Records Of-

fice, Dept. of Va. and N. C., Army of the James, Unentered Papers. At 8:30 P.M. and 9:40 P.M., Rawlins telegraphed to Butler. "It includes all troops whose term of service expire prior to the twenty fifth of August—" "Upon further Consideration the Lt. Genl. has determined not to include the 100 days men in the order. You will therefore not send them—" ALS (telegrams sent), *ibid.*, RG 107, Telegrams Collected (Unbound); telegrams received, *ibid.*, RG 393, Dept. of Va. and N. C., Telegrams Received. See *O.R.*, I, xl, part 3, 361.

To Maj. Gen. Benjamin F. Butler

By Telegraph from City Pt
Dated July 17 *1864.*

To MAJ GEN BUTLER,
COPY SENT TO GEN MARTINDALE,

Several deserters just in on Gen Meades, front, who left the picket line tonight concur in the statement that we are to be attacked tonight. Gen Field[1] visited their line just before they deserted & they overheard him talking with a colonel on the details of the movement. They say it is conceded in their Army that Johnston is gone, unless he can be reinforced, & before they can reinforce him we must be driven back. Have the 10th & 18th Corps duly notified, with caution however that they are to make no demonstration to show that we are expecting any such attack. Be prepared at the same time to take advantage of any abandonment by the enemy of his lines in your front, especially after daylight in the morning   Of course it is not known when the attack is to be, or whether it is to be at all—but we want to be prepared for the enemy if he should give us such an advantage.

U. S. GRANT,
Lt Genl.

Telegram received (at 9:35 P.M.), DNA, RG 94, War Records Office, Dept. of Va. and N. C., Army of the James, Unentered Papers; copies, *ibid.*, RG 108, Letters Sent; *ibid.*, RG 393, 10th Army Corps, Miscellaneous Telegrams Received; (undated) *ibid.*, Dept. of Va. and N. C., Telegrams Sent; DLC-USG, V, 45, 59, 67. Printed as sent at 9:35 P.M. in *O.R.*, I, xl, part 3, 307. On July 17, 1864, 10:20 P.M., Maj. Gen. Benjamin F. Butler telegraphed to USG. "Telegram recieved—Dispositions have been made to meet the exgencies therein mentioned." Telegram received, DNA, RG 94, War Records Office, Dept. of Va.

and N. C., Army of the James, Unentered Papers; copy (undated), *ibid.*, RG 393, Dept. of Va. and N. C., Telegrams Sent. Printed as received at 11:00 P.M. in *O.R.*, I, xl, part 3, 307.

On July 17, Brig. Gen. Robert S. Foster wrote to Col. John W. Shaffer, chief of staff for Butler, enclosing and commenting on a report by Capt. James B. Bell, 24th Mass., of a reconnaissance to Malvern Hill. Copies, DNA, RG 108, Letters Received. *O.R.*, I, xl, part 3, 311–12. On July 18, Butler endorsed these letters to USG. ES, DNA, RG 108, Letters Received.

On July 17, Brig. Gen. Charles K. Graham wrote to Shaffer enclosing and commenting on a report by Capt. Amaya L. Fitch, 13th N. Y. Heavy Art., steamboat *Parke*, of a reconnaissance on the James River. ALS, *ibid. O.R.*, I, xl, part 1, 745–47. On the same day, Butler endorsed this report. "Respectfully forwarded to Lieut General Grant Comdg. The report of Brig Genl Graham approved. The plaudits of Captain Fitchs courage conduct and efficiency are concurred in by the Major Genl Comd'g the Department. This expedition is but another evidence of the efficiency of the armed transports now in the service. The attention of the Lieut General is specially called to the suggestion that no sailing vessel be permitted to come up or go down the river without a tow.   certainly not to come up, because of the ease with which smuggling can be carried on in this length of river and the fact that aid and comfort may be furnished to the enemy as undoubtedly was the case, by this schooner with the torpedos   Sutlers schooners and others have been in the habit of coming up without these tows and I have had numerous complaints of trading with the enemy by them therefore I beg leave again to suggest that the Chief Quartermaster should give the directions required"   ES, DNA, RG 108, Letters Received. *O.R.*, I, xl, part 1, 745.

1. Charles W. Field, born in Ky. in 1828, USMA 1849, taught at USMA for more than four years before resigning from the U.S. Army as of May 30, 1861. After serving as col., 6th Va. Cav., he was appointed brig. gen. as of March 9, 1862, and badly wounded at Second Bull Run. Appointed maj. gen. on Feb. 12, 1864, he commanded a div., 1st Army Corps, under Lt. Gen. Richard H. Anderson in July.

To Maj. Gen. Benjamin F. Butler

By Telegraph from City Pt
Dated July 17th *1864.*

To MAJ GEN BUTLER.

Since my despatch to you two more setts of deserters have come in confirming previous statements, but giving more particulars. The attack if made, is to be principally on Meade's left. The deserters say that a ravine has been cleared out between the respective lines of skirmishers, for the purpose of massing their troops under cover, & out of observation, & that the attack is to be made about four (4) a m or just before day. I very much wish now, that you had a corps ready to make an attack on the enemy, at the same time —it will be adviseable to have Kautz notified to have his cavalry on hand for service on foot.

U. S. GRANT,
Lt Genl

Telegram received (at 11:30 P.M.), DNA, RG 94, War Records Office, Dept. of Va. and N. C., Army of the James, Unentered Papers; copies, *ibid.*, RG 108, Letters Sent; DLC-USG, V, 45, 59, 67. *O.R.*, I, xl, part 3, 307. On July 17, 1864, 11:45 P.M., Maj. Gen. Benjamin F. Butler telegraphed to USG. "Indeed I wish that Corps was here. We shall open with artillery in full blast when they open on the left. Kautz had been notified to report to Brooks on foot before the reciept of your dispatch" ALS (telegram sent), DNA, RG 94, War Records Office, Dept. of Va. and N. C., Army of the James, Unentered Papers; copy (undated), *ibid.*, RG 393, Dept. of Va. and N. C., Telegrams Sent. *O.R.*, I, xl, part 3, 307.

To Maj. Gen. George G. Meade

By Telegraph from City Point 9 20 p m
Dated July 17th *1864.*

To MAJOR GEN MEADE

Your dispatch of 9 p m just received,   No doubt all preparation has been made to repel an attack if one is made—I have duly notified the tenth & eighteenth Corps so that they will be in a state of preparation also—We should be ready not only to repel but to follow up the enemy if he should come out of his lines & especially so if the attack is made near daylight as it likely will be if made at all—It is very reasonable to me that the enemy must come out for if they do not relieve Johnston nothing but unforeseen circumstances can save him—To send such reinforcements they should try to cripple us here—They must feel themselves relatively as strong now as they will be with the return of Earlys Corps besides time is pressing them—I am just in receipt of dispatches to 11 P M last night from Sherman in answer to mine cautioning him of the danger of Johnstons being reinforced from here—He says that he is not all alarmed if Johnston should get twenty thousand 20,000 reinforcements if he will only come out and attack—If you have not done so I think it advisable to notify Sheridan to be in readiness to take the saddle with his Cavalry if he hears heavy firing on your front and to push to the front in that case without further orders

U S GRANT
Lt Gen

Telegram received, DNA, RG 94, War Records Office, Army of the Potomac; copies, *ibid.*, RG 108, Letters Sent; DLC-USG, V, 45, 59, 67; (2) Meade Papers, PHi. *O.R.*, I, xl, part 3, 290–91. On July 17, 1864, 9:00 P.M. and 10:00 P.M., Maj. Gen. George G. Meade telegraphed to USG. "Several deserters have just come in all concurring in the statement that Longstreets corps is to make an attack tonight—One man said Genl. Field had visited the picket line just before he deserted & he overheard him talking with a Col on the details of the movement—The deserters say it is generally believed in their army that Johnston is gone unless he can be reinforced, and before they can reinforce him they must beat us back—Warren & Burnside are warned, and we are all most anxious the experiment should be made.—" ALS (telegram sent), DNA, RG 393, Army of the Potomac, Miscellaneous Letters Received; telegram received, *ibid.*, RG 108, Letters Received. *O.R.*, I, xl, part 3, 290. "The foregoing despatch has been confirmed by several other deserters coming from different parts of the line—Your telegram of 9.30 received—orders were sent to Burnside & Warren to follow up any repulse they might make & Hancock is in readiness to support in any contingency—The orders suggested by you will be immediately sent to Sheridan—If any attack is made it will probably be a general one at several points but I should expect the heaviest to be by Hills Corps attempting to turn my left flank   To meet this we are prepared & Hancock is well placed.—I most earnestly hope they will try the experiment for I think it will relieve us greatly.—" ALS (telegram sent), DNA, RG 94, War Records Office, Army of the Potomac; telegram received, *ibid.*, RG 108, Letters Received. *O.R.*, I, xl, part 3, 291. The enclosure is *ibid.* At 10:45 P.M., Meade telegraphed to USG. "The foregoing seems to confirm my theory, that whilst we are attacked in front by Longstreet—Hill will move around our left—unless it is proposed to move Hill off under cover of the attack—I dont understand what he wants six days rations for otherwise—In any contingency we are quite prepared for them." ALS (telegram sent), DNA, RG 94, War Records Office, Army of the Potomac; telegram received, *ibid.*, RG 108, Letters Received. *O.R.*, I, xl, part 3, 292. Written on a letter of July 17 from John C. Babcock to Maj. Gen. Andrew A. Humphreys. ALS, DNA, RG 94, War Records Office, Army of the Potomac. *O.R.*, I, xl, part 3, 292.

At 9:00 A.M., Meade had telegraphed to USG. "I forward a despatch received from Maj. Genl. Burnside—It appears the enemy have become apprised of his mining operations & are counter-mining—The report made last night informed you it would be a week before operations against the salient, which takes Burnsides mine in reverse, could be commenced—I see no object in exploding this mine, before the advantages gained by it, can be followed up.—Nothing occurred worthy of report on other parts of the line—All the enemys old works have been levelled—" ALS (telegram sent), DNA, RG 393, Army of the Potomac, Miscellaneous Letters Received; telegram received (incomplete), *ibid.*, RG 108,

Letters Received. *O.R.*, I, xl, part 3, 290. The enclosure is *ibid.*, pp. 300–1. At 10:00 A.M., Meade telegraphed to USG. "Despatches have been received announcing the confinement & critical illness of Mrs. Genl. Gibbon. I have uniformly refused all applications for leaves of absences to officers & furlughs to enlisted men, but if you have no objection I will under existing circumstances grant a few days leave to Genl. Gibbon.—" ALS (telegram sent), DNA, RG 393, Army of the Potomac, Miscellaneous Letters Received; telegram received, *ibid.*, RG 108, Letters Received.

To Maj. Gen. Henry W. Halleck

(Cipher) City Point Va. July 18th/64 [*noon*]

MAJ. GEN. HALLECK, WASHINGTON,

Before the 6th & 19th Corps can get to Washington the enemy will have developed his intentions by stopping if he thinks of returning to Maryland. In that case Hunter should stop at Winchester keeping his Cavalry as far out watching the movements of the enemy as he can. If he has not the force to attack with he should not attack but move forward ~~if possible when the ene~~ only as the enemy moves back and always be prepared to get North of the Potomac, without loss, when advanced upon by a superior force. If Louisville is in danger Gov. Morton will send five or ten thousand men at once. Ohio Ia. & Ill. are always ready to send that number of men. Louisville & Nashville must be well guarded. If the enemy have not gone up the valley of course Hunter should not go that way. The idea is he should be between the enemy and Washington, going as far out as he can, never allowing himself to be drawn into an unequal fight south of the Potomac and outside of our defences.

U. S. GRANT
Lt. Gen.

ALS (telegram sent), OClWHi; telegram received (at 8:30 P.M.), DNA, RG 107, Telegrams Collected (Bound). *O.R.*, I, xxxvii, part 2, 374. See telegram to Maj. Gen. Henry W. Halleck, July 16, 1864.

On July 18, 1864, 10:15 A.M., Maj. Gen. Henry W. Halleck telegraphed to USG. "Considering the condition of the garrisons of Washington & Baltimore, I have determined to retain the two heavy Artillery regiments of the 6th corps, unless you direct otherwise." ALS (telegram sent), DNA, RG 107, Telegrams

Collected (Bound); telegram received, *ibid.*; (datelined 10:30 A.M.) *ibid.*, Telegrams Collected (Unbound); *ibid.*, RG 108, Letters Received. *O.R.*, I, xxxvii, part 2, 373; *ibid.*, I, xl, part 3, 312. At 12:45 P.M., USG telegraphed to Halleck. "Your dispatch of 10.30 a. m. in regard to retaining the Heavy Artillery of 6th Corps received. I had just ordered another regiment of this sort from here but will suspend the order unless more than two regiments are required." ALS (telegram sent), OClWHi; telegram received (datelined 12:00 P.M.), DNA, RG 107, Telegrams Collected (Bound). Printed as sent at 11:45 P.M. in *O.R.*, I, xxxvii, part 2, 373; *ibid.*, I, xl, part 3, 312. On the same day, USG telegraphed to Maj. Gen. George G. Meade. "There are 2 Regts of Heavy Artillery with the 6th A C which have been retained for the garrison of Washn This will be enough. The order therefore for you to send another will be suspended" Telegram received, DNA, RG 94, War Records Office, Army of the Potomac; copies, *ibid.*, RG 108, Letters Sent; DLC-USG, V, 45, 59, 67; (2) Meade Papers, PHi. *O.R.*, I, xl, part 3, 314.

To Maj. Gen. Henry W. Halleck

(Cipher)   City Point, Va. July 1~~7~~8th *1864*
MAJ. GEN. H. W. HALLECK, WASHINGTON,

To prevent a recurrence of what has just taken place in Maryland I deem it absolutely necessary that the Departments of "The Susquehanna," "Western" "Va." "Middle," & Washington be merged into one Department under one head who shall absolutely controll the whole. What are now Departments will be Districts, or Corps. The one commander will then controll all troops that co-operate in any movement of the enemy towards Maryland or Pa. I would name Maj. Gen. W. ~~F~~ B. Franklin for such commander.

                                         U. S. GRANT
                                         Lt. Gen.

ALS (telegram sent), OClWHi; telegram received (datelined 1:00 P.M.), DNA, RG 107, Telegrams Collected (Bound); *ibid.*, Telegrams Collected (Unbound). *O.R.*, I, xxxvii, part 2, 374. See telegram to Maj. Gen. Henry W. Halleck, July 20, 1864.

On July 18, 1864, 12:30 P.M., Maj. Gen. Henry W. Halleck telegraphed to USG. "I have just learned from Genl Wright that he formed a junction yesterday at Purcellville, with Genl Crooks command, & that their cavalry struck the enemy's rear near Snicker's gap, capturing a considerable number of wagons & mules, & taking about 60 prisoners. The pursuit will be continued to day to verify enemy's retreat, after which Wright will return." ALS (telegram sent), DNA, RG 107, Telegrams Collected (Bound); telegram received, *ibid.*; *ibid.*, RG 108, Letters Received. *O.R.*, I, xxxvii, part 2, 374.

To Maj. Gen. Benjamin F. Butler

By Telegraph from City Point
Dated July 18 *1864*.

To MAJ GEN BUTLER

Deserters continued coming in last night, all confirming the report that we were to be attacked, the last one in said the order had been given & preparations were made. Longstreet was to attack in front & Hill was to move round to our rear—but before he left he heard his co'l say there would be no attack, because so many deserters had come into our lines & exposed their plans. What was the result of the Flag of truce yesterday?

U. S. GRANT.
Lt Genl

Telegram received (at 10:20 A.M.), DNA, RG 94, War Records Office, Dept. of Va. and N. C., Army of the James, Unentered Papers; copies, *ibid.*, RG 108, Letters Sent; DLC-USG, V, 45, 59, 67. Printed as sent at 10:20 A.M. in *O.R.*, I, xl, part 3, 327. On July 18, 1864, 11:35 A.M., Maj. Gen. Benjamin F. Butler telegraphed to USG. "The flag of truce was recieved and the men have gone to Richmond   Am to send for them Wednesday" ALS (telegram sent), DNA, RG 94, War Records Office, Dept. of Va. and N. C., Army of the James, Unentered Papers; copy (undated), *ibid.*, RG 393, Dept. of Va. and N. C., Telegrams Sent. *O.R.*, I, xl, part 3, 327. An undated telegram from Butler to USG may have been sent the preceding day. "The flag of truce boat is Still up the river   will be down to morrow morning" Telegram received, DNA, RG 107, Telegrams Collected (Unbound).

On July 18, 1:05 A.M., Butler telegraphed to USG. "There are three signal lights in the sky looking like stars one North East by north the other due East and the other nearly West from here" ALS (telegram sent), *ibid.*; copy (undated), *ibid.*, RG 393, Dept. of Va. and N. C., Telegrams Sent. *O.R.*, I, xl, part 3, 327.

To Maj. Gen. Benjamin F. Butler

City Point Va, July 18th/64

MAJ. GEN BUTLER,

Your note of this date is just rec'd. I have made an order suspending Gen. 225 and assigning Gen. Martindale & Terry[1] to the temporary command of the two Corps. Since the late raid into Md I have asked that the Depts of the Middle, Washington The Susquehanna and West Va. be merged into one Dept. and a competant man placed over the whole and have named Franklin as that man. If this is complied with I do not know who I will assign to the 18th Corps.

U. S. GRANT
Lt. Gen

ALS (telegram sent), DNA, RG 107, Telegrams Collected (Unbound); telegram received, *ibid.*, RG 94, War Records Office, Dept. of Va. and N. C., Army of the James, Unentered Papers. *O.R.*, I, xl, part 3, 328. On July 18, 1864, Maj. Gen. Benjamin F. Butler telegraphed to USG. "The General Order No. 225 from the War Deptment has been published directly from the Adjutant Generals office in this and is making irregularity in the Corps and inquiry at these Head Qrs as to whom division commanders are to report   While I grieve to trouble you about such a matter still may I ask that the proper order as I learned it from yourself may be published. It is clearly within your province   Perhaps the an order assignmenting of the 18th to Gen Franklin as son as he shall take to be able to take the field. In the mean time to be under the Command of Gen Martindale would be a gratifying compliment to Franklin and would be appreciated by the Country after his as a sequence to his escape and *had better come from you*   Gen Ord might be also assigned to the tenth   This Corps in the mean time to be under command of Gen Terry who is a good soldier both to report to Department head Quarters—Brooks leaves this morning   All quiet on our lines" ALS (telegram sent), DNA, RG 393, Dept. of Va. and N. C., Telegrams Sent (Press). *O.R.*, I, xl, part 3, 327–28.

1. Alfred H. Terry, born in Hartford, Conn., in 1827, attended Yale Law School and served as clerk of the superior court of New Haven County (1854–60). Early in the Civil War he served as col., 2nd Conn. Militia, and as col., 7th Conn. Appointed brig. gen. as of April 25, 1862, he served in the South Atlantic theater before transfer to the Army of the James in late 1863. For his assignment to command the 10th Army Corps, see *ibid.*, p. 313.

To Maj. Gen. George G. Meade

By Telegraph from City Point
Dated July 18 *1864.*

To MAJ GEN MEADE

I have the report of a refugee who has just come in to the gunboats who says that Lee is said to have left the south side and gone leaving Beauregard & Longstreet   some say he has gone to the valley and others say he has gone south   Have you had any deserters from Hills Corps in the last 24 hours

U. S. GRANT

Lt Genl

Telegram received (at 10:50 P.M.), DNA, RG 94, War Records Office, Army of the Potomac; copies, *ibid.*, RG 108, Letters Sent; DLC-USG, V, 45, 59, 67; (2) Meade Papers, PHi. *O.R.*, I, xl, part 3, 314. On July 18, 1864, 11:30 P.M., Maj. Gen. George G. Meade telegraphed to USG. "Seven deserters from the 64. Georgia regt—Wrights brigade—Mahone's Division Hill's corps came into our lines between 2 & 3 o'clock this morning   They gave no particular information & knew nothing of the contemplated attack of last night beyond rumours that one was to be made.—These men were questioned & knew nothing of any movements or change of position of their corps, nor had they heard of the corps having six days cooked rations issued as reported by deserters from Longstreets Corps last night—I should think the refugee's story was a camp rumour.—" ALS (telegram sent), DNA, RG 393, Army of the Potomac, Miscellaneous Letters Received; copies, *ibid.*, Letters Sent; (2) Meade Papers, PHi. *O.R.*, I, xl, part 3, 314.

At 9:00 A.M., Meade had telegraphed to USG. "The foregoing is forwarded as an explanation of the failure to make the threatened attack. All has been perfectly quiet.—" ALS (telegram sent), DNA, RG 94, War Records Office, Army of the Potomac; telegram received, *ibid.*, RG 108, Letters Received. *O.R.*, I, xl, part 3, 313. Written on a telegram of the same date from John C. Babcock, Office of the Provost Marshal, Army of the Potomac, to Maj. Gen. Andrew A. Humphreys. "A deserter from the 59th Geo. of Anderson's Brigade, Fields Division Longstreets Corps has just been forwarded. He came into our lines about 12 o'clock last night. He states—That orders were issued to the pickets last evening to fire on any man seen going beyond the picket line—These orders were peremptory and have never been given before. That his Col. said that no attack would be made on our lines, as so many deserters came into our lines yesterday, and told us all about it. They did not leave the trenches—Informant says that it was generally understood an attack was to be made last night—Longstreet was to assault us in front and Hill would, make a circuit in our rear. The movement was freely discussed among officers and men and did not meet with much favor. It was looked upon as a foolish and desperate movement. Informant is intelligent and his information corroborates all we have relative to Longstreet's position &c. &c." ALS (telegram sent), DNA, RG 94, War Records Office, Army of the Potomac. *O.R.*, I, xl, part 3, 313.

On July 19, 4:00 P.M., Meade wrote to USG. "The foregoing just received is forwarded." *Ibid.*, p. 335. Meade enclosed a report from a deserter which indicated that the 3rd Corps, Army of Northern Va. (Lt. Gen. Ambrose P. Hill) had not moved from its previous position. *Ibid.*, p. 334.

To Julia Dent Grant

———

City Point, Va. July 18th *1864.*

DEAR JULIA,

I have just rec'd a letter from you which shows that many times letters are a long time on the road between here and Sappington P. O. I presume they get through though ultimately and that you have heard from me frequently since that. I write about twice a week.

I am in most excellent health. Think Richmond will fall before we quit here but cannot say how soon. Until Richmond does fall I do not expect to go home. I do not know what to direct about the children's schooling more than I have directed. I want them though to be at good schools and without loss of time. If you can not make suitable arrangements in St. Louis you may go where you think best, East or West. My kindes regards to all at home and love and kisses for you and the children.

I am sorry Dr. Barrett has been retained in prison. I got the Sec. of War to order his release on bail. But Gen. Rosecrans never obeyed an order in his life that I have yet heard of. In this case he may have been right but I do not know. Dont be perswaded on any account to let White have the farm one moment after his time expires.

ULYS.

ALS, DLC-USG.

To Charles G. Leland

———

City Point, Va, July 178th *1864.*

MY DEAR SIR,

I have to acknowledge the receipt of your letter of the 8th instant.

In reply therto permit me to return through you my grateful

acknowledgements to the ladies and gentelemen who by their generous partiality and contributions have secured for me the celebrated dagger of Garibaldi. I am specially obliged to Miss Anna
M. Lea, Miss Eliza M. Jackson and Mrs. J. W. Sherwood for the
active interest they manifested in conferring upon me this unex-
pected honor.

I shall cherish the dagger as a souvenir of that distinguished
soldier & patriot General Garibaldi, who by his devotion and sacrifices to the cause of liberty in Italy is entitled to the highest respect
and admiration of every American.

Be good enough to send it at your convenience, by Express, to
Mrs. U. S. Grant, St. Louis Mo. care of Mr. Chas. Ford, Agt. U. S.
Ex. Co. St. Louis, Mo.

With the highest personal regard, I am,

> Very respectfully
> your obt. svt.
> U. S. GRANT
> Lt. Gen. U. S. A.

CHARLES GODFREY LELAND, ESQ.
1526 LOCUST STREET
PHILADELPHIA

ALS, OHi. Charles G. Leland, born in Philadelphia in 1824, a journalist and
man of letters, edited a daily newspaper for the Sanitary Fair of Philadelphia,
where a dagger belonging to Giuseppe Garibaldi was voted to the most popular
gen. Charles Godfrey Leland, *Memoirs* (New York, 1893; reprinted, Detroit,
1968), pp. 272, 368; Elizabeth Robins Pennell, *Charles Godfrey Leland: A
Biography* (1906; reprinted, Freeport, New York, 1970), I, 276. On July 28,
1864, Julia Dent Grant wrote to Leland. "Your letter of the 22nd ~~ultimo~~ together
with 'the dagger of Garibaldi, borne by the Italian hero in nearly all his battles'
and presented to my husband by the late Great Central Fair held in Philadelpha
was received to day through Mr. Chas. W. Ford. That I will safely keep the
dagger and cherish with profound gratitude the compliment to my husband, in
the gift to him, of this most celebrated weapon of modern times, assure those
who have thus honored him." ALS, OHi.

To Abraham Lincoln

(Cipher)   City Point Va. July 19th *1864*
A. LINCOLN, PRESIDENT,

In my opinion there ought to be an immediate call for say 300.000 men to be put in the field in the shortest possible time. The presence of this number of reinforcements would save the annoyanc[e] of raids and would enable us to drive the enemy back from his present front, particularly from Richmond, without attacking fortifications. The enemy now have their last man in the field. Every depletion of their Army is an irreparable loss. Desertions from it are now rapid. With the prospect of large additions to our force these desertions would increase. The greater number of men we have the shorter and less sanguinary will be the war.

I give this entirely as my view and not in any spirit of dictation, always holding myself in readiness to use the material given me to the best advantage I know how.

U. S. GRANT
Lt. Gen.

ALS (telegram sent), IHi; telegram received (sent at 10:00 A.M., received at 8:30 P.M.), DLC-Robert T. Lincoln. *O.R.*, I, xxxvii, part 2, 384; *ibid.*, I, xl, part 3, 332. On July 20, 1864, 4:30 P.M., President Abraham Lincoln telegraphed to USG. "Yours of yesterday about a call for 300,000 is received. I suppose you had not seen the call for 500,000 made the day before, and which I suppose covers the case. Always glad to have your suggestions" ALS (telegram sent), DNA, RG 107, Telegrams Collected (Bound); telegram received, *ibid.*, RG 108, Letters Received. *O.R.*, I, xl, part 3, 344. Lincoln, *Works*, VII, 452.

To Maj. Gen. Henry W. Halleck

(Cipher)   City Point July 19th 1864
MAJ. GEN. HALLECK, WASHINGTON

The establishment of recruiting Rendezvous at Fortress Monroe, besides being expensive has called for two officers who cannot be spared from the field, and will not add a man to the service.

Every negro that comes in is taken into the service now, the best specimens physically being enlisted in companies already organized and the others are employed as laborers in some of the Departments or sent North. I will add also that every expedition going out brings back all the negroes they can find.

U. S. GRANT
Lt. Gen.

ALS (telegram sent), OClWHi; telegram received (marked sent at noon, received at 7:45 P.M.), DNA, RG 107, Telegrams Collected (Bound); *ibid.*, Telegrams Collected (Unbound). *O.R.*, I, xl, part 3, 334.

To Maj. Gen. Benjamin F. Butler

By Telegraph from City Pt
Dated July, 19 *1864.*

To GEN BUTLER,

Your communication & despatch relative to recruiting at Ft Monroe & Newberne rec'd. I have telegraphed objecting to the establishment of recruiting rendezvous at either place. I dont want states to get the benefit of recruits obtained in that way besides the men so obtained are worth more in keeping present organizations filled.

U. S. GRANT,
Lt. Genl

Telegram received, DNA, RG 393, Dept. of Va. and N. C., Telegrams Received; copies, *ibid.*, RG 108, Letters Sent; DLC-USG, V, 45, 59, 67. *O.R.*, I, xl, part 3, 339–40. On July 19, 1864, 9:30 A.M., Maj. Gen. Benjamin F. Butler telegraphed to USG. "Supposing it to be the settled policy of the War Dept to establish recruiting Rendezvous at Fortress Monroe and Newberne I desire an alteration of detail of officers   They have detailed Col Draper one of my very best officers in charge at Fortress Monroe. Now if they will detail Brig Gen Wilde who is admirably fitted for it there instead of Draper It will solve many difficulties of organization. Will you please apply for the change: Wilde instead of Draper" ALS (telegram sent), DNA, RG 94, War Records Office, Dept. of Va. and N. C., Army of the James, Unentered Papers; telegram received, *ibid.*, RG 108, Letters Received. Printed as sent at 10:35 A.M. in *O.R.*, I, xl, part 3, 339. On July 18, Butler had written to USG. "I have just recieved an order from the War Department detailing two of my best officers—one Colonel Draper and the other Lieut Colonel Craft, to establish recruiting and rendavous depots at Fort Monroe and Newbern, of course looking at the recruitment of colored men Owing to the state of facts at present here, the great demand for labor, the high prices which any negro can get, either as a servant or as an employee in the Quartermaster or Commissary Department, it is impossible to recruit any faster than we are doing, and that is best done in the field by the regimental officers as negros come in   To establish the depots will be a large cost to the United States besides taking from the field two of my very best officers—I respectfully suggest that that course is inexpedient in the present state of this Department, and desire to make this representation to you for such remarks as you may see fit as to the execution of the order—"   LS, DNA, RG 108, Letters Received.

On July 19, 10:10 A.M., Butler telegraphed to USG. "The new iron clad Tunxis left Philadelphia for Washington the 11th instant. She is said to draw only seven ft of Water. She is the very boat we want here in case we get hold of the Howlett House Batty as she can go up at once through the channel and hold what we get and also can move up and down without danger of getting on Shore and save wooden boats the danger of Picket duty, and protect transports from shore Batteries. If you agree with me might not the Tunxis be applied for"   ALS (telegram sent), *ibid.*, RG 94, War Records Office, Dept. of Va. and N. C., Army of the James, Unentered Papers; copy (undated), *ibid.*, RG 393, Dept. of Va. and N. C., Telegrams Sent. *O.R.*, I, xl, part 3, 340.

Also on July 19, Butler wrote to USG. "I have the honor to forward Brig Genl Grahams report of the expedition to Wilcox Wharf, and Harrisons Landing find and Capture Torpedo Workers"   AES, DNA, RG 108, Letters Received. *O.R.*, I, xl, part 3, 343. The enclosed report is *ibid.*

To Maj. Gen. William T. Sherman

(Cipher)   City Point July 19th/64 [*10:30* P.M.]
MAJ. GEN. SHERMAN, NEAR ATLANTA GA.

I see by Richmond papers of yesterday that Smith has left Tupelo and is moving towards Ripley. Although they call it a retreat I judge from S. D. Lee's dspatch that Forrest has been badly whipped. Smith however ought to be instructed to keep a close watch on Forrest and not permit him to gather strength and move into Middle Tennessee.

U. S. GRANT
Lt. Gen.

ALS (telegram sent), OClWHi; telegram received (on July 20, 1864, 8:35 A.M.), DNA, RG 107, Telegrams Collected (Bound). *O.R.*, I, xxxix, part 2, 182. On July 20, 9:00 P.M., Maj. Gen. William T. Sherman telegraphed to Maj. Gen. Henry W. Halleck. "I have a despatch from Gen Grant; answer him in my name that A J Smith has the very orders he suggests viz: to hang on to Forrest and prevent his crossing to Tennessee: I will however renew The order—I advanced from the Chattahoochee in force on the 17th   On the 18th Smith [*McPherson*] & Garrards Cavalry reached the Augusta road & destroyed about five miles of it East of Decatur   On the 19th The whole line crossed Peach Tree Creek, McPherson occupying Decatur—Today we moved on Atlanta and have been fighting all day   Our line now extends from a point of the railroad two & a half miles East of Atlanta and extends around by the north to the mouth of Peach Tree Creek—We find the enemy in force but will close in tomorrow—By the Atlanta paper we learn that Johnston is relieved and Hood commands, That Rousseau is on the road at Opelika and that most of the newspapers and people have left Atlanta   Thomas is on my right, Schofield centre and McPherson on the left—Garrards cavalry on the left, rear of McPherson and Stoneman & McCook on the west bank guarding our right flank—The enemy still clings to his entrenchments—If Gen Grant can keep Lee from reinforcing this army for a week I think I can dispose of it   We have taken several hundred prisoners & had some short severe encounters but they were partial but we have pressed the enemy back at all points until our rifle guns can reach the town   If he strengthens his works I will gradually swing round between him & his only source of supplies—Macon—"   Telegram received (on July 21, 12:45 A.M.), DNA, RG 107, Telegrams Collected (Bound); *ibid.*, RG 108, Letters Received. *O.R.*, I, xxxviii, part 5, 194–95.

On July 16, USG had telegraphed to Halleck. "The following dispatch is taken from the Richmond Enquirer of this date and is forwarded for your information—. . . 'From Okalona July 14th 1864,   To GEN BRAXTON BRAGG—We attacked a column of the enemy under Smith yesterday on the March from Pontotoc—We attacked him in his position at Tupelo this morning but could not force his position—The Battle was a drawn one & lasted three hours—S. D. LEE Lieut Genl'"   Telegram received, DNA, RG 107, Telegrams Collected (Bound); *ibid.*, Telegrams Collected (Unbound); copies, *ibid.*, RG 108, Letters Sent; DLC-USG, V, 45, 59, 67. *O.R.*, I, xxxix, part 2, 172.

On July 18, Maj. Gen. Cadwallader C. Washburn telegraphed to Secretary of War Edwin M. Stanton, sending a copy to USG. "The expedition of Maj Gen A. J. Smith has been a co~~pm~~plete success, he met Lee ~~for~~ Forrest & Walker near Tupelo, he fought them for three days thoroughly whipping and routing them. I quote the following from his dispatches to me dated yesterday at New Albany Miss. 'We met Lee and Walker at Tupelo & whipped them badly on three different days, our loss is small when compared with the Rebel loss. I bring back every thing in good order   nothing lost,[']   a scout who has since come into Lagrange reports the triumph of our Arms complete and the loss of the enemy at twenty five hundred (2500) men"   Telegram received (on July 20), DNA, RG 108, Letters Received. Printed as received July 20, 10:00 A.M., in *O.R.*, I, xxxix, part 2, 179. On July 20, USG telegraphed to Maj. Gen. Benjamin F. Butler and Maj. Gen. George G. Meade a telegram of July 18, 7:00 P.M., from Sherman to Halleck. "We moved today rapidly & McPherson reached the Atlanta & Dalton road at a point seven (7) miles East of Decatur, about four (4) miles from stony mountain. Gen Garrards cavalry at once set to work to break up the road, & was reinforced by Morgan L. Smiths division of Inf'y & they expect by night to have five miles of road effectually destroyed   Thus far we have encountered only cavalry with light resistance & tomorrow will move on Decatur &

Atalanta,   I am fully aware of the necessity of making the most of time & shall keep things moving." Telegram received (addressed to Butler), DNA, RG 94, War Records Office, Dept. of Va. and N. C., Army of the James, Unentered Papers; (addressed to Meade) *ibid.*, Army of the Potomac; copy (addressed to Butler and Meade), DLC-USG, V, 67. *O.R.*, I, xxxviii, part 5, 169–70.

To Edwin M. Stanton

(Cipher)   City Point July 20th/64
A. L̶i̶n̶c̶o̶l̶n̶, P̶r̶e̶s̶i̶d̶e̶n̶t̶, E. M. STANTON SEC. OF WAR

I must enter my protest against States sending recruiting g̶u̶a̶r̶d̶s̶ Agents into the Southern States for the purpose of r̶e̶c̶r̶u̶i̶t̶i̶n̶g̶ filling their quotas. The negroes brought within our lines are rightfully recruits to the United States Service and should not go to benefit any particular state. It is simply allowing Massachusetts (I mention Mass. because I see the order of the Governor of that state for establishing recruiting agencies in the South and see no such order from any other state authority.) to fill her quota by paying an amount of money to recruits the United States have already got. I must also enter my protest against recruiting from prisoners of War.[1] Each one enlisted robs us of a soldier and adds one to the enemy with a bounty paid in loyal money.

U. S. GRANT
Lt. Gen.

ALS (telegram sent), CSmH; telegram received (at 1:30 P.M.), DNA, RG 107, Telegrams Collected (Bound). *O.R.*, I, xl, part 3, 345. On July 20, 1864, 2:30 P.M. and 4:20 P.M., Secretary of War Edwin M. Stanton telegraphed to USG. "Your telegram of this date is received. The i̶d̶e̶a̶ proposition for recruiting in rebel states by the Executives of other states h̶a̶s̶ was neither reccommended nor sanctioned by this Department—although the President states in a telegram to General Sherman that he was favorable to it. H̶i̶s̶ a̶u̶t̶h̶o̶r̶i̶t̶y̶ t̶o̶ r̶ He also authorized General Butler to recruit from Prisoners of War. It is not permitted in any other instance. For these reasons a̶n̶d̶ a̶s̶ m̶y̶ j̶u̶d̶g̶m̶e̶n̶t̶ your protest has been referred to the President for such instructions as he may be pleased to give." ALS (telegram sent), DNA, RG 107, Telegrams Collected (Bound); telegram received, *ibid.*, RG 108, Letters Received. *O.R.*, I, xl, part 3, 345. "The President directs me to [f]orward to you a copy of the telegram sent by him to General Sherman in relation to recruiting agents." ALS (telegram sent), DNA, RG 107, Telegrams Collected (Bound); telegram received, *ibid.*, Telegrams Collected (Unbound); *ibid.*, RG 108, Letters Received. *O.R.*, III, iv, 528. See *ibid.*, I, xxxviii, part 5, 169. Lincoln, *Works*, VII, 449–50.

1. On July 20, USG telegraphed to Maj. Gen. Benjamin F. Butler. "Can you tell me if recruiting is now going on from the prisoners of war at Pt Lookout? I highly disapprove of recruiting from such source, & even reluctantly admit of the propriety of enlisting deserters & refugees." Telegram received (at 8:15 A.M.), DNA, RG 393, Dept. of Va. and N. C., Telegrams Received; copies, *ibid.*, RG 108, Letters Sent; DLC-USG, V, 45, 59, 67. *O.R.*, I, xl, part 3, 355. At 9:00 A.M., Butler telegraphed to USG. "In answer to your telegram I have the honor to report that recruiting has stopped at Point Look Out.—I am about to go to the front at Petersburgh to day   Shall I have the pleasure of meeting ~~you~~ the Lt General there?" ALS (telegram sent), DNA, RG 94, War Records Office, Dept. of Va. and N. C., Army of the James, Unentered Papers; copy (undated), *ibid.*, RG 393, Dept. of Va. and N. C., Telegrams Sent. *O.R.*, I, xl, part 3, 355. See telegram to Maj. Gen. Benjamin F. Butler, July 20, 1864.

To Maj. Gen. Henry W. Halleck

City Point July 20th 2 P m *1864.*

MAJ. GEN. HALLECK, WASHINGTON

If Gen. Barnard can be spared from Washington I would like to have him ordered back to the field.[1] If he cannot be spared now send him as soon as he can be conveniently spared. I think immediate steps should be taken for completing and connecting the fortifications about Baltimore. The officers in charge of the works about Washington can take charge of those of Baltimore also. I have heard nothing of the determination come to on my recommendation about the merging of the four Departments about Washington into one?

U. S. GRANT
Lt. Gen

ALS (telegram sent), OClWHi; telegram received (at 9:35 P.M.), DNA, RG 107, Telegrams Collected (Bound). *O.R.*, I, xxxvii, part 2, 400; *ibid.*, I, xl, part 3, 344. On July 21, 1864, 11:30 A.M. and 5:40 P.M., Maj. Gen. Henry W. Halleck telegraphed to USG. "Genl Barnard is ordered to report to you. Engineer officers have been sent several times to Baltimore to lay out the works. Some are there now. I think, from personal examination, that they are better located than the defenses of Washington. It appears that Early sent a small force south with his plunder, and massed the rest near Winchester. Genl Averill had a skirmish there yesterday & reports having killed & wounded over three hundred rebels, taken 200 prisoners & four pieces of artillery. Nothing heard from Wright for three days. When he recieved your orders he replied that he would return as soon as assured of rebel retreat. Your telegram about merging Depts is in hands of Secty of War. I see no good reason for removing or superceding Genl Augur. He is capable & efficient. Genl. Franklin would not give satisfaction. The President ordered him to be tried for negligence & disobedience of orders when here before, but Genl McClellan assumed the responsibility of his repeated delays in obeying orders." "When Genl Ord was sent to you he commanded fragments of 8th & 19th corps. The portion of the latter north has no commander. No order has yet been issued assigning him. If after seeing him you wish it for the 10th corps it will be immediately issued." ALS (telegrams sent), DNA, RG 107, Telegrams Collected (Bound); telegrams received, *ibid.*; *ibid.* (the first on July 22), RG 108, Letters Received. *O.R.*, I, xxxvii, part 2, 408, 409; *ibid.*, I, xl, part 3, 360, 361. An undated telegram received of the second telegram is in DNA, RG 107, Telegrams Collected (Unbound).

On July 19, 4:00 P.M., Halleck telegraphed to USG. "I am of opinion that another regiment of Heavy Arty in addition to those with Genl Wright should be sent here as soon as you can spare it. I have written to day at length." ALS (telegram sent), *ibid.*, Telegrams Collected (Bound); telegram received, *ibid.*; (on July 20) *ibid.*, RG 108, Letters Received. *O.R.*, I, xxxvii, part 2, 384; *ibid.*, I, xl, part 3, 332. On the same day, Halleck wrote to USG. "The recent raid into Maryland seems to have established several things which it may be well for us to keep in mind. 1st. It has proved that while your army is south of the James River & Lee's between you & Washington, he can make a pretty large detachment, unknown to us for a week or ten days, & send it against Washington, or into West Virginia, or Pennsylvania or Maryland. 2d. Genl Hunter's army which comprises all troops north of Richmond that can go into the field, is entirely too weak to hold West Virginia & the B. & O. Railroad, & at the same time resist any considerable rebel raid north of the Potomac. 3d. We cannot rely upon aid from the militia of the northern states; they will not come out at all, or will come too late, or in so small a force as to be useless. 4th. The garrisons of Washington and Baltimore are made up of troops entirely unfit for the field, and wholly inadequate for the defence of these places. Had it not been for the opportune arrival of the veterans of the 6th Corps, both cities would have been in great danger. So long as you were operating between Washington & the enemy, your army covered Maryland & Penn., and I sent you all the troops from here and the north which could take the field or guard your depôts & prisoners of war. But the circumstances have now most materially changed, and I am decidedly of opinion that a larger available force should be left in this vicinity. It may be answered that reënforcements can be sent in time from the James River, as was done in this case. This answer would be decisive, if we here, or you there, could always be apprized of the number and position of the raiders, as well as the object upon which their march is directed. But this cannot be done without a superior cavalry force, which we have not got, & are not likely to have. The country is so stript of animals that it is hardly possible to supply demands in the field. If the enemy had crossed the Potomac below Harper's Ferry (and it is now fordable in many places) and had moved directly upon Washington or Baltimore, or if the arrival of the 6th Corps had been delayed 24 hours, one or the other of these places, with their large depôts of supplies, would have been in very considerable danger. Will it be safe to have this risk repeated? Is not Washington too important in a political as well as military point of view, to run any serious risk at all? I repeat that so long as Lee is able to make any large detachments, Washington cannot be deemed safe, without a larger & more available force in its vicinity. What you say of establishing schools of instruction here, at Baltimore & at Harper's Ferry will be applicable when we get troops to be instructed. But we are now not receiving one half as many as we are discharging. Volunteering has virtually ceased, & I do not anticipate much from the President's new call, which has the disadvantage of again posponing the draft for fifty days. Unless our government & people will come square up to the adoption of an efficient & thorough draft, we cannot supply the waste of our army." LS, DNA, RG 108, Letters Received. *O.R.*, I, xxxvii, part 2, 384–85; *ibid.*, I, xl, part 3, 333. On July 20, USG telegraphed to Maj. Gen. George G. Meade. "A call is made for One more Regt of Heavy Artillery for the defences of Washington   You may designate one to be sent back as soon as the 6th Corps begins to return"   Telegram received, DNA, RG 94, War Records Office, Army of the Potomac; copies, *ibid.*, RG 108, Letters Sent; DLC-USG, V, 45, 59, 67; (2) Meade Papers, PHi. *O.R.*, I, xl, part 3, 345. On July 21, 1:10 P.M., Meade telegraphed to USG. "In compliance with your instructions of yesterday I have designated the 6th. New York Heavy Artillery as the regiment to be sent to the defences of Washington. The regiment will leave here as soon as the 6th Corps begins to arrive—The strength of the regiment present for duty is 21 officers and 685 men." Copies, DNA, RG 393, Army of the Potomac, Miscellaneous Letters Received; (misdated June 21) Meade Papers, PHi. Printed as sent at 1:15 P.M. in *O.R.*, I, xl, part 3, 361.

1. On July 21, Bvt. Maj. Gen. John G. Barnard telegraphed to USG. "Orders received to report to you. I have been closely confined all the year & would like to be permitted to take my family to Harford, Md, which will detain me until Wednesday or Thursday of next week. If any-thing important demands my immediate presence I don't ask it. Please telegraph." ALS (telegram sent), DNA, RG 107, Telegrams Collected (Unbound). On July 22, USG telegraphed to Barnard. "I know of no objections to your remaining north until next week as you request—" Telegrams received (2), *ibid.*; (press) *ibid.*, Telegrams Collected (Bound).

To Maj. Gen. Benjamin F. Butler

By Telegraph from City Pt.
Dated July 20 *1864.*

To MAJ GEN BUTLER

I shall be engaged today so that it will be doubtful about my going to the front. If I go it will not be earlier than 3 P M. I have relieved Gen Smith from command of the 18th Corps, & shall place Gen Ord in his place. It is now open to select a commander for the 10th Corps. Do you think of any Maj Gen available who you would like to have?   Birney & Gibbon are with the Army of the Potomac only Comd'g divisions   Gen Ord will meet you today at the 18th Corps HdQrs.

U. S. GRANT.

Lt Genl

Telegram received (at 11:30 A.M.), DNA, RG 94, War Records Office, Dept. of Va. and N. C., Army of the James, Unentered Papers; copies, *ibid.*, RG 108, Letters Sent; DLC-USG, V, 45, 59, 67. Printed as sent at 11:30 A.M. in *O.R.*, I, xl, part 3, 355–56. See telegram to Edwin M. Stanton, July 20, 1864, note 1. On July 21, 1864, Maj. Gen. Benjamin F. Butler wrote to USG. "I am obliged for the assignment of General Ord to the Eighteenth Corps. In regard to the Tenth, of the two major-generals I believe Birney would be the best assignment. Allow me, however, to call your attention to General Martindale. He is a graduate of the class of General Meade, a gentleman of ability, and has shown himself to be a good soldier, a good lawyer, and you will pardon me for believing that he has some of the qualities, therefore, of a soldier. General Martindale is the senior brigadier-general in the active service, and has been during the war in many battles, behaving well, and without promotion. If you think with me, might not General Martindale be assigned to the Tenth Corps? Of course these are suggestions to your better judgment, only saying further that General Martindale would be perfectly agreeable to me, and from what I have seen of him commends himself to my good opinion. I say this without prejudice to General Birney, whom I also much respect. If it be said that General Martindale is only a brigadier, that may be answered by saying that is not his fault, and I have no doubt he will earn his spurs. Allow me to congratulate you upon the good news from Hunter; it is very good." *O.R.*, I, xl, part 3, 376. On the same day, 7:05 P.M., Butler telegraphed to USG. "I have seen Genl Martindale and his health is infirm that he must go home so that I think you will not do better than to assign Birney to the 10th Corps—" ALS (telegram sent), DNA, RG 94, War Records Office, Dept. of Va. and N. C., Army of the James, Unentered Papers; copy (undated), *ibid.*, RG 393, Dept. of Va. and N. C., Telegrams Sent. *O.R.*, I, xl, part 3, 376. On the same day, Capt. Ely S. Parker issued Special Orders No. 64. "Subject to the approval of the President, Maj. Gen. E. O. C. Ord U. S. V. is assigned to the Command of the 18th Army Corps and will relieve Brig. Genl. J. H. Martindale now temporarily commanding. Subject to the approval of the President Maj. Genl. D. B. Birney U. S. V. is assigned to the Command of the 10th Army Corps and will relieve Brig Gen. A. H. Terry temporarily Commanding . . . Col Henry S Burton 5th U S Artillery, is relieved from duty in the 18th Army Corps, and will report to Maj. Genl George G. Meade, Comd'g. Army of the Potomac for orders." Copies, DLC-USG, V, 57, 62, 67. *O.R.*, I, xl, part 3, 361–62.

To Maj. Gen. Benjamin F. Butler

—————

By Telegraph from City Pt
Dated July 20 *1864.*

To GEN BUTLER,

As it will be several days before the balance of the 19th Corps will arrive it will not be advisable to send any portion of it to Deep Bottom at present. Send none of it overe until a complete Division is here, at least, and that is sent over withdraw Foster, so as to hold your line at Bermuda perfectly safe. The 19th such portion of it as you have should be encamped if it is not so already near the line of entrenchments, so as to be ready to take them in case of an attack.

U. S. GRANT.
Lieut General.

Telegram received (at 11:00 P.M.), DNA, RG 94, War Records Office, Dept. of Va. and N. C., Army of the James, Unentered Papers; copies, *ibid.*, RG 108, Letters Sent; DLC-USG, V, 45, 59, 67. *O.R.*, I, xl, part 3, 356.

To Maj. Gen. Henry W. Halleck

—————

City Point July 21st *1864.* [*11:00* A.M.]

MAJ. GEN. HALLECK, WASHINGTON

You may retain Wright's Command until the departure of Early is assured or other forces are collected to make his presence no longer necessary. I have ordered another regiment of Heavy Artillery back to Washington but they will not go whilst the 6th & part of 19th Corps is there. I am now sending back all Veterans whos term of service expires previous to the 25th of August.

U. S. ~~GRANT~~
~~Lt. Gen.~~

If Early has halted about Berryville what is there to prevent Wright & Hunter from attacking him?

U. S. GRANT
Lt. Gen.

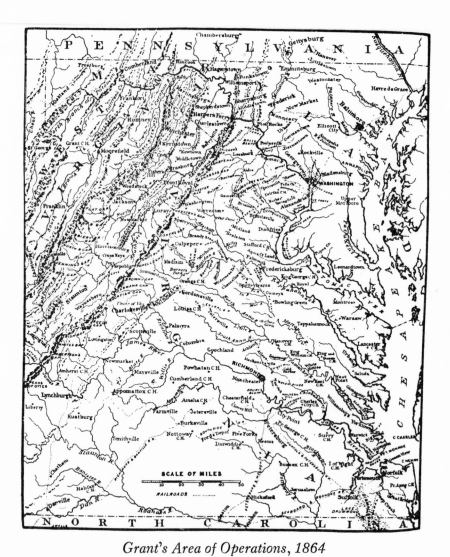

Grant's Area of Operations, 1864

From Robert U. Johnson and Clarence C. Buel, eds., Battles and Leaders of the
Civil War (*New York, 1887*), IV, 494

ALS (telegram sent), OClWHi; telegram received (at 6:00 P.M.), DNA, RG 107, Telegrams Collected (Bound). *O.R.*, I, xxxvii, part 2, 408; *ibid.*, I, xl, part 3, 360. See telegram to Maj. Gen. Henry W. Halleck, July 22, 1864.

To Maj. Gen. Henry W. Halleck

City Point July 21st *1864.*

MAJ. GEN. HALLECK, WASHINGTON

There is no indication of any troops having been sent from here North. Deserters coming in daily indicate nearly the position of every Division of Hill's Longstreet's and Beaurigard's forces. Hill's Corps has withdrawn from its position on the extreme right and was yesterday in rear of the other part of the line held by the enemy. There is a rumor of some force having been sent to Georgia but if this is so it is most likely only regiments detatched from their command.

U. S. GRANT
Lt. Gen.

ALS (telegram sent), OClWHi; telegram received (sent at 11:30 A.M., received at 5:00 P.M.), DNA, RG 107, Telegrams Collected (Bound). *O.R.*, I, xxxvii, part 2, 408–9; *ibid.*, I, xl, part 3, 360.

To Maj. Gen. William T. Sherman

City Point 10 a m
July 21st 1864

MAJ GEN SHERMAN
COMDG D̶E̶P̶T̶ MIL DIST MISS
(COPY TO SEC'Y OF WAR)

Richmond "Whig" of the 20th learns from Macon "Confederate" that but little QrMr or Commissary stores remain in Atlanta all having been removed to safer and more secure points. It also says that it has every reason to hope that Shermans rear will be cut in the next ten days. Johnston has been relieved and Hood takes his

place[1] much to surprise of the army & public, also that this change
indicates that there will be no more retreating but that Atlanta will
be defended at all hazards and to the last extremity

U S GRANT
Lt Genl

Telegram received (at 6:00 P.M.), DNA, RG 107, Telegrams Collected (Bound);
copies, *ibid.*, RG 108, Letters Sent; *ibid.*, RG 393, Military Div. of the Miss.,
Telegrams Received in the Field; DLC-USG, V, 45, 59, 67. *O.R.*, I, xxxviii, part
5, 210–11. On July 21, 1864, 10:00 A.M., Maj. Gen. George G. Meade telegraphed to USG. "Richmond papers of the 20th just received announce the relief
of Joe Johnston and the assignment of Hood to the command of the Army at
Atalanta—no other news—Paper sent by orderly—" ALS (telegram sent),
DNA, RG 393, Army of the Potomac, Miscellaneous Letters Received; copy,
ibid., Letters Sent.

On July 22, Capt. Samuel Bruch, Bowling Green, Ky., telegraphed to Maj.
Thomas T. Eckert, sending a copy to USG. "I teleghed you in cipher of the
Capture of Atlanta the moment I recd the information ~~Did you not get the
msg~~ It is no doubt true though I have recd nothing as yet from Capt Van
Duzer" Telegram received (at 9:00 P.M.), *ibid.*, RG 107, Telegrams Col-
lected (Bound).

On July 23, USG telegraphed to Maj. Gen. Edward O. C. Ord. "I have news
from Atlanta to 9 P. M. last night as late as the rebel account you sent me. The
fighting had all been favorable to us. McPherson was killed and Gushman
wounded but neither life nor limb was in danger. This however was several days
ago" Telegram received, Ord Papers, CU-B.

On July 24, 3:00 P.M., Maj. Gen. William T. Sherman telegraphed to Maj.
Gen. Henry W. Halleck. "On making up reports and examining the field I find
the result of Hoods attack on our left more destructive than I reported, our loss
will not foot up 2000 killed and wounded wheras we have found over 1000 rebel
dead which will make with the usual proportion of wounded, a loss to the enemy
of full 7000 Garrard has returned perfectly successful having completely destroyed the two large bridges near Covington forty miles towards Augusta,
brought in 200 prisoners and some good horses and destroyed the Publec stores
at Covington and Congers including two thousand bales of cotton, a locomotive
and train of cars Our communications are yet all safe and the ~~cavalry~~ Army in
good condition in all respects. As soon as my cavalry rests I propose to swing the
Army of the Tenn round by the right rapidly and interpose between Atlanta
and Macon the only line open to the enemy" Telegram received (on July 25),
DNA, RG 108, Letters Received. Printed as received at 9:50 P.M. in *O.R.*, I,
xxxviii, part 5, 240. After bracketing the final sentence, USG endorsed this telegram. "Telegraph to Army & Corps commanders leaving out the paragraph in
brackets." AES, DNA, RG 108, Letters Received.

On July 25, 8:30 P.M., Sherman telegraphed to USG. "Your despatch of
21st did not come till today—Johnston is relieved and Hood commands. Hood
has made two attempts to strike hard since we crossed the Chattahoochee and
both times got more than he bargained for No doubt he expects to cut to my
rear but I have already cut to his rear having broken the Augusta road out for

fifty miles and his Southern road at Opelika   None remains to him but the Macon road and I think I will have that soon   I would rather that Hood should fight it out at Atlanta than to retreat farther to Macon   If you can keep away reinforcements all well—My army is all in hand and rear well guarded"   Telegram received, *ibid.*, RG 107, Telegrams Collected (Bound); *ibid.*, RG 108, Letters Received; copy, *ibid.*, RG 393, Military Div. of the Miss., Telegrams Sent in the Field. *O.R.*, I, xxxviii, part 5, 247.

On July 26, USG telegraphed to Meade. "I have a dispatch from Sherman up to 3,30 P. M yesterday   as all had been quiet since his last report & no change taken place I did not send it around   Sherman expressed himself very much pleased with the result of Operation[s] since he crossed the Chattahoochie & hoped that Hood would attempt to hold Atlanta   Sherman has today 20,000, more men than he made his first advance on Dalton with. This is after all his losses since crossing the Chattahoochee. He expresses himself perfectly willing to have Hood reenforced by another army Corps if that will induce them to attack. Sherman will probably have the last road remaining to the enemy by tomorrow night"   Telegram received, DNA, RG 393, Army of the Potomac, Telegrams Received; copies (2), Meade Papers, PHi.

1. On July 17, Gen. Joseph E. Johnston relinquished command of the Army and Dept. of Tenn. to Gen. John B. Hood. *O.R.*, I, xxxviii, part 5, 887.

To William T. Blodgett

HEADQUARTERS ARMIES OF THE UNITED STATES,
CITY POINT, Va., July 21. [*1864*]
W. T. BLODGETT, ESQ., CHAIRMAN COMMITTEE ON ARMS, &C.,
NEW-YORK SANITARY FAIR:

DEAR SIR:—Your letter of the 14th instant, informing me that the sword, saddle and horse equipments which a generous public have seen fit to present me with, whilst patriotically donating the proceeds of their sale to the use of the sick and wounded soldiers who are making such noble sacrifices in the cause of their country, is received. Whilst I will always feel glad to meet the loyal citizens of New-York, either here or wherever I may be at any time, yet I should prefer not meeting them as a committee to present this or any other generous token of public approbation. If you please the articles may be sent to me through Adams Express Company, or may be retained in New-York City to such time as I may be able to visit them. Please permit me to thank all subscribers to these pres-

ents, whether voting for me or any other person (the funds all go
to the same noble use,) and I subscribe myself,

> Very truly, your obedient servant,
> U. S. GRANT, Lieutenant-General.

New-York Times, Sept. 4, 1864. William T. Blodgett came to New York City
in 1838 and two years later entered an uncle's varnish business, in which he
prospered, then made more money in real estate. *Ibid.*, Nov. 6, 1875. On July 14,
1864, and, presumably, on Aug. 5, Blodgett wrote to USG. "As Chairman of
the Arms and Trophies Department of the Metropolitan Fair in aid of the United
States Sanitary Commission, I have the pleasure of announcing that your friends
and admirers have designated you as the recipient of the beautiful army sword
contributed to the Fair for the purpose of presentation to the one of our Generals
who should receive the largest number of votes during the continuance of the
Fair. The whole number of votes exceeded 45,000, of which you received 31,200.
A committee from this department proposed presenting this testimonial of your
countrymen in person, but the duties of the active campaign in which you have
been and are now engaged, has suggested the propriety of deferring this pleasure
until you have achieved a consummation of intents and designs of a campaign
in which all the hearts of the nation follow you with patriotic ardor and interests.
As custodian of this testimonial, in which so many of your countrymen have
united, I shall be happy to receive from you any suggestion that prompts itself
in regard to the disposition and manner of conveying the same to you. I am also
intrusted with a military saddle, bridle and mountings complete, of excellent
workmanship, intended for presentation to you by citizens of New-York, and
designed to take the same course as the army sword. Hoping to hear from you
soon, . . ." "I am in receipt of your letter of 21st ultimo. Agreeably with your
wishes, I have the pleasure of enclosing Adams' Express Company's receipt for
the army sword, saddle and horse equipments, presented to you by your countrymen, through the Metropolitan Fair in aid of the United States Sanitary Commission. On their arrival be kind enough to acknowledge the receipt of same,
that the acknowledgement may form part of the history of the great charity in
which so many of our citizens were engaged." *New-York Tribune*, Sept. 3, 1864.
On Aug. 18, USG wrote to Blodgett. "Your favor of the 5th inst., inclosing express company's receipt for the army sword, saddle and horse equipments, generously donated to the Metropolitan Fair for the benefit of our sick and wounded
soldiers, is just received. The articles themselves also reached me this evening.
Permit me, through you, to thank all those loyal citizens to whose partiality I am
indebted for these beautiful presents. The sword I shall endeavor to hand down
to my children untarnished by any act of mine to make them feel ashamed."
New-York Times, Sept. 4, 1864. Concerning the sword, see letter to Julia Dent
Grant, April 24, 1864.

To Maj. Gen. Henry W. Halleck

City Point Va
July 22nd 1864 9 p m

MAJ GEN H W HALLECK
CHF OF STAFF

Your dispatch of ten A M to day received   I telegraphed s[ev]-
eral days ago to retain Wright and the other forces until the retreat
of Early was fully assured, and asked if Wright and Hunter were
not strong enough to attack him. You need not send any troops back
until the main force of the enemy are known to have left the Valley.
Is Wright still where he can act in conjunction with Hunter? If the
first can push the enemy back & destroy RailRoads from Charlottsville to Gordonsville I would prefer that service to having them
here.

U S GRANT
Lt Genl

Telegram received (on July 23, 1864, 7:00 A.M.), DNA, RG 107, Telegrams
Collected (Bound); copies, *ibid.*, RG 108, Letters Sent; DLC-USG, V, 45, 59,
67. *O.R.*, I, xxxvii, part 2, 413–14; *ibid.*, I, xl, part 3, 385. On July 22, 10:00
A.M., Maj. Gen. Henry W. Halleck telegraphed to USG. "A staff officer of Genl
Wright arrived last night with a dispatch dated 1.30 P M of the 21st. Acting on
your previous orders he had given up the pursuit & would reach Washington today. He left the enemy retreating on Front Royal & Strasburg. It is for you to
decide whether he shall remain to cooperate with Hunter's forces, or whether he
shall embark for City Point. In my opinion raids will be renewed as soon as he
leaves, but you are the judge whether or not a large enough moveable force shall
be kept here to prevent them." ALS (telegram sent), DNA, RG 107, Telegrams
Collected (Bound); telegram received, *ibid.*; *ibid.*, RG 108, Letters Received.
Printed as received at 6:40 P.M. in *O.R.*, I, xxxvii, part 2, 413; *ibid.*, I, xl, part
3, 385.

On July 21, noon, USG telegraphed to Maj. Gen. Benjamin F. Butler and
Maj. Gen. George G. Meade. "A dispatch from Gen Hunter of 10 30 a m the
20th states that a dispatch just recvd by him announces that Wright & Crooks
have formed a junction at Snickers ferry have crossed the Shenandoah and are
driving the enemy with every prospect of capturing his whole train   Previous
information announced that Wright had captured eighty wagons & a number
of prisoners   Another dispatch that Crooks had had an engagement with a part
of the enemys force killing & wounding about six hundred"   Telegram received,
DNA, RG 94, War Records Office, Army of the Potomac; *ibid.*, Dept. of Va. and
N. C., Army of the James, Unentered Papers; copies, DLC-USG, V, 67; (2)
Meade Papers, PHi.

To Maj. Gen. Benjamin F. Butler

By Telegraph from City Pt.
Dated July 22 1864.

To GEN BUTLER.

I see firing again in the same direction as last night. Does Foster still hold the position gained today? Has he not been reinforced. Is the firing seen an attack made by the enemy[1]

U. S. GRANT

Telegram received (at 9:20 P.M.), DNA, RG 94, War Records Office, Dept. of Va. and N. C., Army of the James, Unentered Papers. *O.R.*, I, xl, part 3, 400. On July 22, 1864, 9:30 P.M., Maj. Gen. Benjamin F. Butler telegraphed to USG. "Nothing new from Foster since noon. He has not been re-inforced. Have telegraphed to him to ascertain what the firing is. Imagine it to be only picket firing. The enemy as far as heard from have only some cavalry at that particular point." Copies, DNA, RG 94, War Records Office, Dept. of Va. and N. C., Army of the James, Unentered Papers; (undated) *ibid.*, RG 393, Dept. of Va. and N. C., Telegrams Sent. Printed as received at 9:30 P.M. in *O.R.*, I, xl, part 3, 400. At 10:40 A.M., Brig. Gen. Godfrey Weitzel had telegraphed to USG. "Foster proposed this morning to try and retake that position, which the 11th Maine took and had to give up yesterday. This position is the intersection of the New Market and Malvern Hill main road with a branch road leading to the Long Bridge main road. It is an important one, as it cuts the direct communication between the rebel forces at Malvern Hill and those at Chapin's farm. Consequently the enemy would drive him out again as they are stronger than he is now. He has therefore been directed not to make the attempt until re-inforced to-morrow or the day after by a portion of the 19th Corps. That position if held protects perfectly the position at Deep Bottom, the pontoon bridge the navigation of the river, and I think would force the enemy's batteries ~~and force~~ and troops from Malvern Hill. I" ALS (telegram sent), DNA, RG 94, War Records Office, Dept. of Va. and N. C., Army of the James, Unentered Papers; telegram received, *ibid.*, RG 108, Letters Received. *O.R.*, I, xl, part 3, 400. On the same day, Weitzel transmitted to USG telegrams from Brig. Gen. Robert S. Foster and Brig. Gen. Alfred H. Terry about the recapture of the position. *Ibid.*, pp. 404, 405. On the same day, Brig. Gen. John A. Rawlins telegraphed to USG. "Maj Gen Butler telegraphs that Foster has retaken the ~~place~~ position from which he was driven last night, and has directed him to hold it, unless attacked by a superior force, which however he does not apprehend will be attempted—" Telegram received, DNA, RG 94, War Records Office, Army of the Potomac. *O.R.*, I, xl, part 3, 385. At 10:37 P.M., Weitzel telegraphed to USG. "Foster's regiment has fallen back from that position for the night, not having any disposable force to re-inforce it. The firing is below him and is by the gun boats, which are shelling the flanks of that regiment: to keep off the rebels   No symptoms whatever of any pressing or attacking force of the enemy. I have not the least doubt but that, that position can be retaken without loss in the morning. It seems to be sort of neutral ground."

ALS (telegram sent), DNA, RG 94, War Records Office, Dept. of Va. and N. C., Army of the James, Unentered Papers; copy (undated), *ibid.*, RG 393, Dept. of Va. and N. C., Telegrams Sent. *O.R.*, I, xl, part 3, 400.

On July 23, USG telegraphed to Butler. "Is there any thing going on with Genl Foster Command—I see the same evidence of fiting in that direction I did two 2 nights ago" Telegram received, DLC-Benjamin F. Butler. An undated telegram from Weitzel to USG was probably sent the same day. "Foster has been reinforced by one brigade, which is now intrenching on the down stream side of Four Mile Creek. That second bridge from Jones' Neck to the lower side of the creek was laid last night. That Point is now, I think, for good, in our possession, and I suppose some picket firing is going on. I will telegraph at once to Foster." Copy, DNA, RG 393, Dept. of Va. and N. C., Telegrams Sent. On the same day, Weitzel telegraphed to USG a message from Foster. "There is no firing here except an occasional shot by the gun-boats into the woods in front of my line below Four-Mile Creek. The Eleventh Maine hold a position covering the road from New Market to Malvern Hill. All is quiet along my lines." ALS (telegram sent), *ibid.*, RG 107, Telegrams Collected (Unbound); copy (undated), *ibid.*, RG 393, Dept. of Va. and N. C., Telegrams Sent. The message from Foster is in *O.R.*, I, xl, part 3, 419.

1. On July 21, 10:05 P.M., Weitzel telegraphed to Rawlins. "The following despatch just received. 'Deep Bottom   8 45 P. m. 21st   GEN WEITZEL Chf Engr & act. chf staff   Learning that the enemy were at work where they had the battery placed on the 14th inst & knowing that if allowed to entrench themselves they could injure my camps & the pontoon bridge & obstruct navigation I ordered the eleventh (11th) Me. under Lt Col Hill to the bluff below four mile creek with instructions to advance & occupy the enemys position which was done without loss & the ~~eneeys~~ enemys picket as our line advanced   Col Hill now holds the Ground formerly occupied by the enemy which is about a mile and a quarter in front of our work on the bluff and not far from Sweeny's pottery   He has levelled the battery   Col H—— reports quite a force in his front   One Lieutenant & ten enlisted men were captured and have sent to corps Hd qrs R. S. FOSTER Brig Gen'   Will the commandg General please order Genl Benham to send me another bridge six hundred feet long so that I can throw it from Jones Neck to the Down river bank of four Mile creek and thus enable us to re inforce that bank if necessary & thus keep the enemy from erecting batteries on that bank as this attempt was to Command & shell our troops which are in position on the up river bank of that creek" Telegram received, DNA, RG 108, Letters Received. Printed as sent at 9:30 P.M. in *O.R.*, I, xl, part 3, 377. See *ibid.*, p. 389. At 10:45 P.M., USG telegraphed to Butler. "I see constant flashing as if burning powder in the direction of Gen Fosters camp. Do you know what it is   I hear no sound of arty but thought it possible the enemy might be shelling Fosters camp." Telegram received, DLC-Benjamin F. Butler; copies, DLC-USG, V, 45, 59, 67; DNA, RG 108, Letters Sent. *O.R.*, I, xl, part 3, 377. At 10:50 P.M., Weitzel telegraphed to USG. "The General has retired. ~~Genl Foster is~~ The 11th Maine Reg't which had driven the enemy as already reported to you, has in turn been driven, after a fight back into our intrenchments. Nothing serious reported. I have requested the Navy to shell the enemy as they must be in some force, to protect their working parties which will undoubtedly attempt again to erect the battery which the 11th Maine destroyed."

ALS (telegram sent), DNA, RG 94, War Records Office, Dept. of Va. and N. C., Army of the James, Unentered Papers; copy (undated), *ibid.*, RG 393, Dept. of Va. and N. C., Telegrams Sent. *O.R.*, I, xl, part 3, 377. On the same day, USG telegraphed to Weitzel. "If there is any further report from Genl Foster tonight, please forward it to me." Telegram received (at 11:12 P.M.), DLC-Benjamin F. Butler.

To Bvt. Lt. Gen. Winfield Scott

HEADQUARTERS, ARMIES OF THE UNITED STATES,
CITY POINT, Va, July 23, 1864.

LIEUTENANT GENERAL WINFIELD SCOTT, U. S. A.:—

MY DEAR GENERAL—Your letter of the 2d inst., addressed to the Hon. E. B Washburne, in which you informed him that you had heard that some one had told me that you had spoken sl[i]ghtingly of my appointment to my present rank, is just received. Allow me to assure you, General, that no one has ever given me such information. I have never heard of any speech of yours in connection with the present rebellion which did not show the great interest felt by you, both in our eminent success and in the success of all our commanders. In fact, all that I have heard of your saying in relation to myself has been more flattering to me than I probably deserve.

With assurance of great esteem for you personally, General, as well as for the services you have rendered our country throughout a long and eventful public career, I subscribe myself, very respectfully and truly, your obedient servant,

U. S. GRANT,
Lieutenant General U. S. A.

New York Herald, Dec. 9, 1864. On July 2, 1864, Bvt. Lt. Gen. Winfield Scott, West Point, wrote to U.S. Representative Elihu B. Washburne. "I heard a short time ago that some one had informed Lieut. Genl. Grant that I had spoken slightly as an officer. As it is probable that your frank may enable this a letter to reach him I beg leave to say to thro' you that I have never uttered an unkind word about him. The inquiry has frequently been addressed to me—'Do you know Genl. Grant?' I have answered that he made the campaign of Mexico with me & was considered by me & I suppose by all his brothers in commission, as a good officer, & one who attained special distinction at Molino del Rey—Of his more recent services I have uniformly spoken in terms of the highest admiration &

added that, in my opinion, he had richly earned his present rank, & hope he may speedily put down the rebellion." ALS, DLC-Elihu B. Washburne. In late Nov., USG visited Scott, who inscribed a copy of his *Memoirs*, "From the oldest to the ablest General in the world." *New York Herald*, Nov. 22, 1864.

To Maj. Gen. Henry W. Halleck

(Cipher)   City Point July 23d/64 6 p. m.
Maj. Gen. Halleck, Washington,

If Wright has returned to Washington send him immediately back here retaining however the portion of the 19th Corps now in Washington for further orders. Early is undoubtedly returning here to enable the enemy to detach troops to go to Georgia. Hunter's troops must be tired. I would say therefore for him to take up such of the advanced positions suggested by him as in his judgement will best protect the line of the Potomac.

If Wright & Hunter have started after the enemy with the view of following on to the road from Charlottesville to Gordonsville let them go.

U. S. Grant
Lt. Gen.

ALS (telegram sent), OClWHi; telegram received (on July 24, 1864, 7:00 A.M.), DNA, RG 107, Telegrams Collected (Bound). *O.R.*, I, xxxvii, part 2, 422; *ibid.*, I, xl, part 3, 408–9. On July 23, 1:00 P.M., Maj. Gen. Henry W. Halleck telegraphed to USG. "Genl Wright in person arrived this morning, and most of his forces will encamp at our outer line to-night. He says it will take about two days to refit his men with shoes & clothing & to have them paid. Our cavalry yesterday followed the enemy to Strasburg. He is still moving south. Genl Hunter telegraphs to the President that without the assistance of Wright he cannot prevent Early's return, if attempted. A man just in from Gordonsville says the rail road is repaired & the bridge across the Rapidann nearly completed. In regard to Early's force, Genl Wright was assured by union men who saw both armies that Early's was much the larger. The rebels generally said to the country people that as soon as they secured their plunder they would return to Maryland & Penn. for more, & that they expected to meet a force from Richmond to recieve their plunder. They were probably directed by their officers to say this. The President, who has seen all the dispatches on the subject, directs me to say that you alone can judge of the importance of sending the 6th corps to the Army of the Potomac, or of its operating with Hunter against Gordonsville & Charlottsville, and that you alone must decide the question. The part of the 19th corps which returns with Genl Wright will be sent to City Point, as soon as they can be refitted." ALS (telegram sent), DNA, RG 107, Telegrams Collected (Bound); telegram received, *ibid.*; (on July 24) *ibid.*, RG 108, Letters Received. *O.R.*, I, xl, part 3, 408. On the same day, 10:30 P.M., USG telegraphed to Halleck. "Please send back ~~here~~ all Cavalry detachments, whether mounted or not, belonging to regiments here with the exception of those belonging to the 1st Pa 3d Pa 1st N. J. 3d Ia ~~and~~ 6th Pa. ~~These regiments~~ and 8th Pa. These regiments are being sent back having but a short period to serve." ALS (telegram sent), OClWHi; telegram received (on July 24, 7:00 A.M.), DNA, RG 107, Telegrams Collected (Bound). *O.R.*, I, xl, part 3, 409.

On July 23, 2:30 P.M., Asst. Secretary of War Charles A. Dana telegraphed to USG. "A man who left Gordonsville on the 12 inst. arrived here yesterday He is intelligent and seems honest. He reports that when he left the cars were running through from Richmond to Gordonsville Charlottesville Stanton & Lynchburg   The rebels were building a bridge over the Rapidan to get hay from Culpepper" Telegram received, DNA, RG 108, Letters Received. *O.R.*, I, xxxvii, part 2, 422; *ibid.*, I, xl, part 3, 409.

To Elihu B. Washburne

City Point Va. July, 23d *1864*.

HON. E. B. WASHBURN,
DEAR SIR:

Your letter of the 17th enclosing one from Gen. Scott[1] is just received. I enclose to you my answer to the Gens. which please forward to him.—All are well here and bouyant and full of hope. I wish people North [w]ould be as hopeful as our troops who have to do the fighting are.

I cannot write you what I expect to do here. That Maryland raid upset my plans but I will make an attempt to do something before many days.

In regard to the appointment of Capt. Atchison[2] on my Staff to fill the vacancy made by Rowley should he resign I cannot make it. I have now two Staff officers not recognized by any law who have been with me for a long time. As vacancies occur it is but fair that they should be absorbed.

I will save for you some battlefield trophy.

Remember me to the good people of Galena.

Yours Truly
U. S. GRANT

ALS, IHi.

    1. See letter to Bvt. Lt. Gen. Winfield Scott, July 23, 1864.
    2. Probably Charles B. Atchison of Ill., appointed capt. and aide as of July 11, 1862, who served at the close of the war on the staff of Maj. Gen. Edward O. C. Ord. *O.R.*, I, xlvi, part 2, 861.

To Charles A. Dana

                          City Point Va. July 24th *1864*
C. A. Dana, Asst. Sec. of War, Washington,
How does the pursuit after the enemy sum up? Have they been compelled to drop any of their plunder and have we killed captured or scattered any of their force to speak of. What news have you from Foster? We hear nothing from him except through the papers. All quiet here. A Richmond extra of yesterday, claims great victory at Atlanta, capture of a great many prisoners twenty two pieces of artillery, killed large numbers among whom was the celebrated yankee general McPherson, also Genls. G. A. Smith and Wood, that Hardee was in Shermans rear, & they expected victory would be decisive   Shermans dispatches of a day later which of course you have seen places the matter in a very different light, save the death of McPherson.—We will make a move here about tuesday,[1] ~~the exact one of~~ but which one of two that are in contemplation is not yet fixed upon, when it is I will ~~let you k~~ dispatch you.

                                 Jno Rawlins
                         Brig genl—Chf of staff

ALS (telegram sent), OClWHi; telegram received, DNA, RG 107, Telegrams Collected (Bound). Printed as sent at 11:00 a.m. in *O.R.*, I, xxxvii, part 2, 427; *ibid.*, I, xl, part 3, 422–23. USG wrote the first four sentences of the telegram sent; Brig. Gen. John A. Rawlins completed it. On July 24, 1864, 9:00 p.m., Asst. Secretary of War Charles A. Dana telegraphed to Rawlins. "The pursuit of Early on the whole has proved an egregerous failure, relieved only by Averills success at Winchester in which he captured four guns and some prisoners Wright and Crook accomplished nothing and Wright started back as soon as he got where he might have done something worth while. As it is Early has got off with the mass of his plunder and Hunter will hardly be able to break up the railroad beyond what can be repaired in a short time. Had Wright remained in the valley the combined forces might have made a fine campaign at least against the rail roads and the crops. We have no news from Foster nor anything from Atlanta later than VanDuzers despatch of *11 P. M. of yesterday* Will you do me the kindness to let me know what is the matter with John Seitz a baker from this city who has been or is being tried at City Point for some offence, and to have the execution of the sentence suspended if it is in any way severe, at least for the present. Chapman & McIntosh have been made Brigadier Generals. The General's previous recommendation had been mislaid & could not be found McCandless has also been made a Brigadier General Osterhaus has been made a major General" Telegram received, USG 3. *O.R.*, I, xxxvii, part 2, 427; *ibid.*, I, xl, part 3, 423.

On July 25, 3:00 P.M., Dana telegraphed to Rawlins. "I am privately Informed from Gen Wright that the force under Gen Crook in the valley which figures on Hunters Field Return as 8000 Effectives is in reality not over 4000 many of them being also a poor quality of Troops No men of Crooks own Division are there; It looks as if these had not yet all left the Ohio river" Telegram received (on July 26), DNA, RG 108, Letters Received. Printed as received at 11:00 P.M. in *O.R.*, I, xxxvii, part 2, 434. On July 23, USG telegraphed to Secretary of War Edwin M. Stanton. "The order sending Regts, whose times expired by twenty fifth of August to Washington will take Colonel J. B. McIntosh Third Pa. Cavalry & Colonel Geo H. Chapman Third Indiana both Commanding brigades in third Division Cavalry, I have therefore to request their immediate promotion in accordance with previous recommendations." Telegram received, DNA, RG 107, Telegrams Collected (Bound); *ibid.*, Telegrams Collected (Unbound); copies, *ibid.*, RG 108, Letters Sent; DLC-USG, V, 45, 59, 67. *O.R.*, I, xl, part 3, 408. On July 24, 9:05 P.M., Stanton telegraphed to USG. "The appointments of Brigadier reccomendd by you towit Cols McCandless, Chapman Chamberlain, & McIntosh were ordered and have been made and will be transmitted to you by the Adjutant General. The President has appointed General Osterhouse Major General. There are three or four other vacancies of Brigadier awaiting your reccommendation to be filled up." ALS (telegram sent), DNA, RG 107, Telegrams Collected (Bound); telegram received, *ibid.*, Telegrams Collected (Unbound); *ibid.*, RG 108, Letters Received. *O.R.*, I, xl, part 3, 421. At 9:20 P.M., Col. James A. Hardie telegraphed to USG. "The Secretary of War directs me to inform you that General Osterhaus has been, by direction of the President appointed Major General of Volunteers." ALS (telegram sent), DNA, RG 107, Telegrams Collected (Bound); telegram received, *ibid.*, Telegrams Collected (Unbound); *ibid.*, RG 108, Letters Received. On July 26, USG telegraphed to Maj. Gen. George G. Meade. "The Secy of War telegraphs that Col's McCandless Chapman Chamberlain & McIntosh have been appointed Brigadier Generals—Osterhaus at a Major Genl" Telegram received, *ibid.*, RG 94, War Records Office, Army of the Potomac; copies (2), Meade Papers, PHi. On the same day, USG telegraphed the same message to Maj. Gen. Philip H. Sheridan. Telegram received, DNA, RG 94, War Records Office, Army of the Potomac.

1. July 26.

To Maj. Gen. Henry W. Halleck

(Cipher)   City Point Va. July 24th/64 12 m.
Maj. Gen. Halleck, Washington,

Your despatch of 1 p. m. yesterday just received.[1] I presume you had not yet received my dispatch directing the 6th Corps to be returned here and the 19th retained. I would prefer keeping the Army of the Potomac together if possible and if necessary send all of the 19th Corps to Washington. You can retain Gen. Wright until I learn possitively what has become of Early. I would prefer a complete smashup of the enemy's roads about Gordonsville & Charlottesville to having the same force here. If Wright and Hunter can do this job let them do it. Submit the matter to Wright for his views. If they get out to the rail-road every rail ought to be destroyed from Gordonsville back towards Richmond and towards Orange Court House for miles and from Charlottesville towards Staunton and towards Lynchburg in the same way.

U. S. Grant
Lt. Gen.

ALS (telegram sent), OClWHi; telegram received (at 6:00 p.m.), DNA, RG 107, Telegrams Collected (Bound). *O.R.*, I, xxxvii, part 2, 426; *ibid.*, I, xl, part 3, 421–22. On July 24, 1864, noon and 8:00 p.m., Maj. Gen. Henry W. Halleck telegraphed to USG. "The rear of the 6th corps got into camp last night. They are being supplied & paid to day. They will probably begin to embark to-night. Last telegram from Genl Hunter in regard to enemy in the Shenandoah is forwarded." "Genl Wright in accordance with your orders was about to embark for city Point   I have directed him to await your further orders. I shall exercise no further discretion in this matter, but shall carry out such orders as you you may give" ALS (telegrams sent), DNA, RG 107, Telegrams Collected (Bound); telegrams received, *ibid.*; (2nd) *ibid.*, Telegrams Collected (Unbound); *ibid.*, RG 108, Letters Received. *O.R.*, I, xxxvii, part 2, 426; *ibid.*, I, xl, part 3, 421, 422.

On the same day, 5:00 p.m., USG telegraphed to Halleck. "Special order 236 from the Adj. Gen. Office, of date July 13th details Col. A. G. Draper 36th U. S. Colored Troops as commander of ⸮Recruiting Depot at Fortress Monroe, Va. Col. Draper is very much needed here. I would like to have the order changed subsituting Brig. Gen. Wilde for Col. Draper." ALS (telegram sent), OClWHi; telegram received (on July 25, 10:15 a.m.), DNA, RG 107, Telegrams Collected (Bound); *ibid.*, Telegrams Collected (Unbound). *O.R.*, I, xl, part 3, 422. On July 26, 10:00 a.m., Col. Edward D. Townsend telegraphed to USG. "Your

telegram of twenty fourth (24th) suggesting change in Special Orders two
hundred thirty six (236) ~~has~~ is received   The change has been made accordingly
~~Acknowle~~" ALS (telegram sent), DNA, RG 107, Telegrams Collected (Unbound); telegram received, *ibid.*; *ibid.*, RG 108, Letters Received. Dated July
25 in *O.R.*, I, xl, part 3, 436.

On July 24, 5:30 P.M., USG telegraphed to Halleck. "Please direct Gen.
Foster to order Brig. Gen. Wm Birney to report to Gen. Butler if his services
can be dispensed with. His Brigade might be brought here if Foster thinks he
can do without it. Whilst operations continue here much cannot be done in the
Dept. of the South except to hold what we have got." ALS (telegram sent),
OClWHi; telegram received (on July 25, 10:00 A.M.), DNA, RG 107, Telegrams Collected (Bound). *O.R.*, I, xxxv, part 2, 185; *ibid.*, I, xl, part 3, 422. On
July 6, Bvt. Maj. Gen. Montgomery C. Meigs had written to Halleck concerning
a request by Maj. Gen. John G. Foster for armed transports built by Norman
Wiard. *Ibid.*, I, xxxv, part 2, 167. On July 9, Halleck endorsed this letter to USG.
Ibid. On Aug. 10, USG endorsed this letter. "Respy returned. As I have requested
that all troops that can be spared from General Fosters Command be brought
forward; and that, General Foster for the present act purely on on the defensive
at Charleston, there is no necessity for sending these vessels" Copy, DLC-USG,
V, 58. Misdated Aug. 16 in *O.R.*, I, xxxv, part 2, 168. See *ibid.*, pp. 231, 234–
35, 256.

1. See telegram to Maj. Gen. Henry W. Halleck, July 23, 1864.

To Maj. Gen. George G. Meade

City Point, Va, July 24th *1864.*

MAJ. GEN. MEADE,
COMD.G A. P.
GENERAL,

Your note brought by Col. Comstock is received. It will be
necessary to act without expecting Wright. He is now in Washington but it is not fully assured yet that Early has left the Valley and
if Wright was to start back no doubt the Maryland raid would be
repeated.

I am not willing to attempt a movement so hazardous as the one
against intrenched lines against the judgement of yourself and
your Engineer officer, and arrived at after a more careful survey of

the ground than I have given it. I will let you know however in the morning what determination I come to.

> Very respectfully
> your obt. svt.
> U. S. Grant
> Lt. Gen.

ALS, deCoppet Collection, NjP. *O.R.*, I, xl, part 1, 131–32; *ibid.*, I, xl, part 3, 425–26. See following letter.

On July 24, 1864, 11:00 A.M., Maj. Gen. David Hunter, Harpers Ferry, telegraphed to Secretary of War Edwin M. Stanton transmitting a telegram of July 23 from Brig. Gen. George Crook, Winchester. "There are rumors that apparently have foundation that Longstreet is in the Valley. As yet I am not prepared to say how far this may be true" Telegram received, DNA, RG 108, Letters Received. *O.R.*, I, xxxvii, part 2, 428. USG endorsed this telegram to Maj. Gen. George G. Meade. "Is there any word from deserters of Longstreet's Corps within the last day or two?" AES, DNA, RG 108, Letters Received. *O.R.*, I, xl, part 3, 426. On July 24, 8:00 P.M., Meade telegraphed to USG. "The foregoing is sent as all the information we have of Longstreets Corps We have been on the qui-vive to find out any movements of Lees army and question all deserters & others on this point I feel quite sure the Corps has not been moved—" Telegram received, DNA, RG 108, Letters Received. *O.R.*, I, xl, part 3, 426. The enclosure is *ibid.* On July 25, 6:30 P.M., Meade telegraphed to USG. "A deserter from the 19 Missi. Rgt. Andersons old Divn. Hills Corps came into our lines last night He states that Hoods old Division of Longstreets Corps is still in our front on the left of Hills Corps but that McLaws Divn. now commanded by Kershaw moved to the north side of the Appomatox some days since—It was at first rumored they were going to re-inforce Early, but it was subsequently reported they did not go but are still north of the Appomatox.—This confirms the report made to Genl. Foster" ALS (telegram sent), DNA, RG 393, Army of the Potomac, Miscellaneous Letters Received; copies, *ibid.*, Letters Sent; (3) Meade Papers, PHi. *O.R.*, I, xl, part 3, 437.

To Maj. Gen. George G. Meade

City Point, Va, July 24th *1864*

Maj. Gen. G. G. Meade,
Comd.g A. P.
General,

The Engineer officers who made a survey of the front from Bermuda Hundred report against the probability of success from an attack there. The chances they think will be better on Burnsides front. If this is attempted it will be necessary to concentrate all the force possible at the point in the enemy's line we expect to penetrate. All officers should be fully impressed with the absolute necessity of pushing entirely beyond the enemy's present line if they should succeed in penetrating it, and of getting back to their present line promptly if they should not succeed in breaking through. To the right and left of the point of Assault all the aArtillery possible should be brought to play upon the enemy in front, during the Assault. Thin lines would be sufficient for the support of the Artillery and all the reserves could be brought on the flank of their commands nearest to the point of Assault ready to follow in if successful. The fField Artillery & Infantry held in the lines during the first assault should be in readiness to move at a moments notice either to their front or to follow the Main Assault as they should receive orders. One thing however should be impressed on Corps Commanders. If they see the enemy giving way in their front, or moving from it to reinforce a heavily assailed portion of their line, they should take advantage of such knowledge and act promptly without waiting for orders from their Army Commander.

Gen. Ord can co-operate with his Corps in this movement and about five thousand troops from Bermuda Hundred can be sent to reinforce you or can be used to threaten an assault between the Appomattox and James River as may be deemed best.

This should be done by Teusday morning, if done at all. If not attempted we will then start at the date indicated to destroy the rail-road as far as Hicksford at least and to Welden if possible.

Please give me your views on this matter and I will order at once.

In this I have said nothing of the part to be taken by the Cavalry in case the enemy's lines are assaulted. The best ~~they~~ disposition to make of them probably would be to place them on the extreme left with instructions to skirmish with the enemy and drive him back if possible following up any success gained in that way according to the judgement of the commander, or orders he may receive.

Whether we send an expedition on the rail-road or assault at

Petersburg Burnsides ~~m~~Mine will be blown up. As it is impossible
to hide preparations from our own officers and men, and consequently from the enemy, it will be well to have it understood as
far as possible that just the reverse of what we intend is in contemplation.

I am General, very respectfully &c.

U. S. GRANT

Lt. Gen

ALS, deCoppet Collection, NjP. *O.R.*, I, xl, part 1, 129–30; *ibid.*, I, xl, part 3,
424. On July 24, 1864, Maj. Gen. George G. Meade wrote to USG. "I have
received your letter per Lt. Col Comstock.—In reply thereto, I have to state I
yesterday made a close & careful reconnaissance of the enemys position & altho'
I could not detect any positive indications of a second line, yet from certain appearances at different points I became satisfied a second line does exist on the
east of the ridge just in rear of the position of Burnsides mine   I have no doubt
of the successful explosion of the mine & of our ability to effect a lodgment and
compel the evacuation of the line at present held by the enemy; but from their
redoubt on the Jerusalem plank road & from their position in front of the Hare
house their artillery fire would compel either a withdrawal or an advance. The
advance of course should be made but its success is dependant on the question
whether the enemy have or have not a second line on the crest of the ridge—If
they have with the artillery fire already referred to, which sweeps the whole slope
of the ridge, I do not deem it practicable to carry the second line by assault.—
Now from my examination as previously stated, together with the evident necessity for their having such a line, I am forced to believe one will be found and I
do not therefore deem, the assault expedient—Should it be deemed necessary to
take all the risks involved, and there is undoubtedly room for doubt, I would like
a little more time than is given in your note, to place in position the maximum
amount of artillery to bear upon the lines not assaulted. In regard to the assaulting force it would be composed, so far as this army is concerned of the 9th
& 2d corps   The 5th corps have no reserves of any consequence, and would be
required to hold their line & be prepared to meet any attempt to turn our left
flank which in case of an unsuccessful assault I should deem quite probable. Fully
impressed as I am with the necessity of immediate action, and also satisfied that
excepting regular approaches, the assault on Burnsides front is the most practicable, I am compelled as a matter of judgment to state that the chances of success
are not such as to make the attempt advisable—At the same time I do not consider it hopeless & am prepared to make the attempt, if it is deemed of importance to do so.—I enclose you a report of Maj. Duane which confirms my views.—
If Wright is soon to return, and we can extend our lines to the Welden road we
could then advance against the salient on the Jerusalem plank road & make an
attempt to carry these at the same time we exploded Burnsides mine—This was
my idea some time ago & we have been preparing the necessary siege works for
this purpose.—Under your instructions however none of the heavy guns or
material have been brought to the front—it would take perhaps two days to get
them up.—" ALS, Gratz Collection, PHi. Printed with two variant texts in *O.R.*,
I, xl, part 1, 130–31; *ibid.*, I, xl, part 3, 424–25. See preceding letter.

To Julia Dent Grant

———

City Point Va. July 24th *1864.*

DEAR JULIA,

I have just about five minuetes to write you before the mail leaves which is just time enough to say that I am well. I have not heard from you for some time and when I did your letter was an old one. I suppose you have written and your letters will come along after a while. Have you made up your mind where you and the children will go? I want you to exercise your own pleasure about this but want the children to be at a good school. If you like you may go to any Eastern Village where you can get good schools and a pleasant place to board. I would have no objection to Philadelphia. It would cost a greatdeel to furnish a house to go to houskeeping and until I know where we will be I do not want to incur it. Besides if you were housekeeping you would be tied down so that you could not leave home. Boarding at a good place you could always leave the children for a few weeks.

Love and kisses for yourself and children.

ULYS.

ALS, DLC-USG.

To Abraham Lincoln

———

City Point, Va, July 25th *1864*

A. LINCOLN
PRESIDENT OF THE UNITED STATES,
DEAR SIR:

After the late raid into Maryland had expended itself, seeing the necessity of having the four Departments of "The Susquehanna," "The Middle," "Western Va." and "Washington" under one head, I recommended that they be merged into one, and named Gen. Franklin as a suitable person to command the whole.[1] I still think it highly essential that these four Departments should be in one command. I do not insist that the Departments should be broken up, nor do I insist upon Gen. Franklin Commanding. All I ask is that one General officer in whom I, and yourself, have confidance in, should command the whole. Gen. Franklin was named because he was available and I know him to be capable and believe him to be trustworthy.

It would suit me equally well to call the four Departments referred to, a "Military Division," and to have, placed in command of it, General Meade. In this case I would suggest Gen. Hancock for command of the Army of the Potomac, and Gen. Gibbon for the command of the 2d Corps. With Gen. Meade in command of such a Division, I would have every confidence that all the troops within the Military Division would be used to the very best advantage in case of another invasion. He too having no care beyond his own command, would station his troops to the best advantage, from a personal examination of the ground, and would adopt means of getting the earliest information of any advance of the enemy, and would prepare to meet it.

During the last raid the wires happened to be down between here and Fortress Monroe, and the cable broken between there and Cherrystone. This made it take from twelve to twenty-four hours, each way, for dispatches to pass. Under such circumstances it was difficult for me to give positive orders or directions because I could not tell how the conditions might change during the transit of dispatches.

Many reasons might be assigned for the change here suggested some of which I would not care to commit to paper but would not hesitate to give verbally.

I send this by Brig. Gen. Rawlins, Chief of Staff, who will be able to give more information of "the situation" than I could give in a letter.

Hoping that you will see this matter in the light I do, I have the honor of subscribing myself,

> Very Truly & respectfully
> your obt. svt.
> U. S. GRANT
> Lt. Gen.

ALS, DLC-Robert T. Lincoln. *O.R.*, I, xxxvii, part 2, 433–34; *ibid.*, I, xl, part 3, 436.

    1. See telegram to Maj. Gen. Henry W. Halleck, July 18, 1864.

To Maj. Gen. Benjamin F. Butler

> *By Telegraph from* City Pt
> *Dated* July 25 *1864.*

To MAJ GENL BUTLER

The Concentration of the Enemy between the Appo'x and James may result in an attack on your Lines   have you got all your force out near the front? I saw a large Vessel arrive at Bermuda today loaded with Troops   Are they from New Orleans

> U S GRANT
> Lt Genl

Telegram received, DNA, RG 94, War Records Office, Dept. of Va. and N. C., Army of the James, Unentered Papers; copies (sent at 9:15 P.M.), *ibid.*, RG 108, Letters Sent; DLC-USG, V, 45, 59, 67. *O.R.*, I, xl, part 3, 451. On July 25, 1864, 9:15 P.M., Maj. Gen. Benjamin F. Butler telegraphed to USG. "I dont think the concentration of troops between the Appomattox and the James means and attack upon me—I think from the point where the enemys forces are put that it means to repel an advance upon Port Walthal Junction—They are in a convineant position as a reserve either against an attack upon Petersburg or from my lines—About thirteen hundred men arrived to day from New Orleans   they are a portion of the 2d Brigade 2d Division 19th A. C." LS (telegram sent), DNA, RG 107, Telegrams Collected (Unbound); copy (undated), *ibid.*, RG 393, Dept. of Va. and N. C., Telegrams Sent. *O.R.*, I, xl, part 3, 451. At 10:00 P.M., Butler telegraphed to USG. "I have just examined some prisoners and deserters   There are opposite Deep Bottom Johnson's Brigade of Beauregards forces, McGowans Brigade now Conners and Lanes Brigade—These Brigades will average about nine hundred (900) men—On last Saturday McLaws Division of Longstreets Corps came there, consisting of Kershaws old Brigade Kershaw now commanding the Division—Humphrys Brigade about Seven hundred

(700) men Waffords Brigade about Eight hundred (800) Bryans Brigade about 800—Kershaws Brigade about Eight Hundred (800)—They are entrenching themselves in front of Foster between three (3) and four (4) mile creek—I cannot learn that they extend to our right beyond four (4) mile creek   It is reported, but this is not certain, that A P Hill has relieved Kershaw and is in command of all the troops on the North of the James—A refugee left Richmond on Saturday reports no troops in Richmond save the second class militia that is under eighteen and above forty five & the foreign legion of five (5) or six hundred (600) guarding prisoners & bridges—This is also confirmed by two (2) other refugees that left Richmond yesterday—"   LS (telegram sent), DNA, RG 107, Telegrams Collected (Unbound); telegram received, *ibid.*, RG 108, Letters Received. *O.R.*, I, xl, part 3, 451. USG added a note at the end of the telegram received. "The above dispatch just received. It indicates a nervousness about any force going to the N"   AE, DNA, RG 108, Letters Received. *O.R.*, I, xl, part 3, 451.

Also on July 25, Brig. Gen. Godfrey Weitzel telegraphed to USG. "The following despatch has just been received from Genl Foster at Deep Bottom. 'Two prisoners just captured from Humphrey's Miss. Brigade of Kershaw's— formerly McLaws division report their division came to this place Saturday night. It consists of 2 Georgia brigades, 1 S. C Brigade & 1 Miss. brigade, thus making 7 Brigades in my front. I have stirred them up if nothing more. They came from Petersburg they say. A. P. Hill having relieved Kershaw to-day of command of all the forces here.' "   ALS (telegram sent), DNA, RG 94, War Records Office, Dept. of Va. and N. C., Army of the James, Unentered Papers; telegram received, *ibid.* *O.R.*, I, xl, part 3, 450. At 7:45 P.M., 8:00 P.M., and 10:05 P.M., Weitzel telegraphed to USG. "Our signal officers report that the Enemy in some force has just encamped on a hill three miles N W of the Walthall House   This ~~shows that~~ is beyond all doubt a force established as a reserve, midway between our line here and Petersburg and indicates that they are expecting an attack here"   ALS (telegram sent), DNA, RG 107, Telegrams Collected (Unbound); telegram received, *ibid.*, RG 393, Army of the Potomac, Cav. Corps, Telegrams Received. Printed as received at 9:25 P.M. in *O.R.*, I, xl, part 3, 450; (misdated July 20) *ibid.*, p. 356. "Genl Foster reports an appearance of activity ~~on his front~~ by the enemy in his front not before noticed. Clashing &c—The clashing would show that the enemy was preparing for an attack there"   ALS (telegram sent), DNA, RG 107, Telegrams Collected (Unbound); copy (undated), *ibid.*, RG 393, Dept. of Va. and N. C., Telegrams Sent. Printed as received at 8:30 P.M. in *O.R.*, I, xl, part 3, 450. "The following despatch has just been received from Genl. Foster   'Brig. Gen'l Weitzel: I have just captured an Orderly for Col. Corcoran, 17th Miss., who confirms the report that Kershaw's Div. is on my front; he also reports two Miss. Reg'ts advancing in skirmish line towards my pickets, on the lower side of Four Mile Creek; whether for the purpose of attacking in force in the A. M., or to establish 'Picket, can't say—I am inclined to think the latter. I have strengthened my line, and am going to send one of my Veteran reg'ts. over to-night. R. S. Foster, B. G.' "   ALS (incomplete telegram sent), DNA, RG 107, Telegrams Collected (Unbound); copy (undated), *ibid.*, RG 393, Dept. of Va. and N. C., Telegrams Sent.

To Maj. Gen. George G. Meade

City Point July 25th 1864

MAJ GEN MEADE

You may direct the loading of the mine in front of the 9th Corps. I would set no time when it should be exploded, but leave it subject to orders. The expedition ordered may cause such a weakening of the enemy at Petersburg as to make an attack there possible, in which case you would want to spring Burnsides mine. It cannot be kept a great while after the powder is put in, I would say therefore if it is not found necessary to blow it up earlier, I would have it set off during the afternoon of Wednesday.[1]

U. S. GRANT
Lt Gen,

Telegram, copies, DLC-USG, V, 45, 59, 67; DNA, RG 108, Letters Sent; (2) Meade Papers, PHi. *O.R.,* I, xl, part 3, 438.

1. July 27, 1864.

To Maj. Gen. George G. Meade

City Point, Va. July 25th *1864*

MAJ. GEN. G. G. MEADE,
COMD.G A. P.
GENERAL;

Before making an expedition down the Welden road I propose to make a demonstration on the North side of the James River, having for its real object the destruction of the rail-road on that side. To execute this the 2d Army Corps, two Divisions of Sheridan's Cavalry, Sheridan commanding in person, will be required. Kautz' Cavalry will also be ordered to report to Sheridan for the occatsion. This whole force should be got, if possible, to dDeep Bottom without attracting the attention of the enemy and before our own people are allowed a clue to what is really intended.—

There are now two pontoon bridges at Deep Bottom and in the evening before the movement commences a second should be thrown across the Appomattox at Broadway. This would give two roadways ~~of~~ the whole distance to be traveled.

There are now two Brigades at Deep Bottom and on the New Market and Malvern Hill road. These troops will continue to hold their present position thus securing the crossing for our troops on their return. After crossing James River the Cavalry will advance as rapidly as possible in to the Va. Central rail-road, (in fact the bridges over the Chickahominy on both roads should be destroyed) as near to the City as possible. From this point they will work North as far as the South Anna unless driven off sooner. I will direct Gen. Ingalls to send with the expedition two hundred of his rail-road men to aid in the work of destruction.

The 2d Corps will also advance as rapidly as possible from Deep Bottom until they get opposite Chapin's Bluff. Here they will take up a line to prevent the enemy ~~from~~ throwing a force across the river to cut off the return of our Cavalry. If in the judgement of the Commanding officer his whole force is not necessary for this he will advance towards Richmond with his available force and hold such positions as he may think will insure the greatest security to the expedition.

No wagons will be taken with the expedition except to carry necessary intrenching tools and tools for destroying roads. Wagons however to carry forty rounds of ammunition and five days rations, and three days grain, may be sent in advance and parked near the pontoon bridge over the James ready to be forwarded if required. The troops will carry four days rations with them commencing from the time they leave Deep Bottom. To give them these the Com.y at Deep Bottom will be instructed to have on hand sixty thousand rations ready to issue. When the work of destroying the rail-roads is accomplished the whole expedition will return and resume their present places.

It is barely possible that by a bold move this expedition may surprise the little garrison of Citizen soldiery now in Richmond and get in. This cannot be done however by any cautious move-

ment, developing our force and making reconnoisances before attacking. The only way in which it can be done, if done atall, is to
ride up to the City boldly, dismount and go in at the first point
reached. If carried in this way the prize could be secured by hurry-
ing up the 2d Corps and sending back word here so that other disposition could be made.

This expedition has for its object, as first stated, to destroy the
rail-roads North of Richmond. If anything more favorable grows
out of it, it will be due to the officers and men composing it and will
be duly appreciated.

In the absence of the 2d Corps and Cavalry great watchfuness
will be required on the part of the other troops and readiness to
take advantage of any movement of the enemy.

In preparing for this move let it be understood that it is for a
grand raid towards Welden. I do not mean to imply the necessity
of saying anything untrue but simply to make the necessary preparations for starting without giving out the idea of what is to be done
and leave our troops to guess that it is to go South, as they will,
without contradiction.

I should like this expedition to get off to-morrow night, if possible, if not then the night following.

> I am Gen. very respectfully
> your obt. svt.
> U. S. GRANT
> Lt. Gen. Com

ALS, deCoppet Collection, NjP. Printed as received at 8:30 A.M. in *O.R.*, I, xl,
part 3, 437–38.
    On July 25, 1864, 9:45 P.M., Maj. Gen. George G. Meade wrote to USG
transmitting information from a Richmond newspaper. *Ibid.*, p. 444.

To Edwin M. Stanton

(Cipher)   City Point, July 26th/64 2 p. m.
E. M. STANTON, SEC. OF WAR,
    Your dispatch of 29.05 p. m. 24th just received.[1] The vacancies

yet remaining for Brig. Gens. I would like to have given to such men as Sherman may recommend. He has conducted his Campaign with great skill and success I would therefore ~~allow~~ confirm all his recommendations for Department and Corps Commanders. No one can tell so well as one immediately in command the disposition that should be made of the material ~~he has~~ on hand. Osterhaus has proven him self a good soldier but if he is not in the field I regret his promotion.

U. S. GRANT
Lt. Gen.

ALS (telegram sent), CSmH; telegram received (at 8:10 P.M.), DNA, RG 107, Telegrams Collected (Bound). *O.R.*, I, xxxviii, part 5, 260.

1. See telegram to Charles A. Dana, July 24, 1864.

To Edwin M. Stanton

City Point, Va. July 26th *1864*. [*9:00* P.M.]
HON. E. M. STANTON, SEC. OF WAR, WASHINGTON,

I will meet the President at Fortress Monroe at any time that will suit his convenience after about next Friday. I am commencing movements to-night from which I hope favorable results. They may have the effect of drawing the enemy back ~~toward~~ from Maryland. I am also sending the 19th Corps and five or six veteran regiments of Cavalry to Washington.

U. S. GRANT
Lt. Gen.

ALS (telegram sent), OClWHi; telegram received (on July 27, 1864, 5:00 A.M.), DNA, RG 107, Telegrams Collected (Bound). *O.R.*, I, xxxvii, part 2, 444; *ibid.*, I, xl, part 3, 456–57. On July 26, 3:00 P.M., Secretary of War Edwin M. Stanton had telegraphed to USG. "General Rawlins arrived this morning. The Presedent desires you to name if you can a time when it would be convenient for you to meet him in person at Fortress Monroe after Thursday morning." ALS (telegram sent), DNA, RG 107, Telegrams Collected (Bound); telegram received, *ibid.*, RG 108, Letters Received. *O.R.*, I, xxxvii, part 2, 444; *ibid.*, I, xl, part 3, 456. On July 27, 1:30 P.M., Stanton telegraphed to USG. "Your telegram received and is satisfactory. The President will wait your convenience for consultation on the subject of your despatch ~~forwarded~~ brought by General

Rawlins. General Halleck has been ordered to issue ~~such~~ subject to your direction such military orders as may be necessary at the present juncture in accordance with the suggestion made in your telegram of yesterday. I would respectfully beg your own attention as far as possible to Point Lookout for I am apprehensive of an ~~design~~ ef[for]t to release the prisoners there" ALS (telegram sent), DNA, RG 107, Telegrams Collected (Bound); telegram received, *ibid.*, RG 108, Letters Received. *O.R.*, I, xxxvii, part 2, 463; *ibid.*, I, xl, part 3, 501.

On July 28, 9:00 A.M., President Abraham Lincoln had telegraphed to USG. "Will meet you at Fort-Monroe at 8. P. M. on Saturday the 30th unless you shall notify me that it will be inconvenient to you." ALS (telegram sent), DNA, RG 107, Telegrams Collected (Bound); telegram received, Ford's Theatre, Washington, D. C. *O.R.*, I, xxxvii, part 2, 478; *ibid.*, I, xl, part 3, 551. Lincoln, *Works*, VII, 469. On the same day, USG telegraphed to Lincoln, drafting his reply at the bottom of the telegram received from Lincoln. "I think it will be improper for me to leave here befor Monday next in consequence of present and prospective movements." ADfS (telegram sent), Ford's Theatre, Washington, D. C.; copies, DLC-USG, V, 45, 59, 67; DNA, RG 108, Letters Sent. *O.R.*, I, xxxvii, part 2, 478; *ibid.*, I, xl, part 3, 551. On July 29, 8:30 A.M., Lincoln telegraphed to USG. "I have changed my purpose, so that now I expect to reach Fort-Monroe at 10. A. M. Sunday, the 31st" ALS (telegram sent), DNA, RG 107, Telegrams Collected (Bound); telegram received, *ibid.*, Telegrams Collected (Unbound); *ibid.*, RG 108, Letters Received. *O.R.*, I, xxxvii, part 2, 492; *ibid.*, I, xl, part 3, 590. Lincoln, *Works*, VII, 470. On July 30, 10:30 A.M., USG, Hd. Qrs., 9th Army Corps, telegraphed to Lincoln. "I will meet you at Fort Monroe Va. tomorrow at the hour you designated." Telegram received (at 4:15 P.M.), DLC-Robert T. Lincoln; DNA, RG 107, Telegrams Collected (Bound); (2) *ibid.*, Telegrams Collected (Unbound); copies, *ibid.*, Telegrams Received in Cipher; DLC-USG, V, 59, 67. *O.R.*, I, xl, part 3, 636.

To Maj. Gen. Henry W. Halleck

(Cipher)   City Point, July 26th *1864.*
~~E. M. Stanton Sec. of War~~, MAJ GEN. HALLECK
WASHINGTON

Gen. Crooks dispatches idicates the posibility of another raid North by the enemy. It takes a long time for dispatches to come here and go back during which conditions may change. Consequently it is absolutely necessary that some one in Washington should give orders and make disposition of all the forces within reach of the line of the Potomac. ~~Gen. Halleck informs me in a disp~~

No force has gone from here to reinforce Early unless it may be odd regiments. Deserters come in every day enabling us to keep track of every change the enemy makes.

U. S. GRANT
Lt. Gen.

ALS (telegram sent), OClWHi; telegram received (sent at 12:30 P.M., received at 9:00 P.M.), DNA, RG 107, Telegrams Collected (Unbound). *O.R.*, I, xxxvii, part 2, 445; *ibid.*, I, xl, part 3, 457. On July 25, 1864, 10:30 P.M., USG telegraphed to Maj. Gen. Henry W. Halleck. "If the enemy move towards the Potomac, he must be promptly met by Wright and all the force that can be collected—Despatches being so long between here and Washn, orders must be given from there to meet pressing emergencies" Telegram received (on July 26, 2:25 P.M.), DNA, RG 107, Telegrams Collected (Bound); copies, *ibid.*, RG 108, Letters Sent; DLC-USG, V, 45, 59, 67. *O.R.*, I, xxxvii, part 2, 434; *ibid.*, I, xl, part 3, 436. On July 26, 11:00 A.M., Halleck telegraphed to USG. "In view of the return of the enemy with reinforcements, as stated in despatches which have been sent to you, Genl Wright has moved out this morning on the Rocksville road towards the Monocacy, to form a junction with Genl Hunter at such point as the latter may direct. The 6th corps is reduced to a little over eleven thousand. With the detachments of the 19th corps & from here he will have in all about nineteen thousand including cavalry which, being made up of fragments is not very reliable. To give Genl Wright any cavalry at all it was necessary to retain the detachments which you ordered back to the Army of the Potomac. If Early has been reinforced, as stated from several reliable sources, Hunter & Wright will not be strong enough to meet him in the field. I therefore submit to your consideration the importance of sending a force large enough to prevent his again devastating Maryland & Pennsylvania. All information we recieve is immediately telegraphed to you." ALS (telegram sent), DNA, RG 107, Telegrams Collected (Bound); telegram received, *ibid.*; *ibid.*, RG 108, Letters Received. *O.R.*, I, xxxvii, part 2, 445; *ibid.*, I, xl, part 3, 457. On the same day, 7:00 P.M., USG twice telegraphed to Halleck. "I am ordering forward the 19th Corps, several thousand will embark as ~~rapidly~~ as ~~possible~~ to-night and early in the morning." "Six regiments of Cavalry will leave here to-morrow in addition to the 19th Corps." ALS (telegrams sent), OClWHi; telegrams received (July 27, 5:00 A.M.), DNA, RG 107, Telegrams Collected (Bound). *O.R.*, I, xxxvii, part 2, 445; *ibid.*, I, xl, part 3, 457–58.

To Maj. Gen. Benjamin F. Butler

By Telegraph from City Pt
Dated July 26 *1864.*

To GEN BUTLER,

The enemy are again advancing down the Shenandoah valley, & it is said with reinforcements from Lee's army. Everybody is scared, & want reinforcements. Send all of the 19th Corps that can possibly be dispensed with at once. Commence embarking them tonight.

U. S. GRANT
Lt Genl

Telegram received (at 7:16 P.M.), DNA, RG 94, War Records Office, Dept. of Va. and N. C., Army of the James, Unentered Papers; copies, *ibid.*, RG 108, Letters Sent; DLC-USG, V, 45, 59, 67. *O.R.*, I, xxxvii, part 2, 446; *ibid.*, I, xl, part 3, 484. On July 26, 1864, 7:30 P.M., Maj. Gen. Benjamin F. Butler telegraphed to USG. "Dispatch recieved Will Gen Ingalls send me all the transportation he has ~~and~~ to the landing and I will have will ha the troops on board Notify me of the boats sent My QrMaster will give me a list of those already at the landing" ALS (telegram sent), DNA, RG 107, Telegrams Collected (Unbound); copy (undated), *ibid.*, Dept. of Va. and N. C., Telegrams Sent. Printed as received at 7:42 P.M. in *O.R.*, I, xl, part 3, 484.

At 10:00 A.M., Bvt. Maj. Gen. William H. Emory, Washington, telegraphed to Brig. Gen. John A. Rawlins. "I am ordered to City Point where much the largest portion of my Command is, and I shall start by the first boat, unless otherwise directed by Genl Grant, which is made not improbable by the news of the enemy just recieved." ALS (telegram sent), DNA, RG 107, Telegrams Collected (Unbound); copy, *ibid.*, RG 393, 19th Army Corps, Letters Sent. *O.R.*, I, xxxvii, part 2, 458; *ibid.*, I, xl, part 3, 464. At 9:00 P.M., USG telegraphed to Emory. "Remain where you are at present It is more than likely that your Corps will be sent to Washington Some of it goes immediately" Telegram received (on July 27, 5:25 A.M.), DNA, RG 107, Telegrams Collected (Bound); copies, *ibid.*, Telegrams Received in Cipher; *ibid.*, RG 108, Letters Sent; DLC-USG, V, 45, 59, 67. *O.R.*, I, xxxvii, part 2, 458; *ibid.*, I, xl, part 3, 464. Also on July 26, Emory wrote to USG. "I send my aide de camp, Capt. Cooley, to see what has become of the different parts of my command, & to represent to you its disjointed state, & to ask if it can be brought together—When I reached here there were only about 3500 men of the first division, & with these I was sent in pursuit of the enemy leaving orders for the troops as they arrived, to come up— On my return here I found that the troops that had landed after I left for the front, were all sent back to City Point, so that there is here now only a part of the first division—Two of the Brigade commanders, & parts of several regiments, including some of the commanders of the Regiments, have been, by the movement, separated from their division, & the whole of the second division is yet absent from the command—I hope it will suit the convenience of the service to bring the command togethe[r] as I am quite sure it will add to its efficiency—" LS, DNA, RG 108, Letters Received. *O.R.*, I, xxxvii, part 2, 458–59. On Aug. 2, Emory wrote to Rawlins. "The men of this command have left their Woolen Blankets Coats and Over coats at New Orleans. By the time they can be brought here the cold weather will have set in. As they cannot be obtained without Officers, I desire authority from Lieut Gen Grant, to send a commissioned Officer from each Brigade and a Sergeant from each Regiment to New Orleans, to bring them to such place as he may direct. I also suggest if we are to remain north, that the Officers and men of the 1st and 2d Divisions 19th Corps, on detached service, in the Dept of the Gulf, may be ordered to join their commands." Copy, DNA, RG 393, 19th Army Corps, Letters Sent. On Aug. 4, USG telegraphed to Emory. "You are authorized to send a detail of 2 two commissioned officers & six (6) non commissioned officers to New Orleans for the baggage of the (19) corps" Telegram received (press), *ibid.*, RG 107, Telegrams Collected (Bound); copies, *ibid.*, RG 108, Letters Sent; DLC-USG, V, 45, 59, 67.

On July 26, USG telegraphed to the commanding officer, Fort Monroe. "Send all troops from the Dept. of the Gulf passing Fortress Monroe directly to Washington unless you receive other orders." Telegram received, DNA, RG 94, War Records Office, Dept. of Va. and N. C., Army of the James, Unentered Papers; copies, *ibid.*, RG 108, Letters Sent; DLC-USG, V, 45, 59, 67. *O.R.*, I, xxxvii, part 2, 446; *ibid.*, I, xl, part 3, 500.

To Maj. Gen. Benjamin F. Butler

By Telegraph from City Pt
Dated July 26 *1864.*

To GEN BUTLER,

Do you hear anything from Foster?

There seems to be heavy fighting at Deep Bottom,   Has Kautz commenced crossing?

U. S. GRANT,
Lt Genl

Telegram received (at 8:55 P.M.), DNA, RG 94, War Records Office, Dept. of Va. and N. C., Army of the James, Unentered Papers; copies, *ibid.*, RG 108, Letters Sent; DLC-USG, V, 45, 59, 67. Printed as sent at 8:55 P.M. in *O.R.*, I, xl, part 3, 486. On July 26, 1864, 9:05 P.M., Maj. Gen. Benjamin F. Butler telegraphed to USG. "There is nothing new from Foster. Sheridan in person is in Kautz's camp at Gill's landing. The head of Sheridan's column is just passing these head quarters. Kautz has not commenced crossing, that we know of. His orders are to await the arrival of Sheridan's column" Copy, DNA, RG 107, Telegrams Collected (Unbound). *O.R.*, I, xl, part 3, 486. At 10:00 P.M., Butler telegraphed to USG transmitting a telegram of 9:45 P.M. from Brig. Gen. Robert S. Foster, Deep Bottom, to Brig. Gen. Godfrey Weitzel. "All is quiet on my front now   My pickets hold the same position as when I last informed you— About two (2) regiments advanced on the extreme right on the picket line below the creek but were opened on by the Artillery and picket line & retired in haste The columns have not yet arrived—Genl Sheridan is at my HdQrs—I will keep you promptly posted on all that transpires—" Telegram received, DNA, RG 108, Letters Received. *O.R.*, I, xl, part 3, 486.

At 12:15 P.M. and 5:20 P.M., Weitzel had telegraphed to USG. "Genl

Foster has made a good step towards regaining that point He will try and
finish the job this P. M. As it is he is within a hundred yards of it and commands
it" ALS (telegram sent), DNA, RG 107, Telegrams Collected (Unbound);
copy (undated), *ibid.*, RG 393, Dept. of Va. and N. C., Telegrams Sent. *O.R.*, I,
xl, part 3, 483. "At 4.15 P. M. a train of four passenger and six freight cars
loaded with troops passed Port Walthall Junction towards Richmond" ALS
(telegram sent), DNA, RG 107, Telegrams Collected (Unbound); telegram received, *ibid.*, RG 108, Letters Received. Printed as received at 5:20 P.M. in *O.R.*,
I, xl, part 3, 484. At 6:20 P.M., Butler telegraphed to USG transmitting a telegram of 6:15 P.M. from Foster to Weitzel. "The Eleventh (11th) Maine have
taken a position of the Enemys rifle pits and now Command with their muskets
the New Market and Malvern Hill road where the Short Cross road Strikes off
to the long bridge road—They also Command the enemys battery so that not a
man can occupy it—They are about seventy five yards this Side of the road and
about 50 yards from the Battery—The enemy are in Very Strong force on the
opposite Side of the road but have no protection in front at that point—Our loss
in regaining this ground has been about fifteen killed & wounded—" Telegram
received, DNA, RG 108, Letters Received. The Foster telegram is printed as
sent at 5:15 P.M. in *O.R.*, I, xl, part 3, 497.

At 6:06 P.M., Butler telegraphed to USG. "There is delay in the Ponton
Bridge at Broadway. It was not begun till 5.30 this afternoon and the head of
Sheridans column was to be there at six—" ALS (telegram sent), DNA, RG
107, Telegrams Collected (Unbound); copy (undated), *ibid.*, RG 393, Dept. of
Va. and N. C., Telegrams Sent. Printed as received at 6:15 P.M. in *O.R.*, I, xl,
part 3, 484. On the same day, USG telegraphed to Butler. "My orders are that
the cavalry shall not commence crossing, until after dark, & the bridge was to
be commenced as late as could be, & accomplish its purpose." Telegram received
(at 7:15 P.M.), DNA, RG 94, War Records Office, Dept. of Va. and N. C., Army
of the James, Unentered Papers; copies, *ibid.*, RG 108, Letters Sent; DLC-USG,
V, 45, 59, 67. Printed as sent at 7:15 P.M. in *O.R.*, I, xl, part 3, 484. At 8:10
P.M., Butler telegraphed to USG. "Head of Sheridans Column struck lower end
of Ponton bridge at 7.58. P. M" ALS (telegram sent), DNA, RG 107, Telegrams Collected (Unbound); copy (undated), *ibid.*, RG 393, Dept. of Va. and
N. C., Letters Sent. Printed as received at 8:40 P.M. in *O.R.*, I, xl, part 3, 486.

To Maj. Gen. George G. Meade

By Telegraph from City Point [*12:30* P.M.]
Dated July 26 *1864.*

To MAJ GEN MEADE

Your dispatch of 12 M received   I think Hancock will succeed in
getting through the enemys lines or will force them to weaken
Petersburg so that we can take it with the force left behind

Under these circumstances I think it adviseable that Burnside should have all the material at hand in readiness to load his mines in the shortest time—If not discovered by the enemy I would not put the powder in until we think it will be want[e]d—

U S GRANT—Lt Gen

Telegram received (at 1:00 P.M.), DNA, RG 94, War Records Office, Army of the Potomac; copies, *ibid.*, RG 108, Letters Sent; DLC-USG, V, 45, 59, 67; (2) Meade Papers, PHi. Printed as sent at 1:00 P.M. in *O.R.*, I, xl, part 3, 458. On July 26, 1864, noon, Maj. Gen. George G. Meade telegraphed to USG. "More critical examinations from a new signal station would lead to the conclusion that the the enemy have detached works on the ridge in front of Burnside but they have no connected line—This fact increases the chances of a successful assault, and taken in connection with the fact that Genl Burnside does not now think the enemy have discovered his mine, on the contrary believes they are laying the platforms for a battery right over it—I have suspended the order to load & dischage it tomorrow as it may yet be useful in connection with ~~ultim~~ further operations.—I am afraid the appearance of McLaws division together with Wilcox's previously reported, will prevent any chance of a surprise on the part of our people tomorrow—Yesterdays Richmond Examiner also says your strategic movements are known & preparations made to meet them, referring I presume to Fosters operations. There was considerable shelling by the enemy yesterday afternoon all along our lines, brought on I think by Burnside discovering a camp he had not before seen & ordering it shelled—No serious casualties were produced on our side but the 5th corps working parties were very much annoyed, & interrupted.—With this exception all else was quiet.—" ALS (telegram sent), DNA, RG 393, Army of the Potomac, Miscellaneous Letters Received; telegram received, *ibid.*, RG 108, Letters Received. *O.R.*, I, xl, part 3, 458.

Also on July 26, USG telegraphed to Maj. Gen. Ambrose E. Burnside. "Is there any reason to suppose the enemy have found your mine" Telegram received (undated), DNA, RG 107, Telegrams Collected (Unbound); copies, *ibid.*, RG 108, Letters Sent; DLC-USG, V, 45, 59, 67. *O.R.*, I, xl, part 3, 474. On the same day, Burnside telegraphed to USG. "There are no indications that the enemy has discovered the location of the mine, but I am satisfied that they know that we are mining and that they have sunk shafts with a view to ascertaining where our galleries run because they were heard at work there day before yesterday. But the rain of night before last has evidently filled their shafts which has delayed them ~~in their~~ in their work and we have heard nothing of them either yesterday or today except the ordinary work on the surface laying platforms &c. The placing of the charges in the mine will not require us to make any noise so that I hope we will escape discovery until such time as it may be deemed advisable to use the mine   I ~~have~~ am just sending to Genl Meade by his order a statement of my proposition for exploding the mine and the operations to follow it" ALS (telegram sent), DNA, RG 107, Telegrams Collected (Unbound); telegram received, *ibid.*, RG 108, Letters Received. *O.R.*, I, xl, part 3, 474. On the same day, Burnside wrote to Lt. Col. Cyrus B. Comstock requesting 8,000 sandbags for tamping the mine. *Ibid.*, p. 473.

At 9:30 P.M., USG telegraphed to Meade. "The enemy may shew such a force between Deep Bottom & Richmond as to make our movement there more hazerdous than was expected. If so the 2d Corps and Cavalry will be withdrawn to-morrow night and by withdrawing them quietly and rapidly it may be practicable to make an assault on their return." ALS (telegram sent), OCIWHi; telegram received, DNA, RG 107, Telegrams Collected (Unbound); *ibid.*, RG 393, Army of the Potomac, Telegrams Received. *O.R.*, I, xl, part 3, 461. At 11:00 P.M., Meade telegraphed to USG. "I have the Examiner of today. It has another report from Hood claiming 18 colors & 15 guns—dated July 23d—says all is quiet except occasional shells falling into Atlanta.—The paper also states it is understood we have crossed 6000 men at Deep Bottom, with a view of preventing their field batteries interrupting the navigation of the river.—The paper will be sent tomorrow—Two deserters came in today who say there has been no recent movement of troops on their side.—Telegram of 9.30 in cipher just received" ALS (telegram sent), DNA, RG 393, Army of the Potomac, Miscellaneous Letters Received; copies, *ibid.*, Letters Sent; (2) Meade Papers, PHi. *O.R.*, I, xl, part 3, 461.

To Maj. Gen. George G. Meade

(Cipher)						City Point July 26th/64 [*3:00 P.M.*]
MAJ. GEN. MEADE,

The information you have just sent and all information received on the subject indicates a probability that the enemy are looking for a formidable attack either from Bermuda or North of the James and that they will detach from Petersburg heavily to prevent its success. This will make your remaining two corps with the 18th, relatively stronger against the enemy at Petersburg than we have been since the first day. It will be well therefore to prepare for an assault in Burnsides front only to be made if further developements justifies it. If made it would be necessary to abandon most of the front now held by the 5th Corps.

U. S. GRANT
Lt. Gen.

ALS (telegram sent), CSmH; telegram received, DNA, RG 393, Army of the Potomac, Telegrams Received. *O.R.*, I, xl, part 1, 132; *ibid.*, I, xl, part 3, 459. On July 26, 1864, 12:15 P.M., Maj. Gen. George G. Meade telegraphed to USG. "The foregoing is transmitted for your information. You will note it makes no mention of the third division of Beauregard's army, formerly commanded by Ransom, subsequently by Clingman, and which we have hitherto supposed to be in our front." *Ibid.*, p. 459. The enclosure is *ibid.*, pp. 458–59. At 5:30 P.M., Meade telegraphed to USG. "Telegram 3. P M. received.—The only preparation that can be made is the loading of Burnsides mine.—I can not advise an assault with the 2d corps absent, for some force must be left to hold our lines & protect our batteries—The withdrawal of the 5th corps would prevent any attempt te on our part to silence the fire of the enemys guns in front of the 5th corps & unless these guns are silenced, no advance can be made across the open ground in front of the 9th Corps—It is not the numbers of the enemy which oppose our taking Petersburgh, it is their Artillery and their works which can be held by reduced numbers against direct assault.—I have just sent you a despatch indicating an attack on my left flank by the enemy—This is my weak point, and a formidable attack turning my flank would require all my force to meet successfully." ALS (telegram sent), DNA, RG 393, Army of the Potomac, Miscellaneous Telegrams Received; telegram received, *ibid.*, RG 108, Letters Received. *O.R.*, I, xl, part 3, 459–60.

At 4:00 P.M., Meade had telegraphed to USG. "I forward you this telegram just received, for what it is worth.—Hancock is now moving—he leaves a part of our flank entrenchments, on the left of Warrens vacant, but I shall supply his place tonight with a division of Burnside's as soon as it is dark—" ALS (telegram sent), DNA, RG 393, Army of the Potomac, Miscellaneous Letters Received; telegram received, *ibid.*, RG 108, Letters Received. *O.R.*, I, xl, part 3, 460. The enclosure is *ibid.*

To Maj. Gen. George G. Meade

By Telegraph from City Point
Dated July 26 *1864.*

To MAJ GEN MEADE

The enemy are advancing again down Shenandoah valley   They were last night north of Winchester   Hasten off the Cavalry that goes to Washington under my recent order   if they can start tomorrow they may render great service

U S GRANT
Lt. Gen.

Telegram received (at 7:40 P.M.), DNA, RG 393, Army of the Potomac, Telegrams Received; copies, *ibid.*, Cav. Corps, 3rd Div., Telegrams Received; *ibid.*, RG 94, War Records Office, 24th Army Corps; *ibid.*, RG 108, Letters Sent; DLC-USG, V, 45, 59, 67; (2) Meade Papers, PHi. *O.R.*, I, xxxvii, part 2, 446; *ibid.*, I, xl, part 3, 460. On July 26, 1864, 9:00 P.M., USG telegraphed to Meade. "If you wish to send any orders to Gen Wilson about the Cavalry to go North you can telegraph him here now" Telegram received, DNA, RG 393, Army of the Potomac, Telegrams Received. *O.R.*, I, xl, part 3, 461. At 9:00 P.M. and 10:30 P.M., Meade telegraphed to USG. "I will at once sent tee two dispatches to Genl Wilson at your Head Quarters by telegraph" Copies, DNA, RG 393, Army of the Potomac, Miscellaneous Letters Received; *ibid.*, Letters Sent. *O.R.*, I, xl, part 3, 461. "Orders have been sent to Wilson to hurry off all men whose term of service expire by the 25th proxo.—I had supposed they had gone, but I find over 300 of the 3d. Pa. Cav. on duty at these Hd. Qrs who have not been relieved as I had directed, and I have ordered them to proceed immediately to City Point, —and they will be there by morning.—" ALS (telegram sent), DNA, RG 393, Army of the Potomac, Miscellaneous Letters Received; copies, *ibid.*, Letters Sent; Meade Papers, PHi. *O.R.*, I, xl, part 3, 461.

To Maj. Gen. Henry W. Halleck

(Cipher)   City Point, Va, July 27th *1864.* 9 p. m.
Maj. Gen. Halleck, Washington,
The movement this morning to the North bank of James River resulted in the repulse of three Brigades of the enemy from an intrenched position and the capture of four twenty pound parrot guns. The loss was very slight and capture of prisoners small. The troops having marched all night were fatigued and did not follow up their success as they otherwise would. Sheridan's & Kautz' Cavalry is now with Hancock and the two to-gether will try in the morning to push the enemy back into Richmond or South of the James.

U. S. Grant
Lt. Gen.

ALS (telegram sent), OClWHi; telegram received (on July 28, 1864, 7:00 A.M.), DNA, RG 107, Telegrams Collected (Bound); William H. Seward Papers, NRU. *O.R.*, I, xl, part 1, 16; *ibid.*, I, xl, part 3, 502. On July 27, 1:30 P.M., Maj. Gen. Henry W. Halleck telegraphed to USG. "No reports of enemy's movements since yesterday. A scout from the Rapidann says that bridge at that place is complete & cars running to Culpeper C. H. Enemy's cavalry at Culpeper and at the Bridge. Genl Crook has gone to unite with Wright at South Mountain or on the Monocacy, according as the enemy attempts to cross above or below Harper's Ferry." ALS (telegram sent), DNA, RG 107, Telegrams Collected (Bound); telegram received, *ibid.*; *ibid.*, RG 108, Letters Received. Printed as received at 8:45 P.M. in *O.R.*, I, xxxvii, part 2, 464; *ibid.*, I, xl, part 3, 502.

To Maj. Gen. Winfield S. Hancock

Deep Bottom, Va., July 27, 1864—3.30 p. m.
MAJOR-GENERAL HANCOCK:

In passing to the front, I left your headquarters to my left and all the infantry on the same side. Have consequently been riding for near two hours without finding you. In looking at the situation, I do not see that much is likely now to be done. If, however, you can push past the enemy's flank and double him back on Chaffin's Bluff, so as to let the cavalry out to perform their part of the expedition, do so. If you do not find this practicable, remain on the north side of the James until you receive further orders. There has been no further movement of troops from the south side of the river to interfere with you. All there is in your front is supposed to be seven brigades with a small force of cavalry. I will now return to headquarters. Please direct your dispatches to be duplicated, one going to me and one to General Meade.[1]

U. S. GRANT,
Lieutenant-General.

Printed as received at 3:50 P.M. in *O.R.*, I, xl, part 3, 512. On July 27, 1864, 4:00 P.M., Maj. Gen. Winfield S. Hancock telegraphed to USG. "I regret not seeing you having waited at the front where I was told you were coming   I have two Divisions feeling for the enemy's left. It sep takes a great deal of time & seperates my command very much owing to the nature of the woods in which the operations are connected. I shall be as cautious as possible to avoid any bad luck. When night comes I will telegraph you whether I find the left or not. Gen Barlow will either assault what he supposes to be the left, or attack with a regt shortly in way of a reconnoisance. I will try & carry out your views, but doubt whether anything can be done, though it is possible we may frighten the enemy into abandoning his line or reinforcing it. The troops are very tired having no rest since night before last & with no opportunity of making coffee. What is not done this afternoon cannot be done tonight. I would have accomplished more except for weariness of my command this morning consequent on the fatiguing march" Telegram received, DNA, RG 108, Letters Received. *O.R.*, I, xl, part 3, 512–13.

1. On July 28, between 7:00 A.M. and 2:00 P.M., Hancock sent five telegrams addressed jointly to Maj. Gen. George G. Meade and USG or Brig. Gen. John A. Rawlins. Telegrams received, DNA, RG 108, Letters Received. *O.R.*, I, xl, part 3, 560–62. The last four also appear as telegrams received, DNA, RG 94, War Records Office, Army of the Potomac.

To Maj. Gen. George G. Meade

City Point Va. July 27th *1864*. 8.10 p. m,

MAJ. GEN. MEADE,

The enemy only commenced about two hours ago reinforcing Richmond from Petersburg. 29 car loads of troops have been seen to pass the junction within that time.[1] This will make any surprise on Richmond impossible and may prevent our Cavalry reaching the rail-road. I will have this dispatch repeated to Gen. Hancock and let him do what he can in the morning in the way of turning the enemy and driving him from his present position. After that he will be best able to determine whether it will be well to push further.

U. S. GRANT
Lt. Gn

Repeat to Gen. Hancock Gen. Foster's Hd Qrs.

U. S. G.

ALS (telegram sent), PPRF; telegram received, DNA, RG 94, War Records Office, Army of the Potomac; (2) *ibid.*, RG 107, Telegrams Collected (Unbound). Printed as received at 8:50 P.M. in *O.R.*, I, xl, part 3, 504.

On July 27, 1864, 2:00 A.M. and 8:00 A.M., Maj. Gen. George G. Meade telegraphed to USG transmitting messages of 12:30 A.M. and 6:35 A.M. from Maj. Gen. Winfield S. Hancock to Meade concerning his advance. Telegrams received, DNA, RG 108, Letters Received. The enclosures are in *O.R.*, I, xl, part 3, 509–10, 511. On the same day, USG telegraphed to Meade. "In one hour I shall start for Deep bottom despatches addressed to me there will reach me" Telegram received (at 8:25 A.M.), DNA, RG 94, War Records Office, Army of the Potomac; copies (2), Meade Papers, PHi. *O.R.*, I, xl, part 3, 502. At 9:00 A.M., Meade telegraphed to USG. "I send two despatches just received—After reaching Deep Bottom, if you will notify the operater Genl. Hancocks despatches will be handed to you there & the fact recorded when sent to me.—" ALS (telegram sent), DNA, RG 393, Army of the Potomac, Miscellaneous Letters Received; telegram received, *ibid.*, RG 107, Telegrams Collected (Unbound). *O.R.*, I, xl, part 3, 503. The enclosures are *ibid.*, pp. 511–12. Also at 9:00 A.M., Lt. Col. Cyrus B. Comstock telegraphed to USG. "Hancocks Corps is across & one division of Sheridans ~~The~~ Hancock has taken 4 guns & a few prisoners. His picket line supported is pushing forward. A line of rifle pits [a]t places seem well manned is in front & a prisoner reports a line of rifle pits on the Newmarket road. Is General Grant on his way here? It is thought the chance of surprise is over." ALS (telegram sent), DNA, RG 107, Telegrams Collected (Unbound). At 10:15 A.M., Meade telegraphed to USG. "The cavalry on my left reports the enemys infantry in force on the Jerusalem plank road abreast of Lee's Mills.— Also the constant running of trains last night—I infer the enemy have noticed the disappearance of Hancocks camps & expect a raid on the Welden road & have sent troops to meet it. When they find their mistake I should look for a movement on my left & rear.—" ALS (telegram sent), *ibid.*, RG 393, Army of the Potomac, Miscellaneous Letters Received; telegram received (at 10:30 A.M.), *ibid.*, RG 107, Telegrams Collected (Unbound); *ibid.*, RG 108, Letters Received. Implausibly printed as sent at 11:50 A.M., received at 10:30 A.M., in *O.R.*, I, xl, part 3, 503. At 1:15 P.M., Meade telegraphed to USG. "More recent reports from Brig-Genl. McIntosh comdg. cavalry on my left, together with statements of contrabands who left Petersburgh at midnight last night & came into our lines by way of Reams station, tend to disprove the report sent this morning that the enemy had infantry on the plank road to my left & rear.—The contrabands say they could percieve no movement of the enemy last night;—and no indications of any change on my front have been reported up to this moment." ALS (telegram sent), DNA, RG 393, Army of the Potomac, Miscellaneous Letters Received; telegram received (at 1:40 P.M.), *ibid.*, RG 107, Telegrams Collected (Unbound); (at 1:50 P.M.) *ibid.*, RG 108, Letters Received. Printed as received at 1:50 P.M. in *O.R.*, I, xl, part 3, 503. Also on July 27, Meade telegraphed to USG transmitting a message of 7:40 P.M. from Maj. Gen. Philip H. Sheridan to Maj. Gen. Andrew A. Humphreys. Telegram received, DNA, RG 108, Letters Received. The enclosure, datelined 7:50 P.M., is in *O.R.*, I, xl, part 3, 532. At 8:00 P.M., Meade telegraphed to USG. "I forward two despatches just received from Genl. Hancock, which will explain themselves.—Genl Hancock asks for instructions which request is respectfully referred to you—My own opinion from the result of the days operation & Genl. Hancocks reports, is that nothing will be accomplished by his longer continuance across the James.—I have no report from Genl. Sheridan & can form no judgement as to the expediency of his going further" ALS (telegram sent), DNA, RG 393, Army of the Potomac, Miscellaneous Letters Received; telegram received, *ibid.*, RG 108, Letters Received. *O.R.*, I, xl, part 3, 504. The enclosures are *ibid.*, pp. 512–13, 514.

1. On July 27, Maj. Gen. Benjamin F. Butler telegraphed to USG transmitting a signal message of 6:00 P.M. stating that "Eighteen cars loaded with troops just passed the Junction towards Richmond" Telegram received, DNA, RG 108, Letters Received. *O.R.*, I, xl, part 3, 537. At 7:20 P.M., Brig. Gen. Godfrey Weitzel telegraphed to USG. "At 6.45 P. M eleven additional cars ~~passed~~ loaded with troops passed from Petersburg to Richmond." ALS (telegram sent), DNA, RG 107, Telegrams Collected (Unbound); copy (undated), *ibid.*, RG 393, Dept. of Va. and N. C., Telegrams Sent. *O.R.*, I, xl, part 3, 535.

At 9:30 P.M., Butler telegraphed to USG transmitting a signal message of 9:30 P.M. "A train just passed the Junction towards Richmond From the sound I judge that it was heavily loaded" Telegram received, DNA, RG 108, Letters Received. *O.R.*, I, xl, part 3, 538.

At 10:20 A.M., 4:00 P.M., 7:15 P.M., and 9:00 P.M., Weitzel telegraphed to USG. "A few wagons and a few infantry crossed the James river, going towards Foster's front, at 10.10 A. M." ALS (telegram sent), DNA, RG 94, War Records Office, Dept. of Va. and N. C., Army of the James, Unentered Papers; copy (undated), *ibid.*, RG 393, Dept. of Va. and N. C., Telegrams Sent. *O.R.*, I, xl, part 3, 534; (misdated July 28) *ibid.*, p. 572. "At 12.50 P. M five car loads of sick ~~and~~ or wounded rebels passed from Petersburg towards Richmond" ALS (telegram sent), DNA, RG 107, Telegrams Collected (Unbound); copy (undated), *ibid.*, RG 393, Dept. of Va. and N. C., Telegrams Sent. *O.R.*, I, xl, part 3, 535. "A deserter just in from that part of the enemy's line near the upper pontoon bridge, says they heard artillery crossing in the night. They did not know in what direction, and the movement excited no suspision. It is evident that the enemy commenced only about an hour and a half ago to re-inforce Richmond from Petersburg" ALS (telegram sent), DNA, RG 94, War Records Office, Army of the Potomac; copy (undated), *ibid.*, RG 393, Dept. of Va. and N. C., Telegrams Sent. *O.R.*, I, xl, part 3, 534. "Signal officers on the right just report that just before dark the number of rebel troops at Chaffins farm was greater than usual. No movement of troops from west to east bank observed during the day." ALS (telegram sent), DNA, RG 107, Telegrams Collected (Unbound); copy (undated), *ibid.*, RG 393, Dept. of Va. and N. C., Telegrams Sent. *O.R.*, I, xl, part 3, 535.

To Maj. Gen. George G. Meade

City Point, Va. July 27th *1864.*

MAJ. GEN. MEADE,

Gen. Butler sending off the 19th Corps[1] leaves him very weak so that I do not think he can reinforce Hancock much. I will direct him however to send ~~any~~ all the troops he can possibly spare.[2] Gen. Foster now has about 2700 men at Deep Bottom just in position to strike the enemy in flank if he is driven back.

U. S. GRANT
Lt. Gn

ALS (telegram sent), PPRF; telegram received (at 9:00 P.M.), DNA, RG 94, War Records Office, Army of the Potomac. *O.R.*, I, xl, part 3, 504. On July 27, 1864, 9:00 P.M. and 9:45 P.M., Maj. Gen. George G. Meade telegraphed to USG. "I should judge from Hancocks despatches that he does not consider himself in sufficient force to effect much—Can you not re-inforce him from some of Maj. Gen. Butlers troops I make the suggestion because the stronger he is the more powerful the blow he can strike tomorrow.—" "I was not aware the 19th corps had been sent away or was going—indeed referred to theose troops when I made the suggestion I did—I have no doubt Hancock will do all he can but the more troops he has, if he will put them in, the more sure of success he will be" ALS (telegrams sent), DNA, RG 393, Army of the Potomac, Miscellaneous Letters Received; telegrams received, *ibid.*, RG 108, Letters Received. *O.R.*, I, xl, part 3, pp. 504, 505.

1. On July 27, USG telegraphed to Maj. Gen. Benjamin F. Butler. "You will please order the troops of the 19th Corps which arrived today to proceed to Washn. without delay." Telegram received (at 8:15 P.M.), DLC-Benjamin F. Butler; DNA, RG 94, War Records Office, Dept. of Va. and N. C., Army of the James, Unentered Papers. *O.R.*, I, xl, part 3, 535. At 9:00 P.M., Brig. Gen. Godfrey Weitzel telegraphed to USG. "No troops of the 19th Army Corps ar-

rived here to-day. We have sent all of the 1st Division   The troops that did arrive were, seven companies of the 13th New York Heavy Artillery from Yorktown"   ALS (telegram sent), DNA, RG 107, Telegrams Collected (Unbound);
copy (undated), *ibid.*, RG 393, Dept. of Va. and N. C., Telegrams Sent. *O.R.*,
I, xl, part 3, 535.

2. On July 27, USG telegraphed to Butler. "If you can possibly spare any
troops from Bermuda for tomorrows operations send them to Gen. Hancock.
Any that you send should commence crossing as soon after day light as they can."
ALS (telegram sent—facsimile), Joseph Rubinfine, List 64, item 27, [1980];
telegram received (at 9:40 P.M.), DNA, RG 94, War Records Office, Dept. of
Va. and N. C., Army of the James, Unentered Papers. *O.R.*, I, xl, part 3, 536.
At 10:30 P.M. and 10:40 P.M., Butler telegraphed to USG. "I will order Foster
to make as vigorous a demonstration as possible on the right of the enemy from
Buffins house which he now holds to employ all day at least as many of them as
will equal his numbers.—I take leave to suggest that a Division moving with
celerity as far at the left as possible say on or near the Welden road and toward
Petersburgh ~~might~~ if the enemy has weakend his left to send troops to the James
~~either~~ might at least effect a diversion and perhaps achieve ~~a diversion~~ an advantage"   "I will order Brig Genl Birge with his brigade of the 19th Corps,
2900 strong to report to Hancock crossing the Bridge at daylight   I do not know
how to spare them in case of attack but I do not hope for any attack on our
lines—"   ALS (telegrams sent), DNA, RG 94, War Records Office, Dept. of
Va. and N. C., Army of the James, Unentered Papers; copies (undated), *ibid.*,
RG 393, Dept. of Va. and N. C., Telegrams Sent. On the same day, USG telegraphed to Meade, instructing him to send a copy to Maj. Gen. Winfield S. Hancock. "Genl. Butler will send Hancock a brigade twenty nine hundred strong
They will commence crossing soon after day-light, so that he can count on their
assistance—." Telegram received (at 10:50 P.M.), *ibid.*, RG 94, War Records
Office, Army of the Potomac; *ibid.*, RG 107, Telegrams Collected (Unbound);
copies, *ibid.*, RG 108, Letters Sent; DLC-USG, V, 45, 59, 67; (2) Meade Papers, PHi. *O.R.*, I, xl, part 3, 515.

To Maj. Gen. George G. Meade

City Point July 27th *1864*.

MAJ. GEN. MEADE,

The position now occupied by Hancock would give Sheridan
no protection in returning by way of Bottom's Bridge. I do not
want him to go unless the enemy is driven into Chapin's Bluff or
back to the city. Otherwise he would be compelled to return North
of the Chickohominy and it would be two or three weeks before his
Cavalry would be fit for other service. I do not want Hancock to
attack intrenched lines but I do want him to remain another day

and if he can, with the assistence of the Cavalry, turn the enemy's position and drive him away. It looks to me as if the Cavalry might move well out and get in rear of the enemy.

U. S. GRANT

Lt. Gen

ALS (telegram sent), Van Sinderen Collection, CtY; telegram received (at 9:10 P.M.), DNA, RG 94, War Records Office, Army of the Potomac; *ibid.*, RG 107, Telegrams Collected (Unbound). *O.R.*, I, xl, part 3, 505. On July 27, 1864, 9:20 P.M., Maj. Gen. George G. Meade endorsed this telegram to Maj. Gen. Winfield S. Hancock, Deep Bottom. "I forward the foregoing as giving the views of the Lt. Genl. Comd. I You will be governed accordingly by them. I have suggested to the Lt. Genl. Comd. that you be reinforced by any troops Genl. Butler may have to spare so as to make the most vigorous effort possible tomorrow to drive back the enemy—His answer not yet received" AES, DNA, RG 94, War Records Office, Army of the Potomac.

At 11:00 P.M., Maj. Gen. Edward O. C. Ord telegraphed to USG. "There seems from the sound to be trains running on the R Road from Petersburg towards Richmond have been firing thirty pounders to keep trains off the Bridge—" ALS (telegram sent), *ibid.*, Dept. of Va. and N. C., Army of the James, Unentered Papers. *O.R.*, I, xl, part 3, 549. On the same day, USG telegraphed to Ord. "Troops commenced leaving Petersburg before dark and are moving rapidly all the time since. I hope they will weaken the place so as to let us in" Telegram received, Ord Papers, CU-B; copies, DLC-USG, V, 45, 59, 67; DNA, RG 108, Letters Sent. *O.R.*, I, xl, part 3, 548. On the same day, USG telegraphed to Meade. "Genl Ord reports trains running all the time from Petersburg to Richmond. I think we can rely on the place being left tolerably bare." Telegram received (at 11:30 P.M.), DNA, RG 94, War Records Office, Army of the Potomac; copies (marked 12:30 P.M.), *ibid.*, RG 108, Letters Sent; DLC-USG, V, 45, 59, (marked 11:30 P.M.) 67; (2) Meade Papers, PHi. Printed as sent at 12:30 P.M. in *O.R.*, I, xl, part 3, 503. At midnight, Meade telegraphed to USG. "I have had the most careful watch kept up today from all parts of my line to detect any movement of the enemy—The only report indicative of such movement was sent in by the Picket officer on my extreme left who reported the disappearance of camps & evacuation of the lines about the Lead Works on the Welden R. Rd—but the signal officer who commands a view of this portion of the enemys position did not confirm it—If any troops have been moved they are most probably that part of Hills corps Heths Divn. & part of Mahones Divn. occupying the extreme right of the enemy beyond our left front and which have been a kind of reserve for the enemy.—There has certainly been no change in their lines in our immediate front or it would have been reported.—" ALS (telegram sent), DNA, RG 393, Army of the Potomac, Miscellaneous Letters Received; telegram received, *ibid.*, RG 108, Letters Received. *O.R.*, I, xl, part 3, 505.

At 11:40 A.M. (marked P.M.), USG telegraphed to Maj. Gen. Benjamin F. Butler. "D Is any thing seen of the enemy from your observatory? I shall be at Deep Bottom for several hours" ALS (telegram sent), DNA, RG 107, Telegrams Collected (Unbound); telegram received (at 12:30 P.M.), *ibid.*, RG 94, War Records Office, Dept. of Va. and N. C., Army of the James, Unentered

Papers. *O.R.*, I, xl, part 3, 534. At 11:45 P.M., Butler telegraphed to USG. "No reports Have ordered careful observation Will keep you informed At 10 30 A. M. A few infantry and Waggons passed across Chaffins farm—Probably part of the garrison. Any farther reports from Hancock." ALS (telegram sent), DNA, RG 107, Telegrams Collected (Unbound); copy (undated), *ibid.*, RG 393, Dept. of Va. and N. C., Telegrams Sent. Butler wrote the time as 12:45 P.M. on his telegram, which is printed as sent on July [27] in *O.R.*, I, xl, part 3, 534, and on July 28 *ibid.*, p. 573.

On July 28, 9:00 A.M., 9:30 A.M., twice at 10:00 A.M., 11:00 A.M., 12:05 P.M., and 1:50 P.M., Butler telegraphed to USG. "Since daylight about 75 wagons and ambulances, about 100 stragglers and a drove of cattle and mules have crossed Chafin's farm going east One of the rebel rams has moved down the river a short distance Trains were running frequently on the road during the night on the road" "Signal officer at Spring Hill reports that two trains passed towards Richmond one at 12 M and the other at 3.30 A M Signal officer on the high tower reports a train of 27 empty cars passed to Petersburg at 7.45 A. M It is unusual for trains to be passing over the Railroad at night" "A train of twenty seven wagons passed up turnpike to Richmond at 9.30 A M" "The picket officer on the left of our line nearest the railroad reports that nine nine trains of cars moved from Petersburg to Richmond from dark last night until 2 A M this morning. The rebels cheered as the trains passed. I consider this more reliable than the previous report of the signal officer" "The signal officer on being called to account for not reporting as many trains as the officer of the picket says. That the only trains that passed the Junction were the two he reported That trains were moving all night from Petersburg to near the Junction and then back, as if they were shifting the position of their troops." "Three regiments of [ca]valry and ten wagons passed up the turn pike towards Richmond at 11.30 A. M." "At 1.15 P M. five cars loaded with troops passed towards Richmond" Copies (telegrams sent), DNA, RG 107, Telegrams Collected (Unbound); telegrams received, *ibid.*, RG 108, Letters Received. *O.R.*, I, xl, part 3, 571–74. At 4:50 P.M., Brig. Gen. Godfrey Weitzel telegraphed to USG. "The following despatch has just been rec'd from the Sig Offr at Spring Hill—A train of twenty (20) Cars partly loaded with troops just passed the Junction twoards Richmond—" ALS (telegram sent), DNA, RG 107, Telegrams Collected (Unbound); telegram received, *ibid.*, RG 108, Letters Received. *O.R.*, I, xl, part 3, 574. On the same day, Lt. Col. Theodore S. Bowers telegraphed this message to USG. Telegram received, DNA, RG 107, Telegrams Collected (Unbound). At 5:58 P.M., Bowers transmitted a similar telegram (or the same one in variant form) from Weitzel to USG. *O.R.*, I, xl, part 3, 554. USG wrote a note on this telegram, probably intended for Hancock. "Similar dispatches to the above have been coming every hour or two all last night and to-day; look out for them." *Ibid.* On the same day, Butler telegraphed to USG. "The following dispatch has just been received from the Signal officer on the right and is respectfully forwarded for the information of the Lt Genl—A long column of cavalry probably two regiments and an ambulance train are pcrossing Chapins Farm going east over one hundred wagons have gone same route since my last report There is much signalling between Rams and shore—Signed G S DANA Capt & Sig Ofcr" Telegram received, *ibid.*, RG 108, Letters Received. *O.R.*, I, xl, part 3, 575.

To Maj. Gen. Henry W. Halleck

(Cipher)   City Point Va. July 28th/64 3.30 p. m.
MAJ. GEN. HALLECK, WASHINGTON.
The enemy have attempted to drive our Cavalry from the vicinity
of Charles City road near New Market. Casualties are not reported
but I suppose have been small. Torbet's Div.[1] repulsed the enemy
in his front capturing 150 of their number. At last report the enemy
in front of Gregg's Div. were still standing. I am just starting for
the scene of action.[2]

U. S. GRANT
Lt. Gn

ALS (telegram sent), OClWHi; telegram received (at 9:00 P.M.), DNA, RG
107, Telegrams Collected (Bound). *O.R.*, I, xl, part 1, 16; *ibid.*, I, xl, part 3,
551.

1. Alfred T. A. Torbert, born in Del. in 1833, USMA 1855, held the rank of
1st lt. when the Civil War began. Appointed col., 1st N. J., as of Sept. 16, 1861,
he was appointed brig. gen. as of Nov. 29, 1862, commanded the 1st Cav. Div.,
Army of the Potomac, after April, 1864, and engaged C.S.A. forces near New
Market, Va., on July 28, capturing seventy-four prisoners. *Ibid.*, I, xl, part 1,
202.

2. On July 28, 1:15 P.M., Maj. Gen. George G. Meade telegraphed to
USG. "I propose to pay you a visit at City Point if you have no objection—All is
at present quiet here & likely to remain so.—" ALS (telegram sent), DNA, RG
393, Army of the Potomac, Miscellaneous Letters Received; copies, *ibid.*, Letters
Sent; Meade Papers, PHi. *O.R.*, I, xl, part 3, 554. On the same day, USG prepared a telegram for Meade. "I will be at home all day and will be pleased to
have you come down" Copy, DLC-USG, V, 67. Cancellation marks indicate that
this telegram was not sent. At 3:15 P.M., Lt. Col. Cyrus B. Comstock telegraphed
to Maj. Gen. Winfield S. Hancock. "Genl Grant & Meade are just starting up to
your Hdqrs   if your Hdqrs are not near the lower pontoon Bridge will you send
6 horses to meet the Str near the pontoon bridge—" Telegram received, DNA,
RG 107, Telegrams Collected (Unbound). *O.R.*, I, xl, part 3, 562.

To Maj. Gen. Henry W. Halleck

(Cipher)   City Point, Va, July 28th 64 9 p. m. *1864*
MAJ. GEN. HALLECK, WASHINGTON,
I have just returned from Deep Bottom. The enemy evidently

became very sensitive over our move to the North bank of the river and have been moving to meet it ever since they discovered it. The position of our troops to-day was the 2left of the 2d Corps resting at Deep Bottom and extending along Baileys Creek. Greggs & Torberts Cavy Divisions were thrown to the right of the 2d Corps and extend to the New Market road, with one Brigade at Malvern Hill. In getting their position they were attacked by the enemy in heavy force. The fighting lasted several hours resulting in a loss which Gen. Sheridan thinks will not exceed 200 on our side the greater part of whom are but slightly wounded and some are prisoners in the hands of the enemy. We have taken over 200 prisoners besides wounded many of whom were left in our possession. The number could not be estimated because ~~they~~ ambulances were still engaged bringing them in when I left ~~just before sundown~~. the ground. In front of Torberts Division 158 of the enemys dead had been counted. There was equally as much, if not more fighting in front of Greggs Division and probably as many of the enemy's dead were left there.

We have failed in what I had hoped to accomplish that is to surprise the enemy and get on to their roads with the Cavalry near to Richmond and destroy them out to South Anna. I am yet in hopes of turning this diversion to account so as to yeald greater results than if the first object had been accomplished.

U. S. GRANT
Lt. Gn.

ALS (telegram sent), OClWHi; telegram received (on July 29, 1864), DNA, RG 107, Telegrams Collected (Bound). *O.R.*, I, xl, part 1, 16; *ibid.*, I, xl, part 3, 551.

To Maj. Gen. George G. Meade

———

City Point July 28th, 1864

MAJ GEN MEADE

I have given Gen. Hancock no instructions that have not gone to you. My dispatches to you in the night I directed to be taken off at Fosters Hd. Qrs. for Hancock so as to save ~~him~~ time

If Hancock does not crush the enemy this morning I think it will be well to withdraw him, during the night and get him in rear of Burnside before the enemy can return keeping the Cavalry and Butlers troops to occupy the attention of the enemy. This would be with the view of making the assault in front of Burnside.

U S GRANT
Lieut Genl

Telegram, copies, DLC-USG, V, 45, 59, 67; DNA, RG 108, Letters Sent. *O.R.*, I, xl, part 3, 552. On July 28, 1864, 10:00 A.M., Maj. Gen. George G. Meade telegraphed to USG. "Deserters from Finnegan's Brigade Mahones Divn. came in last night   They report that last evening Wrights brigade of their Division relieved Heths Division on the extreme right of their line, and that this Division moved north of the Appomatox—This confirms what I telegraphed you at midnight.—. . . P. S. Have you sent any additional instructions to Hancock?" ALS (telegram sent), DNA, RG 393, Army of the Potomac, Miscellaneous Letters Received; telegram received, *ibid.*, RG 108, Letters Received. *O.R.*, I, xl, part 3, 552.

At 8:30 A.M., Meade telegraphed to USG. "The following despatch just received.—Maj. Gen. Hancock has been advised, he must act on his own judgement, under the instructions received from you, all of which have been transmitted to him—" ALS (telegram sent), DNA, RG 393, Army of the Potomac, Miscellaneous Letters Received; copies, *ibid.*, Letters Sent; Meade Papers, PHi. *O.R.*, I, xl, part 3, 552. The enclosure is *ibid.*, p. 560. At 11:00 A.M., Meade telegraphed to USG transmitting information about C.S.A. movements. ALS (telegram sent), DNA, RG 94, War Records Office, Army of the Potomac; telegram received, *ibid.*, RG 108, Letters Received. *O.R.*, I, xl, part 3, 552.

To Maj. Gen. George G. Meade

By Telegraph from City Point
Dated July 28 *1864.*

To MAJ GEN MEADE

Bringing in Hancock back tonight his corps will too much fatigued for ~~actio~~ve operations in the morning   he can hower hold the ground of the 18th Corps & leave that ready joining 9th in a charge I will hear what you have to say on this subject and then make the necessary orders   Do you think the necessary preperations can be made for an assault in the morning

U S GRANT
Lt. Gen

Telegram received (at 11:30 A.M.), DNA, RG 94, War Records Office, Army of the Potomac; copies, *ibid.*, RG 108, Letters Sent; DLC-USG, V, 45, 59, 67; (2) Meade Papers, PHi. *O.R.*, I, xl, part 3, 553. On July 28, 1864, noon, Maj. Gen. George G. Meade telegraphed to USG. "Your despatch of 11.30 received. An assault can not be made tomorrow as you suggest because there will not be time to in the night to with draw Hancock & relieve the 18th Corps—That being the case, I would suggest Hancock being with drawn tonight & massed in Burnsides rear tomorrow, this would give him the necessary rest, and it could then be determined about assaulting the next morning with the 9th & 2d or 18th as you may desire, adding the available reserves of the corps in line—The assault might perhaps be made tomorrow evening   It could only be made tomorrow morning by putting in the 9th 2d corps & they would hardly reach the scene of action till after daylight." ALS (telegram sent), DNA, RG 393, Army of the Potomac, Miscellaneous Letters Received; telegram received, *ibid.*, RG 108, Letters Received. *O.R.*, I, xl, part 3, 553. See following telegram.

At 12:30 P.M., Meade telegraphed to USG transmitting information about C.S.A. movements. AES (telegram sent), DNA, RG 94, War Records Office, Army of the Potomac; telegram received, *ibid.*, RG 108, Letters Received. *O.R.*, I, xl, part 3, 556–57.

To Maj. Gen. George G. Meade

———

By Telegraph from City Pt. 12 20 P M
Dated July 28 *1864.*

To MAJ. GEN MEADE

Your dispatch of 12 M. received—Unless some thing turns up north of the James between this and night that I do not expect you may withdraw Hancock to be followed by sheridan and make arrangements for assault as soon as it can be made   We can determine by the movements of the enemy before the time comes whether it will be advisable to go on with the assault. I will put in the 18th Corps or not as you deem best

U. S. GRANT
Lt Gnl

Telegram received, DNA, RG 94, War Records Office, Army of the Potomac; copies, *ibid.*, RG 108, Letters Sent; DLC-USG, V, 45, 59, 67; (2) Meade Papers, PHi. *O.R.*, I, xl, part 1, 133; *ibid.*, I, xl, part 3, 553. On July 28, 1864, 1:00 P.M., Maj. Gen. George G. Meade telegraphed to USG. "Your despatch of 12.20 received On reflection I think daylight of the 30th is the earliest time it would be advisable to make the assault—Besides the time required to get up heavy guns & mortars we require the night to make certain preliminary arrangements such as moving troops, removing abattis from the Debouch of the assaulting column etc—I shall make the assault with the 9th corps supported by the 2d.—The reserves of the 18th should be held in readiness to take part & if developments justify it all of Ords & Warrens commands can be put in.—" ALS (telegram sent), DNA, RG 393, Army of the Potomac, Miscellaneous Letters Received; telegram received, *ibid.*, RG 108, Letters Received. *O.R.*, I, xl, part 1, 133; *ibid.*, I, xl, part 3, 553–54.

Also on July 28, USG telegraphed to Meade and to Maj. Gen. Edward O. C. Ord. "I think it will be well to stop all Artillery firing except from field pieces from this time till Saturday morning & to conceal the heavy pieces—This may have an effect in convincing the enemy that we are withdrawing from Petersburg & possibly induce them to come out and see—" Telegram received (at 9:40 P.M.), DNA, RG 94, War Records Office, Army of the Potomac; Ord Papers, CU-B; copies, DNA, RG 108, Letters Sent; DLC-USG, V, 45, 59, 67; (2—misdated July 27) Meade Papers, PHi. *O.R.*, I, xl, part 3, 554. On July 28, Ord telegraphed to USG. "Shall I discontinue the ~~cho~~ cohorn firing. It is well I think to keep it up—" ALS (telegram sent), DNA, RG 94, War Records Office, Dept. of Va. and N. C., Army of the James, Unentered Papers. *O.R.*, I, xl, part 3, 589. On the same day, USG telegraphed to Ord. "You may continue the Cohorn firing" Telegram received, Ord Papers, CU-B; copies, DLC-USG, V, 45, 59, 67; DNA, RG 108, Letters Sent. *O.R.*, I, xl, part 3, 590.

Also on July 28, Ord telegraphed to USG. "Picquet Officers report three or more trains—double-engines—loaded with troops as having passed north last night—a large portion of them taken from Gen. Butler's front." ALS (telegram sent), DNA, RG 107, Telegrams Collected (Unbound); telegram received, *ibid.*, RG 108, Letters Received. *O.R.*, I, xl, part 3, 589. On the same day, USG telegraphed to Ord. "What do you think the fire in Petersburg arises from. Is it probably the work of your shells or of the enemy destroying stores" Telegram received, Ord Papers, CU-B. On the same day, Ord telegraphed to USG. "I think it is an accidental fire of limited extent." ALS (telegram sent), DNA, RG 94, War Records Office, Army of the Potomac.

At 11:50 P.M., Maj. Gen. Benjamin F. Butler telegraphed to USG. "The following dispatch has just been received. 'What instructions Shall be given to Gen Foster   Signed B. F. BUTLER M G' 'Hd Qrs Deep Bottom 11.40 P m 28th to GEN WEITZEL Copy to MAJ GEN BIRNEY—The 2nd Army Corps Commenced with drawing passing up Jones neck about 8.30 this Evening—I have had no notice of their leaving from any official Source but Know they are going by Seeing them pass my Hd Qrs. Sheridans Cavalry is all back on Curls neck & rumor Says all are to With draw tonight—If this is the Case the enemy who are now very Strong on this Side of the river Will no doubt make a reconnoissance in force in the morning to ascertain their whereabouts which will develope the fact that they have only my Small force to oppose them & if they Should Concentrate their forces against me it Cannot fail to result in disaster to my Command & the driving of the Gunboats from the river at this point—I wish you Would Send me Some detailed instructions what Course to pursue in the event of a Strong attack from the Enemys force after the Withdrawal of the troops of the Army of the Potomac—" Telegram received, *ibid.*, RG 108, Letters Received. *O.R.*, I, xl, part 3, 575, 589. At midnight, USG telegraphed to Butler. "I will send you full instructions in the morning   Hancock is only withdrawing one division for purposes which will be explained. Sheridans cavalry all remains nNorth of the river." Telegram received, DLC-Benjamin F. Butler; copies, DLC-USG, V, 45, 59, 67; DNA, RG 108, Letters Sent. *O.R.*, I, xl, part 3, 575.

Also on July 28, Butler wrote to USG. "Allow me to submit to your consideration a thought which has struck me   The rebels have fortified Howlet House bluff with 19. Guns and a very strong work. Trent's Reach is so shallow that our Iron clads cannot get up without great labor in dredging the channels. Now what hinders us from turning the Howlett House Battery by taking the hint from that Dutchman and cut a canal at Dutch Gap   It is but 200 yards from 16 ft watter to 16 ft water across the Gap. The land is but 30 feet high as an average and we should have for a fifty feet cut but about 55000 cubic Feet of excavation—or 10 days labor for a thousand men. By that means our Iron clads could get out and Howlett would be useless. If you will look upon the map you will get my Idea at once. I have made my examination by the Coast Survey Map. I should not depend on the current to do any part of the cutting as at Vicksburgh, although it might help. The Gun-boats cover the place." ALS, DNA, RG 108, Letters Received. *O.R.*, I, xl, part 3, 570–71.

Also on July 28, Lt. Col. Cyrus B. Comstock telegraphed to Brig. Gen. Godfrey Weitzel. "Gen. Hancock told me yesterday that a part of the road over which he moved within your lines was filled with stumps causing much delay. Will you have this corrected? today?" ALS (telegram sent), DNA, RG 107, Telegrams Collected (Unbound). On the same day, between 12:10 p.m. and 3:20 p.m., Weitzel sent five telegrams to Comstock defending the condition of the road. ALS (telegrams sent), *ibid.*, RG 94, War Records Office, Dept. of Va. and N. C., Army of the James, Unentered Papers. *O.R.*, I, xl, part 3, 573–74.

To Maj. Gen. Henry W. Halleck

(Cipher)   City Point, Va. July 29th *1864*
Maj. Gen. Halleck, Washington.

I would approve of making the appointments for corps commands recommended by Gen. Thomas. In relieving Gen. Slocum from command at Vicksburg I would direct Gen. Canby to send a suitable Maj. Gen. from his Mil. Division. Dana would probably be the best man but I would leave this to Canby knowing that he would make a proper selection.

U. S. Grant
Lt. Gn.

ALS (telegram sent), OClWHi; telegram received (sent at noon, received at 6:00 P.M.), DNA, RG 107, Telegrams Collected (Bound); *ibid.*, Telegrams Collected (Unbound). *O.R.*, I, xxxviii, part 5, 289; *ibid.*, I, xxxix, part 2, 209–10. See *ibid.*, I, xxxviii, part 5, 272.

To Maj. Gen. Benjamin F. Butler

City Point, Va, July 29th *1864*

MAJ. GEN. B. F. BUTLER, COMD.G DEPTS. OF VA. & N. C.

GENERAL,

The main object of the expedition North of the James River having failed by reason of the very large force thrown there by the enemy, I have determined to try and take advantage of the diversion made by assaulting at Petersburg before the enemy can get much of his force back there. As the assault must be made promptly on the return of our troops, and a night march being necessary to deceived the enemy, I which will necessarily fatigue them the troops to such an extent as to make their attack weak, I determined to withdraw one Division of the 2d Corps during last night and with it relieve the 18th Corps so as to have all fresh troops for the first assault.

The Division which withdrew last night marched to the neighborhood of Petersburg. They will rest to-day and under cover of night take the place of the 18th Corps. Gen. Meade having studied all the ground over which the assault is to be made, and the 9th Corps, a part of his command, having the advance in the assault, Gen. Ord will report to Gen. Meade for instructions during the assault. Gen. Meade has received verbal instructions from me and is now industriously engaged preparing the details.

As soon as it is dark Gen. Hancock will commence the withdrawel of the balance of his Corps. The Cavalry will follow the Inf.y. The former will reach Petersburg with all dispatch and follow the assaulting Column or take the place now occupied by the 18th Corps as may be found advisable. The Cavalry will make a forced march to the left of our present line and be in readiness to move round the enemy's right.

This movement will leave the Garison at Deep Bottom in presence of a vastly superior force. The Navy will want to dispose of their vessels in such manner as to sweep all the ground in front of our troops.—I wish you would communicate with Capt. Smith, through a staff officer, on this subject. Please caution him to make no changes through the day calculated to attract special interest on the part of the enemy.

Gen. Foster I think had better level the line of rifle pitts we captured from the enemy and move his whole force to the side of the creek first occupied by him. The lower pontoon bridge should also be swung round to the West bank of the river.—It may be advisable for Gen. Foster to move his teams and surplus property to the West bank but these details I leave to you.

If possible I want to leave our withdrawel from the North bank of the river concealed from the enemy until the attack commences at Petersburg.

I have had Gen. Ord informed, verbally, of the fact that he ~~was~~ is to be relieved by the 2d Corps and ~~was~~ is to form a part of the assaulting Column. It only remains to notify him that during the assault he will receive orders from Gen. Meade.

> Very respectfully
> your obt. svt.
> U. S. Grant
> Lt. Gen.

ALS, DLC-Benjamin F. Butler. *O.R.*, I, xl, part 3, 619–20; (incomplete) *ibid.*, p. 628. On July 29, 1864, Maj. Gen. Benjamin F. Butler wrote to USG. "Your instructions are quite clear and perhaps I ought not to trouble you, but fearing that I may misunderstand I venture to ask a word of explanation. You say: General Foster had better level the line of rifle-pits occupied by the enemy, and move his whole force to the side of the creek first occupied by him. General Foster originally held two positions defended by works, one on the north side and one on the south side of the creek, the latter being held to prevent the enemy from commanding the former, which that position does. If Foster abandons the south side and places his whole force on the north side he will be overlooked by the enemy. By leaving a small force in the south work I think he can defend both positions better than one. We will leave some pontoon boats or the bridge, as the enemy cannot cross in face of the gun-boats. Is it your intention that we should literally obey the order or merely that Foster shall hold his old position if he can? If the latter, it may be telegraphed—hold the old position; if the former, obey instructions." *Ibid.*, p. 621. On the same day, USG telegraphed to Butler.

"If it can be done,—hold the old position." Telegram received (at 3:00 P.M.), DNA, RG 94, War Records Office, Dept. of Va. and N. C., Army of the James, Unentered Papers. Printed as sent at 3:00 P.M. in *O.R.*, I, xl, part 3, 621.

Also on July 29, Butler wrote to USG. "I have the honor to send herewith a deserter from the enemy, Thomas J. Powell, who swam the Appomattox and came in last night. Powell gives an account of the departure of a secret armed expedition from Wilmington, supposed to be to release prisoners at Point Lookout. I prefer to send you the information in the 'original package' and so forward the deserter." *Ibid.*, p. 617. At 8:00 A.M., Butler telegraphed to USG. "One train passed towards Richmond from Petersburg last night. At 6 A. M. two batteries and twenty nine wagons were moving along the turnpike towards Richmond" Copy (telegram sent), DNA, RG 94, War Records Office, Dept. of Va. and N. C., Army of the James, Unentered Papers; telegram received, *ibid.*, RG 108, Letters Received. *O.R.*, I, xl, part 3, 617. Butler also transmitted to USG a signal message of 10:30 A.M. from Capt. Gustavus S. Dana to Capt. Lemuel B. Norton. "More trains of wagons & ambulances have just crossed Chapin's farm a few wagons & ambulances are returning from the east towards the enemy's ponton bridge a little this side of Drurys bluff" Telegram received, DNA, RG 108, Letters Received. *O.R.*, I, xl, part 3, 625. During the morning, Butler telegraphed to USG five more times, the last two at 11:10 A.M. and 11:55 A.M. "Birney's officer of the day reports distinct hearing of sound resembling loading of cars with Rail Road iron & moving of trains to Richmond. Also that the force in front of Genl Ferry (the left of our line) is apparently much reduced. Steps have been taken to ascertain more and correctly about this" Copy (telegram sent), DNA, RG 94, War Records Office, Dept. of Va. and N. C., Army of the James, Unentered Papers; telegram received, *ibid.*, RG 108, Letters Received. *O.R.*, I, xl, part 3, 618. "At 9. A. M two trains with thirty nine cars, loaded with troops, towards Richmond Also two baggage trains with 75 wagons went on the turnpike in the same direction Also a regiment of cavalry and a four gun battery just crossed at the pontoon bridge to the North side of James river. In all since day before yesterday after noon at 6 O'Clock there have passed over, to this time, about ten thousand infantry, four regiments of cavalry and three batteries that we know of. Baggage wagons in due proportion" "At sunrise the signal officer on the right saw a long column of troops crossing the pontoon bridge at Chafin's farm to the North bank of the James. Three regiments had crossed when he reported. A General and staff were with the column. This despatch had been mislaid by the Chief Signal officer, and not sent in until just now" Copies (telegrams sent), DNA, RG 107, Telegrams Collected (Unbound); telegrams received, *ibid.*, RG 108, Letters Received. *O.R.*, I, xl, part 3, 618. "In additon to all reported before at 10.30 A. M. three regiments of cavalry and fourteen wagons passed along the turnpike towards Richmond." "Another large force of cavalry was passing up the turnpike at the Junction at 11.10 A. M. at the C This is in addition to all previous reports." Copies (telegrams sent), DNA, RG 94, War Records Office, Dept. of Va. and N. C., Army of the James, Unentered Papers; telegrams received, *ibid.*, RG 108, Letters Received. *O.R.*, I, xl, part 3, 618–19. At 12:15 P.M., USG telegraphed copies of these telegrams to Maj. Gen. George G. Meade. Telegram received (incomplete), DNA, RG 107, Telegrams Collected (Unbound); *ibid.*, RG 94, War Records Office, Dept. of Va. and N. C., Army of the James, Unentered Papers.

At 12:20 P.M., Butler telegraphed to USG. "Eight hundred Cavalry and 40 wagons and ambulances passed the Junction on the turnpike towards Richmond at 11.30 A. M, since last report." Copy (telegram sent), *ibid.*; telegram received, *ibid.*, RG 108, Letters Received. *O.R.*, I, xl, part 3, 619. USG transmitted this telegram to Meade. "The following just recvd from Gen Butler" Telegram received (at 1:00 P.M.), DNA, RG 94, War Records Office, Army of the Potomac; copy, Meade Papers, PHi. At 2:10 P.M., Butler telegraphed to USG transmitting a signal message of 12:35 P.M. from Lt. Alfred G. Simons, Spring Hill Signal Station, to Norton. "Twenty Six (26) baggage wagons have just passed on turnpike near R R Junction going towards Richmond" Telegram received, DNA, RG 108, Letters Received. Printed as sent at 1:00 P.M. in *O.R.*, I, xl, part 3, 619. At 2:15 P.M., 2:25 P.M., and 6:55 P.M., Butler telegraphed to USG. "The following despatch has just been rec'd—Seven (7) cars with passengers, and twelve (12) wagons just passed the Junction twards Richmond" Copy (telegram sent), DNA, RG 94, War Records Office, Dept. of Va. and N. C., Army of the James, Unentered Papers; telegram received, *ibid.*, RG 108, Letters Received. *O.R.*, I, xl, part 3, 619. "Between 11.15 A. M and 12.45 P. M thirty-four (34) wagons have crossed the Ponton over the James going East. They moved towards the river from the P & R. Turnpike by three (3) different roads and across Chapin's Farm by two (2) roads The following rebel message was sent from the Ram to shore, viz: 'I mean the skiffs that came down from Richmond yesterday P. M. Numbers 3 & 4 are mine & you have sent No 2. Is it not a mistake—' " Copy (telegram sent), DNA, RG 107, Telegrams Collected (Unbound); telegram received, *ibid.*, RG 108, Letters Received. *O.R.*, I, xl, part 3, 621. "The following dispatch just recd. 'The enemy's signal officer report about four hundred wagons to have crossed Pontoon over Appomattox going towards Bermuda Hundred (Sgd) G. S. Dana Capt Sig Corps' " Telegram received (datelined 6:50 P.M.), DNA, RG 108, Letters Received; copy (undated, marked as sent at 6:55 P.M.), *ibid.*, RG 393, Dept. of Va. and N. C., Telegrams Sent. *O.R.*, I, xl, part 3, 623.

At 3:00 P.M., Maj. Gen. Winfield S. Hancock telegraphed to USG. "I resp'y suggest that if practicable it would be well to have another bridge thrown here for use tonight A deserter from Kershaws Divn just in reports that Divn as engaged in entrenching in front near the Jennings House probably" Telegrams received (2), DNA, RG 94, War Records Office, Army of the Potomac; copy, Meade Papers, PHi. *O.R.*, I, xl, part 3, 599. Brig. Gen. John A. Rawlins added an endorsement, intended to be telegraphed to Meade. "The above just recvd & Gen Butler has been requested to comply with the request if practicable" Telegram received, DNA, RG 94, War Records Office, Army of the Potomac; copy, Meade Papers, PHi. *O.R.*, I, xl, part 3, 599. On the same day, USG telegraphed to Butler. "If practicable you will have another bridge thrown across the James at Deep Bottom for use tonight." Telegram received (at 4:20 P.M.), DNA, RG 94, War Records Office, Dept. of Va. and N. C., Army of the James, Unentered Papers; copies, *ibid.*, RG 108, Letters Sent; DLC-USG, V, 45, 59, 67. Printed as sent at 4:20 P.M. in *O.R.*, I, xl, part 3, 622. At 4:30 P.M., Butler telegraphed to USG. "In the opinion of the Engineers another Bridge south of the Creek is impracticable because of the steepness of the bluff and the narrowness of the roadway along the Bank of the Creek If it were we have not the Material to Construct it of Shall send down to deep Bottom and if possible to do anything to aid crossing it shall be done Capt Michey has gone for the purpose Shall Birges brigade of the 19th corps leave Bermuda Hundreds with Hancock—Or shall it remain at deep Bottom on this side the James to aid Foster or repel an attempt to Cross" ALS (telegram sent), DNA, RG 107, Telegrams Collected (Unbound); telegram received, *ibid.*, RG 94, War Records Office, Dept. of Va. and N. C., Army of the James, Unentered Papers; *ibid.*, RG 108, Letters Received. *O.R.*, I, xl, part 3, 622. On the same day, USG twice telegraphed to Butler, with the second telegram marked as received at 5:20 P.M. "Genl Benham is already on the way with another bridge" "Birges brigade will remain at your disposal. I have sent word to Gen Benham about the bridge." Telegrams received, DNA, RG 94, War Records Office, Dept. of Va. and N. C., Army of the James, Unentered Papers. *O.R.*, I, xl, part 3, 622, where the second telegram is printed as sent at 5:30 P.M. An undated telegram from USG to Rawlins was sent on the same day, 5:05 P.M. "Call on Gen. Benham to know if he has bridge material for throwing a second bridge across close to the lower one at Deep Bottom. If so to commence the work at once." ALS (telegram sent), DNA, RG 107, Telegrams Collected (Unbound). On the same day, Rawlins telegraphed to USG. "Gen Benham says that by breaking up the Hospital Wharf he can build the bridge. He cannot do it without. Shall it be broken up. He is getting ready." Telegram received, *ibid.*; *ibid.*, RG 94, War Records Office, Army of the Potomac. An undated telegram from USG to Rawlins was sent on the same day, 5:40 P.M. "Break up the Wharf at Hospital. As soon as troops are over the bridge will be taken up and the wharf rebuilt." ALS (telegram sent), *ibid.*, RG 107, Telegrams Collected (Unbound). On the same day, Rawlins telegraphed to Butler. "Gen Benham has been directed to lay the bridge. Please direct Capt Lubey to select the point for laying the bridge & prepare the approaches at once, ~~under the direction~~" Copy (telegram sent), *ibid.*; telegram received (at 6:00 P.M.), *ibid. O.R.*, I, xl, part 3, 622. At 7:00 P.M., Butler telegraphed to USG. "Capt Michie of the Engineers Telegraphs that he is getting ready the approaches for another Bridge at Deep Bottom and that he can get it ready in four hours if Benhams train gets up in time—or if he takes up the Upper bridge to Foster Camp. Had he better do the latter" ALS (telegram sent), DNA, RG 107, Telegrams Collected (Unbound); telegram received, *ibid.*, RG 108, Letters Received. *O.R.*, I, xl, part 3, 623.

To Maj. Gen. Winfield S. Hancock

By Telegraph from City Pt
Dated July 29 *1864.*

To GEN HANCOCK

Has the enemy made any development today. If not it will be well to attract his attention, I would not attack but would keep up the idea of doing so to prevent the withdrawal of the enemy.

U. S. GRANT
Lt Genl

Telegram received, DNA, RG 107, Telegrams Collected (Unbound). *O.R.*, I, xl, part 3, 599. On July 29, 1864, 12:45 P.M., Maj. Gen. Winfield S. Hancock telegraphed to USG, sending a copy to Maj. Gen. George G. Meade. "The enemy are strengthig their works this morning, and have been working all night. They are ~~evidently~~ strengthing their works across all the great road to Richmond, according to the reports of all the videtts. Last night I sent over a Division of Cavalry to get rid of their horses. Gen Sheridan has them concealed along the bank of James River, the division dismounted, returned after daylight giving the appeara[n]ce to the enemy that we were strongly reinforced. The enemy could see the whole movement plainly. The movement of the horses was made during the night. We hold the same ground with our *picket* that the *fights* were on yesterday. I have already sent *Cavalry* out on all the roads this morning—and will do as you suggest, without making an *attack*. . . . No movement of troops has been observed this morning" ALS (telegram sent), DNA, RG 107, Telegrams Collected (Unbound); telegram received, *ibid.*, RG 94, War Records Office, Army of the Potomac; *ibid.*, RG 108, Letters Received. *O.R.*, I, xl, part 3, 599. Other telegrams sent on the same day by Hancock to both USG and Meade are *ibid.*, pp. 598–602.

To Maj. Gen. George G. Meade

By Telegraph from City Point 1 15 P M
Dated July 29 *1864.*

To GEN MEADE

I have not sent Butlers despatches to Gen Hancock. If you have not sent them it will probably be well to send a summary of them

The enemy are evidently piling everything except a very thin line in your front, to the north side of the River—

Hancock was to be careful to have his command well in hand and a strong line to fall behind where the gunboat can have full play along his front. I have no doubt but he has taken ~~themse~~ precautions but it will do no harm to caution him—I am inclined to think the enemy will wait for us to attack unless they discover that we are withdrawing

U S GRANT
Lt Gen

Telegrams received (2), DNA, RG 94, War Records Office, Army of the Potomac; copies, *ibid.*, RG 108, Letters Sent; DLC-USG, V, 45, 59, 67; Meade Papers, PHi. *O.R.*, I, xl, part 3, 591. On July 29, 1864, 2:30 P.M., Maj. Gen. George G. Meade telegraphed to USG. "I earnestly impressed on Hancock yesterday, the necessity of occupying a strong line, entrenching it, & preparing for a heavy attack today, which I deemed probable, when the enemy had accumulated a heavy force—I have now sent him your telegrams. Your note by Capt. Hudson just received—Ord has been with me all the morning—we have been over the line & in conference with Burnside. I will be at my quarters at 4. P. M it being about as near as any part of the line." ALS (telegram sent), DNA, RG 393, Army of the Potomac, Miscellaneous Letters Received; telegram received, *ibid.*, RG 108, Letters Received. *O.R.*, I, xl, part 3, 591.

At 10:00 P.M., Meade telegraphed to USG. "The above intercepted rebel despatch shows Ingalls has made a strike" ALS (telegram sent), DNA, RG 107, Telegrams Collected (Unbound); telegram received, *ibid.*, RG 108, Letters Received. *O.R.*, I, xl, part 3, 591. The telegram on which Meade wrote is printed *ibid.*, pp. 591–92. On the same day, USG telegraphed to Meade. "Gen Butler sent me an intercepted Rebel dispatch of an early hour than the one you sent stating that 400 wagons had crossed the ponton bridge" Telegram received (at 11:00 P.M.), DNA, RG 94, War Records Office, Army of the Potomac; copy, Meade Papers, PHi. *O.R.*, I, xl, part 3, 592.

To Maj. Gen. George G. Meade

City Point, Va, July 29th *1864*.

MAJ. GEN. G. G. MEAD COMD.G A. P.
GEN.

I have directed Gen. Butler to order Gn. Ord to report to you for the attack on Petersburg. The details for the assault I leave for you to make out. I directed Gen. Sheridan whilst we were at Deep Bottom last evening to move his command immediately to the left of Warren from Deep Bottom. It will ~~probably~~ be well to direct the cavalry to endeavor to get round the enemys right flank. Whilst they will not probably succeed in turning the enemy they will detain a large force to prevent it.

I will go out this evening to see you. Will be at your Hd Qrs. about 4 p. m.

> Very respectfully
> your obt. svt.
> U. S. GRANT
> Lt. Gn.

P. S. If you want to be anyplace on the line at the hour indicated inform me by telegraph and I will meet you wherever you may be.

U. S. G.

ALS, NjP. *O.R.*, I, xl, part 1, 134; *ibid.*, I, xl, part 3, 590–91.

On July 29, 1864, 10:30 A.M., Maj. Gen. George G. Meade telegraphed to USG. "From the following despatch and other information it appears quite probable that Heths Division Hills Corps and Fields Division Longstreets Corps have both left my front" Telegram received, DNA, RG 108, Letters Received. *O.R.*, I, xl, part 3, 593. The appended message is *ibid.*, pp. 592–93. At 3:00 P.M., Col. George H. Sharpe telegraphed to Brig. Gen. John A. Rawlins. "In my report this morning of information brought from Richmond I omitted to state that our agent saw day before yesterday in Richmond a large considerable train of waggons by which it was intended to send out of the enemy's lines and throw on our hands large numbers of women, children and decrepid persons, said to be the families of persons who have fled to our lines, or avoided the Confederate service—" ALS (telegram sent), DNA, RG 94, War Records Office, Army of the Potomac. *O.R.*, I, xl, part 3, 593.

Also on July 29, Lt. Col. Theodore S. Bowers telegraphed to Meade, to Maj. Gen. Benjamin F. Butler, and to all corps commanders. "The following despatch from the telegraph Supt. near Atlanta dated 8 P M last evening has just been recvd—'Howards Command got into position on right today & were attacked at once The weight falling on the fifteenth Corps. enemy charged four times in very dense timber and were repulsed as often with what loss I cannot say. Our loss not 100. At this hour the Rebels are massing against right while Schofield & Stanley are ready to attack on our left as soon as our right is pressed heavily' " Telegram received, DNA, RG 94, War Records Office, Dept. of Va. and N. C., Army of the James, Unentered Papers; *ibid.*, RG 107, Telegrams Collected (Unbound); Ord Papers, CU-B; copy, Meade Papers, PHi. See *O.R.*, I, xxxviii, part 5, 288.

To Maj. Gen. Henry W. Halleck

City Point Va
July 30th 10 a m 1864

Maj Gen H. W. Halleck
Chief of Staff.

Finding that my effort to surprise the enemy by sending an army corps and three 3 divisions of cavalry to the north bank of the James river, under cover of night, for the purpose of getting on to the Rail Road north of Richmond, drew all of his forcs from Petersburg except three 3 divisions; I determined to attack and try to carry the latter place. The enemy's earthworks are as strong as they can be made and the ground is very broken and favorable for defences. Having a mine prepared running for a distance of eighty (80) feet along the enemy's parapet and about twenty (20) two

(2) feet below the surface of the ground ready loaded, and covered ways made near to his line, I was strongly in hopes by this means of opening the way the assault would prove successful. The mine was sprung a few minutes before 5. a m this morning throwing up four 4 guns of the enemy and burying most of a South Carolina Regiment. Our men immediately took possession of the crater made by the explosion and a considerable distance of the parapet to the right of it as well as a short work in front, and still hold them. The effort to carry the ridge beyond, which would give us Petersburg and the South bank of the Appomattox failed. as the line held by the enemy would be a very bad one for us, being on a side hill, the crest on the side of the enemy and not being willing to take the chances of slaughter sure to occur if another assault was made, I have directed the withdrawal of our troops to their old lines. Although just from the front I have but little idea of the attack. I think however our linesoss will will be but a few hundred, unless it occurs in withdrawing, which it may not be practicable to do before night. I saw about two hundred prisoners taken from the enemy. Hancock and Sheridan returned from the north side of the river during the night and are now here

U S GRANT
Lt Genl

Telegram received (on July 31, 1864, 7:00 A.M.), DNA, RG 107, Telegrams Collected (Bound); copies, *ibid.*, RG 108, Letters Sent; DLC-USG, V, 45, 59, 67. *O.R.*, I, xl, part 1, 17; *ibid.*, I, xl, part 3, 636.

On July 30, 7:00 A.M., 8:00 A.M., and 9:15 A.M., Lt. Col. Cyrus B. Comstock telegraphed to USG. "Several regiments of Burnsides men are lying in front & in the crater apparently of the mine. In their rear is to be seen a line of Battle of a Brigade or more under cover & I think between the Enemies line & ours. The Volley firing half ½ an Hour ago was from the Enemies works in Warrens front." "About a Brigade more of our men Has moved up to the crater & then filed off to the right along the Enemys line   They are still moving to the right." "I cannot see that we have advanced beyond the Enemys line in the Vicinity of the mine. From here it looks as if the Enemy were holding a line between that point & the crest"   Telegrams received, DNA, RG 94, War Records Office, Army of the Potomac; copies (2), Meade Papers, PHi. *O.R.*, I, xl, part 1, 142, 143, 144; *ibid.*, I, xl, part 3, 637. The third is printed as received at 9:35 A.M. *ibid.*; (printed as sent at 9:35 A.M.) *ibid.*, I, xl, part 1, 144. On the same day, USG telegraphed to Maj. Gen. Ambrose E. Burnside and to Maj. Gen. Edward O. C. Ord. "In reoccupying their his lines haves the enemy captured many of your men?" Copies, DLC-USG, V, 45, 59, 67; DNA, RG 108, Letters Sent. *O.R.*, I, xl, part 3, 664. On the same day, Brig. Gen. Julius White, chief of staff for Burnside, wrote to USG. "The enemy have not reoccupied their lines. General Burnside is at General Meade's headquarters." *Ibid.*

To Maj. Gen. Benjamin F. Butler

By Telegraph from 9th A C [*6:30* A.M.]
Dated [*July*] 30 *1864.*

To MAJ GENL BUTLER

The enemy seem to be in small force   they may to hasten rein-forcements take every thing from your front,   if they do follow in & seize & hold the Road to the last informing me that I may take steps to strengthen you in time   the explosion blew up 4 guns & nearly an entere south Carolina Regt   Our men pushed forward to the Breach without oposition but unfortunatly stoped—I they have been ordered forward again & I am much in hope it is ~~sitil~~ still time to succeed

U S GRANT

Telegram received (at 6:15 A.M.), DNA, RG 94, War Records Office, Dept. of Va. and N. C., Army of the James, Unentered Papers; copies, *ibid.*, RG 108, Letters Sent; DLC-USG, V, 45, 59, 67. *O.R.*, I, xl, part 3, 673. On July 30, 1864, 7:00 A.M., Maj. Gen. Benjamin F. Butler telegraphed to USG. "Dispatch recieved and measures taken to observe the Picket line and promptly—take advantage of any movement   I will move out if there is any stir of the Enemy whatever   The firing you may hear is that of my Colored Troops Drilling" ALS (telegram sent), DNA, RG 107, Telegrams Collected (Unbound); *ibid.*, RG 393, Dept. of Va. and N. C., Telegrams Sent. *O.R.*, I, xl, part 3, 673.

On the same day, USG telegraphed to Butler. "We gained a portion of the enemies lines but cannot hold it,   our men will be withdrawn tonight   the Batteries & guns bearing on the Bridge will open on the enemy if they attempt to cross" Telegram received, DLC-Benjamin F. Butler; DNA, RG 107, Telegrams Collected (Unbound). *O.R.*, I, xl, part 3, 674.

To Maj. Gen. Benjamin F. Butler

By Telegraph from City Pt
Dated July 30 *1864*.

To GEN BUTLER,

I have ordered a Corps of Infy & all the Cavalry to keep on, now that we are in motion, to cut some fifteen or twenty miles of the Weldon R. R. Please order Kautz to report to Gen Gregg at Lee's mills, with his cavy tonight. Ord's corps being the only one out of line will go. They need not take but five (5) days rations with them   I want to do this damage until we rest up & prepare for a bigger operation.

U. S GRANT

Telegram received (at 2:55 P.M.), DLC-Benjamin F. Butler; copies, DLC-USG, V, 45, 59, 67; DNA, RG 108, Letters Sent. *O.R.*, I, xl, part 3, 674. On July 30, 1864, 3:30 P.M., Maj. Gen. Benjamin F. Butler telegraphed to USG. "Your dispatch rec'd and attended to. Genl Ord has been directed to report to you for orders. Two more regiments of infantry crossed Chafin's farm at 2.50 P. M going west" Telegram received, DNA, RG 94, War Records Office, Dept. of Va. and N. C., Army of the James, Unentered Papers. *O.R.*, I, xl, part 3, 674; (misdated July 29) *ibid.*, p. 620.

At 11:25 A.M., Butler telegraphed to USG. "Have just recieved a telegram from Foster that all is quiet in his Front and that he will hold his position   No troops have yet passed to Petersburgh   Might I suggest that as soon as they begin to move If all our batteries and mortars that bear on the bridges should open it might trouble them to get across. How gets on the movement. Nothing has stirred in our front." ALS (telegram sent), DNA, RG 107, Telegrams Collected (Unbound); telegram received, *ibid.*, RG 108, Letters Received. *O.R.*, I, xl, part 3, 674. At 1:20 P.M., Butler telegraphed to USG transmitting a signal message of 1:15 P.M. from Lt. Alfred G. Simons, Spring Hill Signal Station, to Capt. Lemuel B. Norton. "A train of seven empty cars just passed the Junction towards Petersburg. Twenty (20) wagons loaded with forage just passed along turnpike, at Junction, going towards Richmond." Telegram received, DNA, RG 94, War Records Office, Dept. of Va. and N. C., Army of the James, Unentered Papers. *O.R.*, I, xl, part 3, 678. On the same day, Butler telegraphed to USG. "Two infantry Reg'ts Crossed Chafin's farm going west at 2 P. m,   this is the first movement observed to reinforce Petersburg" Telegram received, DNA, RG 108, Letters Received; copy (undated), *ibid.*, RG 393, Dept. of Va. and N. C., Telegrams Sent. Printed as sent at 12:30 P.M. in *O.R.*, I, xl, part 3, 674. At 3:50 P.M., Butler telegraphed to USG. "There is now a ~~continious~~ constance passing of troops—across the ~~ri~~ river going west—with artillery in proportion— Foster has taken another deserter who reports all of Hills corpse except one Brigade—and part of Longstreets corpse—in his front at daylight; with orders to march at moments notice   All quiet in this front—" Telegram received (at 4:00 P.M.), DNA, RG 94, War Records Office, Dept. of Va. and N. C., Army of the James, Unentered Papers. *O.R.*, I, xl, part 3, 675; (misdated July 29) *ibid.*, pp. 621–22. At 6:15 P.M., Butler telegraphed to USG transmitting a signal message of 6:00 P.M. from Simons to Norton. "A train of sixteen (16) cars loaded with troops just passed the Junction towards *Petersburg*." Telegram received, DNA, RG 94, War Records Office, Dept. of Va. and N. C., Army of the James, Unentered Papers. *O.R.*, I, xl, part 3, 679. At 8:15 P.M. (received at 8:30 P.M.), Butler telegraphed to USG. "Have just re-cieved notice from Ord that raid on Weldin road is suppressed and he takes his old positio[n]   Shall I recall Kautz   Can save him a thirty mile march" ALS (telegram sent), DNA, RG 107, Telegrams Collected (Unbound). *O.R.*, I, xl, part 3, 675. On the same day, USG telegraphed to Butler. "Recall Kautz by all means. It was neglect in me not thinking to so direct before" Copies, DLC-USG, V, 45, 59, 67; DNA, RG 108, Letters Sent. *O.R.*, I, xl, part 3, 675. At 8:30 P.M., Butler telegraphed to USG. "A rebel Brigade just crossed the pontoon bridge at Chapins farm going west—A heavily ladend tran just passed the Junction going towards Petersburg" ALS (telegram sent), DNA, RG 94, War Records Office, Dept. of Va. and N. C., Army of the James, Unentered Papers. *O.R.*, I, xl, part 3, 676; (misdated July 29) *ibid.*, p. 623.

Also on July 30, USG telegraphed to Butler. "Send all the remainder of the 19th Corps to Washn. at once & withdraw from the 18th Corps what may be necessary to secure your position. Direct Gen Ord, to send to this place his heavy artillery, or such of it as can be dispensed with, & cannot be rapidly removed in case of necessity." Telegram received (at 10:45 P.M.), DLC-Benjamin F. Butler; copies, DLC-USG, V, 45, 59, 67; DNA, RG 108, Letters Sent. *O.R.*, I, xxxvii, part 2, 510; *ibid.*, I, xl, part 3, 675.

On July 31, 11:30 A.M., Col. John W. Shaffer, chief of staff for Butler, telegraphed to Lt. Col. Theodore S. Bowers. "Troops of 19th Corps all Embarked—and Boats moving off" ALS (telegram sent), DNA, RG 107, Telegrams Collected (Unbound); telegram received (at 12:30 P.M.), *ibid.*, RG 94, War Records Office, Dept. of Va. and N. C., Army of the James, Unentered Papers. *O.R.*, I, xl, part 3, 710. At noon, Butler telegraphed to USG. "~~Remainder~~ Birge's and Molineux' Brigades of the 19th Corps left Bermuda Hundreds for the destination ordered and they are all that were ordered to go at 11 30 A M" ALS (telegram sent), DNA, RG 94, War Records Office, Army of the Potomac; telegram received, *ibid.* *O.R.*, I, xl, part 3, 709.

At 1:20 P.M., Maj. Gen. Edward O. C. Ord telegraphed to Brig. Gen. Godfrey Weitzel. "Shall I send Coherns from trenches. They are useful here, as my front is weak. Shall I take 8 inch mortors from trenches, twould excite suspicion." Telegram received, DNA, RG 94, War Records Office, Dept. of Va. and N. C., Army of the James, Unentered Papers; copy, *ibid.*, RG 393, Dept. of Va. and N. C., Telegrams Sent. Butler drafted a telegram to USG at the foot of this telegram. "The following dispatch has just been rec'd . . . What shall I answer?" ADfS, *ibid.*, RG 94, War Records Office, Dept. of Va. and N. C., Army of the James, Unentered Papers; copy, *ibid.*, RG 393, Dept. of Va. and N. C., Telegrams Sent. On the same day, Capt. Ely S. Parker telegraphed to Butler. "You need not take the Coherns & Mortars from the trenches, until further orders." Telegram received (at 10:00 A.M.), *ibid.*, RG 107, Telegrams Collected (Unbound). *O.R.*, I, xl, part 3, 709. At 8:40 P.M., Col. Henry L. Abbot, Broadway Landing, telegraphed to Bowers. "General Hunt suggests that I notify you that I am loading my train as rapidly as possible at Broadway Landing, this being my understanding of my orders. It can be unloaded faster than it can be put in position, as I do not take the carriages apart. By morning everything not required by General Ord will be here and nearly afloat. Please notify me if this is what you desire." *Ibid.*, pp. 721–22. On the same day, Bowers telegraphed to Abbot. "You have done right. General Grant will return during the night, and his further directions will be telegraphed to you in the morning." *Ibid.*, p. 722.

On Aug. 1, Lt. Col. Cyrus B. Comstock telegraphed to Ord. "Lieut Gen Grant desires me to say that the work to strengthen & perfect your defensive line should be begun at once by your Enginee[r] Officer who will act under the instructions of Gen Barnard Chief Engineer" Telegram received, Ord Papers, CU-B. *O.R.*, I, xlii, part 2, 15.

To Maj. Gen. George G. Meade

By Telegraph from City Point
Dated July 30 *1864.*

To Maj Gen Meade

The enemy have not yet recrossed the James River[1] this will be a favorable opportunity to send a Corps of Infantry & the Cavalry to cut 15 or 20 miles of the Weldon Rail Road   instruct the Cavalry to remain out for this purpose & either Corps of Infantry you may designate   if Ords inform Gen Butler of the fact   5 days rations will be sufficient for them to take along   they should get off by daylight tomorrow & strike the road as near Petersburg as they can to commence work   I cannot yet help feeling that if our Cavalry should get well round the enemys right before our troops are withdrawn from their present position we may yet take Petersburg   I do not feel like giving additional instructions on this subject however

U S Grant
Lt. Gen

Telegram received (at 2:15 P.M.), DNA, RG 94, War Records Office, Army of the Potomac; copies, *ibid.*, RG 108, Letters Sent; DLC-USG, V, 45, 59, 67; (2) Meade Papers, PHi. *O.R.*, I, xl, part 3, 637–38. On July 30, 1864, 2:20 P.M., Maj. Gen. George G. Meade telegraphed to USG. "Despatch of 2.15 just received—I think I shall have to take Ord's Corps, as Hancock is in the trenches and can not be relieved till after dark—Not anticipating your present order, I told

Genl—Gregg Comd. Cav. Corps during sickness of Gen. Sheridan that he might send Kautz back to Genl. Butler   I think it would be advisable to order him to report again to Gregg at Lee's Mills. or" ALS (telegram sent), DNA, RG 393, Army of the Potomac, Miscellaneous Letters Received; telegram received (undated), *ibid.*, RG 108, Letters Received. *O.R.*, I, xl, part 3, 638.

At 2:15 P.M., Meade telegraphed to USG. "I have just received a report from Genl Gregg Comd. Cavalry—He reports his command in presence of the enemy at the Gurley House & at other points near the R. Rd—He does not appear to have made any effort to advance but reports that as the result of his reconnaissance, which he was directed to make, when offensive operations were suspended. At the same time he says his horses have not had water for Forty eight hours & he is in want of forage for his animals & subsistence for his men— Seeing no prospect of the Cavalry being able to do any thing this afternoon, in view of their condition & your orders for a raid tomorrow, I have directed him to with draw & make his preparations for the movement tomorrow.—I find Ords Corps so mixed up with Burnsides, I have concluded it will be quicker work to send Hancock to support the Cavalry & have accordingly ordered Ord to relieve Hancock as soon after dark as possible & allwed Hancock at the same time to move over to the Jerusalem plank road.—" ALS (telegram sent), DNA, RG 393, Army of the Potomac, Miscellaneous Letters Received; copies, *ibid.*, Letters Sent; (2) Meade Papers, PHi. *O.R.*, I, xl, part 3, 638. At 3:30 P.M., Meade telegraphed to USG. "I forward this despatch for your information—Taken in connection with Greggs report of the condition his Cavalry which I send, I have but little hope of effecting any thing in the way of a raid tomorrow—Besides I must think the enemys infantry will be back before night, if not already here. I have however given the necessary orders for the movement tomorrow" ALS (telegram sent), DNA, RG 94, War Records Office, Army of the Potomac. *O.R.*, I, xl, part 3, 648. The enclosures are *ibid.*, pp. 648, 670. At 4:00 P.M., Meade telegraphed to USG. "I send this despatch that you may know the condition of Ord's corps—He seems to think only two divisions can be sent and suggests the other two being retained to sustain Burnside—I had ordered Ord to relieve Hancocks people & Hancock to go on the raid, but there seems to be difficulty & objections all around,—with both Infantry & Cavalry.—" ALS (telegram sent), DNA, RG 94, War Records Office, Army of the Potomac; telegram received, *ibid.*, RG 108, Letters Received. *O.R.*, I, xl, part 3, 639. The enclosure is *ibid.*

On July 30, USG telegraphed to Meade. "A Hospital train of 5 Cars loaded with sick or wounded is just now reported from signal at Point of Rocks as having passed from Petersburg towards Richmond   no troops yet reported going the other way" Telegram received (at 2:45 P.M.), DNA, RG 94, War Records Office, Army of the Potomac; copies, DLC-USG, V, 67; (2) Meade Papers, PHi.

1. Earlier on July 30, USG had telegraphed to Meade. "Gen Butler reports that none of the enemy have yet returned from north of the James" Telegram received (at 1:00 P.M.), DNA, RG 94, War Records Office, Army of the Potomac; *ibid.*, RG 107, Telegrams Collected (Unbound). *O.R.*, I, xl, part 3, 637.

To Maj. Gen. George G. Meade

By Telegraph from City Point
Dated July 30 *1864.*

To MAJ GEN MEADE

It is almost certain that none of the enemys force recrossed the James until since 2 P m today & but 2 or 3 Regiments then. It is nearly as much of an object to draw them back to this side as it is to Cut the road that I want the expedition to go out. I am very much afraid Lee will send an army corps to reenforce Early who I understand from a despatch of last evening had driven Averill out of Hagerstown towards Green castle   since writing the above I have information from signal station on the James that the enemy are now crossing in continues stream   you may therefore suspend the order for movement down the Rail Road   we may get an attack from the enemy tomorrow, evening or next day morning and want to be prepared for it.

U S GRANT
Lt Gen'l.

Telegram received (at 4:50 P.M.—incomplete), DNA, RG 94, War Records Office, Army of the Potomac; copies, *ibid.*, RG 108, Letters Sent; DLC-USG, V, 45, 59, 67; (2) Meade Papers, PHi. *O.R.*, I, xxxvii, part 2, 509; *ibid.*, I, xl, part 3, 639. On July 30, 1864, at 5:00 P.M., 6:00 P.M., and 8:30 P.M., Maj. Gen. George G. Meade telegraphed to USG. "Your telegram suspending raid received. I am of your opinion that we may now expect the enemy to assume the offensive which I think will be by sending a moveable column to turn our left & rear.—I have directed Sheridan to take post to cover our left & rear—Ord will resume tonight his former position & Hancock his, leaving one division on the left rear of our line, the other two in reserve—" "Can you not send Genl. Weitzel & Lt. Col Comstock to confer with Maj. Duane as to the best defenive line to be occupied from the Appomatox to the Jerusalem plank road & decide on the works to be erected.—" ALS (telegrams sent), DNA, RG 393, Army of the Potomac, Miscellaneous Letters Received; copies, *ibid.*, Letters Sent; Meade Papers, PHi. *O.R.*, I, xl, part 3, 640. "Ord reports to me there are many of our dead & wounded lying between our lines & the enemys line. Tho' not officially reported I have reason to believe the enemy got possession of their line including the crater soon after you left—taking I fear a number of prisoners among them Brig Genl. Bartlett—Do you think it worth while to ask for a flag tomorrow to remove our wounded & dead—Ord says there are a number of the enemy whom they can not get off & perhaps they would be more amiable than Beauregard was the last time I applied.—" ALS (telegram sent), DNA, RG 393, Army of the Potomac, Miscellaneous Letters Received; telegram received, *ibid.*, RG 108, Letters Received. *O.R.*, I, xl, part 3, 640. On the same day, USG telegraphed to Meade. "You may exercise your pleasure about asking as a truce to collect the dead & wounded   I leave in the course of an hour or two for Ft. Monroe   Will be back tomorrow night" Telegram received, DNA, RG 94, War Records Office, Army of the Potomac; copies, *ibid.*, RG 108, Letters Sent; DLC-USG, V, 45, 59, 67; (2) Meade Papers, PHi. *O.R.*, I, xl, part 3, 640.

On July 31, Lt. Col. Cyrus B. Comstock telegraphed to Meade. "I have been on Burnsides front today & am told that among the large number of our men now lying around the crater some are still alive—As Gen Grant is now absent at Ft. Monroe, I am unable to report the fact to him with out delay" Telegram received (at 5:00 P.M.), DNA, RG 94, War Records Office, Army of the Potomac; copies (2), Meade Papers, PHi. *O.R.*, I, xl, part 3, 691. At 5:30 P.M., Meade telegraphed to Comstock. "Gen Grant to whom the fact of wounded being left between our lines was communicated last night authorized my asking to remove them under flag of truce   Gen Burnside was authorized this morning to endeaver to make an informal arrangement for the withdrawal of the wounded which if unsuccessful, he was furnished with a letter from my self to Gen Lee asking the privilege—No report has been received from Gen B—" Telegram received, DNA, RG 108, Letters Received; copies, *ibid.*, RG 393, Army of the Potomac, Letters Sent; Meade Papers, PHi. *O.R.*, I, xl, part 3, 691. At 6:00 P.M., Meade telegraphed to Comstock. "The above is the latest report from Genl. Burnside—Shew it to Lt. Genl Grant on his arrival.—" ALS (telegram sent), DNA, RG 94, War Records Office, Army of the Potomac; telegram received, *ibid.*, RG 108, Letters Received. *O.R.*, I, xl, part 3, 705. The enclosed telegram from Maj. Gen. Ambrose E. Burnside, reporting his failure to make arrangements to remove the wounded, is *ibid.*, p. 704.

To Maj. Gen. George G. Meade

By Telegraph from City Point
Dated July 30th *1864.*

To MAJ. GEN MEADE

Our experience of today proves that fortifications come near holding themselves without troops. If therefore the enemy should attempt to turn your position do not hesitate to take out nearly every man to meet such attack   The enemy in such case would be able to leave nothing in his works but a weeak line intintend only to hold it, & ours could be held in turn by a skirmish line. With a reasonable amount of artillery & one Infantry man to six feet I am confi-

dent either party could hold their lines against a direct attack of
the other

U. S. Grant
Lt. Genl

Telegram received (at 10:00 P.M.), DNA, RG 94, War Records Office, Army of
the Potomac; copies, *ibid.*, RG 108, Letters Sent; DLC-USG, V, 45, 59, 67; (2)
Meade Papers, PHi. *O.R.*, I, xl, part 3, 638–39.

To Maj. Gen. George G. Meade

———

By Telegraph from City Pt
Dated July 30 *1864.*

To Maj. Gen Meade

The enemy have Commenced crossing the Potomac at three
different fords above Harpers Ferry.[1] Unless reinforcements are
sent from Lees army I think we have the greatest abundance of
Infantry & artillery there but no cavalry to depend on—Order one
1 division of Sheridans Cavalry to proceed at once to City Point to
embark for Washington   They need not take their transportation
with them nor artillery until the Cavalry is all embarked

U. S. Grant
Lt Gen

Telegram received (at 10:30 P.M.), DNA, RG 94, War Records Office, Army
of the Potomac; copies, *ibid.*, RG 108, Letters Sent; DLC-USG, V, 45, 59, 67;
(2) Meade Papers, PHi. *O.R.*, I, xxxvii, part 2, 509–10; *ibid.*, I, xl, part 3, 640–
41. On July 30, 1864, 10:30 P.M., Maj. Gen. George G. Meade telegraphed to
USG. "Orders in relation to cavalry received & transmitted to Genl. Sheridan.—"
ALS (telegram sent), DNA, RG 393, Army of the Potomac, Miscellaneous Letters Received; copies, *ibid.*, Letters Sent; Meade Papers, PHi. *O.R.*, I, xl, part 3,
641.

On the same day, USG telegraphed to Meade. "Get all the heavy Artillery in
the lines about Petersburg moved back to City Point as Early as possible   It is
by no means improbable the necessity will arise for sending two more Corps
there—" Telegram received (at 10:45 P.M.), DNA, RG 94, War Records
Office, Army of the Potomac; copies, *ibid.*, RG 108, Letters Sent; DLC-USG,
V, 45, 59, 67; (2) Meade Papers, PHi. *O.R.*, I, xl, part 3, 641. At 10:45 P.M.,
Meade telegraphed to USG. "Do you mean City Point, or Broadway where it
came from for the seige artillery & mortars to go.—" ALS (telegram sent),
DNA, RG 393, Army of the Potomac, Miscellaneous Letters Received; copies,

ibid., Letters Sent; Meade Papers, PHi. *O.R.*, I, xl, part 3, 641. At 11:15 P.M., Lt. Col. Theodore S. Bowers telegraphed to Meade. "Gen Grant left an hour ago for ~~City~~ P Fort Monroe. I presume he did not think of Broadway Landing, when he wrote his dispatch. The Artillry can be loaded on boats at City Point, easier than at Broadway, but Col. Abbott is at the latter place and would take charge of it. Please notify Gen Ord of the point you may determine as best, in order that he may send his to the same place." ALS (telegram sent), DNA, RG 94, War Records Office, Army of the Potomac; telegram received (at 11:45 P.M.), DLC-Henry J. Hunt. *O.R.*, I, xl, part 3, 641. At 11:25 P.M., Meade telegraphed to USG. "Genl. Hunt desires to know whether your order includes the seige guns on Ords front & along the Appomatox river   I presume it does, but desire positive instructions" ALS (telegram sent), DNA, RG 393, Army of the Potomac, Miscellaneous Letters Received; copies, *ibid.*, Letters Sent; Meade Papers, PHi. *O.R.*, I, xl, part 3, 641. At 11:30 P.M., Bowers telegraphed to Meade. "The only answer I am able to make to your dispatch of 11:15 is to give you following dispatch from Gen. Grant to Gen Butler: 'Direct Gen Ord to send to this place his heavy Artillery, or such of it as can be dispensed with, and ~~can~~ that can not be rapidly moved in case of necessity.—' Gen. Grant will return here about 4 o.clock to-morrow evening." ALS (telegram sent), DNA, RG 94, War Records Office, Army of the Potomac; telegram received (at midnight), DLC-Henry J. Hunt. *O.R.*, I, xl, part 3, 642.

1. On July 28, 1:00 P.M., Maj. Gen. Henry W. Halleck telegraphed to USG. "The main body of enemy reported yesterday at 20,000 in Martinsburg & that a column had gone towards Cumberland. If this be so, Wright & Crook will form a junction to-night at Harpers Ferry with orders to cross & give battle. If the enemy crosses the river above Harper's Ferry, they are ordered to move against him by South Mountain; if the enemy passes the Blue Ridge, to cross below & meet him. Genl. Hunter reports that he has only eight thousand five hundred men for the field, & that his cavalry & dismounted men are worthless. Experience has shown that new organizations of fragments of regiments are almost useless." ALS (telegram sent), DNA, RG 107, Telegrams Collected (Bound); telegram received (marked as sent at 1:30 P.M.), *ibid.*; *ibid.*, RG 108, Letters Received. Printed as sent at 1:30 P.M. in *O.R.*, I, xxxvii, part 2, 478–79. On July 29, 9:00 P.M., and July 30, 12:30 A.M., Asst. Secretary of War Charles A. Dana telegraphed to USG. "No rebels are any where across the Potomac. On wednesday last Early Headquarters were at Millwood, his men busy threshing & grinding grain.   a day train was then running to Culpeper   great quantities of hay were being taken from there   Gen Wright got to Harpers Ferry today with all his train safe   Gen Halleck had been much alarmed for fear Mosby might cross at Edwards Ferry & cut off Wrights wagon train   Mosby with 400 men was at Leesburg yesterday, has not appeared at either Edwards or Conrads Ferry. ample force to stop him at both places.   no news from Foster or Canby" Telegram received, DNA, RG 108, Letters Received. Printed as sent at 9:30 P.M. in *O.R.*, I, xxxvii, part 2, 492. "Of the 19th Corps 4600 men have arrived here this week made up of fragments of commands. No complete organization has yet arrived" Telegram received, DNA, RG 107, Telegrams Collected (Unbound); *ibid.*, RG 108, Letters Received. *O.R.*, I, xxxvii, part 2, 510.

To Julia Dent Grant

City Point, Va. July 30th *1864*

DEAR JULIA,

Your letter in regard to Fred is received. The promotion you ask for him is not possible now nor until there is a reorganization of the Army. When new regiments are raised, in the regular Army, or new Staff appointments created, the ~~p~~President fills the offices by selection. After they are once filled vacancies occuring are filled by promotion from the next lower grade. In the Inspectors Department Major is the lowest grade and when there is a vacancy the only appointment the President has to give, by selection, is to that grade. As Fred. is now a Maj. high on the list he would not want such promotion. On my Staff he has the rank of Lt. Col. and can remain with as light duties as he could possibly have any where.

We have been having a goodeal of fighting for the last four days but without much loss of life. We have captured four or five hundred prisoners and killed and wounded probably 2000 for the enemy in the time. Our loss has not been near so heavy unless it has been sustained in the last two hours.

The President has telegraphed me to meet him at Ft. Monroe at 10 O'Clock to-morrow. I will leave here at 5 in the morning and return in the afternoon.[1]

Kisses for yourself and the children. Love to all at home. I have but little time now to write and am a goodeal behind hand with my official correspondence. Kisses again for yourself and children. Why dont you make them write to me?

ULYS.

ALS, DLC-USG.

1. On July 30, 1864, 7:00 P.M., Col. John W. Shaffer, chief of staff for Maj. Gen. Benjamin F. Butler, telegraphed to Brig. Gen. John A. Rawlins. "Genl Butler wishes to know wether Genl Grant has gone to Fort Monroe" ALS (telegram sent), DNA, RG 94, War Records Office, Dept. of Va. and N. C., Army of the James, Unentered Papers. *O.R.*, I, xl, part 3, 675. On the same day, Rawlins telegraphed to Shaffer. "He has not" Telegram received, DNA, RG 107, Telegrams Collected (Unbound). On the same day, USG telegraphed to Butler. "I leave here sometime in the course of the night for Ft Monroe, to meet the

President there in the morning. I will return tomorrow night.   should it be necessary to communicate with me during the day telegraph me there." Telegram received (at 8:35 P.M.), DLC-Benjamin F. Butler; copies, DLC-USG, V, 45, 59, 67; DNA, RG 108, Letters Sent. *O.R.*, I, xl, part 3, 676. At 11:00 P.M., Butler telegraphed to USG. "Dispatch received and will meet promptest attention. A pleasant voyage. I could wish I was going with you, but use my house. Mrs. Butler will be happy to entertain you." *Ibid.*

To Bvt. Maj. Gen. Montgomery C. Meigs

Fortress Monroe Va.
July 31st 1864

MAJ. GEN M. C. MEIGS, QR. MR. GEN. U. S. A.
GENERAL

Lt. Col. R. B. Hatch with whom I have been acquainted since the begining of the war, and who has been relieved from duty as Chief Qr. Mr. of the 13th Army Corps, that Corps being broken up, expresses a desi[r]e to be assigned to duty in New Orleans, in charge of water transportation if not as Chief Qr. Mr.

I would in no instance recommend a chief for any Staff Dept. to a Dept. Commander desiring always to be in a condition to hold commanders responsible for short comings within their commands. If however you can assign Col. Hatch to the second choice here, leaving the Dept. Commander to say who shall have the first, I will be pleased.

I am General, very respectfully
your obt. svt.
U. S. GRANT
Lt. Gen

ALS, Mrs. Walter Love, Flint, Mich. On Aug. 1, 1864, President Abraham Lincoln endorsed this letter. "I personally, and heartily concur with Gen. Grant in the within recommendation." AES, *ibid.* Capt. Reuben B. Hatch was next assigned on Feb. 11, 1865, when sent to the Dept. of Miss. *O.R.*, I, xlviii, part 1, 811. See Hatch to Ozias M. Hatch, Feb. 17, 1865, Hatch Papers, IHi.

To Maj. Gen. Henry W. Halleck

(Cipher)   Ft. Monroe July 31/64 8 p. m.
MAJ. GEN. HALLECK WASHINGTON
     The Cavalry going to Washington take all their horses and
equipments with them. They will commence reaching you tomorrow. Will it not be well to land them at Alexandria. I have
given no orders for this.

U. S. GRANT
Lt. Gen

ALS (telegram sent), DNA, RG 107, Telegrams Collected (Unbound); telegram received (on Aug. 1, 1864, 12:55 A.M.), *ibid.*, Telegrams Collected
(Bound). *O.R.*, I, xxxvii, part 2, 527; *ibid.*, I, xl, part 3, 691. On July 30, 10:00
P.M., USG telegraphed to Maj. Gen. Henry W. Halleck. "I have ordered a Division of Cavalry to proceed immediately to Washington." ALS (telegram sent),
OClWHi; telegram received (on July 31, 7:00 A.M.), DNA, RG 107, Telegrams Collected (Bound). Printed as sent at 1:00 P.M. in *O.R.*, I, xxxvii, part 2, •
509; (sent at 10:00 P.M.) *ibid.*, I, xl, part 3, 637. On July 31, 11:30 A.M.,
Halleck telegraphed to USG. "Will the divn of cavalry come armed, mounted and
ready for the field, or must they be remounted & fitted out here?" ALS (telegram
sent), DNA, RG 107, Telegrams Collected (Bound); telegram received, *ibid.*;
ibid., RG 108, Letters Received. *O.R.*, I, xxxvii, part 2, 527; *ibid.*, I, xl, part 3,
690.

To Maj. Gen. Henry W. Halleck

(Cipher)   City Point Va. Aug. 1st *1864*
MAJ. GEN. HALLECK, WASHINGTON.
     I am sending Gen. Sheridan for temporary duty whilst the
enemy is being expelled from the border.
     Unless Gen. Hunter is in the field in person I want Sheridan
put in command of all the troops in the field with instructions to
put himself south of the enemy and follow him to the death. Wherev
ever the enemy goes let out troops go also. Once started up the valley they ought to be followed until we get possession of the Va.
Central rail-road. If Gen. Hunter is in the field give Sheridan di-

rect command of the 6th Corps and Cav.y Division. All the Cavalry
I presume will reach Washington in the course of to-morrow.

U. S. Grant
Lt. Gen.

ALS (telegram sent), CSmH; (facsimile) Grant Cottage, Mount McGregor,
N. Y.; telegram received (sent at 11:30 A.M., received at 10:20 P.M.), DNA,
RG 107, Telegrams Collected (Bound). *O.R.*, I, xxxvii, part 2, 558. On Aug. 2,
1864, 2:30 P.M., Maj. Gen. Henry W. Halleck telegraphed to USG. "Grover's
command of 19th corps landed last night and has encamped on road towards
Rockville. A few companies of Torbet's cavalry are arriving. The transportation of troops in small steamers is slow work, and I presume that several days
will elapse before Sheridan's division is all landed. As it now stands, Wright
commands the 6th corps, Emory the 19th, Crook the troops of Dept of West
Va. and Averill & Duffie the cavalry, Hunter being in general command of
the whole. If Sheridan is not placed in general command, I think he should take
all the cavalry, but not the 6th corps. To make that & the cavalry a single &
separate command, will, in my opinion, be a very bad arrangement. If Sheridan
is placed in general command, I presume Hunter will again ask to be relieved.
Whatever you decide upon I shall endeavour to have done." ALS (telegram sent),
DNA, RG 107, Telegrams Collected (Bound); telegram received, *ibid.*; *ibid.*,
Telegrams Collected (Unbound); (on Aug. 3) *ibid.*, RG 108, Letters Received.
O.R., I, xxxvii, part 2, 573. On Aug. 3, 2:30 P.M., Halleck telegraphed to USG.
"From the best information I can get, Early's force is now about forty thousand,
perhaps a little more. He has about seven or eight thousand cavalry, very well
mounted, the dismounted cavalry about Richmond having been sent up to use
the horses captured on former raid. Genl Sheridan has just arrived. He agrees
with me about his command & prefers the cavalry alone to that and the 6th
corps. How would it do to make a Military Division of Depts of Penn., Washington, Md. & West Va & put Sheridan in Genl command, so far as military operations are concerned? Only about three regts of Sheridan's cavalry have arrived,
& he thinks it will not all be here for several days. It is important to hurry it up,
for if the enemy should make a heavy cavalry raid towards Pittsburg or Harrisburg, it would have so much the start that it could do immense damage before
Sheridan could possibly overtake it. He thinks that for operations in the open
country of Penn. Md & northern Va, cavalry is much better than infantry and
that the cavalry arm can be much more effective there than about Richmond or
south. He therefore suggests that another cavalry Division be sent here, so that
he can press the enemy clear down to the James River. They are now gathering
in their crops in the valley counties & sending them to Richmond by canal &
Rail Road. I concur with Genl. Sheridan and think that much greater damage
can be done to the enemy by destroying his crops & communications north of the
James than on the south." ALS (telegram sent), DNA, RG 107, Telegrams Collected (Bound); telegram received, *ibid.*; *ibid.*, RG 108, Letters Received. *O.R.*,
I, xxxvii, part 2, 582–83. On Aug. 3, midnight, USG telegraphed to Halleck.
"Your dispatch of 2.30 P. M 3rd just received. Make such disposition of Sheridan as you think best" Telegram received (on Aug. 4, 2:00 P.M.), DNA, RG
107, Telegrams Collected (Bound); (garbled) *ibid.*, Telegrams Collected (Unbound); copies, *ibid.*, RG 108, Letters Sent; DLC-USG, V, 45, 59, 67; DLC-

Philip H. Sheridan. *O.R.*, I, xxxvii, part 2, 583. On Aug. 4, 1:00 P.M., USG telegraphed to Halleck. "Another Division of Cavalry has been ordered to Washington from here as suggested by you—The delay in Torbert's Divn has been from transports not returning rapidly." Telegram received (at 1:30 P.M.), DNA, RG 107, Telegrams Collected (Bound); copies, *ibid.*, RG 108, Letters Sent; DLC-USG, V, 45, 59, 67. *O.R.*, I, xlii, part 2, 38. At midnight, Halleck telegraphed to USG. "Had you asked my opinion in regard to Genls Hunter & Sheridan it would have been freely & frankly given; but I must beg to be excused from deciding questions which lawfully & properly belong to your office. I can give no instructions to either till you decide upon their commands. I await your orders, and shall strictly carry them out, whatever they may be." ALS (telegram sent), DNA, RG 107, Telegrams Collected (Bound); telegram received (marked as sent at 10:00 P.M.), *ibid.*; (marked as sent on Aug. 5) *ibid.*, Telegrams Collected (Unbound); (marked as sent at midnight) *ibid.*, RG 108, Letters Received. Printed as sent at 10:00 P.M. in *O.R.*, I, xliii, part 1, 681.

On Aug. 3, 3:30 P.M., Halleck telegraphed to USG. "In order to prevent raids towards Wheeling & Pittsburg, I have directed the roads leading from the cumberland valley through the mountains to be so nearly blocked up that the country people can close them at any time & check the enemy's advance. To do this effectually we want several engineer officers. Please send us some of the large number now about Petersburg." ALS (telegram sent), DNA, RG 107, Telegrams Collected (Bound); telegram received, *ibid.*; *ibid.*, Telegrams Collected (Unbound); *ibid.*, RG 108, Letters Received. *O.R.*, I, xxxvii, part 2, 583.

On Aug. 3, 6:00 P.M., President Abraham Lincoln telegraphed to USG. "I have seen your despatch in which you say 'I want Sheridan put in command of all the troops in the field, with instructions to put himself South of the enemy, and follow him to the death. Wherever the enemy goes, let our troops go also.' This, I think, is exactly right as to how our forces should move. But please look over the despatches you may have receved from here, even since you made that order, and discover if you can, that there is any idea in the head of any one here, of 'putting our army *South* of the enemy' or of pushing following him to the *death*' in any direction. I repeat to you it will not neither be done nor attempted unless you watch it every day, and hour, and force it." ALS (telegram sent), DNA, RG 107, Telegrams Collected (Bound); telegram received (on Aug. 4), *ibid.*, RG 108, Letters Received. *O.R.*, I, xxxvii, part 2, 582. Lincoln, *Works*, VII, 476. On Aug. 4, noon, USG telegraphed to Lincoln. "Your dispatch of 6 to p. m. just received. I will start in two hours for Washington and will spend a day with the Army under Gen. Hunter." ALS (telegram sent), MoSHi; telegram received (at 7:00 P.M.), DLC-Robert T. Lincoln; DNA, RG 107, Telegrams Collected (Bound). *O.R.*, I, xlii, part 2, 38; *ibid.*, I, xliii, part 1, 681.

On July 31, 3:00 P.M., Halleck had telegraphed to USG. "It appears from Genl Averell's reports that while Genl Hunter was collecting his forces at Harper's Ferry to attack the enemy on the south side, the rebel army crossed on the morning of the 29th near Williamsport and moved by Hagerstown into Pennsylvania Their cavalry captured & partly destroyed Chambersburg yesterday. We have no reliable information of the main body, but if it crosed & moved as reported by Averill it would be nearer Baltimore, Harrisburg & York than Hunter was at Harpers Ferry. I consequently directed him to move east of South mountain towards Emmittsburg, and sent last night by railroad to the Monocacy such of Emory's command as had arrived, where he would come immediately under

Hunter's orders. They will probably effect a junction to-night. The weather is so intensely hot that marches will be very slow. It is possible that enemy's infantry is merely covering his cavalry raid. Enemy's cavalry force said to be very large Ours is so weak & poor that it gives us very little information. A very intelligent artificer of 6th corps, captured at the battle of the Monocacy, & who effected his escape in the Shenandoah Valley, has just come in. He says he had several good opportunities to estimate Early's force and actually counted 42 pieces of artillery on their retreat, & thinks that, as compared with our army corps which he has frequently seen on reviews, they numbered at least 30,000. He thinks there were two brigades of Hill's corps with Early. I do not hear that Early recieved any large reenforcements in the valley, but it is said that he greatly increased his cavalry by remounts stolen in Maryland." ALS (telegram sent), DNA, RG 107, Telegrams Collected (Bound); telegram received, *ibid.*; *ibid.*, RG 108, Letters Received. *O.R.*, I, xxxvii, part 2, 527–28; *ibid.*, I, xl, part 3, 690.

To Maj. Gen. Henry W. Halleck

(Cipher)   City Point Va. Aug. 1st *1864*
MAJ. GEN HALLECK, WASHINGTON,

The loss in the disaster of saturday last foots up about 30500 of whom 2450 were killed and 2000 wounded. It was the saddest affair I have witnessed in this war. Such opportunity for carrying fortifications I have never seen and do not expect again to have. The enemy with a line of works five miles long had been reduced by our previous movements to the North side of James River to a force of only three Divisions. Theis line was undermined and blown up carrying a battery and most of a regiment with it. The enemy were taken completely by surprise and did not recover from it for more than an hour. The crater and several hundred yards of the enemys line to the right & left of it, and a short detached line in front of the crater, were occupied by our troops without opposition. Immediately in front of this and not 150 yards off, with clear ground intervening, was the crest of the ridge leading into town and which if carried the enemy would have made no resistance but would have continued a flight already commenced. It was three hours from the time our troops first occupied their enemys works before the enemy took possession of this crest. I am constrained to believe that had instructions been promptly obeyed that Petersburg would have

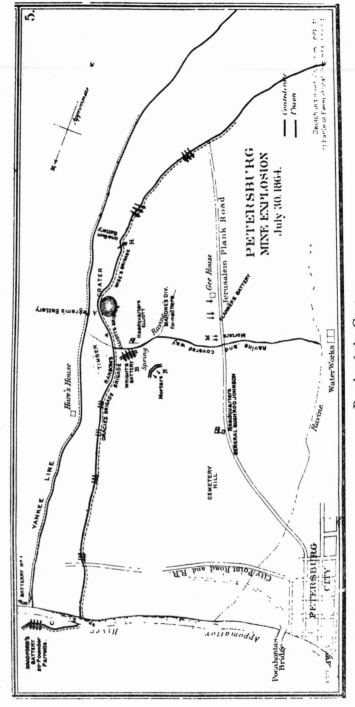

Battle of the Crater
O.R. Atlas, *plate LXXVIII, no. 5*

been carried with all the Artillery and a large number of prisoners without a loss of 300 men. It was in getting back to our lines that the loss was sustained. The enemy attempted to charge our and re-take the line captured from them and were repulsed, with heavy loss, by front by our Artillery. Their loss in killed must be double greater than ours whilst our loss ap in wounded and captured is four times that of the enemy.

U. S. GRANT

Lt. Gn.

ALS (telegram sent), CSmH; telegram received (sent at 2:00 P.M., received at 10:40 P.M.), DNA, RG 107, Telegrams Collected (Bound); (incomplete) *ibid.*, Telegrams Collected (Unbound). *O.R.*, I, xl, part 1, 17–18.

On Aug. 1, 11:20 A.M., and Aug. 2, 8:15 A.M., 1864, Lt. Col. Theodore S. Bowers wrote to Brig. Gen. James H. Wilson. ". . . Gen. Grant and Porter re-turned this morning. Our losses in the late assault will be heavy—and as the evidences of the disgraceful conduct of all concerned develop and thicken, Grant grows sicker at heart. The chances of success were so great—the failure so utter—that all men who understand the whole matter are paralized and pettrified. I suppose an investigation will be ordered to day. . . ." "As the reports of Saturday's operations come in, and the extent of the disaster is developed, the feeling of gloom and despondency that the failure created, deepens and thickens until it threatens to paralize every one. Gen. Meade was to see Grant yesterday. He feels very bad, and insists on a full investigation of the whole affair. . . . I am so sick at heart, that I could make no comments were they even necessary. The Army of the Potomac attach all the blame to the 9th Corps and especially to Burnside. . . . Grant is unwell this morning—so unwell that he has not yet left his bed. His illness is real, and I think resulted from his grief at the disaster of Saturday. . . ." ALS, Wy-Ar. On Aug. 9, Capt. George K. Leet wrote to Lt. Col. William R. Rowley. "The General looks finely and seemed to be in fine spirits notwithstand-ing the disappointment he must have felt at our late failure at Petersburg. Bowers in a letter speaking of the Petersburg affair says 'The plan, the strategy of the movement was the finest I ever saw; the execution of it the most disgrace-ful.' Again—'One good Division would have taken Petersburg: indeed, we had Petersburg and it was only necessary to take possession. There were but three Divisions of rebels there and they were running. We had four Corps in position, but our men refused to move in for fear they *might* be shot at Hence they crowded the Crater full to suffocation, staid there and were captured and killed. Our loss is 4400. My faith in the Army of the Potomac is gone, gone.' Parker says 'I have had the biggest kind of disgust on and dare not express myself on the Potomac Army.' Hudson thinks 'The Army of the Potomac wont do to tie to.' The Staff generally after our repulse on the 31st ulto. seemed to feel rather gloomy and it is not to be wondired at that they did feel so, for every thing pre-vious to the movement seemed to indicate that we would win a brilliant victory. There were screws loose somewhere and the machine would not work . . ." ALS, Rowley Papers, IHi.

On Aug. 2, 9:30 P.M., USG telegraphed to Maj. Gen. Henry W. Halleck.

"I have the honor to request that the President may direct a Court of Inquiry to assemble without delay at such place as the presiding officer may appoint to examine into and report upon the facts and circumstances attending the unsuccessful assault on the enemys position in front of Petersburg on the morning of July 30th 1864, and also to report whether in their judgement any officer or officers are answerable for the failure of the troops to carry into successful execution the orders issued for the occasion and I would suggest the following detail Maj. Gen W. S. Hancock—Br Genl. R B Ayers—Br Genl. N. A. Miles, Col E Shriver Inspr Genl & Recorder" Telegram received (on Aug. 3), DNA, RG 107, Telegrams Collected (Bound); copies, *ibid.*, RG 108, Letters Sent; DLC-USG, V, 45, 59, 67. *O.R.*, I, xl, part 1, 18. On Aug. 3, 4:15 P.M., Col. Edward D. Townsend telegraphed to USG stating that Special Orders No. 258 appointed the court of inquiry as requested. ALS (telegram sent), DNA, RG 107, Telegrams Collected (Unbound); telegram received, *ibid.*; *ibid.*, RG 108, Letters Received. See *O.R.*, I, xl, part 1, 42–43, 171–72. Proceedings of the court of inquiry are *ibid.*, pp. 43–170. See Testimony, Aug. 30, 1864.

On Aug. 3, Maj. Gen. George G. Meade wrote to Brig. Gen. John A. Rawlins requesting that Maj. Gen. Ambrose E. Burnside be removed from duty because he failed to inform Meade of developments on July 30; Meade enclosed charges and specifications. LS, DNA, RG 108, Letters Received; ADf, Meade Papers, PHi. *O.R.*, I, xl, part 1, 172–76.

On Aug. 4, Maj. Gen. Benjamin F. Butler wrote to USG at length urging a court of inquiry to examine the events of July 30 in order to determine whether newspaper accounts blaming the Negro troops for the disaster were justified. *Ibid.*, I, xlii, part 2, 48–49.

On Aug. 4, Burnside telegraphed to USG. "I have permission to visit your Hd Qrs today at City point? Have you any objections to my doing so" Telegram received, DNA, RG 107, Telegrams Collected (Unbound). On the same day, USG telegraphed to Burnside. "I shall be at Home all day—Certainly no objection to your visiting me here" Telegram received, *ibid. O.R.*, I, xlii, part 2, 43. An undated telegram from Burnside to USG may have been sent about this time. "I have permission from Genl Meade to visit City Point this morning will you be at your quarters till 11 o'clock" Telegram received, DNA, RG 107, Telegrams Collected (Unbound). See *O.R.*, I, xlii, part 2, 80, 91, 92; telegram to Maj. Gen. George G. Meade, Aug. 13, 1864.

On Aug. 22, USG wrote to Halleck. "Enclosed herewith I send you reports of the operations of the 30th Ultimo against Petersburg. As the whole matter of our deplorable failure on that occasion has been submitted to investigation I will not make any report myself until after the report of the Court of Inquiry is submitted, and then will probably confine myself to remarks on their proceedings." ALS, DNA, RG 94, War Records Office, Union Battle Reports. *O.R.*, I, xl, part 1, 163. On Aug. 16, Meade had written to Bowers reporting the battle of the Crater. Copies, DNA, RG 393, Army of the Potomac, Letters Sent; Meade Papers, PHi. *O.R.*, I, xl, part 1, 163–66. The other reports transmitted by USG on Aug. 22 are listed in DLC-USG, V, 48.

Site of the battle of the Crater as it appeared in 1865.
Photograph attributed to Mathew B. Brady. *Courtesy National Archives.*
See telegram to Maj. Gen. Henry W. Halleck, Aug. 1, 1864.

Wharf at City Point shortly after the explosion of an ordnance boat. Photograph attributed to Mathew B. Brady. *Courtesy National Archives.* See telegram to Maj. Gen. Henry W. Halleck, Aug. 9, 1864.

To Maj. Gen. Benjamin F. Butler

By Telegraph from City Point
Dated Aug 1st 1864.

To Maj Gen Butler

Have you seen any Rebel Papers of later date than 28th   I would like to hear what they have to say about the advance of shermans Cavalry   The last news I have heard from sherman brought his operations down to Friday[1] night at which time all moved well His Cavalry had been sucsessful in Cutting the Atlanta & main Road leaving Atlanta now without an railroad, or Telegraph with the Balance of the world.

U S Grant
Lt Gen

Telegram received (incomplete), DLC-Benjamin F. Butler; DLC-USG, V, 45, 59, 67; DNA, RG 108, Letters Sent. Two undated telegrams from Maj. Gen. Benjamin F. Butler to USG may have been sent in reply. "I have no late Richmond papers   I will Send out on picket line and try and get one"   Telegram received, *ibid.*, RG 107, Telegrams Collected (Unbound). "I get no Richmond papers of to day   I have Just got those of yesterday a second time in which there are no news"   ALS (telegram sent), *ibid.*

On Aug. 1, 1864, Col. John W. Shaffer, chief of staff for Butler, telegraphed to Lt. Col. Theodore S. Bowers. "Signal Officers at Spring Hill and at Tower report that they See a Column of three to Four thousand Cavalry pass junction going towards Petersburg also baggae & forage train of sixty wagons"   ALS (telegram sent), *ibid.* Printed as sent at 10:30 A.M. in *O.R.*, I, xlii, part 2, 13.

On Aug. 2, Butler telegraphed to USG transmitting a telegram from Brig. Gen. Robert S. Foster to Shaffer. "I forward to Gen Birney three Richmond papers of August 1st to be forwarded to you. The following is an extract from an article in the examiner. The assignment of Gen Joseph E. Johnston to Command of ~~yo~~ our Armies in northern Virginia & the removal to that quarter of a large body of his veteran troops was not known in this city beyond the initiated of the War office elect"   Telegram received, DNA, RG 108, Letters Received. On the same day, Butler transmitted to USG a signal message of 11:35 A.M. "Five (5) cars, loaded with troops, just passed the Junction towards Petersburg." Telegram received, *ibid.*, RG 107, Telegrams Collected (Unbound). *O.R.*, I, xlii, part 2, 22.

On Aug. 3, 10:15 P.M., Butler telegraphed to USG. "A deserter just in from the fourth Alabama reg't. of Law's brigade of Field's Div. reports that Div. with three reg'ts of Wise's old brigade at New Market. Wilcox Div of Hill's corps is between them and Chapin's farm. Kershaw's Div. he reports to have left New Market on Monday for Petersburg. Has not heard of their going south"   Telegram received, DNA, RG 107, Telegrams Collected (Unbound); *ibid.*, RG 108,

Letters Received; *ibid.*, RG 393, Army of the Potomac, Miscellaneous Letters Received. Printed as sent at 10:20 P.M. in *O.R.*, I, xlii, part 2, 34.

1. On Aug. 1, Bowers telegraphed to Butler, Maj. Gen. George G. Meade, and all corps commanders a telegram of July 29, 8:00 P.M., from Maj. Gen. William T. Sherman to Maj. Gen. Henry W. Halleck. "The result of the attack of yesterday chiefly on the 15th Corps is thus reported by Gen Howard 'We have counted 642 rebel dead and there are still others in front of our lines. It is fair to presume that their wounded are five or six times that of the dead. Over 100 are in hand and others being gathered up in the wood' Howard estimates the enemys loss at 5000 and our loss at less than 600. Gen W. H. S Walker was killed on the 22d & it is now reported by prisoners that Wheeler was killed yesterday. Stephen Lee Loring and Stewart severely wounded yesterday. We are so near the enemys line that their artillery prevents our attacking the lines so as to take full advantage of battle. They are gathering into the city wounded and more remote dead. The parapets of Atlanta present a well filled line whenever we approach it. Thomas is making today a strong reconnoissance in force towards east point & Schofield on the left Our Cavalry has now been out three days and must have done its work about Griffin" Telegram received, Ord Papers, CU-B; DNA, RG 393, Army of the Potomac, Telegrams Received; copy, *ibid.*, 10th Army Corps, Miscellaneous Telegrams Received. *O.R.*, I, xxxviii, part 5, 289.

To Maj. Gen. George G. Meade

City Point, Aug 1st 1864.

MAJ GEN MEADE

I see the Artillery belonging to the Cavalry Division is being shipped first My instructions were that the Cavalry should be got off first.

The enemy's Cavalry is now in Pa. and it is important, that we should get a mounted force after them. If Sheridan is able for duty I wish you would send him to report to me in person. I shall send him to Command all the forces ~~after~~ against Early.

U S GRANT
Lieut Genl.

Telegram, copies, DLC-USG, V, 45, 59, 67; DNA, RG 108, Letters Sent. *O.R.*, I, xxxvii, part 2, 559. On Aug. 1, 1864, 10:15 A.M., Maj. Gen. George G. Meade telegraphed to USG. "Your instructions were well understood and were as distinctly conveyed to Genl. Sheridan—viz that the artillery & train of the Division selected to go to Washington should follow the troops—Copy of instructions sent —Genl. Sheridan has been directed to report in person to you & will undoubtedly be able to give some satisfactory explanation of the variation from the orders given. If you will be at your quarters I desire to visit them this a m—" ALS (telegram sent), DNA, RG 94, War Records Office, Army of the Potomac; telegram received, *ibid.*, RG 108, Letters Received. *O.R.*, I, xxxvii, part 2, 559. The enclosure is *ibid.*

On Aug. 2, Lt. Col. Theodore S. Bowers issued Special Orders No. 68. "Maj. Gen. P. H. Sheridan; Commd'g Cavalry Corps Army of the Potomac, is hereby temporarily relieved from duty in the Armies operating against Richmond and will report in person without delay to Maj Gen H. W. Halleck Chief of Staff of the Army, Washington D C. for orders. His Staff will accompany him." Copies, DLC-USG, V, 57, 62, 67. *O.R.*, I, xxxvii, part 2, 572.

To Maj. Gen. George G. Meade

(Cipher)   City Point August 1st 1864
Maj. Gen Meade

Have you any estimate of our losses in the miserable failure of Saturday? I think there will have to be an investigation of the matter. So fair an opportunity will probably never occur again for carrying fortifications. Preparations were good, orders ample and everything, so far as I could see, subsequent to the explosion of the mine shews that all most without loss the crest beyond the mine could have been carried. This would have given us Petersburg with all its artillery and a large part of the garrison beyond doubt.

An intercepted dispatch states that the enemy recaptured their line with Gen Bartlett[1] & Staff, Seventy-five commissioned officers & nine hundred rank & file and recaptured five hundred of their men.

U. S. Grant
Lt. Gn.

ALS (telegram sent), CSmH; telegram received (sent at 9:30 A.M., received at 11:40 A.M.), DNA, RG 94, War Records Office, Army of the Potomac. *O.R.*, I, xl, part 1, 134.

On Aug. 1, 1864, 1:20 P.M., Brig. Gen. Seth Williams telegraphed to USG. "General Meade left here a few moments ago for General Warren's Head-Quarters. I have sent to him your despatch of 1.10 P. M. It will doubtless overtake him at General Hancocks Head Quarters now at the Jones House on the Jerusalem Plank road." ALS (telegram sent), DNA, RG 94, War Records Office, Army of the Potomac; copy, *ibid.*, RG 393, Army of the Potomac, Telegrams Sent. Williams may refer to a different telegram from USG.

At 10:00 A.M., Maj. Gen. George G. Meade had telegraphed to USG. "In reply to my letter to Genl. Lee, I received this morning about 6. o'clock a letter from Genl. Bearegard consenting to a truce from 5 to 9 for the purposes of burying the dead & removing the wounded—The firing has been resumed, but no report yet received from Genl. Burnside as to the numbers on the field—Genl. Burnside reports his losses as amounting to 2000 killed & wounded & 2500 missing—on being called on to explain the occurrence of such a large number of missing, the accompanying despatch was received—As this dated at 9.10 P M July 31. was the first report of any kind made to me since leaving Burnsides quarters with yourself, the justice of attributing this apparently disgraceful flight, to the order authorising the withdrawal, can be judged of.—" ALS (telegram sent), *ibid.*, RG 94, War Records Office, Army of the Potomac; telegram received, *ibid.*, RG 108, Letters Received. *O.R.*, I, xlii, part 2, 3. The enclosure is *ibid.*, I, xl, part 1, 146.

On Aug. 3, 10:00 A.M. and 4:00 P.M., Meade telegraphed to USG. "Comparative quiet reigned along the lines of this army yesterday.—During the night there was considerable musketry firing on the 9. corps front—Yesterday Maj. Genl. Warren reported unmistakable evidences of the enemy mining in his front near the plank road—Genl. W. is countermining & preparing an interior line at the point threatened. About midnight despathes recieved from Maj. Gen. Ord indicating the expectation a mine would be sprung in his front, this army was under arms for an hour before & after daylight this morning. The shorter & defensive line located by the engineers is being constructed.—" ALS (telegram sent), DNA, RG 94, War Records Office, Army of the Potomac; telegram received, *ibid.*, RG 108, Letters Received. *O.R.*, I, xlii, part 2, 26. "A colored scout just in reports that Lee's division of cavalry on Sunday last came from the North side of the Appomatox to Dinwiddie C. H; and on Monday marched back North of Petersburgh—" ALS (telegram sent), DNA, RG 94, War Records Office, Army of the Potomac; copies, *ibid.*, RG 393, Army of the Potomac, Letters Sent; Meade Papers, PHi. *O.R.*, I, xlii, part 2, 26. On the same day, USG telegraphed to Meade. "Have you had any deserters for the last few days fixing Longstreets Corps." Copies, DLC-USG, V, 45, 59, 67; DNA, RG 108, Letters Sent. At 10:00 P.M., Meade telegraphed to USG. "Deserters report Kershaw's Divn as having gone south on monday night—Pickett & Field are reported by Butler as in his front   this accounts for Longstreet. Bushrod Johnston & Hoke which are is all of Beauregard are in our front—Heth & Mahone of Hill are also known to be in our front.—Wilcox is supposed to be north of the Appomatox but not certain. We have had no deserters from Wilcox, but those from Mahone same corps (Hill's) say he has not left.—Fitz Lee's division of cavalry is reported to have gone north of the Appomatox on Day before ysterday—This is our latest information—" ALS (telegram sent), *ibid.*, RG 94, War Records Office, Army of the Potomac; telegram received, *ibid.*, RG 108, Letters Received. *O.R.*, I, xlii, part 2, 26.

1. William F. Bartlett, born in Haverhill, Mass., in 1840, left the junior class at Harvard College in April, 1861, to enlist as a private. As capt., 20th Mass., he was wounded at Yorktown and his leg amputated, but he was appointed col., 49th Mass., later in 1862. Appointed brig. gen. as of June 20, 1864, he was captured at the battle of the Crater on July 30 while commanding the 1st Brigade, 1st Div., 9th Army Corps.

To Julia Dent Grant

City Point, Va, Aug 1st *1864.*

DEAR JULIA,

Since writing to you before about going to Princeton N. J. I have made further enquiries. I find they have as fine schools there as is to be found in the country. It is one of the nicest places to live, the best society, and near to every place in the East. It is close to Long Branch, a favorite Summer resort, near to New York, near Philadelphia, within seven or eight hours of Washington City and within a day, nearly, of here. If you leave for me to decide I say emphatically you will go to Princeton. As soon as I have your say in this matter I will send Col. Porter of my Staff (he was sent to Princeton to school before he went to West Point) to secure you a house. I will leave it to you whether to keep house or board. In my opinion it will be better, if you go there, to keep house. By having a good trusty house keeper you can all ways leave home for a few days and whilst in the East I can always get home, if not in a few hours, in a day at furthest. You would bring Little Rebel with you for the children to ride and I would send you Egyt for you to drive. I know with these, and Jess to *escort*, you would be happy. I could not send you the black pony Jeff Davis. He has got to be one of the most beautiful horses you ever saw, very fleet, and he always was just as easy as a rocking chair. I have been offered $1.000 for him and $1.200 for the horse given to me by Mr. Grant of Cincinnati.[1] Of course I could not sell them but it shows how fine they are regarded.

Love to all and kisses for you and the children. I write, as usual, after every body else is in bed, and with full twelve hours constant wrighting to do, which I must do, before me. Tell Dr Barrett I rec'd his letter this evening. He must not be disappointed if I do not answer him.

ULYS.

ALS, DLC-USG.

1. In early 1864, S. S. Grant gave USG the horse named Cincinnati on condition that the horse would never fall into the hands of anyone who would mistreat him. Frederick Dent Grant in Francis Trevelyan Miller, ed., *Photographic History of the Civil War* (New York, 1911), IV, 296, 298. A photograph of USG and Cincinnati is *ibid.*, X, 301.

To Maj. Gen. Benjamin F. Butler

By Telegraph from City Point
Dated Aug 4th *1864.*

To MAJ GEN BUTLER,

I am compelled to send a second division of cavy to Washn.— this—will leave the cavalry force too weak to protect the flank of the army without the assistance of Kautz. Please order Kautz to report accordingly.[1] Only intending to be absent for a few days, I leave my adj't Genl, & part of HdQrs—but being senior you necessarily would command in any immergency. Please communicate with me by telegraph if anything occurs when you wish my orders.[2]

U. S. GRANT
Lt Genl

Telegram received (at 12:30 P.M.), DLC-Benjamin F. Butler; DLC-USG, V, 45, 59, 67; DNA, RG 108, Letters Sent. *O.R.*, I, xlii, part 2, 48.

On Aug. 4, 1864, Capt. Ely S. Parker wrote to Maj. Gen. Benjamin F. Butler. "Our transports were fired into yesterday at Wilcox's Landing, and to-day at Harrison's Landing. Captain Clitz, commanding gun-boat Osceola, reports that he to-day communicated with females, white, and a contraband at Wilcox's Landing, who agree in saying that an infantry force of about 2,000, and field battery of fifteen guns are encamped from two to three miles from that landing. They say it is Early's troops, but this must be a mistake. I send this for your information." *Ibid.*, pp. 49–50.

On Aug. 5, 9:00 A.M., Butler telegraphed to USG. "I sent Graham up and burnt Seddens house in retaliation for burnig the house of Mr Blair. He went within a mile and a half of Fredericksburgh and saw no enemy   All quiet" ALS (telegram sent), DNA, RG 107, Telegrams Collected (Unbound); telegram received (at 6:15 P.M.), *ibid.*, Telegrams Collected (Bound). *O.R.*, I, xlii, part 2, 62.

On the same day, Parker telegraphed to Brig. Gen. Seth Williams. "If not improper to communicate, I would like to know the cause of the heavy firing this evening, so that it may be communicated to Gen Grant." ALS (telegram sent), DNA, RG 107, Telegrams Collected (Unbound); telegram received, *ibid.*, RG 94, War Records Office, Army of the Potomac. *O.R.*, I, xlii, part 2, 52. At 8:20

P.M., Williams telegraphed to Parker. "The following despatch from General Ord explains the firing you heard this evening. All is ~~qu~~quiet now." ALS (telegram sent), DNA, RG 94, War Records Office, Army of the Potomac; copy, *ibid.*, RG 393, Army of the Potomac, Letters Sent. *O.R.*, I, xlii, part 2, 52. Williams transmitted a telegram (received 8:10 P.M.), from Maj. Gen. Edward O. C. Ord to Maj. Gen. Andrew A. Humphreys. "There was a small mine exploded about 40 yards in front of my left & did not damage my works at all. There was no assault—Loss so far appears trifling except Col Steadman wounded dangerously I have ordered all my reserves back—My lines [inta]ct" Telegram received, DNA, RG 108, Letters Received. *O.R.*, I, xlii, part 2, 64. On the same day, Parker telegraphed to USG. "Rebels exploded a small mine this evening ~~in~~ about 40 yards in front of Ord's left. No damage done to our works. No assault. Loss reported trifling Col. Stedman dangerously wounded. Our lines intact." Telegram received (on Aug. 6, 8:10 A.M.), DNA, RG 107, Telegrams Collected (Bound). *O.R.*, I, xlii, part 2, 52. On Aug. 6, 7:30 A.M., Butler telegraphed to Secretary of War Edwin M. Stanton and USG. "At six thirty (6 30) P. M yesterday the enemy sprang a small mine on front of the eighteenth (18) Corps near Petersburg about forty (40) yards in front of our works—They did not make an assault—A brisk artillery fire was opened along the whole of our line the casualties small—I regret to say that Col Steadman eleventh (11) Conn is dangerously wounded—Beg leave to renew my application that he receive promotion by brevet for gallant & meritorious services—Our lines are ~~ent~~ intact & all is quiet in front of Petersbu[rg] The enemy opened upon us from the Howlett house battery no loss—Col Steadman is dead" ALS (telegram sent), DNA, RG 107, Telegrams Collected (Unbound); telegram received (at 10:15 P.M.), *ibid.*, Telegrams Collected (Bound); *ibid.*, RG 108, Letters Received. Printed as sent at 8:30 A.M. to Stanton in *O.R.*, I, xlii, part 2, 68–69. On the same day, 9:30 P.M., Butler telegraphed to USG. "All has been quiet today. Regular shelling going on before Petersburg. At noon a Thousand Cavalry & Eighty (80) Wagons passed Junction towards Richmond. Richmond papers of this morning. No news save that a landing had been made on Dauphins Island near Mobile & an attack began on Fort Gaines August Third (3rd). Macon confederate late atlanta appeal, says the country will be glad to learn that our army has been reinforced by many thousand veteran troops that all thoughts of giving up ~~at~~Atlanta have vanished" ALS (telegram sent), DNA, RG 107, Telegrams Collected (Unbound); telegram received (on Aug. 7, 6:15 A.M.), *ibid.*, Telegrams Collected (Bound); *ibid.*, RG 108, Letters Received. *O.R.*, I, xlii, part 2, 69.

   On Aug. 7, 1:00 P.M., Meade telegraphed to USG. "The following forwarded for what it is worth." Telegrams received (2—at 9:00 P.M.), DNA, RG 107, Telegrams Collected (Bound); (2) *ibid.*, Telegrams Collected (Unbound). *O.R.*, I, xlii, part 2, 75. The enclosure, with information from three citizens of Petersburg, is *ibid.*, pp. 75–76. On the same day, 10:30 P.M., Butler telegraphed to USG. "All quiet in the lines of our Armies since last advices Enemy moved to Richmond 10 passenger and 3 freight cars filled with troops They did not cross at Drurys bluff. Did not stop in front of us or they would not have been put on cars. 14 Waggons and a drove of Beeves Crossed this Eve at Chaffins Bluff. Kershaws Division is in my front between the Appomattox and James— From the accounts in Rebel papers to Aug 4th I do not credit Heralds report of Farraguts success Would it were true." ALS (telegram sent), DNA, RG 107,

Telegrams Collected (Unbound); telegram received (on Aug. 8, 8:00 A.M.), *ibid.*, Telegrams Collected (Bound). *O.R.*, I, xlii, part 2, 82.

On Aug. 8, 9:00 P.M., Meade telegraphed to USG. "The above just recieved forwarded as the latest information.—" ALS (telegram sent), DNA, RG 94, War Records Office, Army of the Potomac; telegram received, *ibid.*, RG 108, Letters Received. *O.R.*, I, xlii, part 2, 85. The enclosed report of information from deserters is *ibid.*, pp. 84–85.

1. On Aug. 4, USG telegraphed to Maj. Gen. George G. Meade. "Send another Division of Cavalry to Washington at once   I will instruct the Quarter Master to provide transportation as rapidly as it can be got together—I will instruct Gen Butler to send Kautz Cavalry to report to your Cavalry Commander whilst so much of yours is absent"   Telegram received (at 1:15 P.M.), DNA, RG 94, War Records Office, Army of the Potomac; copies, *ibid.*, RG 108, Letters Sent; DLC-USG, V, 45, 59, 67; (2) Meade Papers, PHi. Printed as sent at 12:15 P.M. in *O.R.*, I, xlii, part 2, 39. On the same day, Humphreys telegraphed to Brig. Gen. John A. Rawlins information received from deserters. Telegram received, DNA, RG 108, Letters Received. *O.R.*, I, xlii, part 2, 39. On Aug. 5, 10:00 A.M., Brig. Gen. James H. Wilson telegraphed to Lt. Col. Theodore S. Bowers. "My Divn. is ordered to Washington—please have all the men belonging to it now there, collected and those dismounted, ~~at once~~ supplied with horses at once. I would also like the 8th Ill. cavalry reassigned to me and be put in readiness to join the comd. as soon as it gets there." ALS (telegram sent), DNA, RG 107, Telegrams Collected (Unbound); telegram received, *ibid.*; *ibid.*, Telegrams Collected (Bound). *O.R.*, I, xlii, part 2, 61.

2. On Aug. 4, noon, USG telegraphed to Butler, sending a copy to Meade. "I find it necessary for me to go to Washington for a day or two to give direction to affairs there. In my absence remain on the defensive notifying Gen. Meade that if attacked he is authorized to call in such of your troops as are South of the Appomattox. Only expecting to be absent three days I will not ~~publish any order~~ relinquishing command. ~~and would like if possible that my absence was not generally known.~~" ALS (telegram sent), CSmH; telegram received, DLC-Benjamin F. Butler; DNA, RG 94, War Records Office, Army of the Potomac; *ibid.*, RG 107, Telegrams Collected (Unbound). *O.R.*, I, xlii, part 2, 48.

To Maj. Gen. Benjamin F. Butler

By Telegraph from City Pt.
Dated Aug 4 *1864.*

To MAJ GEN BUTLER,

I think it will be advisable to have all the surplus pontoon material in the hands of Gen Benham,   When any bridging is required he can be called on for it & having it together, it can be kept in quantity sufficient for any immergency,   Divided neither your Engrs, nor Gen Benham, will have enough to throw a bridge over the James or Appomattox. I do not order this if you see any good reason for keeping it as it is.

U. S. GRANT
Lt Genl

Telegram received, DLC-Benjamin F. Butler; copies, DLC-USG, V, 45, 59, 67; DNA, RG 108, Letters Sent.

To Maj. Gen. Benjamin F. Butler

————

City Point Va. Aug. 4th *1864*

MAJ. GEN. B. F. BUTLER,
COMD.G DEPT. OF VA. & N. C.
GENERAL,

Lt. King's communication in relation to closing the port of Wilmington with torpedoes is received. I called Admiral Lee's attention to this matter some time ago thinking myself it was perfectly feasable. The Admiral however thought differently giving as a reason for his views that both channels were commanded by the enemy's guns. All the torpedoes we would plant during the night the enemy would take up during the day. I certainly however would like the experiment tried and if you will arrange with Adm.l Lee for his cooperation what you may do will have my approval.

I am Gen. very respectfully
your obt. svt.
U. S. GRANT
Lt. Gn.

ALS, DLC-Benjamin F. Butler. *O.R.*, I, xlii, part 2, 48. See *ibid.*, p. 210; *O.R.* (Navy), I, x, 145.

To Maj. Gen. Henry W. Halleck

Monocacy Va 8 p m
Aug 5th 1864

MAJ GEN HALLECK

CHF OF STAFF—

I have ordered the concentration of all available forces under Genl Hunter to be concentrated at once at Harpers Ferry and to follow the enemy promptly whereever he may go—

If it is found, as I suspect, nothing but a small raiding force is north of the Potomac, then he is to move up the valley after the main force, detaching sufficient to attend to that left north of him by the enemy. Unless otherwise ordered send all the cavalry yet to arrive as fast as Brigades are complete by Leesburg & the south-side of the Potomac to reach the main army

U. S. GRANT
Lt Gen

Telegram received (at 11:00 P.M.), DNA, RG 107, Telegrams Collected (Bound); copies, *ibid.*, RG 108, Letters Sent; DLC-USG, V, 45, 59, 67. *O.R.*, I, xliii, part 1, 695. On Aug. 5, 1864, 11:30 P.M., USG, Monocacy, Md., telegraphed to Maj. Gen. Henry W. Halleck. "Send Sheridan by morning train to Harpers Ferry calling here on his way to see if Gen Hunter has left. Give him orders to take general command of all the troops in the field within the Division. Hunter will turn over to him my letter of instructions" Telegram received (on Aug. 6, 12:40 A.M.), DNA, RG 107, Telegrams Collected (Bound); copies, *ibid.*, RG 108, Letters Sent; DLC-USG, V, 45, 59, 67. *O.R.*, I, xliii, part 1, 695. See following letter.

On Aug. 5, Secretary of War Edwin M. Stanton wrote to President Abraham Lincoln. "General Grant is at the Department. Shall he call to see you or will you see him here" ALS, DLC-Edwin M. Stanton. At 10:00 A.M., Lt. Col. Cyrus B. Comstock, "Gen. Grants H. Q. Winder Building," telegraphed to "Maj. Gen. Hunter or Maj. Gen Wright Near Monocacy." "Gen. Grant will leave here for Gen. Hunters Hd Qrs about 3 P. M. by rail road. Will you inform me to what point he should come for that purpose and furnish transportation for five from that point to ~~your~~ Gen Hunters Hd. Qrs." ALS (telegram sent), DNA, RG 107, Telegrams Collected (Bound). On Aug. 8, Maj. Gen. Lewis Wallace wrote, probably to his wife. ". . . General Grant dined with me at the Eutaw House, Saturday last. He was unusually kind—even demonstrative to me. He spoke of the Battle of Monocacy, and was Sure we killed and wounded three times as many rebels as our own losses. He had just come from the battlefield. Before leaving, he gave me a warm invitation to visit him at City Point, which I am

Sure to do as Soon as the Shenandoah Valley grows more quiet. . . ." Copy, Wallace Papers, InHi.

Between USG's telegrams to Halleck of 8:00 P.M. and 11:30 P.M., Maj. Gen. David Hunter asked to be relieved because Halleck so distrusted his abilities that another gen. might be more successful. *Memoirs*, II, 320. On Aug. 6, USG telegraphed to Halleck "In relation to bravery and success of Genl. Hunter." DNA, RG 108, Register of Telegrams Received.

On the same day, 10:00 A.M., USG telegraphed to Halleck. "From the dispatches received by Genl Hunter it appears to me evident there is no great force of the enemy, likely not more than two thousand men, North of the Potomac and they engaged in gathering & moving off stock and produce. I believe they will be gone before our troops can get near them" Telegram received, *ibid*., RG 107, Telegrams Collected (Bound). *O.R.*, I, xliii, part 1, 708. At 11:30 A.M., Halleck telegraphed to USG. "One brigade of Torbert's Division of cavalry left last night and another will start this morning for Harpers Ferry via Monocacy. As your telegram of last night says 'send all cavalry *yet to arrive* &c.' I presume you allude to the Division expected from city Point. Do you want an order issued making a Military Division of the four Depts., or shall it await your return here." ALS (telegram sent), DNA, RG 107, Telegrams Collected (Bound); telegram received, *ibid*. *O.R.*, I, xliii, part 1, 708.

On Aug. 8, 12:15 P.M., USG, Fort Monroe, telegraphed to Halleck. "To supply the place of troops going out of service in the Middle Division, the 19th Corps or so much of it as may be necessary can be taken, after Early's forces are expelled. This will obviate the necessity of sending troops from City Point, unless a whole corps is required." Copy (telegram sent), DNA, RG 107, Telegrams Collected (Unbound); telegram received (sent at 1:00 P.M., received at 8:00 P.M.), *ibid*., Telegrams Collected (Bound). Printed as sent at noon in *O.R.*, I, xliii, part 1, 725.

To Maj. Gen. David Hunter

Monocacy Bridge Md
Aug 5th 1864. 8. P. M.

MAJ. GEN HUNTER
COMD'G DEPT WEST VA.

Concentrate all your available forces without delay in the vicinity of Harpers Ferry, leaving only such railroad guards and garrisons for public property as may be necessary. Use in this concentration the RailRoad if by so doing time can be saved. From Harpers Ferry, if it is found that the enemy has moved North of the Potomac in large force, push North following and attacking him wherever found, following him if driven South of the Potomac as long as it is safe to do so. If it is ascertained that the enemy has but a small force North of the Potomac, then push South with the main force, detaching under a competent Commander a sufficient force to look after the raiders and drive them to their homes. In detailing such a force the Brigade of Cavalry now in route from Washington via Rockville may be taken into account.

There are now on the way to join you three other Brigades of the best of Cavalry, numbering at least 5000 men and horses. These will be instructed in the absence of further orders to join you by the South side of the Potomac   One Brigade will probably start to morrow. In pushing up the Shendandoah Valley as it is expected you will have to go first, or last, it is desirable that nothing should be left to invite the enemy to return. Take all provisions, forage and Stock wanted for the use of your Command. Such as cannot, be consumed destroy. It is not desirable that the buildings should be destroyed, they should rather be protected, but the people should be informed that so long as an Army can subsist among them, recurrences of these raids must be expected, and we are determined to stop them at all hazards.

Bear in mind, the object, is to drive the enemy South, and to do this you want to keep him always in sight. Be guided in your course by the course he takes.

Make your own arrangements for supplies of all kinds, giving regular vouchers for such as will be taken from loyal citizens in the Country through which you march.

U. S. GRANT
Lt. Gen.

Copies, DLC-USG, V, 45, 59, 67; DNA, RG 108, Letters Sent. *O.R.*, I, xxxiv, part 1, 26; *ibid.*, I, xxxvi, part 1, 29–30; *ibid.*, I, xxxviii, part 1, 18–19; xliii, part 1, 57–58, 697–98.

To Julia Dent Grant

Washington D. C.
Aug. 5th 1864,

DEAR JULIA,

I received your dispatch after I had got aboard the steamer yesterday to come here. Col. Porter goes at once to Princeton to try to rent you a furnished house. If he succeeds in getting what you want you had better go there at once. I will let you know as soon as he returns.

I have come up here for a day to visit our Army at Harpers Ferry as see what is required to drive the enemy out of Maryland and Northern Va. I shall return here to-morrow night and go immediately back to City Point. I am in most excellent health still. Staff are generally well.

If you go to Princeton get Mr. Ford to ship everything you want to take, including Little Rebel, so that you will have no bother. You have never said whether Lewis bought back the house and lot? I hope he does not want it but still let him have it if he does.—I have but little over an hour in which to get dinner and reach the rail-road depot. If I can get time within this to draw a months pay I will send you a $1,000. Since you left here I have sent one month's pay $1100, and $500 besides to Chicago and have enough on hand to last me a month yet.

Love and kisses for you and the children.

ULYS.

ALS, DLC-USG.

To Maj. Gen. Philip H. Sheridan

(Cipher)   ~~War Department~~
Washington City, Aug. 7th *1864*

MAJ. GEN. SHERIDAN,

Do not hesitate to give commands to officers in whom you repose confidence without regard to claims of others on account of rank. If you deem Torbert the best man to command the Cavalry place him in command and give Averill some other command or relieve from the expedition and order him to report to Gen. Hunter. What we want is prompt and active movements after the enemy in accordance with the instructions you already have. I ~~know am~~ ~~perfectly~~ feel every confidence that you will do for the very best and will leave you as far as possible to act on your own judgement and not embarass you with orders and instructions.

U. S. GRANT

Lt. Gn.

ALS (telegram sent), CSmH; copies (sent at noon), DLC-USG, V, 45, 59, 67; DNA, RG 108, Letters Sent. *O.R.*, I, xliii, part 1, 719. On Aug. 7, 1864, 12:15 P.M., USG telegraphed to Maj. Gen. Philip H. Sheridan. "The Dept's of Washington, The Middle, The Susquehanna and of Western Va have been formed into a Military Division, called the Middle Division and you have been assigned to the temporary Command. Orders will be sent to you by Mail at once. You can assume Command without further authority." Copies, DLC-USG, V, 45, 59, 67; DNA, RG 108, Letters Sent. *O.R.*, I, xliii, part 1, 719.

On Aug. 6, 7:30 P.M., Sheridan telegraphed to USG. "I have the honor to report my command here. I find affairs somewhat confused but will soon straiten them out. I have had a great many reports of the Enemy's movements. There is not much doubt but that some cavalry and Infantry marched from Sharpsburg towards Hagerstown this morning—I hope to be able tomorrow to get more definite information and have ordered Col Lowell with a portion of his command to make a reconnoissance on the south side of the river in the direction of Martinsburg. I am anxiously awaiting the arrival of Genl Torberts command. Gen'l Averill has all the cavalry that belongs here and is following up the Enemy from Springfield in the direction of Moorefield. I have no good reason to think that the Enemy reported as going towards Hagerstown is formidable" Telegram received (at 8:40 P.M.), DNA, RG 107, Telegrams Collected (Bound); *ibid.*, RG 108, Letters Received; copies (2), DLC-Philip H. Sheridan. *O.R.*, I, xliii, part 1, 710. On Aug. 7, 2:00 P.M., Sheridan telegraphed to USG. "I am well satisfied that there is no large force of the Enemy North of the Potomac. Early crossed the river & took dinner at Sharpsburg but returned immediately to Winchester— The Enemy are collecting wheat about Sharpsburg. I have thought it best to let them go on until I can get Torberts Division here then I will strike for Winchester which is the key and pick up the parties on the north side of the Potomac." Telegram received (at 2:30 P.M.), DNA, RG 107, Telegrams Collected (Bound); *ibid.*, RG 108, Letters Received; copy, DLC-Philip H. Sheridan. *O.R.*, I, xliii, part 1, 720.

On Aug. 7, Secretary of War Edwin M. Stanton wrote to USG. "Please let me see you before you leave the city & oblige" ALS, DLC-USG, I, B. For a telegram of the same day from Maj. Gen. Edward O. C. Ord asking if USG were at City Point and the negative reply, see *O.R.*, I, xlii, part 2, 83.

To Maj. Gen. William T. Sherman

(Cipher)   ~~War Department~~
                                   Washington City, Aug. 7th *1864*

MAJ. GEN. SHERMAN,

Your progress instead of appearing slow has received the universal commendation of all loyal citizens as well as of the President, War Dept, and all persons whose commendation you would care for. The enemy detaching a portion of his force to secure the crops of the Shenandoah Valley and raid into Maryland and Pa fto call attention from them has called me here to organize our forces to drive the enemy South. I came from the Monocacy yesterday afternoon after having put all our forces in motion after the enemy and after having put Sheridan in command who I know will push the enemy to the very death.

I will telegraph you in future more frequently than heretofore.

U. S. GRANT
Lt. Gn.

ALS (telegram sent), CSmH; copies, DLC-USG, V, 45, 59, 67; (datelined noon) DLC-William T. Sherman; DNA, RG 108, Letters Sent; *ibid.*, RG 393, Military Div. of the Miss., Telegrams Received in the Field. *O.R.*, I, xxxviii, part 5, 407–8. On Aug. 7, 1864, 8:00 P.M., Maj. Gen. William T. Sherman telegraphed to USG. "I was gratified to learn you were satisfied with my progress Get the War Department to send us recruits daily as they are made for we can teach them more war in our camp in one day than they can get at a rendezvous in a month, also tell the President that he must not make the least concession in the matter of the September draft: It is right and popular with the army and the army is worth considering   I am glad you have given Gen Sheridan the command of the forces to defend Washington; he will worry Early to death   Let us give these southern fellows all the fighting they want and when they are tired we can tell them we are just warming to the work   Any signs of a let up on our part is sure to be falsely construed and for this reason I always remind them that the seige of Troy lasted six years and Atlanta is a more valuable town than Troy   We must manifest the character of dogged courage & perseverance of our race. Dont Stay in Washington longer than is necessary to give impulse to events and get out of it—It is the centre of *intrigue*   I would like to have *Mower* made a Major General, he is a real fighter" Telegram received, DNA, RG 107, Telegrams Collected (Bound); (misdated Aug. 8) *ibid.*, Telegrams Collected (Unbound); *ibid.*, RG 108, Letters Received; copy, *ibid.*, RG 393, Military Div. of the Miss., Telegrams Sent in the Field. Printed as received on Aug. 8, 3:30 A.M., in *O.R.*, I, xxxviii, part 5, 408.

On Aug. 3, 6:20 P.M., USG had telegraphed to Maj. Gen. Henry W. Halleck. "Richmond Dispatch of today contains following—'Macon August 1st 6. P. M—Our Cavalry under Gen Iverson attacked the enemy yesterday near Clinton   The Yankees, commanded by Gen Stoneman were routed, and Stoneman, seventy five officers, & about five hundred prisoners—with two Pieces of Artillery surrendered and have just reached this city—The rest of the Yankees force are scattered and flying toward Eatonton'" Telegram received, DNA, RG 107, Telegrams Collected (Bound); (2—datelined 6:30 P.M.) *ibid.*, Telegrams Collected (Unbound); copies, *ibid.*, RG 108, Letters Sent; DLC-USG, V, 45, 59, 67. Printed as received on Aug. 4, 6:30 A.M., in *O.R.*, I, xxxviii, part 5, 339. On Aug. 4, Halleck transmitted this telegram to Sherman as if USG were telegraphing directly. Copy, DNA, RG 393, Military Div. of the Miss., Telegrams Received in the Field. *O.R.*, I, xxxviii, part 5, 349. On Aug. 4, 10:00 A.M., USG telegraphed to Sherman. "Richmond papers of yesterday announce the capture of Gen. Stoneman and five hundred of his party near Macon Ga. The capture took place the 1st of Aug. Have you heard any thing of this?" ALS (telegram sent), CSmH; copies, DLC-USG, V, 45, 59, 67; DNA, RG 107, Telegrams Received in Cipher; *ibid.*, RG 108, Letters Sent; *ibid.*, RG 393, Military Div. of the Miss., Telegrams Received in the Field. *O.R.*, I, xxxviii, part 5, 350. The date of the capture was altered to July 31 in the telegram sent and copied that way in USG's letterbooks. On the same day, Sherman twice telegraphed to USG, the second time at 11:30 P.M. "Genl Stoneman only had 2.300 men, 900 have got in. I fear the balance are captured as stated in your dispatch. Stoneman was sent to break Railroads, after which I consented he should attempt the rescue of our prisoners at Andersonville." "I have your second despatch about Stoneman. I have newspapers, with dates from Macon of the 1st, speaking of stoneman's capture as a rumor but not as a fact. He started from here, in connection with two other parties, that have got back. He had twenty three hundred (2300) men, and after breaking the Macon road, to was to make an effort to rescue our prisoners. Col Adams, with nine hundred (900) of his men, got back to Marietta today, and telegraphed me he was attacked at Clinton, Ga, by overwhelming numbers, and they fear he is captured. It may be so, but I hope he may, like McCook, dodge and get in. Washburn is moving from Holly springs, on Columbus, Miss. He thinks that Forrest is dead of the wound rec'd in his battle with smith. The country in which I am operating, is very difficult for a large army, and the defensive position very strong, and hard to circumvent, but perseverance will move mountains. I ought to be better advised of your plans and movements— I hear you have blown up the outer bastion of Petersburg, but dont know how near you are to getting full possession of the place, or its [*bearing on*] or [*Richmond*]. Hood uses his militia to fill his lines, and I have a bold front wherever I get at him—" Telegrams received (the first at 10:20 P.M., the second on Aug. 5, 9:00 P.M.), DNA, RG 107, Telegrams Collected (Bound); *ibid.*, RG 108, Letters Received; copies, *ibid.*, RG 393, Military Div. of the Miss., Telegrams Sent in the Field. *O.R.*, I, xxxviii, part 5, 350. The second is printed as sent at 1:30 P.M.

On Aug. 7, 8:00 P.M., Sherman telegraphed to Halleck. "Have recd today the despatches of the Secretary of War and Gen Grant which are very satisfactory. We keep hammering away here all the time and there is no peace inside or outside of Atlanta. Today Schofield got round the flank of the line assaulted yesterday by Gen Reilleys brigade, turned it and gained the ground where the assault was with all our dead and wounded   we continued to press on that flank and brought on a noisy but not a bloody engagement   We drove the enemy behind his main breastworks which cover the rail road from Atlanta to East Point   We captured a good many of the skirmishers which are of their best troops for the militia hugs the breastworks close   I do not deem it prudent to extend more to the right but will push forward daily by paralells & make the inside of Atlanta too hot to be endured. I have sent to Chattanooga for two thirty pounder Parrotts with which we can pick out almost any house in town   I am too impatient for a seige but I dont know but here is as good a place to fight it out as further inland   One thing is certain whether we go inside of Atlanta or not it will be a used up 'community' by the time we are done with it"   Telegram received, DNA, RG 108, Letters Received. Printed as received on Aug. 8, 2:30 A.M., in *O.R.*, I, xxxviii, part 5, 408–9. On Aug. 9, Lt. Col. Theodore S. Bowers telegraphed the text of Sherman's telegram, omitting the first sentence, to Maj. Gen. Benjamin F. Butler, Maj. Gen. George G. Meade, and all corps commanders. LS (telegram sent), DNA, RG 107, Telegrams Collected (Unbound); telegram received, *ibid.*, RG 94, War Records Office, Army of the Potomac; DLC-Benjamin F. Butler; Ord Papers, CU-B.

To Julia Dent Grant

F't. Monroe, Va. Aug. 8th *1864.*

DEAR JULIA,

The day I wrote you last I found time to draw my pay and get a draft for $1,000 for you but not time to mail it before the cars left. I went out to Monocacy Md, set our troops all in motion placing in command an officer, Gen. Sheridan, in whom I have great confidance and have just reached here on my way back to City Point. Col. Porter, who was with me, went on to Princton N. J. to make arrangements for you to go there. I look for him back tomorrow or the day following. You might as well make your arrangements for coming on without waiting another letter. If you can not get a house there I want you to come East any way. You might come on to Philadelphia at once and if satisfactory arrangements are not made at Princeton you can rent a furnished house there and we will make that our permanent home for the war. It will always be convenient to me and it is a pleasant place to live.

My love to all at home. Love and kisses for you and the children.

ULYS.

ALS, DLC-USG.

To Maj. Gen. Henry W. Halleck

City Point 11 45 a m
Aug 9th 1864

MAJ GEN HALLECK
CHF OF STAFF

Five minutes ago an ordnance boat exploded carrying timbers, grape canister and all kinds of shot over this point—Every part of the yard occupied as my Hd Qrs is filled with splinters and fragments of shells

I do not know yet what the casualties are beyond my own Hd Qrs. Col Babcock is slightly wounded in hand and one man mounted orderly is killed and two or three wounded and several horses killed—The damage at the wharf must be considerable both in life & property—As soon as the smoke clears away I will ascertain & telegraph you

U S GRANT
Lt Genl

Telegram received (at 10:30 P.M.), DNA, RG 107, Telegrams Collected (Bound); *ibid.*, Telegrams Collected (Unbound); copies, *ibid.*, RG 108, Letters Sent; DLC-USG, V, 45, 59, 67. *O.R.*, I, xlii, part 1, 17; *ibid.*, I, xlii, part 2, 94–95. On Aug. 9, 1864, 11:50 A.M., USG telegraphed to Maj. Gen. Benjamin F. Butler and to Maj. Gen. George G. Meade. "An ordnance boat blew up at the wharf a few moments ago sending shell & splinters all over the point   The damage to life & property must be great, out of my own yard however I have not yet learned   Col. Babcock was wounded in the hand & an orderly killed & three or four wounded   Several horses were also killed   on the wharf & on other parts of the point the losses must be heavy"   Telegram received, DNA, RG 94, War Records Office, Army of the Potomac; DLC-Benjamin F. Butler.

On Aug. 11, USG telegraphed to Maj. Gen. Henry W. Halleck. "The following is a list of casualties from the explosion of the ammunition barge on the 9th to wit. Killed twelve enlisted men two citizens employees, one citizen not employed by Govt. thirty eight colored laborers,   wounded three commissioned Officers four enlisted men, fifteen citizens employees, eighty six colored laborers, Besides these there were 18 others wounded Soldiers and citizens not belonging about the whf. The damage to property was large, but I have not the means [o]f reporting it." Telegram received (at 9:45 P.M.), DNA, RG 107, Telegrams Collected (Bound); copies, *ibid.*, RG 108, Letters Sent; DLC-USG, V, 45, 59, 67. *O.R.*, I, xlii, part 1, 17; *ibid.*, I, xlii, part 2, 112.

On Aug. 15, Lt. Col. Theodore S. Bowers issued Special Orders No. 74 appointing a board headed by Lt. Col. Horace Porter to investigate the cause of the explosion. Copies, DLC-USG, V, 57, 62, 68; DNA, RG 94, Letters Received, 1368A 1864. *O.R.*, I, xlii, part 2, 197. The board was unable to determine the cause of the explosion and concluded that it was an accident; on Aug. 20, USG endorsed the report. "Respectfully forwarded to the Secretary of War." ES, DNA, RG 94, Letters Received, 1359A 1864. For a description of the explosion and a statement that it resulted from sabotage, see Horace Porter, *Campaigning with Grant* (New York, 1897), pp. 273–75. See also *O.R.*, I, xlii, part 1, 954–56; *ibid.*, I, xlvi, part 3, 1250.

To Maj. Gen. Henry W. Halleck

City Point Aug 9th 1864

MAJ GEN HALLECK
CHF OF STAFF

The 7th [*1st*] Regt U S Vols composed of deserters and prisoners from the rebel ranks is now on duty at Norfolk—

I have ordered it to the Dept of the North West—Please direct Pope to send an equal amount of troops to Genl Sherman and if he can send more to do it. My own opinion is that two or three Regts can be sent from the Dept of the N W. without danger

The 1st Regt. U S Vols. numbers 1000 for duty and is a first class Regiment but it is not right to expose them ~~as~~ where to be taken Prisoners they must suffer as deserters

U S. GRANT
Lt Genl

Telegram received, DNA, RG 94, War Records Office, Miscellaneous War Records; (at 11:00 P.M.) *ibid.*, RG 107, Telegrams Collected (Bound); copies, *ibid.*, RG 94, Vol. Service Div., A716 (VS) 1864; *ibid.*, RG 108, Letters Sent; DLC-USG, V, 45, 59, 67. *O.R.*, I, xli, part 2, 619.

On Sept. 25, 1864, 1:25 P.M. (sent at 3:00 P.M.), Secretary of War Edwin M. Stanton telegraphed to USG. "The President sometime ago authorised a regiment of prisoners of war at Rock island to be enlisted into our service   He has written you a letter of explanation. It was done without my knowledge and he desires his arrangement to be carried into effect. The question now arises how they shall be organized officered and assigned to duty. Shall they be formed into one regiment by companies as other troops or assigned in companies or squads to other organizations. Please favor me with your views on the subject. The Presidents letter is forwarded you by mail." ALS (telegram sent), DNA, RG 107, Telegrams Collected (Bound); telegram received, *ibid.*, Telegrams Collected (Unbound); *ibid.*, RG 108, Letters Received. *O.R.*, III, iv, 744. On Sept. 22, President Abraham Lincoln had written to USG. "I send this as an explanation to you, and to do justice to the Secretary of War. I was induced, upon pressing application, to author[*ize*] the agents of one of the Districts of Pennsylvania to recruit in one of the prisoner depots in Illinois; and the thing went so far before it came to the knowledge of the Secretary, that in my judgment it could not be abandoned without greater evil than would follow it's going through. I did not know at the time that you had protested against that class of thing being done; and I now say that while this particular job must be completed, no other of the sort will be authorized, without an understanding with you, if at all. The Secretary of War is wholly free of any part in this blunder." ADfS, DLC-Robert T. Lincoln; copy, DLC-Edwin M. Stanton. Lincoln, *Works*, VIII, 17. On Sept. 23, Lincoln sent this letter to Stanton endorsed: "Secretary of War please read & forward." AES, DLC-Edwin M. Stanton. On Sept. 25, 6:30 P.M., USG telegraphed to Stanton. "Your dispatch in relation to the organization of troops from prisoners of War just received. I would advise that they be placed all in one regiment and be put on duty either with Gen. Pope or sent to New Mexico." ALS (telegram sent), CSmH; telegram received (at 8:10 P.M.), DNA, RG 107, Telegrams Collected (Bound); *ibid.*, Telegrams Collected (Unbound). *O.R.*, III, iv, 744. See D. Alexander Brown, *The Galvanized Yankees* (Urbana, Ill., 1963).

On Sept. 22, Bvt. Maj. Gen. Alvin P. Hovey, Indianapolis, wrote a letter recommending the enlistment of some C.S.A. prisoners at Camp Morton into the U.S. Army and U.S. Navy. On Oct. 13, USG endorsed this letter. "Respy. returned. I do not deem it advisable to enlist any more of this class of men at present than we have in service" Copies, DLC-USG, V, 58; DNA, RG 108, Register of Letters Received. On Oct. 15, 5:00 P.M., Halleck telegraphed to USG. "The conduct of the regiment of rebel deserters enlisted by Genl Butler & sent to the northwest has been such, that no more of that class should be recieved. Genl Sibley reports that they are entirely untrustworthy and even dangerous." ALS (telegram sent), *ibid.*, RG 107, Telegrams Collected (Bound); telegram received, *ibid.*; *ibid.*, Telegrams Collected (Unbound); *ibid.*, RG 108, Letters Received.

To Act. Rear Admiral S. Phillips Lee

City Point Va Aug 9th 1864.

ADM'L S. P. LEE
DEAR SIR

Your letter of the 24th inst. inclosing communication relative to the withdrawel of Iron Clads from the James River was duly received. Owing to my absence from here most of the time since the receipt of your letter it has not been answered earlier.

Whilst I believe we will never require the amoured vessels to meet those of the enemy I think it would be imprudent to withdraw them. At least two such vessels, in my judgement, should be kept in the Upper James. They stand a constant threat to the enemy and prevent him taking the offensive. There is no disguising the fact that if the enemy should take the offensive, on the Water, altho we probably would destroy his whole James River Navy, such damage would be done our shipping and Stores, all accumulated on the Water near where the conflict would begin, that our victory would be dearly bought.

> I have the honor to be Adm'l,
> Very Respectfully Yours
> U. S. GRANT
> Lieut Gen'l.

Copies, DLC-USG, V, 45, 59, 67; DNA, RG 108, Letters Sent. *O.R.*, I, xlii, part 2, 95; *O.R.* (Navy), I, x, 373. On July 24, 1864, Act. Rear Admiral S. Phillips Lee, Hampton Roads, Va., wrote to USG. "I enclose a copy of a communication received to-day from the Navy Department, relative to the expediency of withdrawing the iron-clads from James River   I request the favor of an early reply, giving your views on the subject . . . Please address your reply to me at Beaufort N. C." LS, DNA, RG 108, Letters Received. *O.R.*, I, xl, part 3, 427; *O.R.* (Navy), I, x, 373. Lee enclosed a copy of a letter of July 22 from Secretary of the Navy Gideon Welles to Lee. "You will inform this Department whether any of the Iron Clads attached to your command can be withdrawn, having due regard to the exigiencies of the public service within the limits of your command; whether they are absolutely essential to the holding possession of James river or other waters of Virginia, and whether the Military forces can maintain their positions in Virginia, assisted and protected by wooden vessels & only in case the iron clads should be withdrawn, or with the assistance and protection of wooden vessels and a portion of the iron clads. Answers to these questions and such other information bearing upon the subjects of inquiry as your Judgement may dictate, can be furnished at your leisure—The opinion of Lieut. General Grant upon the points indicated would be valuabled and the Department would be gratified if you could obtain it—"   Copy, DNA, RG 108, Letters Received. *O.R.*, I, xl, part 3, 427; *O.R.* (Navy), I, x, 296. See *ibid.*, pp. 371–73.

To Maj. Gen. Philip H. Sheridan

From City Point 12 M August 9th *1864.*

MAJ GEN P H SHERIDAN
HARPERS FERRY

Information derived from deserters, refugees and a man sent

from here to Richmond, all corroborating, locate every Division
and Brigade of Hill, Longstreet and Beauregards forces[1]—Not
one Brigade has been sent from here. I shall endeavor to hold them
and rather create a tendency to draw from your front than allow
them to reenforce

U S GRANT
Lt Genl

Telegram received (at 10:00 P.M.), DNA, RG 107, Telegrams Collected
(Bound); copies, *ibid.*, RG 108, Letters Sent; DLC-USG, V, 45, 59, 68. *O.R.*, I,
xliii, part 1, 737.

1. On Aug. 9, 1864, USG telegraphed to Maj. Gen. Benjamin F. Butler.
"How does your information place Longstreets Corps & wilcoxs Div of Hills
Corps   I have the statements of deserters Coming in at Petersburg & wish to
compare—I will be over to see you this P. m," Telegram received, DLC-
Benjamin F. Butler; copies, DLC-USG, V, 45, 59, 67; DNA, RG 108, Letters
Sent. On the same day, 11:30 A.M., Butler telegraphed to USG. "Deserters place
Longstreets corps as follows. Picketts Div. in our front between the appomattox
& the James—Field's Div. is before Foster at Deep Bottom & Mahone on the extreme left in front of Gen Meade. Wilcox Div has Scales' & Thomas' brigades
between Picketts Div. & the appomattox, Thomas on the north & Scales on the
south of Swift creek—Lane & Conner are before Foster at Deep bottom—We had
deserters from all these except Mahones Division yesterday—Three last night
about ten oclock from Scales & Thomas—They report Kershaws div. in reserve
in rear of Pickett   I was about saddling my horse to visit you—I have the boat
waiting   Which shall it be" LS (telegram sent), *ibid.*, RG 107, Telegrams
Collected (Unbound); telegram received, *ibid.*, RG 108, Letters Received. On the
same day, USG telegraphed to Butler. "As you are all prepared come & see me."
Telegram received, DLC-Benjamin F. Butler.

To Maj. Gen. William T. Sherman

(Cipher)   City Point Va. Aug 9th *1864* [*11:30* A.M.]
MAJ. GEN. SHERMAN, NEAR ATLANTA GA.

The enemy having drawn to your front most of his forces West
of Alabama can you not reinforce from your Mississippi garrisons?
~~Would it not be safe for the force moving on to Columbus Miss.
to continue their march Eastward~~   I will ask to have all Western
recruits sent immediately to you. Your views about shewing no
dispondency but keeping the enemy, with his last man now in the

field, constantly employed are the same I have often expressed. We must win if not defeated at home. Every day exhausts the enemy at least a regiment, without any further population to draw from to replace it, exclusive of losses in battle. I would suggest the employment of as many negroes as you can as teamsters, company cooks, Pioneers &c. to keep the enlisted men in the ranks, and the shipment to Nashville of every unemployed negro, big and little. By sending some of your disable officers you might rake a conciderable force from Northern Hospitals also. Deserters coming in daily keep us well posted of the position of Lee's forces. Stories of deserters are not to be relied on but they give their regiment, brigade and Division correctly and many of them coming locates the whole. I think no troops have gone from Lee to Hood.

U. S. GRANT
Lt. Gn.

ALS (telegram sent), CSmH; telegram received (at 9:30 P.M.), DNA, RG 107, Telegrams Collected (Bound); *ibid.*, Telegrams Collected (Unbound). *O.R.*, I, xxxviii, part 5, 433–34. On Aug. 10, 1864, 8:00 P.M., Maj. Gen. William T. Sherman telegraphed to USG. "Your despatch of the ninth is received—It is to replace our daily losses that I propose that all recruits made daily in the Western states instead of accumulating at depots should at once come to Nashville and be sent here on the cars which can bring four hundred a day without interfering with freights   I have ordered Washburne at Memphis to have A. J. Smith, who is now marching on Columbus Mississippi, come to Decatur Ala. whence I can bring to this army certain regiments and fragments that properly belong here and a division that I originally designed to form a part of this army, the balance of infantry & cavalry I would send back via Savannah and Jackson Tennessee My lines are now ten miles long, extending from the Athens road on the left round to East Point on the South   I cannot extend more without making my lines too weak. We are in close contact and skirmishing all the time. I have just got up four 4½ inch rifled guns with ammunition and propose to expend about four thousand rifled shots on the heart of Atlanta   We have already canonaded it with our lighter ordnance. Since July 28 General Hood has not attempted to meet us outside of his parapets   In order to possess and destroy effectually his communication I may have to leave a corps at the RailRoad bridge well entrenched and cut loose with the balance and make a desolating circle around Atlanta. I do not propose to assault the works which are too strong or to proceed by regular approaches   I have lost a good many regiments and will lose more by the expiration of Service and this is the only reason why I want reinforcements—I have killed, crippled & captured more of the enemy than we have lost by his acts" Telegram received (on Aug. 11, 3:30 A.M.), DNA, RG 107, Telegrams Collected (Bound); (incomplete) *ibid.*, Telegrams Collected (Unbound); *ibid.*, RG 108, Letters Received; copy, *ibid.*, RG 393, Military Div. of the Miss., Telegrams Sent in the Field. *O.R.*, I, xxxviii, part 5, 447.

To Emma S. Cameron

City Point, Va., August 9, 1864.
MY DEAR MADAM: Your letter of the 8th of July was duly received, but not so promptly answered. I know yours to be a case
where prompt payment should be made, and am willing to so indorse your claim. I believe your property at Chattanooga has been
appraised by a board of officers. If so, send me the proceedings of
the board, and I will make my indorsement and return them to
you. If you have no such evidence of the claim, inform me, and I
will order a board to assess it, and will indorse the proceedings.
This will be the first step toward a collection.

Yours, truly,
U. S. GRANT.

MRS. CAMERON.

SRC, 43-1-237. On Dec. 7, 1863, Emma S. Cameron had written to USG. "I
understand that a Fort has been, or is to be erected on Cameron Hill, Chattanooga.
As it was my home; and is associated with many happy hours and pleasant antici-
pations, never to be repeated, would it be too great a favor, to ask that the name
of Cameron may be retained for the Fort?" ALS, DNA, RG 393, Dept. of the
Cumberland, Unentered Letters Received. On Dec. 11, USG endorsed this letter.
"Refered to Brig. Gen. W. F. Smith, Chief Eng. Fort Cameron sounds as well as
any other name. . . . P. S. Miss Cameron is strongly Union and the family, for
their Union Sympathies, were forced to leave Chattanooga." AES, *ibid.* On Oct.
25, 1864, USG endorsed a claim for the taking of Cameron Hill, Chattanooga,
by U.S. forces to construct Fort Cameron. "I know the property within described
and the parties owning it *well. Mr Cameron and his wife* have been unflinchingly
friends of the Government from the beginning of our troubles to the present day.
There are no more thoroughly loyal people any where in the north and they are
entitled to protection and pay for their property converted to Government use.
What is now known as *Fort Cameron* Chattanooga, Tenn was the private property of Mr C. From its elevated and commanding position it had to be taken and
fortified   By this means the entire property with improvements has been entirely destroyed for private use   *I would recommend that the property be pur-
chased at a fair valuation for Government* use" Copy, *ibid.*, RG 94, Letters Received, 64G 1865. On Jan. 28, 1865, James Cameron wrote to USG. "I have
just been informed by the Board of claims here that your writing to the Secretary
of War in Washington will validate the *copy* of your kind endorsement of our
claim for damages to Cameron Hill; as the original is in the hands of Ajt. Gen'l
Thomas *without the endorsement* the Board here have informed Gen'l Thomas
of Washington that you endorsed our claim for speedy settlement, and have

sent him a copy of your endorsement. please do us the additional kindness to write to Secry Staunton that you have so endorsed our claim, and Adjt. Genl. Thomas will call upon Secry Staunton in reference to its final settlement. I am aware that I am both trespassing upon your kindness and most valuable time, and only the assurance that the claim cannot be settled without causes me to do so. Genl. Donaldson has ordered an ambulance for my wife's use, and she is busy from morning to night with increased resources at command for the destitute. I trust that the Lord will grant you life, health, and the happy issue of crushing out this vile rebellion; which we believe here you, and your able assistants are doing rapidly. My wife joins me in kind regards to yourself and family." ALS, DNA, RG 108, Letters Received. See letter to Julia Dent Grant, Dec. 28, 1863.

To Maj. Gen. Henry W. Halleck

City Point
Aug 10 1864

MAJ GEN HALLECK
CHF OF STAFF

The Richmond Papers of today contain the intelligence that Ft Gaines had surrendered with 600 men—50 guns and six months provisions

It also says Fort Powell has blown up—Please telegraph Sherman this and the previous news from Mobile

U S GRANT
Lt Genl

Telegram received (at 10:20 P.M.), DNA, RG 107, Telegrams Collected (Bound); *ibid.*, Telegrams Collected (Unbound); copies, *ibid.*, RG 108, Letters Sent; DLC-USG, V, 45, 59, 68. *O.R.*, I, xxxix, part 2, 239. On Aug. 10, 1864, 10:50 A.M., Maj. Gen. Benjamin F. Butler telegraphed to USG. "I have just recieved telegraphic report of contents of Richmond paper of to day which announces the surrender of Fort Gaines off Mobile with six hundred men fifty guns and six months provisions. Also the blowing up of Fort Powell. I will send the official despatch as soon as I recieve it. Please let the operator forward this to the Secretary of the Navy" LS (telegram sent), DNA, RG 107, Telegrams Collected (Unbound); telegram received, *ibid.*, RG 108, Letters Received. At 11:00 A.M., Lt. Col. Theodore S. Bowers telegraphed Butler's message to Maj. Gen. George G. Meade. ALS (telegram sent), *ibid.*, RG 107, Telegrams Collected (Unbound); telegram received, *ibid.*, RG 94, War Records Office, Army of the Potomac. At 1:00 P.M., USG telegraphed to Meade. "Richmond papers of this morning announce that Fort Gaines surrendered to the Yankees with 600 men 50 Guns and 6 months supplies also that Fort Powell was blown up. You know I presume that seventeen of our Gunboats had run the Rebel Batteries at Mobile & had captured or destroyed all but one of the Rebel Gunboats   We have a small Military force near Mobile under Gordon Granger—" Telegram received, *ibid.* Also on Aug. 10, USG telegraphed to Meade and all corps commanders. "The following extracts from the Richmond Enquirer of this A m are respectfully furnished for your information" Telegram received, *ibid.*; copies, *ibid.*, RG 393, 2nd Army Corps, 1st Div., Telegrams Received; Ord Papers, CU-B. The dispatches from Mobile are *ibid.*

On Aug. 8, 3:00 P.M., Butler had telegraphed to President Abraham Lincoln, sending copies to Asst. Secretary of the Navy Gustavus V. Fox and USG. "The following is official report taken from Richmond Sentinel August eighth (8th)" Telegrams received (2), DNA, RG 107, Telegrams Collected (Unbound). Printed as received at 7:00 P.M. in *O.R.* (Navy), I, xxi, 440. Butler appended a message of Aug. 5 from Maj. Gen. Dabney H. Maury, Mobile, to C.S.A. Secretary of War James A. Seddon. "Seventeen (17) of the enemys vessels fourteen (14) ship & three (3) Iron Clads passed fort Morgan this morning   The Tecumseh a monitor was sunk by fort Morgan   the Tennessee Surrendered after a desperate engagement with the enemys fleet   Admiral Buchanan lost a leg & is a prisoner   The Selma was captured   The Gaines was beached near the hospital   The Morgan is safe & will try & run up tonight   The enemy's fleet has approached the city   A monitor has been engaging fort Powell all day" Telegram received, DNA, RG 107, Telegrams Collected (Unbound). *O.R.* (Navy), I, xxi, 440. On Aug. 9, 5:40 P.M., Butler telegraphed to USG, sending a copy to Fox. "The following is from the Richmond Examiner of the 9th—'A despatch from Mobile dated August 7th, two days later than our previous advices, State, that the situation has not materially changed Since the Enemys Victory over Our Ironclads on last friday—The Navy Dept. received a telegram yesterday morning, announcing that, the Morgan the only Gunboat of our fleet which was not either Sunk beached or Captured had Succeeded in getting over the bar & reaching Mobile." Telegram received, DNA, RG 107, Telegrams Collected (Unbound); *ibid.*, RG 108, Letters Received. *O.R.*, I, xlii, part 2, 100; (printed as received Aug. 10, 6:00 P.M.) *O.R.* (Navy), I, xxi, 440.

To Maj. Gen. Henry W. Halleck

(Cipher)   City Point Aug. 10th 1864 [2:00 P.M.]
MAJ. GEN HALLECK, WASHINGTON

Order Gen. Foster to send all the troops he can possibly spare to Washington standing himself purely on the defensive. We must try and get ten thousand reinforcements to Sherman by some means. Can not troops be got by thining out about Columbus Cairo and Paducah and other places leaving them to be filled up afterwards. I would like to hear of 1000 a day going by some means.

U. S. Grant

Lt. Gn.

ALS (telegram sent), CSmH; telegram received (at 11:00 p.m.), DNA, RG 107, Telegrams Collected (Bound); *ibid.*, Telegrams Collected (Unbound). See *O.R.*, I, xxxv, part 2, 231, 256.

To Maj. Gen. Benjamin F. Butler

———

By Telegraph from City Point
Dated Aug 10 *1864.*

To Maj Gen Butler

The navy ought to be apprised of the Despatch taken from the Rebel signal and so station a part of their Boats as to Command the Ground arround our Troops at Dutch Gap—If the Enemy open from Howlets open from our Water Batteries on it—Are our men well Covered from artillery fire   if so and they are the alert a Rebel attack ought to prove Disastreous to them

U S Grant

Lt Gen

Telegram received, DLC-Benjamin F. Butler; copies, DLC-USG, V, 45, 59, 68; DNA, RG 108, Letters Sent. *O.R.*, I, xlii, part 2, 106. On Aug. 10, 1864, 6:10 p.m., Maj. Gen. Benjamin F. Butler telegraphed to USG. "The following has just been received by our signal officer & is forwarded for your Information   It evidently refers to some attack upon our working party at Dutch Gap—I have informed Gen Birney & will inform Capt Smith—Have you any orders. We will endeavor to be ready—" Telegram received, DNA, RG 108, Letters Received. *O.R.*, I, xlii, part 2, 106. The enclosed message, from C.S.A. Lt. Gen. Richard S. Ewell to Gen. Robert E. Lee concerning the placement of art., is *ibid.* At 8:10 p.m., Butler telegraphed to USG. "We are preparing to meet the Rebels if they choose to attack us—I think our men are under cover. The navy have been notified to be ready on their part—A Rebel deserter this afternoon reports a rumor in their camp that their cavalry have been knocked to pieces with a loss of four (4) Guns up in the Shenandoah Valley,   have you any news upon that subject? He also reports that last saturday right smart of cavalry which was in the rear of their line—I presume a brigade between the James & Appomattox left for the Shenandoah" LS (telegram sent), DNA, RG 107, Telegrams Collected (Unbound); telegram received, *ibid.*, RG 108, Letters Received. *O.R.*, I, xlii, part 2,

106–7. On the same day, USG telegraphed to Butler. "Who has Immediate Command of Troops at Dutch Gap   It will require some one there who Can not be Stampeded"   Telegram received, DLC-Benjamin F. Butler; copies, DLC-USG, V, 45, 59, 68; DNA, RG 108, Letters Sent. *O.R.*, I, xlii, part 2, 107. At 8:50 P.M., Butler telegraphed to USG. "That Command is in immediate charge of Maj Ludlow of my staff a Gentleman of experience who will not be stampeded —He is now here—I have explained to him all the circumstances & we shall not leave—I have been able since I sent to you to decipher the enemiey's signals   Put in where the first break is 'Col Carter's' and where the second is 'Cox's overseers house' which place you will find on the map and it will read as follows   'Col Carter is here engaged in locating Artillery at Signal Hill and Coxs overseer's House' "   LS (telegram sent), DNA, RG 107, Telegrams Collected (Unbound); telegram received, *ibid.*, RG 108, Letters Received. *O.R.*, I, xlii, part 2, 107.

At 10:35 A.M., Butler had telegraphed to USG. "If you see no objection I will take up the pontoon bridge at Broadway Landing and turn over the material to Brig Genl Benham"   LS (telegram sent), DNA, RG 107, Telegrams Collected (Unbound). On the same day, USG telegraphed to Butler. "I You may take up the Bridge at B'Way Landing & turn over the material to Brig Genl Benham or if you prefer I will order Genl Benham to take up"   Telegram received, DLC-Benjamin F. Butler; copies, DLC-USG, V, 45, 59, 68; DNA, RG 108, Letters Sent.

To Maj. Gen. Benjamin F. Butler

By Telegraph from City Pt
Dated Aug 10 *1864.*

To GEN BUTLER

The Richmond Enqurer of todays says official intelligence was rec'd on yesterday announcing a disaterous surprise to a portion of our troops in the vally at an early hour on Sunday morning[1]   It appears that McCausland & Bradley Johnsons cavy were in Moorfield in Hardy Co where they were resting after their hard work of the previous week. On Sunday morning while they were sleeping Averills command made a decent upon him capturing four hundred men, 900 horses & four pieces of Arty. The remainder of our two commands scattered among the mountains. Washn. papers of yesterday contain similar statements as coming from Sheridan further than this I have no intelligence

U. S. GRANT
Lt Genl

Telegram received, DLC-Benjamin F. Butler. Misdated Aug. 19, 1864, in *Private and Official Correspondence of Gen. Benjamin F. Butler* . . . (n. p., 1917), V, 77. On Aug. 10, USG telegraphed the same message to Maj. Gen. George G. Meade. Telegram received (at 9:10 P.M.), DNA, RG 94, War Records Office, Army of the Potomac; copies (2), Meade Papers, PHi. See *O.R.*, I, xliii, part 1, 2–7.

On the same day, USG telegraphed to Maj. Gen. Benjamin F. Butler and to Meade. "Order such surgeons & asst. Surgeons as can be spared from the field to report to the secy. of War for the purpose of visiting northern hospitals to send from them to the field all men improperly or unnecessarily detained" Telegram received, DLC-Benjamin F. Butler; (at 10:30 A.M.) DNA, RG 94, War Records Office, Army of the Potomac; copies, *ibid.*, RG 108, Letters Sent; DLC-USG, V, 45, 59, 68; (2) Meade Papers, PHi. On Aug. 9, 3:30 P.M., Maj. Gen. Henry W. Halleck had telegraphed to USG. "Military & medical officers are much wanted to ~~send~~ go to the hospitals in different states to examine convalescents & send those fit for duty to their regiments. The Secty of War wishes you to send to the Adjt Genl such officers & surgeons as you can spare for this purpose." ALS (telegram sent), DNA, RG 107, Telegrams Collected (Bound); telegram received, *ibid.*; *ibid.*, Telegrams Collected (Unbound); *ibid.*, RG 108, Letters Received. On Aug. 13, 1:15 P.M., USG telegraphed to Meade. "Your communication in relation to sending Medical officers to bring men from nothern hospitals is recvd   You need not under the circumstances send any. I will have Wilson placed on that duty as you suggest" Telegram received, *ibid.*, RG 393, Army of the Potomac, Telegrams Received; copies, *ibid.*, RG 108, Letters Sent; DLC-USG, V, 45, 59, 68; (2) Meade Papers, PHi. Meade's letter to USG, enclosing a letter from his medical director, was endorsed by USG some time between Aug. 14 and Aug. 17. "Respy. forwarded to the sec of war. Medical officer cannot well be spared from this Army at this time. The suggestion of Gen Meade that Med. Insp Wilson, now in Washington, be assigned to this duty is appd. and an order to that effect respectfully requested." Copy, DLC-USG, V, 58.

On Aug. 10, USG telegraphed to Butler. "I will not be able to go up the River with you today   will go tomorrow" Telegram received, DLC-Benjamin F. Butler.

Also on Aug. 10, Lt. Col. Theodore S. Bowers telegraphed to Capt. George K. Leet. "We had some information here yesterday that troops supposed to be over a Regt left Richmond last saturday evening by the Central road going North   The attention of the men sent by Col Sharpe should be carefully drawn to them to ascertain which way these troops have passed from Gordonsville and their number" Telegrams received (2—at 10:30 P.M.), DNA, RG 107, Telegrams Collected (Bound); *ibid.*, Telegrams Collected (Unbound). *O.R.*, I, xliii, part 1, 760.

1. Aug. 7.

To Surgeon Henry S. Hewit

———

City Pt. Va. Aug. 10th *1864.*

DEAR DR.

Your letter of the 12th of July is before me. It will afford me great pleasure to aid you in securing an appointment to West Point for your son when the time comes. The appointments for /65 will not be until March next.

The campaign you have been engaged in is a remarkable, and to this point, most successful one. Sherman is one of the very few men, if not the only man, who could have conducted it. I have always felt ~~for~~ in Sherman and McPherson a confidence that I could feel in but few men. They have been free from personal ambition at the expense of others. They have been truly zealous in the performance of their duties and truly great in their intelegence and military skill.

My hearty wishes for your success in life Dr. and I subscribe myself your *Friend*

U. S. GRANT
Lt. Gn.

ALS, ViU. See letter to Surgeon Henry S. Hewit, Feb. 24, 1865.

To Isaac N. Morris

———

City Point, Va. Aug. 10th *1864.*

HON. I. N. MORRIS,
DEAR SIR;

Your letter of the 23d of July was duly received. I hope your nephew, Mr. Crapsey, has not nor will not publish my letter a copy of which you furnished him. I never write any thing intended for publication.

In the matter of furnishing material for my own biography I could not think of such a thing. It would be egotistical and I hope egotism is not to be numbered among my faults.—I have read your sketch in the National Intelligencer.

Except flattering it is substantially correct.

Yours Truly

U. S. Grant

ALS (facsimile), *An Address Delivered by Frank H. Jones before the Chicago Historical Society at the Celebration of the 100th Anniversary of the Birth of General Ulysses S. Grant* (Chicago, 1922), pp. [20–21]. See letter to Isaac N. Morris, July 12, 1864.

To Lydia Slocum

Headq'rs Armies of the United States,
City Point, Va., August 10. [*1864*]

Mrs. Lydia Slocum:

My Dear Madam: Your very welcome letter of the 3d instant has reached me. I am glad to know the relatives of the lamented Major General McPherson are aware of the more than friendship existing between him and myself. A nation grieves at the loss of one so dear to our nation's cause. It is a selfish grief, because the nation had more to expect from him than from almost any one living. I join in this selfish grief, and add the grief of personal love for the departed. He formed for some time one of my military family. I knew him well. To know him was but to love him. It may be some consolation to you, his aged grandmother, to know that every officer and every soldier who served under your grandson felt the highest reverence for his patriotism, his zeal, his great, almost unequalled ability, his amiability, and all the manly virtues that can adorn a commander. Your bereavement is great, but cannot exceed mine.

Yours truly,

U. S. Grant,

Lieutenant General.

Washington Chronicle, Aug. 29, 1864. On Aug. 3, 1864, Lydia Slocum, Clyde, Ohio, wrote to USG. "I hope you will pardon me for troubling you with the perusal of these few lines from the trembling hand of the aged grandma of our beloved General James B. McPherson, who fell in battle. When it was announced at his funeral, from the public print, that when General Grant heard of his death, he went into his tent and wept like a child, my heart went out in thanks to you for the interest you manifested in him while he was with you. I have watched his progress from infancy up. In childhood he was obedient and kind; in manhood, interesting, noble, and persevering, looking to the wants of others. Since he entered the war others can appreciate his worth better than I can. When it was announced to us by telegraph that our loved one had fallen, our hearts were almost rent asunder, but when we heard the Commander-in-Chief could weep with us, too, we felt, sir, that you have been as a father to him, and this whole nation is mourning his early death. I wish to inform you that his remains were conducted by a kind guard to the very parlor where he spent a cheerful evening in 1861, with his widowed mother, two brothers, only sister, and his aged grandma, who is now trying to write. In the morning he took his leave at six o'clock, little dreaming he should fall by a ball from the enemy. His funeral services were attended in his mother's orchard, where his youthful feet had often pressed the soil to gather the falling fruit, and his remains are resting in the silent grave scarce half a mile from the place of his birth. His grave is on an eminence but a few rods from where the funeral services were attended, and near the grave of his father. The grave, no doubt, will be marked, so that passers-by will often pause to drop a tear over the dear departed. And now, dear friend, a few lines from you would be gratefully received by the afflicted friends. I pray that the God of battles may be with you, and go forth with your armies till the rebellion shall cease, the Union be restored, and the old flag wave over our entire land. . . . Aged 87 years and 4 months." *Ibid.*

To Abraham Lincoln

City Point, Va. Aug. 11th *1864.*

A. LINCOLN,
PRESIDENT OF THE U. STATES,
SIR:

Col. J. N. McElroy of the 60th Ohio Vols. has been compelled to quit active Field service after having been on duty since May 1861. The Col. has served under me in the West the greater part of the time and I know him to be an officer of education, zeal and more than ordinary merit. It is for Physical disability that he now quits, but with great desire to be place on some duty where he can serve to the close of the War. He would make a good Asst. Adj. Gen. or Asst. Inspt. Gen. or could command a Veteran Reserve

Regt. I would unhesitatingly recommend him for either of the above named Places.

> With great respect
> your obt. svt.
> U. S. GRANT
> Lt. Gn.

ALS, DNA, RG 94, ACP, M171 CB 1870. On Aug. 22, 1864, President Abraham Lincoln endorsed this letter. "I find this on my table without remembering how, or when it came. Please file." AES, *ibid*. On Aug. 10, Lt. Col. Orville E. Babcock had written to Col. James A. Hardie recommending James N. McElroy for an appointment. ALS, *ibid*. McElroy was appointed maj. and judge advocate as of Sept. 26, 1864.

On March 10, 1866, Governor Jacob D. Cox of Ohio wrote to USG requesting that McElroy be appointed to the U.S. Army. On Dec. 27, 1866, Bvt. Maj. Gen. George A. Custer, Fort Riley, Kan., wrote to Maj. Gen. John A. Rawlins. "Personal . . . I desire to enlist your sympathies and services in behalf of a particular friend of mine—Col J N McElroy, now 2nd Lt 2nd Cav. The Cols case is a peculiar one, he was at West Point two years with me, but was compelled to leave the Academy on account of a simple act of indiscretion. His dismissal was considered by most all at that time as being very unjust. He entered the volunteer service from Ohio at the begining of the war and rose to the rank of Col (60th Ohio) and exercised for a considerable period the command of a Brigade. He served during the war, on many occasions distinguishing himself by his ability and gallantry.   he rendered excellent service during the Wilderness campaign, as well as in many others. At the close of the war he was very desirous to entering the regular Army, but the delay of Congress in providing for an increase of the Army induced Col McElroy, under the advice of friends, to apply for one of the vacancies in the old regiments thinking it would assist him in obtaining higher rank in the reorganization. He obtained a 2nd Lieutenantcy in the 2nd Cav. and at once joined his regiment in this Department, where he has since been serving. When the 7th Cavalry was ordered to be organized at this Post, Lieut McElroy was among the officers detailed to assist in the organization. He has been upon this duty until the past week when he was relieved by officers of the 7th. No officer has labored more diligently or successfully in the organization of this regiment than Lt McElroy.   he has performed the duty usually devolving upon field officers, and in the most able manner. He has applied for a brief leave which if granted will enable him to visit Washington. I as well as every other officer in the 7th Cav am extremely anxious that Lieut McElroy should if possible be commissioned as Captain in this regiment, he having served with it is fully identified with it. . . ." ALS, *ibid*. On Jan. 5, 1867, Babcock wrote to Rawlins. "I take great pleasure in testifying to the ability and efficient services of Lieut McElroy. He entered West Point (U S Mil Acady) in my class, and as Genl Custer states was dismissed without trial or investigation, and for a single act of indiscretion, taking too much liquor on New Years Day, most of it at houses where he had made New Year's Calls. All the members of my class offered the Supt, Genl Delafield, that we would sign a pledge to abstain from the use of intoxicating liquors while on duty as Cadets at the Mil Acady if he would release Cadet McElroy. The Supt would not accept it, though he did accept a similar pledge for another class-mate within a year. All my classmates thought Cadet McElroy unjustly treated—I have never changed my mind. Lieut McElroy was among the first to come forward in 1861, going into the field with the Three Month men, and again with the Three Year Call. He served with distinction about Vicksburg, in East Tenn, and from Culpepper C. H. to Petersburg, Va, leaving the field only when broken down by disease brought on by exposure in the Field—His conduct had been so examplory that Genl Grant and others gave him letters asking the Sect of War to appoint him into the Judge Advocate Genl's department—which was done and he remained in this department with the rank of Major, until the Close of the war. I think Lieut McElroy's age conduct, experience & education fit him for a higher position than he now occupies. I am certain that if appointed a Capt in any regiment he will fill the position to the satisfaction of the Gov't and to the superior officers of the regiment." ALS, *ibid*. On the same day, USG endorsed this letter. "Respectfully forwarded to the Secretary of War, with the recommendation that in case of original vacancy Lt. McElroy be appointed Captain of Infantry." ES, *ibid*. On Jan. 30, Col. Edward Hatch, 9th Cav., wrote to Brig. Gen. Lorenzo Thomas, asking that McElroy, still serving as 2nd lt., 2nd Cav., be promoted in the 9th Cav. ALS, *ibid*. On Feb. 9, USG endorsed this letter. "Respectfully forwarded. Lt. McElroy has previously been recommended for a Captaincy of Infantry. If there is a vacancy in 9th Cavalry the within application is approved." ES, *ibid*. McElroy was appointed capt., 8th Cav., as of March 6, 1867, and resigned and died in 1870.

To Edwin M. Stanton

(Cipher)   City Point Va. Aug. 11th 1864
HON. E. M. STANTON, SEC. OF WAR WASHINGTON.

I think it but a just reward for services already rendered that Gen. Sherman be now appointed a Maj. Gen. in the ~~r~~Regular Army, ~~and~~ W. S. Hancock and Sheridan Brigadiers in the Regular Army. There are three vacancies for Maj. Gen. and one for Brig. Gen. and Sherman's promotion would make the second. All these officers have proven their worthiness for this advancement. I would also recommend the promotion of Brig. Gen. Mower to fill the the vacant Volunteer Major Generalcy that would thus be created.

U. S. GRANT
Lt. Gn.

ALS (telegram sent), CSmH; telegram received (sent at 2:00 P.M., received at 9:00 P.M.), DNA, RG 107, Telegrams Collected (Bound); *ibid*., Telegrams Collected (Unbound). *O.R.*, I, xlii, part 2, 111; *ibid*., I, xliii, part 1, 767. On

Aug. 11, 1864, Secretary of War Edwin M. Stanton telegraphed to USG. "The promotions you reccommend will be immediately made.—and will" ALS (telegram sent), DNA, RG 107, Telegrams Collected (Bound); telegram received, *ibid.*, Telegrams Collected (Unbound); *ibid.*, RG 108, Letters Received. On Aug. 12, Maj. Gen. William T. Sherman telegraphed to Stanton, sending a copy to USG. "Please convey to the President my thanks for the honor conferred on me—I would have preferred a delay to the close of the campaign also for the commission for Genl Mower whose task was to kill Forrest he only crippled him but he is a young & game officer All well" Telegram received, *ibid.*, RG 107, Telegrams Collected (Unbound); (on Aug. 13) *ibid.*, RG 108, Letters Received. Printed as sent Aug. 12, 7:30 P.M., received Aug. 13, 1:30 A.M., in *O.R.*, I, xxxviii, part 5, 471.

To Maj. Gen. Henry W. Halleck

(Cipher)   City Point Va. Aug. 11th/64
Maj. Gn. Halleck, Washington

We have deserters daily from both Hill's & Longstreets Corps fixing a portion of them at least in our front. There is evidence however of some troops having gone North in the th last few days. It is not impossible that there may be two Divisions, one from each of these Corps, now on the way North. Please notify Sheridan of this.

Two regiments from Fosters Dept. have arrived here. I have heard of none others.

U. S. Grant
Lt. Gn.

ALS (telegram sent), CSmH; telegram received (at 10:20 P.M.), DNA, RG 107, Telegrams Collected (Bound). *O.R.*, I, xlii, part 2, 112. On Aug. 11, 1864, 11:00 A.M., Maj. Gen. Henry W. Halleck telegraphed to USG. "I have issued the order to Genl Foster, but as he sent three thousand five hundred men with Genl Birney, and as his force is much diminished by sickness at this season, I very much doubt if he can safely spare many, if any more. I had previously telegraphed to General Washburne to send everything he could possibly spare to Genl Sherman. Instead of there being anything available in the west, I yesterday ordered five regiments from here and Baltimore to guard prisoners of war at Johnson's Island, Chicago Indiannapolis & Rock Island, in place of hundred days men about to be discharged. Eleven regiments in West Va are to be discharged in four or five days; also most of the militia here and in Baltimore. We have no means of replacing them." ALS (telegram sent), DNA, RG 107, Telegrams Collected (Bound); telegram received, *ibid.*; *ibid.*, Telegrams Collected (Unbound); *ibid.*, RG 108, Letters Received.

On Aug. 11, USG telegraphed to Maj. Gen. George G. Meade. "There is very strong Evidence aside from that brought in by deserters that the enemy are sending troops north—I think one Division from Each Hills & Longstreets Corps have gone—Is our line now in condition to be held by two 2 Corps" Telegram received (at 7:30 P.M.), *ibid.*, RG 94, War Records Office, Army of the Potomac; copies, *ibid.*, RG 108, Letters Sent; DLC-USG, V, 45, 59, 68; (2) Meade Papers, PHi. Printed as sent at 7:30 P.M. in *O.R.*, I, xlii, part 2, 115. Meade endorsed this telegram. "Referred to Maj. Duane Chief Engineer" AES, DNA, RG 94, War Records Office, Army of the Potomac. *O.R.*, I, xlii, part 2, 115. At 11:00 P.M., Meade telegraphed to USG. "Reply to telegram of 7.30 delayed to get report of Engineer officer.—Engineers report it will require three days to complete the redoubts & riflepits in the fronts occupied by the 9th & 5th Corps, and three days more to prepare all the abbattis—This work can only be executed at night it being under the enemys fire, and owing to the extreme heat of the weather & other causes, the work is not as rapidly executed as I expected— I have given orders to put on the maximum force & push it—I know nothing of the condition of the work on the 18. Corps line—" ALS (telegram sent), DNA, RG 94, War Records Office, Army of the Potomac; telegram received, *ibid.*, RG 108, Letters Received. *O.R.*, I, xlii, part 2, 115. Also on Aug. 11, Meade sent four telegrams to USG transmitting information of C.S.A. movements derived from deserters, newspapers, and signal station officers, and on Aug. 12 sent two more. Telegrams received, DNA, RG 108, Letters Received. *O.R.*, I, xlii, part 2, 112–15, 124–25.

Also on Aug. 11, Maj. Gen. Edward O. C. Ord telegraphed to USG. "A Deserter came in this A M reports that he heard a cook who came to his Regt last night from the other side of Petersburg say—that—he heard a man just from Richmond say that part of Lees troops were going north through Richmond yesterday—As cars were running on the Richmond R Road during the night there may be something in the report—" ALS (telegram sent), DNA, RG 107, Telegrams Collected (Unbound); telegram received, *ibid.*, RG 108, Letters Received. *O.R.*, I, xlii, part 2, 123.

Also on Aug. 11, Capt. George K. Leet, Washington, telegraphed to Lt. Col. Theodore S. Bowers. "Scout just arrived reports following. The old man, whom he met a Eleven Oclock last night, left Gordonsville yesterday morning & reports that Longstreets entire Corps was passing North through Staunton night before last. Could give no information as to numbers but was certain the whole Corps was moving to join Early & Breckenridge. Two other Scouts are expected tomorrow morning." ALS (telegram sent), DNA, RG 107, Telegrams Collected (Bound).

To Maj. Gen. George G. Meade

By Telegraph from City Point
Dated Aug 11 *1864.*

To MAJ GEN MEADE

Has any discovery been made of the points where the enemy seem

to be mining   if it can be ascertained nearly where they are running their mines I think it would be well to let them run on without counterming in hopes of having them attack us being careful
to have at such places a second line to keep our men & to establish
batteries to meet any breach that might be made by their explosion

U S Grant
Lt Gen

Telegram received, DNA, RG 94, War Records Office, Army of the Potomac;
copies, *ibid.*, RG 108, Letters Sent; DLC-USG, V, 45, 59, 68; (2) Meade Papers,
PHi. *O.R.*, I, xlii, part 2, 114. On Aug. 10, 1864, 4:50 P.M., Maj. Gen. George
G. Meade had telegraphed to USG. "The following just recd from Gen. Crawford
& is forwarded for your information"   Telegram received, DNA, RG 108, Letters Received. Printed as sent at 5:00 P.M. in *O.R.*, I, xlii, part 2, 101. The enclosed message, reporting information from a deserter about C.S.A. mining, is
ibid. On Aug. 11, 3:45 P.M., Meade telegraphed to USG. "I am not aware that
the enemys mining operations are positively known at any point—Maj. Genl.
Warren some time ago thought he had detected evidences of their mining on his
front, but he subsequently concluded he was mistaken—The arrangments referred to by you of a second line &c were at that time made by him." ALS (telegram sent), DNA, RG 94, War Records Office, Army of the Potomac; telegram
received, *ibid.*, RG 108, Letters Received. *O.R.*, I, xlii, part 2, 114.

To Maj. Gen. Henry W. Halleck

(Cipher)   City Point Aug. 12th/64
Maj. Gen. Halleck, Washington,

Inform Sheridan that it is now certain two Divisions of Infantry have gone to Early and some Cavalry and twenty peices of
Artillery. This movement commenced last Saturday night.[1] He
must be cautious and act now on the defensive until movement here
force them to detach to send this way. Early's force with this increase can not exceed 40,000 men but this is too much for Sheridan
to attack. Send Sheridan the remaining Brigade 19th Corps. I have
ordered to Washington all the One Hundred days men.[2] Their
time will soon be out but for the present they will do to sand in the
~~intrenchm~~ defences.

U. S. Grant
Lt. Gn

ALS (telegram sent), Stevens Collection, Washington University, St. Louis, Mo.; telegram received (sent at 9:00 A.M., received at 7:00 P.M.), DNA, RG 107, Telegrams Collected (Bound). *O.R.*, I, xliii, part 1, 43, 775. See *Memoirs*, II, 326–27. On Aug. 13, 1864, 7:30 P.M. and 10:00 P.M., Maj. Gen. Philip H. Sheridan, Cedar Creek, Va., telegraphed to USG. "I was unable to get South of Early but will push him up the valley. Reports from citizens, here, Washington, and Harpers Ferry report Longstreets Corps coming this way from Staunton but I still rely on your telegram that it is not here   There is nothing in the valley but wheat and a few fine mules. The sum total of all Earlys transportation is 250 wagons—he has not sent off or accumulated any supplies   He was simply living off the country   the Sixth (6) Corps now occupies Strausburg" Telegram received (on Aug. 14, 1:30 A.M.), DNA, RG 107, Telegrams Collected (Bound); *ibid.*, Telegrams Collected (Unbound); *ibid.*, RG 108, Letters Received; copies, *ibid.*, RG 107, Telegrams Received in Cipher; DLC-Philip H. Sheridan. *O.R.*, I, xliii, part 1, 783. "Your despatch of aug. 12th recd. At the time the sixth (6) army Corps was occupying the heights at Strausburg: the enemy had taken position about three miles beyond and near the base of Signal Mountain. It did not appear that there was more there than their rear-guard with about twelve pieces of artillery   I was making preparations to attack them when your despatch arrived. It did not appear as though they would make a stand and looked more like an invitation for me to follow them up. I did not think it best to do so and have taken position on the south side of Cedar Creek.   all the reports all the reports that I hear and that I have been hearing for some days confirm your telegram that Longstreet is in the valley and that Fitz Lees Cavalry is making its way up the country and when last heard from was at Orange Court-House. So far as I have been able to see there is not a military position in this Valley South of the Potomac. The position here is a very bad one as I cannot cover the numerous rivers that lead in on both of my flanks to the rear   I am not aware that you knew where my command was when you ordered me to take up the defensive. I should like very much to have your advice   Early accumulated no supplies in this section of the Valley; his trains were very much magnified and will not number more than 250 wagons—he left at winchester about 75 there was no supplies accumulated there   I have a large number of hundred days men whose terms of service expire in a few days   Can they be made to serve for a longer period or shall I allow them to be mustered out   Mosby attacked the rear of my wagon train this morning en route here from Harpers Ferry and burned six wagons" Telegram received (on Aug. 14, 8:00 P.M.), DNA, RG 107, Telegrams Collected (Bound); (on Aug. 16) *ibid.*, RG 108, Letters Received; copies, *ibid.*, RG 107, Telegrams Received in Cipher; DLC-Philip H. Sheridan. *O.R.*, I, xliii, part 1, 783. See telegram to Maj. Gen. Philip H. Sheridan, Aug. 16, 1864.

1. Aug. 6.
2. On Aug. 11, USG telegraphed to Maj. Gen. Benjamin F. Butler. "You may commence immediately shipping to Washington all the one hundred day men" Telegram received (at 8:00 P.M.), DLC-Benjamin F. Butler; DLC-USG, V, 45, 59, 68; DNA, RG 108, Letters Sent.

To Maj. Gen. Henry W. Halleck

(Cipher)   Aug. 12 [1864] 7 P m
MAJ. GEN. HALLECK, WASHINGTON.

I get constant reports of an intention on the part of the rebels to land atrms at Point Lookout to arm the prisoners confined there to aid their escape. I do not think the plan very feasable but it is probably advisable that they should all be removed to places further North and more secure.

U. S. GRANT
Lt. Gen.

ALS (telegram sent), MoSHi; telegram received (at 11:00 P.M.), DNA, RG 107, Telegrams Collected (Bound). *O.R.*, I, xliii, part 1, 775.

On Aug. 14, 1864, 12:15 P.M., Col. William Hoffman, commissary gen. of prisoners, telegraphed to USG. "Deducting from the prisoners of war now at Ponit Lookout those ordered to Elmira there will remain including the sick about six Thousand well guarded by infantry, artillery with field works and four gunboats and are beleived to be safe but if you deem it advisable they will be removed to New York" Telegram received (on Aug. 15), DNA, RG 108, Letters Received; copy, *ibid.*, RG 249, Telegrams Sent. *O.R.*, II, vii, 594. On Aug. 15, 8:30 P.M., USG telegraphed to Hoffman. "You need not move any more Prisoners from Point Lookout so long as you deem them safe there" Telegram received (on Aug. 17, 6:30 A.M.), DNA, RG 107, Telegrams Collected (Bound); *ibid.*, RG 249, Letters Received; copies, *ibid.*, RG 107, Telegrams Received in Cipher; *ibid.*, RG 108, Letters Sent; DLC-USG, V, 45, 59, 68; USG 3. *O.R.*, I, xlii, part 2, 194; *ibid.*, I, xliii, part 1, 799; *ibid.*, II, vii, 594.

To Maj. Gen. Benjamin F. Butler

By Telegraph from City Pt
Dated Aug—12th *1864.*

To GEN BUTLER.

Our ientrenchments are now so strong that with a very thin line they can be held. We have the further security that the enemy have shown that he feels no inclination to attack fortifications. Under this view I have been thinking that with the colored troops alone or at furthest with the colored troops & the white troops of the 10th corps the 18th corps might be got foot loose to rest & fit up for other service which I will make known to you. I think one Inf'y man to six feet the greatest abundance at Bermuda & one (1) to four feet sufficient for the line north of the Appomattox   As soon after the matter about which I addressed you confidentially an hour ago is settled I wish you would take this matter in hand.

U. S. GRANT
Lt Genl.

Telegram received, DLC-Benjamin F. Butler; copies, DLC-USG, V, 45, 59, 68; DNA, RG 108, Letters Sent. *O.R.*, I, xlii, part 2, 136.

To Maj. Gen. Benjamin F. Butler

(Confidential)   City Point Va. Aug. 12th 1864
MAJ. GEN. BUTLER,
COMD.G DEPT. OF N. C. & VA.
GENERAL,

It having become evident that the enemy has sent North two if not three Divisions of Infantry, twenty pieces of Artillery, and one Division of Cavalry, besides the dismounted Cavalry, and a few regiments to Charleston, I have determined to see if we cannot force him to return here or give us an advantage. To do this I have given the same instructions as for the last move from Deep Bottom. There is this difference however in the preparation. The 2d Corps, the only one out of line and foot loose, will march here this afternoon to embark on steamers. They will be under the impression, except the commander, that Washington is their destination. To facilitate embarkation (ostensibly) the Artillery & transportation goes to Bermuda Hundred to-night. After dark to-morrow night the Pontoon bridge will be laid at the same place as on the former occation. As soon as laid, or soon after 12 O'Clock at night, the Cavalry and Artillery will commence crossing. The Inf.y, which will all be embarked here during the day on steamers, will start so as to reach Deep Bottom about 2 a. m. the 14th. I hope to have prompt movements and ~~with~~ favorable results.

What force can you spare from Bermuda Hundred to be used North of the James with this expedition? What ever force you can spare, reducing the force to hold your line to a minimum, I wish you to have ready to follow the Artillery and Cavalry soon after day light on the 14th.

> I am General, very respectfully
> your obt. svt.
> U. S. GRANT
> Lt. Gn.

ALS, DLC-Benjamin F. Butler. *O.R.*, I, xlii, part 2, 136. At 5:30 [P.M.], Aug. 12, 1864, Maj. Gen. Benjamin F. Butler wrote to USG. "Your note of instructions is recieved Owing to the recent arrival of the South Carolina Troops I am unable to say just how many we can spare for the purpose but I think 10 thousand men for a weeks operations and perhaps more if the 18th holds its ground for the present. I will write you in detail and at length as soon as I can ascertain precisely" ALS, DNA, RG 108, Letters Received. *O.R.*, I, xlii, part 2, 136.

On Aug. 11, Butler had telegraphed to USG. "If you like I will be down with my boat at two (2) o'clock when you have finished your dinner" Telegram received, DNA, RG 107, Telegrams Collected (Unbound). On the same day, USG telegraphed to Butler. "The hour named by you to be here will suit me" Telegram received, DLC-Benjamin F. Butler. Also on Aug. 11, USG telegraphed to Butler. "Be so kind as to forward without delay your last Tri Monthly reports, to embrace the organization of your Command." Copy, DLC-USG, V, 68. On Aug. 12, Butler telegraphed to USG. "Telegram receved Our trimonthslys are not made up as early ~~as pr~~ as otherwise would be done be cause we wait for N. Carolina. Report shall be ~~sent by~~ sent in the mornig" ALS (telegram sent), DNA, RG 107, Telegrams Collected (Unbound); telegram received, *ibid.*, RG 108, Letters Received.

On Aug. 12, 5:00 P.M., Butler telegraphed to USG transmitting a signal message reporting railroad cars carrying troops to Richmond. Copy (telegram sent), *ibid.*, RG 107, Telegrams Collected (Unbound); telegram received, *ibid.*, RG 108, Letters Received. *O.R.*, I, xlii, part 2, 138. On the same day, Butler telegraphed to USG. "We have caught enough of a signal message to rebel rams to learn that they have a deserter. Message is as follows: And that they are cutting a canal through. The explosion Tuesday, he says, was a gun-boat." *Ibid.*, p. 137. On the same day, Butler telegraphed to USG transmitting a telegram of the same date from Capt. Lemuel B. Norton to Col. John W. Shaffer. "The Signal Officer at the Water Battery reports that he saw late this P. M. several heavy columns of dust ~~a~~ on the P & R Turnpike near Kingsland Creek, moving towards Richmond." Copy (telegram sent), DNA, RG 107, Telegrams Collected (Unbound).

To Maj. Gen. Henry W. Halleck

(Cipher)   City Point Va. Aug. 13th 1864, 1 p. m.
MAJ. GEN. HALLECK, WASHINGTON,

Is there any recruits going from the Western states to Sherman? I have sent a regiment 1000 strong, a very excellent regiment but composed entirely of deserters and prisoners from the rebel Army, to Pope. The regiment must now be ~~on its w~~ in New York on its way. All the troops that Pope can relieve by this increase I want sent to Sherman. Have Inspectors or Surgeons gone to the Western Hospitals to clear them out and send the convalescents to the front?

U. S. GRANT
Lt. Gn

ALS (telegram sent), CSmH; telegram received (at 7:35 P.M.), DNA, RG 107, Telegrams Collected (Bound). *O.R.*, I, xli, part 2, 680. On Aug. 13, 1864, 9:30 P.M., Maj. Gen. Henry W. Halleck telegraphed to USG. "I presume the regiment asked for by Genl Augur was the 2d New York, Col. Whistler. Boards are sent to examine hospitals as fast as we can get surgeons. In the meantime inspections are being made by local surgeons. The extreme heat has had a very bad effect upon the sick in hospitals   All troops under Genl Pope not actually in the Indian campaign were ordered to Genl Sherman, and special inspection made of his Dept. A new demand for troops to-day from Indianna and fears expressed of an attempt to release prisoners of war." ALS (telegram sent), DNA, RG 107, Telegrams Collected (Bound); telegram received, *ibid.*; *ibid.*, Telegrams Collected (Unbound); (on Aug. 14) *ibid.*, RG 108, Letters Received. *O.R.*, I, xli, part 2, 680; *ibid.*, I, xlii, part 2, 140.

On Aug. 17, Maj. Gen. Henry W. Halleck wrote to USG. "I enclose herewith a copy of a letter just received from Genl. Pope, from which you will see the difficulty of immediately withdrawing troops from his Dept., and the necessary loss of property and increase of Indian difficulties resulting therefrom. It is a very great mistake to suppose that Genl. Pope has retained an unnecessarily large force in his Dept. On the contrary I have found him the most ready of all the Dept. Commanders to give assistance to others when asked—certainly quite a contrast to some of the present and former commanders of the Depts. of Kansas, Missouri and Ohio. In addition to the pressing representations of the Governors of Kansas, Nebraska, Idaho and Colorado, and Genls. Curtis, Blunt, &c., the Indian Bureau and Interior Dept. all urge the absolute necessity of sending *more* troops into the Indian country if we wish to avoid a general Indian war. Undoubtedly much of this is gotten up by Indian Agents and speculators for their own purposes; nevertheless, in view of existing hostilities in that quarter, the breaking up of the overland mail route, the capture of military posts, and the murder of emigrants, the military authorities will be very seriously blamed if they withdraw the troops now there. It is pretended by the Indian Bureau and the Territorial Officers that there is undoubted evidence of a much larger combination, and a much more extensive Indian war pending in the northwest than in 1862." LS, DNA, RG 108, Letters Received. *O.R.*, I, xli, part 2, 739. The enclosure is *ibid.*, pp. 675–76.

On June 10, Lt. Col. Theodore S. Bowers issued Special Orders No. 32. "Lieut Col W. L. Duff (2nd Regt. Illinois Artillery Vols.) Assistant Inspector General, will proceed to the Department of the North West and Inspect the troops of that Department wherever they may be stationed or on duty. Upon the execution of this order he will rejoin these Headquarters—" Copies, DLC-USG, V, 57, 62, 66. On July 2, Lt. Col. William L. Duff, St. Paul, Minn., wrote to Brig. Gen. John A. Rawlins about his inspection tour and expressed doubts that Maj. Gen. John Pope needed a strong force in his dept. ALS, DNA, RG 108, Letters Received. *O.R.*, I, xli, part 2, 29–30.

To Maj. Gen. Henry W. Halleck

City Point Va
Aug 13th 1864

MAJ. GEN H W HALLECK
CHIEF OF STAFF.

The 6th & 10th New York Heavy Artillery are ordered to Washington. Gen Augur made request for a particular regiment giving however only the name of its Colonel "Wheeler." No regiment commanded by Col Wheeler can be found here[1]

U S GRANT
Lt. Genl.

Telegram received (at 4:00 P.M.), DNA, RG 107, Telegrams Collected (Bound); *ibid.*, Telegrams Collected (Unbound); copies, *ibid.*, RG 108, Letters Sent; DLC-USG, V, 45, 59, 68. *O.R.*, I, xlii, part 2, 140. See preceding telegram.

On Aug. 12, 1864, 11:00 A.M., Maj. Gen. Henry W. Halleck had telegraphed to USG. "Please direct one of your staff to send me a list of Heavy Artillery regiments to be sent here, in order that we may retain the convalescents belonging to them." ALS (telegram sent), DNA, RG 107, Telegrams Collected (Bound); telegram received, *ibid.*; *ibid.*, Telegrams Collected (Unbound); *ibid.*, RG 108, Letters Received. On the same day, USG telegraphed to Maj. Gen. Benjamin F. Butler. "Send one regt Heavy Art'y to Washn. and let me know as soon as possible what one you send." Telegram received, DLC-Benjamin F. Butler; DLC-USG, V, 45, 59, 68; DNA, RG 108, Letters Sent. On the same day, Butler telegraphed to USG transmitting a telegram of the same date from Maj. Gen. Edward O. C. Ord to Butler. "The tenth 10th N. Y. Lt Col Arden Comdg will go as they are not in trenches   they are about 900 for duty & will get off in about two hours and are ordered to march to City Point" LS (telegram sent), *ibid.*, RG 107, Telegrams Collected (Unbound). On Aug. 13, USG telegraphed to Maj. Gen. George G. Meade. "Send a regiment of heavy artillery to this place to embark for Washington & let me know the name & number of the regt. as soon as possible" Telegram received, *ibid.*, RG 94, War Records Office, Army of the Potomac; copies, *ibid.*, RG 108, Letters Sent; DLC-USG, V, 45, 59, 68; (2) Meade Papers, PHi. *O.R.*, I, xlii, part 2, 141. At 10:30 A.M., Meade telegraphed to USG. "The 6th N. Y. Heavy Artillery, Col Kitching comdg, will be at once sent to City Point, in compliance with your telegram just received." Copies, DNA, RG 393, Army of the Potomac, Letters Sent; Meade Papers, PHi. *O.R.*, I, xlii, part 2, 141.

1. On Aug. 8, 3:45 P.M., Maj. Gen. Christopher C. Augur telegraphed to USG. "General Halleck informs me that you may send some of the Heavy Artillery regiments for duty in the Forts here. As colonel Whistler is now comg a brigade in these works, I should be glad to have his regiment sent, if it can be spared." LS (telegram sent), DNA, RG 107, Telegrams Collected (Unbound); telegram received, *ibid.*; *ibid.*, RG 108, Letters Received. *O.R.*, I, xlii, part 2, 85; *ibid.*, I, xliii, part 1, 727. The name was changed from Whistler to Wheeler in transmission. Joseph N. G. Whistler, USMA 1846, taught at USMA before his appointment as col., 2nd N. Y. Art., as of May 6, 1863. Wounded at Petersburg in June, 1864, Whistler served afterward in the defenses of Washington. His father, Col. William Whistler, had commanded the 4th Inf. in which USG served.

To Maj. Gen. Benjamin F. Butler

> *By Telegraph from* City Pt
> *Dated* Aug 13 *1864.*

To GEN BUTLER,

Are the Rams firing at working parties at Dutch Gap—If so with what effect. Which do you call Battery Sawyer?

U. S. GRANT.
Lt Genl

Telegram received, DLC-Benjamin F. Butler; copies, DLC-USG, V, 45, 59, 68; DNA, RG 108, Letters Sent. On Aug. 13, 1864, 6:20 A.M., by readdressing and rewriting a telegram he had received from a signal officer, Maj. Gen. Benjamin F. Butler telegraphed to USG. "The Rams have moved down in the next reach beyond Dutch Gap below Cox ferry. Battery Sawyer ~~firing~~ water Battery is replying" LS (telegram sent), *ibid.*, RG 107, Telegrams Collected (Unbound). Printed as received at 6:35 A.M. in *O.R.*, I, xlii, part 2, 158. At 7:55 A.M., Butler telegraphed to USG. "The rebel rams, the rebel battery at Signal station & Howlet house have opened upon the working party at Dutch Gap—The Sawyer

Battery which is the one at Crow Nest Signal Station the water Battery, the morter battery Wilcox, one of the redoubts have opened in reply—5 or 6 men were wounded by a chance shot. I have directed the 100 pounder which is in position at Dutch Gap to open." Copy (telegram sent), DNA, RG 107, Telegrams Collected (Unbound). *O.R.*, I, xlii, part 2, 158.

To Maj. Gen. Winfield S. Hancock

City Point, Va. Aug. 13. 1864.

Maj. Gen. W. S. Hancock
Comd'g. 2d A. C.

In addition to the instructions which you already have, but little can be added. You will have to be guided in Your movements by those of the enemy and his numbers. If You do not succeed in placing the enemy between your Infantry and the James river, it may not be safe to send the Cavalry to the Va. Central Railroad. Of this matter you can best judge. There is no necessity in holding Your connection with Deep Bottom. With the force at Your Command, You will always be able to get back to that point or some other on the James River. Wherever You go consume or destroy all the forage and provisions, except what is housed for family use, if it does not interfere with Military movements to do so. I always regret to see wanton destruction of property, which cannot be used in prolonging the War, and know that you equally oppose such conduct on the part of our troops. No caution on this head subject therefore is necessary. Cattle, horses, forage and provisions however, and especially so near as partially beseiged city, are fair captures and it is a duty we owe ourselves to take them even if they should be the property of Union citizens. In such case, a very improbable one near Richmond, they could be paid for.

Having a force of 9000 men from the 10th Army Corps, in addition to your own Corps, if You can advance beyond Chapins Bluff, keeping that point covered, I think it advisable to do so. Unless forced to return, in order to keep communication with the James, remain at the highest point up the river gained, until the

Cavalry returns, and You receive Orders to return. You can always be supplied by Steamers either at Dutch Gap or Deep Bottom.

Very respectfully
your obdt servt.
U. S. GRANT.
Lt. Genl.

Copies, DLC-USG, V, 45, 59, 68; DNA, RG 108, Letters Sent. *O.R.*, I, xlii, part 2, 148.

On Aug. 13, 1864, Lt. Col. Francis A. Walker, adjt. for Maj. Gen. Winfield S. Hancock, transmitted to USG a copy of orders for the movement the following day. ALS, DNA, RG 108, Letters Received. *O.R.*, I, xlii, part 2, 149–50.

To Maj. Gen. George G. Meade

By Telegraph from City Pt
Dated Aug 13th *1864.*

To MAJ GEN MEADE

If the enemy are reduced as much in numbers as we have every reason to believe they are Hancocks movement tomorrow may lead to almost the entire abandonment of Petersburg—Have this watched as closely as you can & if you find this view realized take such advantage of it as you deem best—Either move to the left with such troops as you can take from the ninth & fifth Corps leaving but a very thin line or draw out the 5th Corps entire to move with according to your judgment—I shall go to Deep Bottom early in the morning myself

U S GRANT
Lt Gen

Telegram received (at 10:10 P.M.), DNA, RG 94, War Records Office, Army of the Potomac; copies, *ibid.*, RG 108, Letters Sent; DLC-USG, V, 45, 59, 68; (2) Meade Papers, PHi. *O.R.*, I, xlii, part 2, 140.

On Aug. 13, 1864, 8:00 A.M., Maj. Gen. George G. Meade telegraphed to USG. "Will you give the necessary orders about the bridges at Deep Bottom—I have directed Hancock to confer with you fully on the proposed plan of operations.—" ALS (telegram sent), DNA, RG 94, War Records Office, Army of the Potomac; telegram received, *ibid.*, RG 108, Letters Received. *O.R.*, I, xlii, part 2, 140. On the same day, USG telegraphed to Meade. "I have given all the orders for bridge &c—Hancock will be reinforced nine thousand 9000 men from Butler"

Telegram received, DNA, RG 94, War Records Office, Army of the Potomac; copies, *ibid.*, RG 108, Letters Sent; DLC-USG, V, 45, 59, 68; (2) Meade Papers, PHi. *O.R.*, I, xlii, part 2, 141. On the same day, Lt. Col. Cyrus B. Comstock twice telegraphed to 1st Lt. Peter S. Michie, the second time at 9:00 P.M. "Gen. Benham has been ordered to build the new bridge at Deep Bottom taking the material from here. The spare boats now at Deep Bottom should be taken below all the ponton bridges and held in readiness for Gen. Hancock if he needs them in landing troops" "Gen Benham's train boats he reports will be at Deep Bottom by 9½ P. M. & the bridge down by 11½ P. M. It will only be necessary to use the boats now at Deep Bottom in case of some extraordinary delay in the above programme." ALS (telegrams sent), DNA, RG 108, Telegrams Sent by Comstock.

At 5:30 P.M., Meade telegraphed to USG transmitting information received from deserters. Telegram received, *ibid.*, Letters Received. *O.R.*, I, xlii, part 2, 141–42.

At 10:00 P.M., Meade telegraphed to USG. "The following is referred for the necessary authority to bring up the 10 inch Mortars as under your orders of the 30th Ult all these Mortars were withdrawn & sent to Broadway landing" Telegram received, DNA, RG 108, Letters Received. *O.R.*, I, xlii, part 2, 142. Meade transmitted a copy of a telegram received by him from Brig. Gen. Henry J. Hunt, chief of art. "The enemy has established a battery of rifled 32 Pdrs just behind the Crest Near the plank road in front of & about 1300 yards from our large Battery near the Tayler house   As yet but one or two Guns have been opened on us   The position is well covered from our direct fire   I would reccommend that 4 10 inch or 8 inch preferably 10 inch Mortars be placed in position near the Taylor house to control it"   Copy, DNA, RG 108, Letters Received. *O.R.*, I, xlii, part 2, 142–43. On the same day, Comstock telegraphed to Meade. "Lt. Gen. Grant desires me to say that he approves the proposition in refence to the mortars and wishes you to call move them up from Broadway accordingly." ALS (telegram sent), DNA, RG 108, Telegrams Sent by Comstock; telegram received (at 10:30 P.M.), *ibid.*, RG 94, War Records Office, Army of the Potomac. Printed as sent at 10:30 P.M. in *O.R.*, I, xlii, part 2, 143.

At 10:30 P.M., Meade telegraphed to USG. "The withdrawal of Greggs division of Cavalry & Kautz small force leaves but little Cavalry to watch between the left of the army & the James—I would therefore suggest the withdrawal of the Cattle herd of the armies in the fiedld as near City Point as practicable—Kautz has been ordered to post a regiment at Sycamore Church.—" ALS (telegram sent), DNA, RG 94, War Records Office, Army of the Potomac; telegram received, *ibid.*, RG 108, Letters Received. *O.R.*, I, xlii, part 2, 143.

To Maj. Gen. George G. Meade

City Point Va. Aug 13 '64.

Maj Gen. Meade.

I gave Gen. Burnside leave of absence. for The leave is only just made out this evening and directions were given to communicate the fact to you, and no doubt it will be communicated in the morning by the A. A. G. Gen. Parke will Command the 9th Corps. He has gone out this evening.

U. S. GRANT
Lt. Genl.

Telegram, copies, DLC-USG, V, 45, 59, 68; DNA, RG 108, Letters Sent; (2) Meade Papers, PHi. *O.R.*, I, xlii, part 2, 142. On Aug. 13, 1864, 10:00 P.M., Maj. Gen. George G. Meade telegraphed to USG. "Brig. Genl. Wilcox informs me he has assumed command of the 9th Corps—No official communication has been received at these Hd. Qrs authorising Genl. Burnside to leave—Has any action been had or taken." ALS (telegram sent), DNA, RG 94, War Records Office, Army of the Potomac; copies, *ibid.*, RG 393, Army of the Potomac, Letters Sent; Meade Papers, PHi. *O.R.*, I, xlii, part 2, 142.

On Aug. 13, Maj. Gen. Ambrose E. Burnside telegraphed to USG. "In accordance with the understanding with you yesterday I request that Lt Col Richmond A. A. G. Lt Col Loring asst Insp Gen & Major Neill A A G be allowed to go with me—Shall I give to them & to my 2 aides & Maj Lydig of Gen Parkes staff leaves of absence for Twenty (20) days by your authority or shall I call early tomorrow morning at your Hd Qrs for the orders. I have made arrangements with Gen Wilcox for the proper & efficient carrying on of the duties at Corps Hd Qrs during my absence—" Telegram received, DNA, RG 108, Letters Received. On Aug. 14, USG telegraphed to Meade. "Special Orders No 73 granting leave of absence for 30 days to Maj Gen A E Burnside & Lieut Col Richmond a. a. G of the 9th Corps are on the way to your Head Quarters also leave of absence to Lieut Col Pierce Clf Q. M for 8 days granted on recommendation of Gen. Ingalls" Telegram received (at 7:50 A.M.), *ibid.*, RG 94, War Records Office, Army of the Potomac; (2) Meade Papers, PHi. *O.R.*, I, xlii, part 2, 168.

On Aug. 25, Burnside, Crawford House, White Mountains, N. H., telegraphed to USG. "Shall I report with my staff at your Head Qrs or shall I wait further orders. We would like a few days more if consistent with interest of service   Please answer at Glen House" Telegram received, DNA, RG 107, Telegrams Collected (Unbound); *ibid.*, RG 108, Letters Received. On the same day, Lt. Col. Cyrus B. Comstock telegraphed to Burnside. "Lt. Gen Grant directs me to say that you are authorized to remain absent with your staff till further orders, notifying him of any change of address." ALS (telegram sent), *ibid.*, Telegrams Sent by Comstock. On Aug. 31, Burnside, Providence, R. I., telegraphed to USG. "My leave of absence expires friday next   Shall we await orders here" Telegram received (press), *ibid.*, RG 107, Telegrams Collected (Bound); *ibid.*, Telegrams Collected (Unbound); *ibid.*, RG 108, Letters Received. *O.R.*, I, xlii, part 2, 603. On Sept. 1, USG telegraphed to Burnside. "Await orders where you are. Your Staff may remain with You." Copies, DLC-USG, V, 45, 68, 107; DNA, RG 108, Letters Sent. *O.R.*, I, xlii, part 2, 1000. On the same day, Lt. Col. Theodore S. Bowers telegraphed to Burnside. "Lieut. Gen. Grant directs me to say to you, that under existing circumstances he does not deem it best to return to you to the Command of thYour Corps at present, but, that he will not relieve You from it, unless to assign You to some other

Command. He therefore desires you to remain at Providence or such other place, as you may select, until further orders from him." Copies, DLC-USG, V, 45, 68, 107; DNA, RG 108, Letters Sent. *O.R.*, I, xlii, part 2, 641. On Sept. 24, 5:00 P.M., Meade telegraphed to USG listing the staff officers with Burnside. Df (telegram sent), DNA, RG 94, War Records Office, Army of the Potomac; copies, *ibid.*, RG 393, Army of the Potomac, Letters Sent; Meade Papers, PHi. On Sept. 28, USG telegraphed to Burnside. "You will please direct the return without delay to the A. of P. of all your Staff, except the personal Aides-de-Camp." Copies, DLC-USG, V, 45, 69, 107; DNA, RG 108, Letters Sent. On Sept. 30, Burnside telegraphed to USG. "Dispatch recieved and the members of my Staff will be ordered back at once. Some have gone." Telegram received, *ibid.*, RG 107, Telegrams Collected (Unbound); *ibid.*, RG 108, Letters Received. *O.R.*, I, xlii, part 2, 1136. On Oct. 3, Lt. Col. Adam Badeau telegraphed to Burnside. "Lieut. Gen. Grant directs me to say that you are at liberty to retain Lt. Col. Richmond" ALS (telegram sent), DNA, RG 107, Telegrams Collected (Unbound); copy, DLC-USG, V, 69. On Oct. 4, Burnside wrote to USG. "I enclose the resignation of Major Neill, who has been with my command from the time we started to N. C. until I left you in August—It is almost absolutely necessary that he should resign, and not knowing exactly how to forward the paper ~~directly~~ I have taken the liberty of forwarding directly to you, with the request that you will send it forward, and thereby confer a favor upon . . . My address for a few days will be 5th Avenue Hotel New York—" ALS, DNA, RG 94, ACP, 216N CB 1864. On Oct. 19, USG endorsed this letter. "Respectfully forwarded to the Adjutant General of the Army, Washington. D. C.—Approved." ES, *ibid.* See letter to Maj. Gen. Ambrose E. Burnside, Oct. 17, 1864.

To Maj. Gen. Henry W. Halleck

Strawberry Plains, Aug. 14 *1864* 10 a. m.

MAJ. GEN. HALLECK. WASHINGTON.

Last night I moved the 2d Corps about 9000 men of 10th Corps and Greggs Division of Cavalry to this side of the river to threaten Richmond from the North and if possible to draw back troops from the valley.[1] We have captured prisoners from four different Brigades of Fields Division Longstreets Corps and also from Wilcox Division of Hills Corps. Fields Division is one that we supposed had gone to the valley. We know two Divisions of Hills Corps to be at Petersburg. This fixes the 3d here as I have hertofore supposed. Picketts Division of Longstreets Corps is opposite Butler at Bermuda Hundred. This leaves but one Division of Infantry to have gone to the vally. I am now satisfied no more has gone. Please forward this to Sheridan.

U. S. GRANT
Lt. Gn

ALS (telegram sent), CSmH; telegram received (sent at 11:00 A.M., received Aug. 15, 1864, 9:00 A.M.), DNA, RG 107, Telegrams Collected (Bound). *O.R.*, I, xlii, part 2, 167; *ibid.*, I, xliii, part 1, 791.

1. On Aug. 14, 5:00 A.M., 8:15 A.M., and 8:25 A.M., Maj. Gen. Winfield S. Hancock telegraphed and wrote to USG. "At this moment not more than half of the troops have landed from the steamers We have been working all night It will be 9 oclock before all of the corps are disembarked. The cavalry are across—I ordered Gen Birney to attack at day light but I have since ordered him to defer it until we are ready here unless he has commenced it—I have not heard his firing yet—" Telegram received (at 10:10 A.M.), DNA, RG 94, War Records Office, Army of the Potomac; *ibid.*, RG 108, Letters Received. *O.R.*, I, xlii, part 2, 172. "Genl Birney has driven in the Enemy's picquets capturing, he says, about one hundred. I have sent to have them questioned. Two of my Divisions are now advancing Genl. Birney's present line is the Kings land road. he will advance with my troops." "I telegraphed you at 5. a. m. but I am informed that 1½ miles of the telegraph line was knocked down last night my telegram was to the effect, that not more than one half of my troops were dis embarked at that hour (5 a m) & that I had directed Genl. Birney to suspend his attack until I sent him further orders—At this hour 2 Divisions are disembarked & about one half of the third." ALS, DNA, RG 108, Letters Received. *O.R.*, I, xlii, part 2, 172. At 1:20 P.M., Lt. Col. Cyrus B. Comstock wrote to Hancock. "General Birney, who is across the creek, will push for the New Market road at once. Apparently General Birney has troops within a few hundred yards of New Market." *Ibid.*, p. 185. At 3:20 P.M. and 6:30 P.M., Hancock wrote to USG, sending a copy of the second to Maj. Gen. George G. Meade. "Gen Barlow attacked the enemys line on the Central Road, took the first line of rifle pits, driving the enemy out but failed to take the 2d & 3d lines though attempting it twice. He is now about to try it again & thinks he will succeed—The troops are not behaving steadily today. A great many are straggling & sunstruck The loss in officers has been heavy. The enemys force did not appear large The point referred to is abut a mile up the Central Road from the Newmarket Road" ALS (2), DNA, RG 94, War Records Office, Army of the Potomac. *O.R.*, I, xlii, part 2, 173. "Gen Barlow has made another attack upon the enemy & has been repulsed with some loss The enemy are massing pretty heavily to their left & I rather anticipate an attack upon Gen Barlow Gen Birney just reported to me that he has captured Six pieces and two mortars. I have ordered all my skirmishers to advance on my left where the enemy commenced ~~making~~ massing on my right including those of Gen Birney" Telegram received, DNA, RG 107, Telegrams Collected (Unbound); *ibid.*, RG 108, Letters Received. *O.R.*, I, xlii, part 2, 173. At 5:05 P.M., Maj. Gen. David B. Birney telegraphed to Maj. Gen. Benjamin F. Butler, who transmitted the message to USG. "I have captured six (6) guns & two mortors. I hope to bring them in after nightfall. they were taken by Gen. Fosters brigade." Telegram received, DNA, RG 107, Telegrams Col-

lected (Unbound); *ibid.*, RG 108, Letters Received. *O.R.*, I, xlii, part 1, 677. At 7:30 P.M., USG telegraphed to Hancock. "No movement of Troops from Petersburg has been observed until this evening. a body supposed to be about a division now seems to be moving so reported by Signal Officer—" Telegram received, DNA, RG 107, Telegrams Collected (Unbound); copies, *ibid.*, RG 108, Letters Sent; DLC-USG, V, 45, 59, 68. *O.R.*, I, xlii, part 2, 173. On the same day, Hancock telegraphed to USG and Meade. "Gen Birney has called upon me for transportation for the six Guns & two Mortars captured by him this evening—I think there is no doubt but they will be gotten off—after dark tonight— Gen Barlow did not find the enemys left flank which was refused, but attacked a salient of their line, He had a presistant fight although he did not carry it, he held the ground passed over The attack was not made in sufficient force— The troops did not fight with their accoustomed vigor, owing to the excessive heat large numbers straggled from the ranks, The loss was considerable—The troops saved their honor by not losing their killed & wounded—Gregg reports the charles city road cut up by the enemy's entrenchments the advanced of which he carried—They were occupied by Hamptons Legion—The lines were thinly held but were re inforced while Barlow was attacking . . . P. S. I shall set Birney at work in the morning as Gen Grant suggested" Telegram received (at 9:30 P.M.), DNA, RG 94, War Records Office, Army of the Potomac; *ibid.*, RG 108, Letters Received. Printed as sent at 9:30 P.M. in *O.R.*, I, xlii, part 2, 174.

On Aug. 15, Butler telegraphed to USG. "My pickets at Dutch Gap report trains running all night from Petersburg to a point just above them & their stopping & whistling probably at Chaffins farm—Signal officer at spring Hill reports two (2) trains have passed from Petersburg & two (2) towards Petersburg the last loaded with Commissary stores up to Seven (7) a. m. at Nine (9) a. m. a regt. of Cavalry has just passed Junction towards Richmond—Birney reports that his Six (6) guns turn out to be four Eight (8) Inch Howitzers— Also that he is ordered to make an assault on the right of Hancocks this morning. Pretty far round from left to right of the 2nd Corps—" Telegram received, DNA, RG 108, Letters Received. Printed as sent at 9:00 A.M. in *O.R.*, I, xlii, part 2, 206. On the same day, USG telegraphed to Butler. "Did Birney secure the Guns reported or are they on ground that could not be reached by either party?" Telegram received (at 11:05 A.M.), DLC-Benjamin F. Butler. *O.R.*, I, xlii, part 2, 206. On the same day, Butler telegraphed to USG. "The following is an answer to my inquiry about Guns taken by Gen Birney yesterday." Telegram received, DNA, RG 108, Letters Received. *O.R.*, I, xlii, part 2, 206. The enclosure is *ibid*. Also on Aug. 15, Hancock telegraphed to USG and Meade. "Gen Birneys Captures yesterday were Eight (8) Inch Sea Coast howitzers Three (3) of them are entirely removed & the fourth partly taken off—but the train is broken. I dont know that any more will be gotten off—Gen Gregg has found the Enemy entrenched on the Charles City Road at Whites House—Their people Came out of their Entrenchments & attacked but I do not think they have much Strength there—I expect to feel along with my infantry to the Charles City Cross road if I do not sooner find a place to attack—" Telegram received (at 1:30 P.M.), DNA, RG 94, War Records Office, Army of the Potomac; *ibid.*, RG 108, Letters Received. *O.R.*, I, xlii, part 2, 197–98.

To Maj. Gen. Henry W. Halleck

(Cipher)   City Point Aug. 14th/64 8. p. m.
MAJ. GEN. HALLECK, WASHINGTON,

The move to the North side of the James to-day developed the presence of Fields Division of Longstreets Corps which I had supposed ~~had~~ gone to the valley. Picketts Division is also here. We captured six pieces of artillery and over one hundred prisoners. Longstreets troops were under marching orders and this move will detain ~~them~~ it, at least for the present. I think Sheridan is still superior to Early in numbers but not sufficiently so to attack fortifications.

U. S. GRANT
Lt. Gn.

ALS (telegram sent), CSmH; telegram received (on Aug. 16, 1864, 3:30 P.M.), DNA, RG 107, Telegrams Collected (Bound). *O.R.*, I, xlii, part 2, 167; *ibid.*, I, xliii, part 1, 791.

To Maj. Gen. Benjamin F. Butler

Strawberry Plains Aug. 14th/64
MAJ. GEN. BUTLER, REPEAT TO GEN. ORD.

Gen. Meade has been directed to watch closely and if present demonstration North of James should force the enemy to weaken his lines at Petersburg so that advantage can be taken of it to do so without waiting further instructions. In such case he has been authorized to call on the 18th Core for co-operation or assistance. Please instruct Gen. Ord that in case of operations against Petersburg he will receive orders from Gen. Meade.

U. S. GRANT
Lt. Gn.

ALS (telegram sent), DNA, RG 107, Telegrams Collected (Unbound); telegram received, DLC-Benjamin F. Butler; Ord Papers, CU-B. *O.R.*, I, xlii, part 2, 180. On Aug. 14, 1864, Maj. Gen. Edward O. C. Ord telegraphed to USG.

"Dispatch received and will be obeyed." ALS (telegram sent), DNA, RG 107, Telegrams Collected (Unbound).

On the same day, 4:45 P.M., Maj. Gen. Benjamin F. Butler wrote to USG. "I inclose the notes just received from Colonel Dandy. He seems to have joined Hancock nearly. Birney says he is forming his line for the night." *O.R.*, I, xlii, part 2, 180. The enclosed messages from Col. George B. Dandy, 100th N. Y., are *ibid.*, p. 181.

To Maj. Gen. George G. Meade

By Telegraph from City Pt 7 20 P M
Dated Aug 14 *1864.*

To Maj. Gen Meade

You may extend the 9th & 18th Corps as you propose. If Parke & Ord will leave a very thin line in the works and have the bulk of their men in reserve it will rest them very much   I am satisfied that a thin skirmish line is plenty to man our works especially when there is a reserve—

U. S. Grant
Lt. Gen

Telegram received, DNA, RG 94, War Records Office, Army of the Potomac; copies, *ibid.*, RG 108, Letters Sent; DLC-USG, V, 45, 59, 68; (2) Meade Papers, PHi. *O.R.*, I, xlii, part 2, 169. On Aug. 14, 1864, 7:10 P.M. and 11:00 P.M., Maj. Gen. George G. Meade telegraphed to USG. "I propose to withdraw Warren tonight & leave his line to be held by Parke, extending Ord as far as the exploded mine.—Warren to be held in reserve either for a movement, or to reinforce any part of the line if attacked.—As Ord was to be used only in case of a movement, I submit this to you before giving orders." "Orders have been given for the withdrawal of the 5th corps & the occupation of the lines by the 9th & 18th corps—The 5th will be held in reserve for contingencies.—No further intelligence has been received from Signal officers that has not been sent you, except that between 5 & 6 P. M the officer on the plank road saw a small body of cavalry with wagons & ambulances moving northward along the Weldon R. Rd.—" ALS (telegrams sent), DNA, RG 94, War Records Office, Army of the Potomac; telegrams received, *ibid.*, RG 108, Letters Received. *O.R.*, I, xlii, part 2, 169, 170.

At 8:30 A.M., Meade had telegraphed to USG. "Have I any authority to call on Genl. Ord for assistance in case of making a movement.—The only movement in my judgment practicable is to take Warren out of his lines & move him around the enemys works till he finds a point he can penetrate—To do this his line must either be occupied by the extension of the 9th & 18. corps or else left unoccupied in which case there are redoubts which should the enemy get possession of it might seriously embarrass us to recover.—I have sent my engineers to examine how Parke's left flank can be covered in case of Warren's line being given up—but should it be deemed best to hold Warrens line, some portion of the 18th if any can be spared must assist in the extension.—" ALS (telegram sent), DNA, RG 94, War Records Office, Army of the Potomac; telegram received, *ibid.*, RG 107, Telegrams Collected (Unbound); (2) *ibid.*, RG 108, Letters Received. *O.R.*, I, xlii, part 2, 168. On the same day, USG telegraphed to Meade. "In case you find it practicable to make any demonstration against Petersburg command the 18th Corps as you deem proper. Gen. Ord will be directed to receive orders from you." ALS (telegram sent), DNA, RG 107, Telegrams Collected (Unbound); telegram received (at 1:50 P.M.), *ibid.*, RG 94, War Records Office, Army of the Potomac. *O.R.*, I, xlii, part 2, 168.

At 7:00 P.M. and 8:30 P.M., Meade telegraphed to USG transmitting information received from a signal officer and from deserters. Telegrams received, DNA, RG 108, Letters Received. *O.R.*, I, xlii, part 2, 168–69, 169–70.

To Maj. Gen. Philip H. Sheridan

Cipher   City Point Aug. 14th 8. p. m. *1864*
MAJ. GEN. SHERIDAN, WINCHESTER VA.

I moved Hancocks Corps, Greggs Div. of Cavalry and part of the 10th Corps to the North side of James last night to surprise the enemy and prevent him sending troops away. We captured six pieces of Artillery and prisoners from four differeent Brigades of Fields Div. Longstreets Corps. This is a Division I had supposed had gone to the valley. It is now positive that Kershaws Division has gone and no other Inf.y has. This reinforcement to Early will put him nearer on an equality with you in numbers than I want to see and will make it necessary to observe some caution about attacking. I would not however change my instructions further than to enjoin caution.

U. S. GRANT
Lt. Gn.

ALS (telegram sent), CSmH; telegram received (on Aug. 16, 1864, 2:00 P.M.), DNA, RG 107, Telegrams Collected (Bound); *ibid.*, Telegrams Collected (Unbound). *O.R.*, I, xliii, part 1, 791–92.

To Maj. Gen. William T. Sherman

(Cipher)   City Point Aug. 14th *1864*

MAJ. GEN. SHERMAN, NEAR ATLANTA GA.

No Division or Brigade has gone from here West and I shall endeavor to keep the enemy so busy that none will go. The great danger has been of troops going from Lee to join Early in the Shenandoah Valley. I attempted a suprise on the North side of the river last night with the hope of getting near to Richmond and getting Cavalry on their rail-roads on that side of the river. The enemy were found fortified and their works maned by a Division of Longstreet Corps which I supposed had gone to join Early. I approve The great danger you have to apprehend is from Kirby Smith getting his men across the Miss. The move you propose is a little hazerdous but I believe it will succeed. If you do not force the enemy out to fight you you will easily get back to your base. U. S. Grant Our move to-day has resulted in the capture of six pieces of Artillery and some prisoners and probably the killing and wounding of five or six hundred of the enemy. In killed and wounded our loss will probably reach four hundred.

U. S. GRANT

Lt. Gn

ALS (telegram sent), CSmH; telegram received, DNA, RG 107, Telegrams Collected (Unbound). Printed as sent at 8:30 P.M. in *O.R.,* I, xxxviii, part 5, 488. See telegram to Maj. Gen. William T. Sherman, Aug. 9, 1864.

To Edwin M. Stanton

City Point Va. Aug. 15th 1864 [*1:00* P.M.]

HON. E. M. STANTON,

SEC. OF WAR,

At this particular time it is of great importance that we should have on the Pacific Coast not only good Military Commanders but men who will give satisfaction to the people. From what I learn, unofficially, we lack this both in the selection of a commander for the Dept. and for the District of Oregon & Washington. I know Alvord well.[1] I do not think he is fit for the command and he ought to be called East. He is a good man in his ~~atte~~ intentions and would do well to place on any kind of a Board but I know of no other duty he is eminently suited for. McDowell,[2] if I am not wrongly informed, is likely to do more harm than good where he is. I am in favor of Halleck for that Dept. He is acquainted with the people and can combine Civil with Military Administration which is required in that Dept. McDowell is only a Soldier and has never been any thing els. ~~U. S. Grant Lt. Gn.~~ It would not be necessary to send any one to relieve Alvord at present. Simply to order him East would be sufficient.

If Halleck ~~cann~~ not be spared from where he is then to restore Wright[3] would do. Have you any information from the Pacific Coast leading you to the same conclusion as to the necessity for a change.

~~Lt. Gn.~~ U. S. Grant

Lt. Gn.

ALS (telegram sent), CSmH; telegram received (on Aug. 16, 1864, noon), DNA, RG 107, Telegrams Collected (Bound); *ibid.*, Telegrams Collected (Unbound). *O.R.*, I, l, part 2, 945. On Aug. 18, 7:00 P.M., Secretary of War Edwin M. Stanton telegraphed to USG. "Frequent Complaints have reached the Department in respect to General Alvord and I had determined to supersede him as soon as a good officer could be spared. But as you think his presence not indispensible he shall be relieved at once. No complaint from any source has been made against General McDowell to the Department and I had not heard that his administration was objectionable to any one. He appears to be acting in entire harmony with the Governor of California. There had been frequent applications for the removal of General Wright but as his administration was acceptable to the Department they were for a long time resisted. McDowell has been in command for a very short period. He is believed to be an officer of good administrative faculty, although unfortunate in the field, and to be rigidly honest. To make a change so soon ought to require some very good reason for its justification. You know as I do that no man can please all sides in any Department much less in California. But in this as in all other matters relating to Military affairs it is the desire of the Department to conform to your judgment. In respect to General Halleck ~~sine~~ it would be extremely difficult to spare him since Canby has gone." ALS (telegram sent), DNA, RG 107, Telegrams Collected (Bound); telegram received, *ibid.*, RG 108, Letters Received. *O.R.*, I, l, part 2, 949. On Aug. 20, noon,

USG telegraphed to Stanton. "I know nothing officially of any dissatisfaction with Gen. McDowells administration in Calafornia but as stated in my previous dispatch have heard that he was not liked. I know the Pacific Coast requires a Commanding officer of firmness enough to do his duty, in spite of opposition, but without interferanc[e] with civil rights and without trying to enforce his own peculiar opinions upon the community. I am not well enough acquainted with Gen. McDowell to judge how he will do and therefore do not ask his removal unless there is something known at your office demanding it." ALS (telegram sent), CSmH; telegram received (at 10:00 P.M.), DNA, RG 107, Telegrams Collected (Bound). *O.R.*, I, l, part 2, 951.

1. On Aug. 26, 1863, Brig. Gen. Benjamin Alvord, Fort Vancouver, Washington Territory, District of Oregon, wrote to USG. "I cannot resist the impulse to write you my most cordial and sincere congratulations on your brilliant successes. . . . You will pardon me if I recur to your service as second lieutenant under my command, and thus that I should have the weakness to claim some slight share in your early training. One thing is certain, you always in my society received a high professional stimulus. . . . I was about to write you after Fort Donelson, but I satisfied myself with messages to you per Captain Dent, who was then here. . . . I was appointed a brigadier-general of volunteers 22d of April, 1862, and accepted, fully expecting to go East, but was quite unexpectedly placed in command of this district, which I have commanded since July, 1862." *Ibid.*, p. 592.

2. Severely criticized for his conduct at the battle of Second Bull Run (Aug. 29–30, 1862), Maj. Gen. Irvin McDowell was removed from field command and served on boards of officers until assigned to command the Dept. of the Pacific on May 21, 1864.

3. George Wright of Vt., USMA 1822, served in the Mexican War, and on the eve of the Civil War was col., 9th Inf., and commanded the Dept. of Ore. Appointed brig. gen. as of Sept. 28, 1861, he commanded the Dept. of the Pacific until replaced by McDowell, then commanded the District of Calif.

To Maj. Gen. Henry W. Halleck

(Cipher) City Point, Va, Aug. 15th *1864* [*12:30* P.M.]
MAJ. GEN. HALLECK, WASHINGTON,

If E. K. Smith succeeds in crossing his troops to the East side of the Miss. as he evidently is trying to do Canby can spare a larger force to operate against Mobile with. Instruct him to put as large a force there as he can. He must be able to spare five to eight thousand colored troops to go to Mobile. I am afraid he is unfortunate in his commander of colored troops and I do not think Granger was a good selection for the command at Mobile. I hope however he may prove better than I give him credit for being.

U. S. GRANT

Lt. Gen.

ALS (telegram sent), CSmH; telegram received (marked as sent Aug. 15, 1864, 2:00 P.M., received Aug. 16, 3:30 P.M.), DNA, RG 107, Telegrams Collected (Bound); *ibid.*, Telegrams Collected (Unbound). *O.R.*, I, xli, part 2, 710. See *ibid.*, p. 725.

To Maj. Gen. Henry W. Halleck

———

(Cipher)   City Point Aug. 15th 1864 [9:00 P.M.]
MAJ. GEN. HALLECK, WASHINGTON,

If there is any danger of an up rising in the North to resist the draft, or for any other purpose, our loyal Governor's ought to organize the Militia at once to resist it. If we are to draw troops from the field to keep the loyal states in the harness it will prove difficult to suppress the rebellion in the disloyal states. My withdrawel now from the James River would insure the defeat of Sherman. Twenty thousand men sent to him at this time would destroy the greater part of Hoods Army and leave us men to send wherever required. Gen. Heintzelman[1] can get from the Governors of Ohio, Ia. & Ill. a Militia organization that will deter the discontented from committing any overt act. I hope the pPresident will call on Governors of States to organize thoroughly to preserve the peace until after the elections.

U. S. GRANT

Lt. Gen.

ALS (telegram sent), CSmH; telegram received (on Aug. 17, 1864, 6:30 A.M.), DNA, RG 107, Telegrams Collected (Bound). *O.R.*, I, xlii, part 2, 193–94. On Aug. 11, 1864, Maj. Gen. Henry W. Halleck had written to USG. "(Confidential) . . . Some forty odd regiments of Ohio hundred days men are to be mustered out before the end of the month. The term of service of a number of regiments from Indianna & other states expires this month and the early part of next. To meet this loss of troops there is scarcely nothing coming in under the President's call, & I fear you will be obliged to send troops from the field to guard certain places, as West Va., the prison camps, &c., which cannot be left without garrisons.

There is another very serious matter for which we must be prepared. Pretty strong evidence is accumulating that there is a combination formed or forming to make a forcible resistance to the draft in New York, Penn. Indiana, Kentucky and perhaps some other states. The draft must be enforced, for otherwise the army cannot be kept up. But to enforce it may require the withdrawal of a very considerable of troops from the field. This possible, and I think very probable, exigency must be provided for. I call your attention to it now in order that you may be prepared for it and make your arrangements accordingly. I have not been a believer in most of the plots, secret societies, &c. of which we have so many pretended discoveries. But the people in many parts of the north and west now talk openly and boldly of resisting the draft, and it is believed that the leaders of the 'Peace' branch of the Democratic party are doing all in their power to bring about this result. The evidence of this has increased very much within the last few days. It is probably thought that such a thing will have an effect upon the next election, by showing the inability of the present administration to carry on the war with an armed opposition in the loyal states. Whatever the object, it is thought that the attempt will be made. Are not the appearances such that we ought to take in sail and prepare the ship for a storm?" ALS, DNA, RG 108, Letters Received. *O.R.*, I, xlii, part 2, 111–12. On Aug. 12, Halleck wrote to USG. "I have just received Genl Heintzelman's report on Genl Burbridge's telegram in regard to arresting certain persons in Ohio, Ind. & Ill. Genl H. does not deem it prudent to make arrests at the present time as a rescue would probably be attempted, and his force is not sufficient to put down an insurrection. He thinks there will be a forcible resistance to the draft, and greatly fears disturbances before that time. He does not deem the prisoners of war as secure, and thinks a combination has been formed to release them and sieze the arsenals. To provide against this he wants ten thousand men in each of the states of Indiana & Illinois, & five thousand in Ohio. Genl Pope & the Provost Marshal Genl of Wisconsin report that there will be armed resistance to the draft in that state, and that, as all the troops there have been ordered into the field, they will have no means to enforce it. Apprehensions of a rebel raid from Canada into Michigan & New York to burn towns are reported. There is also much uneasiness in West Va., on account of the discharge of the Ohio hundred days men, which they say leaves them nearly defensless. The Governor of Colorado makes a requisition to-day for ten thousand men to be sent immediately to Genl Curtis to put down Indian insurrections. Genl Carleton reports that his California volunteers will not reënlist & that troops must be sent to New Mexico & Arizona to replace them. Add these requisitions to those from New York, Penn., New Jersey & Delaware, and I think we can dispose of a few hundred thousand men, if you can spare them from the James river! Seriously, I think much importance should be attached to the representations of Genl Heintzelman in regard to the condition of affairs in the west." LS, DNA, RG 108, Letters Received. *O.R.*, III, iv, 613. On Aug. 17, 10:30 A.M., President Abraham Lincoln telegraphed to USG. "I have seen your despatch expressing your unwillingness to break your hold where you are. Neither am I willing. Hold on with a bull-dog gripe, and chew & choke, as much as possible." ALS (telegram sent), DNA, RG 107, Telegrams Collected (Bound); telegram received, *ibid.*, Telegrams Collected (Unbound); *ibid.*, RG 108, Letters Received. *O.R.*, I, xlii, part 2, 243. Lincoln, *Works*, VII, 499.

1. Samuel P. Heintzelman of Pa., USMA 1826, won a bvt. commission as maj. in the Mexican War and held that actual rank as of March 3, 1855. Ap-

pointed brig. gen. as of May 17, 1861, he fought at First Bull Run, commanded
a corps in the Peninsular campaign and at Second Bull Run, and emerged with
a poor reputation as a commander. He was promoted to maj. gen. but left in the
defenses of Washington until Jan., 1864, when he was assigned to command
the Northern Dept. with hd. qrs. at Columbus, Ohio.

To Maj. Gen. Philip H. Sheridan

From City Point 9 p m Aug 15th *1864.*

MAJ GENL P H. SHERIDAN
COMDG MIDDLE MIL DIV
WINCHESTER VA

Our forces north of the James river are still pressing the Enemy
and capturing a few Prisoners occasionally. the presence of two
Divisions of Longstreets Corps is undoubted[1]—Today some prisoners have been taken from W H F. Lees Division of Cavalry[2]

U S GRANT
Lt Genl

Telegram received (on Aug. 17, 1864, 6:00 A.M.), DNA, RG 107, Telegrams
Collected (Bound); copies, *ibid.*, Telegrams Received in Cipher; *ibid.*, RG 108,
Letters Sent; DLC-USG, V, 45, 59, 68. *O.R.*, I, xliii, part 1, 799.

    1. On Aug. 15, 11:30 A.M., Maj. Gen. George G. Meade telegraphed to
USG. "All quiet on the lines.—The 5th corps in reserve on the left ready for
movement.—No indications of any move ment on enemy's part, but some that
camps previously reported taken up are this morning re-occupied—Despatch
from signal officer sent herewith—" ALS (telegram sent), DNA, RG 94, War
Records Office, Army of the Potomac; telegram received, *ibid.*, RG 108, Letters
Received. *O.R.*, I, xlii, part 2, 194. The enclosure is *ibid.* At 1:30 P.M., Maj.
Gen. Winfield S. Hancock telegraphed to USG. "General Gregg says that the
enemy are making a spirited attack upon him down the Charles City road   They
drove him out of the entrenchments he took yesterday. He has taken a prisoner
who says that ~~the loss~~ there was a large force of Cavalry ~~along~~ with Infantry on
that road this morning six (6) miles this side of Richmond   General Gregg
thinks that Hampton has joined. We have no positive evidence of it. My Brigade
of Infantry that went from the Central road to strike the Charles City road, met
the enemy very soon supposed to be Infantry and repulsed them. Another Brigade
has been added to it, and Genl. Birney will attack them very soon   A Knapsack
was picked up this morning during the Cavalry fight marked 13th Gorgia Wilcox Division and also I think Hagans [*Hagood's*] Brigade" ALS (telegram
sent), DNA, RG 107, Telegrams Collected (Unbound); telegram received, *ibid.*,
RG 108, Letters Received. Printed as received at 3:20 P.M. in *O.R.*, I, xlii, part

2, 198. On the same day, Hancock telegraphed to USG. "I have abot 500 sick & wound[ed] here in hospital & shuld like a boat sent to tak[e] them off. of this number about 300 are wounded" ALS (telegram sent), DNA, RG 107, Telegrams Collected (Unbound). At 3:30 P.M., Lt. Col. Theodore S. Bowers telegraphed to Hancock. "A boat to take on your sick and wounded will be sent immediately. Gen. Grant is on his way to your Headquarters." ALS (telegram sent), *ibid*. *O.R.*, I, xlii, part 2, 198. On the same day, 10:00 P.M., Hancock telegraphed to USG. "I sent in this morning about twenty prisoners taken by the Cavalry including eleven refugees. These refugees left Richmond on saturday night. They say a large number of Cavalry went north & many other troops but they do not know definitely what force. I have ordered them sent to City Point where they can be questioned. A prisoner was captured this morning from the 13th South Carolina which makes the second man captured from McGowans Brigade being of different regts. this latter man says that four brigades of Wilcox Division are in front of Gen Foster's old position. I have no positive evidence of the fact. Gen Birney with a part of Gen Motts Division is feeling for the Enemys left or a place where we can attack if we find such a place I shall attack with heavy force in the hope of clearing them out." ALS (telegram sent), DNA, RG 107, Telegrams Collected (Unbound); telegram received, *ibid*., RG 108, Letters Received. *O.R.*, I, xlii, part 2, 197. Also on Aug. 15, USG telegraphed to Hancock. "I am in receipt of your appointment as Brig Genl in the regular army will forward it to *you* by a staff officer tomorrow morning." Telegram received, DNA, RG 107, Telegrams Collected (Unbound); copy, DLC-USG, V, 68. On the same day, Hancock telegraphed to USG. "Your dispatchs recd. I am much obliged to you for the appointment of Brig Gen in the regular Army. I am also obliged to you for being so anxious today for I am not satisfied with our progress here." Telegram received, *ibid*., RG 108, Letters Received. *O.R.*, I, xlii, part 2, 199.

2. On Aug. 15, Hancock telegraphed to USG three times. "I have just taken a staff officer of Gen Birrenger Comdg Brigade of Cavalry in W H F Lee's Div. The Command came over I dont know in what strength last night. Have also captured a private of 3d Div Cavalry & an officer of the 48th alabama I am sending some infantry to strike the Charles City Road to take this Cav in flank; am also sending some infantry to Gregg to the Junction of the Charles City Road with the long Bridge Gen Birney is also feeling around the Enemys right of where Barlow attacked yesterday." Telegram received, DNA, RG 108, Letters Received. *O.R.*, I, xlii, part 2, 198. "A prisoner just sent in reports that his division of Cavy (W. H. F. Lee's) arrived here this a. m. left Reams station at 11 a. m. yesterday Barrington's [*Barringer's*] Chambliss & Dennings [*Dearing's*] brigades. We have forced the enemy back beyond the cross roads on the Charles City road but so far only to the entrenchments occupied by Gregg early this morning The enemy's work appear well filled General Birney is still operating between the central and if he finds a weak place a strong attack with be made I expect to hear of it before long" Telegram received, DNA, RG 108, Letters Received. Printed as received at 5:45 P.M., copy to Meade, in *O.R.*, I, xlii, part 2, 199. "Every thing is quiet here—Gen Birney did not attack tonight not having encountered the enemy's skirmishers until about dark—he Lost thirty or forty men, the greater number Colored, in his observations—I have ordered a movement on the Charles city road under Gen Miles at day light, Gen Birney will also move towards the central road at the same hour prepared to make a heavy attack if possible—The Cavy will operate on the Charles city road & to

the right   Gen Gregg captured a few prisoners this evening—All from W. H. F
Lee's Div. I have no evidence indicating any greater strength there before"
Telegram received, DNA, RG 108, Letters Received; copy, *ibid.*, RG 107, Telegrams Collected (Unbound). *O.R.*, I, xlii, part 2, 199. William H. F. "Rooney"
Lee, born in Va. in 1837, son of Robert E. Lee, attended Harvard College, served
in the U.S. Army (1857–59), then retired to his Va. plantation. A C.S.A. cav.
officer from the start of the Civil War, he was nominated as brig. gen. on Sept.
26, 1862, wounded at Brandy Station and soon captured. Released in March,
1864, and promoted to maj. gen. as of April 23, he commanded a div. of cav.

Calendar

1864, JUNE 4. To Maj. Gen. George G. Meade. "If you will send me the facts in the case of Gen. Ward I will send a request to the Sec. of War to have him mustered out of service."—ANS, DNA, RG 94, Generals' Papers and Books, Ward. Brig. Gen. J. H. Hobart Ward, commanding the 1st Brigade, 3rd Div., 2nd Army Corps, had been charged with leaving his troops to ride to the rear—allegedly trying to hurry up ammunition—on May 6 and later with being too drunk to command. On June 12, Lt. Col. Theodore S. Bowers endorsed a sheaf of papers concerning Ward. "Respectfully returned to Maj. Gen. Geo. G. Meade. Com'd'g Army of the Potomac, who will releive Brig. Gen. Ward from duty, and order him to proceed to Fortress Monroe. and there await trial."—AES, *ibid.* Undated formal charges against Ward prepared by Maj. Gen. David B. Birney were endorsed by USG on June 28. "Respectfully forwarded to the Secretary of War. The good of the service requiring the immediate disposal of this case, and it being impracticable to convene a court for the trial of Gen. Ward, it is recommended that the accused be mustered out of the service"—ES, Lincoln Collection, IHi. On July 16, President Abraham Lincoln endorsed this document. "Recommendation of Gen. Grant approved"—AES, *ibid.* Ward was mustered out on July 18.

On June 12, noon, Asst. Secretary of War Charles A. Dana telegraphed to Secretary of War Edwin M. Stanton. "Genl Owens is under arrest for misconduct in face of the Enemy and ordered to Ft Monroe where Court will sit to try him. Same court will try Genl Ward—Genl Eustis is relieved of his command and ordered to Washington   He is to be informed that if he does not resign charges of neglect of duty and general inefficiency will be preferred against him. He is said to eat opium . . ."—Telegram received (on June 13, 5:00 A.M.), DLC-Edwin M. Stanton. *O.R.,* I, xxxvi, part 1, 96. Late in June, USG endorsed charges against Brig. Gen. Joshua T. Owen prepared by Maj. Gen. John Gibbon. "Respcy. forwarded to the secretary of war, with the recommendation that Brig Genl J. T. Owen be mustered out of service"—Copy, DLC-USG, V, 58. See Lincoln, *Works,* VIII, 547. Owen was mustered out as of July 18. On June 12, Maj. Gen. Horatio G. Wright wrote to Maj. Gen. Andrew A. Humphreys requesting that Henry L. Eustis be "relieved from duty with this Corps"—LS, DNA, RG 94, ACP, 683W CB 1864. On the same day, Meade endorsed this letter favorably but suggested that Eustis be allowed to resign.—ES, *ibid.* On June 28, USG endorsed this letter. "Respectfully forwarded to the Secretary of War. The recommendation of Maj. Gen. G. G. Meade hereon is fully approved, and I earnestly urge that it be carried out."—ES, *ibid.* Eustis resigned as of June 27.

On Aug. 21, Ward wrote to Lincoln asking that the orders mustering him out be revoked and that he receive a trial.—ALS, *ibid.,* 1519W CB 1864. On Oct. 2, Lt. Col. Ely S. Parker endorsed this letter. "Respectfully returned to Maj. Gen. Halleck, Chief of staff of the Army, inviting attention to enclosed report of Maj. Gen. Hancock. I have no objection to restoration of Gen. Ward, for the purpose of having a trial by Court Martial."—ES, *ibid.* On Oct. 25, Col. Edward D. Townsend telegraphed to USG. "The Secretary of War desires me to say that General J. H. Hobart Ward applied for leave to visit the army near Richmond and was refused on the ground of his having been dismissed the service—This information is given you in case he should nevertheless find his way down—Please acknowledge receipt."—ALS (telegram sent), *ibid.*, RG 107, Telegrams Collected (Unbound); telegram received, *ibid.*; (at 8:00 P.M.) *ibid.*, RG 108, Letters Received. At 8:00 P.M., USG telegraphed to Townsend. "Your dispatch of 8. p. m. this date in relation to Gn. Ward's application is received."—ALS (telegram sent), CSmH; telegram received (at 8:25 P.M.), DNA, RG 94, Letters Received, 1100A 1864; *ibid.*, RG 107, Telegrams Collected (Bound).

1864, JUNE 5, 11:00 A.M. Maj. Gen. Ambrose E. Burnside to USG. "Brig. Genl James H. Ledlie Comdg a brigade ~~of~~ in the 1st Div. of this Corps I understand has not been confirmed. And as congress adjourns tomorrow he will be out of service unless he is confirmed on that day. He has behaved with great energy & gallantry since ~~gaining~~ joining this command and I beg that you will if possible have the senate confirm his nomination tomorrow"—Telegram received (at 11:10 A.M.), DNA, RG 108, Letters Received; copies, *ibid.*, RG 107, Telegrams Collected (Unbound); *ibid.*, RG 393, 9th Army Corps, Letters Sent. *O.R.*, I, xxxvi, part 3, 619.

1864, JUNE 5. USG pass. "Pass Mrs. S. P. Edson, Presdt National Relief Association, and two Assistants to and from all the Armies in the field, free on Government Transports, rail-roads and all other conveyances in the public service. This pass good until revoked."—ADS, CSmH. The words "and two Assistants" are in another hand.

1864, JUNE 6. USG endorsement. "Approved and respectfully forwarded to the Secretary of War."—ES, DNA, RG 94, ACP, M1650 CB 1864. Written on a letter of June 5 from Brig. Gen. Orlando B. Willcox to Brig. Gen. Lorenzo Thomas recommending 1st Lt. George D. Martin, 79th N. Y., for appointment as asst. q. m. of vols.—LS, *ibid.* No appointment followed.

1864, JUNE 6. Maj. Gen. James B. McPherson, Acworth, Ga., to Brig. Gen. John A. Rawlins. "I would write you a long letter but time forbids— I reached this point to day with my Command, in fine health and Spirits and we have established ourselves on the R. R. south of the Alatuna Mts, & hold Alatuna Pass—The Armies of the Cumberland & Ohio are near by and we will soon be after Jos. E. J—We have driven him from one strong position to another,   Have had no general Battle, but plenty of Skirmishing and a good deal of hard fighting—Hardee's Corps made an attack on me at

Dallas but was handsomely repulsed, with heavy loss   We burried near *Four hundred of his dead*—Our loss was less than three hundred, *Killed, wounded* & *missing*   This was on the 28th ult in the afternoon   Two days after that they tried it at night twice, and met with a similar fate, when they concluded to let us alone, & moved off to their right, whereupon I was shifted to our left, which accounts for my being here—What I started to write about particularly is this,   Ransom is Very Anxious to get back to my command & I am quite as anxious to have him.—*Crocker* has resigned— had to give up on account of ill health and I want Ransom to command his Division in *the 17th A. C.*—I want him made a *Maj. General* and know that he merits it and will *fill the bill*,   He writes he will be fit for duty by July 1st   Please have this attended to—My kindest regards to the General—Success attend you all—"—ALS, USG 3.

1864, JUNE 8.   Frederick A. Conkling and thirty-eight cosigners, New York City, to USG enclosing resolutions of thanks passed at a meeting on June 4.—DS, USG 3.

1864, JUNE 9.   Maj. Gen. William F. Smith to Brig. Gen. John A. Rawlins. "I have the honor to forward to you a list of the Staff now serving with me at these Hd. Qrs. I would respectfully state that the *Corps* Staff, excepting the A. A. G. who has never been appointed, are now with Genl. Butler comdg. Dept. Va. and N. C. I find it impossible to detail officers of my own command, the officers most suitable to fill staff appointments, on account of the fearful loss of field officers from the late engagements. I started from Genl. Butlers command, with five Brigades of this Corps, and four (4) of the 10th Corps. I have since consolidated the whole into three divisions of the 18th Corps. I respectfully ask that the Status of this command be settled now, and that, I be allowed either to appoint or send forward names to fill the Corps Staff, or that the names I may send in, may be detailed temporarily with me."—Copies (2), DNA, RG 393, 24th Army Corps, Letters Sent by 18th Army Corps. *O.R.*, I, xxxvi, part 3, 715–16.

1864, JUNE 9.   Lucinda C. Clark, New Berne, N. C., to USG. "It is an old saying that the bravest men are the most feeling and the easiest to be approached, fully believing this, I take the liberty of imploring a special favor of you. My nephew, E. C. Cuthbert was captured on board the steamer Boston last July, while attempting to run the blockade into Wilmington, from Bermuda   He is now a prisoner at Point Lookout, willing, nay even anxious to take the oath of allegiance. Will you please use your influence and get him released? I brought him up from infancy, and he is so dear to me, my comfort, my principal support, my all of earthly happiness. Think of this and do be merciful to me, and excuse my addressing you. He is a severe sufferrer from asthma, and had been advised by the physicians to make a sea voyage. How can it be that so many citizens are released and he yet kept a prisoner, and he so willing to subscribe to the oath? The same Lord over all incline you to use ~~the~~ your vast influence, which He alone has given you, in having the orphan's greatest earthly blessing restored to her. My character and standing can be obtained of Gen. Palmer."—ALS, DNA, RG 109, Unfiled Papers and Slips, E. C. Cuthbert.

1864, JUNE 11. USG endorsement. "Respy. forwarded to the Sec of War with the recommendation that General Meades endorsement hereon be complied with"—Copy, DLC-USG, V, 58. Written on a letter of Col. Emory Upton, 5th Brigade, 1st Div., 6th Army Corps, recommending that Capt. Ranald S. Mackenzie, U.S. Engineers, be appointed col., 2nd Conn. Art.—*Ibid.* Maj. Gen. George G. Meade had endorsed this letter. "Respy. forwarded to the Lieut Genl Comdg. The importance of the duties to be performed by Engineer Officers at the present time, makes me reluctant to dispense with the services of any officer of that Corps, but Capt McKenzie, having agreed if allowed to accept the command of the regiment, that he will in addition to the duties pertaining to that command, discharge, also the duties of a Military Engineer, with the troops with which the regiment may be serving whenever called to do so, I recommend that he be permitted to assume command of the regiment at once, and if commissioned by the Governor of Connecticut that he be granted a leave until further orders."— Copy, *ibid.*

1864, JUNE 11, 8:00 P.M. Maj. Gen. Andrew A. Humphreys to Brig. Gen. John A. Rawlins. "I send to you Mr. Van Lew from Richmond, who claims to be a refugee. He came into our lines to day and was sent to these Head Quarters by Genl. Wilson—He desires to see Lt. Genl. Grant or make known his wishes to him and by direction of Genl Meade I send him to you—"—ALS, DNA, RG 108, Letters Received. *O.R.*, I, xxxvi, part 3, 746. For John N. Van Lew, brother of Elizabeth L. Van Lew, a Richmond Unionist, see Meriwether Stuart, "Colonel Ulric Dahlgren and Richmond's Union Underground, April 1864," *Virginia Magazine of History and Biography*, 72, 2 (April, 1964), 160.

1864, JUNE 13. Brig. Gen. Stephen G. Burbridge, Lexington, Ky., to Maj. Gen. Henry W. Halleck, copy to USG. "I attacked Morgan at Cynthiana at day light yesterday Morning & after an Hours hard fighting Completely routed him Killing three Hundred (300) wounded near as many & capturing nearly four Hundred   Besides recaptured nearly all of Genl Hobson Command & over one thousand Horses   our loss in Killed & Wounded about one Hundred & fifty (150)   Morgans Scattered forces are fleeing in all directions   Have thrown away arms are out of Ammunition & wholly Demoralized"—Telegrams received (2), DNA, RG 108, Letters Received. *O.R.*, I, xxxix, part 1, 20. On June 14, Burbridge telegraphed to Halleck, again sending a copy to USG. "In six (6) days my command has marched over two Hundred (200) Miles fought 2 Severe battles Killing wounding & Capturing over three fourths ¾ of Morgan Command   The remaining fourth is Scattered & being pursued in all directions"—Telegram received, DNA, RG 108, Letters Received; *ibid.*, RG 107, Telegrams Collected (Unbound).

1864, JUNE 15.   Secretary of War Edwin M. Stanton to USG. "A despatch from Mr. Dana mentioned that you desired a half million of Confederate paper, to be used to pay for army supplies required from the rebels; and in reply, after consultation with the President and Secretary of State, I informed him this morning that a million would be sent you. The matter has, however, been reconsidered, and the Secretary of State has transmitted to this Department a note, of which a copy is transmitted with this letter. In accordance with his views, it has been thought best by this Government not to give any circulation to rebel currency, for reasons stated by the Secretary of State."—Copy, DLC-Edwin M. Stanton. See *O.R.*, I, xl, part 1, 19; *ibid.*, III, iv, 432–33.

1864, JUNE 15.   Maj. Gen. George G. Meade to USG. "Respectfully forwarded strongly recommended. Capt Pierce is a most efficient officer and the 9th corps is much in want of a chief in this dept   I would request the Lt. Genl. cmdg. ask by telegraph for the immediate appointment of Capt. Pierce as desired by Maj. Genl. Burnside."—AES, DNA, RG 108, Letters Received. Written on a telegram of the same day, 7:40 P.M., from Maj. Gen. Ambrose E. Burnside to Meade. "I beg to recommend that Capt Peirce be appointed Chief Quarter Master of the 9th Army Corps and that he be ordered to report to us as soon as the interest of this army will permit I mean by this despatch that he be made Chief Qr. Mr. with the rank of Lieut. Colonel"—Telegram received, *ibid.* On July 8, Brig. Gen. Rufus Ingalls wrote to Brig. Gen. John A. Rawlins reminding him of the case of Capt. Luther H. Peirce.—LS, ICarbS. On the same day, USG telegraphed to Maj. Gen. Henry W. Halleck. "Please ask the Prest to appoint Capt L H Pierce A. Q. M. Chief Q. M. Ninth Army Corps with rank to date June fifteenth (15) which is about the time he assumed the duties of Chief. He has been before recommended for the appointment."—Telegrams received (2—on July 9, 8:00 A.M.), DNA, RG 94, ACP, P55 CB 1867; *ibid.*, RG 107, Telegrams Collected (Bound); copies, *ibid.*, RG 108, Letters Sent; DLC-USG, V, 45, 59, 67. Peirce was so appointed. Peirce had been appointed q. m. and capt. as of May 18; on Jan. 18, President Abraham Lincoln had written to Secretary of War Edwin M. Stanton. "To oblige the Vice-President, it would personally oblige me for Luther H. Pierce, now a Volunteer Q. M., to be appointed a Quarter-Master in the regular Army— It is said the Quarter-Master-General, & many others competent to judge, recommend him. Let him be appointed, if it *can* be done—"—ALS, DNA, RG 94, ACP, P55 CB 1867. Ingalls's letter of July 8 also requested certain q. m. assignments; on July 11, Capt. Ely S. Parker issued Special Orders No. 54 making these assignments.—Copies, DLC-USG, V, 57, 62, 67. *O.R.*, I, xl, part 3, 173.

1864, JUNE 16. Special Orders No. 35. "Brig. Gen. Rufus Ingalls Chief Quarter Master Army of the Potomac, is announced as Chief Quarter Master of the Armies operating against Richmond, and will immediately assume the duties thereof in addition to those of Chief Quarter Master of the Army of the Potomac   Lieut Col M. R. Morgan Chief Commissary of Subsistence Dept. of Virginia and North Carolina is announced as Chief Commissary of Subsistence of the Armies operating against Richmond and will immediately assume the duties thereof in addition to those of Chief Commissary of Subsistence of the Dept. of Virginia and North Carolina"— Copies, DLC-USG, V, 57, 62, 67. *O.R.*, I, xl, part 2, 88. On June 17, Lt. Col. Theodore S. Bowers issued Special Orders No. 36. "The Chief Quartermaster of the Armies opperating against Richmond will immediately cause to be repaired and put in proper condition the Wharves at City Point and Bermuda Hundreds and build such new ones at either or both of these places and at such points on the Appomattocks river as he may deem necessary and provide and construct Store houses at the two former places sufficient for the storage of all supplies that may be collected there for the Army   He will repair and put in condition for immediate use the Petersburg and City Point Rail Road   He will also discharge from Government service all water Transportation not absolutely necessary for faciliating Military operations"—Copies, DLC-USG, V, 57, 62, 67. *O.R.*, I, xl, part 2, 120.

On July 6, Bowers wrote to Brig. Gen. Rufus Ingalls. "It having been found by experience that the Armies operating against Richmond can be more easily and economically supplied from City Point than from both City Point and Bermuda Hundred, you will therefore make the former place the main depot for these Armies, and the latter a subordinate one—"—ALS, DNA, RG 94, War Records Office, Army of the Potomac. *O.R.*, I, xl, part 3, 35.

1864, JUNE 18–21. USG endorsement. "I do not think it advisable to build the Shreveport and Vicksburg railroad because—besides the great expense, the time it would consume would in all probability render it of but little use when completed. Our forces once in possession of Shreveport, would for both economy and convenience draw their supplies by way of Red river, which is navigable for boats of light draft, if my memory serves me right (and I was stationed for about 14 months near Grand Ecore) about eight month in the year. If there is the amount of work to do on that road I think there is, it would take 8 months to build it"—Copy, DLC-USG, V, 58. Written on a dispatch from Maj. Gen. Edward R. S. Canby concerning the rebuilding of the Vicksburg and Shreveport Railroad, which Col.

James A. Hardie endorsed to USG on June 18.—*Ibid.* See *O.R.*, I, xxxiv, part 4, 211, 424–25, 528–29, 611.

1864, JUNE 20, 6:00 P.M. To Maj. Gen. Henry W. Halleck. "Please order Br Genl Edward Hatch to report to Genl Washburne for duty. If Captain J. P. Morton can be spared from the [Ca]valry Bureau order him to report to Commanding Officer Eighteenth Army Corps as acting Inspector General. A mustering officer is also required for that Corps, which duty Capt Morton can perform in addition to his duties as Inspector—"— Telegram received (on June 21, 3:30 A.M.), DNA, RG 107, Telegrams Collected (Bound); copies, *ibid.*, RG 108, Letters Sent; DLC-USG, V, 45, 59, 67. On June 17, Maj. Gen. Cadwallader C. Washburn telegraphed to USG. "Genl Edward Hatch is fit for field service as he informs me. Will you order him to report to me for duty?"—Telegram received, DNA, RG 107, Telegrams Collected (Bound).

1864, JUNE 22. To [Maj. Gen. John A. Dix]. "Requests furlough for 30 days for Pvt Walter Comstock, 1st R. I. Cav., now at Gen. Hosp. Portsmouth Grove, R. I."—DNA, RG 393, Dept. of the East, Register of Letters Received.

1864, JUNE 22. Lt. Col. Cyrus B. Comstock to Brig. Gen. Rufus Ingalls. "Yesterday by Gen Grants direction I ordered a man who was running a horse into gateposts trees &c and who had already knocked one of the horses eyes out, into confinement. This morning I learn that he is one of your men, and wish to turn the case over to you for such action as you deem proper."— ALS, DNA, RG 393, Dept. of Va. and N. C., Miscellaneous Letters Received.

1864, JUNE 27. USG endorsement. "Respectfully forwarded to the Secretary of War, Washington, D. C. with the recommendation that Col. Chamberlain, 20th Maine, Col. Chapman, 3rd Indiana Cav. and Col McIntosh 3d Penn'a Cav. be promoted to Brigadier Generals. The other officers named may be equally deserving of promotion, but I think vacancies should be kept open until other armies are heard from."—ES, DNA, RG 94, ACP, M1716 CB 1864. Written on a letter of June 9 from Maj. Gen. George G. Meade to Lt. Col. Theodore S. Bowers. "I have the honor herewith to transmit certain communications recommending Colonel John H. Chapman, 3rd Indiana Cavalry   Colonel J B McIntosh 3rd Penna Cavalry   Colonel D D Bidwell 49th N. Y. S. Vols   Colonel O Edwards 37th Mass Vols   Capt. Frederick Winthrop 12th U. S. Infantry   Colonel J L Chamberlain 20th Maine Volunteers   Colonel E S. Bragg 6th Wisconsin Volunteers   Colonel J W Hofmann 56th Penna Volunteers for the appointment of Brigadier General. I make no special recommendations in these cases as I have not been called upon for recommendations and as I am not aware what vacancies exist at the present time in the grade of Brigadier General and how many of such vacancies, if any, it is proposed to fill from the Army of the Potomac. I would respectfully recommend, however, that when the number of such appointments allotted to the Army of the Potomac has been determined upon, the appointments be conferred upon the most merritorious of the officers whose names have been or may be presented for advancement, as shown by the record of their services and the testimonials of their commanders, without regard to other considerations   It is proper to add that Colonel George H Chapman 3rd Indiana Cavalry and J B. McIntosh 3rd Pennsylvania Cavalry have heretofore been recommended to the War Department for the appointment of Brigadier General."—LS, *ibid.*; ADf, *ibid.*, War Records Office, Army of the Potomac. On June 18, Brig. Gen. James H. Wilson wrote to Brig. Gen. Seth Williams. "I have again to commend in the highest terms Col. John B. McIntosh 3d. Penn. Cavalry, Commanding 1st Brigade, and Col. Geo. H. Chapman, 3d Indiana Cavalry, Commanding 2nd Brigade, 3d Cavalry Division, for special gallantry and good conduct during the recent movement of the Army of the Potomac from its position near Cool Arbor to the James River, and respectfully request that they may be promoted to the grade of brigadier general."—ALS, *ibid.*, ACP, W1294 CB 1864. On June 20, Meade endorsed this letter. "As this communication has been forwarded to these Head Quarters it is respectfully transmitted to the Lieutenant General Commanding with the remark that both the officers named have already been recommended for the appointment of Brigadier General."—ES, *ibid.* On June 22, USG endorsed this letter. "Respectfully forwarded to the Secretary of War, Washington D. C. and recommended"—ES, *ibid.* On June 25, U.S. Senator James R. Doolittle of Wis. telegraphed to USG. "Please inform Cutler Bragg is nominated and confirmed."—*O.R.*, I, xl, part 2, 409. Edward S. Bragg, confirmed that day as brig. gen., commanded the 1st brigade, 4th div. (commanded by Brig. Gen. Lysander Cutler), 5th Army Corps.

On June 29, Maj. Gen. Philip H. Sheridan wrote to Secretary of War Edwin M. Stanton recommending that Brig. Gen. Alfred T. A. Torbert be promoted to maj. gen.—LS, DNA, RG 94, ACP, M1554 CB 1864. On July 5, Meade endorsed this letter. "Respectfully forwarded for the consideration of the Lieutenant General Commanding—As I have not been called upon for nominations for General officers I make no special recommendation in this case—"—ES, *ibid.* On July 6, Bowers endorsed this letter. "Respectfully returned to Maj. Gen. G. G. Meade, Com'd'g Army of the Potomac, who will please send in a list of the names of officers of his Command who deserve to be, and whom he desires promoted."—AES, *ibid.* On July 20, Meade forwarded a "List of Officers recommended for promotion to the rank of Major, and Brigadier General. In 2d Corps. For. Maj Genl.— Brig Genl. Francis C. Barlow   For Brig Genl Liut Col. C. H. Morgan Inspr Genl & Chf of Staff, 2d Corps. Col. Thos W. Egan 40th N. Y. Vols. T. A. Smyth 1st Del   H. L. Brown 145th Penna   James A. Beaver 148

Penna   In 5th Corps—For Major General. Brig Genl Charles Griffin   S.
W Crawford. R. B. Ayers   John C. Robinson   J. J. Bartlett. For Brig
General. Lieut Col. H. C. Bankhead Inspr. Genl 5th Corps—Capt Frederick
Winthrop 12th U S Infty. Col. J. Howard Kitching 6 N. Y. Arty. Col Wm
S. Tilton 22d Mass Vols. J. W. Hofmann 56th Penna   Maj Genl. War-
ren, Com'd'g 5th Corps, also recommends the following Officers, not serving
in the 5th Corps—For Brig General. J. B. Sweitzer late Col. 62 Pa Vols
Wm McCandless 2d Pa Res—Col. H. L. Abbott. 1st Conn Arty—Lt Col.
C. H. Morgan Inspr Genl 2d Corps—In 6th Corps. For Maj General   Brig
Genl D. A. Russell   Geo W. Getty   J. B. Ricketts   For Brig General
Col. D. D. Bidwell, 49th Penna Vols   Oliver Edwards 37 Mass   C. H.
Tompkins 1st R. I. Artilley   Wm H. Penrose 15th N. J. Vols   Lt Col
Martin T. McMahon, Asst Adjt Genl. Col T. O. Seavor 3d Vt Vols—In
9th Corps—For Maj General. Brig Genl O. B. Willcox   Robert B. Potter
For Brig General. Col. Wm Humphrey 2d Mich Vols. Col John J. Curtin
45th Penna Vols   Joshua K. Sigfried 48 Penna   Benj C. Christ 50 Penna
E. G. Marshall 14th N. Y. Heavy Arty—In Cavalry Corps—For Maj General—Brig Genl A. T. A. Torbert   D. McM. Gregg   J. H. Wilson—For
Brig General—Col. Thomas C. Devin 6th N. Y. Cavalry—R. A. Alger 5th
Mich Cavalry—Capt Marcus A. Reno 1st U. S. Cavalry—Col I. Irvin Gregg
16th Penna Cavalry—Jno. B. McIntosh 3d Penna Cavalry—Geo H. Chapman 3d Ind Cavalry—John Hammond 5th N. Y. Cavalry—"—D (altered
from original tabular form), *ibid.* On the same day, Meade endorsed
this list. "The within list of nominations for promotion is respectfully
forwarded for the action of the Lieutenant General Com'd'g in accordance
with the endorsement of the 6th instant on the returned nominations of
Major General Sheridan. Such of these promotions as there are now vacancies for, it is earnestly urged should be made without delay, and where there
are no vacancies, it is most respectfully submitted that appointments by
Brevet and assignment with Brevet rank whilst in the field, would be only
simple justice to many most meritorious officers—I consider it of the highest importance that faithful services and gallantry in the field should be
promptly rewarded—the tone and efficiency of this army would be greatly
improved if services such as are herein recorded were promptly acknowledged"—ES, *ibid.* On July 22, USG endorsed this list. "Respectfully forwarded with the remark, that the Officers herein recommended are worthy
meritorious and deserving of promotion, or to fill any vacancies, that may
exist, but I would respectfully suggest, that if any promotions are to be
made or vacancies filled, justice to the entire Army would demand that they
be not made until recommendations for promotion etc. for meritorious services can also be obtained from the Southwestern Army."—ES, *ibid.*

1864, JUNE 27.   USG endorsement. "Respectfully forwarded to the Secretary of War, Washington D. C. and attention invited to the recommendations of Generals Brooks, Smith and Butler."—ES, DNA, RG 94, ACP,

R62 CB 1865. Written on a copy of a letter of June 12 from Brig. Gen. William T. H. Brooks to USG recommending Capt. Theodore Read for promotion.—ALS, *ibid.* On the same day, Maj. Gen. William F. Smith endorsed the original letter. "I beg leave earnestly to recommend Capt Read to the attention of the authorities for the promotion which he has so often earned under my Command as well as others. I know of no officer of his rank whose services have been so gallant so continuous & so much for the benefit of the Country as have those of Capt Read"—AES, *ibid.* On June 23, Maj. Gen. Benjamin F. Butler endorsed this letter. "Respectfully forwarded. —Approved;"—ES, *ibid.* Read was promoted to maj. as of July 25.

1864, JUNE 27. USG endorsement. "Respy. forwarded to the Secretary of War, Washington D. C. and recommended that the Brevet rank of Maj Genl be conferred upon Brig Gen Jno. C. Robinson, for gallant and meritorious services in the field"—Copy, DLC-USG, V, 58. Written on a letter of June 23 of Maj. Gen. Gouverneur K. Warren concerning Brig. Gen. John C. Robinson. No promotion followed.

1864, JUNE 28. USG endorsement. "Respectfully forwarded to the Secretary of War, Washington, D. C. and recommend the case of Gen'l Bartlette for the favorable consideration of the Government."—ES, DNA, RG 94, ACP, B1184 CB 1866. Written on a letter of June 27 from Maj. Gen. Gouverneur K. Warren to Brig. Gen. Seth Williams regarding the appointment of Brig. Gen. Joseph J. Bartlett, who was originally nominated to rank from Oct. 4, 1862, not confirmed, again nominated from the same date, but finally confirmed as of March 30, 1864.—ALS, *ibid.* On June 27, Maj. Gen. George G. Meade endorsed this letter. "Respectfully forwarded concurring in all that Genl. Warren says. Genl. Bartletts case I consider extremely hard and simple justice, independantly of the value of his services in the present campaign, require the injustice done to Genl. Bartlett should be corrected if practicable."—AES, *ibid.* No action followed.

1864, JUNE 28. USG endorsement. "Respectfully forwarded with the recommendation that Col. C. J. Paine be appointed a Brigadier Gen. to command Colored Troops. We are much in want of suitable commanders for this class of troops and Gen. Butler, who is personally acquainted with the services of this officer believes him eminently qualified for such command."—AES, DNA, RG 94, ACP, 563P CB 1864. Written on a letter of the same day from Maj. Gen. Benjamin F. Butler to Secretary of War Edwin M. Stanton recommending Col. Charles J. Paine, 2nd La., for brig. gen. —LS, *ibid.* Paine was both nominated and confirmed on July 4.

1864, JUNE 28. Lt. Col. Theodore S. Bowers to Brig. Gen. Seth Williams. "Has the 158th Ohio one hundred day men at this place belonging to Butlers command been relieved If not when will it probably be relieved"—Telegram received (at 5:00 P.M.), DNA, RG 94, War Records Office, Army of the Potomac; copy, *ibid.*, RG 107, Telegrams Collected (Unbound). On the same day, 8:00 P.M., Williams telegraphed to Bowers. "Colonel Gates commanding the Provost Guard at City Point has been directed to relieve at once the 158th-Ohio regiment belonging to Genl. Butlers command—We were under the impression that all of General Butlers troops at City Point had been relieved by Colonel Gates."—ALS (telegram sent), *ibid.*, RG 94, War Records Office, Army of the Potomac; copy, *ibid.*, RG 393, Army of the Potomac, Letters Sent. On the same day, Bowers telegraphed to Col. John W. Shaffer, chief of staff for Maj. Gen. Benjamin F. Butler. "Gen Meade has directed the 158th Regiment Ohio Hundred Day Men to be relieved at once. It will await your orders in the morning"— ALS (telegram sent), *ibid.*, RG 107, Telegrams Collected (Unbound). Printed as sent at 9:20 P.M. in *O.R.*, I, xl, part 2, 484. At 10:20 P.M., Shaffer telegraphed to Bowers. "The 158 regt Ohio Vols is under orders to proceed to Norfolk immediately upon being relieved. this will give us a Regt of drilled Cold. Troops from Norfolk"—ALS (telegram sent), DNA, RG 107, Telegrams Collected (Unbound).

1864, JUNE 29. To Abraham Lincoln. "I hope you will not send Dr Worster here with his newly invented Sandal. Our men are well and comfortably clad and we require no new invention. Arms, and men to use them is all we want"—Telegrams received (2), DNA, RG 107, Telegrams Collected (Bound); copies, *ibid.*, RG 108, Letters Sent; DLC-USG, V, 45, 59, 67. On the same day, Lincoln had telegraphed to USG. "Dr. Worster wishes to visit you with a view of getting your permission to introduce into the army 'Harmon's Sandal sock' Shall I give him a pass for that object?"—ALS (telegram sent), DNA, RG 107, Telegrams Collected (Bound); telegram received, *ibid.*, Telegrams Collected (Unbound). Lincoln, *Works*, VII, 416. On April 13, J. Rutherford Worster wrote to Lincoln about and enclosed endorsements of the "wash-leather Sandal-Sock."—ALS, DLC-Robert T. Lincoln. See Johnson, *Papers*, V, 101–3. On Sept. 30, Worster arrived at City Point to promote his socks.—Register of Passes, DNA, RG 109, Union Provost Marshals' File of Papers Relating to Two or More Civilians.

1864, JUNE 29. To Brig. Gen. James B. Fry. "I have this day sent to the Military Governor of Washington George Watson, who was recently forwarded to this place with a detachment of recruits and convalescents and beg to call your attention to his case. It appears from all the information I can obtain that Watson is a citizen of Oxfordshire England, and came to this country in April to visit his son who resides in Ohio. When in New York on his return home, he was enlisted into our service. He is an old, decrepit man wholly unfit for service, and could not have passed a medical examination"—Copies, DLC-USG, V, 45, 59, 67; DNA, RG 108, Letters

Sent; *ibid.*, Letters Received. On Sept. 23, Fry wrote to USG. "I have the honor to enclose copies of papers in the case of George Watson, who was forwarded to this city by your order, with request, that his case would be thoroughly investigated. Private Watson was duly forwarded to N. Y. and there was examined by the Board of Enrolment by whom he was supposed to have been accepted as a recruit. It appears from the enclosed report of the Surgeon of the Board, that Watson had never been before that Board for examination, previous to that time, and the testimony goes to show, that, some other person was fraudulently offered, under Watson's name to the Board, was found duly fit for service and accepted. After the acceptance of this substitute for Watson, the true Watson was put in his place, uniformed, and sent off. Watson has been discharged from the service by order of the Secretary of War."—LS, *ibid.* Accompanying papers indicate that George Watson, a crippled sixty-nine-year-old Englishman, was kidnapped, drugged, robbed, and enlisted in N. Y., and that another man passed the medical examination.—*Ibid.*

1864, JUNE 30.   USG endorsement. "Respectfully forwarded to the Secretary of War, with the recommendation that Company F be broken up as requested within"—ES, DNA, RG 94, Letters Received, 467C 1864. Written on a letter of June 16 from Capt. Avery B. Cain, 4th Inf., to Brig. Gen. Lorenzo Thomas recommending that Co. F be consolidated with other cos. of the regt. because of the small number of privates serving.—ALS, *ibid.* On July 6, Maj. Gen. Henry W. Halleck approved the request.—AES, *ibid.*

1864, JUNE 30–JULY 2.   USG endorsement. "Respy forwarded to the Secretary of War with the recommendation that for gallantry on the field of battle, Private James Coleman, Compy "F" 4th U S Inf. be pardoned and restored to duty. It occurs to me that the action of the Maj General Commanding the Dept of the East, in commuting the sentence of death to imprisonment is irregular. See accompanying order."—Copy, DLC-USG, V, 58. Written on a letter of June 24 of 2nd Lt. John R. Bothwell, Co. F, 4th Inf., concerning Private James Coleman, sentenced by court-martial to be shot, but then the sentence was commuted to hard labor at Dry Tortugas. Bothwell recommended that "for conspicuous gallantry and actions" Coleman be pardoned and returned to his co.—*Ibid.*; *ibid.*, V, 48.

1864, [JUNE].   USG endorsement. "The within order complimentary to Capt. F. R. Leib, late of the 116 Pa. Vols. is heartily endorse."—*The Union Army* . . . (Madison, Wis., 1908), IX, 348. Written on an order of June 1 of Col. Richard Byrnes commending Capt. Frank R. Leib for gallantry, favorably endorsed by Maj. Gen. Winfield S. Hancock.—*Ibid.*, pp. 347–48.

1864, JULY 2.   USG endorsement. "Approved, and respectfully forwarded to the Adjutant General of the Army, Washington, D. C."—ES, DNA, RG

94, Letters Received, 396A 1864. Written on a letter of June 14 from Capt. Charles B. Amory to Col. Edward D. Townsend, AGO, requesting assignment as adjt. to the 3rd Brigade, 1st Div., 10th Army Corps.—LS, *ibid.* The request was granted. See *O.R.,* I, xl, part 3, 370–72, 445.

1864, JULY 3. USG endorsement. "Cadets Adams & Merritt are hereby relieved from duty in the field and are authorized to proceed to their homes to take the benefit of their Cadet furloughs."—Typescript, DNA, RG 94, ACP, A368 CB 1866. Written on a letter of June 20 from Col. Alexander H. Bowman, USMA, to Brig. Gen. Richard Delafield requesting that Cadets Henry M. Adams and Henry A. Merritt be allowed to observe the Army of the Potomac during their furloughs.—Typescript, *ibid.* On June 27, Maj. Gen. Henry W. Halleck endorsed this letter by ordering the cadets to report to USG for duty.—Typescript, *ibid.*

1864, JULY 3, 5:00 P.M. Maj. Gen. Benjamin F. Butler to Lt. Col. Cyrus B. Comstock. "When at Fortress Monroe I prepared a platform car to carry a 13 in mortar and also another to mount a 30 Pdr Parrot The Mortar car worked admirably I can be used with a horizontal archc of fire of 70 Degrees and any elevation. It will be necessary to have the City Point rR Road repaired to Smiths lines to use them is it repaired They guns will be here tomorrow"—ALS (telegram sent), DNA, RG 94, War Records Office, Dept. of Va. and N. C., Army of the James, Unentered Papers. *O.R.,* I, xl, part 2, 614. See *ibid.,* p. 617. On July 5, Butler telegraphed to Brig. Gen. John A. Rawlins. "Will you be kind enough to order a 13 inch Mortar and Car on which it is to be fired now at City Point to be placed on the Rail track and run out to Gen Smith Also a Car with a thirty pounder parrott. I suppose both have arrived"—ALS (telegram sent), DNA, RG 107, Telegrams Collected (Unbound). Printed as sent at 4:00 P.M. in *O.R.,* I, xl, part 3, 19. On the same day, Comstock wrote to Butler. "The track of the rail road is now laid Gen. Ingalls informs me to Gen. Smiths Hd. Qrs. & the mortar is now here ready to be sent forward. Do you wish to have it sent to Gen. Smith?"—ALS, DNA, RG 94, War Records Office, Dept. of Va. and N. C., Army of the James, Unentered Papers. *O.R.,* I, xl, part 3, 19. On the same day, Brig. Gen. Godfrey Weitzel telegraphed to Comstock. "General Butler requested Generals Ingalls and Rawlins in two dispatches to send the mortar and Parrott gun, both on their cars, to General Smith."—*Ibid.* On July 6, Comstock telegraphed to Weitzel. "A mortar of Gen. Butler's is here the Qr. Mr. tells me, who wishes to know what to do with it. I telegraphed to Gen. Butler last night asking if he wished to have it sent to Gen. Smith but have received no reply. If the General has no choice in reference to it, I suppose it should be sent to Gen. Hunt Chief of Artillery for use."—ALS (telegram sent), DNA, RG 107, Telegrams Collected (Unbound); telegram received, *ibid.*

1864, JULY 4. USG endorsement. "Of the services of Lieut George A. Armes, I cannot speak from personal knowledge, but knowing the high and well merited standing of Maj Gen Hancock, both as a soldier and gentleman, I concur in his commendation of his services—"—ES, RPB. Written to accompany a letter of Maj. Gen. Winfield S. Hancock concerning 2nd Lt. George A. Armes, Veteran Reserve Corps.—George A. Armes, *Ups and Downs of an Army Officer* (Washington, 1900), pp. 113–14. On May 30, Brig. Gen. John A. Rawlins had assigned Armes to Hancock for staff duty.—LS (facsimile), *ibid.*, p. 89. On July 16, President Abraham Lincoln endorsed the reverse of USG's note. "Lieut. Armes wishes to be promoted to a Captaincy, and on the recommendations of Gen's Grant and Hancock, I am certainly willing, provided there is any place to which he can consistently be appointed."—AES, RPB. Lincoln, *Works*, VII, 443–44.

1864, JULY 5. To Maj. Gen. Benjamin F. Butler. "It will be necessary to keep up the patrol between Powhattan & Jamestown Island, for the protection of our Telegraph. I learn this morning that two & half miles of wire is gone."—Telegram received (at 9:35 A.M.), DLC-Benjamin F. Butler; copies, DLC-USG, V, 45, 59, 67; DNA, RG 108, Letters Sent. *O.R.*, I, xl, part 3, 19.

1864, JULY 6. USG endorsement. "Approved and respectfully forwarded."—AES, DNA, RG 94, ACP, D475 CB 1864. Written on a letter of June 15 from 1st Lt. Patrick K. Delany, 118th N. Y., to Secretary of War Edwin M. Stanton requesting an appointment as capt. and q. m., already favorably endorsed by several officers.—ALS, *ibid.* Delany was so appointed as of July 23.

1864, JULY 6. Act. Rear Admiral S. Phillips Lee, Norfolk Navy Yard, to USG. "Lieutenant Cushing, commanding U. S. S. Monticello, made a bold and skilful reconnoissance on the 23d ultimo, on which he was absent two days and ~~two~~ three nights, in the vicinity of Wilmington, and obtained the following information, in substance from prisoners taken and from his own observation. Three miles below Wilmington, he found the river obstructed by iron pointed spiles, driven in at an angle, and only to be passed by going into the channel left open about 200 yards from a heavy battery on the left bank. A short distance above is a 10-inch gun, navy battery, and another line of obstructions consisting of diamond shaped crates, filled and supported in position by two rows of spiles, the channel here being within 50 yards of the guns. A third row of obstructions and another battery complete the defenses of the city. The river is also obstructed by spiles at Old Brunswick, and there is a very heavy earthwork there. From dispatches taken from a captured courier it appeared that there are 1300 men in Fort Fisher, its rear is protected by four light batteries. From provision-returns taken, it appeared that the garrison was quite well supplied. Lieutenant

Cushing examined the ironclad Raleigh, beached near Western Bar, and found her, as reported, a complete wreck. The ironclad North Carolina was in commission and anchored off the city, she is little relied on. Both torpedoe boats were destroyed in the recent fire. The wooden propeller Gaskins carrying two guns, patrols the river. I hope this information will prove useful."—Typescript, DNA, RG 45, Area 8, Lee Papers. See *O.R.* (Navy), I, x, 202–4.

1864, JULY 6, 8:00 A.M. Maj. Gen. Benjamin F. Butler to USG. "You spoke to me a day or two since about making Surgeon McCormick the Director of transportation of the wounded and Director of the Medical Dept of the Armies operating against Richmond   Dr McCormic will hand you this note and will if you wish state wherein such centralisation of the Medical arrangements would be beneficial"—ALS (telegram sent), DNA, RG 393, Dept. of Va. and N. C., Telegrams Sent (Press).

1864, JULY 6. Lt. Col. Theodore S. Bowers to Maj. Gen. Benjamin F. Butler. "You will please order Lieut. Col. Herman Briggs, Chief Quarter Master of the 18th Corps, now on duty at Fortress Monroe to report for duty with his Corps on the field   If you have no officer of his Department available to relieve him of his present duties one can be furnished you."—ALS (telegram sent), DNA, RG 107, Telegrams Collected (Unbound); telegram received, *ibid.* *O.R.*, I, xl, part 3, 51. On the same day, 12:20 P.M., Butler telegraphed to Bowers. "Lt Col Biggs is so sick with a very troublesome and dangerous disease as to be entitled to sick leave and go home and when I saw him four days since he told me he would endeavor to hold on where he was   He cannot ride on horse back. I will send Capt. Clark just relieved at Yorktown or the best Qr Master I have in the Corps into the field but Col Biggs is not able to go."—ALS (telegram sent), DNA, RG 107, Telegrams Collected (Unbound). *O.R.*, I, xl, part 3, 51. See *ibid.*, p. 57.

1864, JULY 7. To Maj. Gen. George G. Meade. "Please authorize Gen Pierce Birneys Division to come into City Point today   his sister Mrs Grant is here & will spend the day only"—Telegram received (at 9:15 A.M.), DNA, RG 94, War Records Office, Army of the Potomac.

1864, JULY 9. USG endorsement. "Respectfully forwarded to the Secretary of War for his action—"—ES, DNA, RG 107, Letters Received from Bureaus. Written on a letter of March 30 from William S. Hawkins, Gloucester County, Va., to Capt. James E. Fleming, provost marshal, concerning the burning of fence rails on his farm and the seizure of corn and other supplies by troops of Brig. Gen. Judson Kilpatrick.—ALS, *ibid.* In the months between the writing of the letter and USG's endorsement, other endorsements and attachments had been added which tended to support the allegations but noted that the officer who should have given receipts had since been captured.—*Ibid.*

1864, JULY 9. USG endorsement. "Respy. forwarded to the Secretary of War, with the request that when Captain Martins' Battery can be spared, it be ordered to report to General Sheridan, to take the place of Company "K" 1st U. S. Artillery ordered to Washington to refit."—Copies, DLC-USG, V, 58; DLC-Philip H. Sheridan. Written on a letter of Maj. Gen. Philip H. Sheridan requesting a battery.—*Ibid.*

1864, JULY 10. Maj. Gen. Ambrose E. Burnside to USG. "Have you any news from the North that is proper to Communicate"—Telegram received, DNA, RG 107, Telegrams Collected (Unbound).

1864, JULY 12. USG endorsement. "Respectfully forwarded to the Secretary of War and recommended that the resignation of Gen'l. Smith be speedily accepted, as this is the third time he has tendered it."—ES, DNA, RG 94, ACP, S1011 CB 1863. Written on a letter of June 30 from Brig. Gen. William Sooy Smith, Nashville, to Secretary of War Edwin M. Stanton tendering his resignation.—ALS, *ibid.*

1864, JULY 12. To Maj. Gen. Henry W. Halleck. "The Chief Quartermaster 15th Army Corps having resigned, I most heartily approve of the appointment of Cap't. Greenberry L. Fort to fill the vacancy. Capt Fort has proven himself one of the purest and most efficient Officers in his Dept. serving in the West"—Telegram, copies, DLC-USG, V, 45, 59, 67; DNA, RG 108, Letters Sent.

1864, JULY 12. USG endorsement. "Respy returned, approved with the recommendation that the detail asked for by Governor Seymour be made."—Copy, DLC-USG, V, 58. On June 29, Governor Horatio Seymour of N. Y. wrote a letter requesting that Maj. Frederick Shonnard, 6th N. Y. Art., be assigned to the governor's staff, and on July 9, Maj. Gen. Henry W. Halleck endorsed this letter. "respectfully referred to Lieut Genl Grant for his action. Maj Shonnard is it is understood a nephew of Gov Seymour, and the duties to be performed State and not United States."—Copies, *ibid.*; DNA, RG 108, Register of Letters Received. Shonnard was so assigned.

1864, JULY 12. USG endorsement. "Respectfully refered to Maj. Gen. Butler."—AES, DNA, RG 108, Letters Received. Written on a letter of July 2 from Private Charles Donelly, Co. B, 2nd N. H., Camp Hamilton Military Prison, to USG. "Myself and fellow prisoners hope that by addressing you at atime when you accomplished one of the greatest victories that the Union has yet witnessed your heart may be inclined to greater leniency towards the humble soldiers who by their ready sacrifice of home comforts have joined you and our other great Generals in carrying out the wishes of the nation. There are in this Military Prison some fifty or sixty soldiers who, like myself, have been Kept in dreary confinement for the most trivial offences; some for the too common offense of getting on a spree, and others for perhaps a hasty word to an officer, and others again for a desertion of a few hours: most of them petty crimes which if the Authorities had the time to enquire into would have discharged long ago. The earnest desire of myself and all these men is to be allowed to rejoin our respective regiments and to share in the laurels which the Army has been gathering under your command. Hoping that you will give your favorable notice"— ALS, *ibid.* An endorsement states that Donelly had been returned to duty on July 10. On July 12, USG wrote an identical endorsement on a letter of June 27 from Private J. W. Gilson, Co. F, 17th Mass., "Hard Labor Prison," Norfolk, to USG complaining that soldiers were treated like convicts.—ALS, *ibid.* Attachments state that Gilson, sentenced to be shot for desertion, had his sentence commuted to imprisonment during the war.— *Ibid.*

1864, JULY 12. To J. F. Callan. "The republication of the laws passed by Congress touching our Military organization, proposed by you, cannot prove otherwise than beneficial to the service and will be a source of satisfaction to thousands of others feeling an interest in studying such matters." —ALS, Automatic Retailers of America Historical Foundation, Philadelphia, Pa.

1864, JULY 12. Col. James A. Hardie to USG. "It appearing that the Senate at their late Session ~~failed to~~ adjourned without Confirming the appointment of Brig. Genl. James H. Wilson, U. S. Vols.—The Secretary of War directs me to inform you that a new letter of appointment has this day been issued for that officer, with original date of rank, (October 30, 1863.) which will be forwarded you by mail."—LS (telegram sent), DNA, RG 107, Telegrams Collected (Bound); telegram received, *ibid.*, RG 107, Telegrams Collected (Unbound); *ibid.*, RG 108, Letters Received. *O.R.*, I, xl, part 3, 176.

1864, JULY 13. To Secretary of War Edwin M. Stanton. "Herewith I enclose to You Special Order appointing Capt. Henry Page A. Q. M. as Acting Chief Quartermaster of the Cavalry Corps Army of the Potomac. I would respectfully recommend that he be appointed Lieut. Col. and Chief Quartermaster of that Corps, to rank as such from the date of the Order, July 11th. 1864. He has been recommended for the position by Gen. Sheridan and approved by Gen. Ingalls."—LS, DNA, RG 94, ACP, P139 CB 1869. Capt. Henry Page was appointed as USG requested.

1864, JULY 14. Isaac F. Quinby, Rochester, N. Y., to USG. "Mr. Geo. Wm. Brown is an applicant for the appointment of Asst. Quarter Master U. S. Vols. and I take pleasure in saying that I believe he possesses qualifications which peculiarly fit him for such appointment. He is well educated, honest, and of a temperament which prompts to constant physical and mental activity. He served for several months as clerk in the Q'r Master's office at Memphis and is familiar with most of the varied duties that the appointment he seeks would devolve upon him. In the belief that he would prove a competent and faithful officer of the Gov't, I would respectfully recommend him for the appointment."—Copy, DNA, RG 94, ACP, B1572 CB 1864. Enclosed in a letter of Nov. 28 from George William Brown, New Orleans, to Col. Edward D. Townsend asking if USG had endorsed the original letter.—ALS, *ibid.* Brown received no appointment.

1864, JULY 16, 10:00 P.M. Maj. Gen. George G. Meade to USG. "I forward you a despatch report just received from the Chief of Artillery giving the time it will take to remove the siege guns & materials, in case a sudden withdrawal of the army, should become necessary, after the siege operations have been entered upon. In compliance with you wishes preparations have been continued for commencing the siege—batteries have are being erected for placing guns & mortars in position to silence the enemys fire at the salient on the Jerusalem plank road   The Chief Engineers estimates it will take eight days to finish these works & have them ready for their armament—The chief of artillery will require three days to unload the vessels now containing the siege guns, mortars & materials.—In case of withdrawal besides the three days indicated in his report for withdrawing these guns— if reloaded at the landing where the vessels now are Broadway landing it would require three additional days, but if they are carried to City Point & there reshipped this last element would not enter into the calculations.—I have deemed it proper to lay these facts before you as they may be material to you, in your future plans, and to say that I have directed the siege works to go on & in the course of three or four days shall commence the unloading of the guns & materials.—The mine will be ready in a day or two, but will not be loaded or sprung till the effect of our operations against the salient is ascertained."—ALS (telegram sent), DNA, RG 393, Army of the Potomac, Miscellaneous Letters Received; telegram received, *ibid.*, RG 108, Letters Received. *O.R.*, I, xl, part 3, 276–77. The enclosure is *ibid.*, p. 277.

1864, JULY 18. To C.S.A. Maj. Gen. George E. Pickett. "We are sending congratulations to you, to the young mother and the young recruit."— Arthur Crew Inman, ed., *Soldier of the South: General Pickett's War Letters to His Wife* (Boston and New York, 1928), p. 112. This letter congratulating Pickett on the birth of a son was also signed by Brig. Gen. Rufus Ingalls and Surgeon George Suckley.

1864, JULY 18. Maj. Gen. George G. Meade to "Genl.," presumably USG. "I enclose you a note from the Prov. Mar. Genl—of this army—Do you know any thing of these cases?—My impression is that Capt. Parker in the kindness of his heart & in ignorance of my orders, has given these passes probably without referring to you. I have been very strict in requiring compliance with the order prohibiting officers wives from visiting their husbands in campp, and only recently compelled compliance on the part of a Divn. Comdr. Ladies connected with the Sanitary & Christian Commissions or State Societies are permitted to reside where the the General hospitals are, but are not permitted to come to the front, or be in the camps where the troops are.—If I am right in my surmise that these cases have not been brought to your notice, may I ask that these officers be required to comply with existing orders, as soon as convenient or if it is your wish exceptions should be made in their cases that I may be notified in future when such exceptions are made so that the necessary instructions can be given to my subordinates—"—ALS, James S. Schoff, New York, N. Y. On July 20, Capt. Ely S. Parker endorsed this letter. "Respectfully returned. There was that in the case of each of these Ladies, that seemed to justify the permission given them, especially while the Commands to which their husbands belong remained in Camp, where they then were, and still are. You are authorized however, when these Commands move, to notify these Officers, that the permission for their wives to remain with them in camp, is terminated."—ES, *ibid.*

1864, JULY 18. Mrs. E. M. Danforth to USG. "A lady friend and myself on the 16th were ushered into your lines by your pickets in order to search for subsistence, as all we have has been destroyed by your army, and are still detained without any real cause, consequently I implore you as chief commander to release us forthwith, as each of us has little children that are suffering for our lone attention. We are at a lady's house who has no means, and we are very dissatisfied, as we are not able to compensate her for her kindness. Your immediate attention to this will be considered by us one of the kindest acts of humanity."—*O.R.*, I, xl, part 3, 326. Enclosed in a letter of the same day from Col. Thomas C. Devin, 2nd Brigade, 1st Cav. Div., to Maj. Gen. Andrew A. Humphreys discussing the matter.—*Ibid.*

1864, JULY 20. To Maj. Gen. Ambrose E. Burnside. "Yes!"—Telegram, copies, DLC-USG, V, 45, 59, 67; DNA, RG 108, Letters Sent. On the same day, Burnside received permission from hd. qrs., Army of the Potomac, to visit City Point.—*O.R.*, I, xl, part 3, 352.

1864, JULY 20. To Maj. Gen. George G. Meade. "Capt. A. J. Hall 1st Mich Sharp shooters who has been on leave of absence for the purpose of bringing into service some good riflemen sends in his resignation for the purpose of going to Michigan again to bring into service a new organization   I have given him authority to take the morning boat by sending in his resignation to go through the proper channel to you   Please accept it when it reaches"—Telegram received, DNA, RG 94, War Records Office, Army of the Potomac; copies, *ibid.*, RG 108, Letters Sent; DLC-USG, V, 45, 59, 67; (2) Meade Papers, PHi.

1864, JULY 20.   Lt. Col. Cyrus B. Comstock to Brig. Gen. Henry W. Benham. "Lt. Gen. Grant desires that you detail a proper officer and a squad of men to repair the defenses at City Point, especially the small redoubt and the infantry parapet in its vicinity, completing their revetments. The Comdg Officer at this post will furnish you with a working party in addition to your own, on your requisition."—ALS, DNA, RG 94, War Records Office, Army of the Potomac. *O.R.*, I, xl, part 3, 347–48.

1864, JULY 21.   To Jennette Robertson. "Your letter of the 20 inst. accompanying a beautiful smoking cap and slippers, the work of fair hands generously donated for the wounded and sick soldiers, and presented to me by over-partial subscribers, is received. I do not know that your fair was for the benefit of the soldiers, but suppose it was; but it was either that or the Church; in either case the cause was good. Your present was duly appreciated, and will not be worn earlier than the time prescribed in your note."—Amanda Lowman Bartholomew, "A Memory of Jennette Robertson Higley," *Iowa Historical Record*, XIII, 4 (Oct., 1897), 150–51. Sent after persons attending a Presbyterian fair for the benefit of sick and wounded soldiers voted USG the most popular gen., the package included a note stating that the cap and slippers were not to be worn until Richmond had fallen.—*Ibid.*, p. 150.

1864, JULY 21.   Brig. Gen. Rufus Ingalls, City Point, to Brig. Gen. John A. Rawlins. "Since the navigation of this river is constantly liable to interruption by Rebel Batteries, which, under cover of darkness or woods, can approach its banks at points favorable for firing upon our transports, I would suggest that the Naval Commander be requested to have the river patrolled oftener by his Gun Boats between Harrison's Bar and the mouth of the Chickahominy. These boats can *prevent* the Batteries being established, which will be of greater service than the driving of them away after they have fired upon unarmed vessels laden with troops and supplies. Many of the buoys have been destroyed and displaced. The channel should be well marked. I have the honor to represent that the 'Light Boat' has been removed from Cedar Point on the Potomac River. Our transports bound up and down now have to anchor frequently in that vicinity when they approach it in night time. A Light Boat should be reëstablished there, and the channel of that river as well as this should be better marked."—LS, DNA, RG 108, Letters Received.

1864, July 21.   Capt. Alexander B. Sharpe, City Point, to USG discussing cases of improper conduct by enrolling officers in western Pa.—ALS, DNA, RG 108, Letters Received.

1864, July [22–25].   USG endorsement. "Respy. forwarded to the surgeon General U. S. A. and recommendations of General Meade approved" —Copy, DLC-USG, V, 58. Written on a letter, received July 3, from Asst. Surgeon George E. A. Winans, correspondent for the *London [Canada] Free Press*, asking an interview with USG. The letter was referred to Maj. Gen. George G. Meade, who endorsed it on July 19. "respectfully returned to Head Qrs. Armies U. S. It appears that Dr G. E. A. Winans is in the employ of the Government as a contract physician. I am not aware, whether according to the terms of his employment or under the practice Dr Winans is authorized to wear a uniform. As Dr Winans is simply employed by the Surgeon General; I recommend that the within communication be forwarded to the Surgeon General, with the request that Dr Winans be discharged from the public service"—Copy, *ibid.* Born in Galena but taken to Canada when a child, Winans was a physician and promising poet who died in 1865 at the age of twenty-two. According to his letters, Winans interviewed USG twice, the second time on July 4.—C. VanDusen, *The Prodigy* (Toronto, 1870), pp. 114, 120.

1864, July 22.   To Philip B. Fouke. "I have examined the common, or wedge, tent pattented by R. B. Cullan Esq. and also one variety of his shelter tent. His improvement seems to be particularly in securing ventilation which has proven to be highly essential in crowded tents. This he has done admirably.—I have no doubt but this improvement should be taken advantage of in future purchases of tents to supply the Army."—ALS, DLC-USG, I, B. See telegram to Col. Philip B. Fouke, March 11, 1862.

1864, July 23.   To Maj. Gen. Benjamin F. Butler. "Sec. Seward, son and daughter are here. Will leave here at 1.30 p. m. for Point of Rocks and will be pleased to see you at the landing. As Mr. Seward leaves to-day in time to get through difficult navigation before dark he will not be able to visit you at your Hd Qrs."—ALS (telegram sent), Paul L. Rude, Ridgewood, N. J.; telegram received, DNA, RG 393, Dept. of Va. and N. C., Telegrams Received. On the same day, USG wrote to Butler. "Secretary Seward and party have just left here for Point of Rocks on boat City of Hudson."—*O.R.*, I, xl, part 3, 415.

1864, July 24, 11:00 A.M.   To Asst. Secretary of War Charles A. Dana. "I have no objection to the order prohibiting arms going into Ky. being relaxed so far as to allow the Gov. of the State to receive arms."—ALS (telegram sent), OClWHi; telegram received (at 6:00 P.M.), DNA, RG 107,

Telegrams Collected (Bound). *O.R.*, I, xxxix, part 2, 202. On July 23, 3:00 P.M., Dana telegraphed to USG. "Gov. Bramlette ~~of Kentucky~~ applies to have an order issued in compliance with your request prohibiting the sending of arms into Kentucky, relaxed so far as to allow the state authorities to receive arms ~~the~~ for which they have made contracts & which ha~~ve~~d been partially supplied previous to the order ~~He says~~ The arms are mostly Ballard rifles, and as he says are intended exclusively for Kentucky troops now serving under Gen Burbridge. Ought they to be allowed to go forward" —ALS (telegram sent), DNA, RG 107, Telegrams Collected (Bound); telegram received, *ibid.*, RG 108, Letters Received. *O.R.*, I, xxxix, part 2, 200.

1864, JULY 25. USG endorsement. "Respectfully forwarded, and the within list of recommendations approved—"—ES, DNA, RG 94, ACP, Q161 CB 1864. Written on a letter of the same date from Brig. Gen. Rufus Ingalls to Brig. Gen. John A. Rawlins. "I have the honor of transmitting herewith, in addition to those enclosed in my communication of the 21st inst. the recommendations for the appointment of the Division QrMasters of the 10th & 18th Army Corps, with the rank of Major, under the recent Act of Congress. I have to request, that the Lt. Genl. Commdg, the Armies, will consider them favorably and have them returned to me, to be forwarded to the QrMaster Genl. for reference to the War Department."—ALS, *ibid.*

1864, JULY 25. To Maj. Gen. George G. Meade. "I did not see the individual calling himself Robert W. Fowlke, but saw the Card which I take to be in the genuine hand writing of the President. I send you a~~s~~ similar card from the President which I know to be genuine, with which you can compare the one held by Fowlke. You escercise your own Judgment about letting Mr. F. go through, however even if his pass is all right, I think it will be better to detain him at all events until after the present movements are over."—Copies (2), Meade Papers, PHi. On the same day, 10:25 A.M., Meade had telegraphed to USG. "An individual calling himself Robert W. Foulke has presented himself here with a pass written on a visiting card & signed A. Lincoln authorising his passing our lines into Nottoway Co. Va.— He states he called at your Hd. Qrs, and was there by some officer referred to me—As this proceeding is irregular, and I have no means of either testing the signature of the President or indentyfing the individual bearing it, I shall not allow him to cross the lines without your order to that effect.—"— ALS (telegram sent), DNA, RG 393, Army of the Potomac, Miscellaneous Letters Received; copy, *ibid.*, Letters Sent.

1864, JULY 25. Special Orders No. 66, Armies of the U.S. "The Ordnance Depot at Bermuda Hundred will be broken up and the Ordnance and Ordnance Stores turned over to Lieut. Morris Shaff, Depot Ordnance Officer at City Point Va. Until further orders all Ordnance & Ordnance Stores required by the Troops operating against Richmond will be drawn from the Ordnance Depot at City Point, upon requisitions approved by the Chief of Ordnance of the Army or Department, in which the troops are serving"— Copies, DLC-USG, V, 57, 62, 67. *O.R.*, I, xl, part 3, 439.

1864, JULY 26. Maj. Gen. Edward O. C. Ord to USG. "My Corps Quarter Master, Col. Howard, has been taken by Gen. Butler. The next senior is reported as not fit. Can you send me a good one vice Howard."—ALS (telegram sent), DNA, RG 94, War Records Office, Dept. of Va. and N. C., Army of the James, Unentered Papers.

1864, JULY 26. Capt. Ely S. Parker to Bvt. Lt. Col. James L. Donaldson. "Your communication of the 17th inst, with enclosure has been received, and forwarded to the Secty. of War with the following endorsement: 'I can bear testimony to the zeal, integrity and efficiency of Col. Donaldson as Quartermaster, He is deserving of promotion and I most heartily endorse the within recommendation. (sgd) U S GRANT Lt Gen."—Copies, DLC-USG, V, 45, 59, 67; DNA, RG 108, Letters Sent.

1864, JULY 27, 12:40 P.M. President Abraham Lincoln to USG. "Please have a Surgeons examination of Cornelius Lee Comyges in Co. A. 183rd Vols. made on the questions of general health and sanity."—ALS (telegram sent), DNA, RG 107, Telegrams Collected (Bound); telegrams received (2), *ibid.*, Telegrams Collected (Unbound). Lincoln, *Works*, VII, 465.

1864, JULY 28. "Scout Plew" to USG. "Early on Wednesday the 20th instant at Leesburg—He is waiting in the Valley above Snickners Gap to secure the Crops to send down to Richmond by the way of Lynchburg— with the Stores and plunder they captured in Maryland & Pennsylvania Genl Hampton is now with Early or in that vicinity of country—Genl Early has had no reenforcements from Richmond that I can learn of. His force consists of about thirty thousand (30 000) strong"—ALS (telegram sent), DNA, RG 107, Telegrams Collected (Unbound).

1864, JULY 30. To Maj. Gen. George G. Meade. "Maj Allen Pay master is here with funds to pay the 3d N. Y batty & battery E 1st R I arty are they where they can be paid if the maj Goes out both these batteries belong to the 6th Corps but have been left back"—Telegram received (at 2:00 P.M.), DNA, RG 94, War Records Office, Army of the Potomac; copies, *ibid.*, RG 108, Letters Sent; DLC-USG, V, 45, 59, 67. On the same day, 2:00 P.M., Meade telegraphed to USG. "It appears to be impracticable for Major Allen to pay ~~batteries~~ the 3d New York battery—and battery E. 1st Rhode Island Artillery to day, as I learn that one or both of the batteries are in position—If the Major ~~will~~ will come out to-morrow morning and learn from ~~the~~ Genl. Hunt Chief of Artilly the location of the batteries no doubt he can then pay them,"—Df (telegram sent), DNA, RG 393, Army of the Potomac, Miscellaneous Letters Received; copies, *ibid.*, Letters Sent; Meade Papers, PHi.

1864, [JULY 31]. Maj. Gen. Benjamin F. Butler to USG. "I take leave to forward to Lt Gen Grant this report which shows that 60 men and a little gun boat went by water within 20 miles of the Weldon Road. This will do good as it will lead the enemy to think that any other expedition is only a cotton raid"—AES, DNA, RG 108, Letters Received. *O.R.*, I, xl, part 1, 822. Written on a report of July 31 of Brig. Gen. Innis N. Palmer of an expedition from New Berne to Manning's Neck, N. C.—LS, DNA, RG 108, Letters Received. *O.R.*, I, xl, part 1, 821–22.

1864, JULY 31. Brig. Gen. Godfrey Weitzel to Lt. Col. Cyrus B. Comstock. "Pleas send any orders in reguards to the line of the 18 A. C. to Capt Farquhar—As I leave here tomorrow on account of ill health—"—ALS (telegram sent), DNA, RG 94, War Records Office, Dept. of Va. and N. C., Army of the James, Unentered Papers. *O.R.*, I, xl, part 3, 711.

1864, AUG. 1, 10:30 A.M. To Secretary of War Edwin M. Stanton. "Your dispatch to Secretary Dana inquiring if rebel women can be sent from New York this way is received. Let them come—"—Telegram received (at 10:15 P.M.), DNA, RG 107, Telegrams Collected (Bound); copies, *ibid.*, Telegrams Received in Cipher; *ibid.*, RG 108, Letters Sent; DLC-USG, V, 45, 59, 67.

1864, AUG. 1. To Governor J. Gregory Smith of Vt. "I have the honor to acknowledge the receipt of your communication of date 20th ult. in relation to the Vermont Brigade and to say to you in reply, that there is no present intention to, or probable necessity for moving this Brigade from the vicinity of Washington. No positive promise to continue it there, can however, be made, as troops must go where the exigencies of the service require."— Copies, DLC-USG, V, 45, 59, 67; DNA, RG 108, Letters Sent. On July 20, Smith wrote to USG. "I have the honor respectfully to request, that the 1st Vermont Brigade, now serving in the defence of Washington, may be permitted to remain there for the present, in the event it should be deemed necessary to assign any troops for that purpose. I am induced to ask this courtesy, from the fact that our Brigade has seen very hard service, and lost over two thousand men, in the recent campaign, and, while they are ever willing to do thire duty faithfully and cheerfully, in any position that may be assigned them, still the rest would doubtless by grateful to them, and both the troops and the state would accept it as a just recognition of the gallant services which they have rendered. Will you be pleased to consider the matter and if consistent, grant the request."—ALS, *ibid.*, Letters Received. See *O.R.*, III, iv, 530–31.

1864, AUG. 1.   Capt. Henry C. Robinett, Wilmington, Del., to USG. "I have while here, detached from my regiment on Recruiting Service, received a Commission of Captain & Aide-de-Camp. No Orders were sent with my Commission. Subsequent to the receipt of it I was relieved from duty on Recruiting Service; but again 'no Orders' to report to any person or place reached me. I am extremely anxious, General, to be on duty in the field! I should be delighted to serve again under the eye of 'Our Old Commander' as it was my good fortune to do in the West,—particularly at Vicksburg! ! ! Could you not assign me to duty, General, according to my rank as Capt & A. D. C, near yourself? If so I shall endeavor to justify the bestowal of the favor as I did the first you granted at Millikens Bend, La. in April 1863. I hope sincerely my request ~~request~~ may meet with a favorable consideration, General, at your hands, for I am so weary of, and dissatisfied with my present inactivity. Please excuse the presumption (if it seem such to you) displayed in asking this favor, for my eagerness to see another siege like Vicksburg re-enacted and to be serving with *you* has prompted it. My Commission was forwarded to me from the War Department 2nd of April through Gen. McClerland; it may be he should have sent me orders, but he did not. He is, I learn, absent from his command in a very critical state of health. ~~Can~~ . . . P. S. Direct any communication for me to Wilmington, Del."— ALS, DNA, RG 108, Letters Received. On Sept. 15, Capt. George K. Leet issued Special Orders No. 94 assigning Robinett to duty on the staff of USG.—Copies, DLC-USG, V, 57, 62, 69. *O.R.*, I, xlii, part 2, 831.

Robinett served on USG's staff through the close of the war, then returned to the 1st Inf. By General Court Martial Orders No. 12, Dept. of the Gulf, Dec. 29, 1865, Robinett was dismissed from service following a disorderly scene in a saloon.—Copy (printed), DNA, RG 94, ACP, R816 CB 1865. On Jan. 18, 1866, Asst. Surgeon Charles B. White, New Orleans, wrote to Bvt. Brig. Gen. Cyrus B. Comstock stating his belief that Robinett had acted as he did because of the head wound he had received at Corinth in 1862.—ALS, *ibid.*, RG 108, Letters Received. By General Court Martial Orders No. 119, April 24, upon USG's recommendation, Robinett was restored to duty.—Copy (printed), *ibid.*, RG 94, ACP, R178 CB 1866. In 1867, Robinett submitted papers to a retiring board asserting that he was incapacitated by his wound from active service; the board ruled against him.—*Ibid.*, Letters Received, 270R 1867. He died on April 22, 1868.

1864, AUG. 2.   To Col. John T. Sprague, N. Y. AG. "I have the honor to acknowledge the reciept of your letter of date 24th ultimo requesting me to name an Officer of the regular service suitable to take Command of the 22nd Regt. New. York Vol. Cavalry. I would respectfully recommend Capt. M. A. Reno 1st U. S. Cavalry, as an Officer of experience and ability in the Cavalry Arm of the service, and one whom I believe would give entire satisfaction as the Commanding officer of a Cavalry Regiment. Capt Reno is at present serving on the Staff of Maj. Gen. P. H Sheridan Comd'g Cavalry Corps where any communication would reach him"—Copies, DLC-USG, V, 45, 59, 67; DNA, RG 108, Letters Sent. Capt. Marcus A. Reno did not receive the appointment.

1864, AUG. 2.   Harriet F. L. Gibson, Cleveland, Tenn., to USG. "I came here with permission of Genl Sherman and Schofield.   my husband informs me that Genl Steedman comdg this District has ordered him to encamp with the small portion of his regiment here and that he intends to order all Officers families out of the District   my husbands Command extends over three Railroads from this point & he was ordered by Genl Schofield to establish headquarters here last spring   you promised to grant me a favor   will you now give me permission to remain here as the army is my only home"— Telegram received, DNA, RG 107, Telegrams Collected (Unbound). Mrs. Gibson's husband, Col. Horatio G. Gibson, 2nd Ohio Heavy Art., commanded at Cleveland. On Aug. 12, Lt. Col. Theodore S. Bowers telegraphed to Mrs. Gibson. "You have permission to remain with the Army in Tennessee."—ALS (telegram sent), *ibid.*

1864, AUG. 8.   J. H. Schenck, City Point, to USG complaining of ill treatment on the steamboat *Dictator.*—ALS, DNA, RG 108, Letters Received. On Aug. 14, Col. Theodore B. Gates wrote to Capt. Philip Schuyler, Jr., adjt. for Brig. Gen. Marsena R. Patrick, denouncing Schenck's arrogant conduct on the voyage to City Point.—ALS, *ibid.* See Schenck to President Abraham Lincoln, Jan. 16, DLC-Robert T. Lincoln.

1864, AUG. 9.   USG endorsement. "Respectfully returned to the Secretary of War. Col. C. P. Stone, will report at the expiration of his leave to Maj. Gen. G. K Warren Comd'g 5th corps Army of the Potomac."—ES, DNA, RG 94, Letters Received, 1356S 1864. Written on a letter of July 29 from Col. Charles P. Stone, 14th Inf., Southborough, Mass., to Brig. Gen. Lorenzo Thomas asking where he should report when his leave expired.—LS, *ibid.* See *O.R.,* I, xlii, part 2, 95, 143.

1864, AUG. 10.   USG endorsement. "Respectfully returned. I do not approve of the plan or policy within proposed."—ES, DNA, RG 94, Letters Received, 1564S 1864. Written on a letter of July 20 from Maj. Gen. Cadwallader C. Washburn, Memphis, to Secretary of War Edwin M. Stanton proposing to forbid sales of cotton except to the U.S. government.—LS, *ibid.*

1864, AUG. 11.   USG endorsement. "Respectfully returned to the Secretary of War, and special attention invited to the enclosed report. From an examination of the papers in the case, it appears, that Col. Armstrong has grossly misrepresented the condition of his Command, in his communication to the President, having falsified his own reports, in his subsequent statement. I would therefore recommend, that he be dishonorably dismissed the service"—ES, DNA, RG 94, Vol. Service Div., A727 (VS) 1864. Written on a letter of July 19 from Col. James B. Armstrong, 134th Ohio, "Near Bermuda Hundred," to President Abraham Lincoln. "I send, by the hands of a friend, a statement herewith, which is meant as an appeal to you, the highest authority in the Land, in behalf of my Brigade of Ohio Hundred (100) days men. For obvious reasons this appeal is made directly to your Excellency; though I am aware it is unmilitary—but the excuse must be the urgent nature of the case, which will allow me to claim, in behalf of this command, the special notice of the Executive more as a Citizen than as a Soldier, because of the following reasons. This is the *only* Brigade of this class of troops so near the front. The unusual nature of our fatigue duties has born so heavily upon our unseasoned men, together with the climate, that, unless we are relieved, I have reason to fear our numbers will be so diminished by disease and death as not even to leave skeleton Regiments to take home the middle of August. Not counting casualitis, and deaths by disease, I have the honor to submit the enclosed copy of yesterdays report of the strength of the 130th 132d 134th & 142d O. V. I. of this Brigade, with the further remark that the daily list is increasing 40 to 50 men per diem without adequate Hospital accommodations."—ALS, *ibid.* On July 25, Lincoln endorsed this letter. "Submitted to the Sec. of War."—AES, *ibid.* On Aug. 10, Maj. Gen. Benjamin F. Butler wrote to Lt. Col. Theodore S. Bowers denying charges made by Armstrong.—*Private and Official Correspondence of Gen. Benjamin F. Butler* (n.p., 1917), V, 30–31.

1864, AUG. 11. USG endorsement. "respectfully submitted to the Hon. Sec. of State. I can not call to mind the discharged soldier who writes the within but have no doubt he correctly states his services and the manner of his discharge."—AES, DNA, RG 59, Letters of Application and Recommendation, Lincoln and Johnson Administrations, Thomas P. Orwin. On July 6, Thomas P. Orwin, U.S. Consulate, Newcastle on Tyne, wrote to USG. "You will I am sure be any thing but unkind to the wounded of Fort Donaldson, and as I was one of the 31st you will know how we suffered. I was wounded in the head, and six months after discharged at St Louis Mo. I was clerk or Secy at Logans head quarters and have often been in your office (at Cario) on the Levy, but General you time is precious and I will ask out right but respectfully for what I want a favour you can very soon do. there is a vacent consulate at Sonneburg in Germany, and if you will communicate to Mr. Seward approvingly I am sure I will get it. Brig General Logan will tell you who and what I am or Mrs. Logan or the McCooks. if the Judge had lived I should have had a freind in Washington but alas he is dead, General I was at Belmont and was wounded at Fort Henry and Donaldson and I love my Country and am no in Civil Service as Vice Counsul at New castle If you will help me by just saying a word to the Secy of State, Oh I shall be so grateful beleive me"—ALS, *ibid.*

1864, AUG. 11. USG to an unidentified person. "The hats sent by you to my address have reached. The larger of the two, the felt is just the size I need. I am under many obligations for your kind consideration."—Typescript, Grant Family Papers, USGA.

1864, AUG. 12. Secretary of War Edwin M. Stanton to USG. "I transmit to you a correspondence of line officers of your command with Mr. Harris, a Senator from New York, in regard to the detail of officers on recruiting duty. Much annoyance is occasioned to this Department by military officers irregularly addressing members of Congress, and ~~of~~ other Departments of the Government ~~at large~~, in regard to military affairs. It is an evil which no one can better understand than yourself, and for which you can apply the best corrective. You are aware that it is no uncommon practice for officers to ~~use~~ solicit political & personal influence to get themselves detached from service or relieved from duty in the field; and I regret to say that in this instance it has been countenanced by General Officers. Besides the pertinacious applications which are thus pressed upon the Department, to the delay of its legitimate business, other embarrassments arise from conflicts with the views of commanding officers. You will observe, by a copy of the letter of General Meade, that, while he discountenances the detailing of officers from the field for recruiting service, his subordinates have appealed to the personal influence of a distinguished Senator to accomplish that very object. This is only one of many ~~evils~~ instances that occur almost daily from this irregularity, and which it is difficult to resist when such influences are encouraged and promoted by General Officers in the army. The efforts of this Department have proved unavailing to break up the practice, and I do not know that you can check or restrain it. The subject, however, is submitted to your consideration for such remedy as you may advise, or see proper to adopt."—LS, DNA, RG 108, Letters Received. Stanton enclosed a copy of an endorsement by Maj. Gen. George G. Meade disapproving detachments for recruiting, and copies of letters to U.S. Senator Ira Harris of N. Y. from Capt. Henry Grinton, 2nd N. Y. Cav. (Harris Light Cav.), Brig. Gen. John B. McIntosh, Brig. Gen. James H. Wilson, and Lucien Birdseye, New York City (uncle of 1st Lt. Mortimer B. Birdseye, 2nd N. Y. Cav.), all requesting detachment of recruiting parties for the 2nd N. Y. Cav.—Copies, *ibid.*

1864, AUG. 13. To commanding officer, Fort Monroe. "Give Mrs Walker (Mary) a pass to visit these Headquarters free on Govt service."—Copies, DLC-USG, V, 68; (press) DNA, RG 107, Telegrams Collected (Bound). Dr. Mary E. Walker had recently been released from a C.S.A. prison to which she had been taken after her capture while serving as an asst. surgeon.—Charles McCool Snyder, *Dr. Mary Walker: The Little Lady in Pants* (New York, 1962; reprinted, New York, 1974), pp. 44–47.

1864, AUG. 15. USG endorsement. "Respy refered to the sec of war. It seems to me an order should be issueed exempting deserters (not refugees) from the rebel army, from draft. As stated in the enclosed letter such soldiers would run two risks, and would not do to rely on at a battle. Every soldier who deserts from the enemy, is equal to one soldier added to our strength."—Copy, DLC-USG, V, 58. Written on a letter of Aug. 9 of Charles Braxton and others, Indianapolis, asking that C.S.A. deserters be exempt from the draft.—*Ibid.*

Index
═══

All letters written by USG of which the text was available for use in this volume are indexed under the names of the recipients. The dates of these letters are included in the index as an indication of the existence of text. Abbreviations used in the index are explained on pp. xvi–xx. Individual regts. are indexed under the names of the states in which they originated.